THE CORRESPONDENCE OF

Alexander Pope

Pope's Villa

THE

CORRESPONDENCE

OF

Alexander Pope

EDITED BY

GEORGE SHERBURN

VOLUME V

INDEX

OXFORD

AT THE CLARENDON PRESS

1956

Oxford University Press, Amen House, London E.C.4
GLASGOW NEW YORK TORONTO MELBOURNE WELLINGTON
BOMBAY CALCUTTA MADRAS KARACHI CAPE TOWN IBADAN

———

PRINTED IN GREAT BRITAIN

CONTENTS

VOLUME V

CORRECTIONS

I. LADY MARY WORTLEY MONTAGU'S RETURN FROM THE CONTINENT
(1718)

Vol. i. *pp.* 513, 519, and 522. The last three letters from Lady Mary to Pope before her return to London are clearly misdated by her, and her datings have been wrongly accepted here. Information to this effect came late to the editor from Professor Robert Halsband, when he kindly read the proofs for this part of Pope's correspondence. Lady Mary could not have written from Lyons on 28 September O.S. (p. 513), since the State Papers (78/162) indicate that Lord Stair reported the arrival of Mr. Wortley in Paris on 18 September O.S. She may have 'run about' Paris, but not in October, as she said she did in a doubtful letter from the spurious volume of her *Letters* (1767): here p. 519; and she could not have written to Pope on 1 November shortly after landing at Dover; for she and her husband were back in London not later than 2 October. The precise date of arrival seems a bit difficult to determine, but the small differences in date could not authenticate the datings of the three letters here under consideration. Professor Halsband notes an item of news in *The Weekly Journal ; or British Gazetteer*, 11 October 1718, which reports, under the heading of 'Hampton-Court, October 3' that 'On Thursday 7-night last the Honourable Wortley Montagu, Esq . . . and his Lady arrived in Town; and the next day he waited on His Majesty at Hampton-Court'. The item is confused perhaps; but the *Gazette* for 11 October records that Mr. Wortley waited on His Majesty at Hampton Court on 4 October. 'George Paston' in *Lady Mary Wortley Montagu and her Times*, p. 289, quotes a letter from Montagu Bacon, dated 'London, 2 October 1718', who remarks, 'I am very sorry my uncle Wortley keeps his chamber, but it is less inconvenient in so cheerful a family'. The remark suggests a possible return at the end of September and a report to His Majesty delayed because of slight indisposition.

The proper dating of these last letters from the Continent affects Pope's behaviour in that he certainly intended to rush from Cirencester to London to greet her ladyship upon arrival. He stayed in the country, however, except for one very brief visit to Town, until at least the middle of October. On 11 October he wrote to Lord Burlington (i. 517), 'I went to Town a Fortnight since, in no other view than the hopes to meet you'. Pope's time sense was normally bad, and

if he did greet Lady Mary on her arrival, the 'fortnight since' must be interpreted loosely. The strong emphasis on his sole desire to meet Burlington would be due to the fact that Pope had hung fire all summer on a possible lease of land in Burlington Gardens on which he now decided *not* to build a house. In any case the visit was a very brief one (see i. 518). If he had come to Town literally 'a fortnight back' (27 September) he would have learned of her ladyship's imminent return and should have awaited her. One suspects that his visit was so timed that he very briefly waited on the cheerful household mentioned by Montagu Bacon.

The texts of the letters written from abroad by Lady Mary are here those of the first printing (1763). Professor Halsband, who intends to edit Lady Mary's letters, finds that the texts of 1763 are farther from Lady Mary's autograph transcripts than are the texts given by Moy Thomas (1861). Most of the divergences are of little importance.

II. 'IN POWER YOUR SERVANT'

Vol. ii, *p.* 294. This letter (10 May) to Fortescue is impossibly dated in [1725?] on the hasty supposition that it referred to Pope's gratitude for the grant of £200 secured from the Government in April 1725. The quotation ('In Power your Servant', &c.) comes from Doding-ton's *Epistle to Sir Robert Walpole*, published towards the end of 1725, and the quotation makes May 1725 an impossible date for the letter. The quotation seems to echo *The Craftsman*, 14 October 1727, and hence may well date May 1728 or later. The gratitude might be for Walpole's aid in getting the abbey for Father Southcote (Spence, pp. 7–8 and G. D. Henderson, *Chevalier Ramsay*, p. 90), though 'dispatch' possibly does not describe the negotiations for that affair, or it might be for presenting *The Dunciad* to the King in March 1729. Pope was during the period 1726 to 1732 frequently dining at Sir Robert's table on Sundays. See ii. 368, 441, 530, and iii. 112.

ADDITIONAL LETTERS

(Not known early enough to be placed in their proper chronological sequence)

POPE *to* JAMES TOOKER[1]   18 *December* 1712

Longleat MSS.

Decr 18. 1712.

I receivd yours within an hour after I had sent a Letter to you, with one inclosed to my Lord Lansdowne, which I hope have reachd your hands. The Contents of them I make it my request to you to keep private, in all else to do just as seems best to your Judgment—Your Verses upon Fort Knocke gave me a great deal of Diversion, but of that sort of Laughter which is Rationall; & when we Laugh *with* an Author, not *at* him. 'Tis not the easiest Talent to make another ridiculous without becoming so oneself. I take Mr Tooker in this copy to be of that number which Boileau speaks of

—Qui rit, & qui fait rire,
Qu'on blâme en le lisant, & pourtant qu'on veut lire.[2]

You may depend upon it, you'l never Laugh all alone, in a miserable merry manner, as some do; but whenever you please to you can Laugh quite over the nation, and for many years after your Death: Posterity will take up the Laugh & carry it on. And whoever idolizes the man you ridicule, tho they are never so angry at your Mirth, will be forc'd to confess, they would laugh if the Jest were not too great, & too true an one.

The Elegy from Tibullus is (without flattery) in my opinion extreamly well done; All I can object to is that Triplett,

Some Sov'reign cordial for her ease prepare
Nor plunge her Lover in a deep despair
Who importunes the Gods with fervent prayr.

---

[1] This letter was recently discovered at Longleat by Miss Dorothy Coates, who kindly transcribed it for the editor. The autograph original appears among business papers of the 1st Viscount Weymouth, in whose financial affairs Tooker was concerned. Tooker is mentioned among Pope's friends in Gay's poem 'Mr. Pope's Welcome from Greece' (stanza xx). Another mention in the letter to Caryll of 23 Oct. 1733 is annotated as follows by Elwin (vi. 346): 'This may have been James Tooker, who was described in a deed of 1730 as of 'Woodhouse, in the county of Southampton, Gent'. Woodhouse was, we believe, a house in the parish of Idsworth, adjoining Ladyholt park.' (Caryll lived at Ladyholt, where Tooker was visiting in Oct. 1733.) Lord Lansdowne had (1711) married the widow of Thomas Thynne, the mother of the 2nd Viscount Weymouth.

Tooker would seem to be one of the many gentlemen of his day who wrote verses. Those on Fort Knocke have not been identified. The elegy translated from Tibullus is iv. iv.

[2] Boileau's Seventh Satire, ll. 13, 14.

I think the first of these lines may be omitted without prejudice to
the sence or connexion, (this being added by the translator) and the
Latin of the 3rd Verse has an Epithet which methinks you have not
fully express'd—Votaque pro domina non numeranda facit.) What if it
were—Who wearies Heavn with never-ceasing pray'r—or, Who tires
the Gods—That line which now runs thus,

> Blasphemes the powrs he had adord in vain

will be more harmonious & more full, if it be altered,

> Blasphemes the powrs so late adord in vain.

This is all I can with the utmost Severity of a friend object against,
or more properly doubt of, and I shoud think I falsifyd a Trust if I
did not fairly tell you the least doubt that occurrd to me. It will be
no less in you, if you use not the same freedom with the Poem I may
send you (after I have heard from you). There are several reasons I
have to do this to you, and expect it from you, which the following
Verses express so well that you'l pardon me if I repeat them,

> Te mihi junxerunt nivei sine crimine mores,
> Simplicitasque sagax, ingenuusque pudor;
> Et bene nota fides; et candor frontis honestae;
> Et studia, a studiis non aliena meis.[1]

This is so good a picture of you, that I need no other to be always
mindfull of you, and consequently always | Your most faithfull and |
affectionate Servant, | A. Pope.

Address: To Mr Tooker, att | Mr Reynold's a Hatter's in | Little Russel
Street | Covent garden | London.

CONGREVE *to* POPE[2]   23 *June* [? 1719]

Harvard University

I am very sorry to hear you have been ill. it has not been my fault that
I have not been to wait on you. I shall think it very long till I hear
you are better. I am my selfe but upon a very indiffrent foot. I thank
you a thousand times for your Care of the Spaw water I have sent this
morning to the Custom house about em. I believe I shall not need quite
so many but some friends may be glad of some of them I am Dear Sir
ever your most Obedient humble Servant Wm Congreve

June 23

[1] Here Pope seems to assemble compliments from various authors. The first line is from
Ovid, *Amores*, i. iii. 14.
[2] The year is guessed at because in the summer of 1719 Congreve was visiting Lord
Shannon at Ashley. For letters bearing on matters here mentioned see ii. 12–13 and 27.

THE DUKE OF BUCKINGHAM *to* POPE[1]   [? 1720]

James M. Osborn

I can no more pretend to equal you in complements than in any other writing, and therefore would not have given you this trouble, but to prevent a mistake (I suppose) of my expression. For I only meant, tho to my own loss, saving you the care of one chorus more, about which there was some difficulty in finding a subject for it: because I found an old one of my own since yesterday, which will make up the set, with those two chorus's of yours that I had your leave to put in the Book when tis returnd; which for that reason I wish as soon as you please to send it to | Your very humble servant | Buckingham

[THE EARL OF ISLAY] *to* HENRIETTA HOWARD[2]

11 *August* [? 1726]

Blickling Hall

Whitton. Aug. 11.

Madam: Since I writ my other Epistle I am come to Whitton My Man hapned to stay behind on the road & so I send him from hence: I thought it best to leave Your friend Vernon to himself 2 or three days to see if upon recollection he would be A little more Christian I mean humane. instead of that he Yesterday sent to me to know Your answer, so that I think I am at the end of my string with him: The man that brought your letter to Town to day did not stay for an answer or else you had received it immediately: You are really in love with Your grounds, he knows, & therefore is so cruel God forgive him for I never will   I am your most obt. &c.

Address: To | The Honble | Mrs. Howard

[1] Pope had published in his *Works* (1717), pp. 379–84, 'Two Chorus's to the Tragedy of Brutus, not yet publick'. These His Grace incorporated in his tragedy, and apparently he wished for a third, for which Pope lacked a subject. Pope's care is rendered superfluous by the Duke's discovery of his old chorus. The letter should fall between 1717 and 1721, when the Duke died.

The original letter is inlaid in the grangerized copy of Spence's *Anecdotes* purchased by Mr. Osborn from the Derby Sale at Sotheby's in 1953.

[2] This unsigned letter is clearly in the handwriting of Lord Islay, a friend of both Mrs. Howard and Pope. It relates to Pope's letter about the road (ii. 259—wrongly there placed in 1724) and to the later letter from W. Plomer (v. 19). A letter from John Gay to Mrs. Howard, dated 17 March 1725/6, preserved among the Blickling Hall MSS., indicates that the road was being finished early in 1726. Vernon must have died shortly after this Islay letter was written: he was buried on 31 August 1726. The letter is made available by the kindness of R. W. Ketton-Cremer, Esq., and is printed by permission of the National Trust.

SWIFT *to* POPE¹   [1 *August* 1726]
Harvard University

There have been strange Alterations in the Scheme,—made by Lord Peterb and Dr Arbuthnot, and my Lord said he would give you notice of it. The Opera and some other Affairs have altered their measures; of which I suppose you will here, and I think Wednesday is the day fix, unless they vary again. I am in confusion and will leave the Matter so; I am weary of the Town, and of little Business left in it. So that the kind Lodging in your Heart must be large indeed if it holds me; mine cannot hold the idear and Friendship I have to you   I am ever &c

Monday Morn, past 9.

Address: To Alexander Pope Esqr
Endorsements: from Dr. Swift | a King a Scarecrow of Straw, yet protects the corn.—a fine Lady is like a Catt, when young the most gamesome & lively of all creatures, when old the most melancholy.

POPE *to* BUCKLEY²   20 *February* [1727/8]
Sold at Sotheby's 28 November 1913
                                          Twickenham, February 20th.
[Regrets his inability to see Buckley so soon as Thursday as he is engaged with company, and]

Planting some things wch will otherwise be too late for ye season. . . . On my return to town I will meet you anywhere . . . tho the affair the Dr. mentioned to you I think will keep you cool, etc.

*POPE *to* SAMUEL WESLEY³   6 *January* [1728/9]
Portland Papers (transcript)
                                               January the 6.
Sir,—I hoped long before this to have seen you; but the dangerous Illness of my Mother has confined, and will in probability confine me,

¹ The original of this letter, once in the collections of Locker-Lampson, has recently come to Harvard. The date is based on the assumption that Lord Peterborow is planning a dinner in Swift's honour, but has changed its date to Wednesday 3 Aug. Swift's letter written the day after the dinner (here ii. 384) indicates that Pope was too sick to be present. Ball thought it written in June (see Ball, iii. 447).
² It is impossible to choose a year for so small a fragment as this. If the 'Dr.' is Dr. Mead, the letter probably falls as late as 1728, when Mead was working with Buckley on the edition of Thuanus.
³ This new letter, discovered by Sir Harold Williams among the MSS. of the Duke of Portland and here printed by kind permission of His Grace, seems to be a transcript of the letter that Lord Oxford was asked (iii. 8) to transmit to Wesley. The remarks in the first paragraph about deferring *The Dunciad* can hardly represent more than a momentary intention. Pope's emphasis on his own moral integrity is typical, and the formula for a public repentance imposed on Cooke (but not transmitted to him) is especially interesting. This letter seems to the editor to make very doubtful Norman Ault's interpretation of the personal relations of Pope and Wesley. Ault's error is to take as veracious statements made by Dunces hostile to Pope. For Ault's views see Pope's *Minor Poems* (1954), pp. 294–5.

long, whether or no I shall be so happy at last as to preserve her, God
only knows! but in either circumstance, of her death, or of a lingring
painful life which will demand my daily Care of her; I think it no
way becoming, if not highly indecent; for me to be medling with Fools
& Fooleries at this juncture: and have therefore laid aside all thoughts
of the Dunciad. Its true, I gave a Correct Copy of it with the blanks
filld up, at the request of 2 or 3 Friends, who were willing to attend it
with some Illustrations and pieces of their own. But I have desired
'em now to put it off, and let the Gentlemen write and confederate as
they please, they should for me at present rest (if they are wise enough
to rest) with their Iniquities Cover'd.

Nevertheless, that I may not any way inadvertently be guilty of an
Injury to the Good meaning or repentance (if there be any) of Mr
Cooke, I would beg you to show him this, and tell him plainly from
me: that if his motive of Addressing to me were sincere and that he
really is sensible of having injurd me in his Battle of Poets (I charge
him with nothing but just what he owns himself, nor will mention
some other things which he hath thought fit to deny of a fresh date.)
He ought to consider, that was a *Publick Printed* Reflection on a part
of my *Moral* Character; which can no way be repaird by a *private*
Letter, but as *Publick* a Recantation, of which in a like Instance Mr
Hill has set him an Example.

As for speaking of each others Poetry, I think we are both at liberty.
But on my Morals I insist and I shall think him in earnest if he signes
this Declaration, "That whereas in that Poem he had Reflected on my
Char. as a man movd by Mercenary views and hinting as if I had
impos'd on the Publick by a fraudulent Subscription, he doth hereby
declare that he had no knowledge of the true state of that fact, but
asserted it rashly and since is made sensible of the Contrary."

I do again Sir beg your pardon for renewing this trouble on my
Account, But it is really from a spirit of justice to the Man, as well as
to my self, for fear I may seem to slight him if he has any meaning:
and that I may one way or other do him justice to my Lord Pembroke,
who shews him favor, and whom I have a just respect for. His answer,
Yea or no, will cut the whole matter short.

I hope the time will come when I may have the pleasure of seeing
my Lord Oxford and you, both at his House and at mine. I am with
esteem | Sir | Your most affect: hum. Servant | A. Pope

You'l please to return me those two Letters[1] I gave you, or give
them my Lord.

---

[1] The two letters are presumably those received from Cooke. See ii. 509, 519.

POPE *to* BRIAN FAIRFAX[1]   14 *August* 1730

James M. Osborn

Twick'nam: Aug. 14. 1730

Sir,—The bearer of this imagines that my Recommendation will be
of use to him. I can only say, that if you can find occasion to doe him
any favour, it will be an obligation to me; And that he is one of so good
a character, as I am assured will merit any you may show him, and
acknowledge it with all gratitude. I take this opportunity to tell you
with truth, how much I sincerely have long been, & am, with respect,
| Sir. | Your most Obedient & most | faithful Servant, | A. Pope.

GAY *and the* DUCHESS OF QUEENSBERRY *to* SWIFT[2]

6 *December* 1730

Add. 4806

Both your Letters to my great satisfaction I have receiv'd; You were
mistaken as to my being in town for I have been here ever since the
beginning of May; but the best way is to direct my Letters always to
the Duke's house in London; and they are sent hither by his Porter.
We shall stay here till after the Holidays; you say we deserve Envy.
I think we do, for I envy no man either in town or out of it; We have
had some few Visitors and every one of 'em is such that one would
desire to visit; the Duchess is a more severe check upon my finances
than even you were and I submit, as I did to you, to comply to my own
good; I was a long time before I could prevail with her to let me allow
myself a pair of shoes with two heels, for I had lost one, and the shoes
were so decayd that they were not worth mending; you see by this
that those who are most generous of their own can be the most covetous
for others; I hope you will be so good to me as to use your interest
with her, (for whatever she says, you seem to have some) to indulge me
with the extravagance suitable to my fortune. The Lady you mention
that dislikes you hath no discernment.[3] I really think you may safely
venture to Amesbury, though indeed the Lady here likes to have her

---

[1] This letter was purchased by Mr. Osborn from the Derby Sale at Sotheby's in 1953.
See iii. 124.

Brian Fairfax (1676–1749), a Yorkshireman, was a member of the Burlington circle and
a distinguished art-collector. He is mentioned in the letters and in the will of William Kent
(see Margaret Jourdain, *The Work of William Kent*, pp. 86 and 90). He also is found among
the signers of the petition to Lord Burlington against Kent's project for removing a certain
tree. See here iv. 324. The identity of the person recommended is unknown, and although the
addressee also may be uncertain, Fairfax is altogether probable since he was given as addressee
in the Sotheby catalogue for the sale of 12–15 May 1851. After that sale the letter was inlaid
in the grangerized copy of Spence's *Anecdotes*, where it now remains. The text is from a
transcript kindly made by Mr. Osborn.

[2] By accident this letter was omitted from its proper place, which would be about iii. 154.
Pope printed the answer to this letter, which is here found in iii. 179–82.

[3] The Queen.

own way as well as you which may sometimes occasion disputes, and I tell you beforehand that I cannot take your part. I think her so often in the right, that you will have great difficulty to persuade me She is in the wrong; then there is another thing I ought to tell you to deterr you from this place, which is, that the Lady of the house is not given to show civility to those she does not like; she speaks her mind, and loves truth; for the uncommonness of the thing I fancy your curiosity will prevail over your fear & you will like to see such a Woman. but I say no more, till I know whether her Grace will fill up the rest of the Paper.

[The Duchess:]

write I must, particularly now as I have an oppertunity to indulge my predominant passion, contradiction. I do in the first place contradict most things Mr. Gay says of me—to deterr you from coming here which if you ever do I hereby assure you that unless I like my own way better you shall have yours, & in all disputes you shall convince me if you can, but by what I see of you this is not a misfortune that will always happen for I find you are a great mistaker, for example you take prudence for imperiousness tis fro[m this] first that I determined not to like one who is too gid[dy he]aded for me to be certain whether or no I shall ever be acquainted with. I have often known people take great delight in Building Castles in the Air, but I should chuse to Build friends upon a more solid foundation. I would fain know you, for I often hear more good likeable things than tis possible any one can deserve. pray come that I may find out something wrong, for I, and I believe most women, have an inconceivable pleasure to find out any faults—except their own—Mr Cibber is made Poet Laureat.

I am Sir as much your Humble Servant as I can be to any person I dont know | CQ

Mr Gay is very peevish that I spell and write ill but I dont care for the pen nor I can do no better besides I think you have flattered me & such people ought to be put to trouble.

[Gay:]

I hope you are pleas'd; and that you will allow for so small a summ as 200*l* you have a lumping penniworth.[1]

Amesbury. Decr 6. 1730.

Address: For | The Reverend Dr. Swift | Dean of St Patrick's in | Dublin | Ireland | by way of London.
Postmark: 7/DE
Endorsements by Swift: Decemb. 14th 1730 Mr Gay and Ds of Q——y [repeated in a second endorsement]. Answered.

[1] See iii. 152, where Swift says he would have given £200 to have had three lines more from the Duchess in their last letter.

SWIFT *to* MATTHEW PILKINGTON[1]   22 *July* 1732

Harvard University

Whereas severall scattered Papers in prose and verse for three or four years last past, were printed in Dublin, by Mr George Faulkner, some of which were sent in Manuscript to Mr William Bowyer of London, Printer, which pieces are Supposed to be written by me, and are now by the means of the Reverend Mathew Pilkington who delivered or sent them to the said Faulkner and Bowyer, become the Property of the said Faulkner and Bowyer, I do here without specifying the said Papers, give up all manner of right I may be thought to have in the said Papers, to Mr Mathew Pilkington aforsaid, who informs me that he intends to give up the said right to Mr Bowyer aforsaid.

Witness my hand. Jul. 22. 1732 | Jonath: Swift. From the Deanery-house in Dublin, the day and year above written.

SWIFT *to* POPE[2]   1 *May* 1733

Portland Papers

Dublin, May 1st 1733

I answer your Letter the sooner because I have a particular reason for doing so. Some weeks ago ⌈there⌉ came over a Poem called, *the Life and* ⌈*genuin*⌉ *character of, &c.*[3] *written by himself.* It was reprinted here, is ⌈after a short advertisement⌉ dedicated to you. It is grounded upon a Maxim in Rochefoucault & the dedication after a formal story says that my manner of writing is to be found in every line. I believe I have told you, that I writ a year or two ago near 500 lines upon the same maxim in Rochfoucault, & was a long time about it, as that impostor says in his dedication, with many curcumstances all pure invention. I desire you to believe, & to tell my friends, that in this spurious piece, there is not a single line, or bit of a line, or thought, any way resembling the genuin Copy any more than it does Virgil's Æneis, for I never gave a Copy of mine, nor lent it out of my sight, and although I showed it to all common acquaintance indifferently: & some of them, especially one or two females had got many lines by heart, here & there and repeated them often; yet it happens that not one

---

[1] This curious document, which is not a letter, is here printed by way of annotation of Pope's letter to Pilkington, here found on iii. 323. Publication of the 'third' volume of the *Miscellanies* (1732) was complicated by the fact that some of the same pieces that he here gives to Pilkington and Bowyer Swift has sent for use in the *Miscellanies*, published by Motte.

[2] See iii. 367–9 for Pope's printed text (1741) of this letter, which he badly truncated. Sir Harold Williams, having discovered in the Portland Papers a contemporary transcript (somehow not assembled with the Longleat Harleian transcripts), kindly has secured permission for reprinting the fuller text here. Altered phrasing, apart from omissions, is indicated in footnotes. Omissions by Pope are placed in half brackets.

[3] &c.] of Dr. S. *1741.*

single line or thought is contained in this impostor,[1] although it appears that the knave[2] who counterfeited me, had heard of the true one. But even this trick shall not provoke me to print the true one, which indeed is not proper to be seen till I can be seen no more. I therefore desire you will undeceive my ffriends; and I will order an Advertisement to be printed here, and transmitted to England, that every body may know the delusion, and acquit me, as I am sure you must have done your self, If you have read any part of it, which is mean, & trivial, and full of that cant that I most despise. I would sink to be a Vicar in Norfolk rather than be charged with such a performance. Now I come to your letter. ⌐Only let me add one Vexatious circumstance, that this counter-feit Poem cost me 6 shill. for Postage this day, in a folio edition, after I had been teazed with it this fortnight by the Hawkers for a peny.¬ When I was of your age, I thought every day of Death, but now, every minute, and a continual giddy disorder more or less is a greater addition than that of my years. I cannot affirm that I pity our friend,[3] but, I pity his friends. ⌐I cheifly pity the Dutchess,¬ I pity you, & would at least equally pity myself, if I lived amongst you, because I should see him oftener than you did, who are a kind of Hermit, How great a noise soever you make, by your ill nature in not leting the honest villians of the times enjoy themselves in this world, which is their only hap-piness, & terrifying them with another. I should have added in my libel, that of all men living, you are the most happy in your enemys and your friends: And I will swear you have fifty times more Charity for mankind than I could ever pretend to. Whether the production you mention came from the Lady or the Lord,[4] I did not imagine that they were at least so bad versifyers, Therefore, facit indignatio versum, is only to be applyed when the indignation is against general vilany and never operates when a vilian[5] writes to defend himself. I love to hear them reproach you for dullness; Only I would be satisfied, since you are so dull, why are they so angry? Give me a shilling, and I will ensure you, that posterity shall never know, you had one single enemy, ⌐always¬ excepting those whose memory you have preserved. ⌐All things in verse good or bad that London produces, are printed here. among the rest, the Essay on Man, which is understood to come from Doctor Young. No body names you for it here (we are better judges, and I do not railly) It is too Philosophical for me, It is not equall, but that author our friend, never wants some lines of Excelent good sense. *What is, is best*, is the thought of Socrates in Plato, because it is per-mitted or done by God. I have retained it after reading Plato many years ago. The Doctor is not merry enough nor angry enough for the

---

[1] impostor] imposture *1741*.
[3] our friend, but] our friend Gay, but *1741*.
[5] When a vilian] when some sort of people *1741*.

[2] the knave] they *1741*.
[4] Lady Mary or Lord Hervey.

present age to relish as he deserves.⌝ I am sorry for the scituation of Mr Gay's papers. You do not exert your self as much as I could wish in this affair; I had rather the two Sisters were hangd than see his works swelled by any loss of credit to his memory: I would be glad to see his valuable works printed[1] by themselves, those which ought not to be seen burned immediately, and the others that have gone abroad, printed seperately like Opuscula or rather be stifled & forgotten. I thought your Epitaph was immediately to be ingraved, & therefore I made less scruple to give a Copy to Lord Orrery, who earnestly desired it, but to no body else; and he tells me, he gave onely two, which he will recall. I have a short epigram of his upon it, wherein I could correct a line, or two at most, and then I will send it you (with his permission). I have nothing against yours but the last line, *Striking their akeing*, the two participles seem as they are so near, to sound too like. I shall write to the Dutchess who hath lately honoured me with a very friendly letter, and I will tell her my opinion freely about our friend's papers . . I want health; my affairs are embroyled:[2] but I will break through the latter if the other mends. I am in[3] a course of Medicines, lame and giddy. My cheif design next to seeing you is to be a severe Critick on you and your neighbor, but first kill his father that he may be able to maintain me in my own way of living, & particularly my horses, it cost me near 600ll for a wall to keep mine, & I neer ride without two Servants for fear of accidents; *hic Vivimus ambitiosâ paupertate*; ⌜I drink a pint and half of wine every day, the pint at noon, & the half at night.⌝ You are both too poor for my acquaintance, but he much the poorer. ⌜With you I will find grass, & wine, & servants; but with him not.—The homage you paid, &c. was more your goodness &c. I will pay none:⌝ The Collection you speak of is this. A Printer came to me to desire he might print my works (as he calld them) in 4 volumes by subscription. I said I would give him no leave, & should be very sorry to see them printed here. He said they could not be printed in London, I answerd, they could if the partners agreed. He said he would be glad of my permission, but as he could print them without it, and was advised that it Could do me no harm, & having been assured of numerous subscriptions, he hoped I would not be angry at his persuing his own Interest, &c. ⌜without giving me any just offence;⌝ much of this discourse past, and he goes on with the matter, wherein I determine not to intermeddle, though it be much to my discontent, and I wish it could be done in England, rather than here, allthough I am grown perfectly indifferent in every thing of that kind. This is the ⌜very⌝ truth of the story. ⌜There is no property among Printers here, neither will it be one farthing in my

---

[1] his valuable works printed] the most valuable printed *1741*.
[2] embroyled] enlarged *1741*.   [3] am in] can use *1741*.

pocket; For among us, mony for Copys is a thing unheard of.⌐ My Vanity turns wholly at present in being personated in your *Quae virtus* &c. ⌐But in order to that, I desire to be represented as a man of thrift onely as it produceth Liberty and Independance, without any thoughts of hoarding; and as one who bestowes every year at least one third of his income; though sunk a third by the misery of the Country. I had letters lately from Lord Carteret, Lord Masham & Lord Bathurst. I will answer to the two latter, & have already done the first, so you may spare my service. I will write to Lord Peteb. to be left at your house. Service to Dawley & Mr Poulteney, the Doctor Mr Lewis &c. when you meet them.⌐ You will observe in this letter many marks of an ill head, & a low spirit, but a heart wholly turned to love you with the greatest earnestness & truth.[1] ⌐My humble service to Mrs Pope, & Patty. I love her good nature in being so afflicted for our friend. I cannot but send you Lord Orrery's verses on you. Dr. D— presents particularly his most humble service.

> Entomb'd with Kings though Gay's cold ashes lye
> A Nobler Monument thy strains supply.
> Thy matchless Muse still faithfull to thy friend
> Unaw'd by Courts, his Virtues dare commend.
> Lamented Gay, forget your treatment past,
> Look down and see your merit crownd at last:
> A destiny more glorious, who could hope?
> Belov'd in Life, in Death bemoan'd by Pope.

My Lord altered almost every line from the first Copy, and all for the better, and more than we desired; but his modesty equals his other virtues. Dr Sheridan desires, that if a little staring boy of eleaven years old should happen to appear in your sight, when you come to town, & you let him look round you, and hear you speak, that you will treat him with your usual humanity, & let him boast that he hath seen you, & it happens, that few boys can better deserve such a favour.⌐

Address: To Alexander Pope Esqr at Twitenham in Middlesex. By London.

SWIFT *to* POPE[2]　　　　　　　　　　　　　　　12 *May* 1735

Portland Papers

Your Letter was sent me yesterday by Mr Stopford who landed the same day, but I have not yet seen him. As to my silence, God knows

---

¹ The printed text of 1741 ended here.

² Pope's printed text of this letter (1741), here given, iii. 456, is considerably abbreviated from this present text taken from the transcript made for, but not included in, the group of Harleian transcripts. The present text was discovered by Sir Harold Williams, through whose kind offices, and the gracious permission of the Duke of Portland, it is here printed.

it is my great misfortune; ⌐I never am a day without frequent terrors
of a fit of Giddyness; my head is never well, and I cannot walk after
night-fall. My Memory is going fast; my spirits are sunk nine parts in
ten. You will find in this Letter probably fifty blunders, mistakes not
only litteral & verbal, but half sentences either omitted or doubled.
Besides,⌐ my little domestick affairs are in great confusion by the villany
of Agents, and the miseryes of this Kingdom, where there is no money
to be had: Nor am I unconcern'd to see all things tending towards
absolute Power, in both Nations. (it is here in perfection already)
although I shall not live to see it established. This condition of things
both publick and personal to my self, hath given me such a kind of
despondency, that I am almost unqualifyed for any company, Diversions, or Amusement. ⌐I dine alone four fifths of the week & pass the
whole Evening by my self at home. If I ride, one of my servants carryes
my dinner & wine to some acquaintance at four or five miles distance.
My Eyes will not suffer me to read much, nor at all at night; and as to
writing, I have lost all inclination & ability, even to correct or finish
some things that have many years layn by me. But what is worse, I am
pester'd twenty times a morning with impertinent business, relating
to my station.⌐ The Death of Mr Gay & the Doctor hath been
terrible wounds near my heart. Their living would have been a great
comfort to me, although I should never have seen them, like a Sum
of Money in a Bank from which I should receive at least annual
Interest, as I do from you; and have done from My Lord Bolingbroke.
To show in how much ignorance I live, It is hardly a fortnight since
I heard of the Death of ⌐my dear Friend⌐ My Lady Masham, my
constant friend in all changes of times. God forbid that I should expect
you to make a voyage that would in the least affect your health: but
in the meantime how unhappy am I, that my best friend should have
perhaps the only kind of disorder for which a sea voyage is not in some
degree a Remedy. The ⌐D.⌐ old D. of Ormonde said, he would not
change his dead son [Ossory] for the best living son in Europe. Neither
would I change my absent[1] friend for the best ⌐present⌐ friend round
the Globe. ⌐Lord B— acts a very high part of Friendship in accom-
panying Lord Berkeley. .[2] I am glad he begins to learn frugality, I
hope it is not too late, But as to his breathing after retirement, I fear
he will hardly find it till he breathes his last.⌐ I have lately read a book
imputed to him, called a Dissertation upon Partyes. I think it very
masterly written ⌐but whether it be his or your Neighbor friend's,[3]
or both, is not agreed on here. In a former letter you desired me to

[1] Pope.
[2] *The General Evening Post*, 24 Apr. 1735, reports: 'The Lord Bolingbroke accompanies
the Earl of Berkeley, and his son the Ld Dursley, to Paris.' On 17 Aug. James, 3rd Earl of
Berkeley died at the seat of the Duke of Rutland at Aubigny (France).
[3] William Pulteney?

advise Lord B— to forbear a Frailty which he has no call for. but I had not courage to attempt. It is very wrong in every view as well as that of Immorality, and I wish you who are present would have undertaken the office. Is Lord Berkeley's voyage for Life owing alone to his ill habit of Body, (which I foretold him in his youth, & reminded him the last time I saw him) or is it hastned by any discontent at publick proceedings. Lord E.[1] too did not write to me as you thought he would, by Mr Stopford. I told you one reason against my going either to France or England. . That I cannot now make shifts. I have my own little regular Oeconomy with my very few servants about me; and dare not venture to be a days Journey from this Town, for fear of taking a fit of giddyness that sincks me for a month, & by which I lose ground that I never quite recover. I was caught so some months ago in a Village six miles from hence, & with the utmost difficulty got home.⌐—Pray God reward you for your kind Prayers. you are a good Man, & a good Christian, & I believe your Prayers will do me more good than those of all the Prelates in both Kingdoms, or any Prelates in Europe except the Bp. of Marsailles.—⌐The bearer of this is a young Gentleman who goes to France to study Physick,[2] he is the eldest son of a wealthy Citizen (as wealth is reckon'd here) his Mother hath more sense, wit, & knowledge than the whole Sex here could make up among them. I esteem her very much, and she is my most usefull Friend. The young man hath taken his degrees, is modest & virtuous, & hath a very good Genius & Taste, which I hope he will be wise enough to apply to his more usefull Study. I could not refuse him the Honor of waiting on you, although his stay in London will not be above a week.—I shall with great pleasure receive the present you make me by Capt. Wentworth;[3] especially if I see in a blank page your name and Attestation. If you are mentioned in any writings imputed to me, you must charge it more upon my Pride than Friendship. I pleased you once with a passage in one of Cicero's letters to a Friend: *Orna me.* And I remember in one of your Letters you said you intended that an Epistle should be inscribed to me. You will please to give or send the enclosed to Mr Poulteney, And I must allways charge you with offering my humble service to Lord Oxford, Lord Masham, Lord Bathurst, and Mr Lewis, when you happen to see them. My Lord Peterbourow hath lived longer than I could ever hope, His death will be a new Affliction to me. This is the necessary tax of long life, that we must suffer the loss of our best Friends.⌐ God ⌐Almighty⌐ preserve you for contributing more to mend the world than

[1] Either Egmont or Essex?
[2] Unidentified.
[3] The present presumably is the second volume (quarto) of Pope's *Works*, published in April.

the whole pack of (modern) Parsons in a Lump.—I am ever entirely yours ⌐J. Swift.⌐

⌐May 12. 1735.⌐
Address: To Alexander Pope Esqr.

SWIFT *to* POPE[1]   *3 September* 1735
Portland Papers

This letter will be delivered to you by Faulkner the Printer, who goes over on his private affairs.[2] This is in answer to yours of two months ago which complains of that profligate Rogue Curl, ⌐although I believe I answered it already, and yet my memory decays so fast, that every day I less & less depend upon it.⌐ I heartily wish you were what they call disaffected, as I⌐, who detest abominate & abhor every Creature who hath a dram of Power in either Kingdom. Yet⌐ I may say as David did ⌐to God;⌐ I have sinned greatly, but what have these sheep done? You have given no offence to the Ministry nor to the Lords, nor Commons, nor Qu— nor the next in Power, ⌐I mean the K—although your thoughts of them all are the same with mine.⌐ For you are a Man of Virtue, and therefore must abhor vice & all Corruption, although your discretion holds the reins. ⌐Therefore, you merited a better Treatment from the H. of Lords, than that they should let so infamous & so abandoned a Rogue triumph over you in so publick a manner.⌐ You need not fear any Consequence in the Commerce that hath so long passed between us, although I never destroy'd one of your Letters. But my Executors are Men of Honor and Virtue, who have strict orders in my Will to burn every Letter left behind me.[3] Neither did our letters contain any turns of Wit or fancy, or Politicks or Satyr, but meer innocent friendship; yet I am loth that any Letters from you & a very few other friends should dye before me; I believe we neither of us ever leaned our Head upon our left hand to study what we should write next; yet we have held a constant intercourse from your Youth and my middle age, & from your middle age it must be continued till my death, which my bad state of health makes me expect every month. I have the ambition, & it is very earnest as well as in hast to have one Epistle inscribed to me while I am alive, and you just in the time when Wit and Wisdom are in the height. I must once more repeat

[1] Pope's briefer text (1740) of this letter is given in iii. 491–3. The Harleian transcript, discovered by Sir Harold Williams, is here printed through his kind offices. Pope's omissions are indicated by half-brackets.

[2] Presumably, in part, to further the sale of Swift's *Works*.

[3] Pope, already involved in publishing his letters, was by this unpleasing remark of Swift's doubtless stimulated to beg for the speedy return of his letters. Later, in publishing the letters Pope carefully suppressed all mention of requests for return: the letters were to appear as if printed in Ireland.

Cicero's desire to a friend, *Orna me*. A month ago, ⌜one⌝ William Duncombe sent me over by a friend of mine, the Works of one John Hughes Esqr, ⌜and makes me a subscriber with an Apology sent me in a short Letter.⌝ They are in Verse & Prose. I never heard of the Man in my life, yet I find your Name as a Subscriber too. ⌜However neither you nor I are numbered among his acquaintance in that short sketch of his Life, where Addison, Garth, Steel, Congreve, & some others who are all dead are mentioned.⌝ The Man is too grave a Poet for me, and I think among the mediocribus in Prose as well as Verse. ⌜Tell me whether you know any thing of him; for his Publisher Duncombe absolutely decides for him, as the best Lyrick Poet of the Age.⌝ I have the honor to know Dr Rundle,[1] ⌜and at his desire went to wait on him.⌝ He is indeed worth all the rest you ever sent us, but that is saying nothing, for he answers your Character; I have dined thrice in his company. He brought over a worthy Clergyman of this Kingdom as his Chaplain, which was a very wise & popular Action. ⌜He is to dine with me when I get a healthy day:⌝ His only fault is, that he drinks no wine, & I drink nothing else. ⌜When do you expect my Lord Bolingb: back from France? Will his Estate hold out as long as his life? & is his worthless Father immortal? Is Mr Poultney often your Neighbor? I write to him by the same bearer with [t]his; and to my Lord Oxford, who is surrounded with happiness & great Allyances. We have a Bishop dead Dr Bram of Cork, the most speculative writer of his Age, and as Scholars tell me, excellent in his way, but I never read much of his works. I hope the D. of D.[2] now the Parliament here is to meet, will find a Successor for once among the whig Divines here, & yet those they have named for Candidates are the very worst they could pick up.⌝ This Kingdom is now absolutely starving, by the means of every Oppression that can possibly be inflicted on mankind.—Shall I not visit for these things sayth the Lord. You advise me right, not to trouble my self about the World. But oppressions torture me,[3] & I cannot live without meat & drink, nor get either without Money; and Money is not to be had, except they will make me a Bishop or a Judge, or a Colonell, or a Commissioner of the Revenue; ⌜Patty Blount wrongs me, or the wrong lyes at your door, for I never sent you a letter wherein she is not remembred, with hearty Professions of Service and Friendship. Mr Faulkner tells me that he hath an Intention to print all your works, (except Homer) in two or three volumes in duodecimo, which although you cannot hinder, yet he desires you will not take ill, & he is ready to submit himself in all points to you. Here you are in my case, for it will be done by some

---

[1] On Rundle see iii. 436, 492, 508.
[2] The Duke of Dorset, at this time Lord Lieutenant of Ireland.
[3] One of Swift's most poignant outcries.

other Printers, who may add spurious things, and make many blunders; whereas Mr Faulkner hath many learned and ingenious Gentlemen who befriended him, & therefore I think you had better indulge what you cannot prevent. I am ever Dearest Sir yours, &c.⌐

⌐Dublin Septr. 3d 1735. where and in what health are my Lord Bathurst and Masham and Mr Lewis?⌐

Address: To Alexander Pope Esqr

POPE *to* THE EARL OF ORRERY¹   12 *July* 1737

1752 (Orrery's *Remarks*, p. 228)

My Lord,—The pleasure you gave me, in acquainting me of the Dean's better health, is one so truly great, as might content even your own humanity: and whatever my sincere opinion and respect of your Lordship prompts me to wish from your hands for myself, your love for him makes me as happy. Would to God my weight, added to your's could turn his inclinations to this side, that I might live to enjoy him here thro' your means, and flatter myself 'twas partly thro' my own! But this, I fear, will never be the case; and I think it more probable, his attraction will draw me on the other side, which, I protest, nothing less than a probability of dying at sea, considering the weak frame of my breast, would have hindred me from, two years past. In short, whenever I think of him, 'tis with the vexation of all impotent passions that carry us out of ourselves only to spoil our quiet, and make us return to a resignation, which is the most melancholy of all virtues.

POPE *to* THE EARL OF ORRERY²   7 *November* [? 1739]

1752 (Orrery's *Remarks*, p. 230)

When you get to *Dublin* (whither I direct this, supposing you will see our dear friend as soon as possible) pray put the Dean in mind of me, and tell him I hope he received my last. Tell him how dearly I love, and how greatly I honour him: how greatly I reflect on every testimony of his friendship; how much I resolve to give the best I can of my esteem for him to posterity; and assure him the world has nothing in it I admire so much, nothing, the loss of which I should regret so much, as his genius and his virtues.

¹ In his *Remarks on Swift* (1752) Orrery printed excerpts from three of Pope's letters to himself expressing warm regard for Swift. One of these (2 Apr. 1738) is here found, iv. 92. Two others are here belatedly added under dates of 12 July 1737 and 7 Nov. [1739].

² For similar excerpts see vol. iv (2 Apr. 1738) and vol. v (12 July 1737).

W. PLOMER *to* POPE[1]   10 *August* 1739

Blickling Hall

Sir,—When Mr Ward and I were to wait on you in September last, I then left with you a Narrative of what passed between your Self and me when the Ground of the then Mrs Howard, now Countess of Suffolk, was going to be set out. This Narrative being afterwards shewn to her and Mr Berkeley by your self, I waited on them, and desired they would secure the new way to me, if not I informd them I must insist upon the old way back again. They both then desired I would stay till about March before I proceeded, for they did intend to purchase the Charity Lease of Mrs Vernon, and should a contest arise before they had agreed with her she (Mrs Vernon) might hear of it and then would exact a larger price for her Lease To this I agreed as they desired, and have now staid till this time, but am no nearer being secured than when I first complaind.

Tho I have applied severall times since I can not get them to sign a common Covenant to support me in the use of the new Way, as was promisd to be done when we consented to the laying the old one into her Garden, which my Lady could not have done without our compliance.

I am very desirous to end this affair without any contest if I could. But unless I will trust to a promise which dies with the Person that makes it, I must either prosecute my Right or set down contentedly and lose it, which last I can not comply with.

I must Sir now take leave to inform you, I had never parted with my Property in the manner I did, was it not for the Faith and Trust I repos'd in Your Self. I confided in what you said and thought my self very secure of the performance, beleiving I had to doe with a man of strict Honour. This consideration makes me yet think you will see that Justice done me I have so much reason to expect from You.

I here send a copy of the last drawn paper which was lately sent to Mr Berkeley, which I desier you will take into your consideration. If the Countess and he comes into this it will end all our dispute, and prevent the filing a Bill in Chancery. In consequence of which you know Sir very well that I shall be obliged to make you a party. I am | Sir | Your most obedient Humble Servant | W. Plomer.

London August 10th 1739

[1] This letter, discovered by R. W. Ketton-Cremer, Esq., who kindly furnished the editor with a photostat, concerns the long-prolonged trouble of the owner of Marble Hill with the Vernon family, from whom the grounds were in part purchased for Mrs. Howard. It seems not to have been to the interest of Mrs. Howard (Countess of Suffolk) to settle the matter expeditiously. See here ii. 259 for an early letter relating to the affair, and also Lord Islay's letter, here v. 5.

Least the Narrative I left with you should happen to be mislaid, I have herewith sent another copy of it.

Address: To | Alexander Pope Esqr | Twickenham

POPE *to* [? G.] ARBUTHNOT[1]   [? 1740]

Sotheby 14 March 1912

Sunday.

Dear Sir, may God be your comfort & may all good befall you! no man more truly wishes it than I.

[1] If addressed to George Arbuthnot this letter might date in May 1740 when Margaret Arbuthnot died. She was the sister of George. Since Charles Arbuthnot, son of the doctor, died on Saturday, 4 Dec. 1731, one wonders if this Sunday note might then have been addressed to the doctor.

ALPHABETICAL LIST OF CORRESPONDENCES

This list is designed to enable readers to reconstitute a single correspondence if they so desire. In the entries double-dating for the months of January to March has been abandoned in favour of the modern system; thus 1714/15 becomes 1715. Asterisks (*) are prefixed to dates of letters that have not been printed hitherto in collected editions of Pope's letters. A dagger (†) indicates that the text comes only from Pope's printings; a double dagger (‡) indicates that the letter is a fabrication—made possibly from two or more genuine letters; and parallel lines (‖) indicate that the letter, though printed by Pope, here comes from a more reliable text. The use of italic type in an entry indicates that the letter is *from* and not *to* the person under whose name it is entered.

ANONYMOUS OR UNKNOWN CORRE-
SPONDENTS
1 March 1705 . . .	i. 4	
[10 February 1715?] . .	i. 277	
[Summer of 1715] . .	i. 305	
†[? 1716]	i. 380	
†[?*1716*]	i. 380	
†[? 1716]	i. 381	
*[June 1717]. . . .	i. 413	
†[Summer of 1717] . .	i. 420	
†[? September 1717 . .	i. 431	
*[*October 1717*] . .	i. 433	
*[? October 1717]. . .	i. 436	
1 June 1719. . . .	ii. 5	
*[1719]	ii. 18	
*[? August 1721] . . .	ii. 80	
21 March 1722 (no text) .	ii. 110	
[February 1726] . . .	ii. 367	
*2 September 1731 (to the Duke of ——). . .	iii. 223	

JOSEPH ADDISON
‡30 July 1713 . . .	i. 183	
‡26 *October 1713* . .	i. 196	
†*2 November 1713* .	i. 196	
‡[December 1713?] . .	i. 197	
‡14 December 1713 . .	i. 201	
‡30 January 1714. . .	i. 208	
†10 October 1714. . .	i. 263	

WILLIAM AIKMAN
[1725]	ii. 294	

RALPH ALLEN
*7 April 1736 . . .	iv. 9	
30 April [1736] . . .	iv. 13	
5 June [1736] . . .	iv. 18	
*18 July [1736] . . .	iv. 23	
*30 July [1736] . . .	iv. 24	

RALPH ALLEN (*cont.*)
*8 September [1736] . .	iv. 31	
*7 October 1736 . . .	iv. 36	
6 November 1736 . .	iv. 40	
*14 May 1737 . . .	iv. 68	
8 June 1737. . . .	iv. 74	
*26 July [1737] . . .	iv. 82	
*28 August 1737 . . .	iv. 83	
*11 October 1737. . .	iv. 86	
[24 November 1737] . .	iv. 89	
28 April [1738] . . .	iv. 92	
*[6 July 1738] . . .	iv. 108	
*19 August [1738] . .	iv. 119	
*10 October 1738. . .	iv. 134	
2 November [1738] . .	iv. 144	
*9 January [1739] . .	iv. 157	
*6 February 1739. . .	iv. 165	
*17 April 1739 . . .	iv. 172	
*[5 May 1739] . . .	iv. 175	
*18 May [1739] . . .	iv. 180	
*2 August [1739] . . .	iv. 190	
*14 September [1739] . .	iv. 194	
*25 March [1740] . . .	iv. 230	
*19 April [1740] . . .	iv. 234	
*15 May 1740 . . .	iv. 238	
*27 May [1740] . . .	iv. 245	
*17 June [1740] . . .	iv. 246	
*17 July [1740] . . .	iv. 252	
*[? August 1740] . . .	iv. 254	
3 October [1740] . . .	iv. 273	
*14 October [1740] . .	iv. 280	
*4 November [1740] . .	iv. 290	
*11 November [1740] . .	iv. 292	
*17 November [1740] . .	iv. 297	
*2 December [1740] . .	iv. 299	
*17 April 1741 . . .	iv. 340	

RALPH ALLEN (*cont.*)

*14 May 1741 . . . iv. 343
*5 June 1741. . . . iv. 347
*[? 14 July 1741] . . . iv. 349
*18 July 1741 . . . iv. 351
*23 July [1741] . . . iv. 353
*13 August 1741 . . . iv. 357
*28 August 1741 . . . iv. 360
*24 September 1741 . . iv. 362
*1 October 1741 . . . iv. 363
*[6 January 1742] . . iv. 378
*[9 January 1742] . . iv. 379
*19 January [1742] . . iv. 383
*8 February 1742. . . iv. 386
*[*c*. April 1742] . . . iv. 391
*27 May [1742] . . . iv. 398
*12 June [1742] . . . iv. 401
*19 July [1742] . . . iv. 404
*10 August [1742] . . iv. 411
*[24 August 1742] . . iv. 411
*[13 September 1742] . . iv. 417
*23 September [1742] . . iv. 420
*[? 1 December 1742] . . iv. 428
*8 December [1742] . . iv. 430
*[December 1742]. . . iv. 431
*27 December [1742] . . iv. 432
12 March 1742 . . . iv. 443
*24 March 1743 . . . iv. 449
*[*c*. 30 March 1743] . . iv. 450
*12 April [1743] . . . iv. 452
*14 April [1743] . . . iv. 454
*13 September [1743] . . iv. 471
*30 October 1743 . . . iv. 476
*8 November 1743 . . iv. 479
*17 November [1743] . . iv. 481
*23 November [1743] . . iv. 485
*8 December [1743] . . iv. 486
*3 January 1744 . . . iv. 489
20 January [1744] . . iv. 494
*25 February [1744] . . iv. 502
6 March [1744] . . . iv. 504
*[21 March 1744] . . . iv. 509
*[? 9 April 1744] . . . iv. 517
*20 April [1744] . . . iv. 519
*7 May [1744] . . . iv. 522

GEORGE ARBUTHNOT

1 March 1735 . . . iii. 452
*6 August 1735 . . . iii. 480
[April 1739] . . . iv. 171
3 August [1739]. . . iv. 191
[? 1740] . . . . v. 20
*26 September 1740 . . iv. 267
*[6 December 1740] . . iv. 303
[? 24 October 1741] . . iv. 366

GEORGE ARBUTHNOT (*cont.*)

29 October 1741. . . iv. 367
*[February 1743] (2 letters) . iv. 388
*[April or May 1742] . . iv. 394
*12 February [1743] . . iv. 441
*[1743] . . . . . iv. 442
23 July 1743 . . . iv. 461

DR. JOHN ARBUTHNOT

11 July [1714] . . . i. 233
2 September 1714 (with
  Parnell) . . . . i. 249
†7 September 1714. . . i. 251
†9 July 1715 . . . . i. 305
[*February 1716*] (with Pope
  et al. to Parnell) . . i. 331
[*August 1719*] . . . ii. 9
[*September 1723*]. . . ii. 196
‡10 September [1725] . . ii. 318
23 July 1726 . . . ii. 383
[*c*. 20 September 1726] (to
  Swift) . . . . ii. 401
16 *November 1726* (to Edward, Earl of Oxford) . ii. 411
23 *November 1726* (to Edward, Earl of Oxford) . ii. 417
9 *June 1729* (to Swift) . iii. 36
17 October [1729] (from
  Lady Mary Wortley
  Montagu) . . . iii. 59
[October 1729] (from Lady
  Mary Wortley Montagu) iii. 60
†[*c*. 5 December 1732 ?] . iii. 334
†5 *December 1732* (with Pope
  to Swift) . . . . iii. 334
15 July [1734] . . . iii. 415
†17 *July 1734* . . . iii. 416
‡26 July 1734 . . . iii. 418
2 August [1734]. . . iii. 423
25 August 1734 . . . iii. 428
3 September [1734] . . iii. 431
3 January 1735 (from Lady
  Mary Wortley Montagu) iii. 448

JOHN, 2ND DUKE OF ARGYLE

*25 October [1738 ?] . . iv. 137
*11 July 1739 . . . iv. 189

SIR JAMES ASHE

*[1725] . . . . . ii. 300

FRANCIS ATTERBURY

[*December 1716*] . . . i. 378
||8 *November 1717* . . i. 451
†20 November 1717 . . i. 453
1 *January 1718* . . . i. 459
†18 *February 1718* . . i. 467
3 September 1718 . . . i. 499

FRANCIS ATTERBURY (*cont.*)
8 September 1718 . . i. 499
||*12 September 1718* . . i. 501
August 1720 . . . ii. 51
†23 September 1720 . . ii. 53
||*28 September 1720* . . ii. 54
||*26 March 1721* . . . ii. 73
27 May 1721 . . . ii. 76
2 August 1721 . . . ii. 78
20 August 1721 . . . ii. 79
||*27 September 1721* . . ii. 83
||*15 October 1721* . . . ii. 86
1 January [*1722?*] . . ii. 93
[*? 1722*] . . . . ii. 100
†8 February 1722 . . . ii. 101
||*26 February 1722* . . ii. 104
†14 March 1722 . . . ii. 106
||*16 March 1722* . . . ii. 107
||[*17 or 27 March 1722*] . ii. 108
†19 March 1722 . . . ii. 109
||*6 April 1722* . . . ii. 113
‡*25 May 1722* . . . ii. 119
[*1722*] . . . . . ii. 123
||*15 June 1722* . . . ii. 124
†27 July [*1722*] . . . ii. 127
||[*30 July or 3 August 1722*] ii. 128
August 1722 . . . . ii. 131
||*10 April 1723* . . . ii. 165
||[*20 April 1723*] . . . ii. 166
May 1723 . . . . ii. 168
†May 1723 . . . . ii. 169
||*20 November 1729* . . iii. 76
[1730?] . . . . . iii. 85
23 November 1731 . . iii. 245

HENRY BAKER
[*1723–4*] . . . . . ii. 212
ALDERMAN JOHN BARBER
10 October 1717 . . . i. 444
ALLEN, LORD BATHURST (later Earl
Bathurst)
5 July [*1718*] . . . i. 476
14 August 1718 . . . i. 488
[August 1718] . . . i. 489
†*13 September* [*1719*] . . ii. 13
[*25 July 1722*] . . . ii. 126
21 October 1723 . . . ii. 207
*17 September 1724 . . ii. 257
[*October 1724?*] . . . ii. 262
[*? 1725*] . . . . ii. 292
[*June 1725?*] . . . ii. 298
[*1727*] . . . . . ii. 464
15 September [*1728*] . . ii. 516
7 November [*1728*] . . ii. 524

ALLEN, LORD BATHURST (*cont.*)
*[December 1728] . . ii. 530
11 September 1730 . . iii. 130
19 September 1730 . . iii. 133
1 October [*1730*] . . iii. 136
8 October 1730 (from
Bolingbroke) . . . iii. 139
18 December [*1730?*] . . iii. 156
9 July [*1732*] . . . iii. 295
20 July [*1732*] . . . iii. 299
9 September 1732 . . . iii. 312
6 August 1735 . . . iii. 480
19 August 1735 . . . iii. 483
8 October 1735 . . . iii. 499
[October 1735] . . . iii. 503
14 August 1736 . . . iv. 24
23 November 1738 . . iv. 148
*9 August [*1739?*] . . iv. 192
[28 April 1741] . . . iv. 341
CHARLES BATHURST (bookseller)
29 August [*1740*] . . iv. 259
18 October [*1740*] . . iv. 284
23 October [*1740*] . . iv. 285
*[1740–1] . . . . iv. 324
[3] February 1741 . . iv. 333
[*? May 1741*] . . . iv. 345
15 June [*1741*] . . . iv. 349
[23] July 1741 . . . iv. 352
5 September [*1741*] . . iv. 361
15 November [*1741*] . . iv. 371
EDWARD BEDINGFIELD
16 May 1712 . . . . i. 141
The Rev. GEORGE BERKELEY (later
Dean and Bishop: the philosopher)
†*1 May 1714* . . . . i. 221
7 July 1715 . . . . i. 304
2 November 1717 . . i. 445
[*? 1721*] . . . . ii. 62
The Hon. GEORGE BERKELEY (m. [1735]
Henrietta, Countess of Suffolk)
[*1724*] . . . . ii. 259
HUGH BETHEL
†*12 July 1723* . . . ii. 178
†*9 August 1726* . . . ii. 386
†*24 June 1727* . . . ii. 436
†*17 June 1728* . . . ii. 501
9 June 1730 . . . iii. 113
*[April 1731?] . . . iii. 195
*1 May [*1731*] . . . iii. 196
*28 July 1731 . . . iii. 209
*8 September 1731 . . iii. 227
*[8 October 1731] (with
Martha Blount) . . iii. 232
*[1732?] . . . . . iii. 287

HUGH BETHEL (*cont.*)

*5 May [1732]	. .	iii. 287
†9 August 1733	. .	iii. 380
*[1733 ?]	. .	iii. 388
*6 August [1734].	. .	iii. 426
*28 September [1734]	.	iii. 435
*4 October [1734]	.	iii. 436
Undatable letters.	.	iii. 518–19
*16 June [1736]	.	iv. 21
*2 November 1736	.	iv. 39
*11 February [1737]	.	iv. 57
*[? May 1737]	.	iv. 67
*[May 1737].	. .	iv. 67
*25 September 1737	.	iv. 85
*31 July 1738	. .	iv. 113
19 November 1738	.	iv. 146
*27 November 1739	.	iv. 205
*18 February [1740]	.	iv. 224
[1740] .	. .	iv. 253
*2 August 1740	.	iv. 254
*26 September [1740]	.	iv. 268
28 November [1740]	.	iv. 298
*14 April [1741]	.	iv. 338
*[? 1741]	. .	iv. 354
*1 January [1742]	.	iv. 375
*21–23 May 1742.	.	iv. 395
*[1742] .	. .	iv. 414
*20 March 1743	.	iv. 445
*16 August 1743	.	iv. 467
*5 October 1743	.	iv. 473
*29 October [1743]	.	iv. 475
*20 February [1744]	.	iv. 498
*19 March [1744]	.	iv. 508
25 March 1744	.	iv. 511
[April 1744]	. .	iv. 514

SLINGSBY BETHEL

14 September 1736	.	iv. 33
*30 September 1736	.	iv. 35
*[Early 1737 ?]	.	iv. 65
12 November 1737	.	iv. 87
*18 March [1739]	.	iv. 168
31 October [1739]	.	iv. 197
15 March 1741	.	iv. 335
*[? 14 October 1741]	.	iv. 365
16 June 1742	.	iv. 401
*22 March 1743	.	iv. 447
28 October [1743]	.	iv. 475
23 November 1743	.	iv. 485
[1744] .	. . .	iv. 488
[1744] .	. . .	iv. 496
*6 February [1744]	.	iv. 496
*8 February 1744.	.	iv. 497
26 March 1744	.	iv. 513

FRANCIS BIRD

[? 1720]	. . . .	ii. 26

EDWARD BLOUNT, of Blagdon, Devon

‡27 August 1714	. .	i. 246
†[*September 1714?*]	.	i. 247
†*11 November 1715*	.	i. 320
†21 January 1716.	.	i. 328
‡10 February 1716	.	i. 329
‡20 March 1716	.	i. 337
†*24 March 1716*	.	i. 337
23 June 1716	.	i. 344
‡8 September 1717	.	i. 424
†27 November 1717	.	i. 454
[*June or July 1719*]	.	ii. 7
30 August 1719	.	ii. 10
†3 October 1721	.	ii. 85
†21 October 1721.	.	ii. 88
†27 June 1723	.	ii. 176
†2 June 1725.	.	ii. 296
†13 September 1725	.	ii. 319

TERESA and MARTHA BLOUNT, addressed jointly

[? July 1713]	. .	i. 182
‖[? September 1714]	.	i. 252
‖[23 July 1715]	. .	i. 307
*1 August [1715]	.	i. 310
[Autumn 1715]	.	i. 317
[June 1717].	. .	i. 409
‖13 September 1717	.	i. 426
‖[September 1717]	.	i. 429
[? 1717] (2 letters)	.	i. 435
[24 October 1717]	.	i. 447
[Late 1717 ?]	.	i. 455
[? 1718]	. . .	i. 460
[? 1718]	. . .	i. 467
[August 1718]	. .	i. 490
17 September [1718]	.	i. 512
8 October [1718]	.	i. 514
[1719] .	. . .	ii. 1
[? 1720]	. . . .	ii. 21

MARTHA BLOUNT

25 May 1712	. .	i. 143
‖6 October [1714]	.	i. 259
[Post 24 November 1714]	.	i. 268
†[February 1715 ?]	.	i. 280
3 June [1715]	.	i. 293
[19 August 1715]	.	i. 315
†[? 1715]	. . .	i. 318
[? March 1716]	. .	i. 338
[November 1716]	.	i. 375
[December 1716]	.	i. 379
[*c. 10 November 1717*]	.	i. 452

MARTHA BLOUNT (*cont.*)

6–9 August 1718 . .	i. 479
[? *September 1719*] . .	ii. 11
30 October [1719?] . .	ii. 16
[January 1720] . . .	ii. 30
*[*August 1723*] . . .	ii. 191
†[15 June 1724] . . .	ii. 235
22 June [1724?] . . .	ii. 236
29 February 1728 (from Swift) . . .	ii. 475
7 May 1728 (to Swift) .	ii. 490
‡[September 1728] . .	ii. 511
4 September [1728] . .	ii. 513
[*8 October 1731*] (with Pope: to Hugh Bethel) .	iii. 232
†[? 6 December 1732] . .	iii. 335
†*7 September 1733* . .	iii. 385
11 August [1734] . .	iii. 427
[17 September 1734] . .	iii. 434
25 August 1735 . . .	iii. 487
26 August [1736] (with Pope: to Fortescue) . . .	iv. 28
10 December [1736] (with Pope: to Mrs. Knight .	iv. 47
[? June 1739] . . .	iv. 183
4 July [1739] . . .	iv. 185
[7 July 1739] . . .	iv. 187
[? 19 November 1739] .	iv. 200
24 [November 1739] . .	iv. 204
27 December [1739] . .	iv. 211
8 September 1740 (to Mrs. Price)	iv. 265
[11 August 1741] . .	iv. 355
[*28 July or 4 August 1743*]	iv. 462
[Early August 1743] . .	iv. 463
[25 March 1744] . .	iv. 510

TERESA BLOUNT

‖September [1714] . .	i. 256
‖[Late October 1714] . .	i. 264
[10 February 1715?] . .	i. 277
[? 1716]	i. 349
7 August [1716] . . .	i. 349
[1717?]	i. 434
[*Autumn 1717*] . . .	i. 435
[? 1717]	i. 456
31 December 1717 . .	i. 458
[? 1718]	i. 459
[? 1718]	i. 460
21 February [1718] . .	i. 468
[October 1718] . . .	i. 517
[? 1720]	ii. 25
[? 1720] (two letters) .	ii. 26
[*c.* 2 February 1720] . .	ii. 31
[6 or 13 March 1720] .	ii. 38

TERESA BLOUNT (*cont.*)

[1720]	ii. 57
11 December 1720 . .	ii. 59

HENRY, VISCOUNT BOLINGBROKE

[*August 1723*] (to Swift) .	ii. 186
18 February 1724 . .	ii. 218
9 April 1724 . . .	ii. 226
18 August 1724 . . .	ii. 249
22 March 1725 (to Lord Harcourt)	ii. 290
‖14 December 1725 (with Pope: to Swift) . .	ii. 348
23 July 1726 (to 'the Three Yahoos')	ii. 383
22 September 1726 (to Swift)	ii. 402
†[*February 1728*] (with Pope: to Swift)	ii. 472
†*5 April 1729* (from Swift) .	iii. 27
‖*30 August–5 October 1729* (to Swift)	iii. 47
31 October 1729 (from Swift)	iii. 63
‖*19 November 1729* (to Swift)	iii. 70
†21 March 1730 (from Swift)	iii. 98
‖[*9 April 1730*] (to Swift) .	iii. 101
8 October 1730 (to Lord Bathurst)	iii. 139
†*January 1731* (to Swift) .	iii. 163
[*20 March 1731*] (with Pope: to Swift)	iii. 183
2 August 1731 (to Swift) .	iii. 210
†[*March 1732*] (with Pope: to Swift)	iii. 274
12 April 1734 (to Swift) .	iii. 404
27 June–6 July 1734 (to Swift)	iii. 411
15 September 1734 (with Pope: to Swift) . .	iii. 431
8–24 August 1738 (from Swift)	iv. 115
3 September 1740 . .	iv. 260
[*21 May 1743*] (to Lord Marchmont) . . .	iv. 456
[January 1744] (also to Lord Marchmont) . . .	iv. 490
[*14 February 1744*] (to Lord Marchmont) . . .	iv. 498
[*1744*] (to Lord Marchmont)	iv. 503
[26 March 1744] (also to Marchmont) . . .	iv. 513
[*1744*] (to Lord Marchmont)	iv. 519

WILLIAM BORLASE, D.D.

*9 March [1740] . . .	iv. 228
*8 June 1740. . . .	iv. 245

FRANCIS BOURNE
[*October 1717?*] (a draft
    composed by Pope) . i. 436
JOSEPH BOWLES
*26 September 1721 . . ii. 83
WILLIAM BOWYER, the younger
*[? 1741] . . . . iv. 338
*13 November [1742] . . iv. 426
3 November [1743] . . iv. 477
23 February [1744] . . iv. 501
3 March 1744 . . . iv. 504
*[March 1744] . . . iv. 505
*[March or April 1744] . iv. 514
CHARLES BRIDGEMAN
28 September 1724 . . ii. 261
[1725] . . . . . ii. 327
RALPH BRIDGES
*3 March 1708 . . . i. 41
5 April [1708] . . . i. 43
2 July 1715 . . . . i. 303
CHARLES BRINSDEN
*[15 November 1739] . . iv. 200
*20 November 1741 . . iv. 372
*15 March 1742 . . . iv. 389
JOHN BRINSDEN
*15 December 1739 . . iv. 209
November [1740] . . iv. 289
*[c. 17 January 1741] . . iv. 329
8 June 1741. . . . iv. 348
*[? August 1741] . . iv. 354
*21 January [1742] . . iv. 384
*30 June 1742 . . . iv. 403
HENRY BROOKE
[*November 1739*] . . iv. 198
1 December 1739 . . iv. 207
[*1739–40*] . . . . iv. 212
WILLIAM BROOME
30 May [1714] . . . i. 227
[November 1714] . . i. 266
29 November 1714 . . i. 270
29 January [1715] . . i. 275
10 February 1715 . . i. 276
16 June [1715] . . . i. 297
6 December [1715] . . i. 321
[? 1717] . . . . i. 394
16 February 1719 . . ii. 3
31 December [1719] . . ii. 19
24 March 1720 . . . ii. 40
[1720] . . . . . ii. 48
December [1720] . . ii. 59
16 July 1721 . . . ii. 76
10 February [1722] . . ii. 102
March 1722 (from Fenton) ii. 105
April [1722] (with Fenton) ii. 110

WILLIAM BROOME (*cont.*)
23 May 1722 (from Fenton) ii. 119
29 May 1722 (to Fenton) . ii. 121
7 June 1722 (from Fenton) ii. 122
9 July [1722] . . . ii. 125
12 August [1722] . . ii. 130
18 September 1722 . . ii. 134
22 November [1722] . . ii. 144
13 December 1722 (from
    Fenton) . . . . ii. 147
23 December 1722 (to
    Fenton) . . . . ii. 150
1 January 1723 (from
    Fenton) . . . . ii. 151
1 January 1723 (from
    Fenton) . . . . ii. 152
6 March 1723 (to Fenton). ii. 162
6 April [1723] . . . ii. 163
14 July [1723] . . . ii. 182
3 October [1723] . . ii. 204
24 October 1723. . . ii. 208
24 December 1723 . . ii. 210
28 December 1723 . . ii. 211
9 January 1724 (from
    Fenton) . . . . ii. 214
30 January [1724] (with
    Fenton) . . . . ii. 215
6 March [1724] . . . ii. 223
3 April 1724 . . . ii. 225
24 April 1724 . . . ii. 231
30 April 1724 (from Fenton) ii. 231
31 May 1724 (from Fenton) ii. 233
4 July [1724] . . . ii. 241
19 July 1724 (from Fenton) ii. 244
16 August [1724] . . ii. 247
12 September 1724 . . ii. 256
8 October [1724] . . ii. 264
31 October [1724] . . ii. 269
[November 1724] . . ii. 271
4 December 1724 . . ii. 273
19 December 1724 (from
    Fenton) . . . . ii. 278
13 February [1725] . . ii. 287
5 March [1725] . . . ii. 287
30 March [1725] . . ii. 291
8 April 1725 . . . ii. 292
25 May [1725] . . . ii. 295
29 June [1725] . . . ii. 302
14 September [1725] . . ii. 320
2 November [1725] . . ii. 336
10 November 1725 . . ii. 338
20 November [1725] (from
    Fenton) . . . . ii. 339
22 November [1725] . . ii. 340

WILLIAM BROOME (*cont.*)

1 December 1725 (to Fenton)	ii. 344
21 December 1725 (from Fenton)	ii. 351
30 December 1725 . .	ii. 355
2 January 1726 . . .	ii. 357
13 January 1726 (from Fenton)	ii. 360
20 January 1726. . .	ii. 363
29 January 1726 (from Fenton)	ii. 365
[1726] (two letters) . .	ii. 365
16 April 1726 . . .	ii. 374
20 May 1726 (from Fenton)	ii. 377
4 June [1726] . . .	ii. 378
10 June 1726 (from Fenton)	ii. 379
7 August 1726 (from Fenton)	ii. 384
23 August 1726 . . .	ii. 389
26 August 1726 (to Fenton).	ii. 390
5 September 1726 . .	ii. 396
7 September 1726 (from Fenton)	ii. 397
22 November [1726] (from Fenton)	ii. 415
5 December [1726] . .	ii. 420
17 December 1726 (from Fenton)	ii. 422
28 March 1727 (from Fenton)	ii. 429
26 April 1727 . . .	ii. 431
3 May 1727 (from Fenton)	ii. 432
[5 October 1727] . .	ii. 449
3 December [1727] (from Fenton)	ii. 463
9 January 1728 . . .	ii. 470
3 April 1728 (from Fenton)	ii. 486
7 April [1728] (from Fenton)	ii. 487
3 May [1728] (from Fenton)	ii. 488
15 June [1728] (to Fenton)	ii. 499
15 September [1728] (from Fenton)	ii. 518
12 March [1729] (from Fenton)	iii. 24
24 June [1729] (from Fenton)	iii. 37
11 August [1729] (from Fenton)	iii. 44
28 September [1729] (from Fenton)	iii. 54
22 March [1730] (from Fenton)	iii. 100
2 May 1730. . . .	iii. 105

WILLIAM BROOME (*cont.*)

16 June [1730] . . .	iii. 116
17 August 1730 . . .	iii. 124
29 August 1730 . . .	iii. 128
14 December [1730] . .	iii. 155
19 May [1731] . . .	iii. 198
22 July 1735 (from Curll).	iii. 475
4 August 1735 . . .	iii. 478
26 August 1735 (from Lintot)	iii. 489
22 September 1735 . .	iii. 495
2 October 1735 . . .	iii. 497
29 October 1735 . . .	iii. 506
18 November 1735 . .	iii. 510
1 December 1735 . . .	iii. 512
12 January [1736] . .	iv. 2
25 March 1736 . . .	iv. 4

JOHN (Sheffield), DUKE OF BUCKINGHAM

*[? 1717]	i. 386
[? 1717]	i. 386
*[? 1717]	i. 387
[August 1718] . . .	i. 485
1 September 1718 . .	i. 492
[? 1718]	i. 508
*[? 1720]	v. 5

KATHERINE, DUCHESS OF BUCKINGHAM

†27 January [? 1722] . .	ii. 99
*30 or 31 March [1724] .	ii. 225
[1725]	ii. 286
[? 1725]	ii. 303

SAMUEL BUCKLEY, Gazetteer and bookseller

*12 February 1723 . .	ii. 157
*20 January 1725. . .	ii. 285
*2 February [1725] . .	ii. 286
20 February [1728] . .	v. 6
26 January [1728] . .	ii. 471
*[1728–9?]	ii. 529
*13 November [1729] . .	iii. 69
*16 June [1732] . . .	iii. 294
20 August [1734] . .	iii. 428
*9 April 1735 . . .	iii. 454
[13 July 1735] . . .	iii. 473
*17 August 1735 . . .	iii. 482
*13 April 1737 . . .	iv. 66
[23 November 1737] . .	iv. 88

RICHARD (Boyle), EARL OF BURLINGTON

†[November 1716] . .	i. 371
*[23 October 1717] . .	i. 447
*14 January 1718. . .	i. 461
*26 August [1718?] . .	i. 491

RICHARD (Boyle), EARL OF BURLING-
TON (*cont.*)
*11 October [1718] . . i. 516
*2 February 1719. . . ii. 1
*[3 February 1719] . . ii. 2
*23 December [1728] . . ii. 532
*[1729] . . . . . iii. 4
*[1729] . . . . . iii. 4
*29 October [1729] . . iii. 61
*2 November [1729] . . iii. 67
[2 *November 1729*] . . iii. 67
[*December 1729*]. . . iii. 82
*16 January 1730. . . iii. 86
*22 May 1730 . . . iii. 111
*[? 1731] . . . . iii. 183
*4 April [1731] . . . iii. 187
*1 June [1731] (2 letters) . iii. 200
*21 December 1731 . . iii. 259
[January 1732] . . . iii. 265
*[? 1732] . . . . iii. 272
[*? 1732*] . . . . iii. 273
*[? 28 July 1732]. . . iii. 302
*19 September 1732 . . iii. 313
*8 *October 1732* . . . iii. 322
*6 November [1732] . . iii. 328
*24 November [1732] . . iii. 332
*30 *November 1732*] . . iii. 333
*[1733] . . . . . iii. 341
*[March 1733] . . . iii. 356
*[? 1733] . . . . iii. 364
*20 [August 1733] . . iii. 382
*[March or April 1734] . iii. 403
*25 July [1734] . . . iii. 417
9 Undatable letters . iii. 515-18
*3 *May [1736]* . . . iv. 14
*[4 May 1736] . . . iv. 14
*[? June 1736] . . . iv. 22
*27 November [1736] . . iv. 43
*[July or August 1737] . iv. 82
*17 August 1738 . . . iv. 117
28 November 1738 (from
William Kent). . . iv. 149
*19 December 1738 . . iv. 153
27 January 1739 (from
William Kent). . . iv. 162
*6 *February 1739* . . iv. 164
*[? 12 April 1739] . . iv. 172
*15 October 1739. . . iv. 196
*19 January [1740] . . iv. 220
*[? 30 April 1740] . . iv. 237
*[1741 ?] (The 'tree petition') iv. 323
*[? 1742] . . . . iv. 408
*[? January 1744] . . iv. 490

DOROTHY (Savile), COUNTESS OF
BURLINGTON
*[1729] . . . . . iii. 20
*8 June [1731] . . . iii. 201
*[? 1732] . . . . iii. 271
*[1732 or 3 ?] . . . iii. 273
*[1732-3] . . . . iii. 341
*20 October [1733] . . iii. 389
*[? Late 1733] . . . iii. 396
*5 December [1733] . . iii. 397
Undatable letter . . . iii. 518
*[1736] . . . . . iv. 1
*[*c.* 8 September 1738] . iv. 124
*29 October 1738 . . . iv. 139
15 October [1739] (text
lacking) . . . . iv. 197
The Rev. MATHER BYLES, of Boston,
Mass.
*7 *October 1727* . . . ii. 450
*18 *May 1728* . . . ii. 494
*25 *November 1728* . . ii. 527
*[? *1736*] . . . . iv. 16

MARY (Freeman) CAESAR (Mrs. Charles
Caesar)
*22 July [1722 or 3] . . ii. 126
10 *September 1723* . . ii. 197
*12 September [1723] . . ii. 198
*23 April [1724] . . . ii. 230
*1 June [1724] . . . ii. 235
*[? 1724] . . . . ii. 262
*[April 1725] . . . ii. 293
*4 August [1725 ?] . . ii. 312
*28 August [1726] . . ii. 391
*7 May [1728] . . . ii. 490
10 July [1729] . . . iii. 39
2 September 1729 (from
Jervas) . . . . iii. 50
*30 June [? 1730] . . iii. 118
*15 November 1732 . . iii. 331
*17 November 1735 . . iii. 509
JOHN, LORD CARTERET (later Earl
Granville)
16 February 1723 . . ii. 159
JOHN CARYLL
||31 July 1710 . . . i. 93
25 January 1711. . . i. 113
15 June 1711 . . . i. 117
||18 June 1711 . . . i. 117
||25 June 1711 . . . i. 120
||19 July 1711 . . . i. 126
2 August 1711 . . . i. 131
[Post 4 September 1711] . i. 133
†23 *May 1712* . . . i. 142

JOHN CARYLL (*cont.*)

‖28 May 1712 . . . i. 143
19 November 1712 . . i. 154
[29 November 1712] . . i. 156
5 December 1712 . . i. 160
21 December 1712 . . i. 165
8 January 1713 . . . i. 170
[? February 1713] . . i. 172
30 April 1713 . . . i. 174
12 June 1713 . . . i. 176
23 June 1713 . . . i. 179
14 August 1713 . . . i. 185
31 August 1713 . . . i. 188
20 September [1713] . . i. 190
‖17 October 1713 . . . i. 193
15 December [1713] . . i. 203
9 January 1714 . . . i. 207
25 February 1714 . . i. 209
12 March 1714 . . . i. 214
19 March 1714 . . . i. 214
19 April 1714 . . . i. 218
1 May 1714 . . . i. 219
†8 June 1714 . . . i. 229
29 June 1714 . . . i. 232
‖[13] July [1714] . . i. 235
†25 July 1714 . . . i. 238
16 August 1714 . . . i. 240
25 September [1714] . . i. 255
26 October [1714] . . i. 265
19 November [1714] . . i. 267
‖3 March 1715 (with Gay) . i. 282
[*c.* 19 March 1715] (with
Gay) . . . . i. 286
[April 1715] (with Gay) . i. 288
[June 1715] . . . . i. 292
29 June [1715] . . . i. 302
13 August 1715 (to Lintot) . i. 312
14 August 1715 . . . i. 313
11 October 1715 . . . i. 317
[? December 1715] . . i. 322
10 January [1716] . . i. 326
‖20 March 1716 . . . i. 335
20 April [1716] . . . i. 339
‖22 June 1716 . . . i. 343
7 June 1717 . . . i. 410
[30 June 1717 ?] . . . i. 413
16 July 1717 . . . i. 416
[6 August 1717] . . . i. 417
18 August 1717 . . . i. 418
22 August 1717 . . . i. 419
6 October 1717 . . . i. 442
[28 October 1717 ?] . . i. 448
6 November 1717 . . i. 448
‖28 December [1717] . . i. 457

JOHN CARYLL (*cont.*)

18 January 1718 . . . i. 461
25 January 1718 . . . i. 462
4 February [1718] . . i. 463
18 February 1718 . . i. 464
29 March [1718] . . . i. 471
1 May [1718] . . . i. 474
June 1718 . . . . i. 475
11 August 1718 . . . i. 483
3 September 1718 . . i. 497
18 October 1718 . . . i. 517
[November 1718] . . i. 522
[February 1720] . . . ii. 31
3 March [1720] . . . ii. 37
[*c.* 1 May 1720] . . . ii. 42
19 September 1720 . . ii. 53
28 October [1720] . . ii. 57
12 December 1720 . . ii. 60
28 February 1721 (to
Wright) . . . . ii. 72
30 [28 ?] February 1721 . ii. 72
16 July 1721 . . . ii. 77
2 April [1722] . . . ii. 111
[? May 1722] . . . ii. 117
26 October [1722] . . ii. 139
[*c.* 17 May 1723] . . ii. 172
[Mid-June 1725] . . ii. 299
23 November [1725] . . ii. 341
25 December 1725 . . ii. 352
19 January 1726 . . . ii. 360
[February 1726] . . . ii. 366
[1726] . . . . . ii. 380
30 August 1726 . . . ii. 392
5 December 1726 . . ii. 418
[1726–7] . . . . ii. 423
28 March 1727 . . . ii. 428
10 May [1727] . . . ii. 434
5 October 1727 . . . ii. 448
‖3 February 1729 . . . iii. 12
16 February [1729] . . iii. 17
8 April 1729 . . . iii. 30
30 May 1729 . . . iii. 35
8 July [1729] . . . iii. 38
20 July 1729 . . . iii. 40
12 August 1729 . . . iii. 44
30 August 1729 . . . iii. 46
19 October 1729 . . . iii. 60
13 November 1729 . . iii. 70
20 November 1729 . . iii. 74
February 1730 . . . iii. 88
February 1730 . . . iii. 89
12 February 1730 . . iii. 90
10 May 1730 . . . iii. 109
16 June 1730 . . . iii. 115

JOHN CARYLL (*cont.*)
29 July 1730 . . . iii. 122
18 August 1730 . . . iii. 126
22 October 1730. . . iii. 141
6 December 1730 . . iii. 154
6 February 1731. . . iii. 172
15 April 1731 . . . iii. 189
1 November 1731 . . iii. 237
6 March 1732 . . . iii. 273
29 March [1732] . . iii. 279
4 May 1732. . . . iii. 284
20 May 1732 . . . iii. 284
29 June 1732 . . . iii. 294
27 July 1732 . . . iii. 302
27 September 1732 . . iii. 316
14 December 1732 . . iii. 337
January 1733 . . . iii. 340
31 January 1733. . . iii. 345
8 March 1733 . . . iii. 353
20 March 1733 . . . iii. 358
6 May 1733. . . . iii. 369
2 June 1733. . . . iii. 373
25 June 1733 . . . iii. 375
27 August 1733 . . . iii. 383
4 September 1733 . . iii. 384
24 September 1733 . . iii. 387
23 October 1733. . . iii. 390
1 January 1734 . . . iii. 400
28 February [1734] . . iii. 402
19 April [1734] . . . iii. 405
7 July 1734. . . . iii. 414
[*c.* 5 August 1734] . . iii. 425
15 October 1734. . . iii. 437
31 December 1734 . . iii. 446
8 February 1735. . . iii. 450
18 February 1735 . . iii. 451
12 May 1735 . . . iii. 455
17 July 1735 . . . iii. 474
JOHN CARYLL, junior (d. 1718)
8 November 1712 . . i. 150
5 December 1712 . . i. 163
[? Early 1716] . . . i. 334
EDWARD CAVE
[7 October 1735] . . iii. 499
JAMES, DUKE OF CHANDOS
9 January 1715 (to Hon. S.
Harcourt). . . . i. 274
27 December 1731 . . iii. 262
WILLIAM CHESELDEN
21 November [? 1741] . iv. 372
CHARLES CHEVALLIER
[*c. 11 September 1718*] . i. 500

WILLIAM CLELAND
[*16 December 1731*] (to John
Gay) . . . . iii. 254
RICHARD (Temple), VISCOUNT COB-
HAM
1 November 1733 . . iii. 391
8 November 1733 . . iii. 393
NATHANIEL COLE
18 November 1737 . . iv. 87
[*1737?*]. . . . . iv. 88
*17 March 1741 . . . iv. 335
[? May 1741] . . . iv. 345
JOHN CONDUITT
8 November 1727 . . ii. 457
10 November 1727 . . ii. 458
WILLIAM CONGREVE
‡16 January 1715. . . i. 274
‡19 March 1715 . . . i. 285
‡7 April 1715 (with Gay) . i. 290
[*1719*] . . . . . ii. 12
*23 June [? 1719]. . . v. 4
20 January [1720] . . ii. 27
†6 May [1727] . . . ii. 433
THOMAS ('Hesiod') COOKE
11 August 1728 . . . ii. 509
16 September 1728 . . ii. 519
ANT. CORBIÈRE
28 February 1724 . . ii. 223
[*29 February 1724*] . . ii. 223
JUDITH COWPER
30 September 1722 . . ii. 136
18 October [1722] . . ii. 138
5 November [1722] . . ii. 141
[*1722*]. . . . . ii. 143
[*1722*] . . . . . ii. 144
[*1722*] . . . . . ii. 148
17 January 1723. . . ii. 155
2 June 1723. . . . ii. 174
[13 July 1723] . . . ii. 179
29 August [1723] . . ii. 194
26 September 1723 . . ii. 201
9 November [1723] . . ii. 209
LADY SARAH COWPER
*[30 May 1728] . . . ii. 496
DR. WILLIAM COWPER
5 February 1732. . . iii. 268
JAMES CRAGGS (1686–1721), Secretary
of State
†15 July 1715 . . . i. 306
†2 September 1716. . . i. 360
[*? 1717*] . . . . i. 434
1 October 1719 . . . ii. 16
HENRY CROMWELL
12 or 13 July [1707] . . i. 25

HENRY CROMWELL (*cont.*)

‖19 January 1708 (for 22 Jan.
    1709) . . . . i. 36
‖18 March 1708 . . . i. 41
25 April 1708 . . . i. 46
‡27 April 1708 . . . i. 48
†10 May 1708 . . . i. 48
‖1 November 1708 . . i. 51
22 January 1709 . . . i. 54
‖7 May 1709 . . . . i. 56
†10 June 1709 . . . i. 63
†11 July 1709 . . . i. 66
17 July 1709 . . . i. 69
‖29 August 1709 . . . i. 70
‖19 October 1709 . . . i. 72
‖30 November 1709 . . i. 75
‖15 December 1709 . . i. 76
‖10 April 1710 . . . i. 81
‖17 May 1710 . . . i. 87
‖24 June 1710 . . . i. 89
†*15 July 1710* . . . i. 91
†20 July 1710 . . . i. 92
†*3 August 1710* . . . i. 95
‖21 August 1710 . . . i. 96
‖12 October 1710 . . . i. 98
‖28 October 1710 . . . i. 100
†*5 November 1710* . . i. 102
†11 November 1710 . . i. 103
†*20 November 1710* . . i. 104
‖25 November 1710 . . i. 105
†*5 December 1710* . . . i. 108
†17 December 1710 . . i. 109
†30 December 1710 . . i. 111
‖10 May [1711] . . . i. 115
‖10 June 1711 . . . i. 117
25 June 1711 . . . i. 124
‖15 July 1711 . . . i. 125
24 July 1711 . . . i. 130
†*26 October 1711* . . . i. 134
‖12 November 1711 . . i. 135
†*7 December 1711* . . . i. 136
‖21 December 1711 . . i. 137
†27 June 1727 (from Mrs. E.
    Thomas) . . . . ii. 437
†*6 July 1727* . . . . ii. 439
†*1 August 1727* . . . ii. 440
J. CROOKSHANKS
*20 March 1724 . . . ii. 224
EDMUND CURLL, bookseller
27 March 1733 (from 'E. P.') iii. 359
11 October 1733 (from
    'P. T.') . . . . iii. 387
15 November 1733 (from
    'P. T.') . . . . iii. 395

EDMUND CURLL (*cont.*)

22 *March 1735* . . . iii. 460
[March 1735] (adv.) . . iii. 460
[May 1735] (adv.) . . iii. 461
4 April [1735] (from 'P. T.') iii. 461
29 *April 1735* (to 'P. T.') . iii. 462
[*3 May 1735*] (3 letters to
    P. T.) . . . . iii. 463
12 May 1735 (to P. T.) . iii. 464
15 May 1735 (to P. T.) . iii. 465
16 May 1735 (to R. Smith) iii. 466
23 May 1735 (adv. by P. T.
    and R. S.) . . . iii. 467
12 July 1735 . . . . iii. 471
22 *July 1735* (to Wm
    Broome) . . . . iii. 475
26 *July 1735* (adv. 'To the
    Public') . . . . iii. 476
23 August 1735 (from 'S. E.') iii. 487
15 September 1735 . . iii. 493

JOHN DANCASTLE

[*1715*] . . . . . i. 273
*30 May 1717 . . . i. 403
[*Summer of 1717*] . . i. 404
7 *October 1717* (to Pope sr.) i. 443
5 January [1721] . . ii. 63
THOMAS DANCASTLE
*24 April [1716] . . . i. 340
7 August 1716 . . . i. 351
*18 February [1717] . . i. 393
7 *October 1717* . . . i. 443
18 October [1717] . . i. 445
25 October 1718 . . . i. 518
*16 December 1718 . . i. 524
27 *July [1719]* . . . ii. 8
*9 November 1719 . . ii. 18
ISABELLA, COUNTESS OF DENBIGH
*[? 1742] . . . . iv. 397
JOHN DENNIS
29 *April 1721* . . . ii. 75
3 May 1721 . . . . ii. 75
EDWARD DIGBY, eldest son of the 5th
    Lord Digby
18 *July 1724* . . . ii. 243
†21 April 1726 . . . ii. 375
ROBERT DIGBY, brother to Edward
†2 June 1717 . . . . i. 408
†31 March 1718 . . . i. 472
†17 April 1718 . . . i. 473
1 May 1720 . . . . ii. 43
†*21 May 1720* . . . ii. 47
†*9 July 1720* . . . ii. 49
†20 July 1720 . . . ii. 49

ROBERT DIGBY (*cont.*)
†*30 July* [? *1720*]. . . ii. 51
†*12 November 1720* . . ii. 58
†[May] 1722. . . . ii. 115
†[1723] . . . . . ii. 161
†*14 August 1723* . . . ii. 191
†[27 June 1724?] . . . ii. 240
†1 September [1724] . . ii. 253
‡10 September 1724 . . ii. 254
‡28 December 1724 . . ii. 280
2 July 1725 . . . . ii. 304
†12 August [? 1725] . . ii. 314
†10 October [1725] . . ii. 329
WILLIAM, 5TH LORD DIGBY
*8 September [1729] . . iii. 51
ROBERT DODSLEY
5 February 1733. . . iii. 346
*8 May [1734] . . . iii. 407
*20 August [1737] . . iv. 83
'DORIMANT'
18 November 1722 . . ii. 144
3 December 1722. . . ii. 146
12 December 1722 . . ii. 147
JAMES DORMER, Brigadier-General
22 November 1726 (from
J. Gay) . . . . ii. 415
LIONEL, DUKE OF DORSET
9 November 1721 (to Lady
Suffolk) . . . . iii. 241
JOHN DRUMMOND
*1 August 1724 . . . ii. 245
WILLIAM DUNCOMBE
20 October 1734. . . iii. 437
5 November [1734] . . iii. 441
[23 November 1734] . . iii. 442
[6 May 1735] . . . iii. 454

'E. P.' *See under* Edmund Curll
JAMES ECKERSALL
[*6–13 February 1720*] . ii. 32
*14 February 1270 . . ii. 32
21 [February 1720] . . ii. 33
2 March [1720] . . . ii. 34
*[21 March 1720] . . ii. 39
THOMAS EDWARDS
*28 April [1741] . . . iv. 342
29 April 1741 . . . iv. 342
18 July 1741 . . . iv. 351
ABEL EVANS, D.D.
[*August 1717*] . . . i. 420
[*October 1717*] . . . i. 444
[*November 1717*] . . i. 448
13 May 1719 . . . ii. 5
26 July 1719 . . . ii. 8

BRIAN FAIRFAX
14 August 1730 . iii. 124 and v. 8
GEORGE FAULKNER
27 September 1740 (from
Lord Orrery) . . . iv. 270
[*September 1740*] (to Lord
Orrery) . . . . iv. 270
4 October 1740 . . . iv. 275
14 October 1740 (to Lord
Orrery) . . . . iv, 280
18 October 1740 (from Lord
Orrery) . . . iv. 284
4 November [1740] . . iv. 290
6 November 1740 (to Lord
Orrery) . . . . iv. 291
8 November 1740 (from
Lord Orrery) . . . iv. 292
15 November 1740 (to Lord
Orrery) . . . . iv. 295
15 November 1740 (from
Lord Orrery) . . . iv. 295
19 November 1740 (from
Lord Orrery) . . . iv. 298
ELIJAH FENTON
5 May 1717 . . . i. 402
[*September 1718*]. . . i. 496
29 September 1718 . . i. 514
14 September 1719 (to
Lintot) . . . . ii. 15
‡5 May [1720] . . . ii. 45
See also under Broome *for entries.*
ARABELLA FERMOR
†[1714–15] . . . . i. 271
CHARLES FORD
*19 May [1714] (with
Parnell) . . . . i. 223
*[19 July 1714] . . . i. 237
*2 September 1714 (with
Parnell) . . . . i. 249
2 October [1714] . . i. 258
*[1718] . . . . . i. 521
*5 January 1720 . . . ii. 27
*[1725?] . . . . . ii. 283
*[1725] . . . . . ii. 283
*[1725?]. . . . . ii. 284
*22 October [1738?] . . iv. 137
WILLIAM FORTESCUE
[*1716*] (to Gay) . . . i. 341
24 June 1720 . . . ii. 48
3 July 1720. . . . ii. 49
22 February [1722] . . ii. 104
[February 1724]. . . ii. 216
[? July 1724] . . . ii. 241
[? July 1724] . . . ii. 242

WILLIAM FORTESCUE (*cont.*)		
25 *July 1724*	. . .	ii. 245
10 September 1724	. .	ii. 255
17 September 1724	. .	ii. 257
*18 March [1725]	. .	ii. 289
10 May [1725 ?] .	. .	ii. 294
23 September 1725 (with Gay).	. . . .	ii. 322
[October–November 1725]		ii. 335
[*1725*]	.	ii. 346
[*1725*]	.	ii. 346
[*1725*]	.	ii. 347
5 January 1726 .	. .	ii. 358
17 February 1726	. .	ii. 368
2 April [1726] .	. .	ii. 373
16 May [1727] .	. .	ii. 435
*5 August [1727].	. .	ii. 441
‡17 September 1728	. .	ii. 521
[17 or 24 October 1728]	.	ii. 524
[November–December 1728]	. . . .	ii. 529
[Late 1728] . . .	.	ii. 530
*[? December 1728]	.	ii. 530
[January 1729] .	. .	iii. 5
[*1729*]	.	iii. 6
[? 1729] . . .	.	iii. 7
[*1729*]	.	iii. 11
[15 May 1729] .	.	iii. 33
13 September [1729 ?]	.	iii. 52
*20 February 1730	.	iii. 91
*7 June 1730. .	. .	iii. 112
24 August 1730 .	. .	iii. 127
6 September [1730 ?] .		iii. 129
*[October 1730] .	. .	iii. 139
[? October 1730].	. .	iii. 140
[? October 1730].	. .	iii. 141
[April 1731]	. . .	iii. 193
*1 May [1731] .	. .	iii. 196
*[Spring of 1731].	. .	iii. 198
*[Spring of] 1731.	. .	iii. 198
*[2 September 1731]	. .	iii. 224
[? 1732] . . .	.	iii. 264
[? 1732] . . .	.	iii. 265
*[February 1732 ?]	. .	iii. 270
[? Early March 1732]	.	iii. 271
*[May 1732]. . .	.	iii. 283
[? 1733] . . .	.	iii. 342
[18 February 1733]	.	iii. 350
8 March [1733] .	.	iii. 354
18 March 1733 .	. .	iii. 356
[April 1733]	. . .	iii. 364
7 June 1733. .	. .	iii. 374
[? July 1733] .	. .	iii. 376
[? July 1733] .	. .	iii. 376

WILLIAM FORTESCUE (*cont.*)		
*[July 1733] . .	. .	iii. 377
*[November 1733]	. .	iii. 391
13 November 1733	. .	iii. 395
27 March 1734 .	. .	iii. 403
*[May 1734]. . .	.	iii. 407
[June 1734]. .	. .	iii. 409
*17 June 1734 .	. .	iii. 409
November 1734 .	. .	iii. 440
5 [November 1734]	.	iii. 441
[13 December 1734] .		iii. 443
[? 15 December 1734]	.	iii. 443
January 1735 .	. .	iii. 449
[January 1735] .	. .	iii. 450
22 March 1735 .	. .	iii. 453
[? 22 June 1735].	. .	iii. 469
*[? 13 July 1735].	. .	iii. 472
2 August 1735 .	. .	iii. 477
23 August 1735 .	. .	iii. 486
November 1735 .	. .	iii. 508
December 1735 .	. .	iii. 511
*[January 1736] .	. .	iv. 2
26 March 1736 .	. .	iv. 6
[13 April 1736] .	. .	iv. 10
[? 5] May 1736 .	. .	iv. 15
[11 or 18] May 1736 .	.	iv. 18
[30] May 1736 .	. .	iv. 18
[Post 16 June 1736] .		iv. 21
[June 1736]. .	. .	iv. 22
*16 August 1736 .	. .	iv. 26
26 August [1736] (with M. Blount)		iv. 28
*21 September [1736] .	.	iv. 33
3 September 1737	. .	iv. 84
*[December 1737]	.	iv. 89
31 July 1738 .	. .	iv. 114
*8 September 1738	. .	iv. 125
*25 December 1738	. .	iv. 155
*[February 1739].	. .	iv. 166
*27 March [1739].	. .	iv. 169
*[? 26 June 1739].	. .	iv. 183
26 July 1739 .	. .	iv. 189
17 August 1739 .	. .	iv. 193
*[1 or 8 November 1739] .		iv. 198
*20 November [1739] .	.	iv. 202
*1 January [1740]	. .	iv. 214
*5 January 1740 .	. .	iv. 216
*23 January 1740.	. .	iv. 221
*[May 1740]. . .	.	iv. 243
*17 September 1740	. .	iv. 267
*12 August 1741 .	. .	iv. 355
February 1743 .	. .	iv. 440
March 1743. . .	.	iv. 451
[April 1743]	. . .	iv. 454

WILLIAM FORTESCUE (*cont.*)

[4] June 1743 . . .	iv. 456
*15 March [1744] . .	iv. 507
*[? 7 or 14 April 1744] .	iv. 516

JOHN GAY

†13 November 1712 . .	i. 153
†24 December 1712 . .	i. 168
†23 August 1713 . . .	i. 187
†23 October [1713] . .	i. 195
†4 May 1714 (with Parnell)	i. 222
†23 September 1714 . .	i. 254
‖3 *March 1715* (with Pope to Caryll)	i. 282
[*18 March 1715*] (with Pope to Parnell) . . .	i. 284
[*c. 19 March 1715*] (with Pope to Caryll) . .	i. 286
[*April 1715*] (with Pope to Caryll)	i. 288
‡*7 April 1715* (with Pope to Congreve) . . .	i. 290
†8 *July 1715*	i. 305
[*February 1716*] (with others to Parnell) . . .	i. 331
*[1716] (from Fortescue) .	i. 341
[*January 1717?*] . . .	i. 388
†8 November [1717] . .	i. 449
†9 *August* [*1718*] (to Mr. F—)	i. 482
1 May 1721 (to Charles Lockyer)	ii. 75
†11 September 1722 . .	ii. 133
†[September–October 1722]	ii. 137
22 December 1722 (to Swift)	ii. 149
8 January 1723 . . .	ii. 152
†13 July 1723 . . .	ii. 181
[*2 September 1725*] . .	ii. 316
22 September 1725 (with Pope: to Fortescue) .	ii. 322
[*September 1725*] . . .	ii. 323
23 July 1726 . . .	ii. 383
16 September 1726 (to Swift)	ii. 399
[*September 1726*] (to Swift)	ii. 403
15 October 1726 (from Swift)	ii. 406
22 October 1726 (to Swift).	ii. 409
†*17 November 1726* (to Swift)	ii. 413
22 November 1726 (to General Dormer) . .	ii. 415
†16 October 1727 . . .	ii. 453
†*22 October 1727* (with Pope: to Swift)	ii. 454
‖23 November 1727 (from Swift)	ii. 460

JOHN GAY (*cont.*)

12 February 1728 (to Lord Oxford)	ii. 473
15 *February 1728* (to Swift)	ii. 473
26 February 1728 (from Swift)	ii. 475
20 March 1728 (to Swift) .	ii. 478
28 March 1728 (from Swift)	ii. 481
2 August 1728 . . .	ii. 508
†[1729]	iii. 1
†[1729]	iii. 2
†[1729]	iii. 2
‡[1729]	iii. 3
[February–March 1729] .	iii. 19
9 *November 1729* (to Swift)	iii. 68
20 November 1729 (from Swift)	iii. 72
3 March 1730 (to Swift) .	iii. 94
‖19 March 1730 (from Swift)	iii. 96
4 July 1730 (to Swift) .	iii. 119
†21 July [1730] . . .	iii. 121
†18 August [1730] . . .	iii. 125
†11 September 1730 . .	iii. 131
†1 October 1730 . . .	iii. 134
†October 1730 . . .	iii. 138
†23 October 1730 . . .	iii. 142
8 November 1730 (with the Duchess: to Swift) .	iii. 145
‖10 November 1730 (from Swift)	iii. 147
‖19 November 1730 (from Swift)	iii. 151
‖13 March 1731 (from Swift)	iii. 179
20 *March 1731* (to Swift) .	iii. 185
27 *April 1731* (to Swift) .	iii. 194
‖29 June 1731 (from Swift).	iii. 202
18 *July 1731* (with the Duchess: to Swift) . .	iii. 204
‖28 August 1731 (from Swift)	iii. 218
1 November 1731 (with the Duke: to Swift) . .	iii. 238
†*1 December 1731* (Gay and Pope to Swift). . .	iii. 248
‖[*1 December 1731*] (from Swift)	iii. 250
[16 December 1731] (from Cleland)	iii. 254
[*13 March 1732*] (to Swift)	iii. 276
‖4 *May 1732* (from Swift) .	iii. 285
16 *May 1732* (to Swift) .	iii. 288
‖10 July 1732 (from Swift).	iii. 296
24 *July 1732* (with the Duchess: to Swift) . .	iii. 300
‖12 August 1732 (from Swift)	iii. 303
28 *August 1732* (with the Duchess: to Swift) . .	iii. 307

JOHN GAY (*cont.*)
†2 October 1732 . . . iii. 318
‖3 October 1732 (from
Swift) . . . iii. 319
†7 *October 1732* . . . iii. 321
SAMUEL GERRARD
18 April 1740 . . . iv. 234
17 May 1740 . . . iv. 241
JAMES GIBBS
[*1719?*] . . . . . ii. 4
[*1725?*] . . . . . ii. 298
LAWTON GILLIVER, bookseller
1 (or 17) February 1741 (no
text) . . . . . iv. 333
RICHARD GRAHAM
*29 February 1716 . . i. 333
*[2 November 1716] . . i. 366
FLETCHER GYLES, bookseller
*[27 May 1741] . . . iv. 346

CHARLES (Montagu), EARL OF HALIFAX
3 December 1714 . . i. 271
†ANTHONY HAMILTON (General)
10 October 1713 . . . i. 192
ELIZABETH, DUCHESS OF HAMILTON
[*June 1717?*] (by G. Maddison) . . . . i. 404
October [1717] . . . i. 436
[*October 1717*] . . . i. 439
SIMON, VISCOUNT HARCOURT
*19 December 1721 . . ii. 92
*7 April 1722 . . . ii. 114
27 *April 1722* . . . ii. 115
*[17 July 1722] . . . ii. 126
*[24 November 1722] . . ii. 146
6 December 1722 . . ii. 146
*[27 January 1723] . . ii. 156
20 February 1723 . . ii. 160
[6 May 1723] . . . ii. 171
21 June 1723 . . . ii. 175
*22 August [1723] . . ii. 193
*16 October 1723 . . . ii. 205
*22 March 1725 (from
Bolingbroke) . . . ii. 290
3 July 1725 . . . . ii. 306
*1 March 1727 . . . ii. 427
*April 1727 . . . . ii. 430
The Hon. SIMON HARCOURT (1684–
1720)
9 January 1715 (from the
Duke of Chandos) . . i. 274
[*August 1718*] (to Mrs. Pope) i. 491
EDWARD, LORD HARLEY, *see* Edward,
2nd Earl of Oxford

MRS. [MOLLY LEPELL] HERVEY
†[1720] . . . . . ii. 41
AARON HILL
[*? 1720*] . . . . ii. 35
2 March [1720] . . ii. 36
[September 1726 ?] . . ii. 404
18 *January 1731* . . . iii. 164
26 January 1731 . . . iii. 165
28 *January 1731* . . . iii. 166
5 February 1731 . . . iii. 169
10 *February 1731* . . iii. 173
15 February 1731 . . iii. 176
14 March 1731 . . . iii. 182
4 April 1731 . . . iii. 188
5 June 1731 . . . . iii. 200
1 September 1731 . . iii. 222
3 September 1731 . . iii. 226
17 *September 1731* . . iii. 228
25 September 1731 . . iii. 230
30 *September 1731* . . iii. 230
1 October 1731 . . . iii. 231
[4] October 1731 . . . iii. 231
29 *October 1731* . . . iii. 234
29 October 1731 . . . iii. 235
30 *October 1731* (to the
Countess of Suffolk) . iii. 236
1 November 1731 . . iii. 238
[9 December 1731] . . iii. 253
[11 December 1731] . . iii. 253
17 *December 1731* . . iii. 257
22 December 1731 . . iii. 259
[24] *December 1731* . . iii. 261
5 February [1732] . . iii. 267
16 *January 1733* . . . iii. 342
16 *May 1733* . . . iii. 370
22 May 1733 . . . iii. 371
20 *September 1733* . . iii. 386
7 *November 1733* . . iii. 392
10 *November 1733* . . iii. 394
13 November [1733] . . iii. 394
*11 *May 1738* . . . iv. 94
9 June 1738 . . . . iv. 101
17 *June 1738* . . . iv. 103
20 June 1738 . . . iv. 106
25 *June 1738* . . . iv. 107
*15 July [1738] . . . iv. 110
21 July 1738 . . . iv. 110
31 *July 1738* . . . iv. 111
17 August 1738 . . . iv. 118
29 *August 1738* . . . iv. 120
30 August [1738] . . iv. 121
1 *September 1738* . . . iv. 122
12 September 1738 . . iv. 126
23 *September 1738* . . iv. 128

AARON HILL (*cont.*)
29 September [1738] . . iv. 131
4 *October 1738* . . iv. 132
5 November 1738 . . iv. 145
8 November 1738 . . iv. 146
8 December 1738 . . iv. 151
9 *December 1738*. . . iv. 152
15 *January 1739*. . . iv. 158
*22 January [1739] . . iv. 159
26 *January 1739*. . . iv. 161
[14] February 1739 . . iv. 165
21 *February 1739* . . iv. 167
EDWARD HOLDSWORTH
[December 1737] . . iv. 90
WILLIAM HOLMES, D.D.
*28 March 1742 . . . iv. 390
HENRIETTA HOWARD, COUNTESS OF
SUFFOLK (after 1731)
11 August [1724?] (from
the Earl of Islay) . . v. 5
†20 June [1727] . . . ii. 435
[October 1727] . . . ii. 445
[May 1729]. . . . iii. 34
30 October 1731 (from A.
Hill) . . . . . iii. 236
9 November 1731 (from the
Duke of Dorset) . . iii. 241
JABEZ HUGHES
26 February 1720 . . ii. 34
*16 *May 1720* . . . ii. 46
JOHN HUGHES
19 April [1714] . . . i. 218
7 October 1715 . . . i. 316
*22 January [1720] . . ii. 28
22 *January* [1720] . . ii. 28
[January 1720] . . . ii. 29
18 February 1720 . . ii. 33

[ARCHIBALD, EARL OF ISLAY]
11 August [1724] (to Mrs.
Howard) . . . . v. 5

CHARLES JERVAS
[*Post 27 May 1714*] . . i. 226
†28 July 1714 . . . i. 239
†16 August 1714 . . . i. 243
†20 *August 1714* . . . i. 244
†27 August 1714 . . . i. 244
[? *October 1714*] . . . i. 262
12 *June 1715* . . . i. 295
[*June 1715* (with Pope: to
Lintot) . . . . i. 296
28 *June 1715* . . . i. 300
[July 1715] . . . . i. 303

CHARLES JERVAS (*cont.*)
[? *31 July 1715*] . . . i. 310
2 [*August 1715*] . . . i. 311
12 *August 1715* . . . i. 312
[*February 1716*] (to Parnell) i. 331
[? 1716] . . . . i. 340
‡9 July 1716. . . . i. 346
†14 November 1716 . . i. 370
†29 November 1716 . . i. 376
[June–July 1717] . . i. 410
12 December [1720] . . ii. 23
2 *September 1729* (to Mrs.
Caesar) . . . . iii. 50

WILLIAM KENT
28 *November 1738* (to the
Earl of Burlington) . v. 149
27 *January 1739* (to the
Earl of Burlington) . iv. 162
SIR GODFREY KNELLER
18 February 1718 . . i. 466
16 *June 1719* . . . ii. 6
[1719] . . . . . ii. 9
[1719] . . . . . ii. 15
[1719] . . . . . ii. 17
ANN (CRAGGS) KNIGHT. See also
Newsham or Nugent.
[Spring 1728] . . . ii. 485
*[1728?] . . . . ii. 485
[1734] . . . . . iii. 408
5 August 1734 . . . iii. 425
1 September [1734] . . iii. 430
29 August 1735 . . . iii. 490
25 November 1735 . . iii. 511
17 May [1736] . . . iv. 17
6 September 1736 . . iv. 30
30 October 1736. . . iv. 38
10 December [1736] (Pope
with M. Blount) . . iv. 47
JOHN KNIGHT (2nd husband of Ann
Craggs)
4 September 1724 . . ii. 254
*[5 September 1724] . . ii. 254
30 October 1727 . . . ii. 456
24 November [1727] . . ii. 462
[1728] . . . . . ii. 484
[? 1728] . . . . ii. 485
8 November 1729 . . iii. 67
30 July 1730 . . . iii. 122
20 June [? 1731]. . . iii. 202
23 August [1731] . . iii. 217

GEORGE, LORD LANSDOWNE
†10 January 1713. . . i. 172

GEORGE, LORD LANSDOWNE (*cont.*)
†*21 October 1713* . . . i. 194
*3 November 1732 . . iii. 327
MATTHEW LANT
*20 April 1724 . . . ii. 230
BERNARD LINTOT
10 June 1715 . . . i. 294
[June 1715?] (with Jervas) i. 296
22 June 1715 . . . i. 298
*13 August 1715(from Caryll) i. 312
11 [July] 1719 . . . ii. 7
14 September 1719 (from
Fenton) . . . . ii. 15
[1724] . . . . . ii. 248
7 January 1725 . . . ii. 284
26 August 1735 (to Broome) iii. 489
HENRY LINTOT, son of Bernard
*29 *January 1740*. . . iv. 222
16 May 1740 . . . iv. 240
*31 January [1741] . . iv. 333
CHARLES LOCKYER
1 May 1721 (from Gay) . ii. 75
*1 November 1721 . . ii. 91
GEORGE LYTTELTON (cr. Baron Lyttelton, 1756)
4 December 1736. . . iv. 46
22 December [1736] . . iv. 48
13 July 1738 . . . iv. 109
15 August [1738] . . iv. 116
25 October [1738] . . iv. 138
[*c.* 1 November 1738] . iv. 142
[*April 1739*]. . . . iv. 170
12 December 1739 . . iv. 208
13 June [1741] . . . iv. 348
3 November 1741 . . iv. 367
7 November 1741 . . iv. 368

McKRIE (or MACKENZIE)
10 October 1717 . . . i. 443
G. MADDISON (for the Duchess of
Hamilton)
[*June 1717*]. . . . i. 404
DAVID MALLET
1 November [1729] . . iii. 65
12 December 1729 . . iii. 82
21 December 1729 . . iii. 82
*[*January 1730*] . . . iii. 86
[20 or 27 January 1730?] . iii. 87
29 October [1730] . . iii. 143
*29 December 1730 . . iii. 157
[18 February 1731] . . iii. 177
[Spring of 1731] (2 letters) iii. 189
1 September 1731 . . iii. 221
7 November [1732] . . iii. 329

DAVID MALLET (*cont.*)
[? 1733] . . . . iii. 344
*18 March [1733] . . iii. 357
[May or June 1734] . . iii. 408
2 August [1734] . . . iii. 421
[*1735*] . . . . . iii. 457
19 August [1735] . . iii. 484
[16 February 1739] . . iv. 167
17 December 1739 . . iv. 209
25 January 1741. . . iv. 331
[? 1743] . . . . iv. 451
[? 1743 or 1744]. . . iv. 453
7 May [1744] (from Lord
Orrery) . . . . iv. 522
19 May 1744 (to Lord
Orrery) . . . . iv. 522
1 June 1744 (to Lord
Orrery) . . . . iv. 523
HUGH, EARL OF MARCHMONT
10 January 1740. . . iv. 217
29 February 1740 . . iv. 227
22 June [1740] . . . iv. 248
[October 1740] . . . iv. 271
9 January 1741 . . . iv. 327
[? April 1741] . . . iv. 341
10 October 1741 . . . iv. 363
*13 *March 1743* (with Pope:
to Duchess of Marl-
borough) . . . . iv. 444
[21 May 1743] (from
Bolingbroke) . . . iv. 456
[July 1743] . . . . iv. 458
[January 1744] (to Bolingbroke also) . . . iv. 490
[14 February 1744] (from
Bolingbroke) . . . iv. 498
[1744] (from Bolingbroke) iv. 503
[26 March 1744] (to Bolingbroke also) . . . iv. 513
[1744] (from Bolingbroke) iv. 519
SARAH, DUCHESS OF MARLBOROUGH
[1740] . . . . . iv. 258
[1740] . . . . . iv. 258
5 September [1740] . . iv. 264
13 August 1741 . . . iv. 358
[15 August 1741] . . iv. 359
[22 October 1741] . . iv. 366
18 January [1742] . . iv. 381
19 January [1742] . . iv. 382
[February 1742]. . . iv. 389
13 May [1742] . . . iv. 394
[26 August 1742] . . iv. 412
[September 1742] . . iv. 419
[16 September 1742] . . iv. 419

JOHN, 5TH EARL OF ORRERY (*cont.*)

8 *January 1741* . . . iv. 326
10 *January 1741* (to Mrs.
  Whiteway) . . . iv. 327
12 *January 1741* . . . iv. 328
23 January 1741 . . . iv. 330
29 January 1741 . . . iv. 332
22 *March 1741* (with Pope:
  to Swift) . . . . iv. 336
23 July [*1742*] . . . iv. 406
27 *July 1742* . . . iv. 407
27 August [1742] . . iv. 413
13 January 1743 . . . iv. 436
9 February 1743 . . iv. 440
16 *February 1743* . . iv. 442
12 August [1743] . . iv. 466
[18 August 1743] . . iv. 468
30 September 1743 . . iv. 472
17 November [1743] . . iv. 482
19 March 1744 (from Lady
  Orrery) . . . . iv. 507
30 March 1744 . . . iv. 513
10 April [1744] . . . iv. 517
[*c.* 5 May 1744] . . . iv. 521
19 *May* [*1744*] (to Mallet) . iv. 522
19 May 1744 (from Mallet) iv. 522
1 June 1744 (from Mallet) iv. 523

MARGARET, COUNTESS OF ORRERY

*14 October 1742 . . . iv. 422
*31 October 1742 . . . iv. 423
19 *March 1744* (to Lord
  Orrery) . . . . iv. 507

EDWARD (LORD HARLEY); after 1724
  2ND EARL OF OXFORD

6 February 1722 . . . ii. 101
10 *February 1722* . . ii. 102
[1723 ?] . . . . ii. 156
13 February 1723 . . ii. 158
24 August [1723] . . ii. 193
29 September 1723 . . ii. 203
23 March 1724 . . . ii. 224
*22 May [1724] . . . ii. 232
22 September 1724 . . ii. 259
25 *September 1724* . . ii. 260
29 September 1724 . . ii. 261
8 October 1724 . . . ii. 263
26 *October 1724* . . . ii. 268
6 November 1724 . . ii. 270
[*c.* 7 December 1724] . . ii. 275
12 December 1724 . . ii. 275
17 *December 1724* . . ii. 276
22 December 1724 . . ii. 278
[July 1725] . . . . ii. 310
30 July 1725 . . . ii. 311

EDWARD (LORD HARLEY); after 1724
  2ND EARL OF OXFORD (*cont.*)

30 *August 1725* . . . ii. 315
7 September 1725 . . ii. 316
[*c.* 11 October 1725] . . ii. 331
17 October [1725] . . ii. 334
19 *October 1725* . . . ii. 334
[? November 1725] . . ii. 335
7 November 1725 . . ii. 336
[November 1725] . . ii. 338
14 December 1725 . . ii. 347
27 December 1725 . . ii. 354
7 January 1726 . . . ii. 359
22 January 1726 . . . ii. 364
3 March 1726 . . . ii. 369
10 *March 1726* . . . ii. 371
22 March 1726 . . . ii. 371
26 March 1726 . . . ii. 372
3 April [1726] . . . ii. 373
22 *April 1726* . . . ii. 376
3 July 1726 (with Swift) . ii. 381
17 *July 1726* . . . ii. 381
[15 August 1726] . . ii. 387
21 September 1726 . . ii. 402
[27 September 1726] . . ii. 406
16 November 1726 (from
  Dr. Arbuthnot) . . ii. 411
23 November 1726 (from
  Dr. Arbuthnot) . . ii. 417
8 December 1726 . . ii. 421
[22 April 1727] . . . ii. 430
[23 April 1727] . . . ii. 431
[15 August 1727] . . ii. 443
25 August 1727 . . . ii. 444
[2 October 1727] . . ii. 447
13 December 1727 . . ii. 464
26 December 1727 . . ii. 465
28 December 1727 . . ii. 466
[1728–34] . . . . ii. 467
12 February 1728 (from
  Gay) . . . . ii. 473
6 May 1728 . . . . ii. 489
[14 May 1728] . . . ii. 493
[17 May 1728] . . . ii. 493
[20 May 1728] . . . ii. 495
27 *May 1728* . . . ii. 496
[13 June 1728] . . . ii. 498
17 June [1728] . . . ii. 502
[25 June 1728] . . . ii. 502
1 July 1728 . . . . ii. 504
[17 July 1728] . . . ii. 505
[25 July 1728] . . . ii. 506
27 *July 1728* (to Swift) . ii. 506
[17 August 1728] . . ii. 510

EDWARD (LORD HARLEY); after 1724
2ND EARL OF OXFORD (*cont.*)

10 September 1728 . . ii. 514
14 September 1728 . . ii. 515
[27 November 1728] . . ii. 528
[28 December 1728] . . ii. 533
[6 January 1729] . . iii. 7
20 January 1729. . . iii. 9
[21 January 1729] . . iii. 9
[30 January 1729] . . iii. 10
30 January 1729. . . iii. 10
[31 January 1729] . . iii. 11
[1 February 1729] . . iii. 12
[14 February 1729] . . iii. 16
14 February 1729 . . iii. 17
[20 February 1729] . . iii. 19
[March 1729] . . . iii. 25
[March 1729] . . . iii. 25
[13 March 1729] . . iii. 25
27 March [1729] . . iii. 26
[18 April 1729] . . . iii. 31
[16 May 1729] . . . iii. 33
14 August [1729] . . iii. 45
[*c.* 15 September 1729] . iii. 53
6 October 1729 . . . iii. 55
9 October 1729 . . . iii. 56
16 October [1729] . . iii. 58
29 October [1729] . . iii. 62
22 November 1729 . . iii. 78
24 December [1729] . . iii. 83
[29 January 1730] . . iii. 87
[2 April 1730] . . . iii. 100
[16 April 1730] . . . iii. 103
[24 April 1730] . . . iii. 104
[May 1730] . . . iii. 105
[17 May 1730] . . . iii. 110
2 June 1730. . . . iii. 111
8 June 1730 . . . iii. 112
[June 1730 ?] . . . iii. 114
2 July 1730 . . . . iii. 118
[18 July 1730] . . . iii. 120
[20 July 1730] . . . iii. 120
[3 August 1730]. . . iii. 123
1 October 1730 . . . iii. 135
3 November 1730 . . iii. 144
10 November 1730 . . iii. 146
16 November 1730 . . iii. 149
[*c.* 2 December 1730]. . iii. 153
[? 1731] . . . . iii. 159
[11 February 1731] . . iii. 175
[15 February 1731] . . iii. 176
[2 March 1731] . . . iii. 177
[3 March 1731] . . . iii. 178
[5 March 1731] . . . iii. 178

EDWARD (LORD HARLEY); after 1724
2ND EARL OF OXFORD (*cont.*)

[13 March 1731] . . iii. 179
[3 April 1731] . . . iii. 186
22 April [1731] . . . iii. 193
[27 April 1731] . . . iii. 193
2 May [1731] . . . iii. 197
21 May [1731] . . . iii. 199
15 June [1731 ?] . . . iii. 201
10 August 1731 . . . iii. 216
15 August [1731] . . iii. 216
[30 August 1731] . . iii. 221
[31 October 1731] . . iii. 236
7 November 1731 . . iii. 240
[20 November 1731] . . iii. 245
22 January [1732] . . iii. 266
16 [March 1732] . . iii. 278
28 April 1732 . . . iii. 280
22 September 1732 . . iii. 315
23 October 1732 . . . iii. 324
29 October [1732] . . iii. 325
1 December 1732 . . iii. 333
[1733] . . . . . iii. 359
17 April 1733 . . . iii. 365
25 May 1733 . . . iii. 371
[16 August 1733] . . iii. 381
[21 August 1733] . . iii. 382
20 October 1733 . . . iii. 389
26 December – 7 January
   1733–4 . . . . iii. 397
[1734 ?] . . . . iii. 404
2 July [1734] . . . iii. 410
4 August 1734 . . . iii. 424
30 August 1734 (from Swift) iii. 429
1 September 1734 . . iii. 429
10 November 1734 . . iii. 442
30 December 1734 . . iii. 445
3 March 1735 . . . iii. 452
17 June 1735 . . . iii. 468
[21 July 1735] . . . iii. 474
18 August [1735] . . iii. 483
27 August 1735 . . . iii. 489
25 December 1739 . . iv. 211

ROBERT, 1ST EARL OF OXFORD

*[20 March 1714] (from
   Scriblerus) . . . i. 216
*[April 1714] (from Scrib-
   lerus) . . . . . i. 216
*10 April 1714 (to Scriblerus) i. 217
*[17 April 1714 ?] (from
   Scriblerus) . . . i. 217
[? 5 June 1714] (from
   Scriblerus) . . . i. 228
*5 June 1714 (to Scriblerus) i. 228

ROBERT, 1ST EARL OF OXFORD (*cont.*)
12 June 1714 (from Scrib-
lerus) . . . . i. 230
8 July 1718 (from Scrib-
lerus) . . . . i. 478
8 *July 1718* (to Scriblerus) i. 479
||21 October 1721. . . ii. 90
||*6 November 1721* . . ii. 91
*12 December 1721 . . ii. 91

'P.T.' *See under* Edmund Curll.

THOMAS PARNELL
†*4 May 1714* (with Pope: to
Gay). . . . . i. 222
†*19 May 1714* (with Pope: to
Ford) . . . . i. 223
[25 May or 1 June 1714] . i. 225
2 *September 1714* (to Ford) i. 249
*13 September 1714 . . i. 253
18 March [1715] (with Gay) i. 284
7 April 1715 . . . i. 291
27 *June 1715* . . . i. 299
[February 1716] (with Gay,
Jervas, Arbuthnot) . . i. 331
29 July [1716] . . . i. 348
[1717] . . . . . i. 395
6 July [1717] . . . i. 415

JAMES PEARSE
*19 *April 1724* . . . ii. 230
*[2 May 1724] . . . ii. 232

ROBERT PEIRSON
*29 June 1725 . . . ii. 301

JOHN, LORD PERCIVAL (cr. 1733 Earl
of Egmont)
*22 September [1722] . . ii. 135
25 *September 1722* . . ii. 135
*22 *October 1724* . . ii. 267
*26 October 1724. . . ii. 267
*31 *October 1724* . . ii. 268
*20 *November 1724* . . ii. 272
*21 November 1724 . . ii. 273

CHARLES, 3RD EARL OF PETERBOROW
*12 July [1723] . . . ii. 177
[1723] . . . . . ii. 183
*[August 1723?] . . . ii. 189
[1723] . . . . . ii. 196
*[1723] . . . . . ii. 197
24 August 1728 (for 1732) ii. 510
†[*April 1732*]. . . . iii. 281
†[*Early May 1732*] . . iii. 282
†24 August [1732] . . iii. 306
†[*August 1732*] . . . iii. 310
†[September 1732] . . iii. 311
†[*October 1732*] . . . iii. 317

CHARLES, 3RD EARL OF PETERBOROW
(*cont.*)
[*1733*] (to Lady Mary
Wortley Montagu) . . iii. 352
13 *June 1735* . . . iii. 468
*20 August [1735] . . iii. 485

[NATHANIEL ?] PIGOTT
[1737?] . . . . iv. 79

MATTHEW PILKINGTON
22 July 1732 (from Swift) . v. 10
*17 October [1732] . . iii. 323
*[1732] . . . . . iii. 323

CHRISTOPHER PITT
18 *July 1726* (to Spence) . ii. 382
23 July 1726 . . . ii. 382
2 August 1728 (with Spence) ii. 507

W. PLOMER
10 *August 1739* . . . v. 19

VISCOUNT POLWARTH, *see the* EARL OF
MARCHMONT.

ALEXANDER POPE, senior
[March 1717] . . . i. 394
[1717] . . . . . i. 402
17 September [1717] . . i. 433
25 [September 1717] . . i. 433
*7 October 1717 (from the
Dancastles) . . . i. 443

The Rev. ALEXANDER POPE of Caithness
28 April 1739 . . . iv. 93

EDITHA POPE (the poet's mother)
[August 1718] (from the
Hon. S. Harcourt) . . i. 491
22 March 1719 (from Mrs.
Rackett) . . . . ii. 4
19 April [1719] (from Mrs.
Rackett) . . . . ii. 4
[26 *January 1720*] . . ii. 29
[14 May 1723] . . . ii. 172

ANN (SOMERSET) PRICE (Mrs. Uvedale
Price)
8 September 1740 (from
Martha Blount) . . iv. 265
[8 September 1740] . . iv. 266

MATTHEW PRIOR
*[1718] . . . . . i. 521
[February 1720] . . . ii. 30

WILLIAM PULTENEY (later Earl of Bath)
13 *August 1724* . . . ii. 247
4 *September 1724*. . . ii. 254
*22 August 1727]. . . ii. 443

QUEENSBERRY—see GAY.

LOUIS RACINE
*1 September 1742 . . iv. 415

LOUIS RACINE (*cont.*)
*25 October 1742 . . . iv. 422
CHARLES RACKETT, brother-in-law of
Pope
[7 September 1717] . . i. 424
9 September 1717 (from
John Weston) . . . i. 426
13 July [1723] . . . ii. 181
HENRY RACKETT, son of Charles
*[1733 ?] . . . . . iii. 339
MAGDALEN RACKETT, the poet's half-
sister (Mrs. Charles R.)
*22 March 1719 (to Mrs. Pope) ii. 4
*19 April [1719] (to Mrs.
Pope) . . . . . ii. 4
1 August 1719 . . . ii. 9
[1729] . . . . . iii. 6
9 July 1729 . . . . iii. 39
28 July [1734] . . . iii. 421
22 November [1739] . . iv. 203
[? October 1741] . . iv. 365
MICHAEL RACKETT, eldest son of
Charles and Magdalen
*22 January 1739 . . . iv. 160
ELIZABETH (Griffith), Lady Rich
[July 1716] . . . . i. 345
JONATHAN RICHARDSON (father and son)
*[? 1721] . . . . . ii. 61
*[1721–44] . . . . ii. 61
*[? 1722] . . . . ii. 93
6 February [? 1722] . ii. 100
*6 March [? 1722] . . ii. 106
4 November [1722] . . ii. 140
*1 July [? 1723] . . . ii. 177
[1724] . . . . . ii. 272
20 January [1725] . . ii. 284
10 June 1725 . . . ii. 297
13 January [1731] . . iii. 160
3 October [1731] . . iii. 231
2 November [1731] . . iii. 240
February or March 1732 . iii. 269
[October 1732] . . . iii. 326
‖2 November 1732 . . iii. 326
November [1732] . . iii. 330
9 November [1732] . . iii. 330
[November 1732] (from
Richardson, jr.) . . iii. 330
[November 1732] . . iii. 331
[1733] . . . . . iii. 345
[18 February 1733] . . iii. 350
[February 1733] . . . iii. 351
2 March [1733] . . . iii. 352
†10 June 1733 . . . iii. 374
8 January [1734] . . iii. 402

JONATHAN RICHARDSON (father and son (*cont.*)
*25 June [1734 ?] . . . iii. 410
[? 1735] . . . . iii. 457
*22 August [1735] . . iii. 485
*[February 1737] . . . iv. 54
3 March 1737 . . . iv. 58
17 June [1737] . . . iv. 78
[29 June 1737] . . . iv. 79
[? July 1737] . . . iv. 79
18 July [1737] . . . iv. 80
[? July 1737] (no text) . iv. 81
[4 January 1738] . . . iv. 91
*[? 17 August 1738] . . iv. 118
*[? September 1738] . . iv. 123
*20 September [1738] . . iv. 127
*19 November [1738] . . iv. 147
*December 1738 . . . iv. 151
*[Post August 1739] . . iv. 194
*[1 December 1741] . . iv. 374
*[? 3 June 1742] . . . iv. 399
*10 June [1742] . . . iv. 400
*[30 July 1742] . . . iv. 408
*[? August 1742] . . . iv. 409
*[5 August 1742] . . . iv. 409
*14 November 1742 . . iv. 427
21 November [1743] . . iv. 484
*[1744] . . . . . iv. 487
*20 December [1743] or
3 Jan. [1744] . . . iv. 487
3 January 1744 (no text) . iv. 489
26 March 1744 . . . iv. 513
MRS. D. ROBINSON
*9 October 1725 . . . ii. 329
WILLIAM ROLLINSON
[6 or 13 August 1714] . i. 240
NICHOLAS ROWE
[*August 1713*] . . . i. 184
20 *August 1713* . . . i. 186

RICHARD SAVAGE
*17 October 1736 . . . iv. 37
[*c.* April 1742] . . . iv. 392
15 September 1742 . . iv. 417
GEORGE SELWYN
*29 September [1738] . . iv. 130
HENRY, EARL OF SHANNON (for Congreve)
[*1719*] . . . . . ii. 12
THOMAS SHERIDAN, D.D.
12 August 1727 (from
Swift) . . . . ii. 442
6 September [1727] . . ii. 445
[12 October 1728] . . ii. 523

SIR HANS SLOANE
30 March 1742 . . . iv. 391
22 May 1742 . . . iv. 397
CHRISTOPHER SMART
*6 *November 1743* . . iv. 478
18 November [1743] . . iv. 483
JOSEPH SPENCE
18 July 1726 (from
Christopher Pitt) . . ii. 382
2 *August 1728* (with Pope:
to C. Pitt) . . . ii. 507
**11 *September 1730* . . iii. 132
[1733] . . . . . iii. 380
[1 September 1735] . . iii. 491
4 *September 1735* (to
Spence's mother) . . iii. 493
7 October [1735] . . iii. 498
Spence on Pope's last days iv. 525
SIR RICHARD STEELE
26 *July 1711* . . . i. 131
30 December 1711 . . i. 139
20 *January 1712* . . . i. 141
†1 June 1712. . . . i. 145
†18 June 1712 . . . i. 146
†15 July 1712 . . . i. 147
†7 November 1712 . . i. 149
†*12 November 1712* . . i. 152
†6 November 1712 . . i. 153
‡29 November 1712 . . i. 158
†*4 December 1712* . . . i. 159
†[December 1712]. . . i. 159
6 December 1712 . . i. 165
4 August 1713 (to Lintot). i. 184
REV. JAMES STOPFORD
*16 December [1726] . . ii. 421
*17 February 1727 . . ii. 425
*20 November 1728 . . ii. 527
WILLIAM, 4TH EARL OF STRAFFORD
[1725] . . . . . ii. 300
*[*June 1725*]. . . . ii. 303
6 July [1725] . . . ii. 308
12 August [1725] . . ii. 313
5 October [1725] . . ii. 327
JONATHAN SWIFT, D.D.
8 December 1713 . . i. 198
†18 June 1714 . . . i. 230
†*28 June 1715* . . . i. 301
†20 June 1716 . . . i. 341
30 *August 1716* . . . i. 358
10 *January 1721*. . . ii. 64
22 December 1722 (from
Gay). . . . . ii. 149
‖8 January 1723 (to Gay) . ii. 152
‖[August 1723] . . . ii. 183

JONATHAN SWIFT (*cont.*)
[August 1723] (from
Bolingbroke) . . . ii. 186
‖20 *September 1723* . . ii. 198
19 *July 1725* . . . ii. 310
†14 September 1725 . . ii. 321
‖*29 September 1725* . . ii. 324
‖15 October 1725. . . ii. 331
‖*26 November 1725* . . ii. 342
‖14 December 1725 (from
Pope and Bolingbroke) . ii. 348
3 *July 1726* (with Pope: to
Lord Oxford) . . . ii. 381
[*1 August 1726*] . . . v. 6
†4 [*August*] 1726 . . . ii. 384
†22 August 1726 . . . ii. 387
†[*August 1726*] . . . ii. 393
†3 September 1726 . . ii. 394
16 September 1726 (from
Gay). . . . . ii. 399
[*c.* 20 September 1726]
(from Arbuthnot) . . ii. 401
22 September 1726 (from
Bolingbroke) . . . ii. 402
[September 1726] (from
Gay). . . . . ii. 403
15 *October 1726* (to Gay and
Pope) . . . . ii. 406
22 October 1726 (from Gay) ii. 409
†16 November 1726 . . ii. 411
†17 November 1726 (from
Gay). . . . . ii. 413
†[27] *November 1726* . . ii. 417
†5 *December 1726*. . . ii. 419
†17 February 1727 . . ii. 426
†8 March 1727 . . . ii. 426
12 *August 1727* (to Sheridan) ii. 442
†2 October 1727 . . . ii. 447
†*12 October 1727* . . . ii. 451
†22 October 1727 (from Gay
and Pope) . . . ii. 454
30 *October 1727* (for 1726) ii. 456
23 *November 1727* (to Pope
and Gay) . . . ii. 460
[? January 1728] . . ii. 467
†[February 1728] (from
Bolingbroke and Pope) . ii. 472
15 February 1728 (from
Gay). . . . . ii. 473
26 *February 1728* (to Gay) ii. 475
29 *February 1728* (to
Martha Blount) . . ii. 475
20 March 1728 (from Gay) ii. 478
†23 March 1728 . . . ii. 479

JONATHAN SWIFT (*cont.*)

28 *March 1728* (to Gay) . ii. 481
7 May 1728 (from Martha
  Blount) . . . . ii. 490
†*10 May 1728* . . . ii. 491
†*1 June 1728*. . . . ii. 497
†28 June 1728 . . . ii. 503
†*16 July 1728* . . . ii. 504
27 July 1728 (from Lord
  Oxford) . . . . ii. 506
†12 [October] 1728 . . ii. 521
†*13 February 1729* . . iii. 15
6 March 1729 . . . iii. 20
5 *April 1729* (to Bolingbroke and Pope) . . iii. 27
9 June 1729 (from Dr.
  Arbuthnot) . . . iii. 36
†*11 August 1729* . . . iii. 42
‖20 August–5 October 1729
  (from Bolingbroke) . iii. 47
†9 October 1729 . . . iii. 57
‖*31 October 1729* (to Bolingbroke) . . . . iii. 63
†*31 October 1729* . . . iii. 64
9 November 1729 (from
  Gay). . . . . iii. 68
‖19 November 1729 (from
  Bolingbroke) . . . iii. 70
20 *November 1729* (to Gay) iii. 72
†28 November 1729 . . iii. 79
6 *February 1730* . . . iii. 89
26 *February 1730* . . iii. 92
3 March 1730 (from Gay). iii. 94
†[4 March 1730] . . . iii. 95
‖*19 March 1730* (to Gay) . iii. 96
†*21 March 1730* (to Bolingbroke) . . . . iii. 98
‖[9 April 1730] (from Pope
  and Bolingbroke) . . iii. 101
2 *May 1730*. . . . iii. 107
†[*c*. 19 June 1730] . . iii. 117
4 July 1730 (from Gay) . iii. 119
8 November 1730 (from
  Gay and the Duchess) . iii. 145
‖*10 November 1730* (to Gay) iii. 147
‖19 November 1730 (to Gay
  and the Duchess) . . iii. 151
6 December 1730 (from Gay
  and the Duchess) . . v. 8
15 *January 1731* . . . iii. 160
January 1731 (from Bolingbroke) . . . . iii. 163
‖*13 March 1731* (to Gay
  and the Duchess) . . iii. 179

JONATHAN SWIFT (*cont.*)

‖[20 March 1731] (from
  Bolingbroke and Pope) . iii. 183
20 March 1731 (from Gay) iii. 185
20 *April 1731* . . . . iii. 190
27 April 1731 (from Gay). iii. 194
‖*29 June 1731* (to Gay) . iii. 202
18 July 1731 (from Gay
  and the Duchess) . . iii. 204
20 *July 1731* . . . . iii. 207
2 August 1731 (from
  Bolingbroke) . . . iii. 210
‖*28 August 1731* (to Gay) . iii. 218
1 November 1731 (from
  Gay and the Duke) . iii. 238
†1 December 1731 (from
  Gay and Pope) . . iii. 248
‖[*1 December 1731*] (to Gay
  and the Duchess) . . iii. 250
†[March 1732] (from
  Bolingbroke and Pope) . iii. 274
[13 March 1732] (from
  Gay) . . . . iii. 276
‖4 May 1732 (to Gay). . iii. 285
16 May 1732 (from Gay) . iii. 288
†*12 June 1732* . . . iii. 291
‖*10 July 1732* (to Gay and
  the Duchess) . . . iii. 296
22 *July 1732* (to Matthew
  Pilkington) . . . v. 10
24 July 1732 (from Gay
  and the Duchess) . . iii. 300
‖*12 August 1732* . . . iii. 303
28 August 1732 (from Gay
  and the Duchess) . . iii. 307
‖*3 October 1732* (to Gay and
  the Duchess) . . . iii. 319
†5 December 1732 (from
  Pope and Dr. Arbuthnot) iii. 334
†[1733] . . . . . iii. 343
†16 February 1733 . . iii. 347
[*31 March 1733*]. . . iii. 360
†2[0] April 1733 . . . iii. 365
†*1 May 1733* (*See also* v. 10) . iii. 367
12 *May 1733*. . . . v. 13
†28 May 1733 . . . iii. 372
[? Summer of 1733] . . iii. 376
‖*8 July 1733* . . . . iii. 377
†1 September 1733 . . iii. 383
†6 January 1734 . . . iii. 400
12 April 1734 (from
  Bolingbroke) . . . iii. 404
27 June–6 July 1734 (from
  Bolingbroke) . . . iii. 411

JONATHAN SWIFT (*cont.*)
30 *August 1734* (to Lord
Oxford) . . .   iii. 429
†15 September 1734 (from
Bolingbroke and Pope) .   iii. 431
||*1 November 1734* . .   iii. 438
†19 December 1734 .   iii. 444
†*12 May 1735* (See also v. 13)   iii. 456
†*3 September 1735* (See also
v. 16) . . . .   iii. 491
†*21 October 1735* . .   iii. 505
‡[November 1735] . .   iii. 508
†*7 February 1736* . .   iv. 3
†*25 March 1736* . .   iv. 5
†*22 April 1736* . .   iv. 11
†*17 August 1736* . .   iv. 27
||*2 December 1736* . .   iv. 44
†30 December 1736 . .   iv. 49
†*9 February [1737]* .   iv. 55
18 March 1737 (from Lord
Orrery) . . . .   iv. 60
†*23 March 1737* . .   iv. 62
†*31 May 1737* . .   iv. 71
12 June 1737 (from Lord
Orrery) . . . .   iv. 75
†*[June] 1737 (for 23 July)* .   iv. 76
23 July 1737 (from Lord
Orrery) . . . .   iv. 81
8–24 August 1738 (to Pope
and Bolingbroke) . .   iv. 115
12 October 1738 . . .   iv. 134
28 April 1739 . . .   iv. 174
? *10 May 1739* . . .   iv. 175
17–19 May 1739 . . .   iv. 176
[? May 1740] . . .   iv. 242
8 October 1740 (from Lord
Orrery) . . . .   iv. 277
22 March 1741 (from
Orrery and Pope) . .   iv. 336

JACOB TONSON, senior
20 *April 1706* . . .   i. 17
14 November 1731 . .   iii. 243
[*February 1732*] (to Tonson, junior) . . .   iii. 269
7 June 1732. . . .   iii. 290
4 December 1735 . .   iii. 513
JACOB TONSON, junior
5 *October 1713* . . .   i. 191
11 July 1719 . . .   ii. 7
*[1721 or 1722] . .   ii. 63
*3 September [1721] .   ii. 80
*[? May 1722] . . .   ii. 117
*[16 or 23 May 1722 ?] .   ii. 118

JACOB TONSON, junior (*cont.*)
*[6 August 1722 ?] . .   ii. 130
[1723–4] . . . .   ii. 211
*[? 1724] . . . .   ii. 213
*[21 January 1724 ?] . .   ii. 215
*[February 1724]. . .   ii. 217
*[1724] . . . .   ii. 222
[1724] . . . .   ii. 222
23 *December 1724* . .   ii. 279
*[1725] . . . .   ii. 282
*[January 1725] . .   ii. 285
*[March 1725] . .   ii. 288
*20 January 1727 . .   ii. 424
November [1731] . .   iii. 241
13 *November 1731* . .   iii. 242
14 November 1731 . .   iii. 243
18 *November 1731* . .   iii. 244
[February 1732] (from his
uncle) . . . .   iii. 269
[1733–4] . . . .   iii. 399
JAMES TOOKER
*18 December 1712 .   v. 3
[RICHARD] TOWNE, M.D.
*5 January 1727 . . .   ii. 424
'TOWNLEY'
12 November 1722 . .   ii. 144
SIR WILLIAM TRUMBULL
†*19 October 1705* . . .   i. 10
15 *June 1706* . . .   i. 17
†*9 April 1706* . . .   i. 45
‡*30 April 1713* . . .   i. 176
†*6 March 1714* . . .   i. 212
†*12 March 1714* . . .   i. 212
14 February 1715 . .   i. 281
||*22 February 1715* . .   i. 281
†16 December 1715 . .   i. 323
†*19 January 1716* . . .   i. 327

SIR PETER VANDEPUT
*[1724] . . . . .   ii. 232
JOHN VANDER BEMPDEN
[1715 ?] . . . . .   i. 325
THOMAS VERNON
[*September 1719* ?] . .   ii. 15
VOLTAIRE
[September 1726] . .   ii. 399
M. and R. VYNER (? Mr. and Mrs.)
*7 *June* [1718] . . .   i. 476
*8 *June* [1718] . . .   i. 476

WILLIAM WALSH
†*20 April 1705* (to Wycherley)   i. 7
†*24 June 1706* . . .   i. 18
†*2 July 1706* . . . .   i. 18

WILLIAM WALSH (*cont.*)

†20 *July 1706* . . .	i. 20
†9 *September 1706* . .	i. 21
†22 October 1706 . . .	i. 22
21 *July 1707* . . .	i. 29

HUMPHREY WANLEY

1 July 1725 . . .	ii. 304
31 July 1725 . . .	ii. 312

WILLIAM WARBURTON

*2 February 1739 . .	iv. 163
11 April [1739] . .	iv. 171
26 May 1739 . .	iv. 182
20 September 1739 . .	iv. 195
4 January 1740 . . .	iv. 215
17 January [1740] . .	iv. 219
16 April 1740 . .	iv. 233
*[Late April 1740] .	iv. 236
*[26 April 1740] . .	iv. 236
*[? 5 May 1740] . .	iv. 237
*[7 May 1740] . .	iv. 238
*[c. 23 May 1740] .	iv. 243
24 June [1740] . .	iv. 251
27 October 1740 . .	iv. 288
4 February 1741 . .	iv. 334
14 April 1741 . .	iv. 339
[? April 1741] . .	iv. 341
*27 May [1741] . .	iv. 345
*[28 May 1741] . .	iv. 346
*[4 or 11 June 1741] .	iv. 346
12 August [1741] .	iv. 356
20 September [1741] .	iv. 361
12 November 1741 .	iv. 370
22 November 1741 .	iv. 373
*[? January 1742] .	iv. 379
*[? January 1742] .	iv. 380
*[? January 1742] .	iv. 380
*[? January 1742] .	iv. 380
*[1742]	iv. 384
*[?1742] (five letters) .	iv. 385
*[? 1742] . . .	iv. 386
*[February 1742] . .	iv. 387
[16 February 1742] .	iv. 388
23 April [1742] . .	iv. 393
5 June [1742] . .	iv. 399
*18 June [1742] . .	iv. 402
*[June 1742] . .	iv. 402
18 July [1742] . .	iv. 403
*5 August [1742] .	iv. 410
*1 November [1742] .	iv. 424
*[6 November 1742] .	iv. 425
27 November [1742] .	iv. 427
*4 December [1742] .	iv. 429
28 December 1742 . .	iv. 434
18 January 1743 . .	iv. 438

WILLIAM WARBURTON (*cont.*)

24 March [1743] . .	iv. 447
[? 3 May 1743] . .	iv. 454
21 May [1743] . .	iv. 455
*[4 September 1743] .	iv. 471
7 October [1743] .	iv. 474
*[15 November 1743] .	iv. 480
12 January [1744] .	iv. 491
[1744] . .	iv. 492
*27 January [1744] .	iv. 495
21 February 1744 .	iv. 500
[March 1744] . .	iv. 505
*[8 March 1744] . .	iv. 506
*[12 March 1744] .	iv. 506
*[? 5 or 12 April 1744]	iv. 515
*[? April 1744] .	iv. 515
*[11 or 18 April 1744]	iv. 518
*[April or May 1744] .	iv. 520
*[April or May 1744] .	iv. 520

FRANCIS WATERS

*11 September 1718 .	i. 501

LEONARD WELSTED

†12 *March 1733* . .	iii. 355

SAMUEL WESLEY, junior (1691–1739)

*6 January [1729] .	v. 6
*24 April 1730 . .	iii. 104
21 October [1735] .	iii. 504

MARTHA WHITEWAY

[*June or later, 1739*] .	iv. 184
16 *May 1740* . .	iv. 240
18 June 1740 . .	iv. 248
7 *October 1740* (to Lord Orrery)	iv. 277
20 *December 1740* (to Lord Orrery) . . .	iv. 307
24 December 1740 (from Lord Orrery) . .	iv. 308
30 *December 1740* (to Lord Orrery) . . .	iv. 320
2 [January] 1741 (from Lord Orrery) . .	iv. 325
10 January 1741 (from Lord Orrery) . .	iv. 327

JOHN WESTON

9 September 1717 (to Charles Rackett)	i. 426

WILLIAM WYCHERLEY

†26 December 1704 . .	i. 1
†25 *January 1705* . .	i. 3
†25 March 1705 . .	i. 5
†29 *March 1705* . . .	i. 5
†7 *April 1705* . . .	i. 6
†20 April 1705 (from Walsh)	i. 7
†30 April 1705 . . .	i. 8

WILLIAM WYCHERLEY (*cont.*)

‡23 June 1705 . . . i. 9
†26 October 1705 . . . i. 11
†5 *November 1705* . . i. 12
†5 *February 1706* . . . i. 13
||*22 March 1706* . . . i. 14
†10 April 1706 . . . i. 15
19 *February 1707* . . i. 25
||*11 November 1707* . . i. 29
†20 November 1707 . . i. 31
†22 *November 1707* . . i. 32
†29 November 1707 . . i. 33
6 *December 1707* . . . i. 34
19 *January 1708* . . . i. 38
†28 *February 1708* . . i. 40
†13 *May 1708* . . . i. 49
†18 *May and 28 July 1708* . i. 50
13 *November 1708* . . i. 52

WILLIAM WYCHERLEY (*cont.*)

||*19 February 1709* . . i. 54
17 *May 1709* . . . i. 58
†20 May 1709 . . . i. 60
||*23 May 1709* . . . i. 61
†26 *May 1709* . . . i. 62
14 *June 1709* . . . i. 64
†11 *August 1709* . . . i. 69
14 *February 1710* . . i. 78
||*1 April 1710* . . . . i. 79
†11 *April 1710* . . . i. 82
†15 April 1710 . . . i. 83
||*27 April 1710* . . . i. 84
†2 May 1710 . . . . i. 86

EDWARD YOUNG

8 *June* [*1715*] . . . i. 294
2 *May* [*1723*] . . . ii. 171

INDEX

In a single alphabet entries are here found concerning all persons or places mentioned in the letters. Entries for noblemen will be found, with a cross-reference from the title, under the family name. Addresses to letters and provenances of letters are not indexed. Names of correspondents are printed in capital letters.

A——, Lord Chief Justice (unidentified), at Bath, ii. 521.

Abberley, Worcs., William Walsh, i. 7 n., 29 n. (Pope visits), ii. 10 (Edward Blount visits).

Abbott, Mr. (unidentified), concerned with Mrs. Rackett's legal troubles, iii. 7, 33, 39.

Abdy, Sir Robert, asked to intervene with Lord Petre on behalf of H. Rackett, iii. 154.

Abergavenny, Lord, *see* Neville, George, 14th Baron, iii. 110 n.

Abingdon, Berks., a meeting-place for Pope and Lord Bathurst, iii. 134.

Account of Mr. Wood's Iron, An, &c., iii. 108.

Acheson, Sir Arthur, iii. 15, 20–21; Lady Acheson, iii. 15, 22.

Adderbury, Oxon., 2nd Duke of Argyle, iv. 137 n., 189.

Addison, Charlotte (Rich), Countess of Warwick (Mrs. Joseph Addison), i. 385.

ADDISON, JOSEPH: letters to, i. 183, 197, 201, 208, 263; letters from, i. 196 (2); a lost letter mentioned, i. 165; Pope's letters to A. fabricated, i. 176 n., 193 n., 197, 201, 208, 219–21, 263 n.; A. franks letters to Pope, i. 300 n.; — his relations with Pope: *Spectator* No. 253, i. 113, 141, 263, 264; friendly (1712), i. 141, 170, 197; his reaction to the *Narrative of Dr. Norris*, i. 170, 183, 184; to Pope's *Guardian* No. 40, i. 197; controlled the pens of Buttonians, i. 244 n.; Jervas as intermediary, i. 244, 263, 288, 290; Pope's final sarcastic letter, i. 263; — A. returns Parnell's poem to Pope, i. 284; reads the *Temple of Fame* in MS., i. 152, 154; encourages Pope's *Iliad*, i. 45 n., 196, 209, 220; solicited no subscribers, i. 220 n.; is

ADDISON, JOSEPH (*cont.*)

asked to read the MS. of the first two Books of Pope's *Iliad*, i. 263; prefers Tickell's version, i. 305; — his parallel to Atticus, i. 196 n., 321 n.; the Atticus lines first published, ii. 144; A. quoted in *The Dunciad* (1729), i. 220 n.; — A.'s *Works*: Tickell's ed., ii. 81, 88; *Campaign* quoted by Pope, i. 175; *Remarks on Italy* mentioned by Lady Mary Wortley Montagu, i. 397; *Spectator* cited by Broome, ii. 345 n.; *Cato*: Pope's first opinion of, i. 173; its first performance, i. 174–6; called a party play, i. 175; burlesqued in Gay's farce, i. 287, 289, 290; translated by Salvini, i. 447 n.; quoted by Pope, ii. 480, iv. 429; — A.'s alleged connexion with Tickell's *Iliad* I, i. 423; projected a dictionary, i. 423; author of *Guardian* No. 67 on Tom Durfey, i. 180; author of *Tatler* No. 155, i. 188 n.; a detail in *Spectator* No. 253 corrected by Pope, i. 264; Curll projected an edition of A.'s letters, iii. 459, and of his State Papers, iii. 471; — A. befriended Whiston, i. 185 n.; his manner in company, i. 204; aids Tickell's Lucan subscription, i. 262; Secretary to the Lord Lieut. of Ireland, i. 292; tone of letters about him by friends, i. 306 n.; no epithalamia at his wedding, i. 385; — his character as seen by Lady Mary Wortley Montagu, i. 423; writes to recall Wortley from Constantinople, i. 440 n.; his stepson (Earl of Warwick), i. 450; relations with Swift, ii. 67, 68; on Irish Whigs, ii. 69; criticized by Broome, ii. 345; had Carey or Tickell dangling after him, iii. 191.

Adrian (emperor), *see* Hadrian.

Aelian, mentioned by Broome, ii. 345.

Aeschylus, mentioned by Atterbury, ii. 79.

Aiken, Lucy, *Life* of Addison, i. 139.

AIKMAN, WILLIAM (painter): letter from, ii. 294; given Pope's *Odyssey*, ii. 282, 294; painted Pope's portrait (?), ii. 294 n.; Mallet's epitaph for, iii. 222.

Albery Place, Surrey, Sir Edward Southcote, i. 123 n.

Aldermaston, Newbury, Berks., Lord Stawell, i. 312.

Alexander the Great, i. 9, 114.

Allatius, Leo (Leone Allacci), i. 225.

Allen, B. S., *Tides of Taste* cited on Wm. Kent, iii. 329.

Allen, Joshua, 2nd Viscount, Swift's quarrel with, iii. 92, 362.

Allen, Margaret, Viscountess: impossible for her to send Pope Irish woollens, iii. 72; prejudiced against Swift, iii. 108.

Allen, Mary, niece of Ralph Allen, possibly 'Miss Bounce', iv. 432.

Allen [Philip ?], Postmaster in Bath, brother of Ralph, iv. 371.

ALLEN, RALPH: letters to, iv. 9, 13, 18, 23, 24, 31, 36, 40, 68, 74, 82, 83, 86, 92, 108, 119, 134, 144, 157, 165, 172, 175, 180, 190, 194, 230, 234, 238, 245, 246, 252, 254, 273, 280, 290, 292, 297, 299, 340, 343, 347, 349, 351, 353, 357, 360, 362, 363, 378, 379, 383, 386, 391, 398, 401, 404, 411, 417, 420, 428, 430, 431, 432, 443, 449, 450, 452, 454, 471, 476, 479, 481, 485, 486, 489, 494, 502, 504, 509, 517, 519, 522; — efforts towards the 'authentic' ed. of Pope's *Letters* (1737), iv. 1, 9, 19, 23, 24, 41, 74; the Swift letters (1741), iv. 274; — career and achievements, iv. 9 n.; his brother postmaster at Bath, iv. 371; A.'s second marriage, iv. 68 n.; given a young Bounce by Pope, iv. 175, 181; given Atterbury's Bible by Pope, ii. 169; introduced to Lyttelton by Pope, iv. 144, 190; A. and Hooke in Wales, iv. 204; introduced to Lord Orrery by Pope, iv. 340; Pope invited to 'ramble' with the Allens, iv. 343; they travel with G. Arbuthnot, iv. 367; A. becomes Lord Mayor of Bath (1742-3), iv.

ALLEN, RALPH (*cont.*) 420, 425, 443; his visits to London and Twickenham, iv. 9, 31, 86, 134, 157, 165, 252, 362, 398, 410, 411, 412, 435, 487, 489, 501, 503, 504, 505, 506, 507, 509 (the Good Friday visit of reconciliation), 510, 517; Pope's visits to A., iv. 83–84, 200–1, 206, 208, 215, 221, 230, 280, 362, 363, 378–9, 387, 417, 443, 455, 464, 465, 469, 470; unpleasantness in the visit with Martha Blount in 1743, iv. 436, 454, 461, 463–70; — A.'s new house (Prior Park) in construction, iv. 9; now habitable, iv. 344, 354, 391; Pope helps in choosing pictures for Prior Park, iv. 13, 20, and statues, iv. 253, 351; is interested in A.'s gardens, iv. 37, 41, 239, 247, 254, 413; in how to rear fawns, iv. 413, 452; in a 'pine house' (pineapples), iv. 429, 431, 449; Scot the gardener to visit A., iv. 360; A.'s ill health, iv. 23, 74, 92, 471 (dangerous illness), 476–7, 479, 481, 510; did not at this time employ Dr. Oliver, iv. 486, 489; — benefactions: gave a guinea to an aged woman beggar, iv. 92; to the poor, cold, and hungry, iv. 221–2; kind to Anne Arbuthnot at Bath, iv. 274; asked to aid A. Cleland to a surgeon's post at Bath, iv. 401; gives (through Pope) £20 towards Fielding's *Miscellanies*, iv. 452; acts as banker for Lady Gerard at Bath, iv. 454; — subsidizes N. Hooke's *Roman History*, iv. 36; Hooke his guest, iv. 119; asked to help get young Hooke into the army, iv. 353, 357; Hooke gets £1,000 from Duchess of Marlborough, iv. 383, 386, 404; for Pope A. advances £150 iv. 217; helps Pope to shares in Sun Fire Office, iv. 340; sends Bristol water to Pope, iv. 230, 353, 443, 471; makes stone urns for Pope, iv. 144, 181 n.; sends various cargoes of stone for Pope's grotto, iv. 230, 239, 244, 245, 246, 252, 279, 343, 353, 412, 433 (rustic stone desired), 449, 450; for Savage A. pays £10, per annum, in Wales, iv. 180; invites Warburton to Prior Park, iv. 371; plans to make W. independent, iv. 452; — A.'s

ALLEN, RALPH (*cont.*)
character: prototype for Alworthy in *Tom Jones*, iv. 222 n.; called a Good Man by Pope, iv. 83; his nature sketched, iv. 234, 371; high praise for him, iv. 155, 222; mentioned in 'Epilogue to the Satires' as 'low-born', iv. 93; changed to 'humble', iv. 144–5; A.'s modesty, iv. 400.

Allen, Mrs. Ralph (Elizabeth Holder): commended by Pope, iv. 181, 235, 449; ill in 1744, iv. 485, 509; quarrel with Martha Blount, iv. 462–4; willing to receive Mrs. Bonœuvrier, iv. 219.

Almanacks quoted, i. 81.

Altar of Love, The (1727), Curll publishes pieces by Pope in, ii. 434 n.

Amadis de Gaul, mentioned by Pope, i. 477, ii. 86.

Ambresbury, Wilts, *see* Amesbury.

Amelia, princess, at Bath, Martha Blount to be presented, iii. 435.

Am-Ende, J. J. G., his Latin version of *Essay on Man,* iv. 484 n.

Amesbury, Wilts., *see* John Gay *and* the Duke of Queensberry.

Amhurst, Nicholas, expelled from Oxford (1719), i. 285 n.

Amiens, Dr. (apothecary ?), attends Arbuthnot, ii. 316.

Angel, Mr., of Binfield, a neighbour, i. 403.

Angel, Mr., of London, has coaches and horses for hire, i. 434, 481.

Ann, Lady —, her chariot for Martha Blount, iv. 355.

Anne, Queen, i. 199, 205, 240, 241, ii. 319, 380 n.

Annual Register, The, letter by Pope printed in, i. 436 n.

ANONYMOUS CORRESPONDENTS: letters to, i. 4, 277, 305, 380, 381, 413, 420, 431, 436, ii. 5, 18, 110 (no text), 367, iii. 223; letters from, i. 380, 433, 436.

Ansell, Mr., apothecary of New Brentford, iv. 119.

Anstey, Christopher, Broome wrote for him (1713), ii. 449 n.

Appleby, Leics., *see* Samuel Johnson, iv. 194.

Apollonius, to be translated by Broome, ii. 339, 360.

Apscourt, Surrey, iv. 451.

Arbuthnot, Mr. (?George or his uncle Robert), iv. 89.

Arbuthnot, Anne (dau. of Dr. John): close friend of Pope, iii. 452, iv. 177, 212; seriously ill in 1740, iv. 268; at Bath, iv. 274; urged to use Alderman Barber's legacy to Pope (£100) for trip to Bath, iv. 367; negotiates for Swift's 'singing man', ii. 401; disputes with Wm. Murray, iv. 441; at Twickenham in Pope's last days, iv. 501 n., 511, 526.

Arbuthnot, Charles (son of Dr. John), his death, iii. 250 n., v. 20.

Arbuthnot, George (brother of Dr. John): married to Peggy Robinson (Anastasia's sister), ii. 474; his wife's death (1729), iii. 58.

ARBUTHNOT, GEORGE (son of Dr. John): letters to, iii. 452, 480, iv. 171, 191, 267, 303, 366, 367, 388, 394, 441, 442, 461; — close friend to Pope (1735–44), iii. 452; visits Pope (with Anne), iii. 480, iv. 442, 471; a single vol. of Rymer's *Foedera* offered by him, iv. 51 n.; aids Lady Gerard as to a lease, iv. 186, 191; urged to attend to his sister's health, iv. 268; travels with the Allens, iv. 367; to receive Pope's legacy from Alderman Barber, iv. 367; plans ed. of his father's *Works,* iv. 372; tries to aid Warburton against Mawhood, iv. 385, 388, 475; aids Pope against Lintot, iv. 388, 394; at Bath with Pope, iv. 214; there (and Bristol) again in 1743, iv. 461, 466, 469; his unwillingness to stay at Prior Park a possible cause of quarrel with Allen, iv. 461, 466; takes Pope to Salisbury, iv. 472; as Pope's executor lists his assets for Martha Blount (1745), iv. 340 n.; Pope offers condolence on the death of Margaret Arbuthnot, v. 20.

ARBUTHNOT, JOHN, M.D.: letters from Pope, i. 233, 249 (joint letter, with Parnell), ii. 318, iii. 334, 415, 418, 423, 428, 431; letters to Pope, i. 251, 305, ii. 9, 196, iii. 416; letters from Pope and A., i. 331 (to Parnell), iii. 334 (to Swift); letters from A. to Swift, ii. 401, iii. 36; letters to Edward, Earl of Oxford, ii. 411, 417; letters from Lady Mary Wortley Montagu to A.,

ARBUTHNOT, JOHN (*cont.*)
iii. 59, 60, 448; a letter to him lost, ii. 191; a letter to him fabricated, ii. 341 n., 352; his comment on writing to Swift, ii. 333, 342; doesn't write, Pope says, iii. 176.
Biographical details: in his rooms in St. James's Palace the Scriblerus Club meets, i. 216; later lives in Dover Street, i. 251; still later in Cork Street, iii. 339; in 1724 at Bath with his brother Robert and Gay, ii. 253, 257, 258, 264; there again in 1728, ii. 514; reports on reception of Pope's *Iliad* I, i. 305; plans trip to Devonshire, i. 310; on lunacy of the South Sea Bubble, ii. 54, 60; caned Moore-Smythe for *One Epistle*, iii. 59 n., 106 n., 114; his health, obese, ii. 133; ill (1725), ii. 282, 316, 322, 331; intermittent fevers, ii. 503; convulsive heart, iii. 37; not abstinent in meat and wine, iii. 126, 142, 194, 415; his last illness, iii. 416, 417, 431, 434, 444; his death, iii. 417 n.; his wife, ii. 133, iii. 58 (d. 1730).
His many friends: Atterbury, ii. 165; Martha Blount, ii. 196, iii. 113, 337; Buononcini, ii. 99; Cheselden, ii. 101; Congreve, ii. 27; daily journeys to attend Congreve at Windsor Park, ii. 389, 400, 402; the younger Craggs, ii. 16; John Gay, i. 450; attends Gay in last sickness, iii. 1–2, 335, 337; Lady Mary Wortley Montagu, ii. 6 n., 9 n., 10; her high opinion of him, iii. 59–60; Lord Peterborow, ii. 196; Parnell, i. 284, 332; Pope and A. plan trip to Devonshire, i. 418; Pope's nephew John recommended by A. to J. Drummond, ii. 245; tells Gay Pope has a clap, ii. 290; attended Pope in his fever, iii. 350; final request as to Pope's satire, iii. 417; long, firm friendship with Pope, iii. 416–17; his portrait copied for Pope, iii. 480; prescribed for Pope's mother, i. 394–5, ii. 272; thought well (Warburton said) of Sir Robert Sutton, iv. 493; — Swift, ii. 153, 221, 311, 322, 373 (took Swift about London in 1726), 401; anecdotes about the welcome of *Gulliver*, ii. 411; A.'s minor

ARBUTHNOT, JOHN (*cont.*)
verse on *Gulliver*, ii. 411, 417; could have improved *Gulliver* III, ii. 414, 417; attended Swift in 1727, ii. 443; Swift jokes with Gay about A.'s love to make improvements, ii. 475; one of Swift's singers owes A. money, ii. 479; joke about his brother's bad wines, iii. 102; Wise aided by A. for a scholarship, iii. 141; Swift laments A.'s death, v. 14.
Personality: forgetful, iii. 66; 'the king of inattention', according to Swift, iii. 298; walks badly, ii. 253, 326; highly praised, ii. 272, 326, 331; devoted card-player, ii. 133, 395, iii. 58; his love of mischief, ii. 350; his wit, ii. 401 (anecdote of the Gascon, 'signez'); his life cheerful to the very end, iii. 434.
A.'s Works: Scriblerus, i. 233, 251; collaborates in *Three Hours after Marriage*, i. 388; writes directions against the plague, ii. 104; a Ballad, a poem on Quadrille, the Epistle from Gulliver's Wife, ii. 411, 417; his *Treatise of Aliments*, ii. 333 n.; his *Tables of Ancient Coins*, ii. 333 n., 401, 410, 424–5, 429; *John Bull* to go in the *Miscellanies*, ii. 421; allowed Pope to finish the *Bathos*, ii. 468; paid slowly by Motte for *Miscellanies*, ii. 526; did not insert couplet from Broome in *Bathos*, iii. 116; wrote some notes for *The Dunciad* (1729), iv. 428; *John Ginglicutt's Treatise* a slight thing, iii. 250; a general edition of his *Works* planned by his son, iv. 372; left 'his bastards' (anonymous works?) at others' doors, ii. 133.
Arbuthnot, John (grandson of Dr. John), ill, iii. 428 n.
Arbuthnot, Margaret (dau. of Dr. John): grief at her father's death, iii. 452; died (1740), iv. 268 n., v. 20.
Arbuthnot, Mrs. P. S–M., her *Memories* (1920) cited, iv. 268 n.
Arbuthnot, Robert (brother of Dr. John, and banker in France): his picturesque, indiscreet character, ii. 196, 253, iii. 81; at Bath (1724), ii. 253; nearly shipwrecked (1726), ii. 402; banker for Mrs. Cope, ii. 434;

Arbuthnot, Robert (*cont.*)
death of his wife, iii. 58; sent inferior wine to Swift, who complains, iii. 81, 97, 102; now (1730) gone to China, iii. 102; visits England (1739), iv. 171.

Archer, Sir (unidentified), said to own authorship of things in the *Gazetteer*, iv. 125.

Archibald, Arthur, mysterious name used by Pope once, iv. 93.

Architectural Review, cited for letters of Wm. Kent, iv. 141 n., 149 n., 162 n.

Aremberg, Duke of, Austrian general, iv. 413.

Arendts Collection (New York Public Library), i. 441 n.

Argeville, France, Bolingbroke's residence, iv. 456 n.

Argyle (or Argyll), 2nd Duke of, *see* Campbell, John (1680–1743).

Argyle (or Argyll), 3rd Duke of, *see* Campbell, Archibald (Earl of Ilay).

Argyle (or Argyll), 4th Duke of, *see* Campbell, John (d. 1770).

Ariosto, *Orlando* cited on Astolfo's wife, i. 365.

Aristophanes, i. 28, 492.

Aristotle, i. 488, 492.

Arnall (or Arnold), William: writer for *The British Journal* (?1728), ii. 473 n., for *The Daily Gazetteer*, iv. 179 n.; called a scoundrel by Bolingbroke, iii. 215; in *The Dunciad*, iv. 178.

Arnold, William H., prints and annotates a letter, ii. 285.

Arran, 2nd Earl of, *see* Butler, Charles.

Arthur, Daniel: banker for the Popes (early), i. 155, 180, ii. 6; thought negligent, i. 155, 156, 180, 237.

Arundell, Mr.: married to Lady Fanny, ii. 416; servant recommended to H. Bethel, iv. 473.

Arundell, Lady Frances, has her letter, iv. 150.

Ashe, Sir James, letter from, ii. 300; Twickenham churchwarden.

Ashe, St. George, Bishop of Clogher, commends Parnell's *Bookworm*, i. 371.

Ashley, Walton-on-Thames, Surrey, Lord Shannon, ii. 12.

Aston, Catherine, Lady, aunt of Mrs. Weston, i. 142, 143.

Aston, Walter, Baron, i. 142 n.

Astrop Wells, Northants., Lady Cobham, iv. 188.

The Athenaeum: cited for letters to Buckley, ii. 157 n.; on Mrs. Cope, i. 417, 522, ii. 361 n.; on Mrs. Weston, i. 119 n., 428; on Voltaire's letter to Pope, ii. 399 n.; on attempt of Duchess of Buckingham to give Pope £100, iii. 91 n.; on Mrs. Rackett, iii. 173 n.

Atterbury, Francis, Bishop of Rochester and Dean of Westminster: letters to, i. 453, 499, ii. 53, 101, 106, 109, 127, 166, 168, 169; letters from, i. 378, 451, 459, 467, 501, ii. 51, 54, 73, 76, 78, 79, 83, 86, 93, 100, 104, 107, 108, 113, 119, 123, 124, 128, 131, 165, iii. 76, 85, 245; an unprinted letter fabricated, i. 499; — some papers in Library of Westminster Abbey, iii. 76 n.; various early transcripts of his letters, ii. 165 n., 166 n., iii. 76 n.; transcribed for Harleian Library, iii. 187; farewell letter from the Tower, ii. 165; letter from the Tower to be kept secret, ii. 166 n.; letter printed as by the Duke of Wharton, ii. 166 n.; felony to correspond with him in exile, ii. 169 n.; gossip concerning a letter from Pope, ii. 206; correspondence during exile, iii. 76, 78; letter of condolence on the death of his daughter, iii. 85; his answer to Oldmixon, how published, iii. 245 n.; eager to hear from Pope, iii. 246–7; his correspondence advertised for publication by Curll, iii. 465, 471, 473 n.; Pope plans to print A.'s letters, iii. 494; the correspondence praised by Henry Brooke, iv. 199.

Biographical details: his gout, i. 378, ii. 52, 79, 83, 87; winters spent in the Deanery, i. 451, ii. 86; with Lord Bathurst (St. James's Square), i. 467; suit over the Westminster dormitory, ii. 74, 76; on Dryden's tomb, ii. 51, 55; on South Sea danger, ii. 56; his son elected scholar for Oxford, ii. 108; death of his wife, ii. 107–8, 113; visit to Twickenham, ii. 109,

ATTERBURY, FRANCIS (*cont.*)
113, 117 n.; home over rough
Thames, ii. 119–20; built vault in the
Abbey, ii. 114; affair of his gardeners,
ii. 123, 129, 131; — dislikes present
(plotting ?) employments, ii. 107, 120,
132; contempt for 'the Great', ii. 113,
124; sent to the Tower (1722), ii. 93,
131 n., 133; visited there by Pope and
Caryll, ii. 146; not allowed to see
relatives, ii. 173 n.; his trial, ii. 151, 171
n., 172; prejudged, ii. 165, 168–9;
condemned to exile, ii. 168 n.; goes to
France (19 June 1723), i. 326, ii. 169
n.; in Brussels, ii. 206 n.; death of
Mrs. Morrice, iii. 76–78, 85; health
improved in south of France, iii. 77;
visit from Morrice (1730), iii. 136; his
last days, iii. 246, 247, 248, 274; his
corpse and effects landed at Deal, 29
Apr. 1732, iii. 296 n.; did not die a
Papist, Curll affirms, iii. 471.
Friends and enemies: his amiability,
ii. 174; Dean George Berkeley, ii. 62;
Duchess of Buckingham, ii. 84, &c.;
Cadogan, ii. 386 n.; J. Dart, ii. 258
n.; Lord Harcourt, ii. 146; H. Henchman, ii. 313 n.; J. Morley, ii. 132;
Wm. Morrice, ii. 469, &c.; Lord
Orrery, ii. 115 n., iii. 502; M. Prior,
ii. 84, 85; — friendship with POPE:
on Pope's religion, i. 451, ii. 128;
Pope's visits to A., i. 451, 501, ii. 21,
73, 80, 100, 184; A. at Twickenham,
ii. 78, 115 n., 118; Pope visits him in
the Tower, ii. 146; Pope a witness at
A.'s trial, ii. 165, 171; A.'s exile
lamented by Pope, ii. 179; their part-
ing, ii. 165, 169 n. (gives Pope his
Bible) 169; commended by Pope, ii.
177, iii. 81, 278; urged Pope to burn
Alcander, i. 467; approved Pope's
Preface of 1717, i. 378; commented on
Pope's epitaphs, i. 501–4, ii. 74, 76;
likes the essay on Pastoral Poetry, ii.
80; advises cautiously on Duke of
Buckingham's *Works,* ii. 85, 100,
128; returns Pope's Shakespeare, ii.
87; wants full copy of Pope's lines on
Addison, ii. 104.
A. as a critic: diffident, i. 378; prefers blank verse, i. 378, 504, ii. 97; his
two odes translated from Horace, ii.
93–98; thought contemporaries slight,

ATTERBURY, FRANCIS (*cont.*)
iii. 247; criticism of various authors:
Addison, ii. 88; Cowley, ii. 87; Milton, i. 452 (above Homer and Virgil,
ii. 124 (Milton MS.), wants *Samson
polished*), ii. 124, 165; Sackville's
Gorboduc, i. 467; Shakespeare found
obscure, ii. 78, 79, 129; Waller, ii. 84;
Arabian Tales, ii. 53, 56; Father
Catrou, ii. 79; Huet, ii. 74; Aeschylus,
ii. 79; Cicero, ii. 87; Horace, ii. 123,
129, 176, iii. 247; Virgil, ii. 74, 76,
123, iii. 77, 248; A.'s Discourse
on Iapis, iii. 187, iv. 55, 60; reply
to Oldmixon about Clarendon, iii.
245–6.
Atterbury, Osborn (son of the Bishop);
elected to Oxford, ii. 108; his odes
from Horace, ii. 93–98.
Atticus, T. Pomponius: disparaged by
Cromwell, i. 116; praised by Edward
Blount, i. 321.
Atwell, Mr., tutor to Lord William
Cowper at Oxford, ii. 497.
Atwood, Thomas, attorney concerned
with Lady Gerard's lease, iv. 191.
Audra, Émile, his discovery of Pope's
letter to Louis Racine, iv. 415–16,
422.
Augusta, Princess, quarrels in Court at
her birth, iv. 86.
Augustus, Emperor: his character, i.
116; his regard for Horace, i. 158.
Ault, Norman: transcribes letters, iii.
104, iv. 384, 389, 390, 422; on dates of
letters, ii. 215, iv. 146; his ed. of
Pope's (1717) *Miscellany* cited, i. 13,
321, 328, 410; *New Light* cited: on
Hadrian, i. 159, 178–9; on Prologue
to *Jane Shore,* i. 184; on *Sermon on
Glass Bottles,* i. 295; on epitaphs (esp.
Rowe's), ii. 25, 51, iv. 176; on *Duke
upon Duke,* ii. 85; on 'To a Lady on
her Birthday', ii. 180, 235, iii. 18; on
'The Monster of Ragusa', ii. 334; on
the authorship of the 'poetical soop', ii.
403, 409; on poems appended to
Gulliver, ii. 411; on lines on Pope's
own birthday, iii. 3; on Pope's lines
in answer to Cibber's on glass, iii.
435; on 'Bounce to Fop', iv. 48; on
Pope's dogs, iv. 507.
Aulus Gellius, i. 115, 116, 225.
Austin, St., i. 119.

Austin, Mr., surveyor, in St. Albans Street, ii. 12.

Avery, Emmett, ii. 30.

Avicen, ii. 407.

Avebury (Abery), Wilts., iv. 378.

Ayre, William: *Life* of Pope, i. 246; source of a letter to Gay, i. 388, 482, iii. 19.

Ayscough, Francis, iii. 498.

B——, his suit *in forma pauperis*, i. 320.

B——, discarded by Swift, ii. 414.

B——, Counsellor, at Bath, ii. 521.

Bacon, Sir Edmund, friend of Broome, ii. 320, iii. 507.

Bacon, Francis (Lord Verulam), 'great in disgrace', ii. 167.

Badham, Brettridge, a great knave, Orrery thought, iv. 76.

Baine, R. M., on Jervas's Don Quixote, iv. 455.

Bagshot, Surrey, *see* Hallgrove, home of the Racketts.

BAKER, HENRY, letter to Pope, ii. 212; account of there.

Baker (?Thomas), i. 48.

Balam, Mr.: caused fall to Wycherley, i. 58, 65; Pope's service to, i. 82, 91, 130.

Balch, Elizabeth, on a Pope portrait, ii. 294.

Bald, R. C., a transcript by, ii. 288.

Ball, F. Elrington: his ed. of Swift's *Correspondence*, cited: on Scriblerus verses, i. 233; Alderman Barber and Swift, i. 234; improvements at Cirencester Park, ii. 207; the infant son of the 2nd Earl of Oxford, ii. 317; Gay's 'Steward' (questioned), ii. 343; Swift's projected life of Robert, Earl of Oxford, ii. 374; redating a letter, ii. 417; Dr. Whaley, ii. 523, iii. 21; a letter from Arbuthnot, iii. 36; Pilkington and Bowyer, iii. 323; Macaulay, iv. 184; original of the 'clandestine' Bath letter (1740) to Swift, iv. 242; Swift's mental decay, iv. 305; Faulkner in London, iv. 348.

Ballam, Mr., *see* Balam.

Baller, Katherine: sister and co-heiress of John Gay, iii. 335; Gay's sisters insignificant, Swift thinks, iii. 361, 368.

Balls Park, Herts., Edw. Harrison, ii. 182.

Baltimore, 5th Earl of, *see* Calvert, Charles.

Balzac, Guez de: his letters mentioned by Trumbull, i. 212, by Bolingbroke, iii. 102, by Swift, iii. 505.

Bamber, or Bambers, Mrs., Wycherley's landlady, i. 54.

Bangorian Controversy, i. 461 n.

Barbados, Sir Wm. Codrington, John Rackett, iv. 168–9.

BARBER, JOHN: letter from, i. 444; Swift's attitude towards (1714), i. 234; writes at request of Lady Bolingbroke, i. 444; subscribes to Buononcini, ii. 99; prints Duke of Buckingham's *Works*, ii. 81, 158 n., 159 n. (the licence to print), 160; Fenton's note destroyed, ii. 130; J. Wright's 'Master' (?), ii. 222 n.; Swift's fears as to a legacy from, iii. 74; as Lord Mayor, made Pilkington his chaplain, iii. 293; Swift writes about Wm. Lamb, iv. 135 n.; gives aid to W. Dunkin, iv. 178; seldom seen by Pope, iv. 178; Mrs. Whiteway writes under cover to him, iv. 241; his death, iv. 329; leaves Pope £100, iv. 366.

Barber, Mary, Dublin poet: favoured by Swift, iii. 89, 207, iv. 81; by Dr. Delany, iii. 207; by Mrs. Howard, iii. 194–5; her verses on Gay's *Fables*, ii. 483; reflections on Congreve, ii. 483; goes to England, iii. 107; wishes Pope to revise her poems, iii. 184, 191; in legal difficulties over Swift's *Of Poetry*, iii. 207, 432; Swift's alleged letter to the Queen about her, iii. 207–9; arrested in 1734, iii. 401; gets MS. of *Polite Conversation* to publish, iv. 81.

Barbier, Mrs., a singer, ii. 135 n.

Barbutt, John David, bankrupt post office official, iv. 398, 405.

Barkam, Mr., pays Mrs. Rackett, iii. 39.

Barclay, Mr., object of Pope's charity, ii. 104.

Barnes, Joshua, editor of the *Iliad*, i. 225, 244.

Barnes, Surrey, Jacob Tonson, sr., ii. 223, iii. 185.

Barnstaple, Devon, John Gay, i. 153 n.

Barrow, Isaac, his *Sermons* lent to young Craggs, ii. 81.

Barrow, Samuel, M.D., his Latin lines in 2nd ed. of *Paradise Lost*, i. 452.

Barrowby, Lincolnshire, Rev. Thomas Wood, iii. 329 n., iv. 140–1.

Barry, Sir Edward, M.D., praised by Orrery, iii. 506.

Bassano, Jacopo da Ponte, called 'Bassano', copies of his paintings, i. 443.

Basset, Mrs., Lyttelton's Bath landlady (1738), iv. 139.

Bateson, F. W., cited on Timon-Chandos connexion, iii. 259.

Bath, Earl of, *see* Pulteney, William (cr. 1742).

BATH, Somerset: Pope (q.v.) there in 1714, 1715, 1716, 1728, 1734, 1737, and annually 1739–43; describes the Promenade, i. 259–60; the Roman Bath, i. 257; residents of Bath: *see* Ralph Allen, Dr. George Cheyne, Mrs. Henshew (a landlady), Dr. William Oliver (Westgate Street), Jeremiah Pierce (Lilliput Castle), Dr. David Hartley; — visitors to Bath: Wycherley (1706), i. 15; Cromwell and Wycherley (1711), i. 134; Parnell (with Pope, 1714), i. 254, 258; John Gay (1722), ii. 133, 149; Duchess of Buckingham (1723), ii. 84, 100; Dr. Arbuthnot (1724), ii. 253, 514; Bolingbroke (1728), ii. 498; a large group of friends (all four of Bethel's sisters, Martha Blount, Lady Suffolk, Lord Lovel, Lord Burlington (and wife), Lord Chesterfield, Bolingbroke—and Colley Cibber) in 1734, iii. 434–6; bad roads hurt Pope, iv. 156; Bathampton Manor considered and rejected by Martha Blount, iv. 375, 453; refused Pope and George Arbuthnot (1743), iv. 453.

BATHURST, ALLEN, Baron (cr. 1712), Earl (cr. 1772): letters to, i. 476, 489, ii. 13, 126, 257, 292, 516, 524, 530, iii. 130, 136, 139 (from Bolingbroke), 156, 295, 480, 483, 499, 503, iv. 148, 192, 341; letters from, i. 488, ii. 207, 262, 298, 464, iii. 133, 299, 312, iv. 24; writes Pope at moment when Pope writes him, ii. 258; reproached by Pope for not writing, iii. 130; account of a 'bad' day (a set epistolary piece), ii. 263; complains of weather, ii. 299.

BATHURST, ALLEN (*cont.*)
Personal character: extreme mobility, impetuosity, ii. 410, iii. 133, 176, 405–6, iv. 192; a preserver of ancient honour, ii. 333; superior to physicians, iii. 130, 137, 481; poor health, ii. 207; quotes Horace, iv. 25; his politics: possibly involved in the Atterbury (1722) plot, ii. 87, 93, 120, 123, 132, 200–1; Swift rallies him, ii. 475; Prince Frederick (of Wales) speaks well of him, iii. 137, 500; the Prince visits Cirencester in 1738, iv. 138.

Financial commitments: cashier for Swift and Gay, iii. 69, 94, 96; trustee of Edmund, Duke of Buckingham, iii. 296, 299; co-executor of will of John, Duke of Buckingham, iv. 65 n.; aids Katherine, Duchess of Buckingham in a lawsuit, ii. 282, 303; to POPE has bonds of £2,000, ii. 532, iv. 149 n., 467; discourages Pope in 1718 from building in town, i. 475, 488, 516; co-publisher of *The Dunciad* (1729), iii. 31, 61, 177 n.; Pope plans an Epistle to Lord Bathurst, iii. 157, 291, 325; Pope in Town 'like a porpoise in a storm', iv. 88; B. to have a special copy of the 4to vol. of *Essay on Criticism* and *on Man*, iv. 502; close friendship with Pope, ii. 192, 299, iii. 480–1.

Pope visits B.: at Riskins, ii. 207, 263, 299, 464–5; Riskins sold (1739), iv. 179 n.; Cirencester Park, i. 418, 476, 488, 515, ii. 13, 82, 87; the wood, i. 477, ii. 47, 115; Pope invited to design a wood house, ii. 207; Pope and Swift (1726) to visit there, ii. 373, 381 (at Riskins?), 388, 517, iii. 78 (1729), 130, 134 (Pope's house to be carted off to Oakley Wood), 136, 295, 299, 300 (Brobdingnag style of the Park), 503 n. (Pope's obelisk), iv. 24–25 (1736), 39, 84, 192, 281, 468.

B.'s friends and protégés: his servants, Sanders and Old David, iii. 131; Gay (Bathurst charmed by his 'act'), i. 318, 320; Pope's copy of *Gorboduc*, i. 467; death of the lovers at Stanton Harcourt, i. 482 n., 488; Pope's MS. copy of Lady Mary's

BATHURST, ALLEN (*cont.*)
Eclogues, ii. 39; Curll's covert mention of B., ii. 189 n.; to call on Martha Blount, ii. 127; subscribes to Buononcini, ii. 99; visit to Sir W. Wyndham, ii. 207; work on Mrs. Howard's gardens, ii. 213, 258, 259 n., 292, 298–9, 317; H. Layng, ii. 390; E. Lewis, Cleland, *et al.*, iii. 138; wishes Pope to inquire after Lady Mary's health, iii. 134; dines at Pope's, iii. 176, at Barnes, iii. 185; likes Caryll's Park, iii. 237; first night at *Athelwold*, iii. 253; aided Ryves, iii. 289; venison for the Clelands, iii. 300, for Arbuthnot, iii. 416, 417; urged to visit Peterborow at Bevis Mount, iii. 483; has seen Mme La Touche, iv. 148; wishes to know Warburton, iv. 237, 238; marriage of young Stafford, iv. 341–2; Carteret and Warburton, iv. 439; Allen's illness not reported by B., iv. 477; Swift inquires after B., v. 18.
Bathurst, Catherine, Lady, wife of Lord Bathurst, i. 478, ii. 299.
Bathurst, Benjamin, son of Lord Bathurst, iii. 137 (not in politics in 1730); to be at Scarborough, iii. 197; his marriage projected (1731), iii. 210; is given Riskins (1735), iii. 504 n.
Bathurst, Benjamin (or Peter), brothers of Lord Bathurst—one to stand for Parliament, iii. 137 n.
BATHURST, CHARLES, bookseller, successor to B. Motte: letters to, iv. 259, 284, 285, 324, 333, 345, 349, 352, 361, 371; dates changed here on two letters, iv. 284, 285; Pope offers *Works in Prose*, vol. ii (Swift letters) to B. as publisher, iv. 259; dines at Twickenham, iv. 285; recasts *Miscellanies* for new eds., iv. 284–5, 333, 353, 367, 372; Arbuthnot's *Sermon at the Mercat Cross*, not to be included, iv. 372; piracy by Corbett rumoured, iv. 345; B. owes Pope £26, iv. 361; wishes to become Warburton's publisher, iv. 371; aids Pope with materials for the grotto, iv. 342, 349, 352.
Battalia (or Battaglia), Mr., protégé or employee of Lord Burlington, iii. 87, 329.

Battersea House, *see* Bolingbroke *and* Lord Marchmont, iv. 498.
Bayle, Pierre, *Dictionary*, ii. 302, iii. 176.
Bays, cited from *The Rehearsal*, i. 138.
Beach, Mary (or Mercy), Pope's 'old nurse' and Parnell, i. 225; and young Harcourt, i. 491; her rent unpaid, i. 524; Eckersall, ii. 32; Lord Harcourt, ii. 115; ill, ii. 308, 336; her death, ii. 282, 318, 336.
Bearcroft, Rev. Philip, Lord Percival wishes him to be preacher at the Charterhouse, ii. 267, 269, 272.
Beaufort, Duchess of, *see* Somerset, Frances (Scudamore).
Beaulieu Abbey, Hants., iii. 426, 430 n. (Bewley, to Pope).
Bede, the Venerable, cited by Swift, ii. 326.
Bedford, 3rd Duke of, *see* Russell, Wriothesley.
Bedier, Miss, ii. 476.
Bedingfield, Mr., his death recorded, i. 266.
BEDINGFIELD, EDWARD: letter from, i. 141; account of, i. 91, 141 n.; distributed *Rape of the Lock*, i. 141–2, 145.
Bedingfield, Sir Harry, Caryll's maternal grandfather, i. 266, 411, ii. 392; his wife (sister of Lord Burlington), ii. 392 n.
Begg, Edleen, transcribes Warburton letters, iv. 236 n., 239 n.
Bègue, Comte de, envoy of the Duke of Lorraine, ii. 60.
Behn, Aphra, named to Lady Mary as possibly 'Sappho', iii. 352.
Bell, Col., of the Post Office, deprived by Parliament, iv. 398–9.
Bellenden, Mary, Maid of Honour: married John Campbell (later 4th Duke of Argyle), i. 379 n., 427, 450; account of, iv. 149 n.
Bell-man, — his verses mentioned, iii. 334.
Bellman of St. James's Verses for the Year 1734, mentioned in clandestine Swift letters; omitted in later eds., iii. 401 n.
Bellucci: does monument in the Abbey for the Duke of Buckingham, ii. 99; painted at Cannons, iii. 268.
Bennet, Nelly, ballad by Arbuthnot about her, ii. 411.

Bennington, Herts., Charles Caesar, ii. 197, 198, 202, 262, 313.

Bentinck, Margaret (Harley), Duchess of Portland: aids Mrs. Pendarves, iv. 83; her accouchement awaited, iii. 475. *See also* Harley, Lady Margaret.

Bentinck, William, 2nd Duke of Portland: a good husband, iii. 424; Pope unable to visit him, iii. 446.

Bentley, Richard: most learned man in England, i. 294 n.; his ed. of Horace, i. 372 n., 489, iii. 115; inspires Mallet's 'Verbal Criticism', iii. 66 n.; enemy of C. Middleton, iii. 111; edits Milton (1732) and Manilius (1739), iii. 240 n.; blamed for fire in Cottonian Library, iii. 240; disparaged as a pedant, iii. 241, 244, 267, 269, 291; Pope prefers Richardson's work on Milton, iii. 327, 331; satirized in *Sober Advice* by Pope, iii. 446 n.

Bentley, Richard, jr., son of the scholar, threatens Pope, iii. 446 n.; later apologizes, iii. 451.

Berg Collection (New York Public Library), MSS. cited, i. 191 n., 436, iii. 157, iv. 66, 200, 484.

BERKELEY, GEORGE, Bishop of Cloyne, famous philosopher: letter to, ii. 62; letters from him to Pope, i. 221, 304, 445; his account of first performance of *Cato*, i. 175 n.; praises *Rape of the Lock*, i. 221; chaplain to Lord Peterborow (thanks to Swift), i. 222; letters from Italy, i. 221-2, 445-7; Pope hopes to meet him in heaven, iii. 81; asked to dine with Pope and Atterbury, ii. 62; to spend a week at Twickenham, ii. 62; in London, ii. 62, 149, 324, 329 n., 333; his Bermuda project, ii. 324, 330, 333; concerned about the plague, ii. 104 n.; *Alciphron* too speculative for Swift, iii. 286, and Gay, iii. 289; Pope prefers it to Dr. Delany's book, iii. 276; his *Tar-water* pleases Pope, iv. 514; made Bishop in 1734, iii. 403; Lord Burlington has a party for him, iii. 403.

BERKELEY, Hon. GEORGE, son of 2nd Earl of Berkeley, brother of Lady Betty Germain, 2nd husband of Countess of Suffolk (Mrs. Howard):

BERKELEY, Hon. GEORGE (*cont.*) letter to, ii. 259; marries Mrs. Howard in 1735, ii. 259; supports the pall at Gay's funeral, iii. 338; finds Pope a sickly travelling companion, iii. 409 n.; his marriage, iii. 474; his sister, Lady Betty, iii. 501 n.; goes to France (1736) with Lady Suffolk, iv. 34 n.; has the gout, iv. 212.

Berkeley, James, 3rd Earl, leases Cranford (1726) to Bolingbroke, ii. 400; accompanied to France by Bolingbroke, v. 14; dies there, v. 14.

BERKSHIRE: *see* Aldermaston, Binfield, Bucklebury, Drayton, Easthampstead, Hurst, Letcombe, Mampledurham, Newbury, Oakingham, Reading, Sunning Hill, Windsor, Windsor Forest, Whiteknights.

Bermuda: project of Bishop Berkeley for, ii. 324, 329, 331; the Governor (Sir John Hope Bruce) in trouble, ii. 427.

Bestwick, near Beverley, York, *see* Hugh Bethel.

Bethel, Bridget (Hugh's sister), prepared Pope's broth, iii. 513.

Bethel, Elizabeth (Hugh's sister), married to Sir W. Codrington, iv. 168 n. (*See* Codrington.)

BETHEL, HUGH: letters to, ii. 178, 386, 436, 501, iii. 113, 195, 196, 209, 232 (with Martha Blount), 287, 380, 388, 426, 435, 436, 518, 519, iv. 21, 39, 57, 67, 85, 113, 146, 205, 224, 253, 254, 268, 298, 338, 354, 375, 395, 414, 445, 467, 473, 475, 498, 508, 514; letter from, iv. 511; asked to return Pope's letters (1728), ii. 501; — cousin of the 1st Earl of Cadogan, ii. 386 n.; his four sisters, ii. 513 n., iii. 435; admirable character, iii. 395, 436, iv. 26, 147, 494; his sisters give Pope physic, ii. 513; B. aids Martha Blount concerning the Roberts annuity, iii. 139, 197, 210, 227, 271, 283, 355, 453; later aid to Miss Blount, iv. 39, 467; at Scarborough, iii. 197; told of Pope's rambles, iii. 435; wants Pope's influence in an ecclesiastical matter, iii. 436; Pope sends a chicken for supper, iii. 518; B. aids Mrs. Rackett, iv. 21; friend to Fortescue, Kent, Cleland,

BETHEL, HUGH (*cont.*)
iv. 40; Pope owes him £400, iv. 113;
in danger of being sheriff, iv. 206;
an early will named him as Pope's
executor, iv. 222; advises Pope on
investments, iv. 434; a servant recommended to him, iv. 473, 476;
welcomed back from Italy, iv. 467;
he and Pope exchange portraits, iv.
500, 509, 512; the declining health
of B. and Pope, iv. 498; a final visit
from B., iv. 521.
   B.'s health: bad eyes, iii. 233; his
asthma, iii. 519, iv. 163, 205, 338,
494, 511; in Italy (1741–3) for his
health, iv. 253, 355, 358, 375–7, 395,
414–15, 445, 460; his return, iv.
460 n.; his asthma better in Yorkshire, iii. 113, 195, 287, iv. 57, 164,
186, 225; at Scarborough, iii. 197,
210; his London visits desired by
friends, iii. 3, iv. 39, 113, 354; Pope
hurried from Bristol to greet him, iv.
470.
   Literary connexions: subscribes to
Buononcini, ii. 99; Pope sends him
the *Odyssey*, ii. 179; subscribes (1736)
to S. Wesley's *Poems*, iii. 504; subsidizes Pope's *Letters* (1737), iv. 21,
39; *Essay on Man* mentions him, iii.
209, 227 n., 381, iv. 57 n.; is Ofellus
in Pope's Imitation of Horace, 2nd
Satire of 2nd Book, iii. 209 n., 427,
iv. 150 n.
BETHEL, SLINGSBY, brother of Hugh:
letters to, iv. 33, 35, 65, 87, 168, 197,
335, 365, 401, 447, 475, 485, 488, 496,
497, 513; — gets subscribers for Pope's
(1737) *Letters*, iv. 33, 65; invited to
Twickenham, iv. 33, 35, 197; should
pay M. Blount her interest, iv. 87;
handles investments for Pope, iv. 269,
335, 365, 401, 513; gets wine for
Pope, iv. 33, 39, 87, 515; wine also
for M. Blount, iv. 475; has news of
his brother for Pope, iv. 201, 395,
434, 447, 475; asked to send *The
New Dunciad* to Hugh, iv. 401–2.
Bettenham, James, publishes Hooke's
Roman History, iv. 31.
Betterton, Thomas, actor: Pope sends
'service' to, i. 76; his death, i. 85;
Pope suggests epitaph from Cicero, i.
88; B.'s imitations of Chaucer, i.

Betterton, Thomas (*cont.*)
142; his character by Caryll, i. 142;
papers left in Pope's care, i. 142.
Bettesworth, Arthur, mentioned dis-
paragingly, iv. 407.
Beverley, York, *see* Hugh Bethel, Col.
James Moyser.
Bevis Mount, Southampton, the Earl of
Peterborow, iii. 282, iv. 252, &c.
Bible, quoted by Pope, ii. 54, 472, 521,
531, iv. 208, 247, 252, 412 n.
Bibliothèque raisonnée, prints Atter-
bury's *Vindication*, iii. 246.
Bibury (Glos.), visited by Pope and
Swift (1726), ii. 388, 406.
Bickerstaff, Isaac, *see The Tatler*; *see also*
Richard Steele.
Bickford, Edmund: joining in the trip
to Devon, i. 311; witnesses the *Ody-
ssey* indenture, ii. 217 n.; promiscu-
ously amorous, ii. 255; lame, uses a
staff, ii. 441 n., iii. 126.
Bicknell, Mrs., actress, friend of Gay
and Pope, i. 283 n.
Biggs, stonemason employed by Allen:
lent to Pope, iv. 181, 191, 195, 350;
his brother also employed, iv. 351,
358, 360.
Bindon, Francis, his portraits of Swift,
iv. 233.
Binfield, near Ockingham, Berks.:
Whitehill House, residence of the
Popes, 1700–16, i. 17, 336; neighbours: *see* Angel, Dancastle (Lord
of the Manor), Dancastle, T., Mrs.
Nelson, Mr. Nevill, Mr. Tanner;
Nicholas Rowe visits Pope, i. 329.
Birch, Thomas: his *Life of Atterbury*
cited, ii. 94 n.; transcribes an Atterbury letter, iii. 76 n.; cites a letter to
P. Yorke, iii. 328 n.; for him Pope
reads proofs of *Life* of Gay, iv. 37 n.,
38 n.; he explains the hoax of alleged
Milton lines, iv. 80 n.; his statement
about the clandestine vol. of Swift
letters, iv. 241 n., 242 n.
BIRD, FRANCIS, sculptor: letter to, ii.
26; to make the Pope family monument for Twickenham church, ii.
26–27; works on the Craggs monument for the Abbey, with Guelfi, ii.
457, 463.
Bishop, Sir Cecil, his wife sends the
Blounts a servant, iii. 75.

Blackmore, Sir Richard: a friend of Pope's in 1714, i. 218; attacks Pope in 1716, i. 218 n.; hostile to Swift, i. 358, 371; composed verse in his chariot, i. 373; his *Prince Arthur* not liked, iii. 164.

Bladud, mythical King of Bath, iv. 134.

Blanchard, Rae, cited on Steele, i. 145 n., 148 n., 152 n., 165.

Blandford, Marquess of, *see* Churchill, William Godolphin–.

Blenheim Park: Pope visits it, i. 431–2; Blenheim archives cited, i. 165.

Blewet, Mrs., sister of Mrs. Cope, cousin of Caryll, i. 158 n.

Blome, R., his *History of the Bible*, iv. 20 n.

Blondel, Mr., in the entourage of the Duchess of Hamilton, i. 438–9.

Blount, Mrs. Ann (Cornwallis), demands separation from her husband, iii. 55. (*See* Henry Pope Blount.)

BLOUNT, EDWARD, of Blagdon, Devon: letters to, i. 246, 328, 329, 337, 424, 454, ii. 85, 88, 176, 296, 319; letters from, i. 247, 337, 344, ii. 7, 10; letters to Caryll printed as if to B., i. 240, 246, 329, 335, 337; B.'s widow is asked to return Pope's letters, ii. 423, iii. 79 n; — B. helps on *Iliad* subscription, i. 220, 233 n.; his non-partisan politics, i. 248; on superstition among the Greeks, i. 248; invites Pope and Jervas to Devon, i. 300; arranges the Dunbar marriage, i. 309; his reaction to the invasion of 1715, i. 320–1; on the registration and taxation of Catholic estates, i. 337, 344; decides to live abroad, i. 338; not happy there (1716–17), i. 418, 424–5; visits Pope, i. 411, ii. 7, 10; his rhymes, ii. 10–11; uses Pope's chariot, ii. 10; at Abberley, ii. 10; life in Devonshire, ii. 86, 89, 176 n.; an illness, ii. 88; urged to come to Town for the winter, ii. 320; his death (1726), ii. 387, 392; his daughter Mary marries Hon. Edward Howard, later 9th Duke of Norfolk, iii. 346.

Blount, Henry Pope: Fenton's pupil, ii. 119; spends a summer in Sturston (1722), ii. 122, 147; not desirable for him to stay in Town, ii. 216, 232; Fenton lacks news of, ii. 234; still at

Blount, Henry Pope (*cont.*) his father's, ii. 244; grieved at (false) report of Broome's death, ii. 519; marriage (1728) with Anne Cornwallis, ii. 519, iii. 55, 510; thinks Broome must be writing, iii. 37.

Blount, Judith, Lady: pleased with her son's progress at Sturston, ii. 147; smallpox prevents his early return from Sturston, ii. 214–15, 224.

BLOUNTS OF MAPLEDURHAM (including Mrs. Lister Blount, her son Michael, and her daus. Teresa and Martha): allied to the Carylls, i. 93 n., who send venison, i. 128; they drink (1714–15) Tory healths, i. 252, 265, 308; Mrs. Lister Blount's gift of elderberry wine, i. 315; they leave Mapledurham on Michael's marriage, i. 336; in Bolton Street (1717–38), i. 339 n., 414 n., 430, 458, &c.; will not come to Cirencester (1718), i. 489; visit Twickenham in a bad storm, ii. 57; still gainers in South Sea (Oct. 1720), ii. 58; — going to Sussex (Caryll?), ii. 133; a house in Richmond (summer of 1725), ii. 305; summers in Petersham (1727–33), ii. 435, iii. 113, 370; move from Bolton to Welbeck Street (1738), iv. 113; the mother is badly treated by Teresa and weakly blames Martha also, iii. 41, 45, 47, 127; dangerously ill, iv. 344; her death (1743), iv. 450.

BLOUNT, MARTHA and TERESA: letters addressed to both of them, i. 182, 252, 277, 307, 310, 317, 409, 426, 429, 435, 447, 455, 460, 467, 490, 512, 514, ii. 1, 21; letters to them bound up in 1824, iv. 183 n.; early friendship with Pope, i. 15 n., 113, 137; knew all about *Rape of the Lock* before publication, i. 143, 171, 182, 261; exiles from Mapledurham, i. 327; — Pope tries to buy annuities for them, i. 431, 467 n.; invited on suburban jaunts by Pope (1717?), i. 435; too gay for Pope's period of mourning, i. 456; delayed invitation from the Carylls in 1718, i. 490; Pope offers to show them Blenheim, i. 482; invites them to Cirencester, i. 482; they go to Grinstead, i. 499, 512, 515; Pope wishes them husbands,

BLOUNT, MARTHA and TERESA (*cont.*)
i. 512; Pope meets them at Parsons
Green, ii. 1; they dine (1720) at
Twickenham, ii. 1; coolness between
them and Pope, ii, 25.
BLOUNT, MARTHA: letters to, i. 143,
259, 268, 280, 293, 315, 318, 338,
375, 379, 479, ii. 16, 30, 235, 236,
511, 513, iii. 335, 385, 427, 434, 487,
iv. 183, 185, 187, 200, 204, 211, 355,
463, 510; letters from, i. 452, ii. 11,
191, 490 (to Swift), iv. 28 (to Fortescue, with Pope), 47 (to Mrs. Knight,
with Pope), 462; Pope writes to her
when busy, i. 293; one letter from
Pope not available for publication,
iii. 427; she writes to Swift, ii. 490;
he praises the letter, ii. 498; she
corresponds with H. Bethel, iv. 57;
with Mrs. Price at Spa, iv. 265;
writes for, not to, Pope, i. 351; her
name cut out of a letter, ii. 393.
Her health: has smallpox (1714), i.
264; Spaw water prescribed, iii. 113;
confined for 3 weeks, ii. 491; has a
rash and a fever, iii. 46; ill, iii. 134;
attended now by Dr. Burton, iii.
232; Pope sure she won't take Scarborough waters, iii. 288; ill after
Gay's death, iii. 337; during her
illness her family unsympathetic, iii.
337; in good health, iv. 7; has her
rash again (she's a blonde), iv. 21;
slightly ill, iv. 49; several colds, iv.
225; — Bath prescribed for her
health, i. 257, iii. 434; goes to mass at
Bath, iii. 435; is there (1734) at
expense of Lady Suffolk, iii. 437;
prudish about travelling to Bath
with Pope, iv. 26; there in 1737, iv.
85, 206; ready to go—but doesn't, iv.
365–6; Pope wants her and Anne
Arbuthnot to come at once, iv.
367; tries in vain to interest her in
Bathampton Manor, iv. 375, 430;
her relations with the Allens, iv. 387
(friendly), 398, 452; the unpleasantness at Prior Park, iv. 462, 463; gets
back to London, iv. 467; told by
Pope of Allen's protestations on Good
Friday, iv. 510; causes of the quarrel,
iv. 510 n.
Her finances: Pope sends lottery
tickets, ii. 17; through Burlington is

BLOUNT, MARTHA (*cont.*)
getting a ticket, iii. 518; invests
through Pope in South Sea stocks, i.
379; asks for her Exchequer Orders,
ii. 30; her money re-invested, iii.
449; Pope attempts to get her an
annuity, iii. 530, iv. 467, 473–4;
she is Pope's residual legatee, iv. 160
n.; G. Arbuthnot lists (1745) Pope's
securities, iv. 340 n.; difficulties with
her brother over her quarterly allowance, iii. 112, 139 n., 210, 406, 409,
415, 440, 455, 469, 478; difficulties
over an annuity bought from
Roberts: his life insured, iii. 33, 112;
he does not pay, iii. 5, 91, 197, 198,
225, 271, 283, 427.
Her friendship with Pope: he sends
plays to read, i. 252; *The Rape of the
Lock*, i. 143; has on loan some of
Pope's books, i. 293; he gets her a
3rd night box for *Athelwold*, iii.
253–4; she wants a box for *Mustapha*
on 6th night, iv. 167; sends pamphlets for Caryll to read, i. 472, iii. 173,
370; she won't smile at an epigram
sent to Teresa, i. 349; his verses on her
birthday, ii. 180, iii. 18–19; she sends
Caryll 3rd ed. of 'Of Taste' with its
prefatory letter, iii. 279; sends Caryll
the *Essay on Man*, iii. 340; compelled
the omission of her name from 'On
the Characters of Women', iii. 450;
Curll prints four letters of Voiture as
from Pope to her, iii. 487, 495; she
is thought of in connexion with
Eloisa, i. 338; she invites Pope for
Friday, ii. 11; his absence annoys, ii.
191; his birthday letter to her, ii. 235;
she is at Twickenham, ii. 316; Swift
jokes at her elderly, sickly friends, ii.
476; she sends news of Pope's mother
while he is at Bath (1728), ii. 513;
advises Pope to spend more time in
study, iii. 135; Pope begs Bethel to
help discipline her, iv. 39–40; dines
with Pope, iv. 183; has Pope's first
pineapple, iv. 186; Pope asks her
vainly to come with Fortescue to
Rousham, iv. 189; asked to remember
Pope (at Bath) to Lyttelton, Cornbury, and Cleland, iv. 202; she will
accompany the Arbuthnots to
Twickenham, iv. 443; not known to

BLOUNT, MARTHA (*cont.*)
have been with Pope in his last days, iv. 501 n.; Pope asks when she is coming, iv. 511; hopes (25 Mar. 1744) to be able to come to Town to see her, iv. 511.

Other social connexions: fails to see the Coronation (1715) because of smallpox, i. 264, 268; possibly living in Charles Street briefly, i. 338; has Dr. Arbuthnot's portrait, ii. 196; urged to finish sitting for a picture, iv. 212; reports to Pope on Arbuthnot's health, iii. 415; friendly with Lord Bathurst, ii. 258, iii. 137; gossip about the Duchess of Beaufort subsides (?), iv. 266; Hugh Bethel and his sisters afford warm winter evenings indoors, iii. 233; her esteem for Bethel, iii. 288, iv. 67, 197, 269, 339, 355 (his departure for Italy), 377, 396; she has found a good manservant for him, iv. 473, 476; would have liked Bethel's portrait (Pope has it), iv. 500; Slingsby Bethel a useful friend, iv. 67; gets wine for her, iv. 197, 402, 485; John Caryll her godfather, i. 113; visits to the Carylls, i. 411, 414, iii. 14; never hears from Mrs. Caryll, iii. 451; returns portrait of Judith Cowper after Pope's death, ii. 139 n.; Mrs. Englefield, a virtuous aunt, i. 375; friendship with John Gay, ii. 508, iii. 121, 131, v. 13; in Apr. 1731 Gay in four days breakfasted twice with Martha and Mrs. Howard, iii. 194; tells Pope of Gay's death (?), iii. 335 n.; summer of 1734 at Cheam with Lady Gerard, iii. 425, 426; with Lady Gerard dines at Pope's, iv. 21; an early riser (6 a.m.) at Lady Gerard's, iv. 29; is living with Lady Gerard in 1743, iv. 485; also iv. 488; advised to go with Mrs. Greville to Lady Cobham's, iv. 188; intimate with Mrs. Howard, ii. 446, iii. 474, 478, 491; acquaintance with Mrs. Knight, ii. 457, 485, iii. 68, 450, iv. 47; Lyttelton esteems her, iv. 47; Mallet and young Newsham send service, iii. 485; Sarah, Duchess of Marlborough makes her acquaintance, iv. 412, 414, 419, 457; not invited by the Duchess of Queensberry, iv. 212;

BLOUNT, MARTHA (*cont.*)
Lady Marchmont may invite her, iv. 212; her friendship with Lady Fanny Shirley, iv. 167 n.; Swift her constant admirer, ii. 491, iii. 162, 491, v. 17; dines with Lady Worsley, ii. 191.

Her summers—where spent: Richmond (?), ii. 435; Petersham, ii, 491 (1728), iii. 116 (1730), 193-4; Cheam and Hampshire, iii. 436 (1734); Richmond, 'The Shepherd's Hut', iv. 29 (1736), 34, 35; in or near Twickenham, iv. 67 (1737); at Kew, iv. 113 (1738); Shepherd's Hut, iv. 169 (1739), 170, 183, 189, 190, 193, 267 (1740); not placed in 1741, iv. 348, 355, 363.

Her troubles with her family (as seen by Pope): her reputation may suffer from Teresa's behaviour, iii. 38, 45, 58, 61, 75, 88, 110; harshly treated by her mother and sister, iii. 340, 370; should live apart from them, iv. 26, 85; goes with them to live in Welbeck Street, iv. 113, 188; weakness keeps her with the family, iv. 147, 187, 255, 344, 417; upset by her mother's death, iv. 450, 452, 453; by Pope's will she gets her own house in Town, iv. 508.

Her character: prudent, even prudish, i. 257, 261; not the 'shepherdess' type, ii. 395, 476; Swift jokes about her need of discipline, ii. 476; subservient to her mother and sister, iii. 318, 512; gossip about her and Pope, ii. 353 n., iii. 40 n.; grows older but not wiser (Pope says), ii. 469; unhappy in Town, ii. 16, iii. 218; gives news of Pope's friends when ill, iii. 2, 3; extreme kindness, iii. 237, iv. 177, 414; *semper eadem*, Pope's formula for her, iii. 274, 349, iv. 356; her 'merit', iii. 450, iv. 187; her 'dissipated' social life, iv. 211; prefers a house in Town, iv. 508.

Blount, Mary, dau. of Edward (later Duchess of Norfolk), ii. 86 n., iii. 103 n.

Blount, Michael, brother of Martha and Teresa, i. 265; pretended author of the hermaphrodite letter, i. 279 n.; a special *Iliad* reserved for him, i. 294, 300; his marriage causes his mother and sisters to leave Mapledurham, i.

Blount, Michael (*cont.*)

311, 313, 315; unkind to his mother and sisters, i. 476, ii. 26; his death wrongly reported, ii. 29; dilatory in paying Martha her allowance, iii. 139 n., 406, 409, 437, 453, 455.

Blount, 'Patty', *see* Martha Blount.

BLOUNT, TERESA: letters to, i. 256, 264, 349, 434, 456, 458, 459, 460, 468, 517, ii. 25, 26, 31, 38, 57, 59; letter from, i. 435; her adventurous nature, i. 261, 268; at the Prince's birthday night, i. 375; sends Pope money to invest, i. 375; affronted by his proposed annuity, i. 468; a lottery order, i. 468; Pope offers to give her his coach, i. 517; annuities again, ii. 38; jokes about her discipline of Martha, ii. 476; — Pope comes to dislike her, i. 468, iii. 1; she causes an uproar in the family, iii. 36; her alleged affair with a married man, iii. 40, 41–42, 91, 122; temporarily forsaken by her lover, iii. 142, 173; her love of the Town, iii. 218; the cause of her tears is (?) Moratt, iv. 212; her bad influence on Martha, iv. 500.

Blount, Sir Thomas Pope, of Twickenham, his son to go to Sturston with Fenton, ii. 122.

Blunt, Sir John, Director in the South Sea Company, mentioned in Pope's Epistle to Bathurst, iii. 353.

Boden, Mr., wishes captaincy of a naval vessel and Pope tries to help, i. 443.

Bodleian Library, cited on originals of Cromwell letters, ii. 439 n., and of the four 'S.E.' (Voiture) letters, iii. 487.

Boerhaave, Hermann, prescribed for Wm. Pulteney, iv. 45.

Bohn, H. G., iv. 278 n., 254 n.

Boileau Despréaux: signed his works 'D', i. 49, 192, ii. 498; Épîtres vi and vii cited by Pope, iv. 425–6, v. 3.

Bolingbroke, Henry, viscount, *see* St. John, Henry.

Bolton, 3rd Duke of, *see* Paulet, Charles.

Bolton Street (1717–38), residence of the Blount ladies, i. 339 n.

Bonarelli, Guidobaldo, pastoral poet, i. 18, 19.

Bond, William, his *Spectator* disparaged, i. 276 n.

Bonœuvrier, Mrs., iv. 219.

Book Prices Current, cited on concert at Buckingham House, ii. 134 n.

Booth, Mrs., created the role of Elfrid in *Athelwold,* iii. 232 n.

Booth, Barton: created the role of Cato, i. 175; declined to act in *Athelwold,* end of his career, iii. 232.

Booth, Pennyston, vicar of Twickenham, ii. 313, 328.

Bordoni, Faustina, opera singer, married to Hesse, iii. 216.

BORLASE, WILLIAM, of Penzance: letters to, iv. 228, 245; account of, iv. 228 n.; learns of friendship of Pope and Allen, iv. 222 n.; sends Cornish diamonds for Pope's grotto, iv. 228, 235, 239, 244; thanked by placing his name on the wall of the grotto, iv. 245, 278.

Bosci (or Boschi), Giuseppe, opera singer, ii. 136.

Bossu, Réné Le, i. 63, ii. 216, 226.

Boston, Mass., Pope's *Works* in its libraries in 1728, ii. 494.

Boswell, James, cited on Dr. Barry, iii. 506 n.

Boucher, Mr. (surgeon?), might aid Wise in getting a scholarship, iii. 141.

Boughton, Northants., seat of the Earl of Strafford, ii. 300, 309, 310.

Boulter, Hugh, Archbishop of Armagh, iii. 274 n.

Bounce, Pope's Great Dane, iii. 435, iv. 48; a puppy given to Lord Burlington, iii. 515; another to Ralph Allen, iv. 181; the last Bounce given to Orrery, iv. 406, 422, 508 n.; bitten by a mad dog, iv. 507; Ault's account of, iv. 507 n.

BOURNE, FRANCIS, servant: letter from her written by Pope, i. 436.

Bovy, Mrs., a friend of young Henry Blount, ii. 147.

Bowack, John, Pope aids his selection as secretary to the Commissioners of Westminster Bridge, iv. 82.

BOWLES, JOSEPH, Bodley's Librarian: letter to, i. 421, ii. 83.

Bowles, William Lisle: on Pope's being 'tracked' in Voiture, i. 98; B. the source of a letter, i. 256 n.; on Judith Cowper, ii. 141 n.; on cider, ii. 45 n.; on 'Mrs. H', ii. 136.

Bowry, Pope's waterman: carries messages to and from Fortescue, ii. 346, 373, iii. 11; brings a message from Martha Blount, ii. 191; possibly 'Tom the water fool' in Swift's terms, ii. 407; called Her Majesty's waterman, ii. 473; sent to Aaron Hill and D. Mallet, iii. 189, 235; more than once drunk, iii. 245, 475; sent for cider for Pope, iii. 271.

Bowyer, Jonah (or Jonas), bookseller, handles *Works* (1723) of the Duke of Buckingham, ii. 218 n.

Bowyer, William, sr. (1663–1737), printer of Pope's *Iliad*, iv. 224; his rights in printing Swift's pieces (1732) questioned, iii. 323-4, v. 10; *Miscellanies* (1732) printed in haste to forestall him, iii. 348.

BOWYER, WILLIAM, jr. (1699–1777), printer with his father: letters to, iv. 338, 426, 477, 501, 504, 505, 514; Pope discourages project for a comment on his borrowings, iv. 338; replaces J. Wright as Pope's printer (1742), iv. 392 n.; is printing *Dunciad* I-III, iv. 393, 425, 426, 428; prints a new ed. of Warburton's *Commentary*, iv. 402 n.; to begin to print *Essay on Man* (4to), iv. 434, 448; also the *Essay on Criticism*, with Warburton's comments, iv. 474, 491, 501 (must be entered in the Hallbook); Warburton uses B. as address for letters, iv. 471; to print epistles *On the Use of Riches* while Warburton is in Town, iv. 500, 505; Epistle to Cobham to be printed in 4to, not 8vo, iv. 504; B. must include Warburton's changes in proofs, iv. 514.

Boyle, Charles, Lord, son of the Earl of Orrery: he and his brother Hamilton in Duke Street, iv. 406; brings letter from his father to Pope shyly, iv. 517, 521.

Boyle, Lady Charlot, dau. of the Earl of Burlington, iv. 324.

BOYLE, DOROTHY (Savile), Countess of Burlington: letters to, iii. 20, 201, 271, 273, 341, 389, 396, 397, 518, iv. 1, 124, 139, 197; she is Lady in Waiting to the Queen, iii. 20; is a painter, singer, and wit, iii. 272 n.; at Tunbridge Wells with Gay (1723),

BOYLE, DOROTHY (Savile) (*cont.*) ii. 181; her ill health, iii. 4, 5, 87 n., 342, iv. 29, 237; her copy [portrait?] of Maister Johnson, iii. 272, 341, 329; — Pope works on her family (Savile) papers, iii. 303, 322, 328; Pope is her stray servant, iii. 418; her interest in *The Dunciad*, iii. 4, 20; sends her a pamphlet, iii. 201; she serves as his amanuensis, iii. 272, 273, iv. 1-2, 124; she makes epigrams to have them pass as his, iv. 125; sends him attacks on him in *The Daily Gazetteer*, iv. 124; she signs the tree petition, iv. 324.

Boyle, Lady Dorothy, dau. of the Earl of Burlington, iv. 324; her marriage to Lord Euston, iv. 323 n.; her tragic death, iv. 396; her father's grief, iv. 415.

Boyle, Hamilton, son of the 5th Earl of Orrery, whom ultimately he succeeded: has smallpox in Ireland, iv. 298; returns to England (1741) with his father, iv. 326.

Boyle, Henrietta, 1st wife of 5th Earl of Orrery, her death, iii. 482.

Boyle, Henry, Lord Carleton: Pope visited him at Middleton, i. 375; President of the Council, ii. 110, 113, 289, iv. 183.

BOYLE, JOHN, 5th Earl of Orrery: letters to, iii. 469, 501, iv. 8, 10, 15, 42, 52, 58, 64, 70, 92, 123, 129, 136, 154, 231, 262, 282, 285, 296, 300, 303, 309, 311, 312, 314, 330, 332, 406, 413, 436, 440, 482, 513, 517, 521; letters from, iii. 481, 505, iv. 54, 61, 69, 73, 75, 133, 226 (with Lady Orrery), 275, 276, 279, 287, 291, 293, 294, 304, 306, 307, 326, 328, 407, 442, 466, 468, 472, 522 (to Mallet); letters to O. from Mallet, iv. 522, 523; letters to O. from his 2nd Countess, iv. 507; letters from O. to Faulkner, iv. 270, 292, 295, 298; letters from Faulkner to O., iv. 280, 291, 295; letters from O. to Swift, iv. 60, 75, 81, 277, 336 (with Pope); letters from O. to Mrs. Whiteway, iv. 308, 325, 327; letters from Mrs. Whiteway to O., iv. 277, 307, 320; his letterbooks furnish some texts, i. 198; his *Remarks* also, i. 198 n., v. 18; a letter to him cited, ii. 115 n.; his correspondence

BOYLE, JOHN (*cont.*)
with Pope begins in 1735, iii. 469;
his desire to know Pope, iii. 344, 349
n.; his letters praised by Pope, iv. 517;
the insincerity of his letters, iv. 307 n.
O. in Ireland: fighting a villainous
agent, iii. 363; his rents unpaid, iv.
45; eager to be free from Irish lawyers, iv. 76; spends the year 1735 in
Ireland, iii. 470; recently visited
James Ward, iii. 481; Swift thinks
O. has a genius for verse, iii. 377; feels
isolated—glad of a letter, iii. 482;
praises Dr. Edward Barry, iii. 506;
Fenton his former preceptor, iii. 506;
hopes to know Cornbury, iii. 506;
has been ill, iv. 8; death of Lord
Orkney, iv. 55; O. is co-executor of
will of John, Duke of Buckingham,
iv. 65; leaving Ireland in 1737, iv.
73, 75, 81; O. marries (1738) again,
iv. 116, 123 n.; coach accident near
Coventry, iv. 123; Pope wishes him
to buy Dawley, iv. 136; O. charges
Mallet with plagiarism in *Mustapha*,
iv. 210; isolated at Caledon, iv. 226;
best friend (she says) of Duchess of
Buckingham, iv. 232; his gout, iv.
277; dau. born at Caledon, iv. 287 n.;
sons have smallpox, iv. 305; eager
(1740) to leave Ireland, iv. 306, 307,
329 (1741).
Early services to Pope: delighted to
be Pope's friend, iii. 481; ready to
defend Pope, iii. 470; expects Pope to
defend Atterbury, iii. 502; on Pope's
epitaph for Gay, iii. 361, 368, 372,
502, v. 12, 13; on Cornbury's unpublished lines to Pope, iii. 502, 505;
subsidizes the publication of Pope's
Letters (1737), iv. 53, 55, 65, 69;
necessary to send vols. promptly
because he is leaving Ireland, iv. 69,
70; *Epistle to Augustus* also sent, iv.
70–71; Pope's epigram on Cibber's
'Last Word', iv. 407.
*O. aids in getting Swift letters re-
turned*: Pope asks Swift to turn the
letters over to O., iv. 8, 42, 52; Swift
very 'shy' in regard to the letters, iv.
54; Pope is asked to send Curll's 'New
Letters', iv. 54, 60; forwards Pope's
letter to Swift, iv. 60; returns (1738)
Pope's letters to Swift unread, iv. 287;

BOYLE, JOHN (*cont.*)
Swift's good health, iii. 482; poor
health, iv. 8; O.'s farewell to Swift
(1737), iv. 75; in 1738 he brings Pope
a letter from Swift, iv. 154; Pope and
he write affectionately to Swift (1741),
iv. 336.
O.'s role in the publication (1741) *of
the Swift-Pope letters*: says Gerrard
brought the clandestine vol. from
Bath, iv. 241 n.; can seldom (1737)
see Swift alone, iv. 54; secures the
return of the letters to Pope, iv. 61,
62, 69, 76; is shocked by the chasm
of six years in the correspondence, iv.
73, 75; Pope returns to O. the MS. of
'Verses on the Death of Swift', iv.
130; O.'s comments on the letter of
8 Aug. 1728, iv. 133; sends Pope a
copy of the covering letter that came
with the clandestine vol., iv. 242 n.;
has never seen the original of it, iv.
288, 305; has the clandestine vol.
from Faulkner, iv. 270, 276; returns
it to Faulkner, iv. 284, 291; sends it
himself to Pope, iv. 287, 292, 305;
must return it intact to Faulkner, iv.
306; thinks it was printed in England,
Mrs. Whiteway and Deane Swift involved, iv. 280, 308; publication
stopped in Ireland, iv. 275; thinks the
letters plainly stolen, iv. 276; thinks
private letters should not be published,
iv. 278; advised Swift against publication, iv. 280; agrees with Pope
that letters were printed in Ireland,
iv. 287; explains his 'detaining' the
clandestine vol., iv. 276, 278; if
printed in England, it will be published there, iv. 276; Faulkner may
go on, without mention of Pope's
name, iv. 305; too bad Swift pro-
motes the publication, iv. 309; O.
thinks the letters slight, iv. 308;
attempts to procure original letter
from Bath, iv. 306; sends it to Pope
with the second lot of his letters to
Swift, iv. 326, 327; would like to
study the clandestine vol. with Pope,
iv. 326; received it from Pope minus
first 22 pages, iv. 328; Pope asks permission to use O.'s letters as evidence,
iv. 313, 320, 329.
O.'s dealings with Faulkner: F—

BOYLE, JOHN (*cont.*)
begins printing from the clandestine vol., iv. 270; Pope wants to get the clandestine vol. from Faulkner, iv. 262–4; O. regrets that Faulkner gives Pope uneasiness, iv. 270; gets the clandestine vol. from Faulkner, iv. 276; returns it to be sent to Pope, iv. 287; has confidence in F—'s integrity, iv. 306; will rescue the clandestine vol. from Faulkner after he has finished printing from it, iv. 306; is to read a letter of reply to Faulkner and Mrs. Whiteway, iv. 309; thinks Faulkner was not supposed to be the printer of the letters, iv. 329.

O.'s dealings with Mrs. Whiteway: his ambivalent attitude, iv. 226, 231, 257; insincere, iv. 307 n.; vague talk of 'designing people' close to Swift, iv. 54, 62, 73, 305; thus arouses Pope's suspicions of Mrs. Whiteway, iv. 130 n., 279, 306; she has the Bath letter, iv. 307; O. is sure the letters will be published, iv. 308; in 1737 she said she had no Pope letters, iv. 133; now (1740) she has some that Pope wants O. to send him, iv. 308, 320, 325; assures her that servants must have stolen the Swift-Pope letters, iv. 325; grateful for return of both his and Pope's letters, iv. 328; he asks Pope to thank Mrs. Whiteway for returning the letters, iv. 330.

O.'s later friendship with Pope: jokes about Pope's surfeit of fame, iv. 54; distress at Pope's bad health, iv. 61; invited to Twickenham but the north wind is too cold, iv. 336 n.; leaves Town with Pope and Chesterfield, iv. 338 n.; Pope wishes O. to know Ralph Allen, iv. 340; O. might take Pope to Bath (1741), iv. 350; has a dinner party for Warburton, Pope, and Dr. King, iv. 380; not in good health, iv. 380 n.; commends T. Hooke to Dr. Holmes, iv. 390 n.; Bounce given to O. and sent to Marston, iv. 406; distress over the state of mind of Katherine, Duchess of Buckingham, iv. 407, 442; finds Pope's urns too small, iv. 413; newborn son (1742), iv. 424 n.; futile attempt to help Warburton to an

BOYLE, JOHN (*cont.*)
Oxford degree, iv. 437 n., 442; ill at Bath, iv. 449; improved, he plans to go to Town, iv. 468; must act as executor for Katherine, Duchess of Buckingham, iv. 466, 472; reproached for his retired life, iv. 482; Pope needs help now as to his annuity from the late Duchess of Buckingham, iv. 489; the simple life at Marston, iv. 408, 422, 436, 437, 442, 494 n.; came to Town last week, iv. 494; dinner at Burlington House iv. 497 n.; Pope staying with O. in Duke Street, iv. 497; O. returns to Marston, iv. 513–14; complains of Pope's will, and calls Pope *mens curva in corpore curvo*, iv. 521 n.; writes Mallet about Pope's death, iv. 522.

BOYLE, MARGARET (Hamilton), 2nd wife of John, Earl of Orrery: letter to, iv. 422, 423; letter from her to her lord, iv. 507; called Swift's 'mistress', iv. 336; wishes guinea fowl from the Allens, iv. 422; makes Pope a present, iv. 423; her story of the death of Bounce, iv. 507–8; pregnant, iv. 523.

BOYLE, RICHARD, 3rd Earl of Burlington: letters to, i. 371, 447, 461, 491, 516, ii. 1, 2, 532, iii. 4, 61, 67, 86, 111, 183, 187, 200, 259, 265, 272, 273, 302, 313, 328, 332, 341, 356, 364, 382, 403, 417, 515, 516, 517, 518, iv. 14, 22, 43, 82, 117, 153, 172, 196, 220, 237, 323, 408, 490; letters from, i. 491, iii. 67, 82, 322, 333, iv. 14, 164; — the account of Pope's ride to Oxford with Lintot thought 'merry' by Lintot, iii. 489; undatable letters suggest meetings with Pope, iii. 515–18; iv. 46; B.'s friendship for Pope, iv. 164–5; a patron of John Gay, i. 320, 450, ii. 153; of the Graham family, i. 334 n., of Jervas, ii. 347, of Guelfi, ii. 242 n.; unable to aid Walter Harte, iii. 333, iv. 196; aids Mallet's *Eurydice*, iii. 82; at first performance of Hill's *Athelwold*, iii. 253.

Services to Pope: offers him a site for a town house, i. 516, 475 n. (not used); Pope takes friends to Chiswick gardens (1719, &c., *see under* Pope),

BOYLE, RICHARD (*cont.*)
ii. 2; gets legal advice from Fazacker-ley on *Dunciad*, ii. 532, iii. 4; B. signs document to give Gilliver pro-perty in *The Dunciad*, iii. 59, 61 n., 67; Pope sends B. the MS. of his *Epistle on Taste* (Apr., 1731), iii. 187; apologizes for the Epistle after attacks, iii. 259; B. 'gives Pope laurels', iii. 272; Pope suppresses a pamphlet ('Master Key to Popery'?), iii. 273; B. inspects Pope's portico (1733), iii. 356, 359; Pope gives B. one of Bounce's puppies, iii. 515; congratulates B., iii. 517 n.; B. is getting Pope a ticket, iii. 518; con-sults B. on his 'designs', iii. 515; gets pineapples from B. for Fortescue, iv. 115, but not for Lyttelton, iv. 117; asks for fruit for Bolingbroke (ill), iv. 118; B. lends Pope a horse to ride to Oxford, i. 371; lends a servant when Pope's father dies, i. 447; has Pope frequently as a guest at Chiswick, i. 338, 339 n., 347, 411, 417, ii. 117, iii. 183; Pope dines there (1731) with Bolingbroke, iii. 183, 283; dines there (1734) with Bishop Berkeley, iii. 403; with Sir Clement Cottrell, iii. 516, iv. 22; Commissioners of the Bridge there, iv. 82; no dinner (15. iv. '39) for Bolingbroke, iv. 172; at B.'s Pope could not see S. Gerrard who called, iv. 234; hopes B. asks to bring Warburton (1740), iv. 237; gets J. Richardson a ticket to see the pictures, iv. 409; dines at Chiswick, iv. 490; dines, with Orrery, at Bur-lington House, iv. 497 n.
B.'s rambles: takes Pope to York (1716), i. 350, 351; B. frequently at Lanesboro (Londesborough), i. 491, 518, iii. 233, 303, 313 (York As-sembly Room opened), 328, 333, iv. 91 (long stay), 113, 115, 118, 269, 338; some months (1726) in France, ii. 410, 416; at Bath, iii. 436, iv. 36, 46 (leaves because of smallpox epidemic).
General details: Pope recommends a waterman to B., i. 461; Pope leaves Chiswick for Twickenham, ii. 2; re-commends Atterbury's gardener, ii. 223, B. and Swift at odds over the Boyle monument in St. Patrick's, iii.

BOYLE, RICHARD (*cont.*)
73, 94, 102, 149, 287; B. is made Knight of the Garter, iii. 111; goes into Opposition after the Excise, iii. 339; postpones a visit from Pope on account of Lord Bruce, iv. 14; in-eligible to take Lady Gerard's affi-davit, iv. 183; Pope and B. consider visiting the aged Duchess of Marl-borough (at Windsor Lodge), iv. 408; B.'s grief over death of his dau. Dorothy, iv. 396, 415; his urns designed at Bath by Collins, iv. 413; on rearing fawns, iv. 452; as a gar-dener possibly rivalled by March-mont, iv. 459.
Boyle, Richard, Viscount Shannon, Congreve's host and scribe, ii. 12.
Boyle, Roger, 1st Earl of Orrery, his *Works* ed. by John, 5th Earl, iv. 210 n.
Brady, Nicholas (and Nahum Tate), psalm-writers, i. 307.
Bram, Dr., Bishop of Cork, v. 17.
Brampton-Castle, Herefordshire, seat of Robert, Earl of Oxford, ii. 91, &c.
Bramston, James, his *Art of Politics* ap-proved by Pope before publication, iii. 173.
Brandreth, John: preferments from the Duke of Dorset (Lord Lieutenant of Ireland), iii. 161, 181, 191; asked to aid the *Roman History*, iii. 185.
Brant Broughton, near Newark (Pope spells it *Bruton*), Warburton's parish, iv. 237 n., &c.
Brault, —, translator of the *Odyssey*, ii. 233.
Brennus, a Goth—like Wm. Kent, iii. 417.
Brent, Mrs., Swift's housekeeper, a real 'Walpole', ii. 492, iii. 22, 161 (called 'Sir Robert'), 191.
Brentford, New, Bath waters sent there for Bolingbroke, iv. 119.
Brett, Mrs. Anne, formerly Countess of Macclesfield, Savage's alleged mother, iii. 238 n.
Brewster, Dorothy, cited on A. Hill, iii. 170 n., iv. 131 n.
Briars, John, of Diss, has data on Lady Rich's life, ii. 244, 278.
BRIDGES, RALPH: letters to, i. 41, 43; letter from, i. 303; nephew of Sir

BRIDGES, RALPH (*cont.*)
Wm. Trumbull, i. 29 n., 43 n.; chaplain to Bishop of London, i. 41 n.; corrects Pope's early translation (1708) of Homer, i. 43.

Bridgeman, Old Mr. [not Sir Orlando], his death at Wimpole, ii. 377.

BRIDGEMAN, CHARLES: letters to, ii. 327; letter from, ii. 261; designs Mrs. Howard's gardens at Marble Hill, ii. 213, 261, 327; plans to visit Wimpole with Pope, ii. 264, 327; to see Bolingbroke, ii. 327; employed early by Edward, Earl of Oxford, ii. 327 n., 364; visits Down Hall with Pope, ii. 355; employed by Prince of Wales [George II], ii. 372; makes a 'theatre' in Pope's garden, ii. 372.

Bridgewater, Countess of (Elizabeth [Churchill] Egerton), painted by Pope (after Jervas), i. 187.

Bright, Archdeacon of Lichfield, i. 258 n.

Brindley, James, bookseller: takes subscriptions (1737) for Pope's *Letters*, iv. 41 n., 53, 55, 65; Orrery receives his copies for subscribers, iv. 76; special copy for Hugh Bethel, iv. 67.

BRINSDEN, Rev. CHARLES: letters to, iv. 200, 372, 389; failed to see Pope at Allen's, iv. 200; asked to report on his father's health, iv. 372, 423.

BRINSDEN, JOHN, father of Charles, agent of Bolingbroke: letters to, iv. 209, 289, 329, 348, 354, 384, 403; as agent, forwards letters, &c., to Bolingbroke, iv. 200 n., 329, 369; his ill health, iv. 209, 372, 384, 387, 392, 403; thanked for verses commending *Essay on Man*, iv. 209; accident to his foot, iv. 348; asks Pope to dine, iv. 354; life apparently saved by A. Cleland, iv. 387 n.; furthers, through Pope, appointment of Cleland in Bath Hospital, iv. 401, 405; confined for health in London, iv. 403; his death, iv. 443.

Bristol, 1st Earl of (John Digby), remodelled Sherborne, ii. 237.

Bristol, city: Pope recommended to go there for the waters, iv. 195; describes the city, iv. 201–2, 204–5; Richard Savage there, iv. 210, 418.

British Apollo, i. 56.

British Journal, i. 417 n., ii. 134 n., 164 n., 177 n., 185 n.

Brocas, Mr., i. 26.

Brockes, B. M., translated *Essay on Man* into German, iv. 484 n.

Brodrick, Alan, Viscount Middleton, ii. 66.

Brome, i. 212. *See* W. Broome.

Bromley, William, Speaker of the House of Commons, ii. 11, iii. 360 n.

Bromley, William, alleged schoolmaster of Pope, iii. 360.

Bromley, Kent, Atterbury's residence as Bishop of Rochester, ii. 78–131 *passim*; dinner there for the Duchess of Buckingham, ii. 121.

BROOKE, HENRY: letter to, iv. 207; letters from, iv. 198, 212; — *Gustavus Vasa* banned (1739), iv. 159–60; he retires to Ireland, iv. 198; character commended by Pope, iv. 207; has come to believe Pope the greatest of all poets, iv. 198–9; asks Pope's views as to Christianity, iv. 199; Pope's reply, iv. 207; Pope had revised B.'s *Universal Beauty*, iv. 198; B. pleased by Warburton's *Vindication*, iv. 212–13; grateful for Pope's praise, iv. 213; *Brookiana* cited for text of a letter, iv. 198, 207.

Broome, Mr., vicar of Debenham, his death, iii. 155.

BROOME, WILLIAM: letters to Pope, i. 227, 266, 270, 275, 276, 297, 321, 394, ii. 3, 19, 40, 48, 59, 76, 102, 110 (with Fenton), 125, 130, 134, 144, 163, 182, 204, 208, 210, 211, 215 (with Fenton), 223, 225, 231, 241, 247, 256, 264, 269, 271, 273, 287, 291, 292, 295, 302, 320, 336, 338, 340, 355, 357, 363, 365, 374, 378, 389, 396, 420, 431, 449, 470, iii. 105, 116, 128, 155, 198, 497, 510, iv. 2, 4; letters to Pope, ii. 357, iii. 124, 478, 506, 512; letters from Fenton to B., ii. 105, 110 (with Pope), 147, 151, 152, 214, 231, 233, 244, 278, 339, 351, 360, 365, 377, 379, 384, 397, 415, 422, 429, 432, 463, 486, 487, 518, iii. 24, 37, 44, 54, 100; letters from B. to Fenton, ii. 119, 121, 150, 162, 344, 488, 499; letter from Lintot to B., iii. 489.

B. seems pleased with a letter from

BROOME, WILLIAM (*cont.*)

Pope, ii. 470; sees no harm in the publication (1735) of Pope's letters, iii. 512; a letter to B. thought by Curll to come from Voiture, iii. 495; private letters, B. thinks, are not to be exposed, iii. 479.

Family cares: B. has enemies, Pope says, ii. 205; B. is worried about gossips, ii. 208, 211; grief at death of his dau., ii. 208; his health affected, ii. 224, 226, 234, 271; financial obligations, ii. 338; his brother a London wig-maker, ii. 338; his brother's wedding, ii. 365; birth of B.'s son, ii. 375; his income before the *Odyssey* affluent, iii. 507; Pope buys him lottery tickets, ii. 241, 248, 256; gets a £50 prize, ii. 264; abruptly calls Pope's note for £100, ii. 389, 396, 397.

B.'s ecclesiastical career: Rector of Sturston, i. 181 n., 206, 212 n., 227; gets LL.D. when George II visits Cambridge (1727), ii. 450, 486, 488; refuses a parish in Devon, ii. 486, 519; receives the living of Pulham, ii. 519; preaches at Norwich, ii. 519, iii. 507; his rambles (1735), iii. 506–7.

Life at Sturston: invites Fenton for a summer, ii. 105, asked to receive Fenton and a student (H. P. Blount), ii. 119; does so, ii. 121, 150, 321, 344; Fenton's laziness, ii. 358; Pope urges no communication direct with Lintot, ii. 211, 287 n.; acquaintance with Sir T. Hanmer, ii. 211; dines with Lord Cornwallis, ii. 365; errs in using Lintot as publisher, ii. 211, 385; silently at work, iii. 37; Fenton sends his ed. of Waller, iii. 44; B. laments the death of Fenton, iii. 124; Fenton always praised B., iii. 129; Pope has not seen Lintot on B.'s affairs, iv. 2.

B.'s visits to Town and to Twickenham: invited often by Pope, ii. 3, 19, 48, 59, 77, 144, 204, 208, 224, 232, 295, 344, 390 n., 398; ill in London, ii. 59; unseasonable for B. to visit London while *Odyssey* negotiations with Lintot hang fire, ii. 214, 216 n., 291, 292, 293.

B.'s quarrel with Pope: complains of remarks by Jervas, ii. 471; but B. was

BROOME, WILLIAM (*cont.*)

silent, Pope says, when Lintot was scandalous about Pope, ii. 471; B. is offended by a couplet in the *Bathos*, ii. 269 n., 467, 487; Fenton urges B. to attack Pope openly, ii. 488; B.'s anger, ii. 489, echoes phrasing in attacks on Pope, ii. 489, 499–500; is sure Pope is no master of Greek, ii. 500; attempts at reconciliation, iii. 100, 105–6; Pope wants B. to defend him, iii. 106; alleges ignorance of B.'s authorship of the *Bathos* couplet, iii. 107; Curll asks B. for papers to print against Pope, iii. 475; B. sends the request to Pope, iii. 478–9; reconciliation ensues, iii. 479; B.'s 'ocular demonstration' of Pope's deficiency as a friend, iii. 495–6; pleased to be friends again, iii. 496; estranged from Pope seven years, iii. 498; is taken out of *The Dunciad*, iii. 510, 512, iv. 4; confusion of B. with his namesake of Debenham (deceased), iii. 155.

B.'s work on Pope's Iliad: B.'s blank verse translation mentioned, i. 166 & n.; works on *Iliad* as a friend, unpaid, i. 266 n.; Pope had intended to pay, i. 276; B. extracts notes from Eustathius, i. 266, 270, 276, 297; efforts flag, ii. 295; offers to renew labours, i. 497, ii. 3; works on Index to the *Iliad*, ii. 40; asked to solicit subscribers at Cambridge, i. 227, 266, 297; to forward directions to the printer, i. 394; thanked in 1728 for his labours, ii. 3, 40.

B.'s work on the Odyssey: his Books listed, ii. 103 n.; he and Fenton are 'auxiliars' to Pope, ii. 121; is to do notes for all 24 Books, ii. 121; fights like Teucer behind Ajax, ii. 121; Pope urges industry and secrecy, ii. 103, 106, 125, 256 n.; B.'s Bk. XII approved, ii. 103; has done XI and XII, ii. 110; finds Bk. II wearisome, ii. 110; has finished II, XI, and XII, ii. 122; demands XVI, XVIII, XXIII for his share, ii. 122; to send Bk. II to Pope for revision, ii. 145; not to destroy his work, ii. 163–4; asked to send II and VI if done, ii. 164; should have done Bk. VIII, ii. 182;

BROOME, WILLIAM (*cont.*)
gaps in Bk. II to be filled, ii. 205;
Pope has his Bk. VI, ii. 210; also Bk.
VIII, ii. 231; told what remaining
Books to do, ii. 295–6; Bk. XVIII is
wanted, ii. 336; B. sends Bks. XVI
and XVIII, ii. 302, 338; asked to do
part of Bk. XVII for Pope (ill), ii.
340; works on notes for the *Odyssey*,
ii. 215, 224, 231, 248, 264, 265, 295
(errata on notes), 288, 320, 340, 355;
elation over completion of all the
notes, ii. 357; notes patterned after
those in Pope's *Iliad*, ii. 363; B. reads
proofs, ii. 364, 375; to have copies for
his subscribers immediately on publication, ii. 378; his part in the Postscript to the *Odyssey*, ii. 385 n.; may
apply to Jervas or to Lintot for
Odysseys, ii. 390; is suspicious of
Pope's vague acknowledgements, ii.
390; Fenton and B. are deprived of
credit for the *Odyssey*, ii. 390; B.
wishes to announce the truth about
the number of Books translated: Fenton says 'No', ii. 423; asked by Pope
to refute Lintot's lies, ii. 432; quotes
Pope's expressions (1720) of gratitude
for work on the *Iliad*, ii. 499; B.'s
veracity is questioned as to work on
Odyssey, iii. 479; will do Pope justice,
iii. 497; B.'s translation revised by
Pope, ii. 226, 269, 321; does not revise Pope's work, ii. 321; B.'s list of
subscribers, ii. 271; displeased by
lack of recognition for *Odyssey*, ii.
344, 357; lucrative rewards not despicable, ii. 344; financial terms offered, ii. 271; B. verifies Pope's
account of payments, ii. 293 n., 389
n., iii. 116, 507, 510; happy that his
name accompanies Pope's in the
Odyssey, ii. 358.
   B.'s own poetry: appears in 5th ed.
of Lintot's Miscellany, ii. 269, 295;
projects publication in a separate
vol., ii. 295, 378, 389, 390; published
by Lintot, ii. 385 n., 420, 429 n.; no
appetite for merely posthumous fame,
ii. 391; his concept of poetry, ii.
363, 391; Pope considers using his
critical discourse in last note to the
Odyssey, ii. 363; used as Preface to his
Poems, ii. 363 n.; his phrasing

BROOME, WILLIAM (*cont.*)
queried, ii. 182, 352, 422; plans verses
on Lady Mary and innoculation, ii.
77; Prologue for *Mariamne*, ii. 150,
152, 163–4; congratulates Fenton on
Mariamne, ii. 162–3; slanderous
attacks on the play, ii. 163; 'Melancholy' concerns death of his small
dau., ii. 208; wishes to dedicate 'On
the Seat of the War in Flanders' to
Pope, ii. 211 n.; the poem not acceptable to Lintot, ii. 288; might have
been adapted to Siege of Gibraltar,
ii. 433; sends Pope a poem for criticism, ii. 275; his Epistle to Pope, ii.
275 n., 295, 338, 340, 355; his
Epistle to Fenton, ii. 269 n., 385, 390,
398 n.; an emendation to *King Lear*
sent to Pope, ii. 302; his Prologue
(not used) for Southerne, ii. 340, 358,
360, 365; his imitations of Milton to
be revised by Fenton, ii. 398; writes
a 'Sessions of the Poets' against Pope,
ii. 500; sends Pope his poem on Death,
iii. 513; explains what he wrote for
the Cambridge *Gratulatio . . . de Pace*
of 1713, ii. 449; plans to translate
Apollonius, ii. 339, 360; Fenton
urges him to cultivate Tonson, ii.
429, 430; project of a Virgil by Fenton and B. for Tonson, ii. 429, 433;
Pope had no objection to B.'s blank
verse translation of *Iliad*, iii. 106; B
repents of his poetry, iii. 479; negotiates with Lintot for a reprint, iii. 479,
489, 512.
Broome, Mrs. (William): visited the
Popes with her husband, ii. 295;
liked by Mrs. Pope, ii. 296.
Brown, Mr., chaplain to Caryll, i. 129,
214.
Brown, Mr., considers the purchase of
Hallgrove, iv. 203.
Brown, Antony, of Apscourt, gives Pope
humming-birds, iv. 451 n.
Brown, Sir George, 'Sir Plume' of *Rape
of the Lock*, i. 151 n., 163–4.
Brown, Jeremiah, of Apscourt, where
Pope visits, iv. 451.
Brown, Moses, wins Cave's poetry con-
test (1735), iii. 499 n.
Brownlow, John, Lord Tyrconnel:
possibly mentioned by Swift dis-
paragingly, iii. 162; nephew of the

Brownlow, John (*cont.*)
woman Savage called mother, iii.
238 n.; Pope writes to Hill from T.'s
house, iii. 238; lives not far from
Barrowby, iii. 332; his relations with
Savage, iv. 418.

Broxholm, Noel, M.D.: lives near Pope
at Hampton, iv. 268; drinks R.
Allen's health, iv. 158; thinks Anne
Arbuthnot's health very bad, iv. 268;
attends Pope (1743), iv. 450.

Bruce, Charles, Lord: Pope visits him
at Tottenham for a day (1734), iii.
417; he is brother-in-law to Lord
Burlington, iii. 418 n.; comes to see
Burlington: Pope therefore put off,
iv. 14; marries thirdly (1739) Caroline, dau. of John Campbell and
Madge Bellenden Campbell, iv. 149
n.

Bruce, Sir John Hope: Pope tries to
assist him as Governor of Bermuda,
ii. 424; replaced as Governor, ii. 427;
possible author of *Hardyknute*, ii.
427 n.

Bruneval, Charles, signs at Chiswick the
'tree' petition, iv. 324.

Brussels, Atterbury there (1723), ii. 200
n.

Bruton, near Newark, Trent, *see* Brant
Broughton (Warburton's parish).

Bruyere, *see* La Bruyère, Jean de.

BRYDGES, JAMES, 1st Duke of Chandos:
letters from, i. 274 (to the Hon. Simon
Harcourt), iii. 262 (to Pope); mentioned, ii. 269; wrongly mentioned by
Curll, ii. 14 n.; subscribes to Buononcini, ii. 99; gets an advance copy of
Pope's *Iliad* I, i. 274; subscribes to 10
Iliads, i. 274; false story of his gift of
£500 to Pope, i. 274; complimented
in Preface to Pope's *Iliad*, iii. 256; —
his magnificent qualities stated by
Cleland (Pope?), iii. 256; accepts
Pope's assurance that 'Timon' was
not C., iii. 262; Pope denies to Burlington that 'Timon' meant C., iii.
259; prefatory letter to 'Of False
Taste' showed the Duke's reaction,
iii. 279; C. is omitted from Epistle to
Bathurst, complimented in that to
Cobham, iii. 325 n.

Buckhurst, Lord, *see* Sackville, Thomas
(also Earl of Dorset).

Buckingham, Dukes of, *see* Sheffield,
John and Edmund.

Buckingham, Katherine, Duchess of
Buckingham, *see* Sheffield, Katherine.

Buckingham, Owen, a delinquent subscriber to the *Iliad*, i. 420.

Buckinghamshire, *see* Fawley Court,
Langley, Riskins, Stowe.

Buckland-Filleigh, near Great Tor-
rington, seat of Wm. Fortescue
(q.v.).

Bucklebury, Berks., seat of Bolingbroke's first wife, i. 252.

BUCKLEY, SAMUEL, printer, bookseller,
writer of the *Gazette* (d. 1741): letters
to, ii. 157, 285, 286, 471, 529, iii. 69,
294, 428, 454, 473, 482, iv. 66, 88;
several of the letters printed in *The
Athenaeum*, ii. 157; he lives in Crouch-
end, iv. 66; employed in the Foreign
Office, ii. 157; prints *The Englishman*,
i. 193; thanked by Pope for a present,
ii. 157 (of Mme Dacier's *Odyssey*);
Pope makes him a present of his
Odyssey, ii. 282, 286, 471; prints
Odyssey proposals in *Gazette* and
Courant, ii. 285; B. is invited to view
Pope's garden, ii. 286; — plans a
great ed. of Thuanus, ii. 471; sends
Pope a pamphlet about the ed., ii.
471; Pope makes a Preface for him,
iii. 70; Swift inquires about the ed.,
iii. 73; the ed. is in press by Oct. 1732,
iii. 294 n.; it uses the ornaments from
Pope's Homer with permission, iii.
294; flattering acknowledgements to
Pope in the Thuanus, iii. 294 n.; the
edition is aided by Lord Carteret, iv.
66; Pope's *Works* II called a poor
return for Thuanus, iii. 454; —
before 1735 B. is both printer and
bookseller, iii. 454; in 1735 ceases to
be a bookseller, iii. 482; advertises
in the *Gazette* Pope's plan for an
authorized ed. of his *Letters*, iii. 473;
asked for advice on Pope's troubles
with Tonson (1735), iii. 482; asked to
get data from Knapton on unsold
copies of Pope's *Works*, II, iv. 66;
Pope tries to arrange a dinner with
B., N. Cole, and J. Knapton, iv. 88;
a meeting postponed, v. 6.

Budgell, Eustace: career in Ireland, i.
292, ii. 154 n.; increasing eccentricity,

Budgell, Eustace (*cont.*)
iii. 162 n.; asks Swift's aid in getting
into Parliament, iii. 162.

Buisse, M., confessed years later a plot of
1712 against Harley and St. John, iii.
199.

Bull, John, of Sudbury, an acquaintance of Pope's, iii. 484.

Bullingbrooke, or Bolingbroke, *see* St.
John, Henry.

Bulstrode, seat of the Duke of Portland,
iii. 404, 442.

Bunyan, John: his Sermons distributed
gratis, i. 57; burlesqued in *The
What-d'ye-call-it*, i. 289, 290; like
Pope a wayfarer, i. 427.

Buononcini, Giovanni Battista, composer: charged with plagiarism, ii.
99; his act in the jointly composed
opera, *Muzio Scevola*, ii. 100;
Cantate (1722) and its distinguished
subscribers, ii. 99; *Griselda*, ii. 123
n.; directed concert at Buckingham
House (1722), composed the choruses,
ii. 135 n.

Burford, Oxon., Lord Bathurst's coach
not there, iv. 25.

Burgh, William, Parnell's Dublin address, i. 349.

Burlington, 3rd Earl of, *see* Boyle,
Richard.

Burlington, Mr., of Diss, Norfolk,
friend of Broome and of Fenton, ii.
148, 215, 378, iii. 44; Fenton wants a
rabbit from, ii. 415, 430.

Burnet, Atex (or Aler), author of an
attack on Pope (*Achilles Dissected*),
iii. 355 n., 362.

Burnet, Gilbert, Bishop: burlesque
elegy on him, i. 284; the elegy sent to
Parnell, i. 284; Burnet's death, i.
286, 291; as historian disparaged by
Bolingbroke, iii. 71; his robust frame,
iv. 47.

Burnet, Thomas, son of the Bishop:
attacks Pope in *Grumbler* and *Homerides*, i. 287, 284 n., 285, 291; attacked
in *Sermon on Glass Bottles*, i. 295 n.;
in Swift's list of Pope's enemies, i.
358; supposed author of *Pope Alexander's Supremacy* (1728), ii. 489 n., iii.
33 n.; defends his father's *History*
against Lansdowne's charges, iii.
327.

Burnet, William, also son of the Bishop:
Governor of Massachusetts, ii. 528
n.; M. Byles lends him *The Dunciad*
and a *Key* to it, ii. 528.

Burscough, William, dines at Vandeput's with Pope, *et al.*, ii. 232.

Burton, Simon, M.D.: jokes about Lord
Bathurst's medical skill, iii. 137;
waited in vain on Lord Bathurst, iii.
157; is curious about properties of
Scarborough waters, iii. 197; advises
Martha Blount to take hot waters,
iii. 232; Bathurst urged to consult
him, iii. 481; is Pope's physician, iv.
499, 507, 508, 522; his death, iv. 499
n.

Burward, Mr., Bolingbroke's farm
agent, iv. 148.

Bushey Park, Middlesex, seat of Lord
Halifax in 1714, i. 227; J. Richardson
goes there to paint, ii. 298.

Butler, Col., relative of Lady Arran, i.
427-8.

Butler, Charles, 2nd Earl of Arran,
Chancellor of Oxford University:
suggests Warburton for a D.D., iv.
437; Lady Arran's vagaries, i.
427-8.

Butler, James, 1st Duke of Ormond, v.
14.

Butler, James, 2nd Duke of Ormond, i.
298, 308, 311.

Butler, Thomas, styled Earl of Ossory,
v. 14.

Butler, Samuel (*Hudibras*), Pope's epitaph for, ii. 76; quoted, iv. 247.

Butlers—spoken of as neighbours of
Caryll, i. 156 n.

Butt, John: thanked for a transcript, iv.
390 n.; cited on Pope's version of
Donne's 2nd Satire, ii. 371 n.; on
Thomas Cooke and Pope, ii. 509 n.;
his ed. of 'The Master Key to Popery',
iii. 265 n.

Button, Daniel: his coffee-house, i. 185
n.; Pope called hostile to it, i. 210;
malice there towards *Iliad* I, i. 294,
305; revolution there, i. 290; a
changed place, i. 306.

Byfield, Thomas: converted by French
prophets, i. 35; famous for his sal
volatile, i. 35.

BYLES, MATHER, clergyman and poet
in Boston, Mass.: letters from him to

BYLES, MATHER (*cont.*)
Pope, ii. 450, 494, 527, iv. 16;
flatters Pope, ii. 450–1; sends to Pope
poems printed in a Boston newspaper,
ii. 450–1; praises several of Pope's
works, ii. 450–1; newspaper sent mentions Capt. Jonathan Gulliver, ii. 479
n.; — arranges for conveyance of
Pope's *Works* from Lintot's to Boston,
ii. 494; tells of diffusion of Pope's
poems in New England libraries, ii.
494; asks who is author of the *Key to
the Lock*, ii. 495; arrangements for
bringing over Pope's *Works* failed
and others will be made, ii. 527–8;
B. praises the *Unfortunate Lady*, ii.
528; explains New England taste, ii.
528; — Pope sends his *Works* to B.
without a letter, iii. 7 n.; B. makes his
final bid for a correspondence with
Pope, iv. 16; is sure abuse will never
lessen Pope's character, iv. 16; is
willing to pay for Pope's *Works* in
12's, iv. 17; likes Pope's *Letters*, iv.
17; sends some of his 'little things' to
Pope, iv. 17.
Byng, Mr., Sir Godfrey Kneller's butler, ii. 307 (is this 'Jemmy'?), 308.

C., J., Esq., *see* Caryll, John.
Cadogan, William, 1st Earl: entertain-
ments by him near Reading, i. 351;
his death, and character by Pope, ii.
386; opposed Atterbury, ii. 386 n.;
his house to be taken by Lord Chesterfield or the Duke of Richmond, ii.
416; his collections sold at auction, ii.
416.
Caesar, Caius Julius, i. 90, 165, 440, iv.
127.
Caesar, Charles, account of, ii. 126 n.,
235 n., 262, iii. 149.
CAESAR, M. ADELMAR (Mrs. Charles):
letters to, ii. 126, 198, 230, 235, 262,
293, 312, 391, 490, iii. 39, 50, 118,
331, 509; letter from, ii. 197; some
account of, ii. 126 n.; gets a print of
Pope, ii. 126; gets subscribers to the
Odyssey in 1723, ii. 164 n.; invites
Pope to Bennington, ii. 197; more
subscribers secured, ii. 197, 230; —
is thanked for Miss Cowper's verses,
ii. 198, 209; Pope almost visited
Bennington, ii. 262; her name

CAESAR, M. ADELMAR (*cont.*)
starred among *Odyssey* subscribers, ii.
293; in Town, ii. 312; reports Pope's
desire to visit Wimpole, ii. 317; —
dines at Twickenham with the Oxfords, ii. 490, 496, iii. 40; forgives
Pope's neglect of her, iii. 39; her son
elopes with a great fortune, iii. 40, 56;
asked to send Jervas venison, iii. 50;
silence to be imposed on her, iii. 88;
ill, iii. 118; Swift's letter to her, iii.
378 n.; expected verses from Pope on
Lady Margaret Harley's wedding, iii.
411; Pope sends thanks, iii. 509.
Caithness: Thurso, home of Rev. Alex.
Pope, iv. 94.
Caldwell, Mr., i. 349.
Caledon, Co. Tyrone, Ireland, estate of
Orrery and his second wife, iv. 226.
Callan, N., cited from *RES*, i. 313.
Calvert, Charles, Earl of Baltimore,
selects the Prince's waterman, iv. 348.
Cambis, M., French ambassador, his
death, iv. 216 n.
Cambrai, Congress of, Lord Polwarth a
plenipotentiary, ii. 177, 178.
Cambridge, Richard, his marriage
delays materials for Pope's grotto
(1741), iv. 342, 352.
Cambridge University, *see* Fenton, Jor-
tin, Snape, H. Trumbull, and Whis-
ton; colleges fail to subscribe to the
Odyssey, ii. 271; Fenton and H. Trum-
bull at Trinity Hall, ii. 377; election
of a Master at St. John's, ii. 432.
Cambridgeshire, *see* Wimpole.
Camden, William: on Sir Philip Sidney,
iii. 125; fails to mention Beaulieu
Abbey, iii. 430.
Campbell, Lady Anne, marries the
Earl of Strafford, iv. 341.
Campbell, Archibald, Earl of Ilay
(Islay), succ. (1743) as 3rd Duke of
Argyle: a neighbour of Pope at
Whitton Park, iii. 478; agent for
Mrs. Howard in purchasing land for
Marble Hill, iii. 34 n., v. 5; gets Curll
before the House of Lords concerning
Pope's *Letters*, iii. 464, 478 n.; visit
by Pope and Fortescue deferred, iv.
21; goes to Scotland, iv. 271.
Campbell, Colin, architect protégé of
Lord Burlington, i. 516 n.; plans a
house for Pope in Town, i. 516.

CAMPBELL, JOHN, 2nd Duke of Argyle: letters to, iv. 137, 189; friend of Pope's, i. 217, 379, 417; subscribes to Buononcini, ii. 99; favours Scarborough waters, iii. 232; an obscure request to Pope, iv. 137–8; at Stowe with Pope, iv. 185; Pope visits him at Adderbury, iv. 189, 192; meets Warburton, iv. 238 n.; to dine with Pope, Cobham, and Marchmont, iv. 341; the wedding of his dau., Lady Anne, iv. 341–2; removed from the army, iv. 353, 413.

Campbell, John, later 4th Duke of Argyle, i. 379, iv. 149 & n.

Campbell, John, Lord, his *Lives of the Chief Justices*, iii. 236 n.

Candish (or Cavendish), Admiral, iv. 473.

Cannons, iii. 262.

Canterbury, Archbishop of (Wm. Wake), ii. 269.

Cantillon, Sir Richard, i. 180.

Capell, Lady Elizabeth, marries S. Molyneux (1717), i. 470.

Capell, Lady Jane (Hyde), Countess of Essex, i. 431.

Capell, William, 3rd Earl of Essex: marries Lady Jane Hyde, i. 431 n.; his offer of a pension to his brother-in-law (Cornbury), iii. 277 n.; possibly mentioned by Swift, v. 15.

Carbury, 3rd Earl of, *see* Vaughan, John.

Cardigan, Earl of, ii. 5.

Carew, Mr., Dancastle's nephew, ii. 8.

Carew, Molly, Dancastle's niece (?), ii. 8.

Carey, Henry: author (?) of *Bishop of Ailsbury's Elegy*, i. 284; supposed author of *Namby Pamby*, ii. 343 n.

Carey, Walter: account of, iv. 3 n.; a follower of Addison, iii. 191 n.; reports on Pope's health, iv. 3 n.

Carleton (or Carlton), Lord, *see* Boyle, Henry.

Carlingford, Ireland, Swift lands there (1727), ii. 455.

Carlisle, 3rd Earl of, *see* Howard, Charles.

Carlson, C. L., cited on Cave's poetry contest, iii. 499 n.

Carlton (or Carleton), Lord, *see* Boyle, Henry.

Carnarvon, Earl of, *see* Brydges, James, later Duke of Chandos.

Caroline, Princess of Wales and (after 1727) Queen: Gay hopes for preferment, i. 287, 318 n., 320, &c.; disapproves of masquerades, i. 407; should be *Mater Exercitus*, ii. 116; — admires Swift's wit, ii. 401; likes *Gulliver*, ii. 411; wears Swift's present of Irish silk, ii. 412, 414; summoned Swift 11 times before he attended, iii. 74, 152, 208, v. 8, 16; Swift comments ironically on her disinterestedness, iii. 93; his line about her, iii. 109; his letter to Mrs. Howard about the Princess, iii. 161; sovereigns easily deceived, Swift tells her, iii. 209; Swift thinks her an 'arrant knave', iii. 321; — she goes to *Julius Caesar*, ii. 473; gossip about John Knight's present to her, iii. 80; Secy. Johnstone takes *Eurydice* to her, iii. 158; her death, iv. 88 n., 89.

Carpenter, Mr., friend of Tonson's (?), ii. 118.

Carre, Mr., friend of Marchmont and Bolingbroke, iv. 498.

Carrington, Lady: secretly married to Mr. Mackenzie, iii. 30 n.; Mrs. Rackett's finances involved with her, iii. 39.

Carruthers, Robert, his *Life* of Pope (1857) cited: Pope's alleged 'self-portrait', i. 187 n.; the history of a letter, i. 334 n.; Pope's suggested annuity for Teresa Blount, i. 468; work done at Stanton Harcourt, i. 484 n.; the Rev. A. Pope, iv. 93 n.; fragment of a letter printed by him, iv. 254; Pope's grotto, iv. 278; a letter from Dr. Oliver, iv. 281; Pope's securities in 1744, iv. 340 n.; the death of Mrs. Lister Blount, iv. 450 n.; Pope's bond from S. Bethel, iv. 497 n.; Pope's projected house in Town, iv. 508 n.

Carte, Thomas, his part in Buckley's Thuanus, iii. 73.

Carter, Elizabeth, her translation of Crousaz's *Examen*, iv. 164 n.

Carter, Lawrence, could not admit H. Rackett to practice of law, iii. 153.

Carteret, Mrs., recommends a servant, iv. 473.

Carteret, Edward, in office of Post-master General, dies, iv. 173.

CARTERET, JOHN, Viscount, later Earl Granville: letter to, ii. 159; improbably mentioned to Atterbury, ii. 110 n.; Burscough his chaplain, ii. 232; Pope protests to him about Duke of Buckingham's *Works*, ii. 159–60; C. gets Pope £200 from the government for the *Odyssey*, ii. 160; speaks well of Pope, iii. 65, 81; approves *Beggar's Opera*, ii. 492; visits Amesbury, iii. 145; goes to Bath where Lady C. is recovering, iii. 145; — Swift's friendly relations with, iii. 145, 151, 362; Swift's pieces concerning Lord C., iii. 292 n., iii. 108; C. liked the *Libel on Dr. Delany*, iii. 362; to C. Swift disowned his 'Life and Character', iii. 432; aided Buckley on Thuanus, iii. 73, iv. 66; identified as the 'intending patron' for Warburton, iv. 433, 439 n., 435, 502; thought not to be a true Patriot in the Opposition, iv. 142; death of his uncle Edward, iv. 173 n.

Carteret, Miss, Ambrose Philips's lines on her burlesqued in poem on Miss Hervey, ii. 343.

Cary, Captain: carries letter from New England to Pope, ii. 494; failed to pick up Pope's *Works* for Rev. M. Byles, ii. 527.

Carylls: seven of them subscribe to the *Iliad*, i. 215.

Caryll, Catherine, daughter of Pope's friend: transcribed many of Pope's letters for her father, i. 129, 158, iii. 31 n.; a picture, gift to her from Pope, iii. 415, 402–3, 405.

Caryll, Edward, son of Pope's friend, marries dau. of N. Pigott of Whitton, ii. 367, iii. 88, 110, 115, 274, 284.

Caryll, Henry, son of Pope's friend: in the service of the Duke of Lorraine, ii. 60; his death, ii. 366.

Caryll, John, titular Earl (Jacobite), uncle of Pope's friend, i. 93 n.

CARYLL, JOHN, sr., Ladyholt, friend of Pope: letters to, i. 93, 113, 117, 120, 126, 131, 133, 143, 154, 156, 160, 165, 170, 172, 174, 176, 179, 185, 188, 190, 193, 203, 207, 209, 214, 218, 219, 229, 232, 235, 238, 240,

CARYLL, JOHN, sr. (*cont.*) 255, 265, 267, 282 (with Gay), 286, 288 (with (Gay), 292, 313, 317, 322, 326, 335, 339, 343, 410, 413, 417, 419, 442, 448, 457, 461, 462, 463, 464, 471, 474, 475, 483, 497, 517, 522, ii. 31, 37, 42, 53, 57, 60, 72, 77, 111, 117, 139, 172, 299, 341, 352, 360, 366, 380, 392, 418, 423, 428, 434, 448, iii. 12, 17, 30, 35, 38, 40, 44, 46, 60, 70, 74, 88, 89, 90, 109, 115, 122, 126, 141, 154, 172, 189, 237, 273, 279, 284, 294, 302, 316, 337, 340, 345, 353, 358, 369, 373, 375, 383, 384, 387, 390, 400, 402, 405, 414, 425, 437, 446, 450, 451, 455, 474; letters from, i. 142, 302, 312 (to Lintot), 416, 418, ii. 72 (to Wright); C. letters were transferred, conflated usually, to other correspondents as follows: to Addison, i. 183, 185, 197, 201, 208; to Atterbury, i. 497 n.; to Edward Blount, i. 246, 329, 424; to Congreve, i. 285, 290; to R. Digby, ii. 280; to Steele, i. 158; to Sir W. Trumbull, i. 174; to Wycherley, i. 9; — Pope asks the return of his letters (1712), i. 156 and (1726), ii. 418–19; C. reviews the correspondence with pleasure, iii. 449, iii. 38; will return the letters, iii. 18; Pope's manipulations of texts (1735) would be blamed on Curll, iii. 455 n.; the letters found useless in the 'design' of 1712, i. 161; letters from C. valued by Pope, i. 188; transcripts of these letters err in dates, i. 413 n.; a gap in the correspondence (1716–17), i. 410.

C.'s career, details in: estates of his uncle redeemed, i. 120; Pope's epitaph for the uncle, i. 133; model married life of the Carylls, i. 123; C. attacked in the *Flying Post*, i. 151–2, 154–5; congratulated on being a grandfather, i. 207; has a disabled hand, i. 218; Pope's confidence in C., i. 218; C. has the gout, i. 286, ii. 42, 53; helps arrange Michael Blount's marriage, i. 313; his attitude towards the invasion (1715), i. 322; — his family abroad in 1715–16, i. 265 n., 314, 317; Pope has pictures framed for C., i. 419, 484 ('Black Phil'); Christmas customs at

CARYLL, JOHN, sr. (*cont.*)
Grinstead, i. 457; C. is guardian to
Lord Petre, i. 464; death of C.'s eldest
son, John, i. 474; Pope calls C. 'the
best man in England', i. 512; C.
wishes to sell an estate to young
Craggs, ii. 53, 57; uses Spa waters, ii.
77; writes coldly to Pope, ii. 112;
death of his son Henry, ii. 366; asked
his opinion of the rabbit woman, ii.
418; — Pope consulted on a statue
for C.'s Park, ii. 434, 449; asked impossibly by C. (1729) to paint from
memory portrait of Henry Englefield
(d. 1720), iii. 18; marriage of C.'s son
Edward to dau. of N. Pigott, iii. 88;
a grandson writes verses, iii. 340, 345;
very lame at Pope's house, iii. 373;
Pope advises on staircase at Ladyholt, iii. 402, 406; C.'s death, iii.
474 n.

C.'s kindnesses to others: sends venison to Steele, i. 148 n.; helped Gay's
third-night benefit, i. 282; would
send venison to Atterbury in the
Tower, ii. 140; aids his cousin Mrs.
Cope, i. 522, iii. 13, 17–18, 35–36, ii.
367, 434; urged by Pope to aid Mrs.
Weston, i. 143; the Blount sisters at
Ladyholt, i. 490; gossip about Pope
and Martha Blount discounted, ii.
353; gossip about Teresa's behaviour
real, iii. 40 n., 44, 46, 75, 142, 279;
Martha sends C. pamphlets, i. 472,
iii. 370; asked to send venison for
Martha to Cheam, iii. 425; to help
Martha in difficulties with her
brother, iii. 455.

C.'s kindnesses to Pope: they exchange verses, i. 113; recommends
Pope to Englefield, i. 120; Pope is
grateful for kindnesses, i. 115, 129,
&c.; C. defends Pope against Dennis,
i. 131; recommends Pope to Steele, i.
134; gossip about Pope to be discounted, i. 171; Pope urged to behave
well, i. 179; Pope urged to study
painting, i. 174; commends Pope's
character, i. 230, 269; asks names of
authors of party-papers, iii. 14; sends
venison for Martha Blount, iii. 126;
asked to recommend Henry Rackett
to the Duke of Norfolk, iii. 346; Pope
supposedly at Cobham's, iii. 375; ill

CARYLL, JOHN, sr. (*cont.*)
health keeps Pope from writing, iii.
189–90, 446; financial dealings with
Pope: in France C. checks Pope
investments, i. 155, 180, 241; pays
interest on a loan of £200, i. 155, 318,
449, ii. 37, 72, 111 n., 117, 173, 423;
provides money and wine, i. 442;
treats for an annuity for Pope, i. 293,
449; his interest in the stocks, ii. 43;
involved in the episode of £100 from
Duchess of Buckingham to Pope, iii.
91, 110, 122; pays subscriptions for
the *Iliad*, i. 232.

C.'s interest in books (chiefly
Pope's): his London bookseller is W.
Lewis, i. 113, 144; another to be
chosen, i. 411; thinks Pope had a
hand in *Gulliver*, ii. 423; reports
Catholic attacks on *Essay on Criticism*, i. 119, has seen Hamilton's
translation of it, i. 210; comments on
the Adrian lines, i. 157; asks after
Messiah and *Rape of the Lock*, i. 142;
Rape addressed to C., i. 210; Pope
sends all his *Guardian* papers, i. 194;
sends 'Receipt to Make a Cuckold', i.
267–8; asked, who is the *Unfortunate
Lady?* i. 416, 419; gets subscribers for
the *Iliad*, i. 204, 210, 215, 312, 464;
also to the *Odyssey*, ii. 282, 380, iii.
18; is told of an unfinished poem,
iii. 155; C.'s misinterpretation of the
last line of the *Epistle to a Lady*, iii.
451.

Pope visits C.: for two months, i.
153; visits deferred, i. 219, 289, 318,
343, 403, 416, 442, 448, ii. 393; a visit
achieved, iii. 384.

C.'s rambles: at Old Windsor with
Pope, i. 173; Pope missed him in
London, i. 203, 232, ii. 299; projected
visit to Twickenham, ii. 380, 392,
418; Pope hopes for a glimpse of C.
in Town, iii. 89, 280; wanted for a
week at Twickenham, iii. 284, 358,
370, 373; goes into Warwickshire for
wedding of his son John, i. 144;
coming to London, i. 154, 162, 170;
coming to Mapledurham, i. 293; at
the Lewes assizes, i. 418; in France, ii.
341; might visit Lady Bedingfield, ii.
392; at Ingatestone (Lord Petre's),
i. 518, iii. 18, 284; ill there, iii. 295.

Caryll, Mrs., wife of Pope's friend John, thought to neglect the Blount sisters, i. 481, iii. 451.

CARYLL, JOHN II, eldest son of Pope's friend: letters to, i. 150, 163, 334; his marriage to Lady Mary Mackenzie, i. 144 n.; Pope's advice to a husband, i. 145; an ardent hunter, i. 163, 208; Pope compliments him, i. 150; burlesques Mrs. Nelson's poem on his wife, i. 152; his son born, i. 207; barely seen by Pope, i. 209; also suffers from French investments, i. 242; his death, i. 474; briefly mentioned, i. 162, 177, 204.

Caryll, John III, son of John II, in school in Paris, iii. 340 n.

Caryll, Lady Mary (Mackenzie), wife of John II: helps Pope with his painting, i. 174; commended by Pope as a wife, i. 261, 313; not seen in London by Pope, i. 242, 411, 414; mother of twins, i. 464; visits her mother in Twickenham, ii. 60, 112, 117, 140; accidentally not in the list of *Odyssey* subscribers, ii. 299; in Paris (1725–36), ii. 341 n., 380, 449.

Caryll, Richard, brother of Pope's friend, i. 129, 164, ii. 112.

Cashiobury, Herts., Gay visits Pulteney there, ii. 478.

Catalonians, i. 189.

Catholic disabilities (esp. double taxation), i. 241–2, 326, 337, 338, 344.

Catholic Record Society, i. 122 n.

Cato Censor, i. 28.

Catrou, François, Atterbury's opinion of his Virgil, ii. 79.

Catullus: cited as excellent on trifles, i. 130–1; quoted or adapted by Pope, i. 149, 237, ii. 20, iv. 15, 50.

Causham (Corsham or Caversham?), mentioned by Pulteney, ii. 247.

CAVE, EDWARD, of *The Gentleman's Magazine*: letter to, iii. 499; his poetry contest, iii. 499.

Cavendish, Lady, subscriber to the *Iliad,* i. 300.

Cavendish, William, 3rd Duke of Devonshire, Lord Lieut. of Ireland, iv. 57.

Caxton, William, his Preface to Virgil wanted for *The Dunciad Variorum,* ii. 498.

Cecil, Mrs., gets subscribers for Pope's *Iliad,* i. 300.

The Censor, prints Mrs. Whitrow's epitaph, i. 436 n.

Centlivre, Susannah, i. 88 n., iii. 352.

Cervantes Saavedra, Miguel de: Pope regards *Don Quixote* as 'the true sublime of ridicule', ii. 370; Pope reads it again, iv. 212; thought to be imitated in *Scriblerus,* iv. 239 n.; cited by Pope, i. 10, 114, 477, ii. 23, 141; cited by Swift, iii. 21, 251; beloved by Dr. Cheyne, iv. 208; translated by Jervas, ii. 350, iv. 455.

Chadshunt, Warwickshire, seat of the Newshams, ii. 265, 278, &c.

Chamberlain, Hugh, M.D., of Buckingham House: his poor health, ii. 99; dines at Bromley, ii. 121 n.

Chambers, Lady Mary, her letters published by Curll, ii. 439 n.

Chandler, Knox, ii. 288 n., iii. 357.

Chandos, 1st Duke of, *see* Brydges, James.

Chapman, George, translator of Homer, i. 43, ii. 52.

Chapman, John, alderman of Bath, iv. 432.

Chapman, R. W., transcript made by, ii. 254 n.

Chappel, Judge, a friend of Lintot and witness to articles, iv. 336.

Characters of the Times (1728), i. 48 n.

Charitable Corporation, *see* Sutton, Sir Robert.

Charlemagne, described by Bolingbroke as carried in procession, iii. 103.

Charles I, King of England, i. 75.

Charles II, King of England, i. 6, 78, 169 n., ii. 121.

Charlett, Dr., iv. 278 n.

Charnwood, Lady, iv. 183 n.

Charterhouse, election of a preacher there, ii. 269.

Chartres, (Col.) Francis, iv. 13.

Chaucer, Geoffrey: quoted from Dryden, i. 130; the Cook's tale, i. 169; 'Flower and Leaf' commended by Pope, ii. 202; Pope comments on Chaucer's descriptions, ii. 203; quotes the Knight's Tale, iv. 517; Gay on Wife of Bath's Tale, i. 290; clearer than Shakespeare, Atterbury thinks, ii. 78.

Chauvelin, Marquis de, his disgrace hindered aid to L. J. Hooke by Bolingbroke, iv. 119.

Chavigny, M. de, lived in the Denbighs' house at Twickenham: it burned, iv. 397 n., 409.

Cheam, Surrey, Martha Blount is Lady Gerard's guest there, iii. 425.

Cheddar letter, to Swift, from Pope, Gay, Bolingbroke, Mrs. Howard, Pulteney, and Arbuthnot, ii. 403 n.

Cheek, Tom, i. 36, 48, 116.

Chelsea: J. Brinsden, iv. 403; Philip Miller of the Physic Garden, iii. 451–2; Sir Hans Sloane, iv. 391; Chelsea Hospital, Dr. Tessier, iv. 395; Cheselden, iv. 253 n.; Pope writes from there, iv. 502; goes there in 1744 at times, iv. 497 n.

CHESELDEN, WILLIAM, famous surgeon: letters to, iv. 372; lived in Spring Garden, iv. 234; surgeon at St. Thomas's, iii. 140; at Chelsea Hospital in 1737 ff., iv. 253 n.; will aid Wise to a scholarship, iii. 141; helps on Pope's Shakespeare, ii. 100 n., 106, 177; Pope dines with, iii. 330; Pope stays with him in London, iv. 2, 6, 338; gives account of to Swift, iv. 4, 6, 12; C. reports Buckley as ill, iv. 66; Pope wishes to see C., iii. 486, iv. 79, 89; C. thinks Pope has the gout, iv. 198; acquainted with Mrs. Rackett, iv. 203; removes to the country, iv. 237; operation on Pope's penis, iv. 253, 268; C. Bathurst to call at C.'s for corrected copy of *Miscellanies* (1740), iv. 284; Pope writes to C. laconically, iv. 372; operative cataracts await C. at Bath, iv. 372; treats Pope (bleeding) several times in 1744, iv. 488, 497, 499, 501, 511, 516; C. at Pope's death-bed, ii. 100 n., iv. 525.

Chester, J. L., his *Registers of Westminster Abbey* cited, ii. 200 n.

Chesterfield, 4th Earl of, *see* Stanhope, Philip Dormer.

Chetwood, Knightly, iii. 257 (did not preach at Cannons).

Chetwyn, Mr., of King's College, owned a portrait of Pope, iv. 91 n.

Chetwynd, William Richard, later 3rd Viscount: friend of Bolingbroke's,

Chetwynd, William Richard (*cont.*) iv. 171 n.; lives in Dover Street, i. 443, iv. 518.

CHEVALLIER, CHARLES, writes from the Foreign Office to give news of Lady Mary Wortley Montagu's return, i. 500.

Cheyne, Dr. George: account of, iv. 46; his picturesque character, iv. 46–47, 120, 208, 211–12, 242; physician at Bath, ii. 133; his *Essay of Health*, ii. 179 n.; believes in abstemious diet and much drinking water, iv. 85, 206, 235; tells Samuel Richardson of Pope's delight in *Pamela*, iv. 335 n.; his death, iv. 449 n.

Child, Sir Richard, created Viscount Castlemain, i. 467 n.

Child, Samuel, one of Pope's bankers, iv. 497.

Chiselhurst, residence of Thomas Moore, ii. 200–1.

Chiswick, residence of Lord Burlington, i. 339, ii. 117, iii. 20, &c.; Chiswick House shown only in the afternoon if the family is there, iv. 409; Spencer Compton lives there, ii. 280; the Popes settle in Mawson's New Buildings (1716–19), i. 337 n., 339, 340, 343; Pope there on a visit, 1725, ii. 348.

Christina, Queen of Sweden, i. 257, 261.

Chrysostom, St., ii. 385 (quoted by Fenton).

Chubb, Thomas, read by Pope, iii. 143.

Chudleigh, Lady, some of her letters pub. by Curll, ii. 439.

Churchill, Charles, son of Mrs. Oldfield, marries Lady Mary Walpole, iv. 124.

Churchill, Henrietta Godolphin-: too rich for the simple life, ii. 395; her affair with Congreve, ii. 83, 133; Congreve ill at her house, ii. 402; her compliments to Pope, ii. 508; subscribes £100 for Gay's *Polly*, iii. 24, 52 n.; death of her son, Marquess of Blandford (1731), iii. 227 n.

Churchill, John, 1st Duke of Marlborough: his family painted by Jervas, i. 187 n.; the Duke mentioned by Pope disparagingly, i. 175, 216, 308, 432; his funeral, ii. 127; one of the Juncto that plotted against

Churchill, John (*cont.*)
Harley and St. John, iii. 199; great qualities with a meaner mixture, iv. 36.

CHURCHILL, SARAH (Jennings), Duchess of Marlborough: letters to, iv. 258, 264, 358, 359, 366, 381, 382, 389, 394, 412, 419, 421, 432, 444, 457, 465, 497; at Tunbridge (1730) wins Cleland's money, iii. 126; lyrical over *Gulliver*, ii. 413; joked by Pulteney on her 'approaching marriage', iv. 163; — beginnings of her acquaintance with Pope, iv. 162 n., 178, 258, 264–5; Pope sends her pineapples, asks for venison, iv. 358; her Patriot views make her act for the good of the nation, iv. 359; urged to see Pope's grotto, iv. 359; Pope leaves for Bath in two days, iv. 366; she is ill at Marlborough House, iv. 381; mentions an 'ignoble earl' (Wilmington ?), iv. 382; Pope idle and at her service, iv. 394; all other great ladies angry with Pope, iv. 395; her trust in Socrates as ghostly father, iv. 413, 445, 459; Pope visits her, iv. 411, 417, 419, 420; she is ill in Town, iv. 432; sends Pope venison, iv. 432; because of gout prefers letters to visits, iv. 444; Pope lists her intended kindnesses to him, iv. 457; Pope at Bath wishes to use Chesterfield as address, iv. 465; Pope too ill to wait on her, iv. 498; Pope's executors suppress Atossa portrait, iv. 504 n.; — she employs N. Hooke, iv. 327 n.; rewards him generously, iv. 383, 386, 405; Hooke held in 'slavery', iv. 430; his possible attempts to convert her to Catholicism, iv. 445.

Churchill, William Godolphin-, Marquess of Blandford: solicited by Pope for Dennis's relief, iii. 171; his death, iii. 227 n.

Churchill, Sir Winston, his *Marlborough* cited, iv. 258 n.

Cibber, Colley: *Non-Juror* acted in Dec. 1717, i. 346 n.; Pope attacks it, i. 472 n., 473; *Letter from Mr. Cibber to Mr. Pope* (1742), i. 473 n.; C. said to hate Pope, ii. 334; Pope's lack of influence with C. as manager, iii. 66; C. rejects *Mariamne*, ii. 105 n.; Mal-

Cibber, Colley (*cont.*)
let's *Eurydice* awaits a reading, iii. 86; *The Provok'd Husband* acted for benefit of Dennis, iii. 171 n.; — C. made laureate, iii. 158, iv. 398, v. 9; writes a vile ode, iv. 49; C. a symbol of the bad taste of the time, iii. 158, 192; writes verses at Bath on glass, iii. 435; his *Letter . . . to Mr. Pope* (1742) called impudent and foolish, iv. 415, 425; C. is disparaged by Lord Orrery, iv. 407; C.'s promotion in *The Dunciad* rumoured, iv. 406 n., 415; his father's images for Bedlam called 'brazen', iv. 426 n.; his story about Philips's threat called untrue, iv. 425; a 'canceled' leaf from *Dunciad* sent to him, iv. 448–9; the vanity of C.'s *Apology*, iv. 437–8, 449; C.'s *Another Occasional Letter*, iv. 491 n.

Cibber, Susannah (Arne) (Mrs. Theophilus), iii. 253.

Cibber, Theophilus, mentioned disparagingly, iii. 443.

Cicero, Marcus Tullius: cited on 'Citizen of the World', i. 344 n.; great in disgrace, ii. 167; against hiatus, i. 24–25; exemplifies rhythmus, iii. 140; Pope cites *Pro Archia*, i. 72, 135, iii. 223; *De Senectute*, i. 88; *De Dolore Tolerando*, i. 158, iv. 480; *Tusculan Disp.*, iii. 26 n.; *Ad Herennium*, iii. 140; *Paradoxa*, iii. 227; *Agricultura*, iv. 6; quoted by Atterbury, ii. 55, 87; cited by Bolingbroke: C.'s letters private and revealing, iii. 102–3; *Tusculan Disp.*, ii. 219; *De Natura Deorum*, ii. 220; named by Fenton as a top letter-writer, ii. 398; Swift on C.'s letters, ii. 310, iii. 492, 505 (written to be printed); on *Pro Murena*, ii. 69 n.

Cirencester, Glos., Lord Bathurst's seat: Pope there (1718), i. 475, ii. 81, 83, 388, &c.; its groves, iii. 50; the wood house rebuilt, ii. 207, 314; mentioned wishfully, ii. 258, 259, &c.; Swift and Pope there in 1726, ii. 388; Prince Frederick's visit (1738), iv. 138 n.

Clapp, Sarah L. C., iii. 176 n.

Clarendon, Earls of, *see* Hyde, Edward, 1st Earl, Edward, 3rd Earl, and Henry, 4th Earl.

Clark, Mrs., might take lodgers at Chiswick, i. 402.

Clark, Mrs., a singer, ii. 135 n.

Clarke, Alured, patron of Stephen Duck, iii. 132 n.; writes to Pope about Countess of Burlington, iii. 418 n.

Clarke, George, Fellow of All Souls, M.P. for Oxford University, i. 246 n., 376 n., ii. 81.

Clarke, John, ii. 294, 443 (auctioneer ?).

Clarke, Rev. William, iv. 338 n.

Claudian, mentioned or quoted, ii. 219, 345, 352, iii. 138 n.

Clayton, Charlotte, Viscountess Sundon, Mistress of the Robes and sponsor of Stephen Duck, iii. 132 n., 143 n.

Clayton, Dr. Robert, takes a letter from Lord Oxford to Swift, ii. 506.

Clayton, Thomas, composer, wants libretto from Pope, i. 131.

Cleland, Archibald: J. Brinsden's surgeon at Bath, iv. 384 n., 387 n., 401; appointed, Pope helping, asst. surgeon in Bath Hospital, iv. 401; loses the post, iv. 401 n., 405.

Cleland, Henry, son of William, undergraduate at Christ Church: needs right friends, iii. 144; Lord Oxford to write to Christ Church about Henry, iii. 147, 153.

CLELAND, WILLIAM, of Kingston, Surrey, father of John, the novelist, and Henry an undergraduate at Christ Church, Oxford; his letter to Gay (or Pope's), iii. 254; has often eaten broccoli at Pope's, ii. 425; his 'Letter to the Publisher' in *The Dunciad*, ii. 504, iii. 33 n.; its authorship questioned, iii. 33 n., 162 n.; wrote some *Dunciad* footnotes, iii. 144 n., iv. 428; not attacked in *One Epistle*, but attacked in *Pope Alexander's Supremacy*, iii. 33 n., 114 n.; C. and Savage called Pope's only allies against the Dunces, iii. 37 n.; — friend of Hugh Bethel, iii. 113, iv. 338; at Tunbridge friendly with Sarah, Duchess of Marlborough, and Arbuthnot, iii. 126; visits Pope often, iii. 210, 233, 295, 300; at St. James's Palace, iii. 381; seldom seen by Pope in 1740, iv. 40; is interested in *Don*

CLELAND, WILLIAM (*cont.*)
Quixote, iv. 212; writes Pope a (lost) six-page letter, iv. 218; gets a legacy from the Earl of Scarborough, iv. 225; friend of Chesterfield and Marchmont, iii. 144 n.; Swift sketches his character, iii. 162; C. defends Pope's *Epistle to Burlington* in the *Post-Boy*, iii. 254–7; — dismissed by Walpole: his death, iv. 377; his attitude towards Walpole, iv. 378; his dutiful sons, iv. 378; his widow likely to live in France, iv. 378; John Cleland's novel, iv. 428 n.; Pope's note on C.'s career, iv. 377 n.

Clermont, Thomas Fortescue, Lord, cited as source for a letter, ii. 524 n.

Cleveland, John, his bust at Wimpole should be placed near Pope's (joke), iii. 115.

Clifford, James L., cited, ii. 68 n., 90 n., iii. 265 n., 328 n.

Clifton (Bristol), described by Pope, iv. 201, 204.

Cliveden, Bucks., Earl of Orkney invites Pope to aid 'improvements', iv. 35.

Clogher, Bishop of, *see* Ashe, St. George.

Cloyne, Dean of, *see* Ward, James.

Clye, near Swaffham (Norfolk), *see* Duke of Montrose—and Mallet.

Coates, Dorothy, v. 3 n.

Cobbett, R. S., *Memorials of Twickenham* (1872) cited, ii. 300, 313, iv. 334.

Cobbett, William, *Parliamentary History* cited, i. 307, iii. 282.

Cobham, Viscount, *see* Temple, Sir Richard.

Cobham, Viscountess, *see* Temple, Anne.

Cockburn, Dr. William, ii. 392.

Cockthorpe, Oxon., seat of Lord Harcourt, i. 489, ii. 114–15, 193, &c.

Codrington, Elizabeth (Bethel), Lady, wife of Sir William: Pope's visits to, iii. 427, iv. 224–5, 335, 496, 497; on Hugh Bethel's health, iv. 338; tries to get an annuity for Martha Blount, iv. 473.

Codrington, Sir William, Hugh Bethel's brother-in-law, iii. 195 n.; Pope visits the family at Dodington, ii. 510 n.; a complete courtier at Bath, iii. 435;

Codrington, Sir William (*cont.*) in Town early (1736), iv. 39; his estates in Barbados, iv. 168 n.; his title and death dated, iii. 195 n.

Coghill, Dr. Marmaduke, his death makes a vacancy for the University in the Irish Parliament, iv. 175.

Coigny, Maréchal de, is polite to Mallet, iii. 484.

Coke, Thomas, Lord Lovel: account of, iii. 436 (at Bath); his opinion of Michael Angelo, iv. 163.

Colbatch, Dr. John, opponent of Richard Bentley, iii. 267 n.

Cole, Grace (Miss), dines with Pope and the Caesars, iii. 56 n.

COLE, NATHANIEL, solicitor to the Stationers' Company: letters to, iv. 87, 335, 345; letter from, iv. 88; receives and amends Pope's chancery bill concerning the piracy of Pope's letters, iv. 87–88; consulted about Osborne's sale of 4to *Iliads* and copyrights, iv. 223; speaks to Lintot for Pope, iv. 333, 335–6; invited to Twickenham, iv. 345; dissuades Corbett from a piracy, iv. 345; fails to report on copyrights, iv. 425.

Cole, William: transcribed some of the Pope-Atterbury letters, ii. 166 n., and a part of a letter to Broome about Fenton, iii. 128 n.

Coleman, Mr., a friend of Fortescue's, iv. 203.

Coleshill, Warwickshire, seat of Lord Digby, i. 473, ii. 240, 280 n.

Collection of Pieces on the Dunciad, iii. 241.

Collier, Jeremy, might be shocked by comedy in Vienna, i. 362.

Collingwood, Mr., his 'convent' or house of assignation, i. 269.

Collins, Mr., of Bath: his urns awaited by Pope, iv. 353; designs urns for Lord Burlington, iv. 413.

Common Sense: sponsored by Chesterfield, Lyttelton, *et al.*, iv. 209 n.; Pope will not have verses on *Essay on Man* printed in it, iv. 209.

Compleat Key to . . . The What D'ye Call It (1715) echoed by Broome (1728), ii. 489.

Compton, Sir Spencer, in 1730 cr. Earl of Wilmington, speaker of the House

Compton, Sir Spencer (*cont.*) of Commons (called 'the prater' by Pope's mother, ii. 303), Lord Treasurer, 1742–3, lived in Chiswick: Pope sends respects to, i. 428; he will read the Preface to Pope's Shakespeare, ii. 280; praised in Broome's Epistle to Fenton, ii. 398 n.; Swift's attitude towards, ii. 462, 476; his preferments, ii. 462 n.; solicited by Pope for Dennis, iii. 171; shows Pope some of Wm. Hay's pieces, iii. 173; Pope dines with him at Chiswick, iii. 244; Pope's poor opinion of, iv. 458–9.

Comyns, Sir John, cannot admit H. Rackett to practise law, iii. 153.

Concannen, Mathew: a candidate for the laurel, iii. 151; called a scoundrel by Bolingbroke, iii. 215.

CONDUITT, JOHN, nephew and executor of Sir Isaac Newton: letter to, ii. 458; letter from, ii. 457; account of, ii. 457; Pope revises C.'s dedication to the Queen, ii. 457; Pope dines with in Hampshire, iii. 431; Mrs. Conduitt makes a social uproar at Southampton (1734), iii. 436.

Confucius, called a good moralist by Bolingbroke, iii. 413.

Congreve, Col. (not William !), is dead, ii. 354.

CONGREVE, WILLIAM, dramatist: letters to (all possibly fabricated), i. 274, 285, 290 (with Gay); letters from, ii. 12, 27, 433, v. 4; his amanuensis a blockhead, ii. 433–4; C.'s version of an Ode from Horace quoted, i. 167; bad priests in his plays, i. 106; Curll intends to publish something of C.'s, ii. 434; moral of C.'s 'Letter to Viscount Cobham' offends Swift, iii. 29; C. defends Dryden, i. 2; laughs at A. Philips, i. 229; — C. likes Pope's poetry, i. 238; sorry not to have seen Pope more often, ii. 28; reads Pope's Pastorals, i. 17; favours Pope's *Iliad*, i. 209; it is dedicated to him, ii. 16; copies of the *Miscellanies* sent to him, ii. 439; admires but does not envy Pope *The Dunciad*, ii. 508; holds Dennis's *Original Letters* for Pope, ii. 75; subscribes to Buononcini, ii. 99; — his friends: he visits

CONGREVE, WILLIAM (*cont.*)
Lord Shannon at Ashley, ii. 12; at Bath with Henrietta, Duchess of Marlborough, Gay, and Arbuthnot, ii. 133; Gay saw him in London, ii. 324; he inquires for Gay's health, ii. 433; anxious for the success of *The Beggar's Opera*, ii. 469; Swift appealed to Lord Oxford in C.'s behalf, ii. 67; inquires after C.'s welfare, ii. 153; C. misses seeing Swift (1727), ii. 433; Swift hopes for C.'s health, ii. 452; tries vainly to make Mrs. Barber omit caustic lines on C., ii. 483; C.'s friendship for Pope, ii. 433, v. 4; Lady Mary Wortley Montagu adored by him, i. 357; has written to her, i. 370; sends service to her by Pope, i. 385; writes to her with Pope, i. 405; remembers her even in the midst of gout, i. 442; Lady Mary says C. thought Pope's rhyme and conversation despicable, iii. 449; she mentions C. affectionately, i. 387 n., 413, 423, 460, 524; he talks of her, i. 470; — his health not good, ii. 12–13; bad eyes, ii. 12; uses Spa water, ii. 27, v. 4; ill at Windsor Park (home of Henrietta, Duchess of Marlborough), ii. 389, 402, 408; his death, iii. 3, 9; Swift's grief for, iii. 15, 16.

Coningsby, Thomas, Earl: account of, i. 477 n.; disliked, ii. 240.

Conolly, William, satirized by Swift, iii. 219.

Conquest, Dr., quoted, i. 311.

Conti, Prince of, talks with Mallet of hunting, iii. 484–5.

Conti, Abbé, Lady Mary's friend, i. 520.

Conybeare, John, Dean of Christ Church, visited by Warburton, iv. 357.

COOKE, THOMAS, translator of Hesiod: letters from, ii. 509, 519; Pope sends Wesley a letter to show to C., iii. 8, 9; Pope is troubled about C.'s sincerity, iii. 8; C. protests his admiration for Pope, ii. 509; sends his Hesiod as a present, ii. 509 n.; his answer to Pope's letter delayed, ii. 519; explains his friendships with Dunces, ii. 520; a public recantation from him is asked, v. 7; will omit a passage from

COOKE, THOMAS (*cont.*)
his *Battel of the Poets* (but does not), ii. 520, v. 7; still in *The Dunciad*, ii. 520, 529.

Cooke, William, Provost of King's College, Cambridge, owned a portrait of Pope, iv. 91 n.

Coolings, Thomas, Hugh Bethel's address in York, iii. 114.

Cooper, Mr.: sends marble for Pope's grotto, iv. 244; his name inscribed there, iv. 278; sends Pope cyder, iv. 350.

Cooper, Mary, wife and widow of the bookseller, T. Cooper, pub. sm. 8vo ed. of Pope's Works (vol. III), iv. 478 & n., 502.

Cooper, Thomas, bookseller: P.T. papers deposited with (1735), iii. 458; his name in the imprint of Pope's *Letters* (1735e), iii. 469, iv. 17 n.; he entered Pope's *Letters* in Stationers' Hall, iii. 469, 472 (with Gilliver); Curll serves a process on him, iii. 469, 494; published the sm. 8vo *Dunciad* IV with *Scriblerus*, iv. 426, and *Works* (III, pt. ii), iv. 478 n.

Coote, Thomas, comes from Ireland with note to Pope, iii. 376.

Cope, Mrs., estranged wife of Capt. Cope, her sad state mentioned, i. 113, 129 (a cousin of Caryll's), 158 n.; she goes (1717) to France, i. 416–17; Pope intervenes to help, i. 522; she is with the Carylls (1720), ii. 58; her last illness and destitute state, iii. 13; named as subscriber to the *Odyssey*, ii. 299; Pope reproaches Caryll for not doing more for her, ii. 341, 361, 367; her brother joins her, ii. 380; suffering from cancer, ii. 434; her death, ii. 449, iii. 17–18; Pope had sent £20 a year, iii. 18; apologizes to Caryll for ignorance of Caryll's charity to her, iii. 36.

Copplestone, Mr., has Devonshire cyder, i. 311.

Corbett, Charles, intends a piracy of Pope's *Works in Prose* (1741), iv. 345.

CORBIÈRE, A., employé in the Foreign Office: letters to Pope, ii. 223; arranges for Pope to wait on Mrs. Newsham, ii. 223.

Cornbury, Viscount, *see* Hyde, Henry.

Corneille, Pierre, his diction flags, Bolingbroke thinks, ii. 222.

Cornish, Henry: he and his wife fond of gay and fashionable life, ii. 266, iii. 123; invites the Fortescues and Pope, iii. 198.

Cornwall co., *see* Penzance (Borlase) and St. Mawes (Nugent); the Prince of Wales's estate there neglected, iv. 148.

Cornwallis, Charles, 1st Earl: subscribes to Pope's *Iliad*, i. 270, 297; corresponds with Broome, ii. 365, 378 n.; possibly paying Broome £100, ii. 396; Broome's patron, iii. 498.

Coronell, Mr., aids in Martha Blount's financial troubles, iii. 197.

Cortona, Pietro da, painter, iv. 20.

Coste, Pierre, ii. 88–89 & n.

Cotta, Gaius Aurelius, his difference between *bona ratio* and *mala ratio* unsound, Bolingbroke says, ii. 351.

Cotton, Sir Robert, subscriber delinquent to the *Iliad*, i. 266, 297.

Cottonian Library, burned (1731) in part, iii. 240 n.

Cottrell, Sir Clement, of Twickenham, Master of Ceremonies: subscribes to Buononcini, ii. 99; dines at Vandeput's with Pope, ii. 232; at Court for the Royal Birthday, ii. 233; his health, ii. 415, 432, 463; his mother-in-law just dead, ii. 463; his house full of guests, iv. 468; family adviser to Lady Judith Trumbull, ii. 119 n., 244; talks of Fenton and Broome, iii. 156; gets Fenton a temporary student (young H. P. Blount), ii. 119, 122 (at Sturston with Broome), 130, 135; reports to Fenton on Pope's eagerness as to the *Odyssey*, ii. 147; Fenton returns (with Blount) from Sturston, ii. 208; meets Pope at Sir Clement's, ii. 339; Sir Clement accompanies Fenton and Trumbull to Cambridge, ii. 377; tells Fenton of young Blount's marital troubles, iii. 55; apparently averse to having Fenton's pieces in the Pope-Swift *Miscellanies*, iii. 162; his acquaintance with Broome, ii. 147, 150, 205, 216 n., 358; advises Broome on coming to Town during *Odyssey* negotiations, ii. 214, 216; other mentions, ii. 296, iii. 498; Sir Clement's acquaintance with Lord

Cottrell, Sir Clement (*cont.*) Burlington, iii. 272, 516, iv. 324; with the Dormers, iii. 277, iv. 472; with Caryll, iii. 373, 406; his sister talks very loud, Kent finds, iv. 150.

Cottrell, William, younger brother of Sir Clement, iii. 378 n.; offers (1733) to take Pope to Ireland, iii. 378 n.

Country Life (1950), cited on Cirencester Park, iv. 25 n.

Court Party, The (political), *see* Sir Robert Walpole.

Courthope, W. J., corrected on dates of letters, iv. 264 n., 432.

Coventry, Gilbert, 4th Earl of, his death makes a house available, ii. 38.

Cowley, Abraham, quoted or mentioned, i. 147, 159, ii. 51, 54 n., 87 (by Atterbury), 345 (by Broome), iii. 106.

COWPER, JUDITH, niece of the Lord Chancellor; after 1723, Mrs. Martin Madan: letters to, ii. 136, 138, 141, 143, 144, 148, 155, 174, 179, 194, 201, 209; probably supervised publication (1769) of these letters, ii. 136 n.; her name not used in the edition, ii. 141 n.; friend of Mary Howe (later Countess of Pembroke), ii. 136 n.; friend of Mrs. Caesar, ii. 126 n.; dislikes the Town, ii. 141, 144; ill there, ii. 155, 174; Pope steals her picture, ii. 139 n., 143; hopes to see her come winter, ii. 195; she takes Pope's lines for Martha Blount's birthday for her own, ii. 180 n., iii. 18 n.; Pope never sees her, ii. 198; she has hypochondria, ii. 202; her respect for Pope (1733), ii. 209; marries (1723) Col. Martin Madan, ii. 209; Pope sends messages to her, ii. 235, 313, 392; her verses on Pope, ii. 93, 138; decides to write no more, ii. 143; her description of Bennington, ii. 197, 198, 202; advised to describe actual gardens, ii. 203; declines Pope's suggestions for subject matter, ii. 209; her epitaph for her uncle, Earl Cowper, ii. 209.

COWPER, LADY SARAH, daughter of William, Earl Cowper: letter to, ii. 496; subscriber to the *Odyssey*, ii. 293; called on Pope at Twickenham, ii. 496; now asked to help Walter Harte to a fellowship in Exeter Coll., Oxford, ii. 497.

Cowper, William, 1st Earl: his death and epitaph, ii. 209; mentioned, ii. 496 n.

Cowper, Lord William, son of Earl Cowper, undergraduate in Exeter Coll., Oxford, ii. 497.

COWPER, Dr. WILLIAM: letter to, iii. 268; account of, iii. 268 n.; translated Pope's *Unfortunate Lady* (or *Messiah*) into Latin, iii. 268.

Cox, Lady, Hugh Bethel's sister: ministered to Pope at Durhams, ii. 513; at Bath, iii. 435, iv. 85, 201, 206, 401, 463; would gladly receive Martha Blount, iv. 463, 494.

The Craftsman: mentioned, i. 285, iii. 22 n.; a number (22 May 1731) caused much pamphleteering, iii. 206 n.; attacks *Dunciad*, iii. 220; *Intelligencer* reprints a poem from it, iii. 292 n.; first publication of Bolingbroke's *Dissertation upon Parties*, iii. 456 n.; attacks *Daily Gazetteer*, iv. 179 n.; prints Dodington's *Epistle*, v. 2.

Craggs, James, the elder, died 1721, a possible suicide, ii. 73, 74.

CRAGGS, JAMES, the younger: letter to, i. 306; letters from, i. 360, 434, ii. 16; letters concerning his monument badly dated, ii. 456 n.; C. in France, i. 306, 360; on wit and scandal i. 361; backed the South Sea Bubble, ii. 21; resident (1720) in Twickenham, ii. 16 n.; invites Sir G. Kneller, ii. 15, 16; C.'s education, ii. 45 n.; Fenton his tutor, ii. 45; his death leaves Fenton idle, ii. 45 n.; dies of smallpox, ii. 73 n.; Addison's *Works* were to have been dedicated to, ii. 88; has one volume of Pope's set of Barrow's *Sermons*, ii. 81; his anecdote about the function of porters, iv. 9; his admiration for Lady Mary Wortley Montagu, i. 370, 442, 470; his friendship with Pope: favours the *Iliad*, i. 209, 306; cannot dine with Pope, i. 434; invites Pope to Battersea, ii. 1, 16; lives near Pope in 1720, ii. 21, 45; Pope's high regard for, ii. 73, 134, 160, iii. 81; his sister Anne (Mrs. Newsham-Knight-Nugent), ii. 223 n.; makes a bond between Pope and C.'s memory, ii. 243; Pope supervises the Abbey monument to C., ii. 26

CRAGGS, JAMES (*cont.*) n., 217 n., 242, 243, 246, 266, 457, 484.

Crane River, Pope overturned in it (1726), ii. 357, 401.

Cranford, seat of the Earl of Berkeley, ii. 247; lent or briefly leased to Bolingbroke (1726), ii. 400.

Crank, Mr., can't dine with Pope, iv. 15.

Crashaw, Richard: quoted by Pope, i. 103; discussed by Pope, i. 109–11.

Craster, Sir H. H. E., furnishes text of a new letter, iv. 35 n.

Creech, Thomas, his Lucretius mentioned, i. 374.

Creeke (i.e. Crick), accident to Orrery near there, iv. 123 n.

Croce, Alberto, H. Wanley's wine merchant, ii. 312.

Croix, Petis de la, author of *Arabian Tales*, ii. 56.

Croker, J. W., cited for his work on Pope, i. 27 n., 116 n., 180 n., ii. 446 n., iii. 34 n.

CROMWELL, HENRY, critic and man about town: letters to, i. 25, 36, 41, 46, 48, 51, 54, 56, 63, 66, 69, 70, 72, 75, 76, 81, 87, 89, 91, 92, 96, 98, 100, 103, 105, 109, 111, 115, 117, 124, 125, 130, 135, 137, ii. 437 (from E. Thomas); letters from, i. 95, 102, 104, 108, 134, 136, ii. 439, 440; reproached for not writing to Pope, i. 76; a letter not seen by Wycherley, i. 65, 66; — C.'s manner of life, i. 1; lives at Epsom, i. 15, 27, 38, 40; his deafness, i. 51, 53; called gentle, i. 56, 80; a journey into Leicestershire, i. 51; to Lincolnshire, i. 70; frequents Spring Garden, i. 57; no beau, i. 47, 65; his poor taste in women, i. 28, 65, 67; his housekeeper (Lady Isabella), i. 116; too civil, Wycherley thinks, i. 79; invited to Binfield, i. 43, 116, 117, 124, 125, 130; returns from Bath, i. 134, 135; enjoys Tidcombe's talk, i. 288, 290; introduces Gay (?), i. 113; deafness perplexes him at Gay's farce, i. 282, 285; he sees the hermaphrodite, i. 278; — his literary work: in Ovid's *Amores*, i. 82, 91, 95; a 'Letter . . . on Dryden's Virgil', i. 124; as a critic, rigorous, i. 91; friendship with Pope

CROMWELL, HENRY (*cont.*)
i. 30, 36; asked to correct Pope's translation from Statius, i. 36, 56, 57, 68; on *Pour le Moins* and *Ou vous savez*, i. 95; asked about Pope's imitations of Waller, i. 99; thanked for critical severity, i. 100; on Pope's 'To a Lady with Voiture', i. 109; aids a Pope-Wycherley reconciliation, i. 113, 134; — ceases to write to Pope, i. 153; mentioned disparagingly, i. 185; still friendly to Pope, i. 194; publication of Pope's letters to him: he gave them to Mrs. Thomas, i. 359 n.; she sells them to Curll, who prints them, ii. 297; Pope's slight opinion of the letters, ii. 405, 423; Mrs. Thomas's story, ii. 437–8; C.'s apologetic story, ii. 439–40, 441; — his criticism of others than Pope: fails to understand Juvenal, i. 101; on pathetic fallacy, i. 96; on Rowe's Lucan, i. 102, 104–5, 108, 109, 116.

CROOKSHANKS, JOHN: letter from, ii. 224; thanks Pope for counsel with regard to getting rid of an idiot, ii. 224.

Crouch-end, where Samuel Buckley lived, iv. 66.

Crousaz, Jean Pierre de: replied to by Warburton, iv. 163, 171; translated into English by E. Carter, Forman, and Dr. Johnson, iv. 163–4.; nature of the attack as seen by Pope, iv. 172 n., 208, 213, 216, 402–3.

Croxall, Samuel: account of a visit to old Jacob Tonson, iii. 176; denies authorship of *Essay on Man*, iii. 358.

Cruse, Mr., *see* Cruwys, Samuel.

Cruwys, Samuel, Mrs. Rackett's lawyer, iii. 6 n.; works on the affair with Essington, iii. 33, 39, 91, 141, 196; on the affair with Roberts, iii. 355; assistant to Fortescue, iii. 407, 409, 453, iv. 198; neglectful, iii. 91, 477, 478.

Cunningham, Peter, made transcripts for Elwin, iii. 408 n., iv. 117 n., &c.

Cuperus, Gisbertus, his work half in Greek, i. 225.

CURLL, EDMUND: letters from, iii. 471 (to Pope), 475 (to Broome), 476 (to the Public), 465, 466 (to R. Smith), 493 (to Pope); letters to him, iii. 359

CURLL, EDMUND (*cont.*)
(from E. P.), iii. 387, 395 (both from P. T.); his printing of the Cromwell letters (1726), i. 25, 36 n., 38 n., 41 n., 42 n., 46, 48 n.; his erratic methods: omits a postscript, i. 58 n.; his text altered by Pope, i. 67; his footnotes quoted and corrected, i. 4 n., ii. 14, 66 n., 99 n., 120 n., 184 n., 187 n., 313 n., 315; erroneous anecdotes from E. P. (1733), iii. 359; spices his notes with original acid couplets, ii. 396 n., 478, iii. 495; — C. reports Pope's authorship of a burlesque First Psalm, i. 218 n.; publishes the *Court* Poems (1716), i. 326; is given an emetic by Pope, i. 326, 339; tossed in a blanket by schoolboys, i. 350; Swift names him as enemy to Pope, i. 358, 359; in 1720 C. describes Pope as 'unenvied', ii. 31; C. publishes translation of Mme Dacier's attack on Pope, ii. 157 n.; intends to portray Pope's garden, ii. 263 n.; C. regarded as unspeakable by Fenton, ii. 385; C. exposes Pope's lie about the Dublin ed. of *The Dunciad* being the first, ii. 455 n.; C. claims the *Miscellanies* infringe his copyrights, ii. 477–8; advertises a *Key* to the Dunciad, ii. 496; his race multiplied against Pope, ii. 508; C. parodies Pope's *Imitation* of Satire II. i of Horace, iii. 355.

Publication (1726) of Pope's letters to Cromwell by C., ii. 357, 398 n., 405 n.; C. protests they are not stolen, i. 359; the publication deters Pope from writing letters, iii. 14, 349; leads Pope to ask the return of letters from friends, ii. 419 n.; C.'s advertisements, ii. 438, 439; further similar publication feared by Pope, ii. 419, 449; in 1733 C. shows no interest in more Pope letters, iii. 339, 359; publishes a *Life* of Alderman Barber, with Pope's epitaph on Samuel Butler included, ii. 76 n.; publishes a *Life* of Gay, iii. 359 n.; advertises preparation of a *Life* of Pope, iii. 359 n.

Publication (1735) of Pope's letters, iii. 448, 455, 458–67; his gift of swelling a volume with extraneous

CURLL, EDMUND (*cont.*)
rubbish, iii. 459; *Gulliveriana Secunda* advertised, iii. 459; day of publication busy, iii. 460; will show originals, he says, iii. 460; sends the letters from P. T. to T. Cooper, iii. 461; prints his replies to P. T., iii. 462–4; his advertisements mention letters to lords, iii. 464; summoned before the House of Lords committee, iii. 464–5; is dismissed: 'Where Pope has one lord, I have twenty', iii. 466, v. 16; finds all his copies from P. T. are imperfect, iii. 464, 465, 466; yet sells them all at 5*s*., iii. 467; asserts the letters sent to him ready printed by Pope himself, iii. 476, 493–4; in *Fog's Weekly Journal* tells how the letters got printed, iii. 476; his copyrights questioned, iii. 463, 467, 513; he serves a process on T. Cooper, R. Smythe, *et al.*, iii. 469, 508; announces vol. ii of *Pope's Literary Correspondence*, iii. 471, 476–7; claims to have received letters to Atterbury from Paris, iii. 468 n., 471; solicits letters from Broome, iii. 475, 478; his sign now 'Pope's Head', iii. 477; claims to have Pope's letters to the Duchess of Buckingham, iii. 477, 481; prints four Voiture letters as by Pope, iii. 487, 501; in his vol. iii addresses Pope, iii. 493–4; he advertises in *St. Jame's Eve Post* and Pope replies in the *Gazette*, iii. 494; announces a chancery bill against R. Smythe, Gilliver, and Pope, iii. 494; aware of Pope's use of the sheets of 1729 for the Wycherley letters in 1735, iii. 494 n.; publishes Voiture's *Works*, iii. 495; the 'Initial Anecdotes' of C.'s vol. ii, iv. 1; the 4th 'sham' vol. is published, iv. 7; publishes 'New Letters' (1736), ii. 183 n.; these said to come from Ireland, ii. 349 n., iv. 50; these are sent to Orrery to show to Swift, iv. 54; C. boasts of 'several' letters sent from Ireland, iv. 59 n., 60; his vol. v. on sale early in 1737, iv. 60 n.

C.'s reprint of the Swift–Pope letters: pretends to follow the Dublin text, ii. 189 n., iv. 12; Pope early feared C. would print these letters, iii. 79, 491 n.; Swift will take care against C.'s

CURLL, EDMUND (*cont.*)
getting the letters, iii. 505; C. sued and enjoined for piracy in printing the Swift–Pope letters, iv. 343 n., 350.
Curtius, cited as hero, i. 355.
Cutler, Sir John, the model of parsimony, iii. 186.
Cutts, Lord, i. 120.
Cyrus, his Paradise inferior to Lord Bathurst's, ii. 314.

D—s, charges Cromwell with giving letters to a mistress, ii. 439.
Dacier, André: his comments on the *Iliad*, i. 225; a better scholar than his wife, i. 492, ii. 15.
Dacier, Anne LeFevre: used by Broome in notes, i. 270 n., ii. 363; her ability as critic, i. 485–7; her translation of Homer, i. 485 n.; her attack on Pope, i. 485 n., ii. 15, 157, 248.
Dahl, Michael, his portrait of Pope to be copied for Tonson, sr., iii. 291.
Daily Advertiser, P. T. advertises there (1735), iii. 461–2.
Daily Courant, i. 125 n.; *Odyssey* Proposals, ii. 164 n., 285.
Daily Gazetteer: printed by Samuel Richardson, hostile to Pope, iv. 168; its authors, iv. 179 n.; advertises Hooke's *Roman History* (1738), iv. 31 n.; attacks Pope, iv. 91, 117, 124 n., 178 n.; Osborn advertises 4to *Iliads* and *Odysseys* for sale, iv. 222 n., advertises *Dunciad* of 1743, iv. 474 n., also 4to ed. of essays on *Criticism* and on *Man* (1744), iv. 500 n.; insults the dead and abuses the brave, iv. 250.
Daily Journal: on the Craggs monument, ii. 242 n.; seems to have had access to Lord Oxford's papers, iii. 511, 516; on a successor to Eusden as laureate, iii. 143 n.; prints Hill's epigram against Swift and Pope, iii. 170; announces Theobald's Shakespeare, iii. 241 n.; reprints Cleland's defence of Pope, iii. 254 n., on *Verbal Criticism*, iii. 357 n.; Pope advertises against Curll's ed. of his *Letters*, iii. 476.
Daily Post-Boy: prints defence of the Epistle to Burlington, iii. 254; Pope advertises concerning P. T. and R. S., iii. 460, 464; Pope and Cooper

Daily Post-Boy (cont.)
challenge Curll to produce any original letters, iii. 476.

Dallaway, J., cited for address of Lady Mary Wortley Montagu, i. 339, ii. 22.

Dalrymple, John, 2nd Earl of Stair, commander in the British army, iv. 413; Bolingbroke dines with him, iv. 498.

DANCASTLE, JOHN, of Binfield: letters to, i. 403, ii. 63; letters from, i. 273, 404, 443; friend of the Popes and of Caryll, i. 95, 115, 133, 162, 233, must stay home, in fear of a visitation, i. 273; fruit from his garden wrapped in Pope's MSS. sent to Teresa and Martha Blount, i. 317; Pope's farewell, i. 337; D. to dispose of Pope's palfrey, i. 403, 404; visited at Binfield in 1717, i. 418, 428; Pope's father wants strawberry plants, i. 443, 445; thanked for grapes, i. 519; Pope asks charity for Betty Fletcher, ii. 63.

DANCASTLE, THOMAS, younger brother of John: letters to, i. 340, 351, 393, 445, 518, 524, ii. 18; letters from, i. 443, ii. 8; transcribes Pope's *Iliad* for the press, i. 317 n., 351, 393, 443, 445, 519, ii. 8, 9, 19; asked to make registration of Pope's parents in Chiswick easy, i. 340; Pope hopes to visit Binfield soon, i. 351; visit to Lady-holt impossible, i. 445; asked to help Pope's old Nurse get her rent, i. 524; also ii. 29.

Daniel, Richard, iii. 21.

Darbishire, Helen, iii. 269 n.

Dart, John, ii. 258.

Dartmouth, Earl of, *see* Legge, William, ii. 269.

Daudé, John, i. 35 n.

Davenant, Mr. (the envoy), iii. 370–1.

Davenant, Sir William, iii. 370.

David, 'Old', servant to Lord Bathurst, iii. 131.

Davies, Miles, i. 478 n., 479.

Davies, Robert, *Pope's Maternal Ancestry* cited, i. 433 n.

Davila, A. C., ii. 220.

Davis, Herbert, ii. 64 n.

Davoux, Mr., ii. 409.

Daw, Sir John (in *The Silent Woman*), i. 71.

Dawes, Sir William, Archbishop of York, ii. 164 n.

Dawkes, Ichabod, a newswriter, i. 307.

Dawley, Middlesex: Bolingbroke settles there, ii. 120 n.; but not in 1723, ii. 290, iv. 50; Dawley Farm 4 miles from Twickenham, iii. 193; an 'agreeable sepulchre', ii. 403, 503; it is sold, iv. 148, 177.

Dawson, William, iii. 246 n.

Day, Thomas (?), iii. 113.

Deane, Thomas, former schoolmaster to Pope, ii. 424, 428.

Dearing, V. A., i. 86, iv. 310 n., 495 n.

Deaves, Charles, *see* Doves, iii. 271.

Deboovery, Sir Jacob, iv. 464 n., 472.

Decker, Sir Matthew, his financial dispute with Bolingbroke, ii. 186 n.

Defoe, Daniel, ii. 104 n.

Delany, Mary (Granville) Pendarves, marries Patrick D. in 1743, iv. 83; *see also* Pendarves.

Delany, Patrick: Dublin speculates as to the lady of his choice, ii. 483–4; chaplain to the Hon. Constantine Phipps, ii. 484 n.; his affluence, iii. 109; pestered by younger versifiers, iii. 109; promoted by Lord Carteret, iii. 151; much at his villa, iii. 182; publishes a poem inscribed to a Princess, iii. 286; called a patron to Matthew Pilkington, iii. 293; his new rich wife, iii. 304; his manner of life unchanged by wealth, iii. 344, 363, 378; thought 'every way estimable', iii. 349; an intelligent reader, iv. 278; — his relations with Swift, ii. 468, 476, 498; iii. 65 n., Swift's 'Libel' on, iii. 90; D. complains that Swift's printed letters reflect on the Irish climate, iv. 77; his friendship with Gay, ii. 475, 478, 483, iii. 146; his relations with Pope, iii. 21, 259, 504, v. 13; his *Revelation examined*, iii. 211–12, 274 n., 275, 276, 286, 289.

Delawarr, 1st Earl, *see* West, John, iii. 466.

Deloraine, 1st Earl of, *see* Scott, Henry, ii. 513.

Democritus, iii. 211.

Demosthenes, i. 25, 275 n., ii. 370, iii. 140.

DENBIGH, COUNTESS of, *see* Fielding, Isabella (de Jonghe), iv. 397.

Denham, Sir John, iii. 342.

Dennis, servant to Parnell, i. 225.

DENNIS, JOHN: letter to, ii. 75; letter from, ii. 75; his *Grounds of Criticism*, i. 136 n., 240; a grammarian, i. 185, 202; difficult personality, i. 238, ii. 399; his *Original Letters*, ii. 75; brings about a truce between D. and Pope, ii. 75; D. lied about Wycherley's 'To Mr. Pope', i. 50 n.; without permission D. printed Wycherley's letters, i. 66, 69; — his attacks on Addison, i. 183, 184, ii. 520; attacks Gay, i. 283, 286; attacks Pope's *Essay on Criticism*, i. 113, 115 n., 121, 125 n., 132, 139 n., 155; Pope attacks in his *Narrative of Dr. Norris*, i. 170, 183, 194; D.'s *Remarks on Mr. Pope's Homer*, i. 274 n.; his *Remarks upon the Dunciad*, i. 184 n., ii. 75; possibly had a hand in *Pope Alexander's Supremacy*, iii. 33 n.; thought destined for Bedlam, ii. 3; T. Cooke thinks D.'s opinions weigh nothing, ii. 520; Pope thinks D. stands above other Dunces, iii. 166; Pope would do him service, iii. 166, 169, 171, 174; aided secretly by Pope, iii. 357–8; anecdote of his son and a sword, iv. 364 n.; D. says Pope's aid is due to fear, iii. 171; lacks humanity, iii. 222.

Derbyshire, *see* Eyam, iv. 140, 196.

Dering, Mrs., ii. 485.

Derry, Bishop of, *see* Rundle, Thomas.

Derwentwater, 3rd Earl of, *see* Radcliffe, James, ii. 513.

Descartes, René, i. 488.

Despreaux, *see* Boileau, Nicolas.

Dettingen, battle of, iv. 459.

Devonshire, 2nd Duke of and 3rd Duke of, *see* Cavendish, William.

Devonshire, co., *see* Barnstaple, Exeter, Fallapit, Tiverton, Torbay (Edmund Bickford, Edward Blount, W. Fortescue, J. Gay, and Mr. Copplestone).

Dialogue between Mr. Pope and the Ordinary of Newgate (1733), iii. 355 n.

DIGBY, Hon. EDWARD: letter to, ii. 375; letter from, ii. 243; he, not his sister Elizabeth, is Pope's correspondent, ii. 243; in Paris, ii. 306; death of his brother Robert, ii. 375–6; con-

DIGBY, Hon. EDWARD (*cont.*) cerned about Gay's illness, iii. 3; helps distribute *The Dunciad* (1729), iii. 27, 177 n.; happy, iii. 52.

Digby, Elizabeth, after 1722 Lady Dolben, ii. 243 n.

Digby, George, Lord, iii. 28.

Digby, Mary, sister of Edward, Robert, and Elizabeth, ii. 115, 253, 314–15, iii. 51.

DIGBY, ROBERT, younger son of the 5th Lord Digby: letters to, i. 408, 472, ii. 43, 49, 115, 161, 240, 253, 254, 280, 314, 329; letters from, i. 473, ii. 47, 49, 51, 58, 191, 304; Pope's letters to Robert returned by Lord Digby, iii. 79; letters to Robert fabricated, i. 457–8, ii. 254, 280, 341 n., 352 n.; — biography: undergraduate at Oxford, i. 408 n.; T. Warton, the elder, his tutor, i. 467; his reflections on South Sea, ii. 47; his visits to Lord Bathurst, ii. 58, 192, 258, 314 n.; at Riskins with Pope and Gay, ii. 304, 305; his rural life; ii. 50, 115; writes from Holm Lacy, ii. 304, 305; M.P. for Warwick, 1722– 6, ii. 314 n.; — jokes Pope about courtly depravity, i. 474, ii. 51, 58, 315, 330–1; his friendship for Pope, ii. 47; Pope visits him at Sherborne, ii. 93, 192; in London, ii. 232; Digby at Twickenham, ii. 47, 58, 191–2, 283; on real and artificial rural settings, ii. 305; his health, i. 408, ii. 192, 243, 253; his death, ii. 375–6; Pope's epitaph, iii. 51, 104–5; Pope had Robert's likeness drawn after death, iv. 512.

DIGBY, WILLIAM, 5th Lord: letter to, iii. 51; the epitaph for Robert and Mary Digby, ii. 44, iii. 51.

Dilke, C. W., cited, i. 277 n., 522 n.

Dillon, Wentworth, 4th Earl of Roscommon, i. 503.

Diodorus Siculus, ii. 527.

Diogenes the Cynic, i. 344 n., iii. 152.

Diogenes Laertius, i. 344 n.

Dionysius of Halicarnassus, i. 264; iii. 140.

Disney, or Desaulnais, Henry, called 'Duke', i. 310, 315, ii. 149, 333, iii. 249.

Diss, Norfolk: J. Briars, rector, ii. 244 n.; Mr. Burlington, ii. 148 n.

Dixey (or Dixie), Sir Wolstan, i. 97 & n.

Dodd, or Dod, Mrs., imprint publisher of *The Dunciad*, ii. 496 n., iii. 5 n.

Doddridge, Dr. Ralph, iv. 346 n.

Dodington, George Bubb, iii. 81, 86, 329, 401, v. 2.

Dodington, Glos. (Durhams), ii. 510 n., seat of Sir W. Codrington.

DODSLEY, ROBERT, bookseller and author: letters to, iii. 346, 407, iv. 83; reprints *Gorboduc*, i. 467 n.; Pope his early patron, iii. 346; submits to Pope his verses on the marriage of Lady Margaret Harley, iii. 407; his *Epistle to Pope*, iii. 407 n.; sets up as a bookseller, iii. 454; Pope visits his shop, iv. 38, 380; — D.'s story of the first meeting of Pope and Warburton, iv. 236 n.; helps Savage, iv. 331; helps Lady Orrery, iv. 440; publishes Pope's letters to Judith Cowper, ii. 138 n., 144 n., 202 n.; he takes subscriptions for Pope's letters (1737), iv. 41 n.; delivers a copy to Mrs. Pendarves, iv. 83; a pirated edition offered him, iv. 87; he has the copyright, iv. 88; is one of the publishers of Pope's *Works in Prose*, vol. ii (1741), iv. 259 n.; he and Cooper publish *Dunciad* (1743), iv. 477 n.

Dodwell, Henry, i. 51.

Dolben, Sir John, ii. 243 n.

Dolce, Lodovico, iv. 43.

Dombes, Prince de, grandson of Louis XIV, iii. 484.

Donne, John, i. 16, 26, ii. 371.

Dorchester, Marquess of, *see* Pierrepont, Sir Evelyn (also Duke of Kingston).

Dorimant (pseud. once ascribed to Pope), letters from Dorimant, ii. 144, 146, 147.

Dormer, 5th Lord, ii. 428.

DORMER, JAMES, Brigadier: letters to, ii. 415 (from Gay); at Amesbury, iii. 119, 126; envoy to Lisbon, ii. 415–16; takes Pope to Stowe, iii. 216; takes Gay to Rousham, with Sir C. Cottrell, iii. 277; dialogue between him and Pope, written by Pope, suppressed by Kent, iii. 329; pall-bearer at Gay's funeral, iii. 338; Kent resembles D. but is plumper, iv. 43;

DORMER, JAMES (*cont.*)
D. is 'bronzo-mad', iv. 150; in ill health, iv. 150, 163.

Dormer, Robert, Col., brother of James: Pope dines with him in London, i. 468; D. visits Middleton (Queensberrys), ii. 416; Pope visits him at Rousham, ii. 510 n., iii. 493, iv. 188; Lord and Lady Oxford received at Rousham cordially, iii. 112; Lord Bathurst wants the Dormers to bring Pope to Cirencester, iv. 25; Pope's *Imitation of Horace, Ep. II. ii*, thought addressed to Col. Dormer, iv. 56 n.

Dorset, 1st Duke of, *see* Sackville, Lionel Cranfield (1688–1765).

Dorset, 2nd Duke of, *see* Sackville, Charles (1711–69), styled Earl of Middlesex in our period.

Dorset, 1st Earl of, *see* Sackville, Thomas (1536–1608).

Dorset, 6th Earl of, *see* Sackville, Charles (1638–1706).

Dorset, Mr., rents out horses, iv. 413.

Dorsetshire, Sherborne, Lord Digby.

DOUGLAS, CATHERINE (Hyde), Duchess of Queensberry: letters to her (from Swift), iii. 151, 179, 218, 250, 296, 303, 319; letters from her (and Gay, to Swift), iii. 145, 204, 238, 300, 307, v. 8; perplexing collaboration in letters, iii. 301; she subscribes to Buononcini, ii. 99; called Gay's 'steward', ii. 343 n.; won £1,000 in (Gay's) lottery, ii. 410; — conspicuously Gay's friend in 1728 and after, ii. 474; she has smallpox, ii. 479; Gay's affection for her and the Duke, iii. 19–20; Swift hopes she will teach Gay economy, iii. 74; Gay's blissful life at Amesbury, as Pope sees it, iii. 125; the Duchess's remark on nonsense, iii. 205; the Queensberrys envied in exile, iii. 220; — they are drawn to Sir W. Wyndham, iii. 251; will aid Wm. Reeves, iii. 277; their eldest son has smallpox, iii. 289; her views on Gay's discretion, iii. 301, v. 9; Gay not to live alone, iii. 302; — Queensberrys abroad winter of 1735–6, iii. 501; abroad also in 1738, iv. 149; the Duchess fails to invite Martha Blount to a ball, iv. 212; at

Douglas, Catherine (*cont.*)
Bath, iv. 463; Pope visits Amesbury, iv. 472; — correspondence with Swift: mutual admiration, iii. 69, 96; Swift invited to Amesbury, iii. 145, 146; she is reproved for bad spelling, iii. 181; she and Swift state conditions for a visit, iii. 195, 206; her dd's. identify her handwriting, iii. 220; her retort in jargon, iii. 239, 252–3; Swift at Amesbury might persuade the Duchess to take exercise, iii. 277, 299; she is willing to continue to correspond after Gay's death, iii. 361.

Douglas, Charles, husband of Catherine, and 3rd Duke of Queensberry: subscribes to Buononcini, ii. 99; Gay at Amesbury in 1725 on visit, ii. 316; goes to Scotland (1729) with the Queensberrys, iii. 36 n.; Gay goes to live at Amesbury with the Duke and Duchess, iii. 94; — Swift admires his Grace, iii. 97; Gay reported to be the Duke's chief agent, iii. 148, 180; his Grace adds his invitation to Swift, iii. 239; speaks of Gay as 'our friend John', iii. 239; Gay's effects after his death in custody of the Duke, iii. 335; his Grace oversees the production of Gay's *Achilles*, iii. 337, 347; will set up Gay's tomb in the Abbey, iii. 347; the Duke should (in Swift's opinion) have destroyed poor papers left by Gay, iii. 361.

Dover, Kent, ii. 196 n.

Doves, or Deaves, Charles, iii. 271.

Down Hall, Essex, seat of the 2nd Earl of Oxford, ii. 311; Pope there in Jan. 1726, ii. 358; improved by Harley, ii. 369; also ii. 496.

Drake, James F., dealer, i. 340 n.

Draper, Mr., takes Pope's letter to Bethel (in York), iv. 21.

Drayton, Michael, Selden's notes prolong his life as poet, iv. 428.

Drayton, Berks., James Eckersall, i. 226.

Drelincourt, Mrs., widow of the Dean of Armagh; account of, iii. 233; not responsive to Gay's love, iii. 119, 194, 203; she knows the rascally Roberts, iii. 233.

Drew, Sarah: killed, with her lover, by lightning, i. 479–81; the story retold,

Drew, Sarah (*cont.*)
i. 482–3, 488, 494–6, 497, 499; Lady Mary's reaction to it, i. 523.

Drift, Adrian, Prior's literary executor, ii. 193 n.

Drumlanrigh, Earl of: Douglas, Henry, son of 3rd Duke of Queensberry, has smallpox, iii. 289, 302.

Drummond, Andrew, banker at Charing Cross, iv. 365, 497.

Drummond, John, banker: letter to, ii. 245; agent for Bolingbroke (1723) ii. 186 n.; asked by Pope to aid John Rackett, ii. 246.

Drury Lane Theatre: rejects Fenton's *Mariamne*, ii. 105; Gay's *Captives*, ii. 215; *Beggar's Opera*, ii. 478 n.; Southerne's *Money the Mistress*, ii. 352; accepts Mallet's *Eurydice*, iii. 1.

Dryden, Mrs. (unidentified), venison for Martha Blount consigned to, iv. 185, 188.

Dryden, John, poet: Pope barely saw him, i. 2; Cromwell's rival in love, i. 28; needs masses, i. 200; the Sixth Miscellany, i. 43 n.; his *Aeneid* criticized by Cromwell, i. 91–93; changed from satire to translation, i. 255; his tomb, ii. 51; epitaphs by Atterbury, ii. 55; in error as to *Queen Gorboduc*, i. 408; his remark on Kneller's portraiture, i. 466; Pope's regard for: D.'s portrait in Pope's chamber, i. 120; his art in poetry, i. 24, 34, 44, 57; *Alexander's Feast* praised, i. 23, 108; sea terms in Virgil, i. 101; D.'s dedications, ii. 90 n.; quoted by Pope, i. 99, 130, 194, 198, iii. 244; quoted by Atterbury, ii. 56; by Broome, iii. 512; by Fenton, ii. 487, 488, iii. 55; Swift's hostility to, ii. 483.

Duck, Stephen: his character by Spence, iii. 132–3; likes Pope's *Essay on Criticism*, iii. 133; spoken of as Pope's equal, iii. 143, 146; a candidate for the laurel, iii. 151; a thresher now the emblem of inspiration, iii. 143.

Duckett, George, co-author of *Homerides*, i. 284 n.; did the frontispiece of *Pope Alexander's Supremacy*, ii. 489, iii. 33 n.

Dufkin, Mrs., iv. 367.

Du Fresnoy, C. A., i. 334.

Dunbar, 4th Viscount, i. 309 (Constable, William).

Duncombe, John, not Pope's correspondent (*see* Duncombe, William) but edits Pope's letters to John Hughes, &c., i. 218, 316, ii. 33, 62, iii. 437; sent original letters to the printer, iii. 441 n.

DUNCOMBE, WILLIAM, uncle of John, the editor: letters from Pope, iii. 437, 441, 442, 454; his tragedy, iii. 442; Pope fails to find a Hughes letter, iii. 437, 441, 454; sends Hughes's *Works* to Swift, v. 17.

Dundonald, 4th Earl of (Cochrane, John), i. 308.

Dune [or Downe?], Mrs., of Duke Street, ii. 29.

Dungeness, Kent, engagement with French fleet prevented, iv. 498 n.

Dunkin, William, iv. 178 n., 233 n.

Du Parc, Mlle, iv. 43.

Dupplin, Viscount, *see* Hay-Drummond, Thomas (later 9th Earl of Kinnoull).

Dunmow Priory, its flitch of bacon, ii. 363.

Du Resnel, J. F. de B., his verse translation of *Essay on Man*, iv. 172, 196, 416, 484.

Durfey, Tom, i. 71, 81, 180 (*Guardian* No. 87), ii. 268 (Pope's verses on him).

Durham, Bishop of (Talbot, William), ii. 269.

Durhams, at Dodington, Glos., seat of Sir W. Codrington, ii. 513.

D'Urigny, LaCombe, i. 75.

Dyer, John, newswriter, i. 307.

E., S., initials of person supposedly sending Voiture letters to Curll as Pope's, iii. 487.

Eadnell, Mr., attorney (?) for Roberts, iii. 283, 441.

Easthampstead Park, Berks., *see* Sir Wm. Trumbull, Lady Judith Trumbull, Ralph Bridges, Elijah Fenton, J. Marriott.

East India Company, its motto parodied, i. 333.

Echlin, John, iii. 210.

ECKERSALL, JAMES: letters to, ii. 32, 33, 34, 39; letters from, ii. 32; account of, ii. 32 n.; friend of Jervas also, i. 226

ECKERSALL, JAMES (*cont.*) n.; buys South Sea stock for Pope, ii. 32, 33; lottery tickets, ii. 32, sold to buy South Sea, ii. 38, 39; E. subscribes to S. Wesley's *Poems*, iii. 504.

Edgecombe (or Edgecumbe), Richard, 1st Baron, i. 470, ii. 441.

Edinburgh, University of, Laing MSS. cited, iv. 335 n.

Edwards, Francis, dealer, iii. 427.

EDWARDS, THOMAS: letter to, iv. 342; letters from, iv. 342, 351; his quarrel with Warburton over Shakespeare, later, iv. 342 n.; invited to see Pope's grotto, iv. 342, 361; furnishes materials for the grotto, iv. 342, 349, 351–2.

Edwine, Lady Charlotte, iv. 265.

Edwyn, Mr., iv. 464.

Egmont, 1st Earl of, *see* Percival, John.

Egwood (not located), ii. 317.

Elephants, Danish Order of, i. 75.

Elibank, 5th Baron, *see* Murray, Patrick, iv. 466.

Elliot, Richard, ii. 266.

Elliott, Elizabeth (Mrs. Edward) (sister to Craggs and Mrs. Knight), a Roman Catholic, iii. 218, 426, iv. 30; perhaps with Mrs. Knight, iii. 425, 490; in London, iii. 511, iv. 47.

Ellis, Mr., agent of Orrery's, iv. 325, 327.

Ellis, W. D., i. 288 n., ii. 109 n.

Elrington, Mr., ii. 523.

Elson, Mrs. Van, iv. 509, 515.

Eltham, Kent, Edw. Roper, i. 156 n.

Elwin, Whitwell: his ed. of Pope (1871–2) cited *passim*; for changes in questioned datings of letters see i. 36, 180, 210, 262, 315, 318, 381, 522, ii. 19, 26, 72, 88, 108, 111, 144, 242, 265, iii. 65, 274, 294, iv. 208; small changes in his texts, i. 205, 277, 442, 462, ii. 306, iii. 109.

Elwood, John, i. 259, 331, 410.

Englefields, of Whiteknights (spoken of as a family): visited by Pope, i. 113, 117, 135, 203; allied with the Carylls, i. 93, 133; disapprove Pope's championing of Mrs. Weston, i. 119, 162; cool to Pope about it, i. 162; cool remarks about Martha and Teresa Blount, i. 337; on Miss Fermor's marriage, i. 269.

Englefield, Antony of Whiteknights, grandfather of Martha and Teresa Blount, i. 128; mentioned, i. 15, 31, 115; friend of Wycherley, i. 31–32, 62; also of Cromwell, i. 91, 117; and of Caryll, i. 120, 128.

Englefield, Charles, died 1720, i. 171 n., ii. 29, 31.

Englefield, Edward, i. 144.

Englefield, Henry, died in 1720, i. 171 n.; not civil to Pope's parents, i. 177; did not deliver Caryll's letter to Pope, i. 179; Caryll asks Pope to paint E.'s portrait 9 years after E.'s death, iii. 18.

Englefield, Mrs. Henry, i. 171, iii. 274.

Ennius, Quintus: mentioned by Bolingbroke, ii. 219; his epitaph, ii. 219; his fame comes through Cicero, ii. 387, iii. 26, iv. 261.

Epicurus, iii. 211.

Epistle from Calista to Altamont (1730), iii. 110 n.

Epsom, Surrey, *see* Henry Cromwell, i. 15, ii. 439.

Erasmus, Desiderius: mentioned by Wycherley, i. 69; Pope's model Catholic, i. 118, 122 n., 128, iii. 81.

Essay on the Taste and Writings of this Age, iii. 12.

Essex, 3rd Earl of, *see* Capel, William.

Essex, co., *see* Down Hall (Matthew Prior, Edward, Earl of Oxford), Gosfield (Knight-Nugent), Halstead (J. Morley), Ingatestone (Lord Petre), Leighs (Duchess of Buckingham), Plaistow (Aaron Hill).

Essington, Mr., dilatory agent or debtor to Mrs. Rackett, iii. 5, 7, 33, 112, 196.

Etherege, Sir George, dispute over his *Man of Mode*, ii. 144.

Eu, D', Conte, iii. 484.

Eugene, Prince, i. 420, 421, iii. 199, 503 n.

Euripides, i. 18.

Eusden, Lawrence, i. 346 n., iii. 143, 151.

Eusebius, iii. 212.

Eustas (Eustace ?), Mr., iv. 203.

Eustathius, Archbishop, commentator on Homer: to Pope an obstacle, i. 225; to Mme Dacier, a source, i. 492; used for Pope's notes by Jortin, i. 514; by

Eustathius, Archbishop (*cont.*) Broome, ii. 3, 15, 19, 204, 244, 265, 339, 363.

Euston, Earl of, *see* Fitzroy, George (1715–47).

EVANS, ABEL, D.D., of St. John's Coll., Oxford: letters from, i. 420, 444, 448, ii. 5, 8; reports Pope's concern over R. Digby's health, i. 408; distributes *Iliad*, vol. iii. to Oxford subscribers, i. 420, 444; Pope his guest at St. John's, i. 433; Pope's letter received, i. 444; his books to be bound, i. 444; Lintot most dilatory, Evans thinks, i. 444; reports on the labours of Peche (Peachy ?), i. 448; satirical of the clergy, ii. 5; has visited Pope at Twickenham, ii. 8; speaks of Pope's Duchess (unidentified), ii. 8, 83.

Evans, A. W., *Warburton and the Warburtonians* cited, iv. 164.

Evelyn, Sir John, ii. 78, 112.

Evening Packet, on the fall of Belgrade, i. 420.

Evening Post, i. 25, 345, 350, 426, ii. 519.

Examiner, The, i. 101.

Exeter, city, iv. 156.

Eyam, Derbyshire, iv. 140, 196.

Eyles, Sir John, iv. 512, 522.

FAIRFAX, BRIAN: letter to, iii. 124; Pope recommends a man, iii. 124, v. 8; F. at whist with Kent, iv. 150; mentioned, iv. 154, 324.

Fairfax, Ferdinando, iv. 150, 162, 324.

Fallapit, Devon, seat of W. Fortescue.

Farinelli, opera singer, iii. 484.

Farnham, Surrey, iii. 485.

Facio, N., a French prophet, i. 35 n.

FAULKNER, GEORGE: letters from Pope, iv. 275, 290; letters from Lord Orrery, iv. 270, 284, 292, 295, 298; letters from F. to Orrery, iv. 270, 280, 291, 295; cited for text of a Swift letter, iv. 174 n.; brings Pope a letter from Swift, iii. 491, v. 16;—with Bowyer, F. holds Swift's copyrights, iii. 323, v. 10; prints Dublin ed. of *Gulliver*, ii. 418; his ed. of Swift's *Works*, iii. 369, 404, 429 n., 491, v. 12; plans an Irish edition of Pope's *Works*, v. 17; his ed. (1741) of Swift's *Letters*, ii. 64 n.; adds six letters from London eds.

FAULKNER, GEORGE (*cont.*)
not in clandestine vol., iii. 291 n.;
his statement (1772) about Swift's
wish to publish his letters, iv. 54 n.;
—Pope prefers F. as publisher if the
letters are to be printed, iv. 284; F.'s
theory as to origin of the clandestine
vol., iv. 241 n., 242; asks permission
from Pope for printing, iv. 256, 257,
264, 271, 274; Pope's reply delayed,
iv. 257, 260, 276; the reply stops the
printing, iv. 270; submits the clandestine vol. to Orrery, iv. 270; willing
to send it to Pope, iv. 275, 276, 280,
283, 284, 287; — F. knew Mrs.
Whiteway advised against printing, iv.
277; made Orrery tell Swift that he
(Orrery) had the clandestine vol., iv.
279; a copy of the Bath covering letter
sent to Pope by F., iv. 282; Orrery
convinced of F.'s integrity, iv. 306,
308; Pope sends a reply to Orrery for
F., iv. 311; Pope thanks F. for his
delay, iv. 312; Mrs. Whiteway's
opinion of F., iv. 318; the clandestine
vol. wanted by Pope when F. is
through printing, iv. 332; F. a
friend of J. Brinsden, iv. 348.

Faustina, empress, ii. 116 n.

Faustina, operatic soprano, *see* J. A.
Hesse.

Fawley Court, Bucks., *see* H. Moore,
Esq.

Fazakerley, Nicholas, advises Pope on
dangers of libel in *Dunciad* of 1729,
ii. 532, iii. 4, 25, 236 n.

Fenelon, Archbishop of Cambray, i.
492, iv. 416.

FENTON, ELIJAH: letters from Pope to
him, ii. 45; letters from F. to Pope, i.
496, 514, ii. 15; letters from F. to
Broome, ii. 105, 110, 119, 122, 147,
151, 152, 214, 215 (with Pope), 231,
233, 244, 278, 339, 351, 360, 365,
377, 379, 384, 397, 486, 487, 518, iii.
24, 37, 44, 54, 100; letters from
Broome to F., ii. 121, 150, 162, 344,
390, 488, 499; — letter to F. newly
dated here, i. 402; possibly to him
from Gay, i. 482; letter to F. conflated
with one to J. Richardson, ii. 46; F.'s
post office address in 1722, ii. 106;
seldom writes to Pope, ii. 208, 257,
296, 450; his address given to Broome,

FENTON, ELIJAH (*cont.*)
ii. 302, 384; has no letters from
Broome, ii. 321, 420; has no address
for Broome, iii. 24; ironical about the
merit of the Pope–Cromwell letters,
ii. 398; names Cicero, Pliny, and
Voiture as top letter-writers, ii. 398.

Biographical data: wishes to see
Pope, ii. 15; tutor to the younger
Craggs in Twickenham, ii. 21, 45,
63, 119 n.; discovered Catrou for
Atterbury, ii. 79; F.'s note to Barber
destroyed, ii. 130; accepts Broome's
invitation to Sturston, ii. 105, 110,
111; wishes to bring a pupil with him,
ii. 119; arrives, ii. 122, 130; the return, ii. 204, 208; at Cambridge, ii.
379; projected visit to Pulham, iii. 44,
54.

His residence with the Trumbulls, i.
275 n., ii. 214; at Easthampstead, near
Pope's grove, ii. 233; fails to see
Broome in Town, ii. 231, 233; back
in Town for the winter, ii. 270;
summer of 1728 spent in Twickenham, ii. 486; goes to Cambridge
with young Trumbull, ii. 375, 377,
379, 431–2, 433; asks for a turkey
from Broome and a rabbit from Mr.
Burlington, ii. 415, 422; notes
attacks on Pope in the newspapers, ii.
486; notes false report of Broome's
death, ii. 519; — looking for a successor to young Trumbull as pupil, ii.
488; Lord Gower's son may become
his pupil, iii. 24, 37, 44, 54; F.'s
nephew a lawyer, iii. 37; F. still with
the Trumbulls, iii. 100; F.'s health,
ii. 210, 241; has the gout, ii. 351, 360,
463; bad eyes, ii. 415, 420; gout
again, iii. 107; his death, iii. 121; his
papers claimed by his brothers, iii.
128, 156; Lord Oxford asks details of
F.'s death and burial, iii. 325; F. has
been Orrery's tutor, iii. 506 & n.; —
F.'s personality: a Non-juror, ii.
130, 379; not eligible for a college
post, ii. 379; his even temper, ii. 162–
3; his laziness, ii. 125, 204, 351, 358;
his drowsiness, ii. 234; Pope's glowing
character of F., ii. 389, iii. 326; stood
up for Broome, iii. 129; Pope's
epitaph for F., sent to Broome, iii.
156; — F.'s quotation of classics,

FENTON, ELIJAH (*cont.*)
of Horace, ii. 464, iii. 24; of Ovid, ii. 234; of Virgil, iii. 44, 55; gossip about contemporaries: about John Gay, ii. 216, 487, iii. 24; about Thomas Southerne, ii. 340, 360; about Spence's *Essay on the Odyssey*, ii. 379; — F.'s *Mariamne*: production delayed, ii. 105, 145; wants a Prologue from Pope, ii. 130, 134, 152; gets one from Broome, ii. 147, 150, 151; performed with great success, ii. 151, 162, 163; published by Tonson, not by Lintot, ii. 145; projects another tragedy, *Dion*, ii. 163, 464, iii. 128; revising his life of Milton, ii. 360, 365, iii. 38.
F. *as editor and translator*: Aids Pope on Shakespeare, ii. 63, 130, 213; on the Index, ii. 130, 213, 244; payments for his work, ii. 81, 244; works on Pope's *Odyssey*: translates 4 Books, ii. 103, 119, 182, 231, 233, 244; is secretive as to his share, ii. 274; advises Broome *not* to come to Town during negotiations with Lintot, ii. 214; later urges him to come and make a settlement for their shares, ii. 339, 351, 352, 360, 365, 379; his help on notes for Pope's *Iliad*, i. 496, 514, ii. 15; comments on notes to the *Odyssey*, ii. 216, 244; annoyed by the final note concerning the collaboration, ii. 352, 357, 385; later attempts to reveal the truth unwise, he thinks, ii. 423; fame derived from the *Odyssey*, ii. 429 n.; F.'s edition of Waller, ii. 80, 213, 278, 339, 398; dedicatory verses to Lady Margaret Harley written, ii. 374, 376, 398, 463; the edition published, iii. 24, 37, 44, 55.
F. *supports Broome against Pope* as to the *Bathos*, ii. 487, iii. 37, 100, 107; Broome's project of translating Apollonius, ii. 339; their joint project of translating Virgil for Tonson, ii. 429, 433; F. surprised that Broome will use Lintot as publisher of *Poems*, ii. 385; prefers not to revise Broome's poems, ii. 385, 390; on Broome's Epistle to F., ii. 398, 422; will revise B.'s imitations of Milton, ii. 398; awaits publication of Broome's *Poems*, ii. 429.

Fenton, Lavinia, as 'Polly Peacham', ii. 479.
FERMOR, ARABELLA: letter to, i. 271; *Rape of the Lock* sent to her, i. 145; she is offended, i. 151, and placated, i. 203, 207; her marriage, i. 269, 271, 464 n., ii. 293.
Ferrers, earl, *see* Shirley, Sir Robert, 1st Earl, iv. 167 n.
Fiddes, Richard, D.D., i. 226.
Fielding, Henry: praises *Leonidas*, iv. 72 n.; dislikes the *Gazetteer*, as Pope does, iv. 179 n.; his racial pessimism echoes Pope, iv. 249 n.; Pope gives *Joseph Andrews* to Anne Arbuthnot, iv. 394; piracy of *Joseph Andrews* halted, iv. 425; Pope is a channel for Allen's subsidy of F.'s *Miscellanies*, iv. 451; F.'s compliment to Prior Park, iv. 452.
FIELDING, ISABELLA, wife of William, 5th Earl of Denbigh: letter to, iv. 397; at Twickenham, iii. 113; account of, iv. 397 n.; their house in Twickenham burned, iv. 397 n.
Figg, James, pugilist, iii. 484.
Finch, Anne (Kingsmill), Countess of Winchelsea (1666–1720), i. 203.
Finch, Charles, 4th Earl of Winchelsea, iii. 132 n.
Finch, Lady Betty, dau. of Daniel, 2nd Earl of Nottingham, marries William Murray, iv. 141 n.
Finch, Heneage, 5th Earl of Winchelsea, i. 417.
Finch, Sarah (Nourse), wife of Charles, 4th Earl of Winchelsea, i. 298.
Finch [?William], Lord, i. 308.
Finden (Findon), Sussex, *see* John Caryll, John Stafford.
Fineman, D. A., cited on Welsted's 'lie', ii. 232 n.
Finglass, Ireland, *see* Rev. James Stopford.
Fitzgerald, Mary, Countess Kildare, ii. 17.
Fitzmaurice (later Petty), John, 1st Earl of Shelburne, a friend of Hugh Bethel, iv. 253, 355, 512.
FitzRoy, Charles, 2nd Duke of Grafton: he arrives as Lord Lieut. of Ireland, ii. 66; as Lord Chamberlain he receives Mallet's *Eurydice*, iii. 82, 86; Pope is invited to dine with, iii.

FitzRoy, Charles (*cont.*)
82; chooses Cibber as Laureate, iii.
192; signs the 'tree' petition, iv.
324.

FitzRoy, George, Earl of Euston: signs
the 'tree' petition, iv. 324; is thought
responsible for the death of his wife
(Lady Dorothy Boyle), iv. 396.

Fitzwalter, Lady, *see* Schomberg, Lady
Frederic.

Fitzwilliam, Lord (before 1672), iii.
107.

Flatman, Thomas, i. 159 n.

Fleetwood, Charles, manager of Drury
Lane Theatre, iv. 146, 151, 158, 159,
160.

Fletcher, Andrew, of Saltoun, ii. 89.

Fletcher, Betty, ii. 63.

Fleury, Cardinal, iii. 6 n.

Floyd, Mrs., friend of the Mrs. Blounts,
ii. 1.

The Flying Post: attacks Caryll, i. 152;
violent Whig paper, i. 251.

Fog's Weekly Journal: death of Broome
(of Debenham), iii. 155 n.; prints
defamatory adv. for Curll, iii. 477;
apologizes, iii. 477 n.

Fontaine, Nicolas, iv. 20 n.

Fontenelle, Sieur de, i. 369.

FORD, CHARLES: letters to, i. 223 (with
Parnell), 237, 249 (with Parnell), 258,
521, ii. 27, 283, iv. 137; letter from,
ii. 284; letter to Fortescue earlier
thought to be to F., iv. 507 n.; —
visits Ireland, i. 259, 341, 348, 358,
ii. 154, 200, 283 n., 410, iii. 149,
204; in London, to be at the Duke of
Buckingham's party with Prior, i.
521; Swift (1726) lodges near him, ii.
372 n.; F. reports on *Gulliver* to
Pope, ii. 321 n.; F. (or Pope) dropped
the MS. of *Gulliver* at Motte's door,
ii. 412 n.; F. reports on Pope's gardens, ii. 325; his explanation of
Pope's lady at Court, ii. 343, 350;
Swift mistakes a letter from F. for one
from Pope, iii. 23; — Pope's friendship for Ford, i. 223, 226, 237, 253;
F. invites Pope, i. 249, 259, ii. 27,
283; Pope invites F., ii. 283, 284;
Pope (anonymously) furnishes inscription for a tomb, iv. 137.

Ford, Cornelius, 'Parson', ii. 211.

Forman, Charles, iv. 164 n.

Fortescue, Grace, sister of William, iii.
453, iv. 507, &c.

Fortescue, Joanna, sister and co-heir of
Gay, iii. 335 n., 361.

Fortescue (Miss) Mary, dau. of William,
ii. 257, 322, *and see* Spooner, Mrs.
(John).

FORTESCUE, WILLIAM, Master of the
Rolls: letters to, ii. 48, 49, 104, 216,
241, 242, 255, 257, 289, 294, 322,
335, 358, 368, 373, 435, 441, 521,
524, 529, 530, iii. 5, 6, 7, 11, 33, 52,
91, 112, 127, 129, 139, 140, 141, 193,
196, 224, 264, 265, 270, 271, 283,
342, 350, 354, 356, 365, 374, 376,
377, 391, 395, 403, 407, 409, 440,
441, 443, 449, 450, 453, 469, 472,
477, 486, 508, 511, iv. 2, 6, 10, 15,
18, 21, 22, 26, 28 (with Martha
Blount), 33, 84, 89, 114, 125, 155,
166, 169, 183, 189, 193, 198, 202,
214, 216, 221, 243, 267, 355, 440,
451, 454, 456, 507, 516; letters from,
i. 341 (to Gay), ii. 245, 346, 347; —
a letter wrongly placed, ii. 294 & n.,
v. 2; his endorsement gives date of
receipt, iv. 183 n.; an endorsement
clearly wrong, iv. 456; a letter to him
posted by Gay, ii. 373; he likes
Pope's printed (1735) letters, iv. 7;
his places of residence or business:
Harcourt Buildings, Inner Temple,
ii. 104; Buckland-Filleigh (Devon),
iii. 225, iv. 34, 85; Fallapit, iv. 267,
355, &c.; Richmond, at the Vineyard
(called 'Shepherd's Hut'), iii. 477,
486, iv. 34, &c.; London, Bellyard,
near Lincoln's Inn, iii. 6, iv. 7 (called
'filthy' by Pope).

F.'s family and public career: the
ladies of the family dine at Twickenham, ii. 242; thank Mrs. Pope for
hospitality, ii. 245; all in London, ii.
294, iii. 196; a marriage (that of his
widowed mother?) in the family, ii.
358; Martha Blount, Mrs. Knight,
and Pope wish to dine at F.'s tomorrow, iii. 450; F.'s daughter not
well, iv. 84, 235; death of his sister
Grace, iv. 507; — elected to Parliament (1727), ii. 441, 524; solicitor-
general to the Prince of Wales, iii.
5 n.; attorney-general to the Prince,
iii. 154; rumours make him a

FORTESCUE, WILLIAM (*cont.*)
judge, iii. 351, 356, 364; Baron of
the Exchequer (1736), iv. 2, 6, 26;
Pope hopes (1736) F. may be Master
of the Rolls, iv. 126, 169; becomes
Master, iv. 454 n. (1741); — F.'s
rambles: to Devonshire, ii. 289, iii.
453, &c.; on the circuit, ii. 373, 521,
530, iii. 52, 453, iv. 6–7, 26, 28 n.,
169 n., 183 n.; his ill health: gout
gone, ii. 358, has gout at Fallapit, iii.
127, 129, 139; ill, iii. 350; wants information on a remedy for raving,
iii. 453; ill again, iii. 508, iv. 155; at
Bath for his health, iv. 166, 169, 173;
ill, iv. 193, 235; discusses his epitaph
with Pope, iv. 203; suffers from gravel,
iv. 267.
 Pope's friendship with F.: Pope
wishes to see him, i. 195; F. comes to
Binfield about a suit, i. 320; absent
from the chop-house dinner, i. 332;
has a small horse for Pope, i. 341;
jokingly asked to find estates for
Pope and Gay in Devon, ii. 49; agent
in the Barclay suit, ii. 104; sups with
Pope, ii. 172; visits at Twickenham,
ii. 182, 241, 255, 324, 435, 524, iii.
264–5, 283, 374 (just after Mrs.
Pope's death), iv. 18, 22, 166, 243–4,
355; F. stays away when Bolingbroke
is there, iv. 125, 155, 451, 454, 456,
507; F. of service to Pope in Town,
ii. 322, 335; getting lead to send to
Twickenham, ii. 346; his anecdote of
a real Gulliver at Salisbury assize,
ii. 441, 492; — Pope too sick to dine
with him, ii. 529; hopes to see F.
soon, iii. 11, 193, iv. 166, 169, 189,
355; F. congratulated that Excise
debates are over, iii. 355, 356, 364;
visit by Pope and F. to Chiswick
postponed, iii. 377; Pope sick wants
F.'s coach to go home in, iii. 443; F.
on the pomps of this world, iv. 156;
unable to meet Pope at Rousham,
iv. 189; takes needless trouble to help
Pope borrow £150, iv. 216, 221; F.
asked to express Pope's gratitude for
Jervas's bequest, iv. 222; F. cannot
be Pope's executor, and is omitted
from Pope's will, iv. 222; Pope can't
go out nights, iv. 440.
 F.'s opinion of Tickell's Iliad I, i.

FORTESCUE, WILLIAM (*cont.*)
296; draws up the agreement with
Lintot for the *Odyssey*, ii. 216–17;
witnesses it, ii. 217 n.; advises Lintot
not to go to law, ii. 290; *Miscellanies*, I and II sent to F., ii. 439;
annotates them as to the Mohawks,
ii. 441; Pope's *Imitation of Horace,
Sat. II. i*, not addressed to him in
print before 1751, iii. 351 n.
 F.'s aid to Mrs. Rackett, ii. 530, iii.
5, 6, 7, 91, 112, 407, iv. 214; aids
Martha Blount, in getting an annuity, ii. 530, iii. 5, 33, 53; in the
matter of Roberts's debt to her, iii.
198, 210; urged to action by Pope,
iii. 225, 227, 283, 355, 440; to send
Martha's money to Pope, iii. 449;
F. has advanced money to her, iii.
455; she may stay in the summer in
the Shepherd's Hut, iv. 26, &c.; vague
business relations, iv. 188, 212, 217;
services to Mrs. Howard, ii. 242, 359,
368, iv. 155; a link between Pope and
Sir Robert Walpole, ii. 294, 368, iii.
12, 53, 91 n., 112, 140, 354 n.; his
gratitude to Allen, iv. 181; service
sent to H. Bethel, iv. 40; to Jervas, i.
347; friendship with Gay, i. 300, 340,
341, 449, 482; F. stayed away from
Gay after *Polly* is banned, iii. 52, 126.
Foulet, L., ii. 424.
Fountaine, Sir Andrew, ii. 394 n., 439 n.
Fowler, Mr., i. 26.
Fox, Sir Stephen, ii. 255.
Fox, William, ii. 479 n.
Francis, Capt., iv. 219.
Frederick William I, *see* Prussia, King
of.
Frederick II of Denmark, i. 75 n.
Frederick, Prince of Wales, ii. 281 n.;
his arrival in England, ii. 532; his
visit to Pope, iii. 448, 500; his regard
for Lord Bathurst, 500; festivities
at his marriage, iv. 15; has one of
Bounce's puppies, iv. 48; difficul-
ties with the King in 1737, iv. 86;
Pope sends the Prince a packet (a dog
collar with inscription?), iv. 109;
Pope's alleged influence over the
Prince, iv. 138–9; Pope dines at
Kew with the Prince, iv. 139; the
Prince at Cirencester, iv. 138, 142;
his alignment with the Patriots, iv.

Frederick, Prince of Wales (*cont.*)
142–3, 261; — Pope gives advice, iv.
143–4; the Prince's mines in Cornwall,
iv. 148; made no request as to
Mustapha, iv. 158, 159; at Bath: his
obelisk there, iv. 138, 170, 176; the
Prince offers Pope urns, iv. 170, 178,
181; is Chancellor of Dublin University, iv. 175, 180; Pope sends a
message to, iv. 212; the Princess lies
in (1740), iv. 265; Pope recommends
a waterman for the Prince, iv. 348.

Freeman, Ralph, ii. 126.

French language inferior, i. 486 (Duke
of Buckingham).

French prophets, i. 35.

Froome (Frome), Somerset, post office
for Marston, iv. 441.

Frotherby, Charles, i. 298.

Frowde, Philip, and his brother William, i. 288 n.

Frowde, William, i. 288.

Fulham, Middlesex, Anastasia Robinson, ii. 329 n.

Fulham Bridge lottery (1739), iii.
518 n.

Fuller, Mr., neighbour of Caryll's, i.
499.

G., Sir W., *see* Goring, W.

Gage, Mr., i. 309.

Gage, Joseph, i. 119 n.

Gage, Thomas, 1st Viscount, i. 119
(brother of Mrs. Weston), 260; his
reported recusancy, i. 309; his lady
at Bath, i. 260; said to have travelled
with Bromley, Pope's schoolmaster,
iii. 360.

Gandy, Mr., iii. 477.

Garth, Sir Samuel: read Pope's Pastorals
in MS., i. 17 n.; his wit about *Cato*,
i. 175; on Radcliffe's will, i. 269, 429;
his epigrams on Lady Mary Wortley,
i. 442; his opinion as to the rival
Iliads, i. 305; goes to Italy, i. 309;
his death, ii. 23; his religious temper,
ii. 23 n., 25, iii. 81; Pope has his portrait copied, iii. 291; his Verses to
Lord Godolphin, i. 101; his *Claremont*
(1715), i. 289, 291; his Ovid, i. 418;
revised too much, Fenton thinks, ii.
398.

Gascoin, Mr., i. 260, 402.

Gascoigne, Sir B., i. 6.

GAY, JOHN: letters to, i. 153, 168, 187,
195, 222, 254, 341 (from Fortescue),
449; ii. 133, 137, 453; iii. 1, 2, 3, 121,
125, 131, 134, 138, 142, 318; letters
from (joint letters with Pope): to
Caryll, i. 282, 286, 288; to Congreve,
i. 290; to Fortescue, ii. 322; to Parnell, i. 284, 331 (with Jervas, Arbuthnot, and Pope); letters from himself
alone, i. 305, 388, 482; ii. 75
(to Lockyer), 316, 323 (to Pope), 415
(to J. Dormer), 473 (to Lord Oxford),
508, iii. 19, 321; letters from to
Swift, ii. 149, 399, 403, 409, 413, 473,
478, iii. 68, 94, 119, 185, 194, 248
(with Pope), 276, 288; letters from
Swift to Gay, iii. 72, 96, 147, 202,
218, 285; from Gay and the Duchess
of Queensberry to Swift, iii. 145, 204,
238 (with the Duke, not the Duchess),
300, 307; from Swift to Gay and the
Duchess, iii. 151, 179, 250, 296, 303;
— Gay's letter to Maurice Johnson
on *Cato*, i. 175 n.; his letter to Fortescue in the Morgan Library, i. 181 n.;
letter printed as to Martha Blount
may be to him really, ii. 511–12;
carried off a letter from Pope to
Fortescue, ii. 373; Pope lists some of
Gay's correspondents, i. 450; Gay
complains of no letters, iii. 69; none
from Parnell, i. 284; few from Swift,
iii. 94, 119; seldom from Pope, iii.
120; now obnoxious to Walpole, his
letters are read in the post office, iii.
120; — his addresses: his lodgings in
Whitehall (1724–9), ii. 392, iii. 69;
in care of the Duke of Queensberry,
Burlington Gardens, Piccadilly, iii.
186.

Biographical data: born at Barnstaple, i. 153; appointed secretary to
the Duchess of Monmouth, i. 169; his
unrewarded zeal for Addison, i. 184;
in the Scriblerus Club, i. 195, 216,
217, 228, 230, 250, 478 (1718);
secretary to Lord Clarendon in
embassy to Hanover, i. 229, 230,
250 n., 253, 259; his playful account
of his activities, i. 331; in Devonshire
(1716), i. 349, 350; sends service to
Jervas, Swift, Parnell, i. 371; goes to
France with Pulteney, i. 411, 416,
438, 450; his friendship with Pul-

GAY, JOHN (*cont.*)

teney, ii. 247, 400; — at Stanton Harcourt and Cirencester (1718) with
Pope, i. 477; melancholy 'novel' of the
lovers killed by lightning, i. 479, 482–
3, 488, 489, 490 n.; at the Duke of
Buckingham's party for Prior, i. 521;
abroad in 1719, ii. 48; much at the
Exchange, ii. 48; wrongly thought by
Caryll to be M.P., ii. 140; lodges in
Burlington House, ii. 149, 181 n.; —
at Tunbridge with Lady Burlington
(1723), ii. 181; at Chiswick (1724), ii.
241, 256; sends message to Bolingbroke, ii. 182; at Bath (1722), ii. 133,
257 (1724); reports Arbuthnot ill
but out of danger, ii. 316; goes to the
Bath with Henrietta, Duchess of
Marlborough, and Congreve, ii. 478–
9 (1728), 491; invited to Riskins by
Bathurst, ii. 299; has called on Congreve, ii. 324; — his salary at the
Exchequer, ii. 324; failed to see Mr.
Selwyn, ii. 324; Commissioner of
Lotteries (1723–31), ii. 400, 410, iii.
185; his buttons eaten by mice
(meaning ?), ii. 407, 410; on Voltaire's spoken English, ii. 416;
Italian comedians at the opera house,
ii. 416; has seen Rousham, ii. 416;
Congreve inquires after Gay, ii. 433;
Gay reports Fortescue's marginalia
in re Mohawks, ii. 441; he has made a
proselyte of Will Shippen (meaning ?),
ii. 465; took Delany to see Bathurst
and Bolingbroke, ii. 478; — reported as looking well at Lord
Oxford's, iii. 17; drinks no wine,
iii. 102; hence, Pope thinks, his
depression, iii. 142; his absence from
Town (with the Queensberrys) regretted by Pope, iii. 125, 131; may
become rich through frugality, like
Sir John Cutler, iii. 186; wins an
injunction against pirates, iii. 249;
attends first performance of *Athelwold*, iii. 253; going to Rousham
with Gen. Dormer and Sir C. Cottrell,
iii. 277; not lazy, iii. 277; makes financial report to Swift, iii. 289; at Dawley
finds Lady B. very ill, iii. 289; —
Gay's death, iii. 334, 336 n.; leaves
no will, iii. 347; his sisters his heirs,
iii. 335; account of his funeral at the

GAY, JOHN (*cont.*)

Abbey, iii. 337 n.; his pallbearers
named, iii. 338; Swift's comment on
Gay's death, iii. 343, 368, 432;
Aaron Hill and Fortescue, his early
schoolmates, iv. 38; Pope's small part
in the *Life* of Gay in the *General Dictionary*, iv. 37–38; Gay's illnesses,
ii. 531; seriously ill at Hampstead
(1728–9), iii. 1, 2, 8, 9, 11, 289;
exercise (riding to Somerset and
back) no aid, iii. 321; ill only three
days before he died, iii. 334–5.

Gay's writings: has written a poem
to Lintot, i. 134, 136; his verses in
Miscellaneous Poems and Translations
(1712), i. 134, 138; his *Fan*, i. 188,
195, 210, 214; for his Scriblerus
verses *see under* Scriblerus; writing
pastorals, i. 200 (*Shepherd's Week*);
attacks Philips in them, i. 217, 223,
226, 229; dedicated to Bolingbroke,
ii. 153; Gay's petition to Lord Oxford, i. 228; advised by Pope to
dedicate something to the royal
family, i. 255; his *Letter to a Lady*
(Princess Caroline), i. 267, 318, 320
(its failure); — his *What D'ye Call It*,
i. 282–3; thanks Caryll for aid in the
benefit night, i. 283; sent to Parnell,
i. 284; attacked, i. 285–6, 287, 291;
ironical Preface planned for it, i. 286;
the *Compleat Key* to it, i. 288–90; Gay
burlesques *Cato*, i. 289–90; echoed by
Broome (1722), ii. 121 n.; at work on
Trivia, i. 222, 223, 295; its success,
i. 331; profits from, i. 327, 332;
echoed by Swift later, iii. 286; Gay
attacks Blackmore for Swift, i. 371;
his *Epistle to Burlington*, published
18 Feb. 1717, i. 371 n.; his *Epistle to
William Lowndes*, i. 450; *Three
Hours after Marriage*, i. 379 & n.,
388, 395; 'Mr. Pope's Welcome from
Greece', i. 349 n., 369; — Gay's
Poems (2 vols. 1720) not sent to
Swift, ii. 154; Swift suggests a
Quaker or Newgate pastoral for Gay,
i. 360; *The Captives* acted, ii. 215; the
cancelled epilogue, ii. 215; success of
Captives, ii. 216 & n.; writing Fables
for Prince William, ii. 340, 350;
trouble with the engravers, ii. 400,
410, 416, 417; Mrs. Barber writes

GAY, JOHN (*cont.*)

verses on Gay's *Fables*, ii. 483; Gay regrets dedicating them to Prince William, iii. 20; Motte dilatory in paying Gay for *Miscellanies*, ii. 526, iii. 27; invited to Riskins for the holidays, ii. 465; — *Beggar's Opera* about to be performed, ii. 455, 465, 469; its great success, ii. 473–4, effect on vogue of Italian opera, ii. 474; the play leers upon the Court, ii. 475; continued success, ii. 478, 480; great vogue in Dublin, ii. 482, 492, 493; Duchess of Queensberry conspicuously Gay's friend concerning the opera, ii. 474; *Polly* is 'forbid', iii. 16; — *Polly* published a fortnight before *The Dunciad Variorum*, iii. 4; loss of favour at Court because of *Polly*, iii. 1; Henrietta, Duchess of Marlborough subscribes £100 for *Polly*; Swift disapproves of subscription before performance, iii. 21; the subscription, iii. 17; an injunction against piracy of *Polly*, iii. 37; Fortescue is aloof since *Polly* was banned, iii. 52; attack on the Court in *Polly* embarrassed Fortescue, Mrs. Howard, and even Pope, iii. 52 n.; — Gay rewrites his *Wife of Bath*, iii. 69; it fails again, iii. 69 n., 72, 94; Swift inquires what Gay is now writing, iii. 204; Gay not writing, iii. 206; the letter in defence of Pope in *The Post-Boy*, iii. 254; writing new fables, iii. 248; their character, iii. 288, 297, 301; refuses to write undeserved panegyric on the Queen's Hermitage, iii. 322; — plans a new play, *Achilles*, iii. 289; posthumously staged, iii. 337, 347, 350; some of Gay's papers (letters ?) turned over to Pope, iii. 365; Swift's attitude, iii. 368, v. 12; Swift dislikes *Achilles*, iii. 361; Gay's sisters insignificant compared to Gay's fame, iii. 361; Gay's requests that Pope see to it that his couplet is placed on his tomb, iii. 20; Pope's epitaph for Gay, v. 12.

Gay's place-hunting: in hopes, ii. 322; declines the post of Gentleman Usher (1727), i. 318 n.; liked by the Maids of Honour, i. 379; at Court (1717) for a week, i. 388; complains

GAY, JOHN (*cont.*)

that the Great do not provide, i. 451, ii. 149, 181, 395, 474; ambitious to be in Court, ii. 436, 473; declines to be Gentleman Usher to a two-year-old Princess, ii. 453; tells Swift of his refusal, ii. 452, 455; Swift approves, ii. 460; Gay is still 'attending' but less than formerly, ii. 508; learns that there is no dependence but on one's self, iii. 69; stays from Court, iii. 94.

Gay's character: his appetite for food, ii. 133; for Blouzelindas, i. 255, 331 n.; a hunter, i. 484 n., iii. 146; a fisherman, ii. 305; Swift alleges Gay lacking in 'country skill', iii. 286; in politics an indifferent party-man, i. 254, 259; cares not for quadrille, ii. 410; reads Virgil and Spenser, ii. 410; quotes Milton, iii. 20; Broome thinks him 'a good-natured inoffensive man', ii. 489; his alleged indolence, ii. 305, iii. 286, 289, 293, iv. 177; guilty of inattention, iii. 298, 304; Gay thinks 'indolence and idleness the most tiresome things in the world', iii. 277; still volatile, Swift finds, iii. 285.

Gay's friendships: Henry Cromwell, i. 113, 134, 136; in printing Curll deletes mentions of Gay in Cromwell letters, i. 130 n.; Charles Jervas, i. 340, 341, 347; — Pope's early mentions of Gay, i. 125, 130, 141; Gay invited to Binfield, i. 222; presents Pope to a Duchess, i. 288; Gay and Pope plan to visit Caryll (1715), i. 289; Pope's character of Gay, i. 319–20; grieved at his dependence, i. 319; Gay reports on reception of *Iliad* I, i. 305; he and Pope lie to each other, i. 341; going to see Pope at Chiswick, i. 341; Pope and Gay joke about estates in Devonshire, ii. 49; Gay transfers South Sea stock to Pope, ii. 75; Gay at Twickenham, ii. 245; told as joke that Pope has a clap, ii. 290; on a ramble with Pope, ii. 305; Gay's misfortune is having Tory friends, ii. 332; — Gay's visits at Twickenham, ii. 335, 347, iii. 3; again there with Swift (1726), ii. 381; after Pope's accident in the Crane, ii. 399, 400; writes out the 'poetical soop'

GAY, JOHN (*cont.*)

verses, ii. 403–4, 410; there at Christmas (1727), ii. 466; at Bath (1728), ii. 514; wishes to see Pope in Town, ii. 324; urged by Pope to take exercise, iii. 121; dines with Pope and Lord Oxford, iii. 177–8, 194; at Barnes, with Tonson, *et al.*, iii. 185; later visits to Twickenham, iii. 238, 264–5, 271, 277.

Gay's friendship with Swift: his letters from Swift apparently transcribed by Pope and then returned to Swift (*c.* 1733), iii. 96 n.; renews his correspondence with Swift, ii. 149; has a letter from Swift, ii. 184; Swift thinks Gay's address for letters obscure, ii. 393; Swift wants address of Lord 'B', ii. 408, 410; the Cheddar letter explained, ii. 409; Gay reproaches Swift for not writing, iii. 68, 72, 145, 248; — Swift on Gay's finances (and his own): the roads to patronage indicated, ii. 153, 326; Gay fears he has talked too much to Swift about a career, iii. 151–2; thought financially incompetent by Swift, ii. 505, iii. 43, 58, 107; Gay reports on Swift's money, iii. 94, 185, 194, 205, 206, 300; Swift says Gay needs a fortune of £7,000, iii. 203; Gay's questioned frugality, iii. 248, 251, 285, v. 8; Swift wishes Gay to meet Stopford, ii. 311; — Swift in England (1726), ii. 381, 388, 407, 410; reports on the vogue of *Gulliver*, ii. 413, 414, 416; Gay has new—not borrowed—sheets for Swift in 1727, ii. 400, 479; Gay's account of Swift's return voyage (1727), ii. 454–5; Swift's account, ii. 460; Gay negligent about passing word to Motte, ii. 468; still meditates buying a house for himself and Swift, ii. 508; Swift opposed to revision of *Wife of Bath*, iii. 97; Swift complained to the Queen of bad treatment of Gay, iii. 209; Gay at the height of his powers, Swift says, iii. 220–1, 251; Swift urged to come over in spite of his bad leg, iii. 277, 290; Swift's list of friends, iii. 289; good advice on *Revelation examined*, iii. 289; Swift informed of Gay's death, iii. 334–5;

GAY, JOHN (*cont.*)

— Gay and Martha Blount, i. 513, ii. 316, 508, iii. 194; Gay and Mrs. Howard, ii. 182, 316, 323, 324, 400, 474; Gay's whole trust at Court is in her, ii. 332, 343, 350; Swift's reaction, ii. 409, iii. 194; hopes from Mrs. Howard's influence with the new king, ii. 447; Gay a timid suitor of Mrs. Drelincourt, iii. 119, 194, 203; — Gay and the Queensberrys: with them at times in 1725, ii. 316, 323; travels with them in 1726, ii. 399, 400; his distress at their banishment in 1729, iii. 19–20; goes to Scotland with them, iii. 36; his deep affection for the Duchess, iii. 52, 69; spends the summer with them at Middleton Stoney, iii. 58, 68–69; Gay's misfortune, Swift thinks, adds glory to the Duchess, iii. 74; in 1730 Gay spends winter and summer at Amesbury with the Duke and Duchess, iii. 94, 95; lives in a 'new world', iii. 96, v. 8; — Swift advises much riding, iii. 97; Gay's extreme happiness at Amesbury, iii. 119, 125, 143, 146; Swift supposes Gay to be the Duke's leading agent, iii. 147, 148–9, 204; Gay corrects that idea, iii. 179 206; has four days in Town, iii. 193–4; wishes Swift to come to Amesbury, iii. 195; in 1731 very briefly in Town, iii. 186; the Duke also invites Swift, iii. 239; in 1732 the summer is spent at Amesbury, iii. 288, 301; Gay dies in London in the Duke of Queensberry's house (4 Dec. 1732), iii. 336 n., v. 14.

Gazette, see *London Gazette*.

Gee, Col., iv. 40, 338.

Gelli, —, author of *Circe*, iv. 342 n.

General Dictionary: cited for its article on Atterbury (with a letter to Pope), ii. 94 n., iii. 246; cited on John Gay, iv. 37 n.

General Evening Post: gives Thomas Deane's obituary, ii. 428; reports visit of the Prince to Pope, iii. 500 n.; on Lord Berkeley, v. 14 n.

Gentleman's Magazine: cited on various letters, ii. 26, 30, iv. 351; prints Gay's epitaph, iii. 347; cited on the troubles with Motte over the *Mis-*

Gentleman's Magazine (cont.)
cellanies, ii. 430, 526, iii. 8, 32; on the Prince's visit to Cirencester, iv. 138; on the Warburton–Hanmer quarrel, iv. 438; for various obituary notices, iv. 21, 79, 269, 395, 479.

Geoffrey of Monmouth, *see* Jeffrey.

George, Prince of Denmark, i. 53.

George I: his coronation, i. 205, 262, 264; his German courtiers, i. 271; at Hanover, i. 384; keeps a dull Court, i. 470; on bad terms with the Prince (later George II), i. 407, 462; in his reign Philips gets preferment, ii. 332; a gracious speech to Parliament, ii. 364; his death, ii. 435, 437; his favourite 'Young Turk', iii. 503.

George II (Prince of Wales, 1714–27): as Prince quarrels with his father, i. 407; at Richmond, ii. 1, 14, 372 (employs Bridgeman there), 409; his coronation done over in a puppet show, ii. 462–3; his visit to Cambridge University (1727), ii. 450, 488; wished Compton to succeed Walpole, in 1727, ii. 476 n.; thought to be ruled by his Queen, ii. 472; — the King and Queen present at *Julius Caesar* (1728), ii. 473; expresses a desire for a Key to *The Dunciad*, ii. 502; *Dunciad Variorum* presented to him, 12 Mar. 1729, iii. 20, 26; his birthday night (29 Oct.), iii. 62; makes Burlington Knight of the Garter, iii. 111; Court removes (1730) to Windsor from Richmond, iii. 113; — ironical remarks about the King, iii. 130, 209; the King's remark about Swift's Schomberg monument, iii. 208; returns from Hanover, iv. 47; commands allied armies at Dettingen, iv. 413; Proclamation against Catholics (1744), iv. 504 n.

George, Prince (b. 1738; later George III): no servants for him as yet (1741), iv. 349; his remark to Dr. Johnson about Pope and Warburton, iv. 214.

George William, Prince; his birth and death, i. 451; his christening, i. 465.

George, servant to the Blount ladies, i. 434, 491, 512, ii. 11.

Gerard, Elizabeth (Clifton) Lady, widow of Sir William, 6th Bart., of

Gerard, Elizabeth (*cont.*)
New Hall, Lancashire, a Catholic, close friend of Martha Blount: Pope takes her to Chiswick Gardens, iii. 376; Martha stays with her at Cheam (Aug. 1734), iii. 425, 426, 436; the two ladies dine at Pope's house (1736), iv. 21; — Martha a guest of Lady G., iv. 29, 113; Lady G.'s lease, iv. 183, 186, 191; Martha plans to send Lady G. Pope's gift of pineapples, iv. 186; Lady G. goes to Bath, iv. 454; Martha lives with Lady G. in Welbeck Street, iv. 485; Lady G. had lived before 1739 in Marlborow Street, iv. 488; mentioned, iv. 205, 212, 511.

Geree, John, Rector of Letcombe, Swift stays with him (1714), i. 234 n.

Germain, Lady Elizabeth (Berkeley), wife of Sir John, friend of Swift: she is a relative of the Duke of Dorset, Lord Lieut. of Ireland, iii. 109; stands up for Mrs. Howard, and breaks with Swift on the matter, iii. 363; visited by Mrs. Howard, iii. 501; Sir John mentioned, i. 295.

German courtiers imported, i. 257.

GERRARD, SAMUEL, from Ireland: letters to, iv. 234, 241; tried to see Pope at Lord Burlington's in vain, iv. 234; Pope says he has nothing to send to Swift by G., iv. 241; a packet (the 'clandestine' vol. of Swift letters) left anonymously for G. to take to Swift from Bath, iv. 241 n.; G. recommended by Pope to Dr. Cheyne, iv. 242; left Bath with the clandestine vol. in May 1740, iv. 242 n.; Pope asks Allen if the packet sent to G. reached him duly, iv. 245; G. brings the volume to Dublin, iv. 276; Pope not at Bath with G., iv. 282.

Gervase, Mr., *see* Jervas, Charles.

Gibbs, Mrs., notable for puns, iii. 115.

GIBBS, JAMES, architect: letters from, ii. 4, 298; has 'plans' for Pope (1719), ii. 4; tells Pope where Rysbrack lives, ii. 298; wants to demolish parts of Down Hall: Pope objects, ii. 364.

Gibson, Edmund, Bishop of London, ii. 269, iii. 508 n.

Gilbert, John, later Archbishop of York, iv. 140 & n.

Gildon, Charles: his animosity against Pope, i. 73 n., ii. 334; an object of (medical) charity, ii. 3; best passed over, Pope thinks, in silence, ii. 343, 349.

GILLIVER, LAWTON: letter from, iv. 333; publishes *Dunciad Variorum* with protection against libels, iii. 4, 5 n.; property in *Dunciad* assigned to him by three lords, iii. 37 n., 59; entered by him at Stationers' Hall, iii. 37 n., 59 n.; expiration of his copyright, iv. 223; Pope's favoured publisher in 1731, iii. 238; — publishes for Pope's protégés, Miller, Harte, Hill, *et al.*, iii. 173, 238; he and Bowyer to settle argument over Swift's copies, iii. 323–4; his arrest for publishing a Swift poem, iii. 401 n.; G. and Cooper entered Pope's *Letters* (1735) in the Hall book, iii. 472; G. to follow Fortescue's directions about Curll's vol. ii of Pope's *Correspondence*, iii. 473, 494; admits to Curll that Pope himself had the *Letters* printed, iii. 494; Pope first plans an 'authorized' ed. of *Letters* in sm. 8vo, iv. 17 n.; G. takes in subscriptions for the 1737 *Letters*, iv. 41; Robinson's piracy offered to G. iv. 87; — is allowed (1740) by Lintot illegally to reprint *Iliad*, vol. i in 4to, iv. 223; G.'s evidence in Pope's suit against Lintot, iv. 333.

Gilmore, Robert, iv. 487 n.

Giovanni di Bologna, iv. 150.

Glanvill, Mrs., i. 434.

Gloucestershire, *see* Cirencester (Lord Bathurst), Durhams (Sir W. Codrington), Rentcomb (Sir J. Guise), Stowell (John Howe), Tetbury (on the road to London).

Glover, Richard, iv. 219.

Godalming, Surrey, Mary Tofts, the rabbit woman, ii. 403 n.

Godolphin, Francis, 2nd Earl, i. 101.

Godolphin, Henrietta, wife of 2nd Earl, *see* Churchill, Henrietta Godolphin-; 2nd Duchess of Marlborough.

Goldsmith, Oliver, cited for text of letters to Parnell and Nash, i. 284, 331 n., 348, 395, iv. 176 n.

Goodrich (or Goodridge or Gutheridge), Herefordshire, ii. 455.

Gordon, Thomas, iv. 114 & n.

Gore, Lord, *see* Leveson-Gower, John, 2nd Baron Gower and 1st Earl.

Goring, Sir W., guardian of Mrs. Weston, i, 119, 123, 132.

Gosfield, Essex (the Knights), ii. 457; delighted Martha Blount, iii. 68; Pope there, 1730, iii. 218 n.; rough roads thereabouts, iii. 426; Walter Harte, the vicar, iii. 450 n.; Chesterfield there in 1742, iv. 419.

Gower, Lord, *see* Leveson-Gower, John, 2nd Baron and 1st Earl Gower.

Gower, Hon. Leveson, *see* Leveson-Gower [William ?].

Gracchus, Tiberius, i. 27.

Graevius (Gräve), Johannes G., iii. 29.

Grafton, 2nd Duke of, *see* FitzRoy, Charles.

Graham, Mr., iii. 27.

Graham, James, Duke of Montrose, Lallet's employer, iii. 66, 82.

GRAHAM, RICHARD: letters to, i. 333, 366; his Dedication in DuFresnoy, i. 333–4; asks Pope's advice on an engraving, i. 366.

Grantham, Henry, Earl of, ii. 454.

Granville, Earl, *see* Carteret, John, Lord.

GRANVILLE, GEORGE, Lord Lansdowne: letters to, i. 172, 194; letters from, iii. 327; a letter lost, v. 3; he reads Pope's Pastorals in MS., i. 17 n.; his peerage, i. 172; his marriage (1711), v. 3 n.; accepts dedication of *Windsor Forest*, i. 172; mentioned in *Epistle to Arbuthnot*, i. 172 n.; approves Pope's projected translation of the *Iliad*, i. 194; Pope plans to visit him at Longleat, i. 261; sent to the Tower, i. 287; Lady L.'s last assembly, i. 308; L. friendly to Pope, i. 374–5; L.'s *Thyestes* quoted by Pope, ii. 109; Pope asks L. to aid Dennis, iii. 171; L. sends Pope his comedies for criticism, iii. 327; is embroiled over the text of Clarendon's *History*, iii. 327–8.

Granvilles, might be Greenfields, i. 27.

Gray, Capt. John of Twickenham: sells land for Marble Hill, iii. 34 n.; Pope sees him often, iii. 134; G. tells Lord Bathurst of English elms to be had, iii. 138.

Gray, Thomas, wrote his 'Long Story' for Lady Cobham and Mrs. Speed, iv. 185 n.

Gray's Inn Gate, Tonson's address, i. 17.

Greene, Dr. Samuel, returns from Oxford to London with Pope, iv. 81.

Grenville, George, at Bath, iv. 47, 49.

Grevenkop, iv. 519.

Greville, Fulke, iii. 30.

Greville, Mary (Mrs. Algernon): Pope lends her his house, iii. 480 n.; she and Martha Blount dine at Pope's, iv. 183; her relatives, iv. 188 n.; Martha Blount spends five weeks with her at The Grove, iv. 265.

Grey, Betty, a pretty French prophet, i. 35.

Grey, Henry, Duke of Kent, ii. 65.

Gribelin, Simon, i. 367.

Grierson, Constantia, Dublin scholar and poet, iii. 89, 107.

Griffin, or Griffith, Anne, Maid of Honour, i. 345 n., 381; Pope spent Sunday with her at Staines, i. 428, 470.

Griffin, B., actor, i. 288 n.

Griffith, Col. Edward, i. 345 n., 407.

Griffith, R. H., cited *passim* for bibliographical details; cited for texts of letters, i. 340 n.; iii. 132; on *Dunciad Variorum*, iii. 5; on *Life* of Gay, iv. 38 n.; on 1737 *Letters*, iv. 53, 68, 179, 181.

Grinstead, West, Sussex, Caryll's home, i. 93, 512, ii. 78.

Grolier Club *Catalogue*, ii. 118 n., iii. 291 n.

Gronovius, or Gronov, Johann Friedrich, iii. 29.

Grove, The, home of Mrs. Algernon Greville, iv. 265.

Grub-street Journal: very seldom mentioned by Pope, iii. 85, 111, 173; various news items from, iii. 124, 134, 143, 241, 476.

Grumbler, i. 284, 291.

Guardian, see Richard Steele.

Guarini, G. B., i. 18, 19.

Guelfi, Giovanni Battista, sculptor for the Craggs monument, ii. 242; at work on the clay model, ii. 242, 456; ill, needs Bird's help, ii. 457, 463, 484.

Guevara, Antonio de, ii. 517.

Guicciardini, Francesco, ii. 220.

Guildford, Surrey, ii. 418, iv. 67.

Guise, Sir Christopher, ii. 85.

Guise, Sir John, ii. 85, 86.

Guldeford, Lady, ii. 42.

Gulliver, Capt. Jonathan, of Milton, Mass., ii. 479, 491.

Gulliveriana, by J. Smedly, ii. 523 n.

Gunson, Gamaliel (pseud. for Aaron Hill), iii. 165.

Guy's Hospital, ii. 525.

GYLES, FLETCHER, bookseller: letter to, iv. 346; Warburton's publisher, iv. 237; invited with Warburton to Twickenham, iv. 238; intermediary for Pope and Warburton messages, iv. 339, 341, 346; G.'s death (1741), iv. 237 n., 370.

H—, Mrs., *see* Howe, Mary, or Howard, Henrietta.

Hadrian, his verses imitated by Pope, i. 141, 149, 159, 163, 178.

Hai Ebn Yocktan, ii. 13.

Halifax, 1st Earl of, *see* Montagu, Charles.

Hallgrove, Bagshot, Surrey, home of the Racketts, i. 29, 135, 403, 418, ii. 181; to be leased, one hopes, to a Duke, iii. 223; Racketts advised to sell it, iv. 161.

Halsband, Robert, cited for a transcript, ii. 22; for other information, ii. 194 n., v. 1–2.

Halstead, Essex, John Morley, ii. 148, 156, iii. 382.

Ham, Surrey, the Blounts's summer place, ii. 435.

Hambleton, Widow, her coffee-house is Cromwell's address in Town, i. 43, 51.

HAMILTON, ANTHONY: letter to, i. 192; Pope thanks him for his French version of *Essay on Criticism*, i. 192, 210.

Hamilton, Lord Archibald, iv. 462.

Hamilton, Charles, 2nd Earl of Selkirk, a general object of satire, i. 437 n., iii. 248 n.

HAMILTON, ELIZABETH, Duchess of: letter to, i. 436; letter from, i. 439; invites Pope to music on the Thames, i. 404; other visits, i. 411, 417, 439; Pope compares her to an elephant, i. 437; her portrait painted for Pope, i.

HAMILTON, ELIZABETH (*cont.*)
437; Pope asks her to call on the
Blounts, i. 438; Gay writes to her, i.
450; her untold story about Gay and
Pulteney, i. 450; possibly spoken of
by Abel Evans, ii. 8 n.; subscribes to
Buononcini, ii. 99; given scallops by
Pope, ii. 290.

Hamilton, James, 5th Duke, at Oxford,
i. 490.

Hamilton, Mr., relative of the Duchess, i.
438–9.

Hamilton, Sir F. W., i. 308.

HAMILTON, Lord GEORGE, 1st Earl of
Orkney: letter to, iv. 35; asks Pope's
help on gardens at Cliveden, iv. 35;
is very weak and ill, iv. 47, 48; Pope's
praise pleases him, iv. 35–36, 49, 60;
asked Pope to go to Bath with him,
iv. 60; his death, iv. 47, 55.

Hammersmith, Swift's last refuge in
England, ii. 448.

Hammond, Anthony, iii. 167 n.

Hammond, James, iv. 49 n.

Hammond, Mason, ii. 116, 434, iv. 450.

Hampshire, co., *see* Basingstoke, Beaulieu Abbey, Bevis Mount, Netley
Abbey, Portsmouth, Shawford, Winchester.

Hampstead: a 'soft retreat' in summer,
iii. 123; Arbuthnot ill there, iii. 415.

Hampton Wick, Dr. Broxholm, iv. 268.

Hampton Court, Middlesex, i. 388, 409,
427.

Hampton Court, Herefordshire, seat of
Lord Coningsby, ii. 240 n.

Hanaus, Phil, footman who rescued
Pope from the Crane, ii. 403.

Handel, George F.: musician in charge
of Burlington's music (1716), i. 338;
his Water Music, i. 404 n.; his part
of *Muzio Scevola*, ii. 99; composes for
Chandos, iii. 257; Wm. Kent enjoys
Saul, iv. 163.

Hanmer, Sir Thomas: mentioned disparagingly, i. 216, 234, ii. 14; his
acquaintance with Broome, ii. 211;
to him Pope defends Broome, ii.
211; his remark on the Epistle to
Burlington, iii. 259; Warburton
made uneasy by H.'s forthcoming
ed. of Shakespeare, iv. 438; Pope
investigates the ed. at Oxford, iv.
438–9, 475.

Hanover succession, i. 216.

Hanover Club, their subscriptions to
Pope's *Iliad*, i. 229, 296.

Happy Couple, supposed the name of a
ship, iv. 235 n.

Harcourt, Elizabeth, Viscountess, i.
491 n.

Harcourt, Elizabeth (Evelyn: Mrs.
Simon Harcourt, daughter-in-law
of the Viscount), writes of Mrs. Pope,
i. 490 n.

HARCOURT, SIMON, Viscount: letters
to, ii. 92, 114, 126, 146, 156, 160, 171,
193, 205, 306, 427, 430; letters from,
ii. 115, 146; Pope visits the Harcourts, i. 418, 433, 475–95; Lord
H. suggests a lady as possible wife to
Pope, i. 430–1; will erect a monument to the lovers killed by lightning, i. 481, 495; in London will take
Parnell's *Poems* to 'the Duke', ii. 81,
92; a possible suspect in Atterbury's
plot, ii. 93; — regrets that leaving
town prevents a visit to Twickenham,
ii. 114, 115; invited again, ii. 126;
approves Pope's improvements at
Twickenham (1722), ii. 126; Atterbury writes to him from the Tower,
ii. 146; the epitaph for the Hon.
Simon Harcourt needs 'mending', ii.
146–7; Pope asks advice in his
difficulties over Buckingham's *Works*,
ii. 156, 159, 161; advises Pope on
testimony in the Atterbury trial, ii.
171–2; — his role in the restoration
of Bolingbroke, ii. 175; invited to
Parsons Green (Peterborow?), ii.
183; remembers Swift, ii. 184; aids
Bolingbroke's finances, ii. 186 n.;
gets Kneller portrait of Pope for his
library, ii. 193; Pope conveys to H.
an 'affectionate mention' of him by
Swift, ii. 205; H. interested in cider
and Fortescue, ii. 359; H. and Peterborow to take Swift to wait on Sir
R. Walpole, ii. 373; Pope solicits his
lordship's vote for a preacher at
Charterhouse, ii. 267, 272, 273; —
H. aids Duchess of Buckingham in
her lawsuit, ii. 282, 286; is asked to
contradict gossip (1725) that Bolingbroke and Pulteney are caballing, ii.
291; Pope writes of his troubles with
Lady Kneller, ii. 300, 306–7; asks

HARCOURT, SIMON (*cont.*)
for other legal advice, ii. 430; H.'s
opinion of *Gulliver*, ii. 413; Pope
asks H.'s aid for the Governor of
Bermuda, ii. 427.

HARCOURT, Hon. SIMON (jr.): letter
from him to Mrs. Pope, i. 491; gets
subscribers to Pope's *Iliad*, i. 223,
274, 300; his ill report on Gay's
health, i. 223, inquired after by Pope,
i. 238; his hospitality at Oxford, i.
246, 250; Harcourts are possibly out
of favour (1714) over suspicion of
Jacobitism, i. 252, 259; lacks letter
from Parnell, i. 284; has the gout, i.
286; the Harcourts subscribe for 13
Iliads, i. 298; visits Pope, i. 409, 411;
sends chariot to Stanton Harcourt for
Mrs. Pope and Nurse, i. 491; Pope's
friendship for H. (d. 1 July 1720), ii.
161, 175, 193.

Harcourt Papers, ii. 92, 126, 205.

Hardwicke, 1st Earl of, *see* Yorke,
Philip.

Hare, Francis, i. 462 n., iv. 140.

Harleian Library, *see* Harley, Edward,
2nd Earl of Oxford; *and also under*
Longleat, Portland Papers.

HARLEY, EDWARD, 2nd Earl of Oxford:
letters from Pope to, ii. 101, 156, 158,
193, 203, 224, 232, 259, 261, 263,
270, 275, 278, 310, 311, 316, 331,
334, 335, 336, 338, 347, 354, 359,
364, 369, 371, 372, 373, 381 (with
Swift), 387, 402, 406, 421, 430, 431,
443, 444, 447, 464, 465, 466, 467,
473 (from Gay), 489, 493, 495, 498,
502, 504, 505, 506, 510, 515, 528,
533, iii. 7, 9, 10, 11, 12, 16, 19, 25, 26,
31, 33, 45, 53, 55, 58, 62, 78, 83, 87,
100, 103, 104, 105, 110, 111, 114,
118, 120, 123, 135, 144, 149, 153,
159, 175, 176, 177, 178, 179, 186,
193, 197, 199, 201, 216, 221, 236,
240, 245, 266, 278, 280, 315, 325,
333, 359, 365, 371, 381, 382, 389,
397, 404, 410, 424, 429, 442, 445,
452, 468, 474, 483, 489, iv. 211;
letters from him to Pope, ii. 102, 260,
268, 276, 315, 334, 371, 376, 381,
496, 506 (to Swift), 514, iii. 9, 10, 17,
56, 112, 146, 216, 324; a letter
from J. Arbuthnot to O., ii. 411, 417;
from Swift to O., iii. 429 (No letters

HARLEY, EDWARD (*cont.*)
dating later than 1735 in this correspondence have come down to us,
except the letter of 25 Dec. 1739. The
intimacy, however, continued); two
letters from Pope not preserved, ii.
275, 331; a letter from Dr. Stratford,
ii. 121 n; — the role of the Harleian
Library concerning Pope's letters,
iii. 459; transcripts of the Atterbury
correspondence deposited there, iii.
187; a bound vol. of transcripts asked
for back by Pope, iii. 453; the trans-
scripts in part proof-read by Lord
O., i. 378 n., ii. 105 n., 165 n., 198 n.,
324 n., iii. 360 n.

Biographical data: Edward succeeds as 2nd Earl in 1724, ii. 101 n.;
a son born and died, ii. 317, 335, 342;
subscribes to Buononcini, ii. 99;
improvements at Down Hall, ii. 369,
371; goes through his father's papers,
ii. 371; anxious about the alleged
printing from his papers in *The Daily
Journal*, ii. 515; reports Congreve's
death, iii. 9; Oxford confers on him
the degree of D.C.L., iii. 111; the new
library at Wimpole, iii. 114, 136,
147; the plot of 1712 against Robert
Harley and St. John as told by Pope,
iii. 199; in later years the 2nd Earl
spent much time in the country, iv.
211 n.; — his rambles: to Oxford and
Herefordshire, ii. 315; a wide rambler,
ii. 316, 444; at Rousham and Stowe,
iii. 112; his journey (1730) from
Oxford to Wimpole, iii. 114, 118;
at Down Hall, iii. 216, 221; Pope
lonely in the Dover street house with
the Oxfords away, iii. 280; a ramble
into Norfolk, iii. 325.

Kindnesses solicited from him:
asked to read the Duke of Buckingham's tragedies very privately, ii. 101,
102; a friend to Mrs. Caesar, ii. 126
n., iii. 88; asked to allow Fenton to
inscribe his Waller to Lady Margaret
Harley, ii. 374; Arbuthnot sends him
a Ballad, ii. 417; wants 12 copies
of Arbuthnot's *Tables*, ii. 425;
arranging for a box at *The Beggar's
Opera*, ii. 473; asked for aid in Lady
Howard's cause, iii. 103; promises
aid to Rev. N. Whaley, iii. 104;

HARLEY, EDWARD (*cont.*)
asked Swift to get subscribers for S.
Wesley (sr.) and his *Job*, iii. 109;
asked to interest the dons of Christ
Church in Henry Cleland, iii. 144,
147, 153; asked to aid Henry Rackett,
iii. 150, 153; Pope gives him an
account of Peterborow's last days,
iii. 489; — Prior's papers in Lord O.'s
care, ii. 193, 203; Pope wants to
print *Jinny* by Prior in the Pope–
Swift *Miscellanies*, ii. 466; his friendship for Swift, ii. 184, 331; hopes for
his arrival in England, ii. 333, 334,
350, 372; Swift and Pope (1726)
expect to visit Lord O., ii. 373; they
hope O. will come to Town, ii. 372,
374; O. sees Swift (1726–7) seldom,
ii. 377, 382, 430, 431, 433; receives
the MS. of Swift's *Four Last Years*
and has a transcript made, ii. 387,
402, 496, 502; ¦Swift jokes about
Harleian MSS., ii. 475; Lord O. is
grateful for medals from Swift, ii.
496, 506.
     Lord O. and Pope: considerate of
Mrs. Pope's health, ii. 193, 261, 277,
iii. 146; commends Pope's filial piety,
iii. 17; intermediary with the 1st
Earl concerning Pope's *Epistle* to the
Earl, ii. 90; has (?Rysbrack's) bust of
Pope, ii. 298, iii. 100; asks Pope to
decide whether Fenton should dedicate to Lady Margaret, ii. 376; quotes
Scriblerus verses, ii. 381; his interest
in Pope's concerns appreciated, ii.
464; — sends Pope for Christmas a
collar of brawn, ii. 268, 270, iii. 78,
83, 245, 267, 334; for Christmas
(1727) gives Pope a gold cup and
salver, ii. 465, 470; thinks Pope vs.
Dunces like *Athanasius contra mundum*, ii. 507; — asked if Pope may
deposit some papers in O.'s London
library, iii. 54, 56; expects a visit
from Pope, iii. 87, 382; Pope eager
for news of O. and his library, iii.
240; asked to undertake a mission to
Curll, iii. 359; Lord O. at Bulstrode,
iii. 442; Pope goes to Southampton
without seeing O. first, iii. 483; Pope
stays with O. in Dover Street, iv.
172; a young Bounce waits for Allen,
iv. 175; Pope's last preserved letter

HARLEY, EDWARD (*cont.*)
to O. (25.x ii. 39), iv. 211; rambles
or visits to or with Lord O.: visit
to Wimpole cancelled (1724), ii. 213;
plans to visit Wimpole, ii. 257, 260,
268, 315, 317, 327; unidentified
ramble, ii. 310, 381; Lord O.'s visits
to Pope, ii. 311, 381 (to see Swift),
406 (Lady O. also invited); —
dinners at Twickenham, ii. 467, 490
(with Lady O. and Mrs. Caesar, also
iii. 40), 529 (with Wesley if possible);
Pope's desire to see Wesley about T.
Cooke, ii. 509, 515, 529, iii. 8, 9, 10,
11, 12, 16; asked to fetch Pope to
Town, iii. 19, 26; Pope adds other
invitations, iii. 105, 110; visit deferred
because of Pope's going to Riskins,
iii. 120, 123; dinner with Lord
Bathurst and old Jacob Tonson, iii.
176; dinner at Pope's with Gay, iii.
177–8; dinner at Barnes with Tonson,
Pope, and others, iii. 185; invited
with Mr. Thomas to inspect Pope's
papers, iii. 187, 193; Gay and Pope
dine in Dover Street, iii. 194; other
invitations to Twickenham, iii. 197,
404, 475; Kent reports dinner (1738)
at Dr. Mead's with O., Pope, *et al.*,
iv. 154 n.; — Lord O.'s connexions
with Pope's works: *John Bull*
wanted for the *Miscellanies*, ii. 421;
also five *Intelligencers*, iii. 17; O.'s aid
in subscription for the *Odyssey*, ii.
156, 158, 277; notes errors in commentary, ii. 277; wants Pope's
Verses on Durfey, ii. 268, 277;
finds MS. of Pope's 2nd Satire of
Donne, ii. 371; praises Pope's *Epistle*
to the 1st Earl of Oxford, ii. 382;
O.'s concern in *The Dunciad*, ii. 495;
asks omission of Maittaire from the
poem, ii. 496; wishes for a true Key,
not Curll's, ii. 496; distributes *Dunciad* of 1729, iii. 25, 26; signs the
conveyance to Gilliver, iii. 61, 177 n.;
O.'s connexion with the Wycherley
letters, iii. 55, 58, 80, iv. 330; the
Essay on Man, iii. 153; Pope sends
a poem to be transcribed, iii. 193;
compliments O. in the Epistle to
Bathurst, iii. 241, 281, 325; Harleian Library suspected of concur-
rence in the publication of Pope's

HARLEY, EDWARD (*cont.*)
Letters (1725), iii. 468, 476; — Lord
O.'s character: Pope's eulogy, ii. 261,
369, iii. 82; his interest in old books,
iii. 187; Orrery's opinion, iv. 278.
Harley, Edward, 3rd Earl of Oxford, iv.
443, 520 n.
Harley, Henrietta (Cavendish-Holles),
wife of 2nd Earl of Oxford: subscribes to Buononcini, ii. 99; goes to
Bath, ii. 264, 277, 507, 516; mistaken
message from her to Pope, ii. 348;
loves water to look at, ii. 311; probable godmother to Faustina's child,
iii. 217.
Harley, Lady Margaret, daughter of
2nd Earl of Oxford: her eighth
birthday, ii. 159; at Down Hall, ii.
364; Fenton's Waller is dedicated to,
ii. 374, 376, 463–4; sends service to
Pope, iii. 57, 371; her Thisbean conversation in Dover Street, iii. 187;
seriously ill at Wimpole, ii. 245,
266; remembered Pope's birthday
(21. v. 33), iii. 371–2; marries Duke
of Portland, ii. 467 n., iii. 404, 411
n., 424.
HARLEY, ROBERT, 1st Earl of Oxford
and Mortimer: letters to, ii. 90, 91;
letter from, ii. 91; letters to from
'Scriblerus', i. 216, 217, 228, 230,
478; his reply, i. 479; his correspondence advertised as to be published by
Curll, iii. 465, 471; he lacks letters
from Swift, i. 231, and Parnell, i.
284.
His political career: Lord Treasurer,
i. 199, 207, 234 n.; plot against his
life, iii. 199; his fall from power, i.
252 n., 260, 426 n.; sent to the Tower,
i. 287, 307; his ill health at his trial,
i. 307; his enlargement from the
Tower, i. 478, ii. 332; — his literary
interests, i. 250, 479; Pope's dedicatory *Epistle* to him, iii. 90, 91, 204,
382; O. regrets Pope's long period
of translation, ii. 311, 325; — O.'s
character, i. 420, 426; ii. 67, 68, 201,
233; as seen by Swift, ii. 184, 342,
374 n., iii. 48, 63, 211; Swift's errors
in *Four Last Years*, iv. 177; O.'s
death, ii. 232–3.
Harries, Mr. (possibly an error for
Norris), iv. 516.

Harris, George, iv. 243 n.
Harris, John, wishes to sketch Pope's
garden, iv. 516 n.
Harrison, Edward, ii. 182 n.
Harrison, Thomas, iii. 37 n.
Harte, Rev. Walter: report of his death
is false, ii. 429; a friend of young
Pattison, ii. 440 n.; tries for a
fellowship in Exeter Coll., Oxford, ii.
497; his dutiful career, iii. 332 n.; Pope
recommends H. to Burlington for a
good living, iii. 332, iv. 196; — becomes rector of Gosfield (1734), iii.
430; happy there, iii. 450 n., 491;
deserves added livings, iii. 511, iv. 30;
unsuccessful candidacy for the poetry
professorship, iv. 90; his *Poems* pub.
by Lintot (1727), ii. 429 n., 470 n.;
his *Essay on Satire* approved by Pope,
iii. 173; wrongly thought to be making an Abridgement of Roman
History, iii. 185; his *Essay on Reason*
pub. by Gilliver (1735), iii. 408–9;
approved by Pope, iii. 450.
Harting, Sussex, Ladyholt, Caryll's
place, i. 153 n., &c.
Hartley, Dr. David: at Bath, iv. 449 n.;
prescribes for Martha Blount, iv. 453;
for Allen, iv. 477, 481; for Pope, iv.
470, 471, 522.
Harvard College Library, its holdings
(1728) in Pope detailed by M. Byles,
ii. 494.
Harvard Studies and Notes, i. 70.
Harvest, Mr., ii. 183.
Haslem, Mr., iv. 454, 471.
Hasset, Canon of Saverne, iv. 422 n.
Hasten, Sam, ii. 91.
Hatton, Mr., clockmaker of Duke
Street, i. 465.
Hawkesworth, John, ii. 149 n., iii. 145
n., iv. 58 n.
Hawkins, G., iv. 31 n.
Hawkins, Sir John, iv. 478 n.
Hay, Lord, iii. 478, *see* Ilay, Earl of.
Hay, Lord James, i. 370.
Hay, Robert, iii. 498.
Hay, William, iii. 173.
Hay-Drummond, Thomas, Viscount
Dupplin, iii. 11, 56, 216, 267, 326.
Haym, Nicol., iii. 257.
Haymarket Theatre, i. 12, ii. 474, &c.
Haywood, Eliza, iii. 352.
Head, Richard, i. 474.

Hearne, Thomas: his *Collections* cited, i. 171, ii. 29, iii. 325; in *The Dunciad*, iii. 111; his relations with the 2nd Earl of Oxford, iii. 111 n., 187.

Hebb, Mr., iii. 425.

Heidegger, John James, i. 407.

Heinsius, Daniel, i. 26, 90.

Helsham, Richard, iii. 16.

Hemlow, Joyce, iv. 336 n.

Henchman, Humphrey (D.D.), ii. 313.

Henderson, G. D., i. 123 n., ii. 294 n., iii. 6, v. 2.

Henley, Mrs., iii, 198.

Henley, Anthony, iii. 167 n.

Henry II, of England, iii. 365, iv. 349.

Henshew, Mrs., apothecary, iv. 242.

Herbert, Charles (later, Sheffield, Charles), ii. 303 n.

Herefordshire, *see* Brampton Castle (Robert, Earl of Oxford), Hampton Court (Lord Coningsby), Holm Lacy (Viscountess Scudamore), Goodrich (or Gutheridge) (Swift), Ledbury (Jacob Tonson, sr.); Pope's journey to Herefordshire put off, i. 433.

Heroditus, ii. 219.

Heroi-Comical Epistle in Defense of Punning, i. 376 n.

Hertford, Earl of, *see* Seymour, Algernon, later 7th Duke of Somerset.

Hertfordshire, *see* Balls Park (Edw. Harrison), Bennington (Charles Caesar, Judith Cowper), Cashiobury (William Pulteney), Pishiobury Park (E. Lewis ill there); Hoddesdon, ii. 355.

Hervey, Carr, Lord, i. 295, 361, 381.

Hervey, John, Lord: his marriage to Molly Lepell, ii. 26, 41; satirical of the Earl of Selkirk, iii. 248 n.; his duel with Pulteney, iii. 206 n.; supporter of Walpole, iii. 339; his pretty view of weddings, iii. 411; high opinion of Peterborow, iii. 488–9; — attacks Pope in verses, iii. 364 n., 448 n., iv. 124, v. 11; Pope's scorn of H.'s Latinity, iv. 406; H. and Katherine, Duchess of Buckinghamshire friends of Orrery, iv. 406; is executor to the Duchess, iv. 460; she leaves all papers (including Pope's letters) to H., iv. 446; the Duchess

Hervey, John (*cont.*) leaves a marriage portion to H.'s daughter, Lepell, iv. 446; she marries Hon. C. Phipps, iv. 482 n.; H. gets Buckingham House, iv. 472 n.; his death, iv. 466; his death makes necessary a cancellation in *The Dunciad* (1743), iv. 425 n.

Hervey, Mary (Lepell), wife of John, Lord Hervey: letter to, ii. 41; subscribes to Buononcini, ii. 99; chilly at Bath, ii. 298 n.; her mother (Mrs. Lepell) a friend of Dr. Arbuthnot, iii. 434 n.; caustic remarks (1734) about Pope and Martha Blount, iii. 435 n.

Hervey, (?Lepell), Miss, dau. of Lord Hervey, ii. 349; marries Hon. C. Phipps, iv. 482 n.

Hesiod, ii. 54, 58, 219, 509 n. (translated by T. Cooke).

Hesse, Faustina, opera singer: sends tunes to Lady Cobham, iii. 217; is now a mother, iii. 216.

Hesse, J. A., husband of Faustina, iii. 216 n.

Hewet, John, the rural lover killed by lightning, i. 479, 482, 488, 494, 497, 499, 523.

Hibernian (unnamed), who is 'only a lodger', i. 148, 166, 377.

Highgate, iv. 197.

High-German Doctor, i. 285.

Hill, Mr., of Eggam, i. 312.

Hill, Aaron: letters to, ii. 404, iii. 165, 169, 176, 182, 188, 200, 222, 226, 230, 231, 235, 238, 253, 259, 267, 371, 394, iv. 101, 106, 110, 118, 121, 126, 131, 145, 159, 165; letters from, iii. 164, 166, 173, 228, 230, 234, 257, 261, 342, 370, 386, 392, 394, iv. 94, 103, 107, 111, 120, 122, 128, 132, 146, 152, 158, 161, 167; — his *Collection* of letters (1751), ii. 404 n.; his editings of Pope's letters to him, iii. 175 n.; letters misdated, iii. 228 n., 230 n., 231 n., 235 n., 253, 267; flattering to Mrs. Howard, iii. 236; renews correspondence with Pope in 1738, iv. 91; shop of Samuel Richardson his address for letters, iv. 128; the end of his (preserved) correspondence with Pope, iv. 168; — ambivalence towards Pope: flat-

HILL, AARON (*cont.*)
tery, ii. 35, 36, iii. 164; apologizes for attack in *Northern Star*, ii. 35–36; his letter prefatory to his *Creation*, ii. 35; his public apology called a model for T. Cooke, v. 7; objects to Pope's tone of moral superiority, iii. 166–9; but still loves Pope as a good man, iii. 167; desires to do Pope good by castigation, iii. 169, 174; dislikes Pope's 'vein of civil reproach', iv. 103, 107; glad to help Pope in any difficulty, iv. 132; his attacks on Pope before 1731, iii. 165 n.; *Essay on Criticism* thought defective in diction, iv. 95–99; — H. among the flying-fishes in *Bathos*, iii. 164 n., 167, iv. 99–101; learns that Arbuthnot was (?) the guilty critic of Theobald, iv. 103; the offensive note in *The Dunciad* omitted, iii. 167, 177; on the reception of the *Epistle to Burlington*, iii. 257, 258, 262; on the *Epistle to Bathurst*, iii. 342; awaits the *Essay on Man*, iii. 235; delighted with the *Imitation of Horace's Sat. II. i*, iii. 370; on the *Epilogue to the Satires*, iv. 152; — invited to Twickenham, iii. 188, 226; illness and death of Mrs. H., iii. 201, 222, 228, 228–9; invited to observe his period of mourning at Twickenham, iii. 230, 232; iv. 111, 118; — Pope willing to do any service to Dennis, iii. 165, 166; H.'s reply, 175; H. and Lord Peterborow, iii. 182, 188; on James Thomson, iv. 132, 146; learns that Thomson and Mallet also are writing tragedies, iv. 132; on Mallet, iii. 189, iv. 152, 167; sends Mallet an account of burning the *Essay on Propriety*, iv. 99 n.; Pope first met H. at Dr. Young's, iii. 235; quotes (and revises) Shakespeare, iv. 105; — Hill's non-dramatic works: projected life of Peter the Great, ii. 405; sends Pope the 5th ed. of *The Northern Star*, iv. 158; sends Pope the reprint of the *Plain Dealer* (1730) with complimentary verses by Miss Urania, iii. 164; his *Caveat* corrective, not harmful, to Pope, iii. 168, 174; his Epigram against Pope and Swift, iii. 170; his *Advice to the Poets*, iii. 175, 177, 182, 370; his *Essay on*

HILL, AARON (*cont.*)
Propriety, iii. 168, 175, iv. 95, 99, 103, 108, 121; — dramatic works: *Athelwold* approved by Pope, iii. 200–1, 229, 230, 234; its performance, iii. 234, 235, 253, 254, 258; published by Gilliver, iii. 238; his tragedy about Caesar, to be sent in MS. to Bolingbroke, iv. 105; liked by Pope and Bolingbroke, iv. 111, 120, 121–2, 127, 128, 129; traditional epilogue essential, iv. 129; despondent over getting the play staged, iv. 121, 129, 146, 152, 153, 158–9; gives up all hope of performance, iv. 162, 166, 167–8; gets a hint that Bolingbroke does not require its dedication to himself, if printed, iv. 168; never acted, iv. 105 n.
Biographical data: fantastic classical names for his children, iv. 94 n.; lives in Petty France, near St. James's Park, iii. 371; aided on the *Life* of Gay, iv. 38 n.; owns stock in York Buildings, iv. 94 n.; pleased with Pope's gardening at Bevis Mount, iv. 94; removes to Plaistow, iv. 111; interested in a Davenant theatrical patent, iii. 370; Pope commends his zeal for virtue and his learning, iv. 38.

Hill, (General) John, iii. 249.
Hill, Miranda, wife of Aaron Hill, iii. 222 n.
Hill, Samuel, subscriber to the *Iliad*, i. 300.
Hill, Urania, dau. of Aaron Hill, iii. 164, 172, 175, 177, 230, 231.
Hillhouse, James T., cited in *Modern Language Notes*, i. 182 n.
Hills, Henry, i. 56.
Historical MSS. Commission: Report X, ii. 245, 529; Report on Bath MSS., i. 521; on Montagu House MSS., iv. 14; on Polwarth MSS., i. 345; on Portland MSS., ii. 91, 444, 502.
Historical Register for 1727, ii. 427 n.
History of the Works of the Learned, iv. 163, 171.
Hitchcock, the farmer at Marston, iv. 508.
Hoadly, Benjamin, Bishop of Salisbury, i. 462, iii. 119 n.
Hoadly, John, becomes Archbishop in

Dublin (1730), brother of Benjamin, iii. 119 n., 147.

Hoare, Sir Richard, banker (1648–1718), i. 394.

Hoare, Sir Richard, banker (d. 1754), grandson of the preceding gentleman: serves Gay and Swift, iii. 289, 300; is banker for 'P. T.', iii. 466.

Hobbes, Thomas, i. 43.

Hodges, John C., iv. 151 n.

Hodges, Walter, Vice Chancellor of Oxford, iv. 437, 442 n.

Holder, Elizabeth (becomes Mrs. Ralph Allen), iv. 68 n.

Holderness, Countess of, *see* Schomberg, Lady Frederic.

Holditch, Mr., iii. 38, 489.

HOLDSWORTH, EDWARD, poet: letter to, iv. 90, asking him to vote for Harte as poetry professor.

Hollings, Dr. John, iii. 508.

Holm Lacy, seat of Viscountess Scudamore, ii. 329.

Holman, Mr., i. 253, 309.

Holmes, the Twickenham waterman (The Globe, Hungerford Stairs), iv. 365, 475.

HOLMES, Dr. WILLIAM, President of St. John's Coll., Oxford: letter to, iv. 390, asking him to befriend young Thomas Hooke of St. Mary Hall.

Holt, Mr., ii. 245.

Holt, Lady Jane, sister to the Duke of Wharton, ii. 245 n.

Holt (Wilts. ?), iv. 463.

HOMER: *Pope's first stimulus in poetry*, i. 297; mentioned vaguely, i. 20, 39, 217, 406, 494; his art as seen early by Pope, i. 23, 44, 81, 105, 107, 452, iii. 140; specific passages commented on, or quoted, i. 93, 166, 313, ii. 518, iii. 115 (quoted in Greek); early translations of fragments by Pope, i. 74–75, 166, 191, 220; — Pope's *Iliad*: getting subscribers for it, i. 170, 204, 207, 210, 212, 214, 218–19; aided by Jervas, the Duke of Wharton, Lord Halifax, and others, i. 226; difficulty with A. Philips over subscribers, i. 229 (*and see under* Philips); subscription reveals both friends and enemies, i. 233; thanks Caryll for aid, i. 235; Duke of Chandos subscribes through

HOMER (*cont.*)
young Harcourt, i. 274; Jervas's aid, i. 295, 410 (for Irish subscriptions); later delinquent subscribers, i. 420, 464; copies presented to John Hughes, ii. 46, and the Bodleian Library, ii. 83; — the labour of translation: Pope's lack of skill in Greek, i. 44, 209, 220; the work keeps Pope busy, i. 208, 219, 231 (Bk. I now done, 8 June 1714), 238, 240; the year's task nearly done, i. 250; the daily task of 50 lines, i. 254; works on H. even at Bath, i. 256, 267; at work now (Feb. 1715) on vol. ii, i. 280, 289, 291, 292; two months to be devoted to H., i. 293–4; Bks. V–VIII done (7 Oct. 1715), i. 316; vol. ii soon to be in the press, i. 318; published in Mar. 1716, i. 322 n., 326, delayed because of martial spirit of the moment, i. 332; at work on Bks. X and XI, i. 341, 343; vol. iii published, June 1717, i. 407; Pope servant to Achilles for two months to come, i. 408; weary of the task, i. 409; busy at it, i. 413, 445; at Stanton Harcourt (1718) for uninterrupted work, i. 459, 475; vol. iv. published in June 1718, i. 459; very busy, i. 484 (vol. v finished at Stanton Harcourt); — labour on the commentaries: early commentators tedious, i. 208, 220; Parnell's help valued, i. 225; the enlarged scope of the task, i. 246; study of ancient geography, i. 246; asks aid of Broome on notes from Eustathius, i. 266, 270; Pope's inability to translate Eustathius alleged by Broome, i. 270 n.; Broome at work, i. 275, 276, 297, 323; Parnell's Essay on H. praised, i. 333; Parnell asked for notes on four Books, i. 415; Broome to send directions to the printer, i. 394; Lady Mary on the survival of the Homeric mores in the Orient, i. 406; controversy between LaMotte and Dacier, i. 485–7; Mme Dacier's translation used, i. 485; her *Iliad* uses Eustathius without due acknowledgement, i. 492; consults Sheffield, Duke of Buckingham, i. 493; gets help from J. Jortin, i. 496–7; Broome again available, i. 497; gratitude to Broome,

HOMER (*cont.*)

ii. 3, 40; he works on the Indexes also, ii. 40, 43; some prose essays finally omitted, ii. 43; observations on finishing a book, ii. 43; — problems in publication: Jervas attends to the frontispiece, i. 243, 262; Pope's complete ignorance of Tickell's rival contract with Tonson, i. 196 n.; the rival versions of Bk. I, i. 305; Pope asks Addison to look over Bks. I and II, i. 263; other consultations, i. 265, 266; opinions before publication by 9 judges, i. 267; proof-reading, i. 275, 281; delay in final date of publication, i. 285, 288, 290; Pope retires to Binfield at date of publication, i. 294; Edward Young distributes copies for Pope in Oxford, i. 294; copy sent for the Bodleian Library, i. 294 n., 421, ii. 83; given free to John Hughes, ii. 46; accounts to settle with Lintot, i. 418; later Books transcribed for Pope by T. Dancastle, i. 445, 519; the *Iliad* complete in 1720, ii. 16 n., 27 n., 37, 43; — favourable reception of vol. i of *Iliad*, i. 294, 299, 301, 303, 304, 305, 306; Oxford wits prefer Pope's version, i. 294 n.; Pope's marked copy of Tickell's Bk. I, now at Hartlebury Castle, shows that Pope planned to attack it, i. 296 n.; dangerous praise of Bolingbroke in the Preface, i. 300; temporary fame from Homer expected, i. 396; Lady Mary Wortley's comments, i. 423; — Pope awaits attacks, i. 239; suffers as an author militant, i. 342; needs Parnell's *Frogs* and *Zoilus*, i. 292, 348; his critics burlesqued, i. 374; the 4to *Iliad* immediately a book sought after, iii. 18, 27; Pope's last revision of the *Iliad* (with Warburton's aid), iv. 384, 400, 403; legal troubles with Lintot, iv. 224; — Pope's *Odyssey*: Problems of collaboration, with Broome false claims made, ii. 103, iii. 507 n., 510, iv. 3; his payments to Broome, ii. 293 n., 389 n., iii. 497, 507, 510; his claims as to the notes, iii. 496, 497; Fenton less exigent, ii. 397; help from Henry Layng, ii. 390; from C. Pitt's version, ii. 382; urges

HOMER (*cont.*)

industry on Broome and Fenton, ii. 110, 145, 147, 164, 182; also secrecy, ii. 145, 205, 271-2; the purpose of secrecy is to trick the critics, ii. 205, 273-4; Broome fails in concealment, ii. 273-4; — Pope assigns Books for translation by Broome and Fenton, ii. 103; Fenton completes Bk. XIX, ii. 244; Broome's progress, ii. 210, 269, 302, 336, 338; Broome is asked to complete for Pope Bk. XVII, ii. 340; — Pope's own translation: his varying attitude towards the task, ii. 105, 176, 195, 226, 380; attempts to preserve the true style of the *Odyssey*, ii. 205, esp. in Broome's work, which Pope revises, ii. 103, 226, 321, 356; Pope is thought to steal credit by revising Broome, ii. 385; the collaborators labour (1722) 'to keep Pope on his throne', ii. 121; Pope's translation delayed, ii. 130, 159; does Bk. III, ii. 110, 111; his later work, ii. 131, 151, 182, 211, 213, 225, 248, 265, 302; — Broome's work on the notes: notes on Bk. I done in 1724, ii. 215; on Bk. III, ii. 210, 225, 226; on IV and V, ii. 231, 248; commentators lacking, ii. 248; notes on Bk. VIII, ii. 248; on IX, ii. 270; on XI and XII, ii. 271; printer's proofs sent to Broome, ii. 288; later notes received, ii. 339, 340, 351, 355, 360; surprised to find how often Broome has used Dacier, ii. 363; Pope congratulates Broome on completion of the notes, ii. 363; — Pope does the long critical postscript, ii. 369-70, 372, 375, 377; it has retarded publication, ii. 378; — the *Odyssey* as a project: meditated early, ii. 21, 45, 93; the Proposals planned and deferred, ii. 111; reasons for deferment, ii. 145 n., 156, 158, 159; printed in 1725, ii. 164 n., 274, 275, 385 n.; considers resigning the project to Tickell, ii. 158, 159, 161, 164; grant of £200 from the Ministry, ii. 160 n., 276, 294; subscribers sought, ii. 151, 156, 164 n., 262, 265, 271; Broome's 14 subscribers, ii. 271; plans to print list of subscribers in the Proposals, ii. 275, 279; the major

HOMER (*cont.*)
subscribers, ii. 275, 276, 299; many
names omitted from the printed lists
by accident, ii. 299; — publication of
the *Odyssey*: negotiations with a
bookseller, ii. 210; Broome not
wanted in Town while negotiations
with Lintot proceed, ii, 214; indenture signed, ii. 217 n.; its terms, ii.
290; Tonson consulted on paper and
presswork, ii. 217; proofs are being
read, ii. 217, 257; vols. i–iii published in Apr. 1725, ii. 265 n., 282;
Buckley gives favourable advertising
space in his journals, ii. 285; Lintot's
advertisements objectionable, ii. 285–
6, 287; vols. iv and v published in
June 1726, ii. 360, 374, 380 n.; Pope
will himself send copies for Broome's
subscribers, ii. 287, 288, 291, 292–3;
copies for Pope's subscribers delivered
from Jervas's house, ii. 290, 380; to
Caryll Pope names his collaborators,
ii. 361; gift copies for Mather Byles,
iii. 7, iv. 16; for Buckley, ii. 286, 471;
for Urania Hill, iii. 177; for Stopford, ii. 425; — critical reception of
the *Odyssey*: railing papers, ii. 318,
339 n., 352, 377 n.; Spence's *Essay* a
welcome relief, ii. 321, 379; on Pope's
false 'raising' of Homer's style, ii.
321; Pope thinks his *Odyssey* more
exact than his *Iliad*, ii. 341; his dis-
gust with the public as critic, ii. 341;
— monetary returns from the *Odyssey*: difficult to estimate, ii. 214 n.,
282; Lintot's falsehoods about it, ii.
432; Pope urges a conference for
settlement with his collaborators,
204, 248 n., 271, 339, 344, 365, 470;
Pope is definitely through with translation, ii. 321–2, 325, 341; Swift regretted the *Odyssey* project, ii. 311.
Hooke, Luke Joseph, Catholic son of
Nathaniel, Professor in the Sorbonne,
iv. 119, 353; possibly in London
(1742), iv. 379.
Hooke, Nathaniel: at work on his
Roman History, iii. 185, iv. 181, 281,
495; subscriptions acceptable, iv. 31;
Allen secretly aids the work, iv. 36,
41; H.'s health, iv. 194, 273, 281; his
sons, iv. 353 n.; Gen. Wade willing
to help son Thomas into the army, iv.

Hooke, Nathaniel (*cont.*)
357, 358; Thomas possibly mentioned, iv. 379; his father wishes to
help him at Oxford, iv. 390; the
father goes briefly abroad, iv. 398; —
his friends: Lyttelton, iv. 145; Lord
Marchmont, iv. 358; Warburton, iv.
381, 506; frequently at Bath as protégé of Allen: in 1738, iv. 108, 109,
119, 134, 145; in 1739, iv. 191, 194,
195 (urges Pope to visit Allen), 204,
239; in 1741, iv. 340, 363; in 1742,
iv. 404, 405 (to explain to Allen why
Pope is tied to Sarah, Duchess of
Marlborough); in 1743, iv. 477, 481;
in 1744 (in London), iv. 509, 517;
transcribes for Allen, Pope's 'Prayer
to God', iv. 31; at work in Bath
(1738) on his *Roman History* or the
Travels of Cyrus, iv. 109; — H.'s
employment by the Duchess of
Marlborough: Pope aids the con-
tact, iv. 327, 358, 359; H. her 'im-
partial' historian, iv. 366; her
'prisoner', iv. 375; gets a pension
from her, iv. 383, 386; has 'dressed'
her papers well, iv. 389; possibly
spoken of as Sir Timothy, iv. 412;
he might mend Pope's inscription for
Vernon, iv. 421; he wearies of his
service to her, iv. 430; her health is
better, he says, iv. 432; he and his
dau. now both her prisoners, iv. 434;
H. (Marchmont writes) could bring
her a priest if Socrates proves inadequate, iv. 445; — H.'s (usually
brief) visits to Pope: stays with him,
iv. 230; seldom comes, Pope thinks,
iv. 235; comes with his dau., iv. 259,
350, 360; to have Pope's house while
Pope is with Allen (1741), iv. 366;
at Twickenham in Pope's last days,
iv. 501 n.; ill there, iv. 516; arranges
to have the last rites performed for
Pope, iv. 526.
Hooke, Thomas, Protestant son of
Nathaniel, iv. 353, 390.
Hooker, E. N., i. 136 n.
Hoole, John, iii. 128 n.
Hope, John, *see* Bruce, Sir John Hope.
Hopkins, John (and Sternhold,
Thomas), i. 483.
Horace (Quintus Horatius Flaccus):
Pope plans now to write only Epistles

Horace (*cont.*)
in H.'s Manner, iii. 37; both Whigs
and Tories read H., ii. 199; Second
Satire of the 1st Bk., imitated by
Pope but not owned, iii. 413; H. an
Opposition poet, iii. 420; his gay
tone more suitable for Pope than the
gravity of Lucretius, iii. 433; vague
mentions of, ii. 185, iv. 137; —
quotations by Pope from the Odes,
i. 49, 88, 124, 162, 167, 168, 172,
242, ii. 229, 470, 524, iii. 3, 79, 115,
210, iv. 7, 371, 421; from the Satires,
i. 101, 124, ii. 128, iii. 58, 279, iv.
251; from the Epistles, i. 72, 124, 158,
371, 376, ii. 107, 183, 277, 412, iii.
153, 278, iv. 191, 196, 218, 245, 491;
from *Ars Poetica*, i. 329, ii. 125; —
quoted by Atterbury, i. 502, 503,
ii. 84, 93–98, 129, 176, iii. 247;
quoted by Dr. Arbuthnot, iii. 401;
by Lord Bathurst, i. 489, ii. 207, iv.
25; by Edward Blount, ii. 10; by
Bolingbroke, ii. 218; by Broome, ii.
121, 346, 489, iii. 507; by H. Cromwell, i. 91, 96, 101; Dacier's comments on, i. 492; quoted by R.
Digby, ii. 58; by Fenton, ii. 464, 487,
iii. 24, 100; by Jabez Hughes, ii. 46;
by Parnell, i. 250; by Lord Peterborow, iii. 283; by Swift, i. 301, 302,
358, ii. 152, 153, 311, 420, 453, 493,
iii. 148, 190, 191, 303, iv. 44, 46; by
Sir W. Trumbull, i. 46; by Walsh, i.
20.

Horneck, Philip, i. 295.

Houghton, Arthur, jr., i. 17.

Howard, Lady (unidentified), iii. 103.

Howard, Charles (1674–1738), 3rd
Earl of Carlisle, ii. 146.

Howard, Charles (1675–1733), later
9th Earl of Suffolk, ii. 446; *see*
Howard, Henrietta.

Howard, Edward, later 9th Duke of
Norfolk, iii. 103 n., 346.

HOWARD, HENRIETTA, later (1731)
Countess of Suffolk: letters to, ii. 435,
445, iii. 34, 236 (from A. Hill); Pope
likes her (1717) at Hampton Court,
i. 427; her courtly character, ii. 395;
lack of interest in poetry, iii. 232, 235
(*Athelwold*); no insincere courtier,
iii. 491 (*see below for Swift's contrary
opinion*); subscribes to Buononcini,

HOWARD, HENRIETTA (*cont.*)
ii. 99; possibly friend to Judith
Cowper, ii. 136, 138 n.; Lord
Bathurst's 'prose lady', ii. 258; —
neighbour to Pope, ii. 324, 368;
Pope caught cold calling on her, ii.
403; the birth of Calf-urnia, ii. 435,
436; John Conduitt a friend, ii. 457;
her troubles with Mr. H., ii. 446,
469; articles of agreement with him,
ii. 478, 491, 508; Pope visits her at
Court, iii. 133, 139; she will assist
Pope concerning Lady Walpole's
laver, iii. 140; — becomes Countess
of Suffolk, iii. 205, 209; her unhappiness at Court, iii. 367; dines at
Pope's with Lord Cobham, iii. 377;
her attitude towards Pope, iii. 434;
marries Mr. Berkeley in 1735, ii. 259
n., iii. 474; guests at Marble Hill, iii.
474, 478; Pope dines with her, iii.
480; hopes to go to Stowe with her,
iii. 488; she visits her sister-in-law,
Lady Betty Germain, iii. 501; returns from a stay in France, iv. 34 n.;
gives Pope an eider down, iv. 212;
her health, iii. 401, 408, 514, iii. 53,
141, 434, 440, iv. 8, 47, 49; —
Marble Hill in construction, 1722 (?)-
4, ii. 143 n., 178, 178 n., 183, 257;
Pope's work on her gardens there, ii.
197, 213, 240, 256, 257; a road to be
changed, ii. 259, v. 5, 19; needs
lambs to crop her lawns, ii. 292;
Digby on Twickenham as 'country',
ii. 305; wants more land from Vernon, ii. 323, iii. 34, 35, v. 19; Bridgeman to help her, ii. 327; Peterborow's
affection for her, ii. 178 n., 189, 196,
iii. 281; — Gay very attentive to her,
ii. 133, 182, 316; she is his chief re-
source at Court, ii. 332 (Swift
doesn't think so, ii. 407); she advises
him in declining the Gentleman-
ushership, ii. 454; she reports daily
to Pope on Gay's illness (1729), iii. 2;
embarrassed by Gay's attacks on the
Court in *Polly*, iii. 52 n.; a true
friend to Gay, ii. 400, 474, iii. 52 n.,
121, 131; her loss in his death, iii.
336; — Pope characterizes her for
Swift, ii. 322, 323, 343, 350; Pope
presents Swift to her, ii. 373; Swift
does not write to her, ii. 409; offers her

HOWARD, HENRIETTA (*cont.*)
his cure for deafness, ii. 475, 478, 481;
her 'Sieve Yahoo' letter, ii. 417; contributes to the cheddar letter, ii. 403
n.; Swift wants a recipe from her, ii.
408; her ague, ii. 408; Swift's unfavourable attitude towards her, ii.
461, 476, iii. 93; she forbade him to
go to France, ii. 472; animosity to
her as a courtier, iii. 23, 43, 101, 109;
his reproachful letter to her, iii. 161;
extreme hostility to her, iii. 192, 194,
203, 208, 249, 251; Swift is ironical
about her help to Gay, iii. 286; —
she is defended by Pope, iii. 249; by
Gay and the Duchess of Queensberry,
iii. 205, by Lady Betty Germain, iii.
363; Mrs. Howard helps Mrs. Barber,
iii. 194–5; Fortescue of service to her,
ii. 242, 368, 441, 524, iv. 169; she is
friendly with Martha Blount, ii. 235,
435 n., 446, iii. 194.

Howard, Henry, the crude and un-
dutiful son of Mrs. Howard, later
10th Earl of Suffolk, ii. 446.

Howard, Henry, Lord Morpeth, later
4th Earl of Carlisle, iii. 46, 443.

Howard, Thomas, 8th Duke of Norfolk (thought wrongly (?) to have
been Pope's schoolmate), iii. 346 n.,
360.

Howe, John Grubham, of Stowell, ii.
510 n., 517, 532.

Howe, Mary, Maid of Honour, later
Countess of Pembroke, ii. 136; mentioned as a friend of Judith Cowper,
ii. 136, 138, 141, 155, 195; mistaken
for Mrs. Howard, ii. 143 n.; might
get Miss Cowper to Richmond, ii.
174; at Bath, ii. 174; her portrait of
Miss Cowper returned from Pope after
his death, ii. 139; she wants a copy of
Pope's lines 'To a Lady on her Birthday', ii. 180; her melancholy, ii. 201–
2; Epitaph for Earl Cowper returned
by Miss H., ii. 209.

Howe, Sophia, formerly a Maid of
Honour, ii. 513 n.

Howitt, William, i. 145 n.

Hoye, Mr., of the Blue Periwig in Pall
Mall, Charles Ford's address, i. 522,
ii. 283.

Hubbard, J. H., his piracy of *The New
Dunciad*, iv. 392.

Hucheson (or Hutchinson), Archibald,
iv. 269.

Huet, Pierre Daniel, ii. 74 n.

Hughes, Helen Sard, ii. 257 n., iii. 56 n.,
iv. 355 n.

HUGHES, JABEZ, a translator, brother
of John Hughes: letter to, ii. 34;
letter from, ii. 46; gives Pope a copy
of *The Siege of Damascus*, ii. 34
(letter of condolence for John's
death); thanks Pope for the free copy
of the *Iliad*, ii. 46; is permitted to
print a letter from Pope about John,
iii. 441.

HUGHES, JOHN, dramatist: letters to, i.
218, 316, ii. 28, 29, 33; letter from,
ii. 28; H. aids subscription for the
Iliad, i. 218; permitted to see Jervas's paintings, i. 218; compliments Pope on *Iliad* I, i. 316; his
edition of Spenser given to Pope, i.
316; Pope asked to return at once the
MS. of *The Siege of Damascus*, ii. 28;
Pope cannot write a Prologue, ii. 28;
H.'s death, ii. 33 n.; gift of the *Iliad*
to him, ii. 46; Duncombe edits H.'s
correspondence, iii. 437, 438, 454;
Swift's unawareness of H., iii. 492,
v. 17; Pope's account of H. to Swift,
iii. 508.

Hughes, John, of Stanton Harcourt, *see,
rather,* Hewet, John.

Hulst, Col., iv. 395.

Hume, Alexander, 2nd Earl of Marchmont, Plenipotentiary at Cambrai
(1722 ff.), ii. 177 n.; his death (1740),
iv. 217 n., 228 n.; Nugent's *Ode* to
him, iv. 231.

Hume, Hon. Alexander, younger son of
2nd Earl of Marchmont, iv. 327, 364.

Hume, Anne (Western), wife of the
3rd Earl of Marchmont, iv. 212, 498,
513.

HUME, HUGH, Lord Polwarth: in Feb.
1740 he succeeds as 3rd Earl of
Marchmont: letters to, iv. 217, 227,
248, 271, 327, 341, 363, 456 (from
Bolingbroke), 458, 490 (to Marchmont and Bolingbroke), 498 (from
Bolingbroke), 503 (from Bolingbroke), 513, 519 (from Bolingbroke);
—friend to Wm. Cleland, iii. 144 n.;
to Hooke, iv. 181, 358; to Pope, iv.
178, 209; Pope continually urging

HUME, HUGH (*cont.*)
  him to political activity, iv. 214;
  Pope meets with him and Dr. King,
  iv. 228; M.'s noble public spirit, iv.
  217, 227–8, 261; — Pope's urgency
  upon the death of Sir W. Wyndham,
  iv. 248–51; commended in Pope's
  verses on his grotto, iv. 262; begged
  to return from Scotland to political
  action, iv. 271–3; M. has written to
  Lyttelton of his abstention from
  politics, iv. 271 n.; he is disabled by
  becoming a peer, iv. 272; in 1741 he
  becomes active, iv. 327; asked to dine
  at Pope's with Argyle and Cobham,
  iv. 341; — Pope's high esteem for,
  iv. 364–5; in 1742 spends the Christmas holidays at Twickenham, iv. 431,
  442; to dine (May 1743) with Pope
  and take Bolingbroke back to Battersea, iv. 436; M. and Pope regret that
  gout keeps Sarah, Duchess of Marlborough from seeing them, iv. 444;
  they joke the Duchess about Socrates,
  iv. 445; M.'s skill as a gardener, iv.
  459; in 1743-4 lives with Bolingbroke in Battersea House, iv. 456,
  477, 498.
Hume, Penelope, in 1727 becomes Mrs.
  Charles Jervas, iii. 51 n.
Hunt, Jeremiah, ii. 441 n.
Hunter, Col. (or Brigadier), a director of
  the opera, ii. 135, 136.
Hunter, Mr., i. 325.
Huntington Library, The Henry E.: its
  Quarterly, i. 152 n.; its MS. of
  Spence's *Anecdotes*, iv. 236 n., 525–6.
Hurst, near Ockingham, Berks., Sir
  Wm. Compton, i. 428 n.
Hussey, Christopher, iv. 25 n.
Hutchins, Mr., Fenton's Twickenham
  landlord, ii. 233 n.
Hutchinson, John, iii. 81.
Hyde, Lady Charlotte, dau. of the 2nd
  Earl of Clarendon, iii. 96.
Hyde, Edward, 1st Earl of Clarendon,
  ii. 167, iii. 135, 245 n.
Hyde, Edward, 3rd Earl of Clarendon,
  Gay his secretary on the embassy to
  Hanover, i. 228.
Hyde, Henry, 4th Earl of Clarendon, iii.
  96 n., iv. 266.
Hyde, Henry, Lord Cornbury, son of
  the 4th Earl of Clarendon: corre-

Hyde, Henry (*cont.*)
  sponded with Pope, but no letters now
  known, iv. 52; a later friend of
  Pope's, iv. 178; writes nobly to
  Pope, iv. 218, and Pope has not replied, iv. 218; Pope visits him, i. 431
  n.; — M.P. for Oxford University,
  iii. 277; refused a pension, iii. 277;
  Swift's opinion of C. and of Oxford
  University, iii. 285; Gay praises C.,
  iii. 277; C. is a pall-bearer at Gay's
  funeral, iii. 338; Pope stays with C.
  in Town, iii. 452; C.'s verses on
  the *Essay on Man*, iii. 502, 505–6; C.
  might help Walter Harte, iii. 511;
  Pope's *Letters* for Bethel's subscribers (1737) are at C.'s house in
  Town, iv. 67; Pope also there, iv. 66,
  87; — C. (Aug. 1738) goes to the
  Spa, iv. 117; returns, iv. 149; wants a
  visit from Pope in the country, iv.
  188, 189; at Bath, C. likes Prior Park
  and Allen, iv. 190–1; alarmed needlessly (Dec. 1739) about Pope's
  health, iv. 208, 212; C. (1740) again
  at Spa, iv. 265, 266; he is politi-
  cally relaxed, iv. 272; again at Bath
  (Oct. 1740), iv. 281; at Twickenham (Dec. 1742) with others for the
  holidays, iv. 431; Pope goes to Cornbury in C.'s coach, iv. 472.
Hyde, Jane (Leveson-Gower), wife of
  the 4th Earl of Clarendon and
  Rochester, mother of Lady Jane
  Hyde, Countess of Essex, Catherine,
  Duchess of Queensberry, Henry, Lord
  Cornbury, and others: the beautiful
  mother of two beauties, i. 431 n.;
  Pope visits her, i. 417; Swift's 'mis-
  tress', iii. 97, 148.
Hyde, Lady Jane, Countess of Essex, i.
  431 n.
Hyde, Widow, of Dames St., Dublin,
  iii. 23.
Hyginus, i. 90.

Ibbot, Benjamin, ii. 141–2.
Ilay (or Islay), Earl of, *see* Camp-
  bell, Archibald, later 3rd Duke of
  Argyle.
Ilchester, 6th Earl of, iii. 342 n., 344 n.
Ilive, Jacob, iv. 375, 425, 433 n.
Independent Whig, iv. 114 n. (by
  Thomas Gordon).

Ingatestone, Essex, home of Lord Petre, i. 93, 518, iii. 284.

Innys, W. & J., booksellers, ii. 218 n., 222.

Intelligencer, ii. 523, iii. 17, 292; *see* Sheridan, T., *and* Swift, Jonathan.

Irish, Dr., i. 403.

Irwin, Lady (unidentified among several such), iv. 205 n.

Irving, W. H., i. 175 n., ii. 75 n., 216 n.

Isaac, gardener or servant to R. Allen, iv. 360, 449.

Isabella, 'Lady', Cromwell's housekeeper, i. 116.

Islay (or Ilay), Earl of, *see* Campbell, Archibald, later 3rd Duke of Argyle.

Isleworth, Middlesex, iii. 138.

Jack the Giant Killer, ii. 357.

Jacobite invasion of 1715, *see under* Pretender.

James I, of England, ii. 50.

James II, of England, i. 78.

James, Pope's servant at Bristol, iv. 468.

Jansen, Mrs., ii. 476.

Jefferies (or Jeffery, Edmund ?), bookseller at Cambridge, i. 496 n.

Jeffery of Monmouth, i. 425.

Jeffreys, George, ii. 352 n., 358.

Jehosaphat, valley of, i. 515.

Jemmy, servant to Sir G. Kneller, ii. 289 n.

Jenkin, Robert, ii. 432.

Jennie, (?) servant of Sir W. Trumbull, i. 17.

Jennings, Mrs., i. 431.

Jersey, 2nd Earl of, *see* Villiers, William.

JERVAS, CHARLES: letters to, i. 239, 243, 244, 295, 300, 303, 346, 370, 376, 410, ii. 23; letters from, i. 226, 244, 262, 310, 311, 312, 331 (with Pope to Parnell), 340, iii. 50 (to Mrs. Caesar); a fabricated letter to him, i. 346 n.; he forwards Pope's letters, i. 491; — his servants, Frank (Waters) and Betty, i. 347, 500 n.; Bridgewater House, Cleveland Court, his residence, in disrepair, Pope writes him, i. 377, ii. 24; J. much in Ireland, i. 346 n., 347, 370, 418, ii. 23, iii. 31; hurries home to get venison from Mrs. Caesar, iii. 50; his absence regretted by Fortescue, Gay, and Lord Burlington, i. 347; takes a letter to

JERVAS, CHARLES (*cont.*)
Parnell to Ireland, i. 348; takes 12 copies of Pope's *Iliad*, vol. iii to Ireland, i. 410; takes copies of Pope's *Works* (1717) to Irish friends, i. 416; — subscribes to Buononcini, ii. 99; lends Gay sheets for Swift, ii. 400; says uncomplimentary things about Broome, ii. 471; possibly aids Mrs. Rackett financially, iii. 6; marries Penelope Hume (1727), iii. 50–51; at Hampton Court for his health, near Pope, iii. 271; goes to Italy for his asthma, iv. 126, 156, 177; Pope dines with him, both men ailing, iv. 193; — J.'s death, iv. 177 n.; bequest to Pope, iv. 217, 225; translation of *Don Quixote*, ii. 23 n., 350, iv. 455; — his house in Cleveland Court, long Pope's town address, i. 170, 186, 194, 198, 266, 267, 377, 449, 475, ii. 18, 200, 313; — is Pope's teacher in painting, i. 170, 174, 177, 200; must paint ladies rather than go (1715) to Devonshire, i. 315; paints Teresa and Martha Blount together, i. 332; his valuable collection of Italian paintings, i. 377; urged by Pope to devote himself to historical painting, i. 377; painted Parnell for Pope, i. 395; J. and Pope at Bellucci's, ii. 99; J.'s crayon portrait of Judith Cowper stolen by Pope, ii. 139 n.; — aids Pope in the *Iliad* subscription, i. 218, 220, 226, 295; designs frontispiece for the *Iliad*, i. 243, 244, 262; scorns Tickell's Book I, i. 296; aids Pope with poetical franks, i. 300; urges Parnell to send his *Frogs* and *Pervigilium*, i. 332; Pope's *Odyssey* delivered to subscribers from J.'s house, ii. 290 n.; does not handle the money for the *Odyssey*, ii. 389; Caryll's copies at J.'s house, iii. 18, 30; J. tries to reconcile Pope and Addison, i. 244; gives Addison subscriptions (to Lucan ?), i. 262; his talk with Addison about Pope, i. 263; arranges meeting of the two, i. 288, 290; summons Pope for Lady Mary Wortley, i. 340; his friendship with Eckersall, i. 226, with Parnell, i. 262, 284; his service to Sir W. Trumbull, i. 281.

Jervas, Penelope (Hume), wife of Charles J., iv. 217 n., 222, 225 n.

Johnson, Mrs., iv. 381 (Warburton's landlady ?).

Johnson, Benjamin, actor, i. 283 n.

Johnson, Charles, dramatist, i. 136.

Johnson, Esther, Swift's 'Stella', ii. 445.

Johnson, Maurice, of Spalding, i. 175 n.

Johnson (or Johnston), Pelham, M.D., iv. 338, 436.

Johnson, R. B., ii. 85.

Johnson, Dr. Samuel: disliked Sir W. Dixey, i. 97 n.; his *Dictionary* cited, i. 233 n.; his *Lives of the Poets* cited on Pope, i. 43 n., ii. 379 n., iii. 360 n.; cited on Dryden, ii. 51 n.; on Sheffield, Duke of Buckingham, ii. 73; on Fenton, ii. 162, 211, iii. 128; on Savage, iv. 418 n.; his translation of Crousaz, iv. 164 n.; Pope tries to help J. to a school, iv. 194.

Johnson, T., piratical printer, iv. 87.

Johnstone, James, Pope's neighbour, ii. 44 n., iii. 157, 272 n.

Jones, Inigo, i. 376, iii. 418.

Jones, J. (Rev.), of Welwyn, iii. 376 n.

Jones, Michael, iv. 183 n.

Jones, R. F., iii. 242 n.

Jonghe, Peter de, father of the Countess of Denbigh, iii. 113 n., iv. 397 n.

Jonson, Ben, i. 71.

Jortin, John, i. 496 n., 497, 514.

Joseph, R. Allen's coachman, iv. 379, 449.

Juvenal, i. 100, 189, 508, iii. 420, iv. 257, 450 n.

Kay (or Key), M.D.: Bethel's Yorkshire physician, iv. 375, 395, 473; interested in bees, iii. 114; likes Pope's urns, iv. 474, 512.

Kelsey, 'Young', i. 262.

Kenna, Mrs., iv. 70.

Kennedy, Sir William, i. 278 n.

Kennet, Basil, ii. 54 n.

Kent, Duke of, *see* Grey, Henry.

KENT, WILLIAM: letters to Lord Burlington (only), iv. 149, 162; intermediary between Burlington and Pope, iii. 67, 518; his recipe for mutton steak, iii. 517; friend of H.

KENT, WILLIAM (*cont.*)
Bethel, iv. 40; often with Pope, iv. 43; his reactions to Lady Burlington's epigrams, iv. 125; — K., Bolingbroke, and Pope in 1738 are 'the suffering trio', iv. 125; K. works at Windsor (Oct. 1738), iv. 141 n., and visits Pope, iv. 141; Pope and K. visit Euston, iv. 149; K. at whist, iv. 150; on a rainy Sunday Pope drags K. to see Richardson's new portraits, iv. 150; K. regrets the long absence of the Burlingtons, iv. 150; — 'calumniated' and named (1739) successor to Jervas as principal painter to the King, iv. 154; dines with Dr. Mead, Lord Oxford, B. Fairfax, St. André, and Pope, iv. 154 n.; sends town news to Burlington, iv. 162–3; enjoys Handel's *Saul*, iv. 163; calls on General Dormer, iv. 163; is now His Majesty's face painter, iv. 220; — Pope (1721) engages K. to engrave Addison's portrait (not used ?) for Addison's *Works*, ii. 81; does plates for Pope's *Odyssey*, ii. 288 n.; a portrait of Pope by him (?), ii. 294 n.; does some plates for Gay's *Fables*, ii. 416; sends proofs to Pope, ii. 533; designs the copper ornaments of Pope's Homer, used also in Buckley's Thuanus, iii. 294 n.; in part designs the Queen's Hermitage, iii. 329; Pope's (lost) Dialogue on the Hermitage, iii. 329; K. designs portico for Pope's villa, iii. 322, 329; Pope jokes about K.'s work at Tottenham, iii. 417; Holkham Hall his masterpiece, iii. 436 n.; his work in Chiswick Gardens, iv. 324; praises the quality of Allen's rustic stone, iv. 450; — K.'s personality: a gourmand, iv. 43, 220–1, called the 'Signior', iv. 43; very umbrageous in his drink, iv. 125; jokingly thought qualified for the living of Eyam, iv. 140, 197; speaks truth to kings, queens, and potentates, iv. 140; he and Pope as good Christians as most parsons, iv. 196–7; jokingly called 'agent and attorney of Sathan', iv. 324; delays painting Pope for H. Bethel: will a copy of Vanloo do ? iv. 500, 509.

Kent co., *see* Bromley (Atterbury), Chiselhurst (Thomas Moore), Dover, Dungeness, Eltham (Edw. Roper), Rochester, Rutupiae, Tunbridge Wells, Wickham.

Ker, John, 1st Duke of Roxburghe, iii. 5.

Kew House, after 1730 used by Frederick, Prince of Wales, iv. 139.

Key, Dr., *see* Kay.

Kielmansegge, Baroness von, i. 427 n.

Kildare, Elizabeth (Jones) Fitzgerald, wife of the 18th Earl of, ii. 17.

King, Sir Peter, ii. 269.

King, William (1650–1729), Archbishop of Dublin, i. 284, ii. 418 n.

King, William (1663–1712), author, i. 373, ii. 56.

King, William, D.D. (1685–1763), Principal of St. Mary Hall, Oxford: Orrery brings him the MS. of Swift's *Four Last Years*, iv. 81; in case of K.'s death, his heirs must return the MS. to Mrs. Whiteway, iv. 240, 248; publishes 'Verses on the Death of Dr. Swift', iv. 130 n.; knows of Pope's projected volume of selected Swift things, iv. 259; — thinks well of Deane Swift, iv. 174; K. is a friend of Orrery, iv. 180, 307, 380; of Lord Marchmont, iv. 228; close friend of Hooke, iv. 327, 353 n.; tries to get Warburton's Oxford degree for him, iv. 357, 437, 442, 444; in his absence Pope occupies K.'s Oxford lodgings, iv. 472; Pope must reply to him, iv. 511.

Kingston, 2nd Duke of, *see* Pierrepont, Evelyn.

Kingston, Surrey, home of William Cleland, iii. 144, 425.

Kirk, John, ii. 176 n.

Kirkman, Francis, i. 474.

Knapton, John (and Paul), booksellers: K. has acquired the unsold copies of Pope's *Works*, ii. (1735), iv. 66; takes in subscriptions for the *Letters* (1737), iv. 41 n.; begged to work off the plates carefully, iv. 58; to send copies to Leake at Bath, iv. 68; special copies for the Allens and Gen. Wade, iv. 74, 82; — is among the publishers of the Swift letters (*Works in Prose*, ii. [1741]), iv. 259 n., 285, 333; pub-

Knapton, John (*cont.*) lishes the Pope–Warburton *Shakespeare* (1747), iv. 393, 417; publishes in 1748 the 'death-bed' Moral Essays, iv. 504 n.; succeeds Gyles, upon Pope's recommendation, as Warburton's bookseller, iv. 370, 373; preferred to C. Bathurst, iv. 371 n., 386, to represent Warburton against Mawhood in Warburton's absence, iv. 402, 410, 417, 421.

KNELLER, SIR GODFREY: letter to, i. 466; letters from, ii. 6, 9, 15, 17; Sir G.'s bad spelling, ii. 15–16; friendship with Pope, i. 172, 417, ii. 9, 15–16; K. subscribes to Buononcini, ii. 99; Pope copies K.'s portraits, i. 88 n., 187 n.; Vertue's engraving of K.'s George I is poor, i. 310; — K. gives Pope a picture, i. 417; Pope's portrait by K., i. 466; his Apollo, Venus, Hercules, for Pope, ii. 17–18; to paint Lady Mary for Pope, ii. 21–22; his methods with sitters, ii. 22, 23; Pope defers sittings by himself, ii. 118; his portrait done for Lord Harcourt, ii. 193; 'imploying the pencil, the prayer of the painter', iii. 160; — arranging to lease or sell a house to Mr. Wortley Montagu, ii. 1, 6, 12, 38; the trouble over Sir Godfrey's monument, ii. 27, 282, 300; Pope's account of Sir Godfrey's last hours, ii. 308–9.

Kneller, Susannah (Cawley), Lady, wife of Sir Godfrey: controversy over Sir Godfrey's tomb, ii. 282, 288 n., 289 n., 301, 306–7, 327; is called 'huge' by Pope, ii. 300.

KNIGHT, ANN (CRAGGS) (*see also* Newsham *and* Nugent): letters to, ii. 485; iii. 408, 425, 430, 490, 511, iv. 17, 30, 38, 47 (with Martha Blount); ill, ii. 456; Pope recommends some 'curiosities' brought from the Indies, ii. 485; ill, iii. 123; should see Stowe, iii. 217; patroness of Walter Harte, iii. 450 n., 511, iv. 90 n.; — dines with Pope and Martha Blount at Fortescue's, iii. 450; her health drunk at Bevis Mount (Peterborow's), iii. 491; her London house overrun with builders, iii. 511; sends his epitaph for John Knight,

KNIGHT, ANN (*cont.*)
iv. 17; invitation to Twickenham cancelled by bad weather, ii. 485–6; invited again, iv. 17; — Pope entertains both Mrs. K. and her sister, Mrs. Elliot, iv. 22; building at Gosfield, iv. 30; the term of her widowhood (2 Oct. 1733–23 Mar. 1736–7), iv. 22 n.; Pope will see Mrs. K. at Marble Hill, but not at dinner, iv. 38, 39; he sends good wishes (Christmas) to Gosfield, iv. 48; she marries Robert Nugent, Mar. 1737, iv. 30 n.

KNIGHT, JOHN: letters to, ii. 254, 456, 462, 484, 485, iii. 67, 122, 202, 217; letter from, ii. 254; he asks Pope for a print of the monument to the Duke of Buckingham, ii. 217; wishes Pope to visit Mrs. Newsham (not yet a widow), ii. 254; — Pope has received £55 from K. for the Craggs monument, ii. 456; the monument completed, ii. 457, 484; the Knights now happily married, ii. 462, 484; they are in Warwickshire, iii. 67–68; Pope recommends Mallet as tutor for young Newsham, iii. 202; writes the epitaph for K., iv. 17 n., 176 n.

Knight, Robert, of South Sea fame: though an outlaw he has made the Queen a 'present', iii. 80; his pardon, iv. 414.

Kyrle, John, 'the Man of Ross', iii. 227, 290–1.

LaBruyère, Jean de, Pope on the *Characters*, ii. 142; quoted by Bolingbroke, ii. 472.

Ladyholt, Sussex, estate of John Caryll, leased at one time to Wm. Pulteney, ii. 392 n.

LaFontaine, Jean de, i. 87 n.

Laguerre, Louis, painter, iii. 268.

Lamb, William, singer in Swift's choir, iv. 135, 176, 180.

LaMotte, Houdart de, translated the *Iliad* into French, i. 307, 485–7, 492–3.

Lancelot, Mrs. Patty (Rolt), Swift's relative, ii. 442, iii. 194, 206.

Lancelot, William, husband of Patty, ii. 400, 445 n., iii. 102, 162.

Landa, Louis A., ii. 68 n., 90 n., iii. 265 n.

Lanesboro, Burlington's Yorkshire estate, iv. 26, &c.

Langallerie, Marquess de, i. 342, 359.

Langford, Emanuel, Preacher in the Charterhouse, ii. 267.

Langley, Bucks., Lord Masham, ii. 196.

Lansdowne, Lord, *see* Granville, George.

LANT, MATTHEW: letter from, ii. 230; will come to Twitnam with Pearse, ii. 230, 232.

LaRochefoucauld, François VI de: Wycherley advised to imitate his maxims, i. 34, 86; Pope hostile to LaRochefoucauld, ii. 333; he is Swift's favourite author, ii. 343, iii. 367, v. 10; mentioned by Bolingbroke, iii. 412.

La Source, near Orleans, France, Bolingbroke's residence, ii. 187, &c.

LaTouche, Mme, iv. 148.

Lawson, Capt., ii. 454.

Lawson, Sir Wilfred, iii. 488.

Layng, Henry, ii. 13, 390, iv. 342 n.

Leadham, I. S., iv. 386 n.

Leake, James, bookseller of Bath, iv. 9, 23 n., 41, 68, 407, 459.

Lechmere, Nicholas, Lord, ii. 85, 443.

Ledbury, Herefordshire, home of Jacob Tonson, iii. 243 n.

Lee, George Henry, 3rd Earl of Lichfield, iv. 347.

Legg, Dr., a priest, chaplain to Mrs. Blount, i. 438.

Legge, William, 1st Earl of Dartmouth, ii. 269.

L'Eglise, wine merchant, iv. 87.

LeGrand, William L., i. 420.

LeGrand, Mrs., ii. 485.

Leibniz, or Leibnitz, Gottfried Wilhelm, iv. 164, 416.

Leicester, 4th Earl of, *see* Sidney, Robert (d. 1702).

Leicester, 1st Earl of (in the 6th creation), *see* Coke, Thomas.

Leicestershire, Market Bosworth, Sir W. Dixey.

Leigh, Theophilus, Vice Chancellor of Oxford, iv. 357 n., 437.

Leighs, Essex, Duchess of Buckingham, ii. 259, 262, 297, 457, 462.

LeNeve, Peter (d. 1729), Norroy king-at-arms, iii. 472.

Lennox, Charles, 2nd Duke of Richmond, ii. 416, iv. 34 n.

Lepell, Mrs. (Nicholas), mother of Lady Hervey, iii. 434.

LEPELL, MARY, dau. of Brig. Nicholas Lepell, marries John, Lord Hervey: letter to her (?), ii. 41 (printed as to the 'Hon. Mrs. H—'); Pope sees her at Hampton Court, i. 427; Gay corresponds with her, i. 438, 450, 513; she stays with the Popes, ii. 26 n.; marries the Hon. John Hervey (later Lord Hervey), ii. 26 n., 41.

L'Estrange, Sir Roger, i. 200, iii. 247.

Letcombe, near Wantage, Berks., i. 234, ii. 65.

Leveson-Gower, John, Lord Gower: considers Fenton as tutor for his son, iii. 24, 37; asked by Pope to aid Dr. Johnson, iv. 194; going to Bath, iv. 413; Lord Privy Seal, iv. 414.

Leveson-Gower, Hon. [William ?], supported the pall at Gay's funeral, iii. 338.

Lewes, Sussex, assizes there, i. 418.

Lewis, David, of Westminster School, edits *Miscellaneous Poems* (1730), i. 149 n., 159, iii. 104–5, 123 n.

Lewis, Erasmus: at the Scriblerus Club, i. 228; neighbour to Dr. Arbuthnot, iii. 194; at Sir W. Wyndham's with Arbuthnot and Gay, ii. 479; on Arbuthnot's imposthume, ii. 326; at Cirencester with Pope and Gay, i. 477, 478, ii. 13; his interest in Matthew Prior, i. 521; — friendship with Pope, i. 238, 253; will dine with Pope and Ford, ii. 283, with Pope and Lord Oxford, iii. 10; at Bath (1728) while Pope is there, ii. 515; Pope's characters of L. and Mrs. L., ii. 518, iii. 285; at Bath also in 1731, iii. 285; Pope lodges with him in Town, iv. 177, 237; L. contributes to support Savage, iv. 331, 344; — L.'s friendship with Swift, ii. 153, 350, v. 18; acts for Swift with Motte, ii. 468, iii. 90, 92, 96, 248, iv. 177; is very ill, iii. 295; death of Mrs. L., iii. 501, iv. 51.

Lewis, William, schoolmate and early publisher of Pope, i. 113; may publish for Gay, i. 130; not to be trusted with MSS. not yet to be published, i. 133; had a letter [lost] from Pope, i. 134; to send *Rape of the Lock* to

Lewis, William (*cont.*) Caryll, i. 144; also 2nd ed. of *Essay on Criticism*, i. 152; also *Cato*, i. 175; fails to send Caryll *The Fan*, i. 210; should have sent *Rape of the Lock*, i. 214; is to send Gay's farce, i. 287; sends Pope's emetic pamphlet, i. 339.

Lewis, Will, of Marston, iv. 508.

Lexington, 2nd Lord, *see* Sutton, Robert.

Leyden Gazette, i. 210.

Licensing Act, forbade tragedies of Brooke and Thomson, iv. 162 n.

Lichfield, 3rd Earl of, *see* Lee, George Henry.

Lichfield, Staffs., iv. 194 n.

Lincolnshire, Cromwell goes thither, i. 70.

Lincoln's Inn Fields Theatre, ii. 352, &c.

Lincombe, home of Lord Archibald Hamilton, iv. 463.

Lindsay, Thomas, Archbishop of Armagh, iii. 21 n.

Lindsey, Dame, i. 260.

LINTOT (or [before 1716] LINTOTT), BERNARD, bookseller: letters to, i. 296 (with Jervas), ii. 15 (from Fenton), 248; letters from, i. 294, 298, ii. 7, 284; his letter to Broome, iii. 489; Steele's letter to L., i. 184, apologizing for Pope's *Narrative* on Dennis; — L.'s 'genius', i. 372, 375; his rivalry with Tonson, i. 372; lived in Sussex, i. 372; his young son Henry, i. 372–3, wishes Pope to translate an ode from Horace while riding to Oxford, i. 373; his checks on translators, i. 373–4; his management of critics, i. 374; hopes Lord Lansdowne's trial will afford good copy, i. 374; L.'s opinion of the Oxford letter, iii. 489; — calls at Twickenham when Pope is out, ii. 59; as a publisher: L. asks Pope's opinion on Hill's *Northern Star*, ii. 36; asks Pope to read a proof sheet, ii. 7; not the publisher of Fenton's *Mariamne*, ii. 145; Pope tries to get L. shares in the Duke of Buckingham's *Works*, ii. 218; publishes the *Poems* (1727) of Walter Harte, ii. 429 n.; publishes Broome's *Poems* (1727), ii. 378 n., 420; disparaged by Fenton, ii. 385;

LINTOT, BERNARD (*cont.*)
in 1735 gives Broome estimate of cost of a new edition, iii. 489; Broome to publish, if with L., at his own expense, iii. 512; L. showed Pope Dennis's attack on *Essay on Criticism* before publication, i. 115 n., 125; Gay's poem to L., i. 134, 153; — L.'s publications for Pope: *Miscellaneous Poems and Translations* (1712), i. 36, 68 n., 95, 109 n., 387 n., ii. 488 n.; a new (4th) edition not yet (1724) projected, ii. 269; the 4th ed. (1727) contains 'The Monster of Ragusa', ii. 334 n., 383; *Windsor Forest*, i. 173 n. 5; *Poems on Several Occasions* (1717), i. 321 n., 410; — Pope's *Iliad*: jokes over L.'s returns from it, i. 240; Broome sends notes (from Eustathius) direct to L., i. 270, 276; publication delayed by long rains, i. 290; L. sends Pope Tickell's *Iliad* I, i. 294; projects a vol. containing Dryden, Tickell, Mainwaring, and Pope on *Iliad* I, i. 298; political crisis harms L.'s sales, i. 294, 298; L. reports on distribution of *Iliad* I, i. 295, 298; to send 4 copies to Jervas, i. 296; one copy for Sir J. Shelley, i. 312; record of the Caryll copies, i. 414; L. fears Pope may delay the trade ed. of *Iliad* I, i. 295; L.'s printer also Tonson's, i. 372; Pope to settle year's accounts (1717) with L., i. 418; L. dilatory with Oxford subscribers, i. 444; reports Broome will again work on Eustathius, i. 497; Pope misses Broome in Town, ii. 48; — Pope's *Odyssey*: Broome not to send either text or notes to L. direct, ii. 211; L. normally Broome's publisher, has not yet agreed for the *Odyssey*, ii. 211; bargains for the *Odyssey* like a scoundrel and a fool, ii. 211, 214; permitted to use cheaper paper, ii. 217; urged to fine presswork, ii. 217; and so now again Pope's bookseller, ii. 218; is to send printed notes to Broome for revision, ii. 248; L. himself transcribed *Odyssey* XIV for Pope to work on, ii. 284; his annoying and unscrupulous advertisements of the *Odyssey*, ii. 285; angry that Tonson advertises the Shakespeare as for

LINTOT, BERNARD (*cont.*)
Tonson's benefit, ii. 286; — Pope thinks L. a scoundrel, ii. 287, 290, and a fool, ii. 288; L.'s advertisements undercut the cost of the *Odyssey* in Pope's subscription, ii. 288 n., 290; Broome's notes now sent direct to L., ii. 340; L. delivers copies of the *Odyssey* to subscribers, ii. 389; he indulges in malicious and false gossip, Pope says, ii. 431–2; blamed for estranging Broome from Pope, ii. 470–1; L. alleged to have said Pope urged Dennis to attack *Cato*, ii. 520; — Pope wants a spy to find out if L. sells *Pope Alexander's Supremacy*, iii. 33; did not tell Pope that Broome was in Town, iii. 199; L. to let Buckley have the *Odyssey* copper ornaments for his Thuanus, iii. 294; Pope will never employ L. again, iii. 294; L. (1735) prints small 8vo *Works*, vol. i for Pope, iii. 489; ill of asthma, iv. 2, his death, iv. 4 n.
LINTOT, HENRY, bookseller, son of · Bernard: letters to, iv. 240, 333; letter from, iv. 222; partner of his father after 1730, i. 372 n.; copyrights to Pope's early things in question, iv. 224; his claims on the *Essay on Criticism*, iv. 501 n.; on the *Key to the Lock*, iv. 324, 335–6; obscure difficulties between Pope and H. L., iv. 335–6; L. in vol. iii. of Pope's *Works* (1736) uses pieces copyrighted by Motte, iv. 324; sells Gilliver (and so Osborne) illegally *Iliads* in 4to, iv. 222–3; Pope consults N. Cole about the copyrights, iv. 223; — Pope's memoranda *in re Odyssey* on a letter, ii. 288 n.; L. says he has a receipt concerning the *Iliad*, iv. 394; L. is asked to sell his one-third copyright in *The Dunciad* to no one but Pope, iv. 240, 259, 333; Pope sues in Chancery to recover copyright in *The Dunciad*, iv. 394, 425 n., 455; L. does not reply to request for conference with Pope and counsel (George Arbuthnot), iv. 388, 394; Bowyer asked to note whatever L. may say about copyrights, iv. 502.
Litton, Mr., i. 89.

Livy, Titus, Roman historian, ii. 150, 220.

Lloyd's Evening Post, i. 436 n.

Locke, John, iii. 433.

Lockier, Francis, iii. 132.

LOCKYER, CHARLES, accountant in the South Sea Company: letters to, ii. 75 (from Gay), 91; to transfer Gay's South Sea stock to Pope, ii. 75; to pay the dividend, ii. 91.

Loftis, John, i. 131 n., 152 n.

Logg (or Legg), Dr., a priest, i. 438.

Londesburgh, York, *see* Lanesboro, iii. 323.

London, Bishop of (Gibson, Edmund), ii. 269.

London Daily Post, iv. 12 n., 222 n.

London Evening Post: account of the fire in the Cottonian Library, iii. 240; verses on Lady Margaret Harley's illness, iii. 245 n.; letter from Atterbury to Pope, iii. 246 n.; reports illness of Peterborow, iii. 342 n.; Swift's *Works* advertised, iii. 429; Pope reported ill at Bath (wrongly), iii. 436 n.; — Pope and T. Cooper offer reward for sight of any original letters Curll has, iii. 468; Cooper has entered Pope's letters in Stationers' Hall, iii. 472 n.; announces the death of Tonson jr., iii. 513 n.; comment on the Knight monument, iv. 17 n.; Duchess of Buckingham goes to Spa, iv. 21 n.; Curll advertises for new letters, iv. 50 n.; note on Bolingbroke's arrival from France, iv. 109 n.; — Prince of Wales's visit to Cirencester, iv. 138 n.; Fortescue's assignment in assizes, summer of 1739, iv. 183 n.; Osborne advertises his 1st eds. of Pope's *Iliad*, iv. 222 n.; note on the death of Mrs. Price, iv. 350 n.

London Gazette: on the Peace, i. 61; A. Philips advertises for contributions for a miscellany, i. 276 n.; on the chronology of the Wortley Montagu journey to Constantinople, i. 387 n.; prints Proposals for Pope's *Odyssey*, ii. 285; announces delivery to subscribers to the *Odyssey*, ii. 290; announces Pope's intended authorized ed. of his letters, iii. 473 n.; on lotteries for the bridge, iii. 518 n.; adver-

London Gazette (cont.)
tises Pope's *Letters* (1737), iv. 41; Pope explains in an advertisement the delay in publishing his *Letters*, iv. 65 n.; advertises for subscribers, iv. 65 n.

London Journal, attacks Pope's *Odyssey*, ii. 339, 377 n.

LONDON, environs, streets, theatres, &c. [*The indexing here is eclectic. Where several letters are directed to the same address, normally only one occurrence is noted. Where no reference to page is added to the name of the addressee, the reader should consult entries made under the name of the person mentioned. The London entries as a whole may serve to indicate where in the vaguely defined London 'area' Pope's friends and publishers were to be found.*] — Aldersgate Street, where Swift took coach for Chester, ii. 452 n.; Arlington Street, William Pulteney (1724), ii. 247; Hugh Bethel (his sister's house), iii. 519; Arundell Street, James Pearse, ii. 230; Ashburnham House, iii. 240 n., the Cottonian Library; — Basinghall Street, N. Cole, iv. 336; Battersea, James Craggs, ii. 1; Battersea House, Bolingbroke and Marchmont, iv. 436, 456; Bell Yard near Lincoln's Inn, W. Fortescue, ii. 242; Berkeley Row, Berkeley Square, Pope purchases a lease (1744), iv. 508 n.; Berry (Bury) Street, St. James's, The Greyhound, Charles Ford (1725), ii. 283; Blue Ball, Great Wild Street, near Drury Lane, Mr. Naylor (for H. Cromwell), i. 69; Blue Periwig, next to the George Tavern, Pall Mall, Charles Ford (1714), i. 249; Bolton Street, Piccadilly, the Blount ladies (1717-38), i. 414; Lord Peterborow (1722), ii. 124 (Pope lies there); (1731), iii. 160; Bond Street, the Duchess of Hamilton (1717), i. 405; Bridges Street, John Rich and Drury Lane Theatre, i. 71; Bridgewater House, Cleveland Court, Charles Jervas, i. 227; Buckingham House, the Duke of Buckingham gives a party for Matthew Prior, i. 521; Burlington Gardens, Piccadilly, Duke of Queens-

LONDON (*cont.*)

berry and John Gay, iii. 69; Burlington House, Piccadilly, John Gay, ii. 153; Bury Street (*see also* Berry), The Golden Chair, Swift's town address in 1726, ii. 372; Button's Coffee-house, W. Whiston, i. 185, 187; Philips's rod, i. 229; Pope there, i. 294; reaction there to his *Iliad*, i. 305–6; — Castle Yard, George Arbuthnot, iv. 385; Catherine Street, Strand, Jacob Tonson's shop, ii. 215; Charing Cross, The Blue Periwig, Mr. Robinson, ii. 106; Charing Cross General Post Office, Mr. Robinson, ii. 148; Drummond the banker, iv. 365; Hampton coach leaves from there, iv. 520; Charles Street (St. James's Square?), Lady Mary Wortley Montagu (1716), i. 338; Charterhouse, ii. 267–9; Chartreux (Charterhouse) Square, Samuel Buckley's business address, iv. 66; Cheapside, flower market, iii. 123; Chequer Inn, Charing Cross, coaches leave there for Chiswick, iii. 87; Cleveland Court, St. James's, Charles Jervas, i. 174 n., Francis Waters, Jervas's servant, i. 501; Pope's town address, ii. 200; Viscount Townshend, ii. 290; Cockpit, Whitehall, James Craggs (1719), ii. 16; Conduit Street, Mrs. Cornish, iii. 198; Cork Street, Dr. Arbuthnot (1733), iii. 339; E. Lewis, iv. 165; Covent Garden, Crookshanks, ii. 224; Wright the goldsmith, ii. 72, the Wortley Montagus (1719), ii. 12; Covent Garden Theatre, James Thomson takes a play there, iv. 166, 167; — Devereux Court, Tom's Coffee-house, W. Fortescue, ii. 217; Devonshire Street, 'near Bloomsbury', Pope's school, iii. 359–60; Doctors' Commons, J. Watson's shop near by, iv. 87; Dover Street, Dr. Arbuthnot (1714), i. 251; William Chetwynd (frequent host to Bolingbroke), iv. 171, 2nd Earl of Oxford, ii. 90, &c.; John Knight (and Mrs. Ann [Craggs] Knight), ii. 254; R. Nugent, iv. 233; from Dover Street and Piccadilly at 9 a.m. coaches leave for Chiswick, iii. 87; Downing Street, Viscount Harcourt, ii. 193; Drury

LONDON (*cont.*)

Lane Theatre: *see under* Drury; Drury Lane, 'nymphs' there, i. 47; Duke Street, near Lincoln's Inn Fields, Hatton the clockmaker, i. 465; Duke Street, Westminster, Thomas Gage, i. 309; Matthew Prior, ii. 30; the Earl of Orrery, iv. 130; Durham Yard, J. Brinsden, iv. 354; — East Street and Red Lion Street (corner of), Mr. Eustas, Mrs. Rackett, iv. 203; Euston, 'great works' there in 1738, iv. 149; — Fleet Street, W. Broome stays there, ii. 366; L. Gilliver at Homer's Head over against St. Dunstan's Church, iv. 41 n.; Mead & Co., ii. 183; White Horse Inn (for Twickenham Coach), iv. 506; Frith Street, Mr. Moore (Lady Trumbull's agent), ii. 234; Fulham, Rev. Ralph Bridges (at the Bishop of London's), i. 41, 45; — Genoa Arms, ii. 304; Gerrard Street, for the Stansted Carrier for Ladyholt, i. 419; Golden Ball, 2nd Terrace in St. James's Street, R. Digby, ii. 232; Gray's Inn, Edw. Bedingfield, i. 141; Mr. Mackenzie, iii. 30 n.; Gray's Inn Gate, Jacob Tonson, i. 17; Great Ormond Street, N. Pigott's son, iii. 173 n.; Great Queen Street, Sir Godfrey Kneller, ii. 7; Green Canister in New North Street, Bloomsbury, Henry Rackett (and his mother), iii. 340, 421; Guy's Hospital, its architecture disapproved, ii. 525; — Hammersmith, Swift and the Lancelots, ii. 448; Mrs. Weston, i. 173; Hampstead, Richard Steele, i. 145; Hanover Square, Duke of Montrose and D. Mallet, iii. 144, 189; Lord Cobham, iv. 185, the Earl of Denbigh, iv. 397 n.; Haymarket Theatre, i. 71, 407 (masquerades); Henrietta Street, Covent Garden, the Allens housed there by Mrs. Van Elson, iv. 509; Holborn, over against Gray's Inn, shop of Fletcher Gyles, iv. 237; Holborne Row, Lincoln's Inn Fields, Jonathan Richardson, ii. 298; Hungerford Market, Jacob Robinson's shop, iv. 216; Hungerford Stairs, The Globe, for Holmes the Twickenham waterman, iv. 475;

LONDON (*cont.*)

Hyde Park, military encampments, i. 308, ii. 116; Hyde Park Corner, rendezvous for out-of-town trips, i. 312; — Inner Temple, Harcourt Buildings, W. Fortescue, ii. 104; Lant & Pearse, ii. 230 n.; Islington, a 'soft retreat' in summer, iii. 123; John Street, Westminster, Thomas Cooke's address, ii. 520; — Kensington, i. 434–5; King Street (Covent Garden ?), Daniel Arthur, i. 155 n.; King Street, St. James's Square, Teresa Blount, i. 265; King's Head, Duke Street near Lincoln's Inn Fields, Tho. Thorold, for H. Cromwell, i. 82; — Leicester Fields, Sir William and Lady Judith Trumbull, ii. 214, 245, and Fenton, ii. 270; Leicester Fields, Suffolk Street, W. Aikman, ii. 294 n.; Lincoln's Inn Fields, William Murray, iii. 236 n.; Lord Talbot, iv. 335; Lincoln's Inn Fields Theatre, Fenton's *Mariamne*, ii. 105 n.; Little Britain, Samuel Buckley, iii. 70; Little Russell Street (J. Tooker), v. 4; Ludgate Street, The Crown, J. & P. Knapton's shop, iv. 41 n.; — Marlborough Street, Lady Gerard, iv. 488; Middle Temple Gate, B. Lintot, iii. 489; Moorfields, Bedlam, ii. 3; — New Bond Street, J. Brindley's shop, iv. 41 n.; Mrs. Caesar, iii. 509; Wm. Lancelot, ii. 445 n.; Newgate Street, The Greyhound, Pigott the druggist, ii. 77; Norfolk Street, Strand, J. Drummond (East India Co.), ii. 246; — Ormond Street, Queen Square, Jonathan Richardson, iii. 352; Oxford Chapel, Lord Cornbury lived near it, iii. 452; — Painters Tavern, where Wycherley fell down stairs, i. 58; Pall Mall, Bolingbroke, ii. 399 n., 410; Tully's Head, R. Dodsley's shop, i. 467 n., iv. 41 n.; C. Ford, at Mr. Hoyes's at the Blue Periwig over against the Coco Trees, ii. 283; G. Lyttelton, iv. 238, 368; Pall Mall Coffee-house, T. Parnell (1714), i. 253; Prince's Sadler's, J. Stopford, ii. 422; Viscountess Scudamore, iii. 27; Park Place, Westminster, C. Ford, iv. 137; Parsons Green, Lord Peterborow, ii.

LONDON (*cont.*)

183, iii. 169; Peckham, Edmund Curll, iii. 494; Petty France, Aaron Hill, iii. 371; Piccadilly, Burlington House (Lord and Lady Burlington, Handel, John Gay, *et al.*); the Black Bear (coaches for Southampton from there), iii. 429–30; Lord Peterborow, ii. 285 n.; Poland Street, near Golden Square, Mrs. Caesar, ii. 231; Pope's Head, Rose Street, Covent Garden, Curll's shop, iii. 475; Princes Court, near Story's, Westminster, Samuel Buckley, iii. 294; Prince William Tavern, where Moore Smythe was caned, iii. 114 n.; Pudding Lane, near the Tower, Mr. Ruth's, where Capt. Francis may be heard of, iv. 219; — Queen Square, Alderman Barber and his 'relique', Mrs. Dufkin, iv. 367; Jonathan Richardson, ii. 61; Queen Street, Mr. Pond, iv. 352; — Rathbone Place, near Soho, James Brinsden, iv. 209, and Charles Brinsden, iv. 456 n.; Red Lion Street, Holborn, against East Street, John Hughes, ii. 29; Red Lion Street, Bloomsbury, Lord Harcourt, ii. 175; Rose Street, Covent Garden, E. Curll, iii. 460; Russell Street, Covent Garden, W. Lewis, i. 210; — St. Albans Street, Duchess of Hamilton, i. 439; St. James's Palace, Dr. Arbuthnot, i. 216 n.; St. James's Park, i. 338; Buckingham House, iv. 472; St. James's Place, Little Cleveland Court, Charles Ford (1728 ff.), iv. 137 n.; St. James's Square, Lord Bathurst, ii. 117; St. James's Street, R. Digby, ii. 232; St. James's, near Daniel Pulteney's house, ii. 502; St. John's Gate, Edward Cave (*Gent. Mag.*), iii. 499; St. Martin's-in-the-Fields, Allen married there (1737), iv. 68 n.; St. Paul's, Covent Garden, Wycherley buried there, i. 86 n.; St. Peter's Hill, J. Wright's printing house, iv. 58; St. Thomas's Hospital, W. Cheselden, surgeon, iii. 140 n.; Saracen's Head, trunks forwarded to Pulham from there (Fenton), iii. 44; Savile Row, Dr. Simon Burton, iv. 499; Soho, Mrs. Drelincourt, iii. 119; Spring Garden, Charing Cross, W. Cheselden, iv. 234 n.;

LONDON (*cont.*)

Spring Garden, Vauxhall, H. Cromwell and Sapho, i. 57; Stockwell (1 mile from 'Foxhall'), N. Rowe, i. 187; Strand, Jacob Robinson, bookseller, iv. 87; Jacob Tonson, ii. 81; Stretton Street, Lady Sarah Cowper, ii. 497; — The Temple, Dr. William King, iv. 307 n.; 'Temple Bar to St. James's' the area (Swift says) of Pope's satire, iv. 115; Temple Bar, B. Lintot, i. 419, B. Motte, iii. 9; Tom's Coffeehouse, Devereux Court, W. Fortescue, ii. 48; The Tower, Robert, Earl of Oxford, i. 307 n., ii. 71 n.; Atterbury, ii. 151; Tower Hill, S. Bethel, iv. 67; Tully's Head in Pall Mall, R. Dodsley, iv. 210; Tyburn Road, Vere Street, John Michael Rysbrack, ii. 298; — Warwick Court, Mrs. Johnson: Warburton's lodging, iv. 381; Warwick Lane, James Roberts's shop, iii. 34; Welbeck Street, the Blount ladies after 1738, iv. 113; Westminster Abbey, Samuel Butler's tomb, ii. 76; Rowe's epitaph, ii. 25; Prior's funeral, ii. 84–85; Atterbury's tomb, ii. 114; Thomas Moore (the Cloisters), ii. 201; The Deanery, Atterbury, ii. 73, &c.; Westminster Bridge, lottery for (in 1739), iii. 518 n.; the Commissioners of the Bridge headed by Lord Burlington, iv. 82; Westminster School, Henry Lintot (1716), i. 372; John Bowack, writing master, iv. 82; Whitefriars, Wm. Bowyer jr., iv. 338; Whitehall, office of the *Gazette*, Charles Ford, i. 238; Gay's lodgings (to 1729), ii. 392, iii. 69; White Horse Inn, Fleet Street, Twickenham coach leaves there about 2 p.m., iv. 346; William's Coffee-house, near St. James's, Gibbs and Pope meet there, ii. 298; Will's Coffee-house, i. 11; revolution at, i. 288, 290; Wimbledon, *see* Sarah, Duchess of Marlborough, iv. 358, &c.; Woolwich, the arsenal there, iii. 322; — York Buildings, Steele's Music Room, i. 131 n.; Aaron Hill owns stock in the buildings, iv. 94 n.; London: its walls like those of Jericho ready to fall, iv. 441; 'the land of perdition', iv. 423.

Long, Captain, iv. 353.

Long, Miss, elopes (1729) with young Caesar, iii. 56 n.

Long, the Misses, iv. 265.

Long, Anne, ii. 439 n.

Longleat, Lord Lansdowne (1714), i. 261.

Longueville, Charles, ii. 76.

Longueville, William, ii. 76.

'Longus', *Daphnis and Chloe*, iv. 525.

Lord Privy Seal, *see* Pierrepont, Evelyn, Duke of Kingston.

Lords, Journals of the House of, iv. 266 n.

Lorraine, Duke of, iii. 237 n.

Lorraine, Paul, i. 52, ii. 350.

Louis XIV, of France, i. 61, 208 n., 312, 514, iii. 484 (his grandsons).

Louis XV, of France, ii. 318, 341.

Louisa, Princess, dau. of King George II, ii. 455.

Lovel, Lord, *see* Coke, Thomas.

Lovell, Sir S., i. 78 n., 409.

Lucan (Marcus Annaeus Lucanus): criticized, i. 104; translated by Tickell, i. 262; quoted by Pope, i. 371; his death, iii. 420; Rowe's translation attacked by Cromwell, i. 108–9; profited by Virgil's work, ii. 219.

Lucian, i. 353, ii. 23.

Lucilius, Gaius, ii. 219.

Lucretius (Titus Lucretius Carus): cited by Pope, i. 48, ii. 19; model for the *Essay on Man*, iii. 433; quoted by Fenton, ii. 487; by Lyttelton, iv. 49; translated by G. Sewall (?), i. 374 n.

Ludlow, Edmund, iii. 107.

Luke, St., as a painter, i. 187, 189.

Lumley, Henry, Lord, son of the 1st Earl of Scarborough, i. 89.

Lumley, Richard, 2nd Earl of Scarborough, iii. 15, iv. 225, 226.

Lyddel, Richard, iii. 110 n.

Lynn, Lord, *see* Townshend, Charles, later 3rd Viscount Townshend.

Lyra, Nicholas de, i. 403.

LYTTELTON, GEORGE, later Lord Lyttelton: letters to, iv. 116, 142, 208, 348, 367; letters from, iv. 46, 48, 109, 138, 170, 368; lines by Pope possibly addressed to him, iii. 226 n.; nephew of Lord Cobham, iii. 244 n.; visits Pope with L.'s cousin R. West, iii.

LYTTELTON, GEORGE (*cont.*)
480; affectionate family relationships, iv. 116; his father's ill health (1741) precludes invitations to Hagley, iv. 349; — L. at Bath: happy (1736) there with Burlington, iv. 43; Pope's use of an amanuensis alarms him there, iv. 46; now healthy, iv. 46, 48; at Bath in 1738: to see Hooke there, iv. 145; returning to Town, iv. 149; at Bath in 1740, iv. 281; his politics, iv. 138–9, 261, 342 n.; court life vs. quiet, iv. 368; — L. urges Pope to exercise his real influence over the Prince of Wales, iv. 138–9; *Common Sense* sponsored by L., iv. 209 n.; his esteem for Bolingbroke, iv. 369; friend of Pope from 1730 on, iii. 244 n.; drinks Allen's health with Pope and Broxholme, iv. 157–8; sends service to friends by Pope, iv. 47; Bolingbroke's illness keeps Pope from seeing L. (1738), iv. 117; they may meet at Stowe, iv. 117; — L. for the Prince offers Pope urns, iv. 170; L. takes Pope from Stowe to Hagley (1739), iv. 185; L. cannot come to Twickenham as desired, iv. 348; he hopes that in 1742 Pope and Lord Bathurst will visit Hagley, iv. 349; esteemed by both Bolingbroke and Pope, iv. 367–8; his last visit to Pope, iv. 525; — L.'s relations with Swift: Pope praises him to Swift, iv. 134–5; L. recommends a place for W. Lamb in Swift's choir, iv. 134–5; Swift asks that Prince Frederick nominate M'Aulay for the Irish Parliament, iv. 175; L. eager to help M'Aulay, iv. 178, 180; L. praises *Leonidas*, iv. 72 n.; has read in MS. Pope's Dialogue ii of *1738*, iv. 109; L.'s *Henry II* (4 vols., 1767–71), will take 2 or 3 years, iv. 348; Warburton reads parts of it in MS., iv. 348; Pope introduces Warburton to L., iv. 238; L. and Lord Marchmont, iv. 251, 271 n.

Lyttelton, Sir Thomas, father of George, Lord Lyttelton: Pope uses his office in the Admiralty as an address for letters, iii. 70; Pope wishes to send him pineapples, iv. 117; Sir Thomas is of the 'old patriot' group,

Lyttelton, Sir Thomas (*cont.*)
iv. 143; Sir Thomas comes from Hagley (1739) to Adderbury with Pope, iv. 189; Pope was with him at Hagley, iv. 185, 190; retires in bad health in 1741, iv. 349.

M'Aulay (or MacAulay), Alexander: wishes nomination from Prince of Wales for the Irish Parliament, iv. 175, 178, 180, 184; may bring Pope additional letters from Swift and Mrs. Whiteway, iv. 241, 248, 257; might also bring the 'clandestine volume,' iv. 275; but M. is not able to come, iv. 307, 320.

Macclesfield, 1st Earl of, *see* Parker, Thomas.

Mace, Mrs. Charles (Pope's aunt), i. 433 n.

Mace, Rev. Charles, i. 433 n.

Macfarland, Mrs., who shot her would-be lover, i. 367.

Mack, Maynard, ii. 166 n., 168 n., iv. 310 n., 384 n., 439 n.

Mackay, Donald, iv. 93 n.

Mackenzie, Frances (Herbert), wife of the 4th Earl of Seaforth, mother of Lady Mary Caryll, ii. 60; lives in Twickenham at times, i. 144 n., ii. 78; Mrs. Pope's favourite neighbour, ii. 117; away from Twickenham, ii. 173.

Mackenzie, Kenneth, 4th Earl of Seaforth: his dau., Lady Mary, marries John Caryll, jr., i. 144 n.; his title changed in list of subscribers, i. 221.

Mackenzie, Mr. (unidentified), iii. 30.

Mackenzie, Kenneth, husband of Lady Carrington, indebted to Mrs. Rackett, iii. 39.

Mackenzie, Lady Mary, marries John Caryll, jr., i. 144 n.; *see* Caryll, Lady Mary.

Mackenzie, William, 5th Earl of Seaforth, ii. 392.

Mackenzie, —, *see* McKrie.

McKillop, A. D., iii. 86, iv. 335 n.

MacKinnon, Daniel, i. 308 n.

McKRIE, —(or Mackenzie): letter from, i. 443, regretting his inability to help Mr. Boden to a ship.

Macray, W. D., i. 294 n., 421 n.

Macro, Dr., ii. 399 n.

Macrobius, Ambrosius Theodosius, i. 90, 116, 225.

Madan, Falconer, ii. 93 n., 136, 139, 195 n.

Madan, Mrs. (Capt.) Martin (*née* Judith Cowper), ii. 262; *see also* Cowper, Judith.

Madden, Samuel, his thanks to the dramatist Southerne, iii. 25 n.

MADDISON, G., letter from, i. 404, inviting Pope, for the Duchess of Hamilton, to music on the Thames, i. 404.

Maggs Bros., their catalogues cited, iii. 403 n., iv. 229.

Maids of Honour: a letter, supposedly to one of them from Pope, i. 380; her supposed reply, i. 380–1; sad life of such Maids, i. 427.

Mainwaring, Arthur, reads Pope's Pastorals in MS., i. 17.

Maittaire, Michael, left out of *Dunciad* at Lord Oxford's request, ii. 496.

Malebranche, Nicolas, iii. 433.

Malherbe, François de, i. 25, 57.

MALLET, DAVID: letter to, iii. 65, 82, 82, 87, 143, 157, 177, 189, 221, 329, 344, 357, 408, iv. 167, 209, 331, 451, 453; letters from Orrery to M., iv. 522; from M. to Orrery, iv. 522, 523; letters from M. to Pope, iii. 86, 421, 457, 484; letters from M. descriptive of travels, iii. 408, 421–3 (South Wales), 430; sketches of Paris and Geneva, iii. 457–8; of Hanover, iii. 484; — increasing friendship with Pope, iii. 1, 457–8, 511, iv. 451; invited to Chiswick by Burlington, iii. 87; knows Walter Harte, iii. 408; his kindness to A. Hill, iii. 189, iv. 99 n., 151, 152; helps raise money for Savage's support, iv. 331, 418; — is tutor in the family of the Duke of Montrose, iii. 143 n., 189, 218 n.; to be tutor to James Newsham (Mrs. Knight's son), iii. 218, 426; ill at Mrs. Knight's in Dover Street, iii. 344–5, on the Continent with Newsham (1735), iii. 457 n.; trains young Newsham admirably, iv. 30–31; — his friendship with Orrery, shown in letters about Pope's last days, iv. 518 n., 522–3, 524; promises Orrery an account of Pope's will, iv. 524; his

MALLET, DAVID (*cont.*)
friendship with Bolingbroke, Pope arranges early meetings, iii. 177, 330, 358, 408; publishes Bolingbroke's *Works* after B.'s death, iii. 433 n.; — M.'s works: *Eurydice*, aided by Pope, iii. 1, 65 n., 82, 86, 157–8; performed Feb. 1731, iii. 177 n.; *Of Verbal Criticism*, iii. 66 n.; Savage sees it first and tells Pope of it, iii. 66; ready to be published and dedicated to Pope, iii. 327; publication deferred by Pope because of Theobald, iii. 357; poem approved by Pope, iii. 329–30; *Mustapha*, iv. 145; now completed, iv. 151; Pope declines to do the epilogue, iv. 132; Prince Frederick interests himself in *Mustapha*, iv. 158; performed Feb. 1739, iv. 165 n.; M.'s troubles with Fleetwood, iv. 159, 162; M. seems to be charged with plagiarism, iv. 210; M.'s epitaph for W. Aikman, iii. 222; possibly edited Algernon Sidney's letters (1742), iii. 328 n.

Man, Jenny (at Bath), i. 260.

Manilius, Marcus, ii. 487.

Manly, Mary, named to Peterborow as possibly 'Sappho', iii. 352.

Manners, John, 3rd Duke of Rutland, i. 296, iii. 511.

Manners, Lady Katherine, ii. 416.

Mannock, William: account of, ii. 29 n.; gave anecdotes to Spence, ii. 29 n.; chaplain and cousin to the Racketts, i. 426.

Mansfield, 1st Earl of, *see* Murray, William.

Mansfield, Earls of, still have Pope's portrait of Betterton, i. 88 n., 187 n., 189.

Mapledurham, Berks., *see* Mrs. Lister Blount, Michael, Teresa, *and* Martha Blount.

Marble Hill, Twickenham, home of Henrietta Howard, Countess of Suffolk, after about 1724; process of construction, ii. 178 n., 183; done except for the roof, ii. 257; the gardens, ii. 197, 213, 292; trouble over title to the land, iii. 34–35; many guests there after the wedding (to Hon. G. Berkeley) in 1735, iii. 474.

Marchmont, Earls of, *see* Hume,

Marchmont, Earls of (*cont.*)
Alexander (2nd Earl) *and* Hugh (3rd Earl).
Marchmont Papers, iv. 341 n., 419.
Marcus Aurelius, ii. 116 n., 440.
Marino (i.e. Giovanni Battista Marini), i. 110.
Marion, Elias, i. 35 n.
Market Bosworth, Leicester, i. 97 n.
Market Hill (Ireland), ii. 522 n.
Marlborough, Duke of, *see* Churchill, John, 1st Duke; Sarah, his Duchess, and Godolphin-Churchill, Henrietta, 2nd Duchess.
Marlborough, Wilts., its rocky roads, iv. 156.
Marot, Clement, i. 90.
MARRIOT, Mrs., or her dau. Elizabeth: letters to, i. 149, 180, 205, 211, 277; in a letter Pope borrows from Voiture, iii. 495; Pope dreams of Betty, i. 181; flatters her, i. 205; sends *Rape of the Lock* to, i. 211; apologizes for 'absurdities' to, i. 227; thinks of 'Mrs. Marriots', i. 270; they come to Town, i. 276; Pope sends greetings to, i. 297, 322; they move to Town, ii. 3; Pope not asked to visit them, i. 298; to call on Betty at the Vyners', i. 476; other mentions, ii. 19, 41.
Marriot, John ('Jack'): account of, i. 275 n. 5; presumptive author of the 'hermaphrodite' letter, i. 277–9; as curate at Easthampstead behaves well, ii. 340.
Marryat, Thomas, betrays Pope's dissent from judges in Cave's poetry contest, iii. 499 n.
Marseilles, Bishop of, iii. 456, v. 15.
Marsham, Sir J., Delany wishes to correct his views on chronology, iii. 212.
Marshgate, Surrey, J. Knapton, iv. 285.
Marston, Somerset, the Earl of Orrery, iv. 81.
Martial (Marcus Valerius Martialis), quoted by Pope, i. 42, 101, 432 n., ii. 23, iii. 115.
Martland, Mrs., called Sappho by Cromwell, i. 57 n.
Martyn, John, helps write the *Grub-street Journal*, iii. 240 n.

Masham, Abigail, Lady, iii. 456; her son gets legacy from Disney, iii. 249; the son marries, iv. 51; her death, v. 14.
Masham, Samuel, 1st Lord, v. 18.
Masson, John, i. 26.
Maubrun, —, his epic, ii. 79.
MAWHOOD, COLLET: letters to, iv. 409, 416; executor of the will of F. Gyles, Warburton's bookseller, iv. 379 n., 380; difficulties over Warburton's copyrights, iv. 385, 388; Pope worries because Warburton is not paid, iv. 393, 398, 400, 402; no pretence for Warburton's paying the executor's own fees, iv. 409; M. still dilatory, iv. 410, 416, 417; settlement reached, iv. 425 n.
Mawley, Salop, ii. 11.
Mawson's New Buildings, Chiswick, Pope's home, 1716–18, i. 339.
Maximus Tyrius, ii. 248.
Mead, Richard, M.D.: Pope dines with him, ii. 529, iv. 154 n.; M.'s patronage of Buckley's Thuanus, ii. 471, v. 6; a friend of Mrs. Caesar, iii. 331; to have a portrait of Pope by Richardson, iv. 91; Pope consults him, iv. 484; illness keeps Pope from waiting on M., iv. 487; — M. gives medical advice: to H. Bethel, iv. 338, 375, 512; to Fortescue, iii. 453; to Harcourt's grandson, ii. 115; to Lady Margaret Harley, iii. 245 n., 278; to Pope, iv. 200, 202, 205, 206, 338, 461, 467, 499, 522.
MEAD & CO., bankers (goldsmiths): letter to, asking payment of £12, ii. 183; will pay Broome his £100, ii. 389, 396; will pay Dr. Towne, ii. 424.
Mee, or My, Mr., keeper of Ladyholt Park, i. 465.
Ménage, Gilles de, i. 18, 25.
Mencius, cited by Bolingbroke, iii. 413.
Mendez, Moses, withdraws support from Savage, iv. 418.
Mennes, Sir John, iii. 108.
Mercurius Rusticus, cited on Swift's family history, iv. 174.
Meredith, General, Swift at his father's funeral, iii. 286–7.
Merrill, John, a subscriber to the *Iliad*, i. 296.

Methuen, Sir Paul: praised by Pope, i. 275; Pope's letters to Lady Mary forwarded by his [Foreign] Office, i. 405; talks of Lady Mary, i. 470; has a sketch of Cortona's Scipio and the Captive, iv. 20.

Mews, Betty, Battaglia's mistress, iii. 87.

Meyerstein, E. H. W., ii. 76 n.

Michael Angelo, Lord Lovel's poor opinion of, iv. 163.

Middlesex, Earl of, *see* Sackville, Charles (later 2nd Duke of Dorset).

Middlesex co., *see* Bushey Park, Chiswick, Marble Hill, Cranford, Dawley, Fulham, Hammersmith, Hampstead, Hampton Court, Isleworth, Kew House, Staines, Twickenham, Whitton.

Middleton, Viscount, *see* Broderick, Alan, ii. 66.

Middleton, Conyers: incorporated at Oxford, iii. 111; at Wimpole, iii. 147; relations with Pope, iii. 216, 217 n.; iv. 400; M.'s hostility to Bentley, iii. 267 n.; his 'Letter to Waterland', iii. 280; Warburton writes to him, iv. 236 n.; M.'s dispute with Warburton, iv. 369.

Middleton (Middleton Stoney), a seat of the Duke of Queensberry, ii. 416, iii. 69.

Midhurst, Sussex, Caryll's place, Ladyholt, i. 152.

Mildmay, Carew Hervey, iv. 395.

Milford-Haven, iii. 422 (described by Mallet).

Millar, A., iv. 425.

Miller, James, iii. 173.

MILLER, PHILIP: letter to, iii. 451; foreman in Chelsea Garden, iii. 451 n.; his Dictionaries, iv. 459.

Mills, Mr., friend of Wm. Kent, iv. 150 n.

Milton, John: his portrait in Pope's chamber, i. 120; not to be imitated in his blindness, i. 39; Pope lends the Minor Poems to Trumbull, i. 10; *Paradise Lost* quoted, i. 167, 213, 450, ii. 89, 295; *Paradise Regained*, ii. 110; — M. thought above criticism, iii. 291; his head in R. Allen's library, iv. 351; Atterbury's regard for M., i. 452, ii. 124, 165; H. Brooke's reaction to, iv. 199; Fenton's interest, ii. 365;

Milton, John (*cont.*) 398; Gay quotes M., iii. 20; — J. Richardson's work on M., iii. 240, 327, 330, 331; joke played on Richardson by lines taken from Chalfont window, iv. 80–81; engravings of M., iv. 150; Swift quotes M., i. 358; translations into Italian, i. 222; Milton MSS. in Tonson's hands, ii. 124.

Minshul, Miss, (?) dau. of Richard, ii. 268.

Minshul, Richard, ii. 268 n.

Mist's Weekly Journal: cited on the lovers killed by lightning, i. 479 n.; attacks Pope, ii. 486; on Fenton's *Marianne*, ii. 162; on Swift, ii. 383 n., 414 n.; prints 'Memorial to Dean Swift', ii. 493 n.; *Mist* becomes *Fog*, iii. 334 n.

Mitford, John, a transcript by him used, i. 334.

Modern Language Notes, i. 182 n.

Modern Language Quarterly, i. 229 n.

Modern Philology, i. 388 n., iii. 56 n.

Mohun, Elizabeth (Lawrence), Lady, *see* Griffith, Col. Edward (her first husband) *and* Mordaunt, Col. Charles (her third husband), i. 407.

Molineax, Lord (for Molineux?), ii. 5.

Molyneux, Samuel, i. 308, 470.

Monk, J. H., his *Life of Bentley* cited, iii. 240 n.

Monmouth, Duchess of, *see* Scott, Anne, iv. 38.

Montagu, Elizabeth (Wilmot), wife of the 3rd Earl of Sandwich, i. 261.

Montagu, John, Duke of, i. 297.

Montagu, Lady Mary Churchill, Duchess of: painted by Pope, i. 187, 189; at Beaulieu, iii. 426.

MONTAGU, CHARLES, Earl of Halifax: letter to, i. 271; his patronage of Pope's 'Pastorals', i. 17; of Pope's *Iliad*, i. 199, 209, 220, 226, 227, 263, 270 n.; lends his Eustathius, i. 270, 297; offers Pope a pension, i. 271; mentioned, i. 275, ii. 68.

MONTAGU, EDWARD WORTLEY: letter from, ii. 6; letter to, ii. 12; Pope sends service to, i. 496, 508; his embassy to Constantinople, i. 326, 382 n., 440; places of residence, ii. 12 n.; negotiates with Kneller for a house, ii. 6,

MONTAGU, EDWARD WORTLEY (*cont.*) 38; Rémond affair kept from him, ii. 62; he subscribes to Buononcini's *Cantate*, ii. 99.

MONTAGU, LADY MARY WORTLEY: letters to, i. 345, 352, 355, 363, 367, 382, 388, 405, 417, 439, 505, ii. 21, 22, 38, 52, 62, 82; letters from her to Pope, i. 361, 365, 387, 390, 396, 411, 421, 460, 469, 513, 519, 522, ii. 194, 204; letters from her to Dr. Arbuthnot, iii. 59, 60, 448; letter from Lord Peterborow to her, iii. 352; — a letter to her wrongly thought to be from Pope, i. 338–9; some of her letters misdated, v. 1–2; her notion of Pope as a forger, i. 242 n.; — Pope's letters to her in Turkey, how forwarded, i. 275 n., 405, 407; lack of letters from her complained of, i. 309, 382; slowness of posts, i. 411; letters now lost, i. 417, 460, 469; the *Additional Volume* of her letters spurious, i. 421 n., 519 n.

The embassy correspondence: departure from Charles Street, i. 338, 340 n., 345, 368; not seasick in the Channel, i. 356; amusements in Vienna, i. 361, 362, 365, 366, 368–9; detour to Hanover, i. 384; — dangers in crossing Hungary, i. 363, 364, 387, 390–3; experience of oriental life, i. 393, 396, 397–9, 412; the fall of Belgrade, i. 421; manners of the Turks, i. 422; the return journey, i. 423, 440, 493; in Genoa, i. 500, 501 n.; disadvantages in returning, i. 513; at Lyons, i. 513–14; in Paris, i. 519–21; home, v. 1–2.

Life in England: King George's playfellow, i. 271; not surprised at Addison's appointment as Secretary of State, i. 423; residence in Twickenham, ii. 1, 6, 12 n., 21 n., 38; to be painted by Kneller, ii. 21–23; — buys South Sea shares, ii. 52; difficulty with Rémond, ii. 62; the state of Nuripan, ii. 83; delighted with Pope's Great Walk, ii. 62; her taste in music doubted, ii. 82; may not have Pope's harpsichord, ii. 82; subscribes to Buononcini's *Cantate*, ii. 99; her later reputation in Italy, iv. 377. *Pope's passion for Lady M.*, i. 326,

MONTAGU, LADY MARY WORTLEY (*cont.*) 356, 357, 439–42; she summons Pope through Jervas, i. 340; her conversation commended, i. 354; her empty house saddens Pope, i. 354; Pope's professions are pleasing, i. 361; her head-dress remembered by Pope, i. 368; also her eyes, i. 369; — he might join her in Italy, i. 370, 385; she praises Pope's *Iliad*, i. 398–9; Asiatic simplicity expected of her, i. 494; her return longed for, i. 470; he asks her to notify him upon arrival, i. 505, 515; the fate of the lovers killed by lightning commended to her tenderness, i. 496; she wishes to see Pope, ii. 204; — he cannot decipher her 'fiction', ii. 258; at times suspected as part author of *A Pop upon Pope*, ii. 502 n., iii. 53 n.; challenges Pope to produce a libel in her handwriting, iii. 60; her defence against the charge of writing *One Epistle*, iii. 59–60; her warm sense of Pope's injustice, iii. 60, 106 n.; — Pope complains to Walpole of her libels, iii. 53; her early causes of wrath against Pope, iii. 53 n.; her quarrel with Mrs. Murray, iii. 82 n.; Pope reports on her to Lord Bathurst, iii. 137; Bathurst wishes Pope to be her friend, iii. 134; Pope to pay no attention to her anger, iii. 327; Peterborow's letter to her about 'Sappho', iii. 352; — her protest against the *Epistle to Arbuthnot*, iii. 448; her supposed authorship of *Verses to the Imitator of Horace*, iii. 354, 366 n., 448, v. 11; her opinion of Pope's mother, iii. 449; asks Arbuthnot to show her raging letter to Pope, iii. 449; she regards Pope as a mere libeller and hack writer, iii. 449.

Her literary interests: her pastorals asked for by Pope, i. 370, 441; her specimens of Turkish poetry, i. 399–400, 401–2; Pope sends her his *Works* (1717), i. 385, 407; she thinks the three happiest poets are Addison, Congreve, and Pope, i. 423; failure of Addison and Tickell in the *Iliad*, i. 423; her opinion of Achilles and perfect heroes, i. 424; her comments on the lovers killed by lightning, i. 522–4; she is glad to be honoured in

MONTAGU, LADY MARY WORTLEY (*cont.*)
verse by Broome, ii. 77; she returns *Arcadia* and wishes to borrow Shakespeare, ii. 194.

Montaigne, Michael Eyquem de: his cat, i. 73; his *Essais* quoted: by Pope, i. 201, 489, ii. 88, by Bolingbroke, ii. 472, iii. 48, by Swift, iii. 92.

Montfaucon de Villars, Abbé, i. 268.

Monthly Chronicle, iii. 33 n.

Montrose, 1st Duke of, *see* Graham, James.

Moor, H., of Fawley Court, i. 182.

Moore, Mr., of Frith Street, Fenton's early town address, ii. 234.

Moore, Mrs., sister of the Dancastles, ii. 9, 63.

Moore, Arthur, ii. 290, 291.

Moore, C. A., on Pope and Leibniz, iv. 164 n.

MOORE, THOMAS: letters from, ii. 200, 201; account of, ii. 200 n.; forwards Atterbury letter to Pope, ii. 200; thanks Pope for Atterbury's portrait, ii. 201.

Moore, Tom, ii. 288 n.

Moore-Smythe, James: not a friend of the Blounts, i. 182 n.; speaks well of Pope, ii. 520; uses Pope's verses in his *Rival Modes*, iii. 18 n.; his part in *One Epistle*, iii. 59, 106 n., 114; satirized after his death in the *Epistle to Arbuthnot*, iii. 449.

Moratt, — (unidentified), iv. 212.

MORDAUNT, CHARLES, 3rd Earl of Peterborow (his spelling of the name): letters to, ii. 177, 189, 510, iii. 306, 311; letters from, ii. 183, 196, 197, iii. 281, 282, 310, 317, 352 (to Lady Mary Wortley Montagu), 468, 485; a letter wrongly ascribed to him, ii. 204; his letters to Swift thought opened and intercepted, iii. 281–2.

Biographical data: Berkeley the philosopher his chaplain, i. 222; P. forbidden the Court, i. 289; wishes to meet Bolingbroke, Harcourt, and Pope at a party, ii. 183; goes to the Continent, ii. 1, 185 n., 189, 190 n., 196; dines with the Mrs. Robinsons and Dr. Arbuthnot, ii. 196; a dinner for Swift *et al.*, v. 6; 'enamoured' of Robert Arbuthnot, ii. 196; — at Bath, ii. 514; his attitude towards the

MORDAUNT, CHARLES (*cont.*)
Court, iii. 281; calls London 'the place of corruption', iii. 282; cynical about Sir Robert Sutton, iii. 282; quotes Horace, iii. 283; explains about 'Sappho' to Lady Mary, iii. 352; his wanderings make it difficult to arrange Pope's visit (1734) to Bevis Mount, iii. 414, 425.

His friendships: he cancels an appointment with Pope, ii. 197; Pope meets Mrs. Blounts at P.'s house in Parson's Green, ii. 1; Pope lodges with P. in town, ii. 144, 151, 185, 200, 286, iii. 160; Pope visits him at Southampton, iii. 218, 282; Pope has a voyage on Southampton Water, iv. 179–80; — Aaron Hill compliments P. in a poem, iii. 177, 182, 188; Hill and P. planned to go together to the West Indies, iii. 188; P.'s affection for Mrs. Howard, ii. 178; asks Pope to measure the field at Marble Hill, ii. 183; helps plan Mrs. Howard's gardens, ii. 197, 259 n.; gets political aid (Walpole) on her property there, ii. 323; his attitude towards Mrs. Howard, iii. 281; — his friendship for Swift: takes him (1726) to Sir R. Walpole, ii. 373; gives a dinner for him, with Pope absent, ii. 384, v. 6; Pope begs Swift to correspond with P., ii. 413; P. writes to Swift, ii. 420, 427; speaks well of Swift always, ii. 58, 282; Swift is proud of his friendship, iii. 363, 401, v. 15; P. a friend of Dr. Towne, ii. 424; subscribes, through Pope, for Samuel Wesley's *Poems*, iii. 504.

P.'s personality: too witty for a general, i. 21, ii. 185, 189, 190; may banish himself, ii. 184–5; his courage, i. 493; placates operatic singers, ii. 190; a knight errant, ii. 196; Swift's opinion of, ii. 198–9; as ambassador too mobile, iii. 147; P. and Bathurst 'the two most impetuous men' Pope knows, iii. 405–6; Lord Hervey's opinion of P., iii. 489 n.

His ill health: mentioned, ii. 196, iii. 23, 105 n.; narrowly escaped death (1733), iii. 342–3, 349; goes to Bath for health, iii. 468; thought desperately ill, iii. 455, 470, 474; still

MORDAUNT, CHARLES (*cont.*)
hopes to write about the reign of
Queen Anne, iii. 188, 487; Pope visits
him in his last days, iii. 489–90; owns
his marriage with Mrs. Robinson, iii.
487, 490; active in gardening to the
very last, iii. 487–8; wishes Bathurst
would visit him, iii. 483; summons
Pope for a farewell visit, iii. 483;
Pope's account of P.'s last days, iii.
484, 485, 488, 508–9.

Mordaunt, Col. Charles, nephew of
Peterborow: marries Lady Mohun,
i. 407, ii. 196 n.; visits Peterborow in
1735, iii. 488.

Mordaunt, Elizabeth, Lady Mohun, ii.
196–7.

Mordaunt, Mrs. Lewis, ii. 496 n.

Morgan, a fictitious name in the
Epistle to Bathurst, iii. 353.

MORICE, WILLIAM: letter from, iii.
206; revises a letter, i. 501 n.; a channel permitted for writing to Atterbury, ii. 169 n., iii. 246; an account of,
ii. 201 n.; quits Will's coffee-house
(doubtfully the same Morice ?), i. 288,
290; abroad to visit Atterbury, ii.
201, 206, iii. 76 n., 76–78 (death of
Atterbury's dau.), 90; Wesley's elegy
on Mrs. M., iii. 104; goes again to
the Continent, iii. 136, 247; has compliments for Swift from Atterbury, ii.
469; his service sent to Caryll, iii. 90;
transcripts of his letters for Lord Oxford, iii. 187; will let Vandiest copy
a picture for Allen, iv. 13.

MORLEY, JOHN: letters to, ii. 148, 156,
362; writes to Atterbury, ii. 132; his
connexion with the 2nd Earl of
Oxford, ii. 148 n.; sends Pope oysters,
ii. 148, 156; subscribes to the *Odyssey*,
ii. 156; knows well the Black Bull
Inn, ii. 355; injures his leg and is laid
up in London, ii. 359, 362; Pope
jokes about M.'s activity in selling
land, ii. 372; Pope sees M.'s 'image'
at Halstead, iii. 382.

Morpeth, Viscount, *see* Howard,
Henry.

Morrice, William, *see* Morice.

Morris, Mr. (unidentified), ii. 4.

Morris, R., i. 282 n.

Morris, Robert, an architect, friend of
Dodington, iii. 329.

MOTTE, BENJAMIN: letters to, ii. 438,
526, iii. 8, 23, 27, 32, 306; letter from,
ii. 477 (to R. Woodford); *Miscellanies* i and ii (1727) to be sent to Congreve and Fortescue, ii. 439; may
begin printing *Miscellanies* iii (but
does not), ii. 439; *Dunciad* designed
for vol. iii of the *Miscellanies*, ii. 438;
M. troublesome over the *Miscellanies*,
iii. 1; — dilatory in his payments for
copy, iii. 8; disputes with Curll over
copyrights, ii. 477–8; annoyingly
dilatory in payments, ii. 526, iii. 23–
24, 27, 32, 90, 92; mysterious conveyance of *Gulliver* to M., ii. 412;
unwilling to allow items in the
Miscellanies to be reprinted in *Works
in Prose* (1737), iv. 68, 324.

Motteux, Pierre, his version of *Don
Quixote*, iv. 455 n.

Mowat, Janette, iv. 458.

MOYSER, COL. JAMES: letter to, iv. 460;
Pope's service to (usually sent via H.
Bethel), iii. 197, 228, 427, iv. 40, 207,
225, 255; Martha Blount hopes M.
will not detain Bethel in Yorkshire,
iii. 233; his father (John M.) dies,
iv. 113; the Colonel a sympathetic
friend, iv. 269; in Italy with H.
Bethel, iv. 375, 395, 401; at Bath, iv.
433, 434, 446; receives denial from
Pope of Pope's authorship of a
*Character of the Duke of Bucking-
ham*, iv. 460; other mentions of M.,
iv. 474, 512.

Mulgrave, Lord, *see* Phipps, Constantine.

Murray, Mrs., subscribes to Buononcini, ii. 99.

Murray, Sir Alexander of Stanhope, iii.
82 n.

Murray, Lady Elizabeth (Finch), wife
of William Murray, iv. 141.

Murray, Grisel Baillie, iii. 82 n.

Murray, (General) James, iv. 466.

Murray, John, publisher, ii. 509 n.

Murray, Patrick, Lord Elibank, iv.
466.

Murray, William, later 1st Earl of
Mansfield: hardly yet in 1731 a
'successful youth', iii. 226 n.; pos-
sibly served as counsel in *Craftsman*
(Francklin) libel suit, iii. 236 n.;
Solicitor-general in 1742, iv. 441 n.;

Murray, William (*cont.*)
like Tully may plead a bad case, iv.
466; encourages C. Smart to translate into Latin the *Essay on Man*, iv.
478; ill, iv. 511, 516; to have a copy
of the 4to *Essay on Criticism* and
Essay on Man, iv. 502; — Pope's *Imitation of Horace, Ep. i. vi*, dedicated
to M., iii. 277 n.; Pope met him at
Oxford, iii. 498; gives Pope legal
advice on copyrights, iv. 87, 425;
the friendship of the two men, iv. 178,
516; M. becomes Pope's executor, iv.
497 n.; — Pope's many visits to
M.'s London house, iv. 29, 150, 175,
332, 380, 381, 383, 489, 498 n., 505;
M. visits Pope at Twickenham, iv.
389, 431, 442; M. advises in Mrs.
Rackett's chancery case, iv. 203, 214,
245; the sad life of a lawyer, iv. 368;
aids Warburton against Mawhood, iv.
385, 386, 387, 410, 411, 427, 455;
a friend of Robert Nugent, iv. 344.
Muses Mercury, i. 56.
Muzio Scevola, a composite opera, ii.
99.
My, Mr., *see* Mee.

Nando's Coffee-house, in Fleet Street,
next door to Lintot's shop, iv. 394.
*Narrative of the Method by which
Pope's Letters have been . . . pub-
lished*, iii. 458–67.
NASH, RICHARD (Beau): letters to, iv.
170, 176; N.'s impudent air, i. 260;
Pope will ask him to take Martha
Blount to mass on Sundays, iii. 435;
Pope's inscription for the obelisk in
honour of Prince Frederick, iv. 170,
176.
Needham, Mr., friend of Broome, ii,
379.
Needham, Francis, iii. 104 n.
Nelson, Mrs., of Binfield: called 'Sappho',
i. 42, 47, 100; cool to Pope about
Elizabeth Weston, i. 119 n., 132, 171;
approves Pope's Catholic doctrines,
i. 127; her lines on Lady Mary
Caryll burlesqued by Pope, i. 152; a
trouble-maker, i. 171 n.; Pope critical
of her, i. 173; a Jacobite sympathizer,
i. 309.
Netley Abbey, visited by Pope, iii. 427,
430.

Nevill, Mr., of Binfield, i. 443.
Nevill, George, 14th Baron Aber-
gavenny, iii. 110 n.
Newark upon Trent, Notts., *see* William
Warburton (at Brant Broughton).
Newbury, John, publisher, iv. 478 n.
Newbury, Berks., second night out
from Bath on journey to London, iv.
379.
Newcastle, 1st Duke of, *see* Pelham-
Holles, Thomas, ii. 269.
Newcome, John, later Master of St.
John's College, Cambridge: friend of
Fenton's, ii. 245; complains of the
Odyssey, ii. 377, 385; at first unsuc-
cessful in candidacy as Master of St.
John's, ii. 432.
New England Weekly Journal (1727), ii.
451 n., 479 n.
Newgate, Ordinary of, *see* Lorraine,
Paul.
NEWSHAM, ANN (Craggs), Mrs. John
Newsham (*see also* Knight *and*
Nugent): letters to, ii. 242, 246, 265,
278; account of, ii. 217 n., 223 n.;
she wishes to see Pope, ii. 223, 254;
passes a day at Twickenham, ii. 242;
gives Pope as agent money to erect
a monument to Secretary Craggs (her
brother), ii. 242, 246; Pope desires
friendship without ceremony with
her, ii. 247; she is kept from Town by
Mr. N.'s ill health, ii. 266; a widow
1724–7, ii. 456 n.
Newsham, James, son of John and Ann
Newsham: his age in 1727, ii. 242 n.;
in Westminster School, ii. 266 n.;
Pope recommends Mallet as his
tutor, iii. 202; his boyish occupations,
iii. 218; Pope inquires after his
whereabouts, iii. 426; he takes a letter
to his mother from Bevis Mount, iii.
430; makes the Grand Tour with
Mallet, iii. 457 n., 485, iv. 30.
Newsham, John, husband of Ann
(Craggs), his bad health and death,
ii. 242 n., 266, 278.
Newton, Mrs. A. E., has Pope's 'self-
portrait', i. 187 n.
Newton, Sir Isaac: cited, i. 488 n.;
Bolingbroke thinks he should have
written in English, ii. 220; Pouilly
his disciple, ii. 221 n.; Pope and N.'s
Chronology of Ancient Kingdoms, ii.

Newton, Sir Isaac (*cont.*)
457–9; Warburton called Pope's
'Newton', iv. 213.

Nicholas V, Pope, i. 122 n.

Nichol Smith, D., *see* Smith.

Nichols, John, second master in Westminster, *see* Nicoll, J.

Nichols, John, printer and author: ed.
of Atterbury's *Correspondence* (1783)
cited, i. 499 n., 500 n., 501–4, ii. 104,
106, 110, 120, 173, iii. 76, 85; his
Bibliotheca Typographica, i. 175; his
Literary Anecdotes, i. 496, ii. 244, 284,
313, iii. 128, 294, iv. 228, 324, 390,
402, 404; his *Literary Illustrations*, iv.
507.

Nichols, John G., *Letters to Atterbury in
the Tower* (1859), ii. 166, 168.

Nicole, Pierre, his *Essais de Morale*, ii.
43.

Nicoll (or Nichols), John, 2nd master
in Westminster School, a protégé of
Atterbury, ii. 266.

Noden, Ralph, author of *A Key to the
Tale of a Tub*, i. 359.

Noel, Mr., a Templar, iii. 236.

Noell, Mr., has horses for hire, iv. 47.

Norfolk, 9th Duke of, *see* Howard, Edward.

Norfolk co., *see* Pulham (Broome),
Sturston (Broome, Mrs. Marriot),
Diss (Briars and Mr. Burlington).

Norris (illegible name), Mr., friend of
Fortescue's, iv. 516.

Norris, Sir John (Admiral), iv. 498.

Norris, John, of Bemerton, ii. 439 n.

Norris, Dr. Robert, Pope's *Narrative*
on the madness of Dennis, i. 183, 184.

Norse, J., iv. 23 n.

Northamptonshire co., Boughton (Lord
Strafford), Astrop Wells (Lady Cobham).

Norton, Richard, his will, iii. 432.

Norwood and Battersea, Lord Bolingbroke's estate, iv. 483.

Nostradamus, Johan de, i. 278, 441 n.

Notes and Queries: cited for the inven-
tory (1744) of Pope's personal effects,
i. 187 n., iii. 341 n.; on Addison's
marriage, i. 385; on Spence, ii. 379
n.; on the Duchess of Queensberry's
'coptic' lines, iii. 239 n.; on Woodfall's accounts, iii. 489; on Lady
Gerard's lease, iv. 183 n., 488 n.

Nottingham, 3rd Earl of, *see* Finch,
Daniel.

Nottinghamshire co., Newark on Trent
(Warburton).

Nugent, Ann (*see also* Newsham *and*
Knight): Ann Arbuthnot a friend
of hers, iv. 212; does not quarrel with
Pope, iv. 231, 260, 344.

NUGENT, ROBERT, 3rd husband of
Ann (Craggs): letters to, iv. 230,
256, 257, 260, 344; letter from, iv.
233 (to Mrs. Whiteway); some
account of, iv. 230 n.; wishes Pope's
portrait, iv. 212; also Swift's by
Bindon, iv. 233; — Mrs. Whiteway
offers to return to him additional
Pope letters, iv. 230–1; he agrees to
receive them, iv. 233; she prefers to
send them by M'Aulay, iv. 257; N.'s
compliments to Mr. and Mrs. Deane
Swift, iv. 233; Pope sends N. a letter
now unknown, iv. 235; — N. helps
Pope to mundicks, iv. 257; asked to
forward by private hand Pope's
reply to Faulkner about printing the
Swift letters, iv. 257–8; the letter is
returned to Pope, iv. 276; N. is
elected to Parliament, iv. 344;
Chesterfield at Gosfield, iv. 419 n.;
N.'s *Odes and Epistles* (1739), iv. 231;
Pope commends an ode in MS. by
N., iv. 260; W. Dunkin's *Epistle* to
N., iv. 233 n.

Nut-Cracker (1751) prints verses by
Pope, iii. 100 n.

Oakingham, Berks., near Binfield, i. 121.

Observator, i. 25.

Ockley, Simon, his *Hai Ebn Yocktan*, ii.
13 n.

Ogilby, John, i. 462.

Olaus Magnus, cited by Swift, ii. 407.

Oldfield, Ann: acts Cato's dau., i. 175;
acts Lady Jane Grey, i. 288, 290;
Charles Churchill her son, iv. 124 n.

Oldham, John, i. 408.

Oldisworth, William, i. 166 n., 373.

Oldmixon, John: his Miscellany contains 'Receipt to Make a Cuckold', i.
267 n.; gave his publisher his horse by
way of payment, i. 372; his *Timo-
thys*, i. 373; his attack on Clarendon's
History, iii. 71, 245 n., 328; one of the
heroes of *The Dunciad*, iii. 247.

OLIVER, WILLIAM, M.D., of Bath: letters to him, iv. 218, 219, 227, 229, 244, 278, 374, 469, 470, 480; letters from, iv. 229, 281; prescribes for Pope, iv. 206, 522; does not attend Allen (1743), iv. 477, 480, 481; his angry letter forwarded to Allen by Pope, iv. 486, 489; Pope breakfasts with O., iv. 218; O.'s 'castle', iv. 239; he is eager to see Pope, iv. 282; a joker (?), iv. 340; sends Pope cyder, iv. 349–50; Pope (1741) sees little of him, iv. 374; Tillard's book attacking Warburton is dedicated to O., iv. 404; helps Pope (1743) get through Bath without seeing Allen, iv. 470; he helps get materials for Pope's grotto, iv. 219, 222 n., 228 n., 239, 244; a bath in the grotto to be dedicated to O., iv. 278–9, 281.

Omer, a stonemason employed by Allen (and Pope), his work on the grotto (1740), iv. 230, 235, 239, 245, 246, 274.

One Epistle to Mr. Pope (1730), iii. 106 n. *See also* James Moore-Smythe, Lady Mary Wortley Montagu, *and* L. Welsted.

Orange, Prince of, marries Anne, Princess Royal, iii. 411 n.

Orange, Anne, Princess of, iv. 49.

Orchard Wyndham, Somerset, *see* Sir Wm. Wyndham.

Orford, Earl of, *see* Russell, Edward.

Original Weekly Journal, i. 350 n.

Orkney, 1st Earl of, *see* Hamilton, Lord George.

Ormond, 1st and 2nd Dukes of, *see* Butler, James.

Orrery, 5th Earl of, *see* Boyle, John (1707–62).

Orrery Papers (1903), cited, iv. 56 n., 497 n.

Orsini, Princess, ii. 461.

Osborn, overseer at Binfield (?), i. 524.

Osborn, James M., i. 123 n., ii. 379 n., iv. 354 n.

Osborne, Francis, pseudonym for James Pitt, iv. 179 n.

Osborne, Thomas, bookseller, iv. 222.

Ossory, Earl of, *see* Butler, Thomas.

Ovid (Publius Ovidius Naso); mentioned, i. 81, 96, 106; H. Cromwell and the *Amores*, i. 91, 92, 99;

Ovid (*cont.*)
Heroides, i. 96, 100; *Ars Amatoria* quoted by Orrery, iv. 306; *Metamorphoses*, i. 47, 171, ii. 121, 234 (Fenton); *Tristia* quoted by Gay, i. 287; *Ex Ponto*, i. 99.

Owen, Sir Arthur, iii. 422–3.

Oxford University: visited by Pope, i, 244, 314, 371–5 (with Lintot), 429, 475, ii. 80, 81; the Bodleian Library, ii. 83; colleges mentioned (q.v.) as subscribing to the *Iliad*, i. 421; All Souls, Balliol, Corpus Christi, Magdalen, Merton, New, Pembroke, Queen's, Trinity; other colleges mentioned: Christ Church (Lord Edward Harley, Dr. Stratford, Henry Cleland), Exeter (Lord William Cowper, Mr. Atwell), Hart Hall (George Augustus Selwyn), St. John's (Abel Evans), St. Mary Hall (Walter Harte, Thomas Hooke, William King); Oxford more ready to subscribe than Cambridge, ii. 271; other Oxonians mentioned, *see* R. Adderley, George Clarke, Simon Harcourt (jr.), Walter Hodges, Dr. Leigh, Christopher Pitt, William Rollinson, Joseph Spence, Aaron Thompson, Edward Young. *See also* Lord Cornbury, iii. 277; honorary degrees mooted for Pope and Warburton, iv. 357 n., 436, 440, 442.

Oxford: The Cross Inn, Pope there (1735), iii. 491; Bagley Wood accident, iii. 493.

Oxford, Earls of, *see* Edward Harley (2nd Earl) *and* Robert Harley (1st Earl).

'Oxford Papers', cited obscurely by Elwin as provenance of letters, i. 488, ii. 207, 464 n.

Oxfordshire, *see* Blenheim, Cockthorpe, Cornbury, Middleton, Rousham, Stanton Harcourt, Stonor Park, 'Wattleton' Park.

Oxonian (nameless) at *Cato*, i. 175–6.

Ozell, John, i. 166 n.

P—, Judge, at Bath, ii. 521.

P—, Mrs., at Bath, iv. 212.

P., E., fabricates anecdotes about Pope's school days for Curll, iii. 359.

PMLA (*Publications of the Modern Language Association*), cited for its printings of letters, ii. 144, 450 n.

'P.T.', his role in the publication (1735) of Pope's *Letters*, iii. 460–7.

Pack, Richardson, helps the dramatist Southerne, ii. 352.

Packington, Lady, her letters published by Curll, ii. 439.

Page, Sir Francis, iv. 189–90.

Palladio, Andrea, ii. 50, iii. 187, iv. 151.

Parham, Sussex, Sir Cecil and Lady Bishop, i. 302, iii. 75, 122.

Parker, Thomas, Earl of Macclesfield, ii. 161, iii. 132.

Parliament: its sittings, ii. 106 n., 145, iv. 341 n., 376; called 'the devil's divan', iv. 424; Bill for raising money from papists (1723), ii. 173; copyright law considered but thrown out (1737), iv. 65, 69.

Parnell, Mr., a Curll author, ii. 157 n.

PARNELL, THOMAS: letters to, i. 225, 253, 284 (with Gay), 291, 331 (joint letter from Pope, Gay, and Arbuthnot), 348, 395, 415; letters from, i. 222 (to Gay), 223 (with Pope to Ford), 249 (with Pope to Ford), 249 (with Pope to Arbuthnot), 299; he is at Binfield with Pope, i. 237; he had hoped to be Clarendon's chaplain, i. 228; a favourite in the Pope household, i. 225; returns to London and Arbuthnot, i. 225, 226, 249; hopes to see the Coronation, i. 249; at the Pall Mall coffee-house, i. 253; overstays his leave from his parish, i. 249, 262; — returns to Ireland, i. 205, 262, 269; fails to write to his friends, i. 284, 348; his political situation, i. 284; might be exchanged for Eusden (fabricated letter), i. 347; his last visit to England, i. 415 n., 478–9; called at Jervas's, i. 501; his death (Oct. 1718), i. 346 n., 415, ii. 23 n., 24; remembered with regret by Lord Oxford, ii. 382; — his help on Pope's *Iliad*, i. 205, 226; at Bath with Pope, i. 257, 258, 259; Pope lacks his help on Homer, i. 299; Tickell's mistake as translator, i. 299; asked to work on notes for the *Iliad*, i. 395, 415, 497 n.; — P.'s works: in Tonson's Miscellany, i. 195; his 'Essay on the Life and

PARNELL, THOMAS (*cont.*)
Times of Homer', i. 226 n.; — a poem of his returned by Addison, i. 284, 292; 'Essay on Different Styles of Poetry', i. 292; Pope praises 'Pandora' and 'Eclogue on Health', i. 396; his *Batrachomuomachia*, i. 253, 284, 377, 395, 410; his *Life of Zoilus*, i. 299 n., 371, 395; gives the copy money on it to Gay, i. 395 n., 396; his *Pervigilium Veneris*, i. 332; his 'Bookworm', i. 371; 'To Mr. Pope', i. 416; — Pope praises his poems, i. 415; edits them after P.'s death, ii. 23, 24, 61, 92; dedicated to Robert, Earl of Oxford, ii. 90.

Parsons, Robert, sold land for Marble Hill property, iii. 34 n.

Partridge, John, almanac-maker, i. 87 n.

Pascal, Blaise, i. 129, iii. 173, iv. 416.

Paston, George, see Symonds, E. M.

Pate, W., i. 218.

Pattisson, William, ii. 440.

Paulet, Charles, 3rd Duke of Bolton, ii. 154 n., 479.

Paulet (or Pawlet), Lord Will, ii. 38.

Pausanias: mentioned by Bolingbroke, ii. 219; quoted by Broome, iii. 124.

Paxton, Nicholas, iv. 124, 179.

Peace negotiations of 1709, i. 59, 61.

Peach, R. M., iv. 253 n.

Peche (or Peachy), William, Pope's Oxford helper on the *Iliad*, i. 448 n., 497 n.

Pearce, Dr., see (probably) Dr. Jeremiah Pierce of Bath.

PEARSE, JAMES: letter to, ii. 232; letter from, ii. 230; will visit Pope at Twickenham, ii. 230, 232.

Pearson (a proctor), see Peirson, Robert.

Pecket, Mrs., H. Bethel's York address, iii. 197, 427.

PEIRSON, ROBERT: letter from, ii. 301; concerning the Pope monument in Twickenham church.

Pelham, Hon. Henry (1695?–1754), a friend and patron of W. Kent, iv. 149, 163; his marriage, ii. 416.

Pelham-Holles, Thomas, 1st Duke of Newcastle, ii. 269, 306.

Pembroke, Mary, Countess of, see Howe, Mary.

Pendarves, Mary (later Delany): her account of the rebuilt 'woodhouse' at Cirencester, ii. 207 n., iii. 136 n.; her story of Pope's near drowning, iv. 28 n.; she gets 4to *Letters* (1737) from Dodsley, iv. 83.

Pentlow, Mr., i. 26.

Penzance, Cornwall, *see* Rev. William Borlase, iv. 228.

PERCIVAL, JOHN, Viscount: letters to, ii. 135, 267, 273; letters from, ii. 135, 267, 268, 272; his *Iliad* III lacking, i. 413; visited by Pope, i. 417; asked by Pope (for the Duchess of Buckingham) for opera singers, ii. 135; asks Pope's aid in choosing a preacher for the Charterhouse, ii. 267, 268, 269, 272; concerned in prison reform, ii. 268 n.; sends his son the 'coptic' lines used by the Duchess of Queensberry, iii. 239 n.; mentioned by Swift, iii. 252.

Persian Tales, commended by Pope, i. 393, ii. 202.

Persius (Aulus Persius Flaccus), i. 99, ii. 231, 523, iii. 420.

Peter Alexiowitz 'the Great': his character, ii. 405; as Aaron Hill saw it, iv. 158.

Peterborough (or Peterborow), 3rd Earl of, *see* Mordaunt, Charles.

Peterborough, Dean of, *see* Lockier, Francis.

Peterborow (his spelling of the name), 3rd Earl of, *see* Mordaunt, Charles.

Petersham (Petersum), *see* the 3rd Duke of Queensberry, the Mmes Blount, William Pulteney.

Petrarch, iii. 10.

Petrarchi,—a translator, iv. 484 n.

Petre, Robert, 7th Lord: related to Caryll, i. 93 n., not known by Pope, i. 123; the Baron in *The Rape of the Lock*, i. 142, 145, 464 n.; Caryll visits Lord P., i. 131, 518; approaches him concerning employment for H. Rackett, iii. 172.

Petre, Robert James, 8th Lord, his marriage, iii. 284.

Petre, Catherine, Lady, her *Iliad* III lacking, i. 464.

Petronius Arbiter, i. 324 n., 413.

Petworth House, Sussex, iv. 91 n.

Philips, Mr. (unidentified), ii. 241.

Philips, Father, Dancastle's chaplain, i. 393, 403, 443.

Philips, Ambrose: mentioned, i. 156 n., 217; his Pastorals, i. 100, 101; his *Epistle to the Earl of Dorset*, i. 167–8; warfare against Philips, i. 217, 229; his hostility to Pope, i. 229, 235, 245; story of the rod put up at Button's, i. 229, ii. 489, iv. 425; secretary to the Hanover Club, i. 229, 296; has kicked his mistress, i. 255; his projected miscellany, i. 276; his *Persian Tales*, ii. 56 n.; — his trochaics on Miss Carteret, ii. 326; his reasons for not seeing Swift, ii. 342–3; thinks of going into the Church, ii. 342; to be passed over in silence, ii. 349; won't like Gay's writing for children, ii. 350; Pope's lines on him in *The Dunciad*, ii. 332; a burlesque of his trochaics ascribed (wrongly?) to Pope, ii. 343; 'an unsuccessful complainer', Swift says, ii. 326.

Philips, Sir Erasmus, drowned in the Avon, iv. 479 n.

Philological Quarterly: on Lady Mary Wortley, ii. 194 n.; on Cave's poetry contest, iii. 499 n.

Philostratus, Flavius, his *Heroicks*, i. 448.

Phipps, Dr., of Doctors' Commons, ii. 301.

Phipps, Sir Constantine (1656–1723), ii. 484.

Phipps, Constantine (1707–80), iv. 482.

Pierce, Jeremiah, surgeon at Bath, iv. 89, 227, 372, 401; Pope sends him a 'bundle of willows', iv. 412; hopes to see him Saturday, iv. 469; failed to write of Allen's illness, iv. 477.

Pierrepont, Sir Evelyn, Marquess of Dorchester and 2nd Duke of Kingston: reads Pope's Pastorals in MS., i. 17; subscribes to the *Iliad*, i. 296; is Lord Privy Seal, ii. 291; mentioned, iv. 148.

Pierrepont, Lady Mary (dau. of 2nd Duke of Kingston), *see* Montagu, Lady Mary Wortley.

Pierson, Col. Richard, reports on Bethel's health in Italy, iv. 375, 395.

PIGOTT, [Nathaniel ?]: letter to, iv. 79; son of the counsellor next listed, for whom Pope sends an epitaph.

Pigott, Nathaniel, of Whitton, counsellor at law: a son (unnamed) a druggist, ii. 77, 78; Catherine Caryll's painting consigned to the druggist, iii. 405; one son dies, iii. 173; a dau. marries Edward Caryll, ii. 367; Mrs. P. is ill, iii. 142; Rev. Edward P. (son ?) administered the last rites for Pope, iv. 526 n.; — the counsellor is active in Pope's case against Lady Kneller, ii. 301 n., 307, 309; Pope taken from the river Crane to P.'s house, ii. 401 n.; P. gives Pope a letter with £100 in it from the Duchess of Buckingham, iii. 88, 91, 110, 122; P. had served the Duchess in her suit (1727) against Ward, iii. 122; Pope visits P., iii. 127, 237, 284; P.'s opinion on Mrs. Howard's trouble with Mrs. Vernon, iii. 34; abused in an attack on Pope's 'learned council', iii. 355; his health declines, iii. 437; his death and epitaph (by Pope), iv. 79 n., 79–80.

Pilkington, Letitia, iii. 99 n., 432 n.

PILKINGTON, MATTHEW: letters to, iii. 323; Swift's account of, iii. 293; he longs to see Pope, iii. 293, 323; if modest, Swift says, P. may hope for Pope's protection, iii. 363; Bolingbroke's low opinion of P., iii. 405; chaplain to Alderman Barber when Lord Mayor, iii. 405 n.; — his rights in Swift's pieces offered to Bowyer, iii. 323–4, v. 10; a sentence about P. omitted in Dublin texts of Swift letters, iii. 344; P. attributes pieces to Swift without warrant, iii. 432.

Pindar, ii. 465.

Pinkethman, William, actor, i. 283 n.

Pishiobury Park, Herts., Erasmus Lewis ill there, iii. 295.

PITT, CHRISTOPHER: letters to, ii. 382, 507 (with Spence); letters from, ii. 382 (to Spence); wishes to print his translation of *Odyssey* XXIII, which he had given to Pope to use, ii. 382; his flattering verses to Pope, ii. 383; some of his things to be printed in Lintot's miscellany, ii. 383; Spence inquires as to P.'s authorship of a poem, ii. 507.

Pitt, Harrietta: a toast of Charles Ford's, iii. 204; a friend of Martha Blount and Mrs. Price, iv. 265.

Pitt, James, journalist ('Mother Osborne'), ii. 473, iv. 179 n.

Pitt, William, at Bath, iv. 139.

Pitt diamond, sold to France, i. 440.

Place-Newidd, Denbighshire, Major Roberts, iii. 233 n.

Plain Dealer, a reprint of it sent to Pope by Hill, iii. 164.

Plaistow, Essex, Aaron Hill, iv. 111.

Plato, i. 104, 173, 344 n., 487, ii. 360–1, 470 (Pope's seal); quoted by Pope on anger, ii. 516.

Plautus, Titus Maccius, i. 492, iii. 251.

Pleydell, Sir Mark, at whist with W. Kent, iv. 150 n.

Pliny the Elder, ii. 345, 407.

Pliny the Younger: his two houses, i. 508; translated by Sacy, ii. 218, 226; his letters written to be published, iii. 92, 102, 505; quoted by Pope, iv. 331; adapted by Bolingbroke, ii. 220–1.

PLOMER, W., letter from concerning Pope's involvement in the trouble over Mrs. Howard's new road, v. 19.

Plowden, Edmund, ii. 272.

Plowden, Will, ii. 282, 327, 464.

Plutarch: mentioned by Pope, i. 75, by Bolingbroke, ii. 219, by Broome, iii. 512; called by Pope the 'greatest of moralists', i. 75; Pope cites *Themistocles*, i. 75; *Moralia*, i. 42, 147, 498.

Poems on Several Occasions (1717), contains 'The Monster of Ragusa', ii. 334 n.

Political State of Gt. Britain, i. 275 n.

Polworth, Lord, *see* Hume, Alexander (2nd Earl of Marchmont) *and* Hugh (3rd Earl of Marchmont).

Polwarth MSS., cited from Hist. MSS. Comm., i. 345 n.

Poole, Benjamin, i. 278 n.

Pond, —, of Queen Street, forwards a letter, iv. 352.

Pop upon Pope (1728), ii. 502 n.

POPE, the Rev. ALEXANDER of Caithness, letter to, iv. 93.

POPE, ALEXANDER, senior, father of the poet: letters to, i. 394, 402, 433; Wycherley normally sends his service to him, i. 30, 39, 40, &c., to 85; he reprimands Wycherley, i. 35; a gardener, i. 17; — his investments in

POPE, ALEXANDER, SR. (*cont.*)

France, i. 155, 156, 180, 208 n., 394; his rent charge of Ruston for sale, i. 325; employs his son in a legal matter, i. 174; — Englefields not cordial to, i. 177; asked by his son to find summer lodgings near Mawson's in Chiswick, i. 402; forwards a letter to his son (at Hallgrove?), i. 428; wishes white strawberry plants, i. 443; his death, i. 439, 447, 448, 450, 455, 469.

ALEXANDER POPE (1688–1744)

The numerous entries under the poet's name are classified under the following headings: I. Biographical Data (pp. 111–35), II. Works (pp. 135–44), III. Pope's Letters (pp. 144–51), IV. Pope's Villa, Gardens, and Grotto (pp. 151–2), V. Pope's Rambles and Visits (p. 152), VI. Pope's Character: his Favourite Topics (pp. 152–61), VII. Pope's Reading (pp. 161–3), VIII. Portraits of Pope and his Friends (p. 163).

I. BIOGRAPHICAL DATA

Early years (to 1709): Account of P.'s school days by 'E.P.', iii. 359–60; saw Dryden, i. 2; exchanges MSS. with Wycherley, i. 3, 7, 15, *and passim* to 96; exchanges with Cromwell, i. 36, 77, &c.; Tonson (1706) asks to print P.'s *Pastorals*, i. 17; consults R. Bridges about translations from Homer, i. 41, 43–44; — early coffee-house life, i. 25–29; visits Walsh at Abberley, i. 29; detained from London by his father, i. 30; returns to Binfield for Easter, i. 41; is expected in Town, i. 52, 53; complains of bad eyesight, i. 39; on the *Pastorals* and the translations from Statius, *see* Pope II (WORKS); on the early Homeric translations, *see under* Homer.

1710: P. in Town before Lent, i. 82; ill in May, i. 87, 89; begins correspondence with Caryll, i. 93; revises for Wycherley, i. 80, 83; Wycherley limits the revisions, i. 85, 96; the two are temporarily estranged, i. 98; P. defends Rowe's Lucan, i. 103.

1711: For *Essay on Criticism, see* Pope II; P. visits Caryll at Ladyholt,

POPE, BIOGR. DATA (*1710 cont.*)

i. 115, 117; visits the Englefields, i. 135; newly formed acquaintance with Steele, i. 131–2; with Gay, i. 138; with Mrs. Weston, i. 119, 132; with Mrs. Cope, i. 129; — attacked by John Dennis, i. 121, 122, 125, 132; reconciled with Wycherley, i. 134–5; Cromwell visits Binfield, i. 124, 125; Pope paints in oils, i. 115; is urged to write a tragedy, i. 136.

1712: For *Rape of the Lock, Messiah,* and Adrian's 'Verses' *see* Pope II; he visits Ladyholt, i. 145, 148; asks the return of his letters to Caryll, i. 161; annoys relatives by sympathy for Mrs. Weston, i. 144; corrects verses for J. Tooker, v. 3–4; Cromwell correspondence ceases, i. 153; acquaintance with Addison begun, i. 141, 154; anxiety over French investments, i. 155, 156 (also 180, 208).

1713: For *Windsor Forest, The Guardian,* the *Iliad* Proposals see under Pope II and under Homer; the project of *Works of the Unlearned,* i. 195; Addison's reaction to the *Narrative concerning Dennis,* i. 183, 184; P.'s attitude towards *Cato,* i. 173, 175; Tonson's generosity concerning P.'s copyrights, i. 192; — P. in Town at Jervas's house, i. 172 (for some years hereafter this is his normal town address); instructed in painting by Jervas, i. 174, 177, 187, 189, 198; at Will's coffee-house, i. 172; at Button's coffee-house, i. 181; — visits the Blounts of Mapledurham, i. 203; invited by Rowe to Stockwell, i. 187; Rowe visits Binfield, i. 190, 194; P.'s zeal for Mrs. Weston estranges Mrs. Nelson and the Englefields, i. 173, 177, 179; — party violence of the time, i. 175, 179, 189, 194; trouble still over French bonds, i. 180.

1714: For *Rape of the Lock, see* Pope II and for the *Iliad, see under* Homer; — P. spent the winter of 1713–14 in Town, i. 205, 212, 214; his health affected by wine and taverns, i. 212, 214, 215, 219; spent the summer in Binfield, i. 205, 222, 237; trip to Ladyholt projected in the summer, i.

POPE, BIOGR. DATA (*1714 cont.*)
210, 215, 219, 256; made in Dec., i. 265, 267; — Swift visited in Letcombe, i. 230, 234, 250; Oxford visited, i. 244, 246, 250, 253; Mapledurham visited, i. 253; at Bath with Parnell, i. 242, 253, 255–62; projected visit to Longleat (Lord Lansdowne), i. 261; — in London for the Coronation, i. 249; the Scriblerus Club meets, i. 216–17, 228, 230, 233, 250; — wits of Button's coffee-house unfriendly to P., i. 210, 223, 229; relations with Addison, i. 244, 245, 263; Gay returns from Hanover, i. 254; P.'s alternating passion for Teresa and Martha Blount, i. 258, 261, 264, 268; French investments still worry, i. 208, 236–7, 242; party violence of the year, 209, 220, 238, 241, 245; Steele's role, i. 210, 215; the death of Queen Anne, i. 241, 247, 248, 251, 254.

1715: For the *Iliad*, *see under* Homer; for *The Temple of Fame, Key to the Lock*, *see* Pope II; — P. in Town, i. 275, 291, 322; at home, i. 275, 322; projected journey to the southwest, i. 309–15 *passim*; in Oxford, i. 315; projected visit to Bath, i. 285, 313, 314, 317; hostility of the wits at Button's, i. 274 n., 284, 287, 288–9, 294, 305; the role of Addison, i. 288, 290, 300 n.; of Tickell, i. 299, 304, 305; counterattack in *Zoilus*, i. 284, 292; — political turmoil, i. 287, 298, 301, 306, 308, 324; Lord Oxford's fate, i. 293, 307; Bolingbroke's, i. 295, 301; Lansdowne's, i. 287; Wyndham's, i. 310 n.; Steele's, i. 286; — examination of a hermaphrodite, i. 277–9; a rent-charge for sale, i. 325; P. wishes to buy an annuity, i. 293.

1716: *See under* Homer for the *Iliad*; — the *Life of Zoilus*, i. 333; the *Court Poems* published by Curll, i. 339, 350; removal from Binfield to Chiswick, i. 334, 336–7, 338, 339, 343; social life of P., i. 351–2; journey to the North delayed, 350, 351, 370; at Bath, i. 370; journey to Oxford with Lintot, i. 371–5, 376; trip to Ladyholt

POPE, BIOGR. DATA (*1716 cont.*)
planned, i. 326, 340, 343; at Jervas's house, i. 377; — Lady Mary goes abroad (to Constantinople), 340, 345, 354; the Blount ladies move to London, i. 327; P.'s account of Wycherley's death, i. 328–9; — the Jacobite rebels, i. 322; anti-Catholic legislation, i. 344, 345, 347; society in Chiswick, i. 351, 352; P. purchases South Sea stock, i. 379.

1717: For the *Iliad*, *see under* Homer; P.'s *Works* (1717), i. 394, 396, 403, 407, 410 (*and see under* Pope II); — Parnell's *Frogs*, i. 415; P.'s ramble to Oxford, &c., i. 404, 418, 424, 426, 427–33; life at Hampton Court, i. 427; projected visit to Ladyholt, i. 413, 414, 419, 442, 445; — the Blounts settle in Bolton Street, 409, 414; P.'s troubles with Martha and Teresa, i. 455, 458; Lord Harcourt picks a wife for P., i. 430–1; social activities, i. 404–5, 407, 409, 411, 417, 442, 450; death of an unnamed aunt, i. 433–4; his desire for a fair Circassian from Lady Mary, i. 441; fails to serve Mr. Boden, i. 443; his palfrey sold, i. 403–4; — his South Sea stock, i. 394–5; would invest £2,000 in an annuity, i. 415, 419; political prejudices, i. 416; complains of bad eyesight, i. 405; the death of P. sr., i. 447, 448, 450, 453, 454–5, 469; the poet will not change his religion, i. 453–4.

1718: On the *Iliad*, *see under* Homer; — P. burns *Alcander*, i. 467; spring spent in London and Chiswick, i. 467; the summer spent at Stanton Harcourt and Cirencester, i. 475, 476–8, 481, 484, 488, 489–90, 500, 508–11, 514–15; in July back in London, i. 476, 477, 478; death of the rustic lovers at Stanton Harcourt, i. 480–83, 494–504 *passim*, 523; — a visit to Atterbury at Bromley, i. 467; returns from Cirencester briefly towards the end of Sept., i. 517; brings his mother home in Oct., i. 517; troubles of and with the Misses Blount, 459, 460, 468, 484; Lady Mary's return, i. 500, 505, 517, and v. 1–2; — a meeting of the Scriblerus

POPE, BIOGR. DATA (*1718 cont.*)

Club, i. 478-9; acquaintance with Hatton the clock-maker, i. 465; aid to Matthew Prior, i. 521; writes of Mrs. Cope, i. 522; polite society regards the *Iliad*, i. 464, 470; — projected house in Town not to be built, i. 488, 516; P. ill, i. 461, 469; his watch over his failing mother, i. 463; politics thought absurd or corrupt, i. 462, 470, 472.

1719: For P.'s *Iliad, see under* Homer; Dancastle copies the Books for P., ii. 9, 19; Broome is thanked for aid on Eustathius, ii. 3, 19; P. thinks of retiring as poet, ii. 3; — P. visits five country houses annually, ii. 3; removes from Chiswick to Twickenham, ii. 8; acquires gardens there, ii. 18; the Thames in flood, ii. 59; brief visits to London, ii. 7, 18; in danger on the water by night, ii. 11; James Gibbs draws plans for P.'s improvements of his villa, ii. 4; P. and Sir G. Kneller help the Wortleys find a house in Twickenham, ii. 6, 10, 12; — P. visits Peterborow at Parson's Green, ii. 1; dines with the younger Craggs at Battersea, ii. 1, 16; visits Burlington's Gardens, i. 2; visits Lord Bathurst at Cirencester, ii. 13, 14; Edward Blount visits P. and uses his chariot, ii. 7, 10; A. Evans visits P., ii. 8; Congreve visits P., ii. 12; Mrs. Rackett comes to Twickenham, ii. 9; P. visits his neighbours with Thos. Vernon, ii. 15; visits Kneller, not to play cards but to watch K. paint, ii. 9; — his comments on the advisers of the Prince as to gardens, ii. 14; his interest in Martha Blount's lottery tickets, ii. 16-17.

1720: For the *Iliad* and the *Odyssey, see under* Homer; Pope's epitaph for Rowe, ii. 25; — P. designs, with Bird, the family tomb, ii. 26-27; is at leisure so far as writing goes, ii. 45-46; gardening and building, ii. 23, 44, 48, 58; visits to Town, ii. 27, 28, 38; goes to Tunbridge with the Duke of Buckingham, ii. 48; his care of his mother, ii. 46-47; — Lady Mary Wortley Montagu: her eclogues, ii.

POPE, BIOGR. DATA (*1720 cont.*)

39; P. to have her portrait, 22-23; she has a house in Twickenham, 38; P. advises her to purchase South Sea stocks, ii. 52; the younger Craggs takes a house in Twickenham and employs Fenton as tutor, ii. 45; P. intervenes with Craggs for Caryll, ii. 53, 57; — P. is reconciled with Teresa, ii. 25, 26, 30, 38, 59; the Misses Blount dine at Twickenham, ii. 21, 57; Mary Lepell the guest of the Popes, ii. 41; marries John, later Lord Hervey, ii. 41; P.'s praise of the Digby family life, ii. 44; — his interest in John Hughes's tragedy, ii. 28, 29, 33, 34, 46; Aaron Hill apologizes, ii. 35, 36; P. reads Prior's *Conversation* in MS., ii. 30; his dealings with Eckershall, ii. 32, 33, 34, 38, 39; the deaths of several friends, ii. 24, 29, 31; — his South Sea stocks, ii. 38, 42, 48, 49, 51, 52, 53-54, 56, 57, 60; his connexion with Dryden's tomb in the Abbey, ii. 51, 55; now affluent, P. talks of purchasing an estate in Devonshire, ii. 49.

1721: P. edits Parnell's *Poems* and prefixes his 'Epistle to the Earl of Oxford', ii. 90-92; composes an epitaph for young Harcourt, ii. 74; his connexion with Addison's *Works,* ii. 81; with the *Works* of the Duke of Buckingham, ii. 63, 81, 85; his comment on Buckingham's epitaph, ii. 73; considers editing Waller, ii. 80, 84; — his work on Shakespeare begins, ii. 78, 81; gives a copy of his *Iliad* to the Bodleian Library, ii. 83; his villa is enlarged, ii. 61; his gardens admired by Lady Mary, ii. 82; his journey to Oxfordshire (Harcourt?), ii. 80; to Gloucestershire: to Cirencester, ii. 79, 80, 82, 85; to Rentcomb, ii. 85; — Mrs. P.'s declining state, ii. 73; P.'s agitation over Lady Mary, ii. 62; Broome will dedicate verses on smallpox to her, ii. 77; P. is not allowed to lend her his harpsichord, ii. 82; invites to Twickenham: Richardson, ii. 61; Dean Berkeley, ii. 62; Tonson jr., ii. 63; — Atterbury sends him criticisms, ii. 74, 79; Prior's funeral

POPE, BIOGR. DATA (*1721 cont.*)
ii. 84; a truce made with John
Dennis, ii. 75, 76; the character
of young Craggs, ii. 73, 81; —
Edward and Mrs. Blount greeted
from Rentcomb, ii. 86; Blount's
projected self-exile, 89; Caryll is
helped to Spa waters, ii. 77;
P. urges the Dancastles to extend
charity to Betty Fletcher, ii.
63–64; his concern in the Abbey monument
to Samuel Butler, ii. 76; Gay turns
over South Sea stocks to P., ii. 75, 91.
1722: Verses (and letters) to Judith
Cowper, ii. 139, &c.; Lines on P.'s
grotto, ii. 142; the Harcourt epitaph to be revised, ii. 146; for work
on the *Odyssey*, *see under* Homer;
work on the Duke of Buckingham's
Works, 100, 101, 102, 117, 123, 125,
127–8; the Duke's monument, ii. 99;
— work on Shakespeare, ii. 102, 106,
117, 118; aided by Cheselden, ii.
101; by Fenton, ii. 130; P. gets subscriptions for Buononcini, ii. 99;
helps arrange the Duchess of Buckingham's concert, ii. 135–6; declines
to write prologues for the Duke and
for Fenton, ii. 134; — catches cold
on the river coming from Bromley, ii.
131; attends the funeral of the Duke
of Marlborough, ii. 127, 129; much
at home on account of Mrs. Pope's
fragility, ii. 112; — his friendship
with Atterbury, ii. 101–2, 106, 107,
120; Atterbury's opinion of the lines
on Addison, ii. 104; to visit P. after
the death of Atterbury's wife, ii. 109,
113, 115 n., 116; Atterbury's plot, ii.
120; P. visits him in the Tower, ii.
146; Atterbury's opinion of *Samson
Agonistes*, ii. 124; — Caryll piqued
for lack of a visit, ii. 112; Lady Mary
Caryll in Twickenham, ii. 140; Lord
Harcourt invited to Twickenham, ii.
114, 115, 126; P.'s projected visit to
the Digbys, ii. 115; P. is painted by
Kneller for the third time, ii. 118 n.;
he thanks Morley for oysters, ii. 148;
new friendship with Mrs. Caesar, ii.
126; P. asks Lord Bathurst to call on
Martha Blount, ii. 127.
1723: For the *Odyssey*, *see under*
Homer; for personal relations of the

POPE, BIOGR. DATA (*1723 cont.*)
year *see* (ii. 151–212) especially under
Mrs. P., Lord Bathurst, John
Sheffield (Buckingham), Henry St.
John (Bolingbroke), Charles Mordaunt (Peterborow), Bishop Atterbury, Swift, Fenton, Broome, *et al.*;
— P. sends 'To a Lady on her Birthday' to Judith Cowper, ii. 180, who
compliments him in her verses, 197–
8; P.'s relations with Lady Mary still
cordial, ii. 194; he is attacked in
Mme Dacier's *Odyssey*, ii. 157–8; —
P.'s deference to Tickell as to the
Odyssey, ii. 158, 159, 161; Mrs.
Caesar gets subscribers to the *Odyssey*, ii. 197; P. thanks Morley for
Oysters, ii. 156; reads Prior's MSS.
for Lord Harley, ii. 193, 203; wishes
to copy the Rigault portrait of Prior,
ii. 204; — Lord Harcourt advises P.
concerning testimony at Atterbury's
trial, ii. 156, 161, 171, 172, 206;
Carteret appealed to regarding political difficulties over the Duke of
Buckingham's *Works* and the *Odyssey*, ii. 159–60; P. on the corruption
of public life, ii. 182–3; added taxes
on Catholics, ii. 173; — P. much
from home, 173, 194, 204; R. Digby
visits P., 162, 191; E. Young makes
a request to P., ii. 171; Kneller's portrait of P. goes to Lord Harcourt, ii.
193; J. Richardson helps on Shakespeare, ii. 177; Martha Blount feels
neglected, ii. 191.
1724: On the *Odyssey*, *see under*
Homer; on personal relations *see*,
especially, Robert and Edward Harley, Earls of Oxford, Broome,
Fenton, Mrs. Caesar, Marquise de
Villette (Lady Bolingbroke), Thos.
Tickell, *et al.*; on the edition of
Shakespeare (now being completed)
see ii. 213, 222, 270, 279–80; on
Buckingham's *Works*, Pope wishes
Lintot added to the sharing booksellers, ii. 218, 222; — Bolingbroke
wishes P. to give up translation in
favour of original work, ii. 219–20;
in Town P. stays with Lord Bathurst,
ii. 260, 298; is invited to Ashley
by Pulteney, ii. 247; visits the
Digbys at Sherborne, ii. 236, 240;

Pope, Biogr. Data (*1724 cont.*)
plans to visit Lord Oxford at Wimpole (does not go), ii. 257, 270; Tonson visits him at Twickenham, ii. 223; Fortescue asked to draw up agreement with Lintot, ii. 216–17, is offered Pope's villa for small-pox inoculations, ii. 255; — P. aids Mrs. Howard at Marble Hill, ii. 242, 256, 259, 261, v. 19; discharges his servant Robert, ii. 257; thinks Lady Mary undecipherable, ii. 258; the death of Robert Harley, Earl of Oxford, ii. 232–3, 235; P. is reconciled with Tickell, ii. 223; the Epilogue to Gay's *Captives*, ii. 215–16; a dinner party at the Vandeputs, ii. 232; — P. health, ii. 224–5, 248; his mother's bad health, see *passim*, ii. 261–79; his work on the Duke of Buckingham's monument, ii. 217–18; on the Craggs monument, ii. 217, 223, 242–3, 246, 254, 266; tries to get a berth for his sailor nephew, John Rackett, ii. 246; helps Crookshanks in passing an idiot, ii. 224; helps elect a Preacher for the Charterhouse, ii. 267, 268, 269, 272, 273; his views on political corruption, ii. 269.

1725: On the *Odyssey, see under* Homer; the edition of Shakespeare completed, ii. 282, 286; projected anti-Rochefoucauld maxims, ii. 333; lines quoted, later found in *Dunciad*, ii. 332; — the Lines on Miss Hervey not by P., ii. 343, 349; Swift regrets Pope's engrossment in translation, ii. 311; in Town P. stays at Lord Oxford's, ii. 313, 335, 348; at home he works in his garden and grotto, ii. 296, 297, 328; — a long ramble in July, ii. 314; at Stowe, ii. 302, 310; at Leighs, ii. 297, 299, 303; invited, with Gay, to Riskins, ii. 299, 304; invited to Cirencester, ii. 305; his trouble with Lady Kneller about Sir Godfrey's tomb, ii. 289, 300, 301, 306–7, *and see under* Strafford; — at Christmas time goes to Down Hall, ii. 327, 355; P. invites to Twickenham: Buckley, ii. 286, R. Digby, 283, Ford, 283, 284, Lord Oxford, 311, J. Richardson, 298; Lord Bathurst as gardener, ii. 292, 298–9, 314–15; —

Pope, Biogr. Data (*1725 cont.*)
Broome is desired to stay from Town during negotiations with Lintot, ii. 291; his verses on P., ii. 302, 338, 340; problems in settling for the *Odyssey*, ii. 292–3, 295, 344; — Mercy Beech (P.'s old nurse) dies, ii. 282, 336–7; illness of Arbuthnot, ii. 316, 322, 335; P. helps the Duchess of Buckingham in her suit against Ward, ii. 286–7; Bolingbroke settles at Dawley, ii. 290, 332; P. asks Fortescue to thank Sir R. Walpole for him, ii. 294; — Edward Harley, now Earl of Oxford, ii. 259, 310; his rambles, ii. 316–17, 336, 338, 355; Lintot's bad behaviour, ii. 287, 290, 291; Mrs. Howard, ii. 292, 298–9; Mrs. Caesar, ii. 293, 312; a copy of the *Odyssey* presented to W. Aikman, ii. 294; Dodington quoted, ii. 294; Caryll's copies of the *Odyssey*, ii. 299; death of Mrs. J. Richardson, ii. 284; — P.'s busto by Rysbrack, ii. 298; the Robinsons move to Fulham, ii. 329; Ambrose Philips, ii. 326, 332, 342; Lord Strafford, ii. 300, 308–9, 313–14, 327–8; P. advertises that the Shakespeare subscription is for Tonson's benefit, not for his own, ii. 286; — P.'s health, ii. 289, 290, 319, 323, 329, 346, 352; his mother's health, ii. 287, 329, 334; has jaundice, ii. 335–6, 338, 340, 346; Pulteney and Bolingbroke thought to be 'caballing', ii. 291; Gay hunts a place, ii. 322–3.

1726: On the completion and publication of the last vols. of the *Odyssey, see under* Homer; on the Postscript to the *Odyssey, see*, ii. 369–70, 377, 378, 385; collaboration problems, ii. 365, 390; P.'s version of Donne's *Sat.* ii discovered by Lord Oxford, ii. 371; P. denies a connexion with Lintot's Miscellany, ii. 383; *A Receipt for Stewing Veal*, ii. 403–4; the poems appended to *Gulliver*, ii. 411, 417; — his letters to Cromwell printed by Curll, ii. 404–5; P. asks Caryll, and all others, to return his letters, ii. 419, 423; the Pope–Swift *Miscellanies* in preparation, ii. 420; P. visits Down Hall, ii. 358, 361; with Swift at Cirencester, ii. 388; at

POPE, BIOGR. DATA (*1726 cont.*)
Bibury, 406; in Town frequently at Lord Oxford's, ii. 359, 360, 421; not at Peterborow's dinner for Swift, ii. 384, v. 6; — improves his gardens at Twickenham, ii. 372; he entertains all comers for Swift, ii. 380, 386; P.'s various illnesses, ii. 384, 402; his coach accident in the Crane, ii. 399–409 (*passim*); — invites to Twickenham: Broome and Fenton, ii. 365; H. Bethel, 387; Fortescue, 368; Stopford, 421–2; the death of Edward Blount, ii. 387, 423; of R. Digby, ii. 375; Bridgeman with P. at Down Hall, ii. 364; — Broome is tactless with P.'s note for £100, ii. 389, 396–7; P. refunds to a poverty-stricken subscriber to the *Odyssey*, ii. 391; asks Caryll to send venison, ii. 392; his concern for Mrs. Cope, ii. 361, 367, 380; Fenton's laziness, ii. 357–8; Fenton's Waller to be dedicated to Lady Margaret Harley, ii. 374, 376; P.'s ill opinion of Lintot seconded by Fenton, ii. 385; Morley is thanked for oysters, ii. 362; — Spence's *Essay on the Odyssey*, ii. 379; Swift's summer visit, ii. 372, 373, 381, 384, 387; the welcome of *Gulliver*, ii. 412, &c.; P.'s unlucky remark at Walpole's dinner, ii. 368; P. at Sir W. Wyndham's house, ii. 359; the stock market is bad, ii. 372.

1727: *Miscellanies* i and ii printed, ii. 426, 439; the last vol. in preparation, ii. 425, 426, 438, 444, 466; vol. iii projected, ii. 439; lines quoted from the dedication of *The Dunciad* to Swift, ii. 456; verses appended to *Gulliver*, ii. 426; Curll publishes the Pope–Cromwell letters, ii. 437, 439–41; — Swift visits P. at Twickenham, ii. 435; leaves there, 442; P. has sent him fennel and broccoli seeds, ii. 425; P. and Swift plan to dine at Lord Oxford's in London, ii. 430, 431; they visit him at Wimpole, ii. 441, 442; — Stella is reported ill, ii. 445; Swift leaves for Ireland, ii. 445, 447; P. saw him at Hammersmith, ii. 448; P. plans but does not make a trip to Leighs and Gosfield, ii. 457, 462; dines frequently on Sundays at Wal-

POPE, BIOGR. DATA (*1727 cont.*)
pole's house, ii. 441, v. 2; is invited to Riskins for Christmas, ii. 464–5; — Lintot quarrels over Broome's work on the *Odyssey*, ii. 432; Caryll repays P. £200, ii. 428; P. advises Caryll on statues, ii. 434; tries to get Clarke (auctioneer) the sale of Lord Lechmere's goods, ii. 443; Cleland eats broccoli at P.'s, ii. 425 n.; — Conduit aided by P. in a dedication, ii. 457–9; Mrs. Cope's last illness and P.'s charity to her, ii. 434, 449; Congreve urges P. to give Curll another emetic, ii. 434; P. plans financial relief for his old schoolmaster, Dean, ii. 428; Gay is congratulated on declining to be gentleman usher, ii. 453, 454, 455, 460; his opera is written, ii. 455; P.'s comments on the death of the King, ii. 437; — Lord Harcourt is asked for legal advice, ii. 430; Lord Oxford gives P. a gold cup, ii. 465; P. tries to aid Sir John Hope-Bruce, ii. 427; Mrs. Howard is consoled by P., ii. 445–6; is aided against Mrs. Vernon, ii. 446; P. intervenes on behalf of Mrs. H.'s maid, ii. 447; presents Stopford with the *Odyssey*, ii. 425; pays Dr. Towne a debt, ii. 424; — Mrs. P. is ill, ii. 435, 436, 448; P. supervises finishing the Craggs monument, ii. 456, 457, 463; sells his stocks, ii. 444; comments on political warmth, ii. 426–7.

1728: *Miscellanies*, 'last' vol., ii. 468; Curll's complaints of copyright infringement, 477–8; P.'s *Dulness* or *Dunciad*, ii. 468–533, *passim*; *Dunciad Variorum*, ii. 498, 502, 503, 520; Swift 'properly the author' of it, ii. 523; approved by Congreve, ii. 508; aid from Ireland asked, ii. 523; Fazackerley consulted, ii. 532–3; P.'s worries over Cooke, ii. 509, 510, 519, v. 7; the *Bathos*, ii. 468, 484, 487; Broome offended by it, ii. 487–8, 499; — P. asks H. Bethel to return his letters, ii. 501; P. is attacked by Mist and others, ii. 486; not whipped as his enemies say, ii. 502; stands 'Athanasius contra mundum', ii. 507; P.'s early repute in America, ii. 494–5; — his alleged mobility, ii.

POPE, BIOGR. DATA (*1728 cont.*)

472; seldom in Town, ii. 474, 490, v. 6; a ten-day trip planned, ii. 504; invites the Oxfords to Twickenham, 467, 490 (with the Caesars); at Dawley among the haycocks, ii. 503; goes to Bath, ii. 510, 516, 521, 524; at Stowe, ii. 513; takes physic at Durhams, ii. 513–14; at Cirencester (?), ii. 511–12, 517; — his health, ii. 467–8, 479, 529, 530; his mother's health, ii. 468, 479, 480, 484, 498, 533; the Blount ladies at Petersham, ii. 491; Broome offended, ii. 470–1, 487–8, 489, 499; P. aids Buckley and Mead on Thuanus, ii. 471, 529; — Gay's success with his opera, ii. 469; his illness, ii. 531; P. tries to help Harte to a fellowship at Oxford, ii. 497; Mrs. Howard's sad state, ii. 469; her happy adjustments, ii. 491; P.'s appointments with Mrs. Knight, ii. 485; E. Lewis and wife at Bath with P., ii. 518; M. Maittaire out of *The Dunciad* at Lord Oxford's desire, ii. 496; — Motte dilatory in paying for the *Miscellanies*, ii. 526; Lord Oxford's gold cup, ii. 470; Oxford wishes a Key to *The Dunciad* (as does the King), ii. 502; — *The Daily Journal* seems to print from Oxford's Pope papers, ii. 511, 515–16; his amanuenses employed on *The Dunciad*, ii. 504, 506; P. wishes to dine with Oxford and Mr. Wesley, ii. 529; Mrs. Rackett's troubles over her husband's estate begin, ii. 530; P. dines of a Sunday with Walpole, ii. 530; S. Wesley intervenes for P. with Cooke, ii. 510, 515, 529; last touches on the Craggs monument, ii. 484; — P.'s income increased, ii. 469; he gets an annuity from the Duchess of Buckingham, ii. 525; the political temper of the time, ii. 472–3.

1729: P. sends lines on his birthday, iii. 3; includes them in lines on Martha Blount's birthday, iii. 18; *Miscellanies* (1732), iv, P. collects pieces for, iii. 17, 22 (*see also* Motte, *below*); — *The Dunciad Variorum*, its publication, iii. 4 n., 25, 31; presented to the King by Walpole, iii. 26; Fazackerley consulted on libel, iii. 4;

POPE, BIOGR. DATA (*1729 cont.*)

Lady Burlington sponsors the poem, iii. 4, 20; notes partly by friends, iii. 31, 36; a defensive advertisement projected, iii. 31–32; a piracy stopped, iii. 37; assigned by three lords to Gilliver, iii. 59, 61, 62, 67; 8th ed., iii. 79; — the Digby epitaph, iii. 51; P. now intends to write nothing but imitations of Horace, iii. 37; asks Caryll to return his letters, iii. 14, 31, 38; reasons for not writing letters, iii. 14; Wycherley letters published from the Harley Library, iii. 54, 55, 56, 58, 80; — P. attacked (few defenders), iii. 37; attacked in *Pope Alexander's Supremacy*, iii. 33–34; in *One Epistle*, iii. 59, 60; P. in Town, iii. 6; Caryll visits him, iii. 35; Lord Oxford invited to Twickenham, iii. 10, 11, 12; P. is much at home, iii. 83; the Caesars visit him, iii. 40; he goes to Essex, iii. 36; — dines in Town with Buckley at Dr. Mead's, iii. 70; dines with the Caesars and Miss Cole, iii. 56 n.; uses Sir T. Lyttelton's London address, iii. 70; is invited by the Duke of Grafton, iii. 82; Bolingbroke goes to France, iii. 48–50; Jervas back from Ireland, iii. 50; Bathurst helps distribute *The Dunciad*, iii. 31, 78; — Martha Blount's regard for her family, iii. 13; P. has no *tendresse* for her, iii. 70, 75; her Roberts annuity, iii. 33; P.'s gossip about Teresa Blount, iii. 36, 38, 40, 42, 44, 46, 61, 70; he reproaches Caryll for meagre aid to Mrs. Cope, iii. 12–13, 18; asks Caryll to return his letters, iii. 14; Congreve's death, iii. 3, 9, 10, 15; — Gay's illness, iii. 1, 2, 3, 9, 17; Gay is 'very busy', iii. 17; his subscription, iii. 24; the 'exile' of the Queensberrys, iii. 19–20; Mrs. Howard's troubles with Mrs. Vernon over land, iii. 34–35, v. 5, 19; P. aids Mallet with *Eurydice*, iii. 65 n., 66, 82; Lady Mary Wortley Montagu is said to be libelling P., iii. 53, 59, 60; Moore-Smythe pretends authorship of P. lines, iii. 18; is satirical of P., iii. 59 n.; — Motte dilatory in his payments for the *Miscellanies*, iii. 8–9, 23, 27, 32; Lord Oxford asked to purchase,

POPE, BIOGR. DATA (*1729 cont.*)
through an agent, *Pope Alexander's Supremacy*, iii. 34; sends P. a collar of brawn, iii. 78; he and P. the objects of gossip, iii. 83; — Henry Rackett limited as lawyer in being a Non-Juror, iii. 52 n.; Mrs. Rackett's estate troubles, iii. 5, 6, 39; Swift plans to come over in the spring of 1730, iii. 71; — Horatio Walpole thanked by P., iii. 6; Sir Robert Walpole asked to identify an author, iii. 12; seen once this season by P., iii. 53; his civil treatment of P., iii. 81; — S. Wesley tries to intervene with Cooke, iii. 8, 9; Whalley is aided by P., iii. 21; P.'s bad health, iii. 17, 45–46, 60, 62, 67; Mrs. P.'s ill health, iii. 1–80 *passim*; a religious duty on Monday makes visitors inconvenient, iii. 11.

1730: P. at work on his Ethic Poems, iii. 99, 117, 139, 153; his lines on his busto, iii. 100; his epitaph on Fenton, iii. 156; busy arranging fragments, iii. 155; his comments on the rhythmus, iii. 140; his dissatisfaction with Swift's 'Libel', iii. 91, 101; his reactions to *One Epistle*, iii. 106, 107, 114; *The Grub-street Journal*, iii. 85, 110; — P. lives at home 'in retirement', iii. 118, 123, 134, 136, 138, 151; guests at home: Robert Arbuthnot, iii. 88, Mallet, 87, 144, Lord Oxford, 123–4; in London stays with Lord Oxford, iii. 87, 118, 136; missed Caryll in Town, iii. 89, 90; goes on a short journey, iii. 109; is six days from home, iii. 157; goes to Riskins, iii. 120; is at Court two days, iii. 131, 133 n., 135, 139; urged to visit Cirencester, iii. 134; invited to live with Swift in Dublin, iii. 109; Mrs. Barber is introduced by Swift, iii. 89; — Martha Blount's family troubles, iii. 88; her income, iii. 112, 139; she spends the summer in the country, iii. 113, 136; Teresa Blount does not scandalize Sussex, iii. 122; — Broome, after a lapse, resumes writing to P., iii. 100, 116; Broome is urged to answer libellers of P., iii. 106; P. not the person who put Broome in the *Bathos*, iii. 106, 107, 116; false report

POPE, BIOGR. DATA (*1730 cont.*)
of Broome's death, iii. 155; P. proudly refuses £100 from the Duchess of Buckingham, iii. 91, 110, 116, 122; Burlington is made Knight of the Garter, iii. 111; — P. applies to Cheselden for a scholarship for Mr. Wise, iii. 141; P. tries to aid Cleland's student son, iii. 144; Cibber, not Savage, made laureate, iii. 158; S. Duck called to P.'s attention, iii. 132–3, 143; recommends a man to B. Fairfax, v. 8; Fenton's death lamented, iii. 121, 124, 128; Fortescue ill of the gout, iii. 127, 129; — Gay's remote, exquisite exile at Amesbury lamented, iii. 119, 125, 131, 138, 142; Hearne hostile to P. because of *The Dunciad*, iii. 111; Lady Howard's cause aided by P., iii. 103; Mallet's *Eurydice* furthered by P., iii. 86, 87, 158; Bathurst wishes P. to inquire of Lady Mary's health, iii. 134; Motte has paid Swift completely, iii. 90; — Lord Oxford's new library at Wimpole, with P.'s bust in it, iii. 115, 136, 147, 153; Lord Oxford gives P. a lamprey, iii. 105, and a collar of brawn, iii. 144; — Henry Rackett's inability to be admitted to the bar, iii. 150, 153, 154; delays in the affairs of Mrs. Rackett, iii. 91, 112, 141; — Swift plans to visit England (1730), iii. 93; he sends P. usquebaugh, iii. 97; P. goes to Walpole's levee, iii. 112, P.'s private opinion of Walpole, iii. 113, 125; to get Lady Walpole a laver, iii. 140; — P. tries to get subscribers to Samuel Wesley [sr.]'s *Job*, iii. 95; again aids Whalley's case, iii. 102, 104; P.'s health, iii. 91, 113, 127, 156; his mother's condition, iii. 117, 127, 135; her fall into the fire, iii. 141, 142, 144.

1731: P. at work on the *Essay on Man*, iii. 163, 183–4, 213–14 (summarized), 227, 232, 247; the character of Marlborough, iii. 227; the *Epistle on Taste* (to Burlington), iii. 187–8, 254–63; *Epistle to Bathurst*, iii. 227, 241, 244; thinks *The Grub-street Journal* diverting at times, iii. 173; his lines to a 'successful youth', iii. 226; his epitaph on Charles, Earl of

POPE, BIOGR. DATA (*1731 cont.*)
Dorset, iii. 241; — his aim is correction by ridicule, not by preaching, iii. 173; Swift doubts Cleland's authorship of the letter before *The Dunciad,* iii. 162; Bramston's *Art of Politics* commended, iii. 173; Harte's *Essay on Satire* commended, iii. 173; so also Miller's *Harlequin Horace,* iii. 173; P. is pleased by Mallet's epitaph on Aikman, iii. 222; learns that Tonson will publish Theobald's Shakespeare, iii. 241–4; — Hill sends P. *The Plain Dealer,* iii. 164, and his *Caveat,* 165, 174; he complains of a passage in *The Dunciad,* 164–5; he attacks P.'s defence of it, 166–9; P. conciliates him, 169–72; praises Hill's *Advice to the Poets,* iii. 175, 177, 188; aids in getting Hill's *Athelwold* staged, iii. 200–58, *passim*; condoles with Hill on Mrs. Hill's death, iii. 222–3; Hill is invited to visit P. iii. 230, 231; suggests the title 'Of False Taste', iii. 257.

As guests at Twickenham P. has Cleland, iii. 210, Lord Bathurst, 175, A. Hill, 188–9, Lord Oxford, 178, 193, 197, 202, Mallet, 189, Gay, 227; Tonson sr. fails to come, iii. 176; — P. at Parson's Green (Lord Peterborow), iii. 169, 177; at Chiswick (Lord Burlington), 183, 200, dines there with Lord Wilmington, 244; at Dawley (Bolingbroke), 189, 201; at Gosfield (Knight), 218; at Stowe (Cobham), 216, 244; plans to go to Southampton, iii. 218; — at the first performance of *Athelwold,* iii. 253; in London P. visits J. Richardson, iii. 160; Mrs. Cornish, iii. 198; Lord Oxford, iii. 187; Lord Peterborow, iii. 177; breaks an engagement in order to confer with lawyers, iii. 236; sends Lady Burlington a pamphlet, iii. 201; his mother's condition, iii. 160, 187, 196, 209, 226, 228, 241; his own health, iii. 159, 175, 176, 181, 182, 186, 190, 193, 209, 240, 249; drinks asses' milk, iii. 184–97, *passim.*

He blames Bentley for the Cottonian fire, iii. 240; Martha Blount's worries over the Roberts annuity, iii. 197, 198, 227, 233; her family troubles, iii. 237; Teresa Blount's

POPE, BIOGR. DATA (*1731 cont.*)
gallant returns, iii. 173; — P. recommends Brandreth to Swift, iii. 161; P. would gladly aid Dennis, iii. 166; but Dennis says P. does it through fear, iii. 171–2, 174; P. wishes Essington replaced as Mrs. Rackett's trustee, iii. 196; Mrs. Howard becomes Countess of Suffolk, iii. 205; — P. and Mallet invited to dine in Town with Bolingbroke, iii. 177; P. recommends Mallet to Mrs. Knight as tutor, iii. 202; Lord Oxford sends P. a collar of brawn, iii. 245; P. loses one of Oxford's books, 221; — H. Rackett recommended for a place, iii. 172–3; Mrs. Rackett hopes to lease Hallgrove to a Duke, iii. 224; P. lends J. Richardson an ed. of Milton, iii. 231, 240; Swift is unable to come to England this year, iii. 202; — P. makes use of Lord Oxford's chaplain (T. Thomas), iii. 187, 193; P. sends Atterbury transcripts to Lord Oxford, iii. 187; Mrs. Barber wishes aid from P., iii. 184, 191; she has letters of recommendation to the Queen (? from Swift), iii. 207–8; P. wishes for Dr. Burton an analysis of Scarborough waters, iii. 197; the Duke of Chandos's reaction to the *Epistle on Taste,* iii. 262–3; P. advises Fortescue on building, iii. 225.

1732: Parts of the *Essay on Man* being transcribed, iii. 271, 312; *Miscellanies* iii in preparation (Swift's items), iii. 292–3; Motte wishes to publish, iii. 306, 318; *Epistle to Burlington* (its title), iii. 268; its Preface, iii. 267, 279 (the noise it makes); *Epistle to Bathurst,* publication delayed, iii. 267; the Man of Ross, iii. 290–1, 316; tailpieces from P.'s Homer used by permission in Buckley's *Thuanus,* iii. 294; suppressed dialogue on Kent between P. and Gen. Dormer, iii. 329; — Dr. Cowper's translation of the *Messiah* (?), iii. 268; P. and Tonson on Bentley's Milton, iii. 269, 291; Lady Burlington transcribes something for P., iii. 272, 273; — as guests at Twickenham P. has Fortescue and Gay, iii. 264, 265, 283; Jervas, iii. 271, Caryll fr.,

POPE, BIOGR. DATA (*1732 cont.*)
284, Caryll sr., 302, Cleland, 302, Pilkington, 323; P. stays home 'all the winter', iii. 274; — in London he sees Fortescue, iii. 270, Cheselden, 330, and stays at Lord Oxford's (Dover Street), iii. 278, 280, 315, 323; is at Parson's Green, iii. 283, Chiswick, 283, is urged to come to Cirencester (Bathurst), 299–300; in Sept. Burlington is three weeks from home, iii. 322. The death of Atterbury, iii. 278; Bathurst's 'improvements' in gardening, iii. 295; Martha Blount's family difficulties, iii. 279; she was very ill after Gay's death, iii. 337; Bowyer tries to claim Swift copyrights, iii. 323–4; the Duchess of Buckingham's sudden trip to France, iii. 296; — Lord Burlington in Yorkshire, iii. 313–14; he advises concerning P.'s portico, iii. 314–15, 322, 329; P. works on Lady Burlington's family [Savile] papers, iii. 303, 314, 328; P. regrets not having Mrs. Caesar dine at Twickenham, iii. 331; Mrs. Englefield marries P.'s schoolmate, Webb, iii. 274; Gay declines P.'s request for eulogy of the Court, iii. 322; Gay's death, iii. 334–6; — P. tries to get from Burlington a parish for Harte, iii. 332; is given vol. ii. of Lansdowne's *Works*, iii. 327; E. Lewis is dangerously ill, iii. 295; Mallet's *Verbal Criticism* is to be inscribed to P., iii. 327, 330; — Lord Oxford sends collars of brawn to P., iii. 267, 334; Oxford is mentioned in the *Epistle to Bathurst*, iii. 267; Lord Peterborow on the corruption of the time, iii. 282; Pilkington and Swift's copyrights, iii. 323; — J. Richardson has done a portrait of Bolingbroke for P., iii. 326; R. writes verses on the *Essay on Man*, iii. 326–7; P. wishes to see R. at Cheselden's, iii. 330; P. aids the Richardsons in their work on Milton, iii. 331; — Tonson sr. is to have a copy of Dahl's portrait of P., iii. 291; Mrs. P.'s feeble condition, iii. 267, 268, 270, 274, 281, 288, 331; political conditions, iii. 276, 282, 307.
1733: *Epistle to Lord Bathurst*, iii. 340, 342, 343, 345; *Miscellanies* iii

POPE, BIOGR. DATA (*1733 cont.*)
(1732), iii. 347–8; *Imitation of Horace, Satire i, Bk. II*, iii. 348, 350, 351, 352, 353; Walpole tries to intervene for Lady Mary, iii. 354, in vain, 355; P.'s epitaph for Gay, iii. 347, 360, 368; — *Essay on Man*, its anonymity, iii. 350, 356; the reception of Epistle I, iii. 351, 352, 355–6 (Welsted); of Epistle II, iii. 358; the doctrines of the poem, iii. 354, 390; care to finish the work, iii. 381, 395; *Epistle to Viscount Cobham*, iii. 390, 391, 393; *Imitation of Horace, Satire ii, Bk. II*, iii. 358, 366, 369; *Epistle to a Lady* ('On the Characters of Women'), iii. 349, 363; *A Letter to a Noble Lord*, iii. 396 n.; P. is attacked by Lord Hervey and Lady Mary Wortley Montagu, iii. 366, 397 n.
Much in the country (Twickenham), iii. 359; invites Caryll to visit him there, iii. 358, 373; Cobham and Lady Suffolk dine at P.'s, iii. 377; Spence is invited to visit, iii. 380; P. ill in Dover street (Lord Oxford's), iii. 344–5; alone in Oxford's house, iii. 359, 388; — with Lord Bathurst in St. James's Square, iii. 376; spends ten days together in Town, iii. 350; has a week of business, not poetical, in Town, iii. 357, 358; away from home much after his mother's death, iii. 381; — is at Peterborow's bedside in Kensington daily, iii. 343; visits Chiswick and shows the Gardens, iii. 376–7, 382, 390; goes into Essex (Halstead?), iii. 382; at Stowe, iii. 383; at Ladyholt, iii. 383, 384; at Cirencester, iii. 385; at Southampton for 3 weeks, iii. 387, 401.
P. works on the Savile papers for Lady Burlington, iii. 341; builds a 'new room' and a portico, iii. 341, 353, 356, 358; he takes a sudden cold, iii. 344, 350, but in general his health is good, iii. 357; — Mrs. P.'s last days, iii. 344, 349, 357, 358; she desires to thank Lady Oxford and Lady Margaret in person, iii. 372; her death, 373, 374; Richardson asked to draw a postmortem likeness, iii. 374; P.'s grief, iii. 374, 375, 384, 385; Swift's condolence, iii. 378.

POPE, BIOGR. DATA (*1733 cont.*)

The Blounts give up their summer place at Petersham, iii. 370; Martha Blount's submissiveness to her family, iii. 340; Bethel an agent in the Roberts annuity for Miss Blount, iii. 355; — Lord Burlington furnishes P. with building stone, iii. 341; he advises P. on stucco, 356; meetings of the two men are difficult to arrange, iii. 364–5; Lady Burlington gives P. a picture, iii. 341; does transcribing for P., iii. 397; — Caryll expected in Twickenham in Whitsun week, iii. 370; Caryll asked to recommend Henry Rackett, iii. 346; P., through Mallet, wishes to alleviate the pitiful state of John Dennis, iii. 357–8; P. hears a moving account of Dennis, iii. 394; a benefit for Dennis arranged at Drury Lane, iii. 394 n.; — P. will recommend Dodsley's *Toy Shop*, iii. 346; anecdotes of P.'s early life sent to Curll by 'E. P.', iii. 359–60, and by 'P. T.', iii. 395; 'P. T.' offers Curll 'a large collection of letters', iii. 395; — Fortescue sought in vain in London, iii. 351, because of the Excise debates, iii. 355, 356, 364; the marriage of Fortescue's dau., iii. 391, 395; Swift's grief over Gay's death, iii. 343, 365; Gay's *Works* discussed, iii. 347, 361, 372; the run of *Achilles*, iii. 347, 350; — Hill wishes to give P. shells for an obelisk, &c., iii. 393; Hill's *Zaire* approved of by P., iii. 394; Mallet is asked, for Theobald's sake, to postpone *Verbal Criticism*, iii. 357; — Lady Mary Wortley protests to Peterborow concerning 'Sappho', iii. 352; Pope will not reply to her *Verses address'd to the Imitator of Horace*, iii. 354, 357; Swift wishes P. to make Orrery's acquaintance, iii. 344; Swift gives Orrery a copy of P.'s epitaph for Gay, iii. 365; — complains of the 'Life and Genuine Character' dedicated to P., v. 10; Lord Oxford is asked by P. to send by a 'sober person' a letter to Curll, iii. 359; Oxford is asked to return King Henry's Prayerbook, iii. 365; Oxford remembers P.'s birthday, iii. 371; he and P. plan a ramble, iii. 381; — Henry

POPE, BIOGR. DATA (*1733 cont.*)

Rackett wishes a place with the Duke of Norfolk, iii. 346; John Rackett is in trouble with the law, iii. 339–40; — P., in Town, ill, wishes to see J. Richardson, iii. 345; P. apologizes for going to Cheselden's house instead of Richardson's, iii. 352–3; the Countess of Suffolk unhappy at Court, iii. 367; — Swift's lines on P. in the 'Libel on Dr. Delany' most pleasing to P., iii. 372; Swift thinks Dr. Young the author of the *Essay on Man* and 'not merry enough', iii. 372, v. 11; Swift wishes to visit P. and Bolingbroke, iii. 369; he urges P. to come and live in Dublin, asks P. to be kind to young Thomas Sheridan (11 years old), iii. 369, v. 13, 14; — James Thomson reads (from MS.?) a new poem of his to P., iii. 395; Walpole gets Fortescue to intervene for Lady Mary as Sappho, iii. 354.

1734: The doctrines of the *Essay on Man*, iii. 400, 403; P.'s larger ethical plan, iii. 405; his purpose in the anonymous publication, iii. 438; obscurity of the poem, iii. 439–40; Swift's opinion of the *Imitation of Horace, Satire ii, Bk. II*, iii. 429; *Sober Advice* (Horace, *Sat. II. ii*), iii. 413–14, 447; — P. writes no verses on Lady Margaret Harley's marriage, iii. 411; P. is attacked by Lord Hervey, iii. 400, 401, who is well answered by the Parish Bellman, iii. 401; a group of attacks on P. to be bound up for him, iii. 399; P. states his theory of satire to Dr. Arbuthnot, iii. 419–20, 423, 445.

At home P. has as dinner guests, Lord Oxford, iii. 404, Lady Suffolk and Fortescue, 409; returns from Town because of a fire in his neighbourhood, iii. 409; in Town he sits to Richardson, iii. 402; stays alone in Lord Oxford's town house, iii. 442; is ill there, iii. 443; — a long summer ramble planned, omitting Ladyholt, iii. 405, 408, 413, 425; he goes to Stowe for a week, iii. 409; to Rousham, 410; to Cirencester, 410, 414, 415; to Tottenham (Lord Bruce), 417–18; to

POPE, BIOGR. DATA (*1734 cont.*)

Bevis Mount (Southampton), iii. 416–36 *passim*; Netley Abbey, iii. 427, 430; 'Bewley' Abbey, iii. 426, 430; returns to London and Hampstead (Dr. Arbuthnot), iii. 434; goes at once to Bath, iii. 434–6; returns home in Oct., iii. 437.

P. feels he has little leisure, iii. 402; he has his house stuccoed over, iii. 406; advises Caryll about a staircase, iii. 402, 406; presents Catherine Caryll with a picture, iii. 402–3, 405, 406; his health is indifferent, iii. 414, but much better at Bevis Mount, iii. 426; in Town has a bad cold, iii. 443–6.

Dr. Arbuthnot's last illness, iii. 415, 416, 431; his remarks on his friendship with P., iii. 416, 423; his last request of P., iii. 417, 419, 423; — Bishop Berkeley dines at Chiswick with P. at Burlington's, iii. 403; Martha Blount's difficulty with her brother over income, iii. 406, 409, 415, 427, 440; P. asks Caryll to send her venison at Cheam, iii. 425; she goes to Bath with Lady Suffolk, iii. 434; P.'s gratitude to Lady Burlington, iii. 418; P. dines with Conduitt when at Bevis Mount, iii. 431; passes to Lord Oxford Dodsley's verses on Lady Margaret Harley's wedding, iii. 407; — W. Duncombe is permitted to print a letter from P. to John Hughes, iii. 441; P. is unable to use tickets for Duncombe's *Junius Brutus*, iii. 442–3; P. asks for Fortescue's coach to take him home (ill), iii. 443; P. sends Harte's *Essay on Reason* to press, advising anonymous publication, iii. 408; P. asks Mallet to see Bolingbroke in Town, iii. 408; James Newsham is at Bevis Mount when P. is, iii. 430; — P. congratulates Lord Oxford on Lady Margaret's wedding, iii. 424; P.'s happiness at Bevis Mount with Lord Peterborow, iii. 426; Mathew Pilkington wants morals and conduct, Bolingbroke warns Swift, iii. 405; P. lends Mrs. Rackett £300, iii. 407; is interested in family news, iii. 421; P. eager to see Swift's *Works*, iii. 401, 429, 433; Swift failed to recog-

POPE, BIOGR. DATA (*1734 cont.*)

nize P. as author of *Essay on Man*, I, iii. 433.

1735: Gay's epitaph in Lord Orrery's hands, iii. 502; Lord Cornbury's verses on the *Essay on Man*, iii. 506; *Sober Advice* is disowned, iii. 450; Bentley's threats concerning it, 451; *Epistle to Dr. Arbuthnot* causes Lady Mary to protest, iii. 448; *Epistle to a Lady* sent to Caryll, iii. 450; the last line of the poem does not intend marriage, 451; P.'s *Works*, vol. ii (in quarto) sent to Buckley, iii. 454, who is offered 150 copies at 18s. each; sent also to Caryll, 455, 474; pirated, iii. 477; *Works*, vol. i in sm. 8vo printed by Lintot, iii. 489; — *Letters of Mr. Pope and Several Eminent Persons* published by Curll, iii. 455, 464; P. asks Oxford for bound MSS. of letters, iii. 453; complains of their publication, iii. 455; the advertisement of 12 May, iii. 464; Curll taken before the Lords, iii. 465, 466; P. says the texts have been tampered with and cannot be owned as his, iii. 467; he advertises an authorized edition (*Gazette*, 15 July 1735), iii. 473; — Curll's reply, 494; Curll's correspondence with 'P. T.' and 'R. Smith', iii. 460–5; P. connived at the Cooper ed. of the letters, which is entered in the Stationers' Book, iii. 469; Curll sues Cooper, iii. 469, 494; Curll publishes vol. ii. of *Mr. Pope's Literary Correspondence*, iii. 471; he publishes a print of P.'s house and gardens, 472; asks Broome for data on the *Odyssey*, 475; alleges P.'s connexion with *The Grub-street Journal*, iii. 476; — announces vols. ii and iii of the *Literary Correspondence*, iii. 476–7; P. asks Lord Oxford to return to him the Wycherley MSS., iii. 469; P. asks Spence to return his letters, iii. 498; he also asks Broome, iii. 510; Lintot finds P.'s account of their journey to Oxford 'merry', iii. 489; *A Narrative of the Method by which the Private Letters of Mr. Pope have been Procur'd and Publish'd*, iii. 458–67.

At home P. builds an obelisk, and

Pope, Biogr. Data (*1735 cont.*)
a hot-house for pineapples, iii. 453;
dines with Lord Islay, iii. 478; with
Lady Suffolk, 480; misses visit from
George and Anne Arbuthnot, iii.
480, but urges them to come again
soon; — entertains Lord Oxford, iii.
468; Fortescue and Lady Suffolk,
473; the friends of Lady Suffolk and
Mr. Berkeley, iii. 478; Lyttelton and
West, 480; urges Bathurst to visit
him, 480-1; thinks he may die of
hospitality, iii. 486; is visited by the
Prince of Wales, iii. 500; — in Town
he stays with Lord Cornbury, iii. 452;
at Lord Oxford's, iii. 454, 468, 473;
wishes to see J. Richardson, iii. 485-
6; rambles to Cobham at Stowe, iii.
480, 482, 488, 491; but first to Southampton to bid farewell to Peterborow,
iii. 483, 485; he sees Spence in Oxford,
iii. 491, 493 (accident in Bagley
Wood), 498.
Deaths and sicknesses depress P.,
iii. 452; he attends on Peterborow's
illness in Kensington, iii. 455; recommends to Richardson and in-
directly to Walpole a young gentleman, iii. 457; works on improvements of Fortescue's place (The Vineyard) at Richmond, iii. 477, 486; —
refuses to serve as a poetry judge in
Cave's contest (but does!), iii. 499; is
ready to get Scots cattle for young
Bathurst, iii. 504; is busy planting
and his shell temple has fallen down,
iii. 511-12; at times his health keeps
him from Town, iii. 475.
P. sends condolences to George
Arbuthnot on the death of his father,
iii. 452; Atterbury's letters falsely
advertised by Curll, iii. 471; P. regrets not visiting Bathurst at Cirencester, iii. 499-500; Bathurst is begged
to go to Southampton with P., iii.
483; — Martha Blount's money now
in the hands of a friend (Bethel ?) who
will pay 4%, iii. 449; her brother is
still in arrears, iii. 478; she visits at
Marble Hill after the wedding of Lady
Suffolk and Mr. Berkeley, iii. 478; —
Bolingbroke's *Dissertation on Parties*
approved by Swift, iii. 456, v. 14; P.
wishes Swift to reprove Bolingbroke

Pope, Biogr. Data (*1735 cont.*)
for a moral frailty, v. 14-15; Bolingbroke's conversation missed by P., iii.
483; — Broome forwards Curll's
letter (iii. 475) to P. with assurance of
good will, iii. 479; P. and Broome are
reconciled, iii. 495-6; P. protests he
never claimed the notes to the *Odyssey*
as his, iii. 497; P. asks Broome for a
formal statement as to their relations
on the *Odyssey* project, iii. 497;
Broome gives it in a letter, iii. 507; P.
thanks him, 510; — Curll falsely
advertises to publish P.'s letters to the
Duchess of Buckingham, iii. 477,
481; Buckley has given P. a copy of
his Thuanus, iii. 454; Congreve is
said (falsely) by Lady Mary to have
scorned P.'s abilities, iii. 449; Duncombe gives P. a copy of John
Hughes's *Poems* and P. gives D. his
own quarto *Works*, iii. 454, v. 17; —
P. wishes to see Fortescue *today*, iii.
449; Martha Blount and Mrs. Knight
wish to dine at Fortescue's, iii. 450;
Fortescue's place at Richmond put in
order by P., iii. 477-8; Fortescue is
asked to return P.'s letters, iii. 478;
Fortescue asked to act against Curll's
piracy, iii. 472; — Walter Harte's
Essay on Reason taken to be P.'s, iii.
450; a 2nd ed. of it sent to Caryll, 451;
P. approves of the poem, 455; P.
eager to get Harte an added benefice,
iii. 511; from Dr. Mead P. gets medical advice for Fortescue, iii. 453; from
Philip Miller P. asks for cuttings of
fruit trees, iii. 452; — James Moore-
Smythe attacked by P. shortly after
his death, iii. 449; Wm. Murray seen
by P. at Oxford, iii. 498; correspondence with Lord Orrery begins, iii.
469; — Lord Peterborow begs P. to
come to Bevis Mount, iii. 483, 485;
P.'s account of Peterborow's condition, iii. 487-9; Peterborow owns his
marriage to Mrs. Robinson, iii. 490;
his death, iii. 508-9; — Pulteney is
visited by P. in Twickenham, iii. 474;
Peter Andreas Rysbrack paints pictures for Curll of P.'s house and gardens, iii. 477; 'S. E.' sends Voiture
letters to Curll as if by P., iii.
487, 495; P. disowns them, 501; —

POPE, BIOGR. DATA (*1735 cont.*)

Savage's *Progress of a Divine* disapproved of by P., iii. 504; Lady Suffolk marries the Hon. George Berkeley, iii. 474, 478; Jacob Tonson jr. dies, iii. 513; P. subscribes for 5 people to Wesley's *Job*, iii. 504.

1736: P.'s large ethical plan, iv. 5; the Broome passage in *The Dunciad* cancelled, iv. 2–3, 4; the epigram 'To One who Wrote Epitaphs', iv. 14; the epitaph for John Knight, iv. 17; 'A Prayer to God' (*A Universal Prayer*), iv. 31–33; given to the Duke of Shrewsbury 20 Years ago, iv. 31; *Works* (sm. 8vo), i and ii, sent to Broome, iv. 5; — P.'s *Letters*: Broome is again asked to return P.'s letters, iv. 3; an addition to the Preface of 1737 (not used), iv. 1–2; the edition of 1735 liked by Fortescue, iv. 7; publication of letters deters from writing them, iv. 2, 16, 17; — the offer of an authorized ed. not supposed to be taken seriously, iv. 7, 11; proposals sent to Fortescue, iv. 10, to Lord Orrery, 11, to others, 19; the subscription pushed, iv. 23, 35; the authorized ed. to be called *Works in Prose*, iv. 10; problems in 'editing', iv. 19–20; the size of the ed. debated, iv. 20, 24; in the press, iv. 37, 39, 41, 43; its motto, iv. 50; Curll's 'New Letters' from Ireland reported to Swift, iv. 50.

P. is ill at Cheselden's in town, iv. 2, 6; at Chiswick, iv. 14, 18 (ill there), with Mrs. Knight and Mrs. Eliot, iv. 22; at the 'Shepherd's Hut', iv. 26; — his guests at home characterized, iv. 34; he dines with Wm. Kent, iv. 43; he is visited by Ralph Allen, iv. 9, by Fortescue, 15, 22, by Martha Blount and Lady Gerard, 21; P. and Fortescue visit Lord Islay, iv. 21; — P. goes to Southampton (Lady Peterborow), iv. 13, 18, 21, 33, 34, 36; he visits Windsor Forest (Binfield?), iv. 24; Bathurst gets him to Cirencester, iv. 24, 28, 33; invited to go to Bath with Lord Orkney, iv. 35 (cannot go).

P. is busy improving his gardens, iv. 6, 31, 40; the shell temple rebuilt, iv. 22, 30; works on the gar-

POPE, BIOGR. DATA (*1736 cont.*)

dens at Bevis Mount, using Allen's bath stone, iv. 37; as Allen's agent passes money to Hooke, iv. 36; — corrects the 'Life' of Gay for T. Birch, iv. 37–38; his new friends spoken of as 'weeds', iv. 50–51; his moral capacity has conquered his poetical, iv. 51; is ill in town, iv. 2, 6, 18; has rheumatism, iv. 7; headaches, iv. 31; bad health prevents his dining with others, iv. 38.

Allen visits P., iv. 9 (admires P.'s letters); is aided by P. in choosing pictures for his house, iv. 13, 20, 23; uses P. as agent in aiding Hooke, iv. 36, 41; Bathurst's 'improvements' in his Park, iv. 25; Slingsby Bethel gets P. Madeira, iv. 33, 39; — arranges for Martha Blount to use the Shepherd's Hut, iv. 26, 29; despairs of influencing her to her own good, iv. 39–40; Bolingbroke reported at work writing; he is called 'the greatest man in the world', iv. 6; P. reproves Swift for gossip about Bolingbroke, iv. 27; — Broome wants P. to persuade Lintot to reprint Broome's *Poems*, iv. 2, 4; has not thanked P. for cancelling the *Dunciad* lines, iv. 4; Lady Burlington again P.'s amanuensis, iv. 1–2; she is in bad health, iv. 29, 36, 43; Cheselden is characterized for Swift, iv. 6; — Fortescue serves as judge at Monmouth, iv. 7; P.'s friends in Yorkshire receive Fortescue kindly, iv. 26; Prince Frederick accepts a whelp from Bounce, iv. 48; Mrs. Knight is rebuilding Gosfield, iv. 30; Leake calls, but P.'s servants refuse to let him see the gardens, iv. 9; — B. Lintot dies, iv. 4; P.'s private opinion of John, Duke of Marlborough, iv. 36; Mrs. Rackett loses £150 in a lawsuit, iv. 21; — Swift tells P. all his letters will be returned after Swift's death, iv. 11, 50; Orrery alarms P. as to Swift's health, iv. 8, 11, 15, and leads P. to try to recover his letters, iv. 8, 42; an epistle in verse to be dedicated some day to Swift, iv. 5, 12, 45; Swift is urged to come and live with P., iv. 6; P. vows to preserve memorials (i.e. letters) of their in-

Pope, Biogr. Data (*1736 cont.*)
timacy, iv. 28; — Tickell reported as concerned over P.'s ill health, iv. 3. *1737*: P. sends part of his *Imitation of Horace, Ep. II. ii* and part of Ep. II. i to Swift, iv. 56; completed work sent to Orrery, iv. 70, 72; P.'s inscription for the tomb of N. Pigott, 80; Atterbury's *Iapis* wrongly ascribed to P., iv. 55, 60; — lines supposedly written on glass by Milton, iv. 80; P.'s LETTERS: Swift is again urged to return P.'s letters, iv. 52, 58; Swift's silence on the matter, iv. 52, 54, 59; Curll's 'New Letters' from Ireland reported to Orrery and Swift, iv. 52, 54, 59, 60; Swift agrees to return the letters, iv. 61, 62, 64, 69, 76; Swift's varying account of the number of letters in his hands, iv. 72, 73, 76; P. gets the letters, iv. 81; P.'s clear intention to publish them, iv. 53, 60, 64–65; — P. now diffident about writing letters for fear of publication, iv. 63; his pretended low opinion of the letters in print, iv. 53; the prose pieces to be omitted from the authorized vol. of letters (called *Works in Prose*), iv. 53, 55, 68; — Orrery's work on the subscription, iv. 53, 55, 70–71; Hugh Bethel's aid, iv. 65; S. Bethel's aid, iv. 33, 65; Allen's aid, iv. 68, 74; the publishers are: J. Brindley, iv. 53, 65, 67, 70; Knapton, 58, 66, 68, 74; Dodsley, 41 n., 83, 87, 88; Leake, 68; J. Wright is the printer, iv. 58; — problem of the size of the ed., iv. 66; the engraving for the title-page, iv. 54, 58; the edition pirated by James Watson, iv. 87–88; Swift likes the morality of the letters but regrets their reflections on Ireland, iv. 77; the publication is delayed in hopes of a new copyright law, iv. 65, 66, 69.

In town P. stays at Lord Cornbury's, iv. 66, 67, 81, 88; at home he finds no quiet, iv. 78; invites H. Bethel, iv. 67; invites Richardson, iv. 78, 79; will see Richardson in town, iv. 79; — a long ramble takes him to Oxford, iv. 81, 82–84; Southampton and Portsmouth, 84–85; Cirencester, iv. 83–85; Bath, 84–85; — he is occu-

Pope, Biogr. Data (*1737 cont.*)
pied with law business (for others in part), iv. 68, 70, 78, 87, 88; his health is poor, iv. 58; better, 64, 74; has bad eyesight, iv. 64.

Allen subsidizes the *Works in Prose*, iv. 74; P. visits Allen at Bath and Allen brings him back to London, iv. 86; P. wishes H. Bethel and he might live together, iv. 57; — S. Bethel asked for more Madeira and claret, iv. 87; P. aids John Bowack to a post with the Commissioners of the Bridge, iv. 82; P. wishes to dine with Buckley and Knapton, iv. 89; the death of Queen Caroline, iv. 89; — P. asks Edw. Holdsworth to vote for Harte as Poetry-Professor, iv. 90; the death of Lord Orkney, iv. 60; Lady Peterborow gets a copy of *Works in Prose* for Mrs. Pendarves, iv. 83; — Orrery stresses Swift's decay of memory, iv. 52, 54, 62; Swift is urged to come and live with P., iv. 63–64, 75, v. 18; he again begs for a verse epistle addressed to him, iv. 71–72; Pope's affection for Swift, v. 18.

1738: 'Epilogue to the Satires' ('*1738*') mentions Allen as 'lowborn' or 'humble', iv. 93, 145; it is read in MS. by Lyttelton, iv. 109; Hill likes it as printed, iv. 112; it compliments Walpole, iv. 114; P.'s anti-Court utterance, iv. 117; he plans '*1740*', iv. 114; he gives an epitaph (unidentified) to Ford, iv. 137; — Swift mistakenly says all P.'s letters to him are in Mrs. Whitehead's hands, iv. 115–16, 130, 133; — P. is attacked in *The Daily Gazetteer*, iv. 124–5, 154; Hill criticizes the *Bathos*, iv. 99–101; Hill's *Essay on Propriety* nearly ready, iv. 95–101, 108; P.'s defence against Hill's attacks, iv. 102.

Bolingbroke at Twickenham keeps P. also there, iv. 113, 117; P. is little in town, iv. 154; at home drinks Walpole's health (Bolingbroke being absent) with Thomas Gordon, iv. 114; to be found at Allen's lodgings in town, iv. 123, 134; — P. and Bolingbroke and Wm. Kent are a 'suffering triumvirate', iv. 125; P. dines at Kew (with Prince Frederick),

POPE, BIOGR. DATA (*1738 cont.*)
iv. 139; friends begin to gather (Nov.) in town, iv. 149; P. is gay there with Kent, iv. 150.

P. sits to Richardson and so does Bolingbroke, iv. 91, cancels a sitting, 119; Richardson has three portraits of Bolingbroke and two of P. in his studio, iv. 150; the disposal of these, iv. 91, 128, 151; — P. builds a 'stove' and needs help of Burlington's man Scot, iv. 118; P. helps publish a mangled text of the 'Verses on the Death of Dr. Swift', iv. 130; he tries to persuade Orrery to buy Dawley, iv. 136; he orders urns from Allen, iv. 144; — he reports on a political conference with Sir W. Wyndham to Prince Frederick, iv. 142–4; P. comments on the extreme corruption of the time, iv. 109, 139; calls himself 'virtue's trumpeter', iv. 142; Kent calls him a glutton, iv. 150.

P. flatters Allen and his new wife, iv. 92; tells Allen that he will allow a yearly stipend to a beggar woman whom Allen aided, iv. 92; asks Allen to send Bath waters for Bolingbroke, iv. 119, 134; Allen sends P. 'oil and wine', iv. 145; P.'s dark design with the name 'Arthur Archibald', iv. 93; the Duke of Argyle's request to P. comes too late, iv. 138; P. longs for Hugh Bethel's arrival in town, iv. 147; — P. longs for Bolingbroke's arrival from France, iv. 106–7, 109; Bolingbroke approves Hill's *Roman Tragedy*, iv. 106–7, 110, 111; Bolingbroke is at Twickenham, iv. 113, and briefly ill there, 117, 118; P. reports Bolingbroke's efforts on behalf of Hooke's son in France, iv. 119; P.'s affection for Bolingbroke, iv. 125; the sale of Dawley not easy, iv. 136, 148, 153; — P. jokingly solicits of Lady Burlington the gift of Eyam to Wm. Kent, iv. 140–1; P. grieves over the ill health of Fortescue, iv. 155; — P. sends a packet to the Prince of Wales, iv. 109; P.'s great influence over the Prince alleged, iv. 138–9; unfortunately P. was not at Cirencester when the Prince visited Bathurst, iv. 138, 142; — Hill's

POPE, BIOGR. DATA (*1738 cont.*)
criticisms of P., iv. 95–101; P. replies, iv. 102, 106; Hill rejoins, iv. 103, 107; Hill's *Roman Revenge* read and approved by P. and Bolingbroke, iv. 105, 110, 121–3, 126–7, 128–9; P. declines to write an epilogue, iv. 131–2; P. tries to help in finding the best time to submit the tragedy, since both Mallet and Thomson are Hill's rivals, iv. 145, 151, 152; Hill's critique of Thomson's *Agamemnon* to be Hill's, not P.'s, iv. 146, 152; — P. grieves that Jervas must go to Italy for his health, iv. 126; G. Lyttelton thanks P. for service with Swift, iv. 138; P. wishes to send pineapples to Sir Thomas Lyttelton, iv. 117; wishes to stand well with Murray and Lady Betty, iv. 141; advises G. Selwyn as to translating Cicero's letters, iv. 130–1; — is distressed over reports of Swift's health, iv. 92; gets Swift to give Lyttelton's protégé a place in his choir, iv. 134–5.

1739: A new passage to be added to the next *Dunciad* on the Gazetteers, iv. 178; P. declines to write, and then does write, the inscription on Nash's obelisk at Bath for the Prince of Wales, iv. 170, 176; is revising 'some papers' (Swift correspondence?) for publication, iv. 195; — Warburton's letters in *Vindication* of the *Essay on Man* gratefully received, iv. 163–4, 171–2; they are revised and collected, iv. 182, 196; P. wishes the work translated into French, iv. 196; Brinsden's complimentary verses not to be published in *Common Sense* or any 'party' paper, iv. 209.

P. invites Allen to Twickenham, iv. 157, 165, 173; P. from home, iv. 159; will soon settle at Twickenham, iv. 169; almost constantly at home, iv. 181; not from home in 5 weeks, iv. 195; in London one day in 3 months, iv. 197; — Martha Blount and Mrs. Grenville to visit P., iv. 183; A. and G. Arbuthnot invited to come, iv. 192; — Kent is calumniated, iv. 154; P. at Kent's in liquor, iv. 163; at first performance of *Mustapha*, iv. 166, 167; P. stays with E. Lewis

Pope, Biogr. Data (*1739 cont.*)
(Cork Street) a week, iv. 165, 177;
at Lord Oxford's, iv. 172; at Orrery's
with Dr. King, iv. 180.

His summer rambles projected, iv.
183; goes to Stowe, iv. 183 n., 185–
6; to Rousham, iv. 188; to Hagley, iv.
185; to Adderbury (Duke of Argyle),
iv. 189; to Cornbury, iv. 189; home
after a month of rambling, iv. 191; —
apologizes for not visiting Cirencester,
iv. 192–3; plans to go to Bath in
Nov., iv. 195, 200; goes to Bristol
(described), iv. 200–3, 204–5; returns
to Bath, iv. 206; delighted by its
quiet, iv. 208.

His manner of life at home, iv. 179;
receives urns for his garden from the
Prince of Wales, iv. 170, 178, 181; his
portico is repaired, iv. 181; a new
pavement laid, iv. 191; — he suffers
from rheumatism, iv. 171, 173; and
from bad kidneys, iv. 193; is very
well in the summer, iv. 187; gout
keeps him from dining at Richmond
with Fortescue, iv. 198.

Allen is given a young Bounce,
iv. 175, 181; Ann Arbuthnot now
one of P.'s closest friends, iv. 177; he
dines with her at Bath, iv. 212;
George Arbuthnot gives legal aid to
Lady Gerard, iv. 186, 191; S. Bethel
asked to procure Madeira for Martha
Blount, iv. 197; P. sends her venison,
iv. 185; also sends her good advice, iv.
187, 211; she goes to Richmond, iv.
193; — Bolingbroke has sold Dawley
and leaves for France, iv. 171, 172,
173; Henry Brooke inquires after P.'s
orthodoxy, iv. 198–200, 207–8, 212–
13; P. (facetiously) asks Burlington
to give the benefice of Eyam to Wm.
Kent, iv. 196–7; Fleetwood's chic-
anery is deplored, iv. 159–60; Fortescue at Bath in ill health, iv. 169, 193;
Prince Frederick gives P. busts of
poets and some urns, iv. 170, 178,
181; P. aids Lady Gerard in an affi-
davit necessary to a lease, iv. 183, 186;
she is to have pineapples from P., iv.
186, 191; — A. Hill is still apologetic
over his *Northern Star*, iv. 158; angry
over Fleetwood's treatment of his
Caesar, iv. 159, 162; and so is P., iv.

Pope, Biogr. Data (*1739 cont.*)
165; P. advises against dedicating the
play to Bolingbroke, iv. 166; —
Jervas returns to England and friends,
iv. 177; P.'s attempt to aid Samuel
Johnson, iv. 194; P. is reported by
Kent as 'in liquor', iv. 163; soothes
Mallet concerning the supposed
charge of plagiarism in *Mustapha*, iv.
210; P. involved in the continuing
disputes over the Marble Hill road, v.
19; M'Auley comes over to thank the
Prince, iv. 184; — P. introduces John
Rackett to S. Bethel as one knowing
the condition of the Codrington
estates in Barbados, iv. 168; advises
Michael Rackett because of debts and
outlawry to sell Hallgrove, iv. 160–1;
the place not sold, iv. 203; P. will
advance to Michael Rackett £150, iv.
160; — complains to Hill of Hill's
friend Samuel Richardson, publisher
of the *Gazetteer*, iv. 168; is sending
Richard Savage to Wales to live,
iv. 180; — Swift recommends
M'aulay to the Prince of Wales, iv.
175, 180, 184; Swift will promote
Lyttelton's protégé in his choir, iv.
176; Deane Swift is introduced to
P., iv. 174; — Warburton is thanked
for a mention of P. in the *Vindication
of . . . the Divine Legation*, iv. 182; he is
thanked warmly for his defence of P.,
iv. 196.

1740: Pope's *Odyssey* advertised by
T. Osborne, iv. 222; P. raises questions as to his copyrights with Tonson and Lintot, iv. 223–4; especially
The Dunciad copyrights, iv. 240; a
Latin version of the *Essay on Man*
projected at Cambridge, iv. 251–2,
288; — Warburton's *Vindication*, collected, is well liked by P. and his
friends, iv. 215; to be translated into
French, iv. 216, 219; remarks added
on Epistle IV, iv. 219; Pope's lines
on his grotto, iv. 262; the *Miscellanies* to be reconstituted and reprinted, iv. 284–5, 289.

The Pope–Swift Correspondence: Mrs. Whiteway offers to return added P. letters through Nugent,
iv. 230; or by M'Aulay, iv. 241, 248;
Swift is asked for prose pieces (for the

POPE, BIOGR. DATA (*1740 cont.*)
volume of correspondence or for the *Miscellanies*), iv. 240; — Gerrard takes from Bath an anonymous packet (the Pope–Swift letters) to Swift, iv. 242–3, 245, 276; Faulkner (29 July) writes to P. about this vol. of letters, iv. 256; he waits 2 months for P.'s reply, meanwhile starting to print, iv. 257–8, 270; P. offers C. Bathurst a chance to be the publisher, iv. 259; — P.'s specious history of the affair sent to Orrery, iv. 263–4; he asks Orrery to get hold of the clandestine vol., iv. 264; Faulkner brings it to Orrery, iv. 270; P. greatly vexed, iv. 273; asks Faulkner to send him the clandestine vol. with its covering letter from Bath, iv. 275; Faulkner anxious to please P., iv. 276; — both Orrery and Mrs. Whiteway oppose publication, iv. 276, 277, 278, 301; Mrs. Whiteway is sure the vol. comes from P., iv. 279, 305; Faulkner now wishes to have the clandestine vol. in order to send it to P., iv. 280; P.'s comment, blaming Mrs. Whiteway, on the covering letter from Bath, iv. 282; he suggests that Orrery send him the clandestine vol., iv. 284, 292, 294; wishes the printed letters sent to him at Bath (c/o Allen) and MS. letters sent to him in care of Lord Oxford, iv. 291; Mrs. Whiteway disapproved of the volume without reading it, iv. 285; — P. says any letters in the vol. that were returned earlier by Orrery must have been copied before they were returned, iv. 286; Faulkner says the clandestine vol. had no title-page, iv. 291; P. feels 'monstrously used', iv. 296; the Bath covering letter, Faulkner reports, Mrs. Whiteway sent to Orrery, iv. 295; Orrery says it never came to him, iv. 298, 305; P. wants it, iv. 302; Mrs. Whiteway now says the Bath letter is with the other letters that she will return to P. (she cannot send it to Orrery), iv. 307; Orrery demands all these P. letters from her, in order to return them to P., iv. 308; she asks Orrery to send a trustworthy agent to receive the letters personally, iv. 320; — P. not averse to letting Faulkner

POPE, BIOGR. DATA (*1740 cont.*)
publish, iv. 301; has the clandestine vol. finally and finds it unworthy to be published, but innocuous, iv. 303, 310; finds interlineations in Swift's hand, iv. 303; will keep the first sheets already printed by Faulkner, iv. 303–4; — wants the original covering letter and the other letters of his that Mrs. Whiteway has, iv. 304; Orrery suspects Mrs. Whiteway and Deane Swift are behind the printing of the clandestine vol., iv. 308; he tells her the letters are sure to be published since in print, iv. 308; — P. will tolerate no Preface reflecting on London booksellers, iv. 309–11; P. talks of interpolated half- and quarter-sheets, marked with asterisks, iv. 310; Swift's long letter inserted is really a pamphlet, not a letter, iv. 310; P. notes that the clandestine collection suppresses all his requests for the return of his letters, iv. 311; returns the clandestine vol. to Orrery, iv. 311; — P. says (threateningly ?) that if compelled to vindicate himself he will do to Mrs. Whiteway and Deane Swift the same justice they have done him, iv. 312, 330; has prepared a 'Narration' covering the whole intrigue of the letters, iv. 313; sends it to Orrery, iv. 314–20; Mrs. Whiteway tells her story of the Dean's epistolary habits, iv. 321–2.

P. is at Bath in Jan., iv. 214–22; his little green chair there, iv. 229; comes back to London and home in Feb., iv. 227, 230; Hooke is to join him at home, iv. 230; — Warburton's trip to London anticipated, iv. 220, 233–4; W. is urged to stay at Twickenham, iv. 233; P. dines at Chiswick, iv. 234; goes to Windsor Forest, iv. 234; Warburton arrives in London, iv. 236; — P. lodges with Cheselden in Spring Garden, iv. 236; takes Warburton to Lord Bathurst, iv. 236, 237; they go to Twickenham, iv. 236 (the first dinner there); P. takes Warburton to Lord Burlington, iv. 237; in town P. is now with E. Lewis, iv. 237; has to cancel an invitation to Warburton to dine there, iv. 238; Lyttel-

Pope, Biogr. Data (*1740 cont.*)
ton invites P. and Warburton, iv. 238; Warburton goes to Cambridge and P. goes home from Town, iv. 243; — is expected at Chiswick on Sundays, iv. 244; his visit to Allen at Bath is deferred, iv. 252, 267, 297; accompanies a friend to Southampton, iv. 252; can't go alone in a coach to Bath, iv. 273; agrees to meet Allen's coach at Newbury, but fails to do so, iv. 290, 292; must stay in Town (at Murray's) for a fortnight yet on his sister's chancery case, iv. 290, 292; arranges to go to Bath with G. Arbuthnot, iv. 300, 303; the death of Margaret Arbuthnot, v. 20.

P. is concerned in his sister's chancery case, iv. 214, 245, 258, 290, 292; is putting his papers in order, iv. 280; at work on his gardens, iv. 247; especially the grotto for which Borlase sends minerals, &c., iv. 228, 235, 239, 244, 245–6; B. is rewarded, iv. 254, 278; Dr. Oliver also helps, iv. 228, 229, 247, is rewarded by a bath dedicated to him, iv. 254, 279, 281; — Allen contributes stone, iv. 230, 235, 239, 252; Omer is to work on the grotto, iv. 239, 245, 246, 254, 274; Cooper sends a cargo of specimens, iv. 244, 247; his reward, iv. 278; the motto of the grotto, iv. 245 n.; Nugent sends mundics, iv. 257; P. describes the grotto to Bolingbroke, iv. 261; it is called finished (but not perfect), iv. 267, 274.

After the quiet of Bath, London upsets P., iv. 225; intends to dine alone and always at 2 p.m., iv. 225; has pain and difficulty in urinating, iv. 253; submits to an operation by Cheselden, iv. 255–6, 268–9.

Anne Arbuthnot in bad health, iv. 268; goes to Bath, iv. 274, 290, 293; — Allen is called the link between P. and Hooke, iv. 235; P. sees Vandiest for Allen, iv. 247, 253; urges Allen to come and see the grotto, iv. 247; will send 2 pineapples, iv. 253; Allen lends P. £150 for Michael Rackett, iv. 215, 217; Allen's charity in the bitter winter is praised, iv. 221; he

Pope, Biogr. Data (*1740 cont.*)
sends P. many 'benefits', iv. 235; — Slingsby Bethel to invest P.'s money, which he is taking out of stocks, iv. 299; Martha Blount spends part of the summer at the Vineyard, iv. 267; P. sends a box to Borlase, iv. 298; Fortescue's bond for a loan of £150 is unacceptable to P., iv. 215, 216–17, 221; it is no longer convenient for Fortescue to be P.'s executor, iv. 222; Fortescue is troubled with gravel, iv. 267; — S. Gerrard tries to see P. at Burlington's, iv. 234; P. uses Gerrard to take the printed vol. of letters over to Swift, iv. 241–2, 242–3, 245, 276; — Phil Hanaus who in 1726 saved P.'s life wishes a place as footman, iv. 289; Jervas's will leaves to P. a conditional legacy of £1,000, iv. 217 n., 225; Kent is made His Majesty's face painter, iv. 220; Dr. King has been desperately ill, iv. 301, 307; P. complains of Lintot's loose procedure with regard to copies of Homer, iv. 222–3; — P. is constantly urging upon Hugh, Earl of Marchmont, his public duty, iv. 217, 227–8, 249–51, 261, 271–2; has difficulty in making appointments with Sarah, Duchess of Marlborough, iv. 258, 259, 264–5; — Robert Nugent is now married to Mrs. Knight, iv. 231; P. likes Nugent's *Ode to Marchmont*, iv. 231; Nugent to bring over from Ireland the letters that Mrs. Whiteway has offered, iv. 233; P. sends his reply to Faulkner for safe carriage to Nugent at Bath, and it is returned, iv. 235, 260; P. reads one of Nugent's odes in MS., iv. 260; P. breakfasts with Dr. Oliver, iv. 218–19; — Michael Rackett and his mother in chancery, iv. 214, 245, 290; Hallgrove is not sold, iv. 290; the death of the Earl of Scarborough, iv. 225; — Warburton under attack for his *Divine Legation*, iv. 216; P. with veneration and wonder travels through Warburton's book, iv. 251; Mrs. Whiteway notes that Swift's *Four Last Years*, now in Dr. King's hands, has commercial value, iv. 240, 248; Sir William Wyndham dies, iv. 249;

POPE, BIOGR. DATA (*1740 cont.*)
Bolingbroke's reaction, iv. 272; Zeeman's portrait of P. sent to H. Bethel, iv. 299.

1741: *Miscellanies* (prose) offer copyright difficulties, iv. 324; new pieces to be included, iv. 333–4; Arbuthnot's *Sermon* not to be included, iv. 367, 372; P. is eager to see the vol. reprinted, iv. 353; draws upon C. Bathurst for small sums, iv. 361; — the line on Caesar in the Epistle to Cobham irks Warburton, iv. 339; Warburton is to be the commentator of an ed. of the poems, iv. 361, 362; — P. queries Lintot's right to the *Dunciad* copy, iv. 333; would aid Lintot in a new ed., iv. 333; has new hints for matter from Warburton, iv. 357; considers completing the poem (*Dunciad*), iv. 362; — the SWIFT–POPE LETTERS a major concern for the year, iv. 323; the 'several' letters that Mrs. Whiteway has are returned to Orrery, iv. 325, who sends P. the original of the Bath letter, iv. 326, 328; the packet of 'several' letters is too large for the post: Orrery will bring it, iv. 326; — P. returns all but pp. 1–22 of the clandestine vol. to Orrery, iv. 328; Orrery will give Faulkner a neutral permission to publish the letters, iv. 328; Orrery thinks P.'s 'Narration' skilful, iv. 329; he permits P. to print any of his letters relevant, iv. 329; — P. comments on Mrs. Whiteway's story of the letters, iv. 330; wishes a copy of Faulkner's vol. immediately upon publication, iv. 332; also wants the 'foul copy'; (clandestine vol.) when Faulkner has printed, iv. 332; — tells Warburton that the letters are printed in Ireland at Swift's direction, iv. 334; writes to Swift regretfully about the letters, which, nevertheless, are a monument to their friendship, iv. 337; — Curll's piracy of the letters causes a chancery suit, iv. 343, 350; Corbett plans a piracy, iv. 345; P. sends the letters (*Works in Prose*, ii) to Nugent, iv. 344; he is now done with expensive eds., iv. 350.

P. returns from Bath in Feb., iv.

POPE, BIOGR. DATA (*1741 cont.*)
335; spends a week at Murray's in town, iv. 335, 345; visits Orrery in Duke Street, iv. 336; stays with Cheselden 2 or 3 days, iv. 338; will be available to Warburton all May and June, iv. 341; — at home has a dinner for Cobham, Argyle, and Marchmont, iv. 341; Lyttelton visits P., iv. 342; so do H. Layng and Lord Bathurst, iv. 342; Thomas Edwards is invited, iv. 342; P. is busily 'grottofying', iv. 354; G. West and his family are his guests for a week, iv. 354; P. is to entertain lawyers, iv. 358; — will be at Murray's to greet Warburton, iv. 345, 346; will call on Warburton at Gyles's, iv. 346–7; plans a journey with Warburton to Oxford, iv. 347; the mooted honorary degrees, iv. 357, 362; P. unable to 'ramble' with the Allens, iv. 343–4; asks Warburton to accompany him to Stowe, iv. 346; — now outlines a ramble for himself and the Allens, iv. 347; will not go to Hagley because Sir Thomas Lyttelton is very ill, iv. 349; spends a week at Cirencester, iv. 350; may accompany an unnamed friend to Bristol, iv. 350; Allen will come to fetch P. to Widcombe, iv. 363, 366; P. at Bath (iv. 367) invites Warburton to come to Allen's, iv. 370–1; Warburton comes by way of London, iv. 373.

P.'s 'tree' petition, iv. 323–4; his troubles with Lintot over copyrights, iv. 335–6; his chancery suit against Curll, iv. 343; his annuities in South Sea to be sold, iv. 335; he wishes to buy shares in Sun Fire Insurance, iv. 340, 350, 357, 363; George Arbuthnot is to receive for P. the legacy of Alderman Barber, iv. 366, 367; Lyttelton's view of the important influence of P.'s 'moral song', iv. 369; — P.'s continuing work on his GROTTO: T. Edwards can furnish material, iv. 342–3, 349, 351; Allen's stone will be needed, iv. 343, 351, 353; the stucco of the portico to be covered with stone, iv. 343; Vandiest unable to paint 'grotesques' for the grotto, iv. 340, 343; Cooper also

POPE, BIOGR. DATA (*1741 cont.*)
sends minerals, &c., iv. 350; C.
Bathurst is thanked, and asked for
more stone, iv. 349, 352; — P. asks
Fortescue for scallop shells, iv. 356;
Biggs works slowly on the grotto, iv.
360; it will be completed by Oct., iv.
362; the motto over Pope's door,
'Libertati & Amicitiae', iv. 365.

P. sends the Allens 2 pineapples, iv.
349; Scott (Burlington's gardener)
will help build a 'pine house' at Widcombe, iv. 360; Vandiest soon expected to visit there, iv. 340; a 4th
head for the library there to be
chosen (Ralegh ?), iv. 351; Roubiliac
is making 'heads' for Allen at £20
each, iv. 360; Allen is asked to aid
(through Wade) Hooke's son to get
into the army, iv. 353, 358; — Anne
Arbuthnot urged to seize Ald. Barber's legacy and come at once to
Bath, iv. 367; the legacy, iv. 329; P.
cannot recommend C. Bathurst to
Warburton because W. prefers Knapton as bookseller, iv. 371; — P. is
grieved at H. Bethel's ill health, iv.
338-9; as Bethel leaves for Italy, P.
urges Martha Blount to go and bid
him farewell, iv. 355, 358; Lyttelton
can find no summer lodgings for
Martha at Kew, iv. 348; she sends (by
P.) sincere services to the Allens, iv.
363; she plans to go to Bath but does
not, iv. 365 n.; — W. Bowyer, jr. projects a commentary on P.'s echoes of
others, iv. 338; P. and Martha
Blount both regret not seeing Fortescue, iv. 355; the careers of N. Hooke's
sons, iv. 353 n., 357; P. aids Hooke in
getting employment with the Duchess
of Marlborough, iv. 327, 366; —
Lyttelton, flattered by P., sends service to Allen, iv. 368; Lyttelton will
take 'monkish history' (Henry II)
for his field, iv. 348; P. is content now
with Marchmont's politics, iv. 327,
363-4; P. sends pineapples to Sarah,
Duchess of Marlborough and hints
that he wants venison, iv. 358; he gets
the venison, iv. 359; visits with Hooke
the Duchess at Wimbledon, iv. 358;
invites her to sup in his grotto, iv.
359; — P.'s ill health has kept him (at

POPE, BIOGR. DATA (*1741 cont.*)
Bath) from seeing Dr. Oliver, iv. 374;
P. sends Mrs. Rackett venison and
says that whenever in town he sees her,
iv. 365; J. Richardson possibly at
Bath in Dec., iv. 374; Savage's
finances exasperate, iv. 331, 344, 347;
— P. is pleased that Warburton's
Divine Legation, ii, advances, iv. 334;
P. reads it in sheets, iv. 341; Warburton's anecdote about Waterland, iv.
334; a copy of P.'s *Works in Prose*, ii
(i.e. the Swift–Pope letters) sent to
Gyles for Warburton, iv. 339; P.
wishes a patron would settle Warburton nearer London, iv. 356, 361;
Warburton's Oxford degree not
granted, iv. 357; P. is glad Warburton
drops his dispute with Middleton, iv.
369, 370; Gilbert West and family
are at P.'s for a week, iv. 354.

1742: P. is writing a poem that
abuses travelling (i.e. *The New Dunciad* (*Dunciad* iv) at Bath, iv. 377;
four friends wish the poem published,
iv. 387; a copy is sent to H. Bethel in
Italy, iv. 401-2; it is pirated by J.
Ilive, iv. 392, who is sued in chancery,
iv. 425; and the sale is stopped, iv.
433; P.'s own characterization of the
poem, iv. 393, 396; — P. revises all
four books of *The Dunciad*, and it is
in press, iv. 393, 425-6; has troubles
threatened by Lintot over copyright,
iv. 388, 394, 425; Warburton is to be
called editor of the revised poem, iv.
427-8, 429; earlier notes ascribed to
Cleland and Dr. Arbuthnot, iv. 428;
the prefatory discourse by Aristar-
chus is Warburton's, iv. 431, 434; P.
thanks Warburton for the encour-
agement and aid given in the work
of revision, iv. 434; complains that
Bowyer prints slowly, iv. 428; —
Pope's epigram on Cibber's 'last
word', iv. 407; his inscription for the
bust of Vernon (for Sarah, Duchess
of Marlborough), iv. 421; — he is
reprinting Warburton's *Commentary
on the Essay on Man*, iv. 379-80;
defends his doctrine against the
charges of Louis Racine, iv. 415-16,
422-3; Bowyer is to print the *Essay
on Man* with Warburton's notes, and

POPE, BIOGR. DATA (*1742 cont.*)
later print the other poems thus annotated, iv. 434; P. asks Warburton
to revise the Preface and Life of
Homer, iv. 384, 400, 403.
   In bitter Jan. weather P. and Warburton return from Bath, iv. 378–9;
P. stays in London with Murray, iv.
380, 381, 386; P. (with Warburton)
is invited to dine at Orrery's with Dr.
King, iv. 380; P. breakfasts at
Richardson's, iv. 380; dines at G.
Arbuthnot's, iv. 385; — Bolingbroke
comes to Twickenham, iv. 394; is ill
there, 398; P. thinks a trip to Bath
with Bolingbroke and Warburton
possible, iv. 393; plans to spend June
in London, iv. 402; he invites
Richardson to Twickenham, iv. 408;
Lord Chesterfield is ill at P.'s house,
iv. 411–12, 413; — Warburton arrives,
iv. 412, and goes to Bath with Allen,
iv. 417; P. makes many plans to go to
Bath, iv. 398, 402, 405, 410, 420, 421;
returns from Bath in late Nov., iv. 427,
428; is to have lodgings of his own in
London, iv. 429, 433 n.; spends the
holidays at Twickenham with Murray, Marchmont, Cornbury, and
others, iv. 431.
   P. and Bolingbroke both sit to
Richardson for portraits, iv. 399, 400;
Bounce is given to Lord Orrery and
sent to Marston, iv. 406; work on the
grotto continues, iv. 391, 397, 412,
433; P. gets his Sun Fire shares, iv.
387; — the death of Mrs. Vernon
makes the purchase of his villa possible, iv. 387, 433; P. offers S. Bethel
£300 more to invest for him, iv. 401;
lends Warburton £100, iv. 427; talks
of settling at Widcombe, if Martha
Blount will settle near by, iv. 430; —
his concern with the political changes
in progress, iv. 376, 377–8, 413, 414,
431; on the Patriots, iv. 382; his reserve in commenting, iv. 383–4, 386,
404, 412; he professes a willingness to
submit all opinions to the decision of
the Church, iv. 416; P.'s health is
much as usual, iv. 378; is better for
regular dining, iv. 433.
   Allen arrives at Twickenham 20
Aug. and takes Warburton back to

POPE, BIOGR. DATA (*1742 cont.*)
Bath with him, iv. 411, 413, 417;
Sarah, Duchess of Marlborough sends
Allen a buck, iv. 413; P. sends him pineapples, iv. 420; Allen's new pine house
smokes at first, iv. 429, 431; he sends
P. birds to eat, iv. 431; — P. gives
Anne Arbuthnot a copy of *Joseph
Andrews*, iv. 394; sends medical
advice from Dr. Mead to H. Bethel in
Italy, iv. 375, 395; Martha Blount
thanks the Allens for their kind intention, iv. 398, 417; ill health keeps
her from waiting on Sarah, Duchess
of Marlborough, iv. 414, 419; — the
death of his father brings Bolingbroke to England, iv. 393, 395; he
soon returns to France, iv. 400, 402;
Katherine, Duchess of Buckingham
sat in her coach at P.'s door, iv. 406;
Orrery's pity for her, iv. 407; Burlington's dau. Dorothy, Countess of
Euston, tragically dead, iv. 396, 415;
P. suggests that he and Burlington
visit Sarah, Duchess of Marlborough,
iv. 408; — Cibber is printing an ex-
postulatory letter to P., iv. 406;
Orrery's comment on it, iv. 407; P.
avows that he has (Sept. 1741) written all about Cibber that he ever will,
iv. 415; does not wish to be thought in
any way serious about Cibber, iv.
434; — Archibald Cleland urged by
P. for a place on the staff of Bath
Hospital, iv. 401, 405; William Cleland, dismissed by Walpole, dies, to
P.'s great grief, iv. 377–8; — N.
Hooke now financially easy, P. reports, iv. 383, 386; P. approves
Hooke's *Account of Sarah, Duchess of
Marlborough*, iv. 389; Hooke feels
himself a slave to the Duchess, iv. 430,
434; Thomas Hooke is recommended
to Dr. Holmes by P. and Orrery, iv.
390; — from Sarah, Duchess of Marlborough P. has taken what he never
did from another, and is now 'discarded', iv. 381; she is or has been ill,
iv. 381–2; P. flatters her, iv. 389, 394–
5; she keeps P. from going to Bath,
iv. 405, 411; business has kept him
from her in London, iv. 419, but he
will come to her on Friday with Lord
Chesterfield, iv. 419; he is not allowed

Pope, Biogr. Data (*1742 cont.*)
to leave for Bath with Chesterfield, iv.
420; she later sends P. presents but
does not summon him, iv. 432; — P.
asks Bethel the Continental reputation of Lady Mary Wortley Montagu,
iv. 377; gets Murray to advise Warburton in his difficulty with the
executors of Gyles, iv. 383; is to get
Lady Orrery a pair of guinea fowl
from the Allens, iv. 422, 424; thanks
her for a fine present, iv. 423; Lord
Orrery wishes to copy some of P.'s
urns, iv. 407; — P. is disillusioned
with Pulteney, iv. 382; P. and
Richardson are to see Chiswick
House and Burlington, iv. 409; P. is
much plagued by Savage, iv. 391–2,
417–18, 431, 432; Sir Timothy
(unidentified) is depressed by Duchess
Sarah, iv. 382–3, 412; — Warburton
has troubles with the executors of F.
Gyles, iv. 380–1, *and passim* to iv.
417; Warburton's ed. of Shakespeare
envisaged, iv. 393; W. visits Bath with
Allen, iv. 417, and returns to London,
iv. 424; P. works to find Warburton a
patron, iv. 433; Carteret wishes to
make W.'s acquaintance, iv. 435; P.
thinks W. should complete *The Divine
Legation* before working on Shakespeare or P., iv. 434–5; — Sir Robert
Walpole's downfall, iv. 376; he was
needlessly severe on P.'s friends, iv.
377–8; Gilbert West and his family
visit P., iv. 403.
1743: Publication of *The Dunciad*
delayed because of Lintot's claim on
the copyright, iv. 439, 448; it is half
printed, iv. 456; is published the last
of Oct., iv. 474; a copy is sent to H.
Bethel, iv. 476; Bowyer urged to
watch for any piracy, iv. 477; P. complains that the sm. 8vo ed. is not
divided rightly: Bk. IV should be
with the others, iv. 477, 478; the
Ethic Epistles (i.e. 'Moral Essays')
are to be put to press, iv. 439, 448;
Warburton makes textual emenda-
tions, iv. 480; the *Essay on Man* is
being revised to suit Warburton, iv.
439–40, 448; the first 3 sheets of proofs
received, iv. 455; — Christopher
Smart wishes to make a Latin transla-

Pope, Biogr. Data (*1743 cont.*)
tion, iv. 478, 483; the *Essay on Criticism* with Warburton's commentary
given to the press, iv. 474; the 'Ethic
Epistles', the *Essay on Man*, and the
Essay on Criticism are to be published
in a small ed. to see how they 'take',
iv. 480; the problem of P.'s alleged
character of the old Duke of Buckingham—and of the Duchess, iv. 460.
Among those invited to Twickenham are the Arbuthnots, iv. 441–2;
Murray, 442, 456; Bolingbroke and
Marchmont, 442, 456; Mallet and
Thomson, 453; — P. plans his visit
to Bath for the summer, iv. 441, 443;
in Bath he dines with Chesterfield, iv.
459; leaves the Allens in anger, iv.
463–4, 465; visits Bathurst at Cirencester, iv. 466; goes with G. Arbuthnot to Bristol, iv. 466, and to Wales,
iv. 467; returning to London he pauses
briefly in Bath without seeing Allen,
iv. 469; on return pauses in London
4 or 5 days, iv. 470; — goes from
home with Arbuthnot to Amesbury
and to Salisbury, iv. 472; goes also to
Cornbury, Rousham, and Oxford,
iv. 472; — intends to stay in London
during the winter, iv. 465; will not
settle at Bath, iv. 484; lives much at
Battersea with Bolingbroke and
Marchmont, iv. 486.
P. gets Lord Orrery to work towards
Warburton's Oxford degree, in vain,
iv. 436–7, 440, 442, 456; for Lady
Orrery P. subscribes for a book, unidentified, iv. 440; P. still works on
his grotto, and needs more of Allen's
rustic stone, iv. 443, 449, 450; the
grotto will not be finished before
Easter, iv. 444, 448; P. disparages his
leaden urns, iv. 474; could now purchase his villa, iv. 446, 467; asks
S. Bethel for interest due, iv. 447;
thinks of buying a house in town, iv.
457; anxious to get the arrear on his
annuity from the estate of the
Duchess of Buckingham, iv. 482; —
by another hand P. has passed £20 to
Fielding from Allen for the *Miscellanies* of Fielding, iv. 452; P. tells
Allen how to deal with fawns, iv. 452;
in health P. suffers from weak eyes,

POPE, BIOGR. DATA (*1743 cont.*)
iv. 437 (he employs someone to read to him), 443, 482; from asthma, 445 (and dropsy), 449, 486, 487; asthma and piles make coach travel painful, iv. 467; he cannot dine out, iv. 433, 454.

From the Allens P. gets delicious oysters, iv. 450; Allen assures P. that he will secure Warburton's (financial) independency, iv. 452; Allen declines to let P. and Arbuthnot have a house for the summer at Bath, iv. 461; P. and Martha Blount angry at Allen, iv. 462, 463–4; — Allen, ill, has not written to P., iv. 477, 479; P. explains his hasty passage through Bath en route to London, iv. 481; P. wishes to preserve a sincere friendship with Allen, iv. 485; Allen's coolness with Dr. Oliver, iv. 486; — P. visits Lord Bathurst from Bath, without Warburton, iv. 462, 466; wishes that in their decline he and H. Bethel might pass a year or two together, iv. 447; H. Bethel returns from Italy, iv. 467; — H. Bethel seems not to approve P.'s terms for an annuity to Martha Blount, iv. 473–4; S. Bethel is asked to get more Madeira for Martha Blount, iv. 475, 485; Martha's mother dies, iv. 450, 452; she will not at once go to Bath, iv. 452–3, 454; her great anger later at the Allens, iv. 462; she stays with Lady Gerard in Welbeck Street, iv. 485; — Bolingbroke embarks for France, iv. 456; he returns to England in Nov., iv. 483; P. visits Jeremiah Brown at Abscourt for a day, iv. 451; the illness and death of Katherine, Duchess of Buckingham, iv. 440, 442, 446; P. comments on Cibber's *Apology*, iv. 437–8; a leaf supposedly from *The Dunciad* sent to Cibber, iv. 448–9; Fortescue difficult to see, iv. 440; not expected while Bolingbroke is with P., iv. 451; — Lord Hervey is bequeathed all the Duchess of Buckingham's papers (including P.'s letters?), iv. 446; the death of Lord Hervey, iv. 466; P.'s suit against Lintot is finally ended, iv. 455; — Marchmont and P. beg Sarah, Duchess of Marlborough, to send for

POPE, BIOGR. DATA (*1743 cont.*)
them, iv. 444–5; P. and Martha Blount plan to visit the Duchess, iv. 457; P. enumerates his many debts to the Duchess, iv. 457; she sends P. money for Janette Mowat, iv. 458; P. asks her to send a buck to Bristol for the brother of Lord Elibank, iv. 466; — P. is anxious to see J. Richardson, iv. 487; soothes Warburton's suspicions as to Hanmer's Shakespeare, iv. 438, 475; Lord Carteret said to intend serving Warburton, iv. 439; P. will even flatter in order to get Warburton a patron, iv. 448; Allen repeatedly has undertaken to assist Warburton, iv. 452; Warburton contributes a dissertation on chivalry to Jervas's *Don Quixote*, iv. 455; Warburton plans to leave Allen's in Aug., iv. 462; P. and he dine together every day W. is in London, iv. 471; Warburton is back home in Newark, iv. 474; — P. visits G. West in Kent, and the West family visit P. for a fortnight, iv. 451; P.'s reflections on the death of the Earl of Wilmington, iv. 458–9, 465; other remarks on politics, iv. 437, 441.

1744: A passage in *The Dunciad* offends the clergy, iv. 492; Lintot's remarks on his copyrights to be noted, iv. 502; P. delays the trial publication of the *Essay on Man* and *Essay on Criticism*, iv. 491; 'goes on softly' with the Great Edition with Warburton's comments, iv. 491; Wright employed as printer of the sm. 8vo ed. of the *Essay on Man*, iv. 502; — Epistle to Cobham to be done in 4to not 8vo, iv. 504; wants the MS. of the Epistle on Women returned by Warburton, iv. 515; changes made, iv. 516; the Epistle to Bathurst offends Warburton by its mention of Sir R. Sutton, iv. 492–4; the epistles to Burlington and to the Lady offer few problems except the reinsertion of omitted lines in the latter, iv. 495; both Epistles on the Use of Riches are revised, iv. 500, and are to be finished by Bowyer while Warburton is in Town, iv. 500, 506; — P. plans to add to the

POPE, BIOGR. DATA (*1744 cont.*)
Epistles that addressed to Dr. Arbuthnot and some of the best imitations of Horace, iv. 491; in his bad condition he would gladly resign all concern with his works, iv. 501, 506.
P. (3 Jan.) is at Murray's in town, iv. 489; plans to go to Chiswick in Burlington's coach, iv. 490; goes to Battersea, iv. 490, 491; returns from Town to Twickenham (*c.* 27 Jan.), where he sleeps better, iv. 495; is at Orrery's in Duke Street, iv. 497, 498; wishes to go from Town to Battersea, iv. 498; is back at Twickenham, iv. 501; Bolingbroke to spend part of a day there, iv. 503; — the Proclamation against Catholics obliges P. to stay at Twickenham, iv. 504, 505, though he may risk going to Battersea; would like to go to Murray's, but is too ill, iv. 505; the Allens spend Good Friday with P., iv. 509 n.; — various visitors expected at Twickenham, iv. 511; P. goes to Chiswick (30 Mar.), iv. 514; goes to Cheselden at Chelsea, iv. 516, 522; — Hooke is ill at Twickenham, iv. 516; Lord Boyle brings a letter from Orrery, iv. 517, 521; Bolingbroke at Twickenham, iv. 519, 520; the 3rd Lord Oxford and Sir John St. Aubyn dine there, iv. 520 n.
P. wishes to collect the arrear of £150 from the Duchess of Buckingham's estate, iv. 489; owes Warburton a small debt, iv. 492; again offers S. Bethel £300 to invest, iv. 496, 497; plans to purchase a house with H. Bethel, iv. 496, 509; is buying a house in Town, iv. 508, 509; sat once to Kent for a portrait for H. Bethel, 509; sends S. Bethel £200, iv. 513; has read Berkeley on *Tar Water*, iv. 514; learns of the death of Bounce, iv. 507–8, 517.
P.'s health is extremely worse on account of asthma, iv. 489, 503; has gone to Chelsea to be let blood, iv. 497; is too ill to go from Duke Street to Marlborough House, iv. 498; Cheselden lets blood for P. at Battersea, iv. 499, 501; — P. envisages this

POPE, BIOGR. DATA (*1744 cont.*)
as his 'last' winter or spring, iv. 499–500; has been confined to his chamber for 3 weeks past, iv. 507; speaks of swellings in his legs, iv. 508, 518; had hoped to lodge with Cheselden at Chelsea and so get to Town, iv. 511, 515; — Dr. Thompson is recommended, iv. 512, 514, 521; the diagnosis is now dropsy, iv. 521, 522; has been confined to his chamber for a month now, iv. 513; rides in a chariot for an hour or two on warm days, iv. 518; his death, 524; his last days as recorded by Spence, iv. 525–6.
His disillusionments in his last days, iv. 499; a visit from Allen in Mar. is awaited, iv. 489, 491, 505, 506, 509 n.; P. can see Allen only at Twickenham because of the Proclamation, iv. 504, 515; Mrs. Allen upon arrival in Town is not well, iv. 509; the Good Friday visit reported to Martha Blount, iv. 510–11; P. can't see Allen as he returns to Bath, iv. 517; Allen reaches home safely, iv. 519; — H. Bethel has sent P. his portrait by a painter in Rome, iv. 500, 512; Bethel still prefers Kneller's portrait of P., iv. 512; Martha Blount's quiet still hindered by Teresa, iv. 500; P.'s coloured report to Martha of his meeting with the Allens, iv. 510–11; — Bolingbroke's stay feared brief, iv. 495; he is a comfort to P., iv. 499; Bolingbroke, unwell, cannot come to Twickenham to meet Warburton, iv. 518; — Cibber is reportedly publishing an abusive pamphlet, iv. 491; P. condoles with Fortescue on the death of F.'s sister, iv. 507; Orrery gets reports on P.'s last days from Mallet, iv. 522–4; P. is most anxious to have Warburton and Bolingbroke meet, iv. 491, 495, 505, 506, 520; — Warburton arrives in Town, iv. 505; he desires (P. says) to wait on Lord Bolingbroke, iv. 513, 515; W. is ill in town, iv. 515; is asked to call on Bolingbroke at Chetwynd's, iv. 518.

II. POPE'S WORKS
For their publishers *see* C. Bathurst, J. Brindley, T. and M. Cooper, E.

POPE, WORKS (*cont.*)

Curll, R. Dodsley, G. Faulkner, L.
Gilliver, J. and P. Knapton, W.
Lewis, B. and H. Lintot, B. Motte,
T. Osborne, J. Tonson, sr. and jr.;
— for piracies of the *Works, see* J. H.
Hubbard, J. Ilive, T. Johnson, J.
Robinson, J. Watson; — for printers
employed *see* J. Barber, J. Watts, H.
Woodfall, J. Wright; copyright diffi-
culties real or imagined concerned
The Dunciad, iv. 333; the *Letters*
(1735), iv. 88; the subscription edi-
tion of the *Iliad,* iv. 223; and certain
early works, iv. 223–4, 502.

COLLECTED WORKS: ed. of 1717,
i. 264 n., 396, 410, 411; *Works,* vol.
ii (1735), iii. 433, 444; copies sent to
W. Duncombe, iii. 454; to Caryll,
iii. 455, 474; to Buckley, who is
asked to sell 150 copies, iii. 454; to
Swift, v. 15; the vol. is pirated, iii.
477; P. has troubles marketing the
vol., iii. 454, 477, iv. 66; prints copies
of poems later than 1735 to bind into
the vol., iv. 66; — the projected
'Great Edition' with Warburton's
notes, iv. 361, 434, 491; Pope feels
that he can no longer work on the ed.,
iv. 500–1; the 'death-bed' ed. of the
Moral Essays, iv. 504 n.; issued in
1748, iv. 504 n.; eager to have Warburton plan the ed., iv. 506, 514; —
the trade eds. in sm. 8vo, iii. 489, 502
n., iv. 87, 229; Faulkner projects an
Irish ed., v. 17; *Works in Prose* (1737),
see below under Letters; so also for
Works in Prose, ii (Swift correspondence, 1741).

MISCELLANIES contributed to by
Pope: *Poetical Miscellanies* the Sixth
Part (Tonson, 1709), *see* 'Episode of
Sarpedon' and 'Pastorals'; — *Miscel-
laneous Poems and Translations* (Lin-
tot, 1712, 1714, 5th ed. 1727), *see*
Statius *Thebais,* Bk. I, 'To a Young
Lady with the Works of Voiture',
'On Silence' (in imitation of Roches-
ter), 'Verses design'd to be prefix'd to
Mr. Lintott's Miscellany', 'The Rape
of the Lock' (shorter form), 'Two or
Three; or a Receipt to make a
Cuckold' (first in ed. of 1714); 'The
Monster of Ragusa' (probably not

POPE, WORKS (*cont.*)

P.'s; first found in the ed. of 1727);
P. helped assemble this miscellany for
Lintot, i. 141, ii. 269, 378, 383; —
Poetical Miscellanies (Steele–Tonson,
1727 ed.), *see* 'Lines to Sir G. Kneller
on his painting for me the Statues of
Apollo, Venus, and Hercules'; —
Original Poems and Translations
(Curll, 1714), *see* 'Upon the Duke of
Marlborough's House' (probably not
by P.); — *Court Poems* (Curll, 1716),
i. 326, 339, ii. 39; — *Poems on Several
Occasions* (Pope–Lintot, 1717), *see*
'Imitations of Waller' and 'Ode on
Solitude'; *also see* i. 386 n., 410; —
Pope's Miscellany (Burleigh, 1717)
Part II, 'A Roman Catholic Version
of the First Psalm'; — *Miscellanea in
Two Volumes* (Curll, 1726–7), *see*
Pope's letters to Cromwell, 'Argus',
'You Know Where', 'Verses on Dur-
fey'; — *Atterburyana* (Curll, 1727),
see 'Mr. Pope's Receipt to Make
Soup'; — *Miscellaneous Poems* (D.
Lewis–Watts, 1730), *see* 'Epigram:
When other Ladies', 'Adriani Morien-
tis', 'Cristiani Morientis' ['The Dying
Christian'], Epitaph for Robert
Digby.

The Pope–Swift *Miscellanies in
Prose and Verse* (1727–32): vol. ii
cited for the maxim on Party ('the
madness of the many'), i. 247 n.;
Swift has sent good pieces for the
Miscellanies, ii. 419; he gives P.
carte blanche for revision of them, ii.
420; — P. asks Lord Oxford for
John Bull, &c., ii. 421; asks Swift if
Cadenus and Vanessa should go in, ii.
425; tells Swift the first (prose) vol. is
now printed (Feb. 1727), ii. 426; —
the verse vol. ('last') is now being
arranged, ii. 426; an agreement with
Motte for the *Miscellanies* (10 Apr.
1727) is signed, ii. 430 n.; *The Dunciad* should be ready before winter for
the 'last' vol. of the *Miscellanies,* ii.
438; — P. is proof-reading the vol., ii.
438; it should be published at the
time of the Coronation, ii. 444, 466;
P. lacks verses to fill the 'last' vol., ii.
466 n.; — Curll claims copyrights
to pieces in the *Miscellanies,* ii. 477–8;

POPE, WORKS (*cont.*)
    the *Miscellanies* link P. and Swift
as inseparable friends, ii. 480; Motte
proves dilatory in his payments for
the *Miscellanies*, ii. 526; the three vols.
of *Miscellanies* reach New England,
ii. 528; — *The Art of Sinking in
Poetry* is designed for the third (1732)
vol., ii. 439; it substitutes for *The
Dunciad* in the 'last' vol., 466, 468;
it was originally a project of the
Scriblerus Club, ii. 468 n., iii. 106; it
shows P.'s lack of fear (he says) of the
Dunces, ii. 480; — P. hopes J. Knight
has read the 'last', ii. 484; the
Bathos annoys Broome, ii. 432 n., iii.
106, 116; Hill suspects 'A.H.' means
him, iii. 165, 169; the cruelty of P.'s
satire in the *Bathos* alleged by Hill, iv.
99–101; P. says Arbuthnot was responsible for much of it, iv. 102; —
P. has troubles with Motte and has no
idea (1729) when the third vol. (1732)
will be ready, iii. 8; reproaches
Motte over his dilatory payments,
iii. 8–9, 23, 32; payments not finished
until 1730, iii. 90; — collects material
for the final (1732) vol., iii. 1, 17, 19,
162, 301; political pieces to be ruled
out, iii. 22 n.; the final vol. hastily
brought out to forestall trouble with
Pilkington and Bowyer, iii. 323, 348;
P. questions their authorization to
publish, iii. 324; — P.'s Preface to
the 'third' (1732) vol., iii. 347 n.; he
owns a few loose *jeux d'esprit* in the
Miscellanies, iii. 347; defends his in-
clusions and exclusions, iii. 347–8;
hated to omit the 'Libel on Dr.
Delany' with its (best) panegyric on
himself, iii. 348; 'The Capon's Tale'
his first overt attack on Lady Mary,
iii. 53 n., 352 n.; — the revision and
rearrangement of the *Miscellanies*
(1740–1), iv. 284–5; the reasons for
the changes, iv. 285 n.; some pieces
are to be transferred to the *Works in
Prose* (vol. ii: the Pope-Swift letters),
iv. 333, 349, 353; the 'last' vol. is supposed to contain all the verse, iv.
353; — P. has promised not to include Arbuthnot's 'Sermon at Edinburgh' in the *Miscellanies*, iv. 367;
for P.'s verse pieces found in the

POPE, WORKS (*cont.*)
Miscellanies, see also under 'MINOR
POEMS' (below).
    MAJOR POEMS AND TRANSLATIONS
(arranged alphabetically): 'Atticus'
lines, *see Epistle to Dr. Arbuthnot*;
Bounce to Fop, iv. 1, 48 n.; *The
Second Satire of Donne Translated*, ii.
371, 372; — *The Dunciad* (1728), pre-
monitory phrases to occur in, i. 462;
the early lines on Philips, ii. 332; its
design to be kept secret, ii. 333, 438;
early called 'The Progress of Dulness', ii. 438 n.; will be published
separately, not in the *Miscellanies*, ii.
466; P. daren't trust the MS. to the
post, ii. 468; his 'Dulness' flourishes,
ii. 472; hereafter to be called *The
Dunciad*, ii. 480; — comments on its
reception, ii. 496, 498, 502 n.; it is
approved at Court, iii. 1; P. is still
troubled about Cooke and *The Dunciad*, iii. 8, v. 7; lines inscribing the
poem to Swift composed and sent to
Swift early, ii. 468–9; — *The Dunciad Variorum* (1729), projected before the first publication of the poem
in 1728, ii. 467; P. dares not send the
MS. to Ireland, ii. 455–6; quotes part
of the Inscription to Swift, ii. 456;
thinks the poem 'will rid me of those
insects', ii. 481; asks Lord Oxford for
Caxton's Preface to Virgil, ii. 498; at
work on the *Variorum*, ii. 502; —
King George II 'commands' a Key
to the poem, ii. 502; the Variorum
ed. Pope's substitute for a Key, ii.
502 n.; contents of the poem listed for
Swift, who is asked to contribute
notes, ii. 503; Lord Oxford asked for
aid in transcribing the poem, ii. 504;
notes for Bk. II sent to Lord Oxford,
ii. 506; — the text is printed, ii. 522;
P. wishes some Irish epigrams to add
to the notes, ii. 523; P. momentarily
hesitates to publish the poem, v. 7;
now says the edition soon to be published, ii. 523; — Fazackerley consulted as to possible libel suits, ii.
532, iii. 4; F. is not to be told P. is the
author, iii. 4; P. insists the notes are
written by friends, ii. 505, iii. 31, 36,
165, iv. 428, v. 7 (Cleland and Arbuthnot named as aids); *Dunciad*

POPE, WORKS (*cont.*)

Variorum first placed on sale 10 Apr.
1729, iii. 19 n.; presented to the King
and Queen 12 Mar. 1729, iii. 20 n.;
Lord Oxford distributes copies, iii.
25, 26; — the need to protect Gilliver
as publisher, iii. 31 n.; the role of
noblemen as distributors, iii. 1, 31;
P. suggests the lords protect Gilliver
by a formal announcement, iii. 31–
32; — asks Caryll's opinion of the
footnotes, iii. 36; his petition against
piracies denied since he proves no
property in the poem, iii. 37; a conveyance of copyright to Gilliver is
prepared, iii. 59 n.; P. says the 8vo
ed. is better than the 4to, iii. 57; asks
Swift's opinion of the text and comment, iii. 57; the assignment to Gilliver now preserved as Egerton MS.
1951. f. 7, iii. 59 n.; — P. sends to
Lord Oxford the (unpublished) 8vo
ed. of *The Dunciad* with vol. ii of
Wycherley's *Posthumous Works*, iii.
62; the assignment to Gilliver is sent
to Burlington for signature, iii. 67;
an ed. (the second, so called, and the
best) is sent to Swift, iii. 79–80; Swift
thinks the revised 8vo ed. not likely
to be reprinted in Dublin, iii. 92; —
Pope's statement in *The Dunciad* concerning his payments to Broome, iii.
106 n.; Hearne offended by *The Dunciad*, iii. 111 n.; Hill complains of a
passage in *The Dunciad*, iii. 164, 165,
170, 174; the passage is omitted in
later eds., iii. 177; P. speaks of 'two
lords and one gentleman' as responsible for the variorum *Dunciad*, iii.
177 n.; the publishers said to be
attacked in *The Craftsman*, iii. 220;
P. takes Broome out of *The Dunciad*,
iii. 510, iv. 2–3; the provocation given
by the Dunces unknown to Hill, iv.
104; — *The New Dunciad* written at
Widcombe, iv. 387; it attacks travelling and 'the polite world', iv. 377; its
publication, iv. 387; its kind reception, iv. 396, 415; it is pirated, iv.
392, 433; Warburton thanked for his
aid on the poem, iv. 393; P. sends
The New Dunciad to H.Bethel, iv. 396;
— *The Dunciad in Four Books* (1743)
early projected, iv. 178–9, 357, 362;

POPE, WORKS (*cont.*)

the revision of Bks. I–III well under
way, iv. 393 n.; further changes, iv.
425, 426, 434; proofs to be sent to P.
at Bath, iv. 426; 'brazen' image to
stand, iv. 426; Warburton's aid to be
acknowledged publicly, iv. 427, 428;
P.'s impetuosity in printing, iv. 428,
429, 430, 431; his gratitude to Warburton, iv. 433, 439; Hanmer's
Shakespeare in *Dunciad* iv, iv. 438 n.;
— P. has written all he has to say
about Cibber, iv. 415, 449; a 'cancelled leaf' from *The Dunciad* sent to
Cibber, iv. 448–9; — P. requests Lintot not to sell his share in the copyright of *The Dunciad* to any but P.
himself, iv. 240; expresses doubts as to
Lintot's rights, iv. 333; offers to revise *The Dunciad* for Lintot upon conditions, iv. 333; publication delayed
because of copyright difficulties, iv.
439, 448; the four Books are half
printed, iv. 455–6; to be published
the last of Oct., iv. 474; — P. wishes
to send the poem to H. Bethel, iv.
476; asks Bowyer to watch for
piracies, iv. 477; Dodsley and
Cooper publish the poem, iv. 477 n.; in
the sm. 8vo ed. the two vols. are not at
first properly divided, iv. 477–8; Pope
wishes to know when 500 copies are
sold, iv. 478; the clergy are offended
by two lines in the poem, iv. 492.

ELOISA TO ABELARD, its composition, i. 338; its sentimental conclusion,
i. 338; P. suggests Dr. Cowper translate it rather than the *Unfortunate
Lady*, iii. 268; Caryll asks the identity of the 'Unfortunate Lady', i. 419.

The Epilogue to the Satires (originally *One Thousand Seven Hundred
and Thirty Eight*) disparages the
Latinity of Conyers Middleton, iii.
217 n.; Lyttelton reads Dialogue I
in MS., iv. 109; it is praised by A.
Hill, iv. 112; the lines about Allen
are revised, iv. 93, 144–5; — Dialogue
II is published in July, iv. 114 n.;
praised by Swift, iv. 115; attacked
for its compliment to Bolingbroke,
iv. 154 n.; compliments Bolingbroke
and Walpole in the same passage, iv.
114; quoted by A. Hill, iv. 152; the

POPE, WORKS (*cont.*)
fragment of *One Thousand Seven Hundred and Forty* is quoted concerning Cornbury, iv. 272 n.

P.'s EPISTLES (*see also* 'Moral Essays'): his publications in 1735, iii. 442; Swift hears of a series of epistles projected, and wishes one addressed to himself, iii. 344, iv. 5, 12; P. agrees to add some epistles to the great ed. of the Moral Essays, iv. 500; — his *Epistle to Dr. Arbuthnot*: a MS. in the Huntington Library, iii. 428, 444 n.; written (like *Sober Advice*) at Bevis Mount, iii. 424 n., iv. 33; put together piece-meal, iii. 428; its defensive aim, iii. 428; P. reports that it is finished, iii. 431; — the 'Atticus' lines early conceived, i. 196 n. 4, 306–7; they are published in *St. James's Journal*, ii. 104 n., 144, 147; before publication they are much in demand, ii. 104; — other lines included in the poem are sent early to A. Hill, iii. 226; the source of a line in the poem, i. 450 n.; a line cited, ii. 56 n.; P. wishes an advance copy for Lord Oxford, iii. 446; intends to add it to the great ed., iv. 491; he suggests to Warburton a type of comment, iv. 495; — P.'s *Epistle to Robert, Earl of Oxford*, i. 252 n., ii. 90–92, 382; — his *Epistle to a Young Lady* [Teresa Blount] *on her Leaving Town*, i. 264 n.; — his *Epistle to Jervas*, i. 133 n., 187 n., 198 n., 334, 369 (on Wortley's eyes); — his *Bounce to Fop*, iv. 1, 48; P. hopes to dedicate his second book of epistles (never written) to Swift, iv. 5.

MORAL ESSAYS: One of them finished 'last week', iii. 366; the *Epistle to Cobham* published, iii. 401; A. Hill wishes the lines about the Czar excised, iv. 158; Warburton later disapproves the change, iv. 339; Warburton's general comments approved by P., iv. 495; proofs of the final edition to be in 4to and 8vo, iv. 504; — *Epistle to a Lady* [Martha Blount], *Of the Characters of Women*, its publication, iii. 363; its central theme, iii. 274 n., 349; Bolingbroke's praise of it, iii. 349; a copy sent to

POPE, WORKS (*cont.*)
Caryll, iii. 450; P.'s explanation of the last line, iii. 451; the lost 'character' of the Princesse des Ursines, ii. 461 n.; — the omitted characters (Atossa, Cloe, &c.) replaced in the final ed., iv. 495; the character of 'Atossa' suppressed by Pope's executors, iv. 504 n.; P. asks Warburton to return the MS. of the poem, iv. 515; he instructs Warburton to say that no *living* examples are in the poem, iv. 516; — the *Epistle to Bathurst, Of the Use of Riches*, planned carefully, iii. 157, 241; uses real names of persons, iii. 266; its compliment to Edward, Earl of Oxford, iii. 241; Chandos not finally joined with Lord Oxford in the poem, iii. 325; P. gathers data on the Man of Ross, iii. 290, 291; — worked on the poem for 2 years, iii. 353; it is to appear in the holiday season, iii. 334, 337; a copy sent to Caryll, iii. 340; Hill's comment on P. and the Man of Ross, iii. 342; — the reception of the poem good, iii. 345; a copy sent to Swift, iii. 348; the name Morgan is fictitious, iii. 353; Swift thinks parts will be obscure to Dublin readers, iii. 362; Warburton's commentary, iv. 480; P.'s final revisions, iv. 500; the final printing is delayed, iv. 505–6; — the *Epistle to the Earl of Burlington, Of the Use of Riches* (also *Of Taste* and *Of False Taste*) is sent to Burlington in Apr. 1731, iii. 159, 187, 188; it will not attack 'little offenders', iii. 182; is sent to Lord Oxford for transcription, iii. 193; — promptly defended from attack, iii. 254–7; only malice identifies Timon with the Duke of Chandos, iii. 256; Hill suggests the title 'Of False Taste', iii. 257; it is adopted by P., iii. 260, 265, 267, 268; a piracy reported, iii. 257–8; P. apologizes to Burlington, denying that Chandos was intended as Timon, iii. 259; *The Huntington Library Bulletin* cited on Chandos, iii. 259 n. — P. shows Hill that Chandos is not like Timon, iii. 260, 261, 262; Pope's prefatory letter in the 3rd ed., iii. 265–6; P. is pleased by the attitude of

POPE, WORKS (*cont.*)

    Chandos towards the poem. iii. 266, 268, 279; *The Master Key to Popery* defends the poem, iii. 272 n.; P. explains the scandal over Chandos to Caryll, iii. 279; P.'s final revision of the poem, iv. 500.

    AN ESSAY ON CRITICISM published, i. 113; a first ed. of 1,000 copies, i. 128; Dennis's attack, i. 121, 122, 132; lines offensive to Catholics, i. 118, 122, 126–9; Wycherley praises the poem, i. 134; Cromwell urges P. to undertake the higher poetry, i. 136; P. assures Steele and Addison that he is willing to excise passages of ill nature, i. 139, 264; the 2nd ed. does not excise lines offensive to Catholics, i. 151, 152; a line borrowed from the Duke of Buckingham to be printed in italic, i. 394; — A. Hill criticizes the phrasing of the poem, iv. 97–99; it is translated into French, i. 192; Warburton's commentary on the poem, iv. 455, 474.

    The ESSAY ON MAN, possibly projected as early as 1725, ii. 321; P. is at work on it in the summer of 1730 (i.e. 16 months ago), iii. 247; he works under supervision of Bolingbroke, iii. 71–72, 163; P. tells Swift he is at work on 'a system of ethics in the Horatian way', iii. 81; Swift hopes it is nearly completed, iii. 94; Pope's aim is 'to put morality in good humour', iii. 117; to make mankind less admirers and more reasoners, iii. 250; — P. and Bolingbroke have parallel projects, iii. 249; P. has many fragments to fit together, iii. 85, 153, 155, 271; a phrase in a letter by Bolingbroke parallels a line in the poem, iii. 163 n.; Bolingbroke quotes and summarizes the poem for Swift, iii. 183–4, 213–14; — P. has finished Epistle III of the poem, iii. 209; new ideas and characters occur to him, iii. 227; not nearly ready to publish, iii. 232; Fortescue has one Epistle to be transcribed for P., iii. 270–1; P. quotes a line from Epistle IV, iii. 326; now being published anonymously, iii. 327; P. thanks J. Richardson for complimentary verses on the poem,

POPE, WORKS (*cont.*)

    iii. 326–7; in a letter to Richardson P. pretends ignorance as to the author of the poem, iii. 351; — Epistle I is published in Feb. 1733, iii. 351 n.; its reception helped by anonymity, iii. 352, 356, 433, 438; Croxall and Secker deny authorship of the poem, iii. 358; Swift thinks Dr. Young is the author, v. 11–12; P.'s fear that passages may be heterodox, iii. 354; P.'s enemies praise the poem as better than his own work, iii. 355; — Epistle II appears in Mar. 1733, iii. 356 n.; P.'s care now is to finish the *Essay*, iii. 381; he praises H. Bethel in Epistle IV, iii. 381; is pleased by Caryll's opinion of the poem, iii. 403; paraphrases a passage from the poem in a letter, iii. 403; sends the collected 4to ed. (1734) to Caryll, iii. 405; — expresses doubts as to preserving the grave, lofty tone of the poem, iii. 433; some parts of the poem are obscure, iii. 439; Swift surprised at the depth of P.'s moral insight, iii. 439; — Warburton is thanked for his defence of the *Essay* against Crousaz, iv. 163–4, 171; Warburton's letters on the Essay are collected to form his *Vindication*, iv. 182; P. hopes the *Vindication* may be translated into French, iv. 172, 216, 219; thinks that either he or Warburton must read proofs of the *Vindication*, iv. 182; P.'s gratitude to Warburton, iv. 196; Warburton adds a letter of comment on Epistle IV, iv. 219; P. thinks some flattery of himself might be omitted from the *Vindication*, iv. 220; — thinks Crousaz malicious, iv. 164, 219; says he has never read Leibniz, iv. 164; thinks Warburton understands the poem better than P. himself does, iv. 171–2; urges Fortescue to read the *Vindication*, iv. 203; sends a copy to Henry Brooke, iv. 208, 213; — thanks J. Brinsden for verses on the poem, iv. 209; P. parodies the second couplet of the poem, iv. 247; Warburton is finding a translator to put the poem into Latin, iv. 251–2, 288; P. wishes he had Bolingbroke as a commentator (as Ennius had Tully!), iv. 261; —

POPE, WORKS (*cont.*)

P.'s deference to Warburton slightly qualified, iv. 288 n.; he wishes certain comments and discarded verses used in an ed. rather than in the *Vindication*, iv. 288, 361; approves of Warburton's placing of some lines, iv. 362; suggests small changes in Warburton's commentary on the *Essay*, iv. 379–80; — now plans a 4to ed. of the *Essay on Man* and the *Essay on Criticism* with commentary by Warburton, iv. 428; sets Bowyer to printing the *Essay on Man* for this ed., iv. 434, and also the Ethic Epistles ('Moral Essays'), iv. 439; wishes to announce Warburton's general editorship of a final ed., iv. 439; submits lines from the *Essay* for Warburton's criticism, iv. 439–40; — feels sure he will show to best advantage in the Epistles and the *Essay on Criticism*, iv. 448; will try the taste of the town by placing the *Essay on Man* and the *Essay on Criticism* together in a trial vol., iv. 480, 491; eventually the Moral Essays and the *Essay on Man* are to be in the same vol., iv. 480; — Christopher Smart projects a translation of the *Essay on Man* into Latin, iv. 483; P. lists the languages into which the poem has been translated, iv. 484; — the 4to ed. of the *Essay on Criticism* and the *Essay on Man* is advertised, iv. 500; he would defer publication in quarto of the two Essays, iv. 500; he specifies personages to whom advance copies are to be sent, iv. 502.

HORACE, IMITATIONS OF (chronologically arranged—N.B. Only a few are mentioned in the letters): *The First Satire of the Second Book*: its date of publication, iii. 350 n.; it was 'the work of two mornings' while P. was ill in town at Lord Oxford's, iii. 348, 350, 353; his true object was a score of lines near the end, iii. 348; — a copy sent to Swift, iii. 348; a panegyric of all his friends in one line, iii. 350; Lord Peterborow conveys to Lady Mary the surprise expressed by P. at her taking the character of 'Sappho' as her own, iii. 352; Swift praises

POPE, WORKS (*cont.*)

the poem, iii. 362; Hill praises its 'honest vivacity', iii. 370; Page is satirized in the poem, iv. 190–1; a line of the poem paraphrased, iv. 484; — *The Second Satire of the Second Book*, composed in Mar. 1733, iii. 358; P. informs Swift that he will appear in the poem, iii. 366; Swift assumes that he is to be Ofellus, iii. 369, 429, v. 12–13; the poem is advertised in July 1734, iii. 429 n.; not at once sent to Bethel, iii. 427; — *Sober Advice from Horace* (i.e. *The Second Satire of the First Book*), written at Bevis Mount, iii. 424, iv. 33; is sent to Bolingbroke, iii. 413–14; reflects on Bolingbroke's vices, iii. 414; publication of the poem, iii. 446 n.; P. does not own the poem, iii. 413 n., 446–7; his account of Bentley's anger at the footnotes, iii. 451; P. does not approve of the poem, iii. 450; — *The Second Epistle of the Second Book*, iv. 55, 56, 68; — *The First Epistle of the Second Book* (To Augustus) is sent to Allen, Orrery, and Swift, iv. 68, 70, 72; P. regards it as one of his best, iv. 491; it was written at Bevis Mount, iv. 1, 33; its date of publication, iv. 56 n.

P.'s rhymed letter to Cromwell, i. 25–29; *see also* i. 46; *Messiah* is published in *The Spectator*, i. 141, 144; is an imitation of Virgil's *Pollio*, i. 142; praised by Steele as better than *Pollio*, i. 146; possibly translated into Latin by Dr. Cowper, iii. 269.

The PASTORALS mentioned early, i. 5, 7, 9, 17; said to be written in 1704, i. 17; read in MS. by several critics, i. 17; the third was the last written, i. 17; they are published by Tonson, i. 17, 41; P. fears they may seem too derivative, i. 20; the third Pastoral is dedicated to Wycherley, i. 41, 49; P. eagerly awaits publication, i. 56; a copy sent to Wycherley, who praises P.'s work, i. 59, 62; P. thinks Wycherley's 'puffing' the work has helped, i, 60.

THE RAPE OF THE LOCK is mentioned, i. 125 n., 133 n.; it appears in Lintot's Miscellany (1712), i. 141,

POPE, WORKS (*cont.*)

142; advance copies sent to Lord Petre and Miss Fermor, i. 141–2; Sir Plume is angry, i. 151, 163–4; Miss Fermor is reported to be offended, i. 151; the reception of the poem, i. 151; — the enlarged version promptly undertaken, i. 153, 201; its dedication, i. 203, 207; Caryll not named fully in the poem, i. 210; enlarged version published in Mar. 1714, i. 210 n.; it is generally praised, i. 212; P. uses sylphs from the *Comte de Gabalis*, i. 268 n.; Miss Fermor's marriage causes stares, i. 269; directions for printing the poem in 1717, i. 394; the *Key to the Lock*, i. 251, iv. 324.

WINDSOR FOREST in preparation, i. 141; is thought to be anticipated by Tickell, i. 157; is revised, i. 162, 168; is published, i. 170, 173 n. 5; Lord Lansdowne is thanked for allowing dedication to him, i. 172; Caryll knows the poem by heart, i. 173; it is praised by Garth, i. 289 n.

TRANSLATIONS AND MODERNIZATIONS: for the complete *Iliad* and *Odyssey*, *see under* Homer: the lines about Argus (*Odyssey*) sent to Cromwell, i. 74–75; the 'Episode of Sarpedon' (*Iliad*) added to Tonson's *Miscellany Poems*, i. 46; phrases from Dryden are noted in it, i. 44; P. consults R. Bridges because of his deficiency in the Greek, i. 41, 43, 44, 45; PIECES FROM OVID: *Sappho to Phaon*, i. 77 n., 141; *The Fable of Dryope*, i. 418 n.; —STATIUS, *Thebaid*, Bk. I: the history of the translation, i. 36–38; a first instalment sent to Cromwell, i. 36; a continuation done in 3 days, i. 56; P. suggests methods for Cromwell in his criticism, i. 57; thanks Cromwell for aid, i. 63, 68, 76; — asks Cromwell to return the translation, i. 76–77; wishes to show it to Sir W. Trumbull, i. 77 n.; has written 'Arguments' for the poem, i. 82, 91; on the word 'paradise', i. 95, 96; — modernizations of CHAUCER: *The Wife of Bath Her Prologue*, i. 191 n.; *The Temple of Fame* in preparation, i. 141; sent in MS. to Steele, i. 149 n., who ap-

POPE, WORKS (*cont.*)

proves of it, i. 152; and is thanked by P., i. 153–4; Addison's opinion is awaited, i. 154; the poem is mentioned in *The Spectator*, i. 162, 168; published in 1715, i. 162 n.; it is mentioned in a letter now lost, i. 165; a copy is sent to Martha Blount, i. 280; also one to Trumbull, i. 281, and another to Parnell, i. 284; — P.'s version of *The Second Satire of Dr. John Donne*, ii. 371, 372.

MINOR POEMS: P. burns his *Alcander*, i. 467; his *Capon's Tale* angers Lady Mary, iii. 53 n.; his Choruses for the Duke of Buckingham's plays, ii. 134, 135, v. 5; publication of the *Court Poems*, i. 326, 339, ii. 39; his *Dialogue* [between himself and General Dormer] on Kent's work on the Queen's Hermitage is suppressed by Kent, iii. 329; *Duke upon Duke*, ii. 85 n.; *The Dying Christian*, i. 141; P.'s comment on Hadrian's verses, i. 149, 159 n.; *Adriani Morientis* printed, i. 150, 157; P.'s exegesis of Hadrian, i. 158; he is asked by Steele for a song of a cheerful dying spirit, i. 159, 160; his deceit concerning the three versions of Hadrian's lines, i. 178, 179; P.'s EPIGRAMS: one in praise of Wycherley, i. 54, 'The Ballance of Europe', i. 130; on the journey to Letcombe, i. 235; on Fame and Reputation, i. 280; 'Upon the Duke of Marlborough's House at Woodstock', i. 432 n.; on Lady Kneller's size, ii. 309; an indecent epigram sent to Teresa Blount, i. 349; on his busto by Rysbrack, ii. 298 n., iii. 100; 'On Certain Ladies', iii. 123; on Cibber's verses written on glass, iii. 435 n.; on Cibber's having the last word, iv. 407; 'On one who made long epitaphs', iv. 14; the Epilogue for *Jane Shore*, i. 184 n., 205.

P.'s EPITAPHS: For Edmund, Duke of Buckingham, iv. 460 n.; for John, Earl Caryll, i. 133; the Digby epitaph, iii. 51; for Charles, 6th Earl of Dorset, iii. 241; for Fenton, iii. 125, 128, 156; — for John Gay, iii. 347; the epitaph criticized by Swift, iii. 360–1, 368, v. 12; who

POPE, WORKS (*cont.*)

gives Orrery a copy of it, iii. 363, 365; — the epitaph for the Hon. S. Harcourt, ii. 74, 146; — the epitaph for the lovers killed by lightning: the account of their deaths, i. 479-81, 488; various texts of the epitaph, i. 479 n., 481, 483; the epitaph in six lines, i. 483; that in ten lines printed, i. 479 n., 490 n., 495, 498; — the epitaph for Sir G. Kneller, ii. 309; that for John Knight, iv. 17; that for N. Rowe, ii. 25; for Sir W. Trumbull, i. 133 n.; P. is attacked concerning epitaphs for the Duke of Buckingham, John Gay, and Shakespeare, iv. 137 n. — P.'s 'Farewell to London', i. 295; his parody of the *First Psalm* is attacked by Blackmore, i. 371; its publication, i. 341 n.; P.'s 'genteel equivocation' concerning it, i. 350; *see also* i. 326, 342; P.'s verses in Thompson's Geoffrey of Monmouth, i. 425 n.; lines on his grotto, ii. 142, 297, iv. 262; verses to be appended to *Gulliver's Travels*, ii. 426; the question of their authorship, ii. 426 n.; for Hadrian's verses *see under The Dying Christian*; 'A Hymn Written in Windsor Forest', i. 429; — P.'s IMITATIONS: 'Artimisia' (Earl of Dorset), iii. 241 n.; Martial (X. 23), i. 328 n.; 'Silence' (Rochester), i. 87; his imitations of Waller, i. 97-99; — INSCRIPTIONS (normally prose) done anonymously, iv. 176 n.; one done for Allen, iv. 360; on Samuel Butler, ii. 76; on the Craggs monument, ii. 266; one done at Ford's request, iv. 137; for the tomb of N. Pigott, iv. 79-80; for the Prince's obelisk at Bath, iv. 176; on Vernon's bust, for Sarah, Duchess of Marlborough, iv. 421; 'Lines to Sir Godfrey Kneller on his Painting for me the Statues of Apollo, Venus, and Hercules', ii. 17 n.; — P. evades the authorship of 'Some Colinaeus praise', i. 138 n., 139; 'Verses to Miss Judith Cowper', ii. 139; 'To Mrs. M. B. on her Birthday', sent to Miss Cowper, ii. 180, iii. 18; lines on his own birthday, iii. 3; the lines on 'Moco's happy tree', i. 125; 'The Monster of Ragusa', ii.

POPE, WORKS (*cont.*)

334; 'Ode on the Longitude', i. 288, 290; the 'Ode on St. Cecilia's Day', iv. 478 n.; translated by C. Smart, iv. 484; — the 'Ode on Solitude' sent to Cromwell, i. 68-69; its possible relation to Claudian, iii. 138 n.; the source (?) of one line of it, i. 450 n.; P.'s 'song' about Mrs. Howard, ii. 178 n.; — P.'s PROLOGUES: for *Cato*, i. 170, 175, 184 n.; he revises Broome's Prologue, ii. 130; has declined to write a Prologue for the Duke of Buckingham, ii. 134; will not write a Prologue for Fenton or anyone, ii. 134; Rowe wishes to read P.'s (unidentified) Prologue, i. 184; — the Prologue for Dennis's benefit (1733), iii. 171 n., 358 n.; — 'Receipt to make a Cuckold', iii. 267-8; 'A Rondeau to Phillis' ('You know where'), i. 129 (*see also under* Voiture); — 'A Prayer to God' ('The Universal Prayer'), iv. 31-33; revised to reconcile Freedom and Necessity, iv. 31; — his rondeau from Voiture ('You know where'), i. 90, 95, 98, 129; 'A Tale from Chaucer', i. 50 n.; 'To a Young Lady with the Works of Voiture', i. 109, iii. 487; his Verses on Lying in Rochester's Bed, iv. 189 n.; his Verses on Durfey, ii. 268, 276; the Verses from the Chalfont window alleged to be by Milton, iv. 80-81.

PROSE WORKS: P. says he sinks from poetry to prose, iv. 178; 'The Art of Sinking in Poetry' (Bathos), *see* Pope-Swift MISCELLANIES; *A Full and True Account of the Revenge on Curll* (emetic), i. 339, 359 n.; *God's Revenge against Punning*, i. 350 n., 376; the *Heroi-comical Epistle on Punning*, i. 376; P.'s alleged connexion with *The Grub-street Journal*, iii. 159; ESSAYS, &c.: *Guardian* papers, i. 176-7, 180, 190, 217, 229 n. (on Pastorals); his essays known as his, i. 193, 198; he decides not to continue writing for Steele, i. 194; possible writing for 'The Censorium', i. 156, 159; regrets that Steele printed P.'s name in *Spectator* No. 532, i. 157, 158 (on Hadrian); is reproached for writing for Steele, i. 170, 174, 177,

POPE, WORKS (*cont.*)

197, ii. 75 (attack by Dennis); — *A Key to the Lock*, i. 251, iv. 324; 'A Letter to a Noble Lord', iii. 273; possible reference to 'A Master Key to Popery', iii. 273; *Memoirs of Scriblerus*, i. 205, 250, 339; the work is read to Warburton, iv. 239 n.; printed in *Works in Prose* (ii), iv. 334 n.; *Narrative of Dr. Norris concerning Dennis*, i. 170, 183; submitted (?) to Addison before publication, i. 184; P. denies authorship of it, i. 194; — P.'s PREFACES: he has made one for Buckley, iii. 70; 'Reflections on Pastoral Poetry', ii. 80; Preface to his *Works* (1717), i. 411; for Prefaces to the *Iliad, see under* Homer; for that to Shakespeare, *see under* Shakespeare; for Prefaces to editions of his Letters, *see below under that heading*; — the *Sermon on Glass Bottles*, i. 295; his letter to *The Spectator* No.457, i. 195 n.; 'Thoughts on Various Subjects' cancelled from the 1737 *Letters*, iv. 53 n.; *Three Hours after Marriage*, i. 339, 379, 388; — PROJECTED WORKS: he is asked by Steele for a libretto for Clayton, i. 131; is urged to write a tragedy, i. 136, 138; *The Works of the Unlearned*, i. 195, 339; plans anti-Rochefoucauld maxims, ii. 333; thought by Dr. Cheyne to meditate translating the Psalms into spiritual hymns, iv. 335; — P. objects to an incorrect libel by him against Pride and Covetousness as given out by Lord Chesterfield, iv. 212; denies authorship of prose characters of the Duke and Duchess of Buckingham, iv. 460.

For WORKS EDITED BY POPE *see* John Sheffield (Duke of Buckingham); Thomas Parnell; William Shakespeare, *and* William Wycherley.

III. POPE'S LETTERS

The unreliability of the posts: miscarriage of letters, i. 36, 58, iv. 176; the clerks in the office open and read letters, iv. 187, 363; letters are lost in the post, i. 117, ii. 369, 371, iii.

POPE, LETTERS (*cont.*)

482; or retarded, i. 131, ii. 409; — difficult to find safe messengers, iv. 364; hence P. is slow in writing, i. 275, 281, 292, 346, ii. 249, 448; he also (after 1726) fears publication of his letters, iii. 13–14, 459; private correspondence unfit for publication, iv. 278, 286.

THE PUBLICATION OF POPE'S LETTERS: ostensibly to prevent publication P. in 1726 and thereafter asks for the return of his letters (iii. 459) from the following friends: Caryll, i. 156, 160–1, ii. 418–19, 423, 449, iii. 14, 31; Hugh Bethel, ii. 501; (Mrs.) Edward Blount, ii. 423; Lord Digby, iii. 79; Fortescue, iii. 478; Joseph Spence, iii. 498; Swift, iii. 505 n.; and Broome, iii. 510.

EARLY PUBLICATION: a letter is printed in *Spectator* No. 532, i. 149; another in *Guardian* No. 132, i. 147; — P.'s letters to H. Cromwell are published by Curll, ii. 398, iii. 458–9; P.'s pain at Curll's vol., ii. 419, 423; Mrs. Thomas's story as to the publication, ii. 437–8; — P. publishes his correspondence with Wycherley in W.'s *Posthumous Works*, ii (1729), iii. 1, 459; in preparation he deposits Wycherley letters and MSS. in the Harleian Library, iii. 1, 38 n.; asks permission to make the deposits, iii. 54, 55; gets permission to use the Library as he likes, iii. 56; — other deposits are 'fairly written' for deposit there, iii. 59; many of the Harleian transcripts are proof-read by Lord Oxford, ii. 198 n.; inconsistency in one of these transcripts, ii. 304 n.; P. in transcripts does not expunge uncomplimentary remarks about the first Lord Oxford, iii. 63 n.; — sends some transcripts of Atterbury letters to Lord Oxford, iii. 187; asks his Lordship to return to him the Wycherley deposits, iii. 469; 'two books' of deposits mentioned, iii. 459; both P. and Lord Oxford employed amanuenses for making transcripts, iii. 459; the printed texts (1735) were not made from these transcripts, iii. 453 n.; P. asks Lord Oxford to send

POPE, LETTERS (*cont.*)
the bound vol. of transcripts, iii.
453.

THE EDITIONS OF 1735: P. (1733)
plots through 'P. T.' to entrap Curll
into publishing for him, iii. 339; the
Narrative of the Method by which the
letters were published, iii. 458–67; iii.
273 n., 458 n.; P. T. lists the correspondents proposed for the ed., iii.
460; — Curll wishes to advertise that
P. had revised the Cromwell letters
for a 2nd ed., iii. 460; P. replies to
Curll in *The Daily Post-Boy*, iii. 460;
P.'s advertisement concerning 'P. T.'
and 'R. S.', iii. 461; P. T. explains
how the sheets printed in 1729 happen to appear in 1735 for the Wycherley letters, iii. 465; P. T. dangles
before Curll P.'s correspondence
with Atterbury and Bolingbroke, iii.
465; — P. thinks a Bill should be
passed to protect private letters from
publication, iii. 467; he says his
original letters with postmarks on
them are still (23 May 1735) in the
Harleian Library, iii. 467; tells Lord
Oxford he has new tricks to play on
Curll, iii. 468; his 'agent' in the publication, iii. 470; — Curll's announcement of vol. ii of P.'s *Literary
Correspondence* worries P., iii. 471–2;
plans to destroy Curll's 2nd vol., iii.
472; says he and not Curll will
print genuine letters to Atterbury, iii.
473 n.; announces his intention to
publish an authorized ed. of his
letters, iii. 473; — Curll now says P.
had his letters printed and sent to
Curll to publish, iii. 476; P. challenges Curll to produce any original
P. letters, iii. 476; all copies of the
printed *Letters* sent to Curll by P. T.
were imperfect, iii. 476; — Curll announces his vol. iii for 'next month',
iii. 477; that vol. (he says) will contain P.'s letters to the Duchess of
Buckingham, iii. 477; P. asks Lord
Bathurst to investigate what letters
of the Duchess Curll has, iii. 481; —
P.'s 'authorized' ed. is delayed, iii. 478
n.; Curll prints four letters by
Voiture as if P.'s, iii. 487; Gilliver is
said to have made admissions to

POPE, LETTERS (*cont.*)
Curll concerning the printing of P.'s
letters, iii. 494; P. betrays a knowledge of 'R. Smythe', iii. 494; in an
advertisement in the *Gazette* P. replies to Curll, iii. 494; — P. wants an
attorney to defend Gilliver against
Curll's suit in Chancery, iii. 508;
would rather have Curll print his
letters than get none, iii. 349; complains of Curll's publishing his letters,
iii. 455, v. 16; hopes an Act of Parliament may curb Curll's procedure in
printing private letters, iii. 458.

NEW LETTERS (1736) published by
Curll in vol. v of *Mr. Pope's Literary
Correspondence* (i.e. two letters or a
joint letter from P. and Bolingbroke
to Swift) used by P. to influence
Swift, ii. 183–4, 349 n., iv. 50; he
has Orrery tell Swift of these two
letters 'from Ireland', iv. 52, 59.

LETTERS (1737), called *Works in
Prose*: the relations of the 8vo ed.
(Roberts) to the 4to and folio ed.
(with imprint of Knapton, Gilliver,
and Brindley), i. 453 n., ii. 13 n.;
P. probably preferred the smaller
format for his authorized ed., iv. 10
n.; many letters omitted by him from
the 4to or folio ed., e.g. i. 3, 4, 5, 6,
etc.; — P. asks Lady Burlington to
insert two new sentences in her MS.
copy of the Preface to 1737a, iv. 1–2;
he is (he says) unwillingly forced to
fulfil his promise of an authorized
ed., iv. 11; — the subscription for it
starts slowly and P. hopes it may fail,
iv. 11, 13; it is chiefly promoted by
Ralph Allen, iv. 19, 23; H. and S.
Bethel, iv. 21; Fortescue, iv. 7; Lord
Orrery, iv. 60; no money yet taken
from subscribers, iv. 19–20; P.
thanks Allen for his interest in the ed.
but thinks he overvalues the letters,
iv. 9, 18–19; — cannot accept from
Allen a complete subsidy, iv. 19; for
Allen's sake will be more active in
regard to the subscription, iv. 19;
will take from Allen money for
actual subscriptions, iv. 23; Allen
subscribes 50 guineas, iv. 24; — P.
asks reports from the Bethels as to
their subscribers, iv. 21, 33, 35, 39;

POPE, LETTERS (*cont.*)

sends S. Bethel receipts for 20 small folio copies, iv. 65; explains the status of the subscription to Fortescue, iv. 7, 10; — plans to send his *Letters* to the press in three weeks, iv. 23; the problem of the size of the ed., iv. 20, 24; the first sheet is now printing, iv. 24; P. hopes to publish about Lady Day, iv. 39, 41, 43; Richardson engraves an ornament [P.'s head] for the title-page, iv. 58; P. delays publication in hope of a new copyright law, iv. 65, 69; — is ashamed that he publishes his letters only to serve himself, iv. 39; considered as a book P. thinks his *Letters* is 'nothing', iv. 39, 53; — will send Orrery his 60 copies in Apr. or May, iv. 60; Orrery sends money from his subscribers to Brindley, iv. 65, 69–70; P. sends Orrery 50 copies of the book, iv. 70–71; — advertises for subscribers in the *Gazette*, iv. 65 n.; he prepares to deliver copies to subscribers, iv. 66; a further delay occurs when Motte refuses permission to reprint the 'Tracts', iv. 53, 68; — P. sends extra-fine copies for Allen and General Wade, iv. 68, 74; tells Allen 50 additional copies are due to him, iv. 74; remarks in the letters derogatory to Ireland displease Delany and others in Ireland, iv. 77; — P. never admits any connexion with the publication of his early letters except in the case of the 4tos and folios of 1737, iv. 330 n.; the letters said to make him £200 in arrears to his printer, iv. 350; declares himself done forever with large expensive formats of his works, iv. 350; — will come to Bath when he has settled with the printer, iv. 358; fears Lord Hervey may publish P.'s letters to the Duchess of Buckingham, iv. 446; feels sure Hugh Bethel burns all letters received, iv. 446.

THE SWIFT–POPE CORRESPONDENCE, printed (1741) as *Works in Prose*, vol. ii; in the London eds. of 1741 passages are placed in quotation marks to indicate significant connexion with the history of publication, iii. 369, 492, 505, iv. 11, 72, 76, 116;

POPE, LETTERS (*cont.*)

— Swift says their letters contain nothing but 'innocent friendship', iii. 492, and hence are to be burned after Swift's death, iii. 492, 505, v. 16; P. wishes Orrery had the letters in his safe hands, iv. 8; — Swift now promises that P. may have the letters after Swift's death, iv. 11–12; Swift says he has 'every scrap' of letter that P. ever wrote to him, iv. 42, 52; P. has expressed to Swift his hope that the letters might be entrusted to Orrery, iv. 42, 52; P. wishes Swift would mark over passages and return the original letters, iv. 53; — P. tells Orrery that he has three times asked Swift to return his letters and got no answer to the request, iv. 59; P. fears unfriendly publication of letters, iv. 58–59; he fears some of those about Swift wish to seize his letters, iv. 59; — wishes to make the Pope–Swift letters a memorial to their friendship, iv. 58–60, v. 18; Orrery seconds P.'s plea for return of the letters, iv. 59, 60; P. avows his desire to publish the letters, iv. 59; continues uneasy about the Swift letters, iv. 61; is assured by Orrery that Swift will return the letters, iv. 62, 64; out of the correspondence P. will erect a memorial to their friendship, iv. 64 (i.e. his intention to publish is overt); offers to return to Swift transcripts or censured originals, iv. 65; — has not yet received the letters or word direct from Swift, iv. 69; fears unedited publication, he tells Swift, iv. 63; has thanked Swift for the promised return of the letters, iv. 71; Swift (accepting the intention to publish?) says there is nothing that need be omitted, iv. 72; — Swift not very careful in preserving letters, iv. 71 n., 72 n.; Swift can find no letters from P. for 1717–22, iv. 72; discrepancy in the number of letters returned by Swift, iv. 72 n.; Orrery stimulates suspicion that Swift's friends have secreted some of P.'s letters, iv. 73; Orrery receives P.'s letters from Swift, iv. 76; puts them into P.'s hands, iv. 81, 83; — P.'s summary account of his efforts to get

POPE, LETTERS (*cont.*)
the letters back, iv. 314; he says he burned at once the letters Orrery brought over in 1737, iv. 285-6, 310 (they had been copied in Ireland before the return, P. pretends); letters from P. asking the return of his letters have been suppressed by the 'conspirators' (actually P. is the conspirator), iv. 311.

The 'clandestine' vol. of printed Pope–Swift letters is sent to Swift, iv. 241 n.; P. tells Gerrard that he has nothing to write to Swift, iv. 241; anonymously the clandestine vol. is sent to Gerrard's lodgings in Bath, iv. 242; P. asks Allen if Gerrard got the packet sent to him before he left Bath, iv. 245; — Orrery tells how the clandestine vol. got to Ireland (by Gerrard), iv. 276; P. says he never saw Gerrard at Bath and was not there when Gerrard was, iv. 282; the history of the covering letter sent with the clandestine vol. (called the 'Bath' letter), iv. 242-3; — P. wishes to examine the handwriting in the letter, iv. 282-3; the letter apparently has disappeared, iv. 305; Mrs. Whiteway will send the 'Bath' letter with her second lot of P. letters, iv. 307; P. finds tokens of Irish origin in the letter, iv. 282, 318; it implies that P. and Bolingbroke are unlikely ever to publish the letters, iv. 243; the 'Bath' letter is transcribed in Pope's narrative giving his version of the manœuvres with regard to the Swift letters, iv. 317; Orrery sends him the letter, iv. 326; — P. now requests that the clandestine vol. with the sheets printed by Faulkner be sent to Twickenham, iv. 275; Orrery tells Swift he is sure P. had no hand in the clandestine vol., iv. 278; Mrs. Whiteway thinks P. promoted the vol., iv. 279; Orrery believes it was printed in England, iv. 280; the vol. is to be sent to P. by Faulkner, iv. 280; — P. is much perplexed, he says, by the affair, iv. 282; is sure it was *begun* in Ireland no matter where the vol. was printed, iv. 282, 286; wishes to see the vol., iv. 282, 283, 284, 318; com-

POPE, LETTERS (*cont.*)
ments on the long letter inserted by Swift, iv. 283, 310; if the book is to be published in London, Faulkner might, P. thinks, as well do it in Dublin, iv. 284; — the letters in the vol. cannot be (P. says) those sent to England in 1737: he burnt those, iv. 285-6; P. asks Orrery to revise the vol., iv. 286; asks Orrery's true opinion of the vol., iv. 286; Orrery says it's not worth printing, iv. 310; — the clandestine vol. is sent to P., iv. 287, 305; it is to be returned unrevised, iv. 305, 306; it is returned in five packets, iv. 311; P. is not convinced that London printers are involved, iv. 311; says he had a copy of the clandestine vol. taken before returning it, iv. 311; objects to the insinuation that the clandestine vol. came from him, iv. 319; returns the volume to Orrery, iv. 328; but keeps pp. 1–22, iv. 328, 331; — asks Orrery to get Faulkner to send the original copy of the clandestine vol. to P. when through reprinting it, iv. 332; P.'s need of this 'foul copy', iv. 332 n.

Swift in his letter of 8 Aug. 1738 assures P. that all their letters are sealed up and in a safe hand, iv. 115–16; Mrs. Whiteway attests this highly puzzling statement, iv. 116; P. assumes the safe hand is not that of Mrs. Whiteway, iv. 130, 316.

P.'s manœuvres to make the 1741 vol. seem to come from Ireland, iv. 130 n.; he suppressed letters that would betray his desire to recover and publish the correspondence, iv. 256 n.; suggests that Swift's vanity is what causes the publication, iv. 256; becomes hypocritically 'innocent', iv. 256; — sends by way of Nugent his reply to Faulkner's request for permission to print, iv. 257, 260; Orrery is asked to help rescue the clandestine vol., iv. 262-4, 314-20; P. in a 'Narrative' summarizes the negotiations with Swift, iv. 262-4, 314-20; in this 'Narrative' P. omits the fact that Orrery in 1737 brought back the Swift letters to P., iv. 263; — P. is 'vexed' at the proceedings, iv. 273-4;

POPE, LETTERS (*cont.*)

is now offered from Ireland a (second) lot of original letters, iv. 274; would like a line in the Dean's own hand, iv. 275; — at R. Allen's in 1739 P. evidently plans to work on *Scriblerus* and the Swift letters, iv. 195; P. wishes to finish 'one little work' before he goes to Bath, iv. 280; P. pretends that he urged Swift for years to *prevent* publication of their letters, iv. 256.

P.'s alleged suspicions of Mrs. Whiteway, iv. 130; she has said she has no Pope letters, iv. 133 n.; she and Deane Swift are suspected, iv. 214; P. wishes the return from Mrs. Whiteway of the second lot of his letters, iv. 231, 241, 248, 257; now suspects her offer of returning the letters is not in good faith, iv. 257; — she seems 'romantically impertinent', iv. 232; P.'s grounds for suspicion of Mrs. Whiteway, iv. 241 n.; her officious services to the Dean, iv. 241, 248, 283, 286; P. is astonished at the alleged theft of 10 vols. of Swift MSS., iv. 283; — suspects that his letters were copied before they were returned from Ireland, iv. 286; Orrery regards the letters as a 'vile attempt' against P., iv. 307; P. promises the same justice to Mrs. Whiteway and Deane Swift as they have shown to him (a threat ?), iv. 312, 330.

Faulkner, behaving justly, asks P.'s permission to reprint the clandestine vol., iv. 256; P. tells Nugent that Faulkner is printing, iv. 256; cannot give permission until he sees the vol. to be printed, iv. 264; pretends to blame Swift's condition for the publication, iv. 264; — is offered a chance to revise the letters if he wishes, iv. 274; Faulkner claims to have been at great charge for these letters, iv. 274; P. thanks him for ceasing to print, iv. 275; Mrs. Whiteway says she deferred printing the vol., iv. 277; P. is sure the vol. will be published, iv. 283; revision of copy already in print is impracticable, iv. 283, 311; with Swift's consent the letters may be published—if P. is not men-

POPE, LETTERS (*cont.*)

tioned as consenting, iv. 286, 305, 312; — P. asks Orrery to send him 'the sheets' without Faulkner's knowledge, iv. 287; plans a final answer to Faulkner, iv. 309, 311; encloses an advertisement to be used in the *Letters*, iv. 310; will not tolerate suggestions that he is privy to the publication, iv. 310; 'those about Swift' the objects of his alleged suspicion, iv. 310; — Faulkner must follow P.'s provisos or the law may intervene, iv. 312; P. stops Deane Swift from writing a Preface, iv. 283, 309, 311, 318; textual differences between the Dublin and London eds., i. 359 n., ii. 326 n.; the long letter inserted by Swift was formerly a pamphlet shown to P., iv. 310; the problem of the correspondence of Swift with Gay and the Duchess of Queensberry, iii. 96 n., iv. 311, 314; — P. has finished a detailed 'Narration' concerning the publication of the Swift letters, iv. 313; it charges no one with guilt, iv. 313; if a defence is needed P. may print the 'Narration' with some of Swift's and Orrery's letters, iv. 313; — P. never printed the 'Narration', iv. 313 n.; the 'Narration' here found, iv. 314–20; the two surviving texts are similar, iv. 314 n.; P. did not preserve Faulkner's letter of 29 July 1740 concerning the clandestine vol., iv. 317 n.; the letters at least show the strict friendship of P. and Swift, iv. 320; — Mrs. Whiteway thinks P.'s letters were sold by his servants, iv. 321; she misinterprets a remark about the Wycherley letters, iv. 321, 330; she speaks of a fine letter taken from the stitched vol. of Swift MSS., iv. 322; the second lot of P. letters sealed up and sent by her to Orrery, iv. 326, 328; — Orrery commends P.'s 'Narration', iv. 329; Orrery gives P. permission to print any of his letters, iv. 329; P. asks Orrery to thank Mrs. Whiteway for the return of the letters, iv. 330; thanks Orrery for permission to use his letters, iv. 332; reports to Warburton on the Swift letters, iv. 334.

POPE, LETTERS (*cont.*)
P. plans his own London ed. of the
letters, iv. 312; earlier desired to have
some of Swift's 'tracts' to fill out the
vol., iv. 240 n.; plans to add Scriblerus items, iv. 259; — offers C.
Bathurst a chance to treat for the ed.,
iv. 259; the publishers of the vol.
(called *Works in Prose*, vol. ii) are
named, iv. 259 n.; sheets printed in
1737 are used for the 'tracts' in the
4to ed., iv. 259 n., 285 n.; the 4to
Letters (1741) were imposed by the
printer before the folio, iii. 347 n.,
432; — the London eds. of the letters
(1741) add six letters not in the
clandestine vol., iii. 291 n.; P. expresses to Swift his attitude towards
their published letters, iv. 337; sends
copies of his ed. to Allen, iv. 340, to
Warburton, iv. 339, to Nugent, iv.
344.
P.'s suits in Chancery against
Curll for piracy of the letters, ii.
189 n., iv. 343 n., 349 n.; Corbett
stopped from a piracy, iv. 345; P.
reissues sheets of the clandestine vol.,
with some alterations, as *Works* (sm.
8vo), vol. vii in 1741, iv. 340 n.
POPE'S EDITING OF HIS LETTERS:
TYPICAL EXAMPLES: puzzling postmarks, i. 191, iii. 82 n., iv. 200; his
normal dating for the months of
Jan., Feb., and Mar. is 'Old Style', i.
41 n., 214 n., iv. 327 n.; his misdating
of letters, i. 254, 255, 341, 447; ii. 23,
137, 426, 521, iii. 26, 95, 441; assigns
impossible date for the affair at Pres-
ton Pans, i. 320, 343; — misdatings by
later editors, ii. 259, iii. 250; prob-
lematic dating of the letters concerning the Craggs monument, ii. 456,
242, 246, 265; difficult date on a letter
to Edward Blount, i. 424; a fabricated
letter is misdated, ii. 254-5, 318.
P.'s rhetorical revisions of his
letters: i. 1 n., 51, 67, 131; he transfers verses from one Cromwell letter
to another, i. 42; revisions in the
account of his Sunday at B— Park
(1717), i. 427; two varying texts of an
Atterbury letter, i. 501 n.; his revision of a letter to Swift, ii. 460; —
he believes some details should be

POPE, LETTERS (*cont.*)
omitted in printing, iv. 19; he conceals names frequently, i. 309, 352
(Lady Mary called 'A Lady Abroad');
omits names of lords and ladies, i. 450
n.; conceals Caryll's name in a letter
reproving Caryll, iii. 12 n.; a leaf
cancelled to omit Dodington's name,
iii. 81 n.; — a possible omission in
a Digby letter, ii. 376 n.; political
details softened or omitted, iii. 149,
321 (on booksellers); 'idle passages'
must be omitted, iv. 19; P. tells Allen
that every offensive word in the
letters will be omitted, iv. 23; he
disapproves of many things he has
written in letters, and will omit, iv.
39, 53; a probable omission, iv. 50;
omitted probably from his letters to
Swift all requests for the return of
letters, iv. 63 n.
P. transfers letters from one correspondent to another: from Caryll to
Atterbury, i. 497 n., 498 n.; to Addison, i. 154, 177, 179, 183, 185, 193;
a letter from Addison possibly
fabricated, i. 196; transfers from
Caryll to Edward Blount, i. 190, 337,
343; transferred to Congreve, i. 215;
a conflated letter taken from Caryll
and given to Arbuthnot or Digby, ii.
280, 318; part of a Caryll letter used
to Arbuthnot or Digby, ii. 341; a
Caryll letter remade and given to
Steele, i. 156 n., 158 n.; a Caryll
letter transferred to Sir W. Trumbull,
i. 174 n.; Caryll letters transferred to
Wycherley, i. 93; — a sentence from
a Cromwell letter appears also in a
letter to Steele, i. 42 n.; P. borrows
sentences in a letter from Lord Oxford for his own letter to Mrs. Newsham, ii. 278; shifts a postscript to a
wrong letter, iii. 117 n.
P. openly conflates two letters
from Wycherley, i. 50; conflates two
letters to Caryll, i. 117, 120; conflated letter to Blount, i. 246; to Congreve, i. 274; to the Blount sisters, i.
307; a fabricated letter to Jervas, i.
346 n.; P. conflates two letters to
Teresa Blount, i. 349 n.; to Teresa and
Martha, i. 428, ii. 511; — a revised
or conflated letter from Atterbury, ii.

POPE, LETTERS (*cont.*)
73 n.; a conflated letter to Atterbury, ii. 119; a letter to Digby possibly conflated, ii. 191; composite letters to Gay, ii. 460, 475, iii. 3; one to Swift, ii. 481, iii. 508–9; one to Richardson here remade into two letters, iii. 326; a composite letter made by Warburton from three by P., iv. 455 n.

P. echoes himself in letters, i. 140 (cf. i. 5, 94); sends almost identical letters to two recipients, i. 277 (hermaphrodite letter), 459, 505 (cf. 508: description of Stanton Harcourt); a phrase from a letter to the Misses Blount is used on Lady Mary also, i. 429 n., 470; passages in a Richardson letter are identical with a letter to Fenton 12 years earlier, iii. 270; P. evidently likes to write joint letters with others, i. 284, 331–3, 345, &c., iii. 81; at times he writes ineptly careless footnotes to his letters, i. 274 n.; an unauthorized note gets into the late eds. of his time, i. 280.

THE CHARACTER OF POPE'S LETTERS: as seen by his correspondents: Wycherley thinks P.'s letters should be published, i. 66, 69; Hill likes the letters to Cromwell, ii. 404–5; Swift thinks P. ambitious of epistolary fame, iii. 92, 101; Broome commends P.'s letters as agreeable trifling, iii. 512; Mather Byles finds the letters lead 'into the First thoughts and Domestick Character' of a great man, iv. 17; — P.'s own opinion commends their moral quality, iii. 54, iv. 19, 23; Swift could derive from the *Letters* (1737) 'the best system for the conduct of life ever written', iv. 77; P. shudders at having 'secret opinions' betrayed in print, iv. 53; strong emotions transcend words, iv. 16, 154, 262, 396, 405.

'Set pieces' in letters were probably written for publication: i. 48 (on 'Nothing'); with Parnell writes of sunshine and moonshine, i. 223–4; his joint letter, with Lady Mary, to Lady Rich, i. 345; his letter 'In the Style of a Lady', i. 381; the (lost) Cheddar letter to Swift, ii. 388 n.; — his cheering letter to Morley, ii. 362;

POPE, LETTERS (*cont.*)
Peterborow's (or P.'s!) ironic letter to Lady Mary, iii. 352; his journey to Oxford with Lintot made, so Lintot thought, a 'merry' letter, iii. 489; Curll accuses P. of 'pillaging' Voiture, iii. 495, 501.

P. regards his letters as 'shadows' or images of his mind, i. 355, 367; the 'representations of a free heart', i. 352–3, ii. 258; it tears his heart to write to Swift, iii. 511; writes to Lady Burlington in 'sincerity of heart', iii. 518; letters are 'expressions of the heart', iv. 16, 39, 62; he tries to say only what can be felt, iii. 511; praises Orrery's letters as 'emanations of the best mind and the kindest heart', iv. 517.

P. is no 'brother of Dyer and Dawkes' (i.e. of news writers), i. 307, 479; he writes love and esteem, not news items, iii. 490; only lovers value trivial details, iv. 30; knows no news to send to Italy for Bethel, iv. 415; writes 'long letters about nothing', i. 211; at the last P. thinks letter-writing fruitless, iv. 30, 267; — all that letters say is 'si valeas, valeo', iii. 425, iv. 40, 187, 190, 356, 448; friendly letters are 'meer howd'yes', not news letters, iv. 193–4; but he takes pleasure in re-reading all letters to and from his friends, i. 161, iii. 38, iv. 15; likes letters that hurt no one's character, ii. 419; finds the letters returned to him innocent, unimportant, and virtuous, iii. 38; — P. recognizes the use of 'the complimental part of a letter' but objects to excessive compliment, i. 1, 5, 165, 180, 471, ii. 120, 136–7, 141, iv. 251.

In style a letter should be familiar and informal, ii. 41; his habitual 'neglect of method and style', i. 180; apologizes for a 'tedious long letter' and for 'careless' writing, i. 38, 155, 161, 204, iv. 20, 411; his familiar style in writing to Craggs, i. 307; his letters to Lady Mary he thinks 'artless and natural', i. 405; proper epistolary style is just 'talking upon paper', i. 105, 238, 353, iii. 433; he writes 'without reserve', i. 155, 274; —

POPE, LETTERS (*cont.*)

letters show men in undress, ii. 405, iii. 512; P. favours epistolary simplicity, i. 185, 201–2; on 'wit' in letters, iv. 1, iii. 79, 519, iv. 120, 193, 370; the easy, negligent style not good enough for Curll, iii. 79; — P.'s quality of brevity, iii. 10, 71, iv. 40; the laconic style, iv. 27, 372, 454, 495; he writes 'in folio' only to Swift and Bolingbroke, iv. 27; writing to absent friends makes one melancholy, iii. 433; the 'dedicatory' style illustrated, i. 239; his informal clippings of words mended in the Dublin eds., iv. 77 n.; P. says he did not keep copies of his letters, iv. 53.

IV. POPE'S VILLA, GARDENS, AND GROTTO

The removal to Twickenham, ii. 8; P. improves the villa, ii. 21, 23, 37, 44; now a 'Little Whitehall', ii. 50, 53, iii. 406; the villa in a flood, ii. 59, 60; the villa is poetical but not sufficiently retired, iii. 188; — P. builds a new portico, iii. 322, 329, 341, 353; a new room is added (1733) to the villa, iii. 341; Burlington is asked to inspect the portico before stucco-ing begins, iii. 356; stucco applied to the house, iii. 406; P. lends the house to Mrs. A. Greville (Aug. 1735), iii. 480 n.; — his designs need Burlington's approval, iii. 515; he is (1736) making improvements on the house, iv. 10; a motto for his gate, iv. 34; 'thrice dispossest' of his house by Courtiers from Hampton Court, iv. 134; is pleased with his place, iii. 441.

Pope's GARDENS enlarged by 2 acres, ii. 18; at work planting, ii. 23, 24, 37; his mount has been constructed, ii. 86; his gardens admired, ii. 109, 257; he is to get lime trees from Riskins, ii. 263; his gardens now finished, ii. 286, 296; — Digby mentions the shell temple, the greenhouse, and the grotto, ii. 305; the 'features' of the garden enumerated, ii. 328; a new 'Bridgmannick' theatre is added to the garden, ii. 372; also a new triumphal arch leading into the garden, iii. 358; P. is building a hot-

POPE, VILLA, GARDENS, GROTTO (*cont.*)

house for ananas, iii. 453; asks for grafts for pear trees and grapevines, iii. 451–2; erects an obelisk to his mother, iii. 453; his shell temple falls down, iii. 512; it is rebuilt, iv. 22; — P. grows his own melons and pineapples, iv. 6; sends pineapples to friends, e.g. Martha Blount, iv. 188; Allen, iv. 253; Sarah, Duchess of Marlborough, iv. 358; P.'s high opinion of gardening, iv. 6, 31, 40; — receives urns for the garden from the Prince of Wales, iv. 170 n.; will pay Biggs: Allen is not to do so, iv. 195.

The GROTTO: P.'s pride in it, ii. 125, 142; he describes it to Edward Blount, ii. 296, 297; Swift's comments on Ford's account of the grotto, ii. 325; — P. in 1740 begins the development of the grotto, iv. 214, 227, 254; it is now a museum for virtuosi, iv. 261–2; unwholesome weather keeps P. out of the grotto, iv. 230; the place is unhealthy in cold weather, iv. 267; Oliver suggests it might make a noble tomb for P., iv. 282; grottos should be summer work, iv. 444; the grotto is comparable, says P. ironically, to the Queen's Hermitage, iv. 244; — Allen many times sends stone, &c., for the grotto, iv. 230, 235, 239, 257; P. asks for more stone, iv. 245, 247, 252, 253, 274, 279, 343; P. thanks Allen for 6 tons of stone and two urns, iv. 353; Allen sends more stone, iv. 401, 412, 433, 443, 449; P. wishes Allen, Oliver, and Borlase could see the grotto, iv. 244; he thanks Borlase and Dr. Oliver for stones and ores, iv. 228, 229, 235, 244, 281–2, 351; P. wishes they could see the grotto, iv. 239, 246; in gratitude is placing inscriptions to their honour in the grotto, iv. 245, 254, 278; — wishes more marbles from Plymouth, iv. 247; asks Fortescue to send a hogshead of scallop shells, iv. 356; doubtful aid from Omer, iv. 245; Omer's gold-cliff rock is not received, iv. 254, 274; Thomas Edwards invited to see the grotto, iv. 342; P. thanks

POPE, VILLA, GARDENS, GROTTO (*cont.*)
C. Bathurst and Edwards for minerals, iv. 349, 352; the minerals eventually come from Richard Cambridge, iv. 352; — Vandiest found the grotto too cold and damp for painting, iv. 343; P. has a motto from Horace for his grotto, iv. 245; work on the grotto is half finished, iv. 245, 247; P. hopes the Allens will come to see the grotto, iv. 247, 252; P. is still 'quietly grottofying', iv. 354; is paving the porch to the grotto, and building pedestals for two urns, iv. 360; now has three waterfalls in the grotto, iv. 267; — his autograph ground plan of the grotto, iv. 278 n.; P. said to plan a printed description of the grotto, iv. 281; P. says the grotto is finished, iv. 340; then plans two rooms in the grotto, iv. 352; it will be completed in Oct., iv. 362; the motto, *Libertati et Amicitiae*, carved over the door, iv. 365; — Sir Hans Sloane offers a specimen, iv. 391; P. is grateful, iv. 397; the grotto is said to be 'natural': it owes nothing to chisel or polish, iv. 397; — P. invites Sarah, Duchess of Marlborough to sup with him in the grotto, iv. 359; urges Sir Hans Sloane to see the grotto, iv. 391; defers a visit from Thomas Edwards because of his maid's illness, iv. 361; — successors, not progeny, will enjoy the villa, iv. 34, 40, 247; will not purchase the place, iv. 508.

V. POPE'S RAMBLES AND VISITS

In 1707 he visits Walsh at Abberley, i. 29; in 1715 returns from a ramble, i. 316; his ramble to Oxford, &c., in 1717, i. 424; — in 1719 he records the fact that annually he visits five country houses in five counties, ii. 3; in 1725 he and Gay ramble together, ii. 305–6; his rambles of 1733 listed, iii. 339; his usual ramble in 1734, iii. 408; he summarizes his ramble of 1737, iv. 85; briefly describes the rambles of 1739, iv. 179, 191 n.; in 1743 he goes to Amesbury and Salisbury with G. Arbuthnot, iv. 472; — *major places visited*:

POPE, RAMBLES AND VISITS (*cont.*)
Basingstoke, iv. 37; — Bath, *in 1714*, i. 255, 259, 262; *in 1715*, i. 314, 317; *in 1716*, i. 370; *in 1728*, ii. 509, 514; *in 1734*, iii. 433; *in 1737*, iv. 84, 86; *in 1739*, iv. 198 n., 206, 214; *in 1740*, iv. 267 n., 335; *in 1741*, iv. 362, 378–9; *in 1742*, iv. 404, 421, 427; *in 1743*, iv. 443, 466, 470; — Bevis Mount (Southampton), iii. 218, 375, 401, 416, 427–8, 431, 483, iv. 18, 33, 36, 252, 350; — Binfield (after 1716), i. 194, 428, iv. 234, 410; Blenheim, i. 431–2; Bristol, iv. 200–6, 219, 472; Cambridge, ii. 441; — Cirencester, i. 459, 489, 517, ii. 81, 87, 518, iii. 410, iv. 26, 39, 349, 466; Devonshire, i. 309–15 (not finally visited); Down Hall, ii. 354–5; Gosfield, ii. 457; Hagley, iv. 185; Hallgrove, i. 404, 428; Hampton Court, i. 427; Holm Lacy (not finally visited ?), ii. 314, 329; Kent (G. West ?), iv. 451; Ladyholt, i. 115, 148, 267, iii. 384; Letcombe, i. 205, 234; Leighs, ii. 282, 297, 457; — Mapledurham, i. 203, 253, 409, 433, iii. 427–8; — Oxford, i. 246, 315, 371 n., 426 n., 429, ii. 80, iii. 491, iv. 81, 346, 347, 472; Rousham, ii. 513; iii. 410, 493, iv. 81; Sherborne, ii. 93, 236, 237–9; Southampton: *see* Bevis Mount; Stanton Harcourt, i. 484, 505–11; — Stowe, ii. 282, 513, iii. 217, 222, 375, 409, 481, iv. 183, 347, 404; Tottenham, iii. 417; Tunbridge, ii. 48; Wales, iv. 467; Whiteknights, i. 135; Wimpole (no visit recorded: plans were made), ii. 213, 257, 327; Yorkshire, i. 350, 370.

VI. POPE'S CHARACTER: HIS FAVOURITE TOPICS

PERSONAL TRAITS: enjoys being 'a country putt', ii. 31; jokes about his transformation into a man of the world, i. 352; 'elegant company' at Chiswick, i. 351; his dislike of cards, ii. 9, iii. 191, iv. 178; sleeps in company, i. 204, 342, iii. 134, iv. 259; Fenton (1725) finds P. 'brisk as a wren', ii. 351; — P.'s early love of dogs, i. 28, 73–75; as happy in a small fortune as Sarah, Duchess of Marlborough is in a great one, iv.

Pope, Character (*cont.*)
395; expects to die of hospitality, iii. 486; writes 'when drunk' to the Duchess of Hamilton, i. 436; — trusts surgeons more than doctors, iv. 390; on ill health in general, i. 147–8; ill health is not endearing, i. 158; Swift finds P. as host 'too sickly and complaisant', ii. 442; — a lame thigh keeps P. from parties for Swift (1726), ii. 373; P. a gourmet, i. 484; ill when he eats or drinks too much, ii. 384; his friends criticize his habits of excessive eating, iii. 409, 414; is called a 'gluttonous pretender to philosophy', by Dr. Cheyne, iv. 46; is called 'the greatest glutton I know' by Kent, iv. 150; is reported drunk at dinner at the Murrays, iv. 150; comes to W. Kent 'in liquor', iv. 163; — advised by Swift to seek diversions, iii. 191; when ill P. likes his friends about him, iii. 249; P. philosophizes about sickness, iii. 250; reproached for lack of care for his health, iii. 299; the effect of ill health on memory, iv. 473; on old age, iv. 484; P. is said by Orrery to suffer with cheerfulness and fortitude, iv. 518 n.

P.'s 'unpoetick modesty', i. 33, 113–14; he objects to compliments, i. 33, 193, ii. 356; jokes about the deaths of those of his pigmyan make, i. 89, 438; — is thought to treat Broome and Fenton like a Caesar or 'King of Parnassus' who does not share honours, ii. 345, 385, 390; accused of pride by A. Hill, iii. 168; women he thinks subject to flattery, i. 9; — his sexual jocosity, i. 42, 47; his crude letter about the hermaphrodite, i. 277; he lives the life of a rake, i. 289, 291; he scants decorums at times, i. 384; his passion for Lady Mary Wortley Montagu, i. 389–90; a friend recommends Oxford prostitutes to Pope, i. 428, 430; his light regard for feminine character, i. 516; — he jokes about matrimony, i. 313, 345–6; has no intention of marrying, ii. 134, iii. 1; calls himself 'abhominably epicoene', ii. 189; regards masquerades as the epitome of folly, i. 407; on feminine melancholy, ii.

Pope, Character (*cont.*)
202; on masculine tenderness, ii. 270; lacks ability to charm the ladies, ii. 290; most ladies 'run after music and play at cards', he thinks, iv. 178.

Pope's good deeds (a selection: for his kind offices to his closer friends *see* in this Index under their names): his knack of getting improbable services from his friends, iii. 26 n.; offers his villa for smallpox inoculations, ii. 255; on Christmas charities, ii. 280; his lack of avarice, ii. 391 n.; gives the *Odyssey* free to an impoverished subscriber unable to continue payments, ii. 391; makes a yearly allowance to an aged beggar woman, iv. 92; drafts a letter for a servant, i. 436; intercedes for Mrs. Howard's maid at Marble Hill, ii. 447; tries to get Phil Hanaus a place as footman, iv. 289; — his charity to Barclay, ii. 104; his aid for Mrs. Cope, ii. 434; for Janette Mowat, iv. 458; aids the Duchess of Buckingham in her suit against Ward, ii. 286–7; aids Lady Howard, iii. 103; — helps Allen select pictures for Prior Park, iv. 13, 20, 23; advises Caryll on a staircase, iii. 402–6; advises Fortescue on improvements in his Richmond house, iii. 477, 486; tries to get Boden a ship, i. 443; gets Bowack a place, iv. 82; tries to aid Cleland's son at Oxford, iii. 144; supervises the erection of the Craggs monument, ii. 456, 484; — helps N. Hooke with the Duchess of Marlborough, iv. 327, 366; tries to aid Hooke's son Thomas, iv. 353 n., 390; tries to help Sir John Hope-Bruce, ii. 427; tries to help Samuel Johnson to a school, iv. 194; gets Lady Orrery guinea fowl from the Allens, iv. 422, 424; — can get Scots cattle for Lord Bathurst's son, iii. 504; tries to get his nephew Henry employment as a lawyer, iii. 52 n., 150, 154; aids in getting a scholarship in surgery for Wise, iii. 141; — revises poems or plays by Wycherley, i. 3–96, *passim*; for Harte, iii. 408; for Mallet, iii. 65 n., 82, 158, and for Hill, iii. 201, iv. 111, &c.; aids Buckley's ed. of

POPE, CHARACTER (*cont.*)
Thuanus, ii. 471, 529, iii. 454; aids Dennis in old age, iii. 357-8, 394; recommends Dodsley's *Toy-Shop*, iii. 346; tries to get Harte elected poetry professor, iv. 90; works on the Savile Papers, iii. 341.

Pope's OBSERVATIONS ON POETRY as art and as career: on the USE of poetry, i. 191; no other aim but doing good, iii. 340; poets may be the most moral of mankind, iii. 347, 361; the vanity of mirth, i. 330; — on the 'pleasing parts of poetry', i. 110, 243; limitations of poetry, i. 236; in a crisis poetry seems trifling, i. 324; one should write to please one's self or friends, ii. 190; the arts 'are mere groping in the dark', i. 330; poetry a jingling of bells, i. 330, ii. 176, 209; poets are fiddlers to the tone-deaf, ii. 195; poetry should be enjoyed, not anatomized, ii. 228; — on the NATURE of poetry: design is 'the soul of poetry', i. 110; how the Muses stimulate, i. 135; on fancy or conceit, i. 34; on lying in wait for the imagination, i. 185, 201; on surprise or admiration in poetry, i. 97, 110; on consopition of the senses, ii. 315; — on effective small details, i. 161, 187; in praise of simplicity, i. 19; on classical plainness and naturalness, ii. 289; on fiction and honesty, ii. 210, 302; on the fictitious and wonderful in poetry, ii. 228; — the problem of Truth in poetry, iii. 290-91, 445; one is 'not less a poet for being a man of sense', ii. 229; the necessity of good thought in poetry, ii. 378; the problem of example vs. precept, iii. 419, iv. 13; Nature is preferred to artifice, iii. 384; — on poetic style, ii. 369-70; on the use of description, ii. 202, 203; the picturesque, i. 167; on poetic immortality, i. 49.

OBSERVATIONS ON WIT: wit defined, i. 2; discussed, i. 5, 11, 16, 19, 20, 34, 38, 69; wit and pretty thoughts, i. 110, iii. 79, iv. 120; the best wit not self-conscious, i. 113; excesses of wit, i. 155; on ridicule, v. 3; wit and the heart, i. 213, 280, ii. 139; on men of wit, i. 408; wit and

POPE, CHARACTER (*cont.*)
virtue compared, ii. 137; P. says, jocosely, that wit is the best thing he has, i. 426.

OBSERVATIONS ON THE POETICAL CHARACTER, i. 10, ii. 294; the poet not always inspired, iii. 281; on genius, i. 466, ii. 138; good nature superior to poetry, ii. 274, iii. 222; a poet closes the door to riches, i. 60, 73; how far a poet may borrow from others, i. 19-20; the vanity of poets, i. 114; — a poet in P.'s day writes while stones are thrown at him, i. 416; P. finds writing in his day ineffectual, i. 473; bad writers have more power than good ones, ii. 227-8, iii. 143; on writers and posterity, ii. 227, iii. 135.

OBSERVATIONS ON TYPES OF COMPOSITION: on pastoral comedy, i. 19, ii. 80; on the unities, i. 71; avows himself no judge of dramatic poetry, i. 66; the importance in tragedy of raising the passions, iii. 201; the declamatory style of tragic actors, ii. 370; on epistolary verse, iii. 348-9; P.'s dislike of elegies, iii. 128-9; on epitaphs, iii. 222, iv. 13, 137; P.'s distaste for inscriptions on tombs, iv. 137; dislikes prologues and epilogues, iv. 127; his rule against writing prologues and epilogues, iv. 131-2; unlike Swift, P. despises riddles, ii. 420; his opinions of miscellanies, i. 60, ii. 295, 426; his poor opinion of his letters, iii. 455 (insincere ?).

OBSERVATIONS ON SATIRE: it makes one merry but uneasy, i. 211; his satirical disposition makes enemies, i. 284; satire on 'things' is not personal, iii. 255; the good-natured dislike satire, iii. 255; the real objects of satire evade its effect by fixing it on others, iii. 256; the dangers of pseudonymous satire, iii. 266; good rulers have tolerated satire, iii. 420; satire based purely on the score of party is disapproved, iii. 276; — P.'s ideas of his own spirit and method in satire, iii. 366; on personal vs. general satire, iii. 423; satire now is useless since shame does not exist, iv. 437; he is grateful for the liberty to tell freely his opinions on the highest

POPE, CHARACTER (*cont.*)
subjects and greatest men, iv. 364; defends his satire, iii. 417, 419, iv. 126, 364, 370.

OBSERVATIONS ON VERSIFICATION: those sent to Walsh, i. 22–25; as sent to Cromwell, i. 106–8; on expletives, i. 23, 107; against Alexandrines, i. 23–24, 74, 107; on monosyllabic lines, i. 24, 107; on placing the caesura, i. 23, 107; monotony in repeated rhymes, i. 24, 107; against triple rhymes, i. 24; on hiatus, i. 24, 57, 106; — the sound should echo the sense, i. 22, 107; on poetic diction, i. 101; on Pindaric numbers, i. 110; on rhyme vs. blank verse, i. 500; P. comments on the rhythmus, iii. 139–40; classical examples here important, iii. 140.

OBSERVATIONS ON TASTE: on poetry and painting, i. 19; P. painted a Madonna for Mrs. Caryll, i. 115; is advised by Caryll to study painting, i. 174; paintings as examples have a moral effect, iv. 13; Reformers erred in taking paintings out of churches, iv. 13; comments on 'taste' in gardening, poetry, and religion, ii. 14–15; P. reproves Lord Bathurst's projects in building, ii. 14; private gardeners thought better than professionals, ii. 309, 314; P. is advised by Swift to divert himself by designs for gardens, iii. 191; bad taste employs more hands than good taste, iii. 255; true taste is not confined to the Court, iii. 333.

POPE'S OWN PROBLEMS: Early thinks himself weary of poetry, i. 210, 236; is an heroic poet, not a writer on occasions, i. 465; is urged to a discipleship of Virgil, ii. 219; writes when he thinks of nothing else to do, iii. 270; is incapable, he says, of resentment, ii. 25, iii. 372; — is weary of translating, i. 292, 297, 318, 324; as a poet thinks he has lost all romantic ideas, i. 406; a translator is not a poet, i. 347; Bolingbroke's wish that P. do original writing, ii. 218, 226, 321; P. thinks himself unable to 'fix' the English language, ii. 209, 226, 227; — P.'s early fear of critics, i. 2, 51;

POPE, CHARACTER (*cont.*)
on the public as critic of literary merit, ii. 271–2, 273; is half inclined to write no more because of malignant critics, iii. 266; — likes exotics (Provençal poets), ii. 202; writes (like others) of nothing, ii. 190; wakes to make others sleep, i. 462; his precocity, i. 7; is praised for excellence in diversity by Brooke, iv. 199; — plans, being dispirited, to spend more time in study (i.e. writing), iii. 157; Bolingbroke thinks him greater in reflective poetry than was Horace, iii. 72; his comments on descriptions of winter, i. 166–8; on the character of the Emperor Augustus, i. 116; dislikes the sea-terms in Dryden's Virgil, i. 101; commends Milton's shorter poems, i. 10.

EXPRESSED ATTITUDES TOWARDS ATTACKS: P. thanks Caryll for reporting attacks, i. 119; they imply vogue, i. 132; thinks enemies to his writings are fools, i. 151; takes no pleasure in seeing enemies expose themselves, i. 164, 286; Swift's list of P.'s negligible enemies, i. 358; P. has not replied to attacks, ii. 185–6; thinks himself hated by all bad poets, ii. 334; — attacks on P. reprinted in the *Compleat Collection* (June 1728), ii. 486 n.; Fenton urges Broome to attack P., ii. 488; P. has *not* been beaten, ii. 502; stands like 'Athanasius contra mundum', ii. 507; wishes Walpole's opinion of the author of an attack, iii. 11–12; — the authors of *Pope Alexander's Supremacy*, iii. 33–34; he is much attacked in the newspapers, ii. 507, 508; named in *The Leyden Gazette* as hostile to Button's, i. 210; attacked in *Pasquin*, ii. 160 n.; in *The Daily Gazetteer*, iv. 91, 154, 220; believes that all geniuses are calumniated, iv. 154; — attacked by ministerial writers but has no quarrel with Walpole, iv. 178. See also under Cibber, Thomas Cooke, Curll, Dennis, Gildon, Lord Hervey, Lady Mary Wortley Montagu, A. Philips, *et al.*

OBSERVATIONS ON COMMENTATORS (pedants): P.'s ambivalence with

POPE, CHARACTER (*cont.*)

regard to pedantry, i. 1; on verbal critics (like Bentley), iii. 241, 244; Scriblerus, as editor of *The Dunciad*, is the forerunner of Bentley and Theobald, iii. 244; P.'s low opinion of commentators, i. 493, ii. 140; — the commentator is a crutch to prolong the author's life a bit, iv. 362; on good commentators, iv. 399, 428; the malignity of academic dullness is seen in the matter of Warburton's Oxford degree, iv. 440; P. believes in passing all scribblers in silence (1725), ii. 185, 349; he thinks Virgil erred in writing of Maevius, ii. 349.

OBSERVATIONS ON HOSTILE CRITICS: critics are birds of prey, i. 2, 161; on the pleasure of being abused by bad writers, ii. 523; receives but does not feel injuries, he says, iii. 276; Swift calls P. a hermit who attacks 'honest' villains, iii. 368; P. replies without rancour to Hill's strictures, iv. 102; Hill's attack on the *Bathos*, iv. 99–101; P. replies that Hill knows him as a poet but not as a man, iv. 102; his critics are malignant about 'Timon', iii. 266; — at the start of his career, he says, he got undeserved envy and opposition; later, undeserved flattery, iv. 208; on sincerity in criticism, i. 100; 'fools (in one sense) are the salt of the earth', ii. 315; a dull blockhead galls more than a cunning rogue, ii. 328; thunderbolts preferable to pisspots: great rogues to little, ii. 350; — writers as enemies, i. 236, 239; the ease in making enemies, i. 277, ii. 205; if left alone enemies die of themselves, ii. 350; P.'s spleen and ill nature as seen by Broome, ii. 489; seen by others, ii. 349–50, iii. 166, 359; — Hill thinks pique and contempt P.'s only defect in character, iv. 103–4; P.'s defence to Hill, iii. 171 (he asks Hill to specify one man of merit whom P. has not praised), iv. 102, 104, 106; — P. hates no human creature, iv. 203, 364; hates the incapacity and insincerity of dunces, ii. 481; is disillusioned by the meanness and dirtiness of many, iv. 499; questions whether to continue writing for

POPE, CHARACTER (*cont.*)

a public that does not understand and misapplies, iii. 279; the dullness of the age is shown by the reception of his *Epistle to Burlington* and Hill's *Athelwold*, iii. 260; 'E. P.' thinks P. incapable of correction, iii. 360.

FAME stimulates ENVY and CALUMNY: P. the victim of gossip in Binfield, i. 168, 170–1; called a knave in a pamphlet, i. 289, 290; on envy and calumny, i. 154, 183; calumny best overcome by perseverance in right conduct, i. 177, 198; he is defended by the Blount sisters, i. 183; scandal about himself and his old nurse has been printed, iii. 84; — merit, like the sun, puts an end to stinks, ii. 349, 352; on the rancour of true divines, iv. 334–5; praise is like ambergris — too much is offensive, ii. 349; on fame's short continuance, i. 52; — Falstaff quoted on fame, i. 60; envy results from fame, i. 179; Milton quoted on fame, i. 213; contentment preferable to fame, ii. 226–7, iii. 250; P. is tired of the 'vanity of fame', iv. 53.

OBSERVATIONS ON POLITICS: on political events: the siege of Barcelona, i. 245, 246, 248; P. commends Burlington's compassion for the Jacobite rebels, i. 334; P.'s opinion of the 'horrid' parliament, ii. 269; on the bitterness of party spirit (1727), ii. 426–7; the new era of George II, ii. 437; P. disapproves of Irish politics, iii. 80; — after the Excise turmoil P. rejoices to find all his friends are of the same sentiment in politics and religion, iii. 384, 503; is distressed over the quarrels (1737) between the King and the Prince of Wales, iv. 86; —P. is not much pleased by the turn of affairs in 1742, iv. 396; P. despises the great world (he says), i. 227, 238, 247, 344; contrasts the chaos of politics with the beautiful order of nature, i. 331; the princely virtues have replaced the cardinal virtues, i. 472, 473, ii. 281; the Atterbury trial makes him despair as to the state of the nation, ii. 167; his contempt for the no-wisdom of Parliament, ii. 331;

POPE, CHARACTER (*cont.*)
'in England virtue dwells not with power', iii. 101; the 'courtesy of England', iii. 118; excessive party spirit disrelishes private enjoyments, iii. 383; — disillusionment with the Patriot opposition, iv. 169, 248–51; he meditates retiring to France, iv. 250; nowadays love of one's country is a joke, iv. 269, 351; he awaits England's funeral, iv. 365; his 'sphere' is resignation, not action, iv. 398; he is concerned but doubtful over Public Virtue, iv. 404; — on 'driving out boars', iv. 412; calls London 'the land of Perdition' and Parliament is 'the devil's divan', iv. 423–4; in 1742 public affairs make him long for quiet, iv. 431; calls the King's poet and historiographer 'the two greatest liars in literature', iv. 440; depressed by public affairs, iv. 437, 441.

OBSERVATIONS ON 'PARTY SPIRIT': P. not a politician, i. 210; increasingly tied to the Tories, i. 170, 205; his middle politics, i. 179; he is by report assigned to either Whig or Tory group, i. 194, 209, 220; is criticized by conservatives for working on *The Guardian* for Steele, i. 197–8; is also reputed to be anti-Whig, i. 229; — later calls himself the only scribbler without government patronage, ii. 160; urges Swift to write with dignity about politics, ii. 413; is against the principles in vogue as to patronage, ii. 453–4; is one who 'owed not a sixpence to any party', iv. 169; regrets that politics hinders Bolingbroke from writing for the universe, iii. 445; — P.'s alleged political influence, ii. 158, iv. 214; he hates the party spirit of his day, i. 220, 241, 245, 416; regrets the narrow party 'healths' now in fashion, i. 324; he is a benevolist — for all men, not for a faction, i. 241, 247, 263; does not meddle in politics, i. 323; admires 'public' spirit, i. 357; is congratulated by Swift as of no party, ii. 199, v. 16; the corrupting power of faction, ii. 227–8; — is really an anti-Bermudanist, ii. 331; on the ideal millennial state, ii. 332; anti-party opinions, ii.

POPE, CHARACTER (*cont.*)
332; on 'patriotism', ii. 333; indifferent to both the 'ins' and the 'outs', ii. 395; his ideas on party approved but not followed by Swift, ii. 419; he stays aloof from politics, ii. 427; — Swift thinks all parties and interests indifferent in P.'s eye, ii. 497; as a neutral he has never thought he deserved the money of any party, iii. 81; his neutrality, iii. 81, 276, 401; on the 'young Patriots', iv. 6; the party of honest men the only good party, iv. 143–4; — his friends warm in politics, he is a bystander, iv. 281; speaks scornfully of the Great Leader of Patriots (Pulteney ?), iv. 382; not a party man, only wants honest men in office, iv. 387.

OBSERVATIONS ON THE COURT AND COURTIERS: the emptiness of the Court in 1717, i. 427; P. protests his loyalty to the King, ii. 160, 165, 206, iii. 81; on kings, queens, and liberty, ii. 453; P. has nothing to do with Courts or Courtiers, ii. 469; thought by Broome to have written passages in *The Beggar's Opera* against Courts and ministers, ii. 489; — his relations (1729–32) with Walpole, iii. 81, 85; the embarrassing nature of his 'character' in the 'Libel on Dr. Delany', iii. 90 n.; in 1735 P. prints a sarcastic letter about Sir Robert Walpole, iii. 125; P. is thought not to love the Royal Family, iii. 132 n.; he is joked by Lord Bathurst on being a Courtier, iii. 133; 'Mobs can spoil a gude king', as was said of James I, iv. 144; P. is out of fashion, no courtier, iii. 367; kings are only bestowers of titles (e.g. Walpole and Pulteney), iv. 387; the Court a bad reason for coming to Town, iii. 426.

The great lack of honest men: P. reproaches Lord Bathurst for lack of 'Patriotism', iii. 137; urges Hugh, Earl of Marchmont to act in his country's service, iv. 227–8; praises Bolingbroke's public spirit, iv. 260–2; — England is profligate and poor, iv. 396; worthy men daily fewer in England, iv. 342, 414; P. wishes nothing so much as the welfare and

POPE, CHARACTER (*cont.*)

friendship of honest men, iv. 415; the corruption of high society, ii. 176; the Great are Little Creatures, ii. 181, iv. 135; a mercenary period (1720), ii. 50, 57; all is 'an ocean of avarice and corruption', ii. 182; the casting weight in all matters is money, iv. 367; the scandal of the Charitable Corporation, iii. 280; — reflections on South Sea, ii. 53–54, 60, 107; on the state of law courts, iii. 501–2, iv. 7, 26–27; a profligate nation seldom wins a war, iv. 207; the English called 'the most dirty, rascally race on earth', iv. 249; on the manners of the past ['good old'] times, iv. 269, 363.

POPE'S OBSERVATIONS ON RE-LIGION: attacked for his Faith, i. 209, 220–1; pressure in 1716 on Catholics to abjure, i. 335–6; P. jokingly states to Swift conditions for changing his religion, i. 198–201; as a Protestant he might be made City Poet, i. 309; — answers Atterbury's suggestion that he change his religion, i. 453–4; his early reading in religious polemics, i. 453; Louis Racine's comment on P.'s religion, iv. 423; P. submits his doctrines to the decision of the Church, iv. 416; on his death-bed P. repents of anything said or written by him against the Catholic Faith, iv. 526 n.; — P. on good and bad priests, i. 106; on Catholic tolerance, i. 241; his Catholicism not superstitious, i. 246–7; he wishes to include remarks on 'papists' in his Atterbury testimony, ii. 171–2; explains 'call me papist or protestant', iii. 354; his religion is that of Erasmus, iii. 81; his liberal Catholicism, i. 113, 126–9, 151, 162, 454; — his observance of Holy Week, i. 81; his Lenten observances, i. 115, 214; he frequently speaks of a priest as 'Mr.', i. 122 n.; asks Lord Oxford to defer a visit because of a Christian duty to be performed by his mother and himself on that day, iii. 11; his wish to go to Rome not likely to be realized, iv. 113; he lists friends whom he hopes to meet in heaven (all Protestants), iii. 81; — remarks on superstition, i. 498; on his religion, as fools

POPE, CHARACTER (*cont.*)

see it, iii. 354; against bigotry and persecution, iv. 7; he doubts if he and Richardson are orthodox, iv. 81; is questioned by H. Brooke as to his religion, iv. 199; his creed as given to Brooke, iv. 207; on the joys of separate spirits, i. 190; — P.'s joking idea of heaven, i. 269; on heaven's judgements as punishments, i. 497–8; P. believes in Particular Providence as well as General, iii. 144, 155; in the case of futurity we are curious impertinents, i. 190–1, 330; believes in an after-life, ii. 337, 376; on the millennium, ii. 186, 315; — P. prefers the Christian virtue of charity to doctrines of philosophy, ii. 531; the religious aspects of the death of the lovers killed by lightning, i. 497–8; P. affects to like the Turks: other religions seem declining, i. 342; is attacked for his religion, i. 342; is a good Christian, i. 327, v. 15; a religious liberal, i. 331; writes a sacrilegious letter to the Blount sisters, i. 310–11.

The CHARACTER OF POPE'S MIND: his body and mind, he thinks, are ill matched, i. 369, iv. 15; his heart not like a great warehouse, i. 383; his heart is 'a very uncorrupt witness', ii. 25; his defects are in his head: none in his heart, iv. 426; he regards himself as something of a philosopher, i. 227, 327; the *aequum animum* cultivated ('the fair weather of the soul'), i. 275, ii. 306; — he is a 'citizen of the world', i. 344; his interest in astronomy and Whiston, i. 185, 288, 290; the 'right English climate' of his mind, i. 202, 292, ii. 429; his volatile spirits, ii. 465, 472; 'like a porpoise in a storm', iv. 88; — his character viewed in opposites by some, i. 269; melancholy is, P. thinks, 'the real colour of my mind', ii. 337, iii. 5; the effect of long attendance on his aged mother, iii. 65, 80; on filial affection, ii. 265–6, 436, 480, iii. 17; he is less a patriarch than Caryll, ii. 392–3; thinks his lack of ambition and vanity an ingredient in happiness, iv. 187; he begins to dislike things (Swift gladly

POPE, CHARACTER (*cont.*)
finds), iii. 505; — his zeal for truth
supports him in face of attack, iv. 377;
on lies and excuses, ii. 319; on honesty
and peace of mind, ii. 318; P.'s un-
reliable statements about the passing
of time, iii. 366 n.; his perversions of
statement illustrated, iv. 283; — P.
says his life in thought and imagination is superior to his actual life, iii.
156; wants to be a better man, i. 297;
his moral character disparaged at
Button's, i. 305; his love of un-
designing men, ii. 46; his disdain of
vice, iii. 419; he wishes to be valued as
a man rather than as a poet, ii. 137;
wishes to be known as an inoffensive
person, ii. 138; his morals attacked, ii.
318; — his confidence in the superiority of his moral life, ii. 339; annoyed by critics only when they
attack his morals, i. 274, iii. 166, 168,
172, 372, iv. 102; he will go on his
quiet moral course taking no notice of
attacks, iii. 327; notes the very little
that his enemies can say against his
character, iii. 357; — denies any
debt on his part to posterity or to the
present age, ii. 227; Lyttelton urges the
effectiveness of P.'s 'moral song', iv.
369; P. values the opinion of the
worthy, and perhaps of the great, iii.
420.

P.'s character as seen by his contemporaries: he is highly praised for his
moral poetry by Atterbury, iii. 76; he
seems to Broome dishonest and insincere, ii. 489, 499–500; his personal
qualities are highly praised by R.
Digby, ii. 47, 191–2; Mallet's high
opinion of P.'s character, iv. 523–4;
Orrery's application to P. of *mens
curva*, &c., iv. 521; — Spence praises
P.'s humanity, iv. 526; Swift reproaches P. for pride, ii. 393; P.
despises the world more than Gay or
Swift, ii. 473, 480; Swift thinks P.
better natured than himself, ii. 497;
Swift congratulates P. on his liberty,
ii. 505; — Swift thinks P. talks like
a retired philosopher, iii. 151; Swift
commends P.'s fortitude, patience,
and filial devotion, iii. 190; Swift's
character of P. in the 'Libel on Dr.

POPE, CHARACTER (*cont.*)
Delany' is at times approved by P., iii.
348 n.; — P. begs Swift not to laugh
at his philosophizing, iii. 433; Swift
thinks P. excels 'all mortals on the
subject of morality', iv. 72; Swift
says P. stands above all other poets, iv.
73.
POPE'S GENERAL OBSERVATIONS
ON MORALITY: on the Good Man, ii.
139, 178, 320 (*paulo minus ab angelis*);
the good opinions of such highly
valued, iii. 270; the death of a good
man, iv. 113; the good mind, iii. 182;
P. is glad good men have not been
ashamed of him, iv. 364; on gratitude
(higher than love), ii. 337, 347–8; —
narrow souls scorned, i. 177; 'experience is a downright whore',
i. 318; the idea of a window in one's
bosom, ii. 23; his ninth beatitude
about not expecting, ii. 323, 453;
'Falsehood is folly', Homer says, ii.
353; resignation is the most melancholy of all virtues, iii. 470, 501; in-
discretion and credulity our worst
faults, iii. 497; — philosophy as fruit
succeeds poetry as flowers, iv. 5; P.
honours merit in all professions and
in all parties, iv. 36; inferior men like
inferior pictures sometimes 'glare at
first sight', iv. 43; 'unhappy is he
who must ramble in search of happiness', iv. 134; habit and opinion,
iv. 147; — Man an incongruous animal, i. 185–6, 202; only charity leads
honest men to notice lawyers or
courtiers, iv. 181; impossible to know
the motives of men, iv. 479; the vanity
of human sciences, i. 236; on pleasing
melancholy, i. 172–3; on admirers and
reasoners, iii. 250; — good deeds not
based on self-interest, iii. 74; 'all we
have in this world is no more than
an annuity, as to our own enjoyment',
iii. 79; on philosophy and freedom of
the mind, ii. 531; reflections on death
and perpetuity, ii. 386; Good Works
now unfashionable, ii. 280; on satisfaction from the approbation of good
men, ii. 279; — mortality clouds all,
ii. 45; on animosities within a family,
i. 475; moods of depression, ii. 43; re-
veries, i. 323; on happiness, iv. 356;

POPE, CHARACTER (*cont.*)

'tenderness is the very emanation of good sense and virtue', i. 496; on vanity, iv. 525; his life divided between carelessness and care, iv. 526 (among his last recorded words).

OBSERVATIONS ON THE RETIRED LIFE: P.'s disrelish of town life, i. 319, 461, ii. 24, 315; on winter 'hiving in cities', ii. 319, 329, 364; on the vanity and emptiness of the world, ii. 109; one may live too much in the world, ii. 302; on 'the great', ii. 179, 185, 195; — 'virtue in retirement is either not allowed or not seen', iii. 450; when 'the great world sleeps' there is no news, iv. 29; the pomps of the world unknown to P., iv. 156; like Cato he is 'sick of this bad world', iv. 429, 431; his avoidance of courtiers, iv. 178; on the quiet life, i. 147, 472; ii. 31, 141, 185, 295; — he and Swift are qualified for life in the Welsh mountains, ii. 395; stays home and sees no one, iii. 80; to be at ease is the greatest happiness; to be idle the greatest unhappiness, iv. 36; quiet preferred to honour and title, iv. 126, 156; private life pleasant: the public outlook depressing, iv. 363; — P. is thankful for the freedom in which he has lived, iv. 364, 368; envies Edward Blount his peace and quiet, ii. 176; also envies the Orrerys, iv. 406, 413; — the evening of our days is generally the calmest, iv. 447; on greatness in disgrace, ii. 167–70; he urges Atterbury in exile to work for posterity, ii. 170, iii. 76; — recalls a peaceful walk in St. James's Park, i. 74; on 'the beauties of nature' as a preparation for heaven, i. 319; on moonlight contemplation, i. 330; autumn not the decay of the year but a beautiful time, ii. 330; he recalls his early strolls about Binfield Wood and Bagshot Heath, i. 393; — his thoughtful life in 1723, ii. 185; P. and cardplaying, ii. 9, iv. 186; he enjoys quiet with the Allens at Bath, iv. 208.

OBSERVATIONS ON FRIENDSHIP: on self-love, i. 8, ii. 437; friendship based on similarity of disposition, i. 8; it avoids ceremony, i. 84, ii. 57;

POPE, CHARACTER (*cont.*)

implies equality of obligation, i. 128–9, 330; is an emanation of felicity, i. 213; conduces to the honour of eminent persons, i. 465; 'the conversation of a friend brightens the eyes', ii. 162; — ironical remarks on friendship, i. 235; P.'s yearning for friends, i. 119, iii. 138; on the defence of friends absent, i. 230; absence increases friendship, ii. 349; P.'s dependence on friends, iv. 5–6; — sympathy as basis for friendships, ii. 333; on friendship and humanity, ii. 337; on friends and compliments, ii. 41; friendships easily destroyed, i. 98, 177, 233; on the loss of friends by death or exile, ii. 72–73, 179–80, 227, iii. 470, 474, iv. 49–50; — P.'s great esteem for Bolingbroke, ii. 175; and for all friends, ii. 175; a friend is the height of well being, ii. 180; friendship and letter-writing, ii. 184; on friendship with superiors, ii. 185; his notions of friendship criticized by Swift, ii. 199; P. flatters Lord Oxford, ii. 260, 347; on friendship and hospitality, ii. 298; P. thinks Martha Blount's prayer might be, deliver me from my friends — esp. relatives, ii. 361; — felicity in friendship, ii. 481; on the choice of friends, ii. 501; on fame and friendship, iii. 172; P. is lectured by Swift on the value of 'middling' friends over those in high society, iii. 191; P. thinks friends should come to his defence, iii. 260; — friendship founded on good principles, iii. 419; the pleasures of reconciliation, iii. 497; P. desires most 'the good opinion of reasonable men', iv. 23; his greatest honour in posterity, he feels, will be the regard shown him by Swift and Bolingbroke, iv. 28; friends are props: no one stands alone, iv. 63; without friends along, France and Italy would not be worth visiting, iv. 177; — his first principles: general benevolence and fixed friendships, iv. 208; Bethel shows the value of friendship, iv. 269; P. thinks he understands the duties of friendship in private life, iv. 339; pleasures from friends who are far away, iv.

POPE, CHARACTER (*cont.*)
364; his friendship with Ralph Allen, iv. 404, 427; friendship is the next blessing after liberty, iv. 412; nothing is meritorious but virtue and friendship, iv. 526; P.'s general good will to all men of good will, i. 323, 324, 326, ii. 333.

VII. POPE'S READING: AUTHORS MENTIONED OR QUOTED

[*Pope did much reading and revising for friends. Not all these services are here indexed but see Pope I (Biographical Data). For his chief contemporaries (e.g. Addison, Steele, Gay, Swift, Wycherley, and others) the reader is advised to consult the entries under their names in addition to entries here given.*]

Addison, Joseph: *The Campaign*, i. 175; *Cato*, i. 173, 174–6, ii. 480, iv. 429; *Letter from Italy*, i. 245; see also *The Spectator*; *Amadis de Gaul*, i. 477, ii. 86; Aristophanes (Greek scholia on), i. 492; Ariosto, i. 365; Aulus Gellius, i. 115, 116, 225; Austin, Saint, i. 119.

Barber, Mary, iii. 184; Barrow, Isaac, ii. 81; Bayle, Pierre, ii. 302; *The Bellman of St. James's Verses*, iii. 401; Berkeley, George, iii. 276, iv. 514; Betterton, Thomas, i. 142; — the Holy BIBLE [*quoted, frequently, in Pope's modified phrasing*], *Job*, ii. 366; *Psalms*, i. 466, ii. 209, 465, 516, iv. 252, 412; *Proverbs*, ii. 104; *Ecclesiastes*, ii. 426; *The Wisdom of Solomon*, i. 148, ii. 366; *Daniel*, ii. 86; *Habakkuk*, ii. 86; *St. John*, iv. 208; *I Peter*, ii. 521; *St. Paul*, i. 411, ii. 472 (*I Cor.*), 531 (*I Thes.*), iv. 15 (*Rom.*); *Revelation*, iv. 247; the Canon of the Mass quoted, ii. 89; — Bossu, Réné le, i. 63, ii. 216; Bramston, James, iii. 173; Broome, William, ii. 152, 182, 275, 338, 340, 355, 389, 431, iv. 2; Buckley, Samuel, ii. 471; iii. 294; Bunyan, John, i. 57; Butler, Samuel, iv. 247.

Caesar, Caius Julius, iv. 127; Catullus, i. 130–1, 149, 237, ii. 20, 289, iv. 15, 50; Cervantes, i. 10, 114, 477, ii. 23, 141, iv. 212, 455; Chapman, George, i. 43; Chaucer, Geoff-

POPE, READING (*cont.*)
rey, i. 130, 169, ii. 202, 203, iv. 517; Dr. Cheyne, ii. 179; Chubb, Thomas, iii. 143; — Cibber, Colley: *The Non-Juror*, i. 473; *Letter to Pope*, iv. 406, 415, 425; *Apology*, iv. 437–8, 449; *Another Occasional Letter*, iv. 491; — Cicero, Marcus Tullius: eloquent but not poetical, ii. 370; *Ad Herennium*, iii. 140; *Agricultura*, iv. 6; *De Dolore Tolerando*, i. 158, ii. 480; *De Senectute*, i. 88; *Paradoxa*, iii. 227; *Pro Archia*, i. 72, 135, iii. 223; *Tusculan Disp.*, iii. 26; — Clarendon, 1st Earl of, iii. 135; Claudian, iii. 138; Cleveland, John, iii. 115; Congreve, William, i. 106, 167; Cooke, Thomas, ii. 509, 520; Cornbury, Lord, iii. 502; Cowley, Abraham, i. 147, 159, ii. 54, iii. 106; Cowper, Judith, ii. 195, 202, 209; Crashaw, Richard, i. 103, 109–11.

Dacier, André, i. 492; Dacier, Anne LeFevre, i. 270, 492–3, ii. 157, 248, 363; *The Daily Gazetteer*, iv. 124–5, &c.; *Daphnis and Chloe*, iv. 525; Delany, Patrick, iii. 211, 276; Demosthenes, ii. 370; Dennis, John, i. 113, 121, 132, 155, 184, 274, ii. 75, iii. 33; Dionysius of Halicarnassus, i. 264, iii. 140; Dodsley, Robert, iii. 346, 407; Donne, John, i. 16, 26, ii. 371; Dryden, John, i. 23, 44, 92, 99, 101, 108, 124, 130, 194, 198, 408, iii. 244; Duncombe, William, iii. 442; Durfey, Tom, i. 71, 81.

Erasmus, i. 118–19, iii. 81.

Fenton, Elijah, ii. 105, 145, 151, 162, 374; Fielding, Henry, iv. 394, 452; Fontenelle, i. 369.

Gay, John: Scriblerus lines, ii. 292; *The Fan*, i. 188; *The Shepherd's Week*, i. 217, 229; *A Letter to a Lady* [the Princess], i. 269; *The What D'ye Call It*, i. 282–3; *Poems*, ii. 53; *The Captives*, ii. 215; *The Beggar's Opera*, ii. 469; *Achilles*, iii. 337; the Life of Gay, iv. 37–38; — R. Graham, iii. 333–4, 367; Granville, George (Lord Lansdowne), ii. 109; *The Grub Street Journal*, iii. 110; Guevara, Don Antonio de, ii. 517.

Hai Ebn Yocktan, ii. 13; — Harte, Walter: *Poems*, ii. 429; *Essay on Satire*, iii. 173; *Essay on Reason*, iii.

POPE, READING (*cont.*)
408–9, 450, 455; — Heinsius, i. 26, 90; Hervey, John (Lord), iii. 364, 448, iv. 124; Hervey, (Lepell), Verses on her, not by Pope, ii. 343, 349; Hesiod, ii. 54, 58; — Hill, Aaron: *The Northern Star*, ii. 35, iv. 158; *The Plain Dealer*, iii. 164; *Advice to the Poets*, iii. 177, 182, 188; *The Progress of Wit*, iii. 165; *Athelwold*, iii. 200–1, 223, 258; Hill's complimentary verses, iii. 371; his *Caesar* (i.e. *Roman Revenge*), iv. 110, 118, 131; — Hobbes, Thomas, i. 43; — HOMER, *see under Homer in the main index*; — Hooke, N., his *Roman History*, iv. 31; his *Account of Sarah, Duchess of Marlborough*, iv. 389; — HORACE: *Carmina*, ii. 229, 388, 470, 524; iii. 6, 79, 115, 210, iv. 7, 371, 421; *Epistolae*, i. 72, 162, 371, ii. 107, 183, 412, iii. 153, 279, iv. 191, 196, 218, 245, 491; *Sermones*, ii. 128, iii. 58, iv. 251; *Ars Poetica*, i. 329, ii. 125; — Hughes, John: *Siege of Damascus*, ii. 29, 34; *Poems*, iii. 454; Hyginus, i. 90.
The Intelligencer, ii. 523.
Jeffery of Monmouth, i. 425; Johannes Secundus, i. 331; Johnson, Samuel, iv. 194; Juvenal, i. 100, 101, 189, 508, iii. 420, iv. 257, 450.
LaBruyère, ii. 142; LaFontaine, i. 87; LaRochefoucault, i. 34, 86, ii. 333; Lucan, i. 104, 371; Lucian, i. 353; ii. 23; Lucretius, i. 48, ii. 19, iii. 433.
Macrobius, i. 90, 225; Malherbe, i. 25, 57; — Mallet, David: *Eurydice*, iii. 1, 65–66; epitaph for Aikman, iii. 222; *Verbal Criticism*, iii. 66, 329–30, 357; *Mustapha*, iv. 166; — Marino, Giambattista, i. 110; Marot, Clement, i. 90; Martial, i. 42, 101, ii. 23, iii. 115; *Mass, The Canon of*, ii. 89; Miller, James, iii. 173; — Milton, John: *Lycidas*, i. 213; *Paradise Lost*, i. 167, ii. 89, 295; *Paradise Regained*, ii. 110; — Moore-Smythe, James, iii. 60, 106, 113–14; Montagu, Lady Mary Wortley, i. 370, iii. 357, 366; Montaigne, i. 73.
Newton, Sir Isaac, ii. 457–9; Nicole, Pierre, ii. 43; Nicholas de

POPE, READING (*cont.*)
Lyra, i. 403; Nugent, Robert, iv. 231, 260.
Orrery, John Boyle, 5th Earl of, iii. 372; Osborne, F., ii. 50; Ovid, i. 47, 92, 96, 99, 100, 171, ii. 42.
Palladio, ii. 50, iii. 187, iv. 151; — Parnell, Thomas: Tonson's *Miscellany* (1714), i. 195; 'Essay on Homer', i. 226; *Batrachomuomachia* and *Zoilus*, i. 253, 284, 292, 395, 410 n., 415; 'Pandora' and 'Eclogue on Health', i. 396; *Poems*, ii. 23 n., 24, &c. to 92; — Pascal, i. 129, iii. 173, iv. 416; *Persian Tales*, i. 393, ii. 56, 202; Persius, i. 99, ii. 231, 523, iii. 420; Petrarch, i. 110; Petronius, i. 413; — Philips, Ambrose: 'Winter Piece', i. 101; *Pastorals*, i. 100, 101, 103; *Epistle to Dorset*, i. 167–8; his trochaics, ii. 326; — Pindar, ii. 465; Pitt, C., ii. 382–3; Plato, i. 104, 173, 344 n., 487, ii. 360–1, 516; Pliny the Younger, i. 508, ii. 226, iv. 331; Plutarch, i. 42, 43, 75, 147, 498; Prior, Matthew, i. 178, 459, ii. 30, 193, 203, 336–7, 355, 466; Propertius, ii. 481; Pythagoras, i. 321, 323–4.
Quarles, Francis, ii. 109.
Reuchlin, Johann, i. 122 n.; Richardson, Jonathan, ii. 140; Richardson, Samuel, iv. 335 n.; *Riders Almanack*, ii. 531–2; Rowe, Nicholas, i. 104, 211, ii. 214; Rymer, Thomas, i. 440–1.
Sackville, Thomas (Earl of Dorset), i. 408, 467, iv. 37 n.; St. John, Henry (Bolingbroke), iv. 108–9; Sallust, ii. 531; Savage, Richard, iii. 37 n., 504; *The Savile Papers*, iii. 322, 328, 341; Scaliger, J. J., i. 225; Scudery, Mlle, i. 375, 379, iv. 397; Seneca, Lucius Annaeus, i. 99, 147, 195, ii. 109, 140, 253, 302; Shakespeare, William, i. 60, 186, 202, 427, ii. 329, iv. 208, 475, *see also the main index under* Shakespeare; Sheffield, John (Duke of Buckingham), i. 343, 387, ii. 81, 93, 101, 159, iii. 105; *The Spectator*, i. 1, 139, 162, 195, 276 n.; Spence, Joseph, i. 467, ii. 357, 379, iii. 241 n., iv. 37; Sternhold, Thomas (and Hopkins), i. 368, 483, ii. 334; Strada, F., i. 60, 103; Suetonius, i. 90, ii. 80, iii. 420;

POPE, READING (*cont.*)

Swift, Jonathan: *Gulliver's Travels,* ii. 412, 423, 441; *The Intelligencer,* ii. 523; *A Libel on Dr. Delany,* iii. 85, 90 n., 95, 348; *The Life and Character of Dr. Swift,* iii. 367, 372, 384; *Verses on the Death of Dr. Swift,* iv. 130; recent doubtful works, iii. 304; *The Four Last Years,* ii. 387, 402, 493, 502, iv. 248; *see also* the main index under Swift.

Tasso, i. 19; *The Tatler,* i. 61, 70, 87, 93, 101, 188, ii. 369; Temple, Sir William, ii. 522, iii. 53, 62, 291; Theobald, Lewis, i. 32, 86, 147, 288, ii. 486, iii. 59, iv. 102; Theocritus, i. 101, 116; Thuanus, ii. 471; Tibullus, i. 173, 369, v. 3–4; Tickell, Thomas, i. 109, 157, 196, 264, ii. 88; Tourreil, Jacques de, i. 275; *The Turkish Spy,* ii. 355.

Valerius Maximus, i. 371 n.; Valterie, Abbé, i. 225, 492; Vanbrugh, Sir John, i. 106; *Verses Address'd to the Imitator of Horace* (*see* Lady Mary Wortley Montagu *and* Lord Hervey), iii. 354; Vida, Marco Girolamo, i. 23, 107–8, 317 n., ii. 383; Villiers, George (Duke of Buckingham), i. 26, 138, 161, ii. 23; — VIRGIL: *Georgics,* i. 167, 411; *Eclogues,* i. 146, 337, ii. 190, 293, iii. 118; *Aeneid,* i. 23, 28, 44, 107–8, 122, 317, 453, 464, ii. 24, 302, 364, 380, 465, 532, iii. 118, 142, 255, iv. 448, 521; *Culex,* i. 103, 376; —Voiture, Vincent, i. 44, 89, 90, 98, 130, ii. 41, iii. 495; Voltaire, ii. 228–9, 354.

Waller, Edmund, i. 23, 107, 147; — Warburton, William: *Vindication of the Essay on Man,* iv. 157, 163, 171; *Commentary on the Essay on Man,* iv. 400, 455; *The Divine Legation,* iv. 182, 219, 251, 341; — Wesley, Samuel (1662–1735), iii. 95; Wesley, Samuel (1691–1739), iii. 504; Wilmot, John, Earl of Rochester, iii. 502; Wollaston, William, ii. 179; Wycherley, William; *The Plain Dealer,* i. 57, 187; 'Lines on Mr. Pope', i. 41, 50, iii. 106; P.'s revisions of Wycherley's verses, i. 3, 13, 15, 30, 31, 33, 79, 82, 83, 147, iii. 55; P. advises Wycherley to use the form of *pensées,* i. 34.

VIII. PORTRAITS OF POPE AND HIS FRIENDS

Prints and pictures of P. in the Boston (Mass.) area in 1728, ii. 494–5; Kneller paints P., i. 466, ii. 118, 193; paints Lady Mary's portrait for P., ii. 21–22; — P.'s bust at Wimpole (by Rysbrack), iii. 115; Dahl's portrait of P. to be copied for Tonson sr., iii. 291; P. sits to Richardson, iii. 402; Richardson paints P. for Dr. Mead, iv. 91; Richardson paints P. with his garden and obelisk in the background, iv. 150; Richardson has engraved three portraits of P., iv. 150; P. gives Richardson directions about the 'blue' picture, iv. 150; the 'enamel' portrait by Richardson, iv. 147–8; Richardson engraves P.'s head for the title-page of *Works in Prose,* iv. 54, 58; P. postpones a sitting to Richardson, iv. 399; — will sit for a portrait for Nugent, as he did for Mrs. Nugent, iv. 212; has a noble present from Richardson (Bolingbroke's portrait?), iv. 487; Richardson makes a post-mortem drawing of P.'s mother, iii. 374; — P. offers H. Bethel a copy of Vanloo's portrait, iv. 500; P. has had one sitting to Kent for H. Bethel, iv. 509; H. Bethel prefers Kneller's portrait of P., iv. 512; — a painting of P.'s house and gardens by A. Rysbrack to be published by Curll, iii. 477; portraits of Bolingbroke, iii. 326, iv. 128, 148; P. has a copy made of Dr. Arbuthnot's portrait, iii. 480; has H. Bethel's portrait by an Italian artist, iv. 500, 509; — P. himself copies various Kneller portraits, i. 88 n., 187 n.; one is a portrait of Betterton, i. 88 n.; P.'s design for the family tomb at Twickenham, iii. 58.

POPE, EDITH (or Editha), the poet's mother (1642–1733): letters to, ii. 172; letters from, ii. 29; — carries a letter from her son to Wycherley in Town, i. 58; Wycherley in writing to Pope habitually sends his 'service' to Mrs. Pope, i. 30–85 (*passim*); — Arbuthnot prescribes medicines for her, i. 394–5, ii. 272; she suffers from rheumatism, i. 456, ii. 375; her

POPE, EDITH (*cont.*)
dangerous illnesses, ii. 161 (Feb. 1723), 257 (Sept. 1724), 261, 270 (Nov. 1724); ill of a jaundice, ii. 335–8 (Nov. 1725); very ill, ii. 434–5 (May 1727), ii. 468 (Jan. 1728), ii. 531, v. 6 (Nov. 1728 to Jan. 1729), iii. 2; her languishing state, iii. 9 (Jan. 1729); still in bed, iii. 15 (Feb. 1729); seriously ill, iii. 33 (May 1729); — her fall (Oct. 1730) into the fire, iii. 141, 142, 144, 153, 155; Pope thinks a 'particular Providence' saved her life, iii. 144; thought desperately ill, iii. 226 (Sept. 1731), 254, 259; her extreme weakness, iii. 288; her death (7 June 1733), iii. 374; Pope is confined at home by her illnesses, ii. 261, 270, 273, iii. 3, 11, 14, 19, 53, 145, 160, 254, 259, 279, 288, 331–2; she views *semen masculinum* through a microscope, i. 465; — at Stanton Harcourt (1718), i. 478, 490, 517; her reciprocated affection for Lord and Lady Harcourt, ii. 114, 115; her rent-charge, ii. 5 n.; she sends confused news to her son, ii. 29; because of the storm she will wait on the Blount ladies, not they on her, ii. 57; her favourite neighbours, ii. 117; dusty roads and shortness of breath keep her from visiting Hallgrove, ii. 181; — she and her son dine with the Vandeputs, ii. 232; she likes Mrs. Broome very much, ii. 296; she calls the Speaker (Spencer Compton) 'the Prater', ii. 303; she prays for Swift's conversion, ii. 394; his 'service' to her, v. 13; — her memory is decayed, iii. 53; her death would decrease Pope's income, iii. 74; the poet's erroneous idea of her age, iii. 117, 278; her state does not prevent P.'s having a guest, iii. 284; Richardson is asked to make a post-mortem drawing of her, iii. 374; her funeral, iii. 374 n.; Lady Mary Wortley Montagu's good opinion of, iii. 449.
Pope, Sir Thomas, i. 430 n.
Pope Alexander's Supremacy (1729), i. 229 n., iii. 33–34.
Portales, Charles (a French prophet), i. 35 n.
Porter, Mary, actress, iii. 232.

Portland, 2nd Duke of, *see* Bentinck, William.
Portland, Duchess of (Lady Margaret Harley), i. 479 n.
Portsmouth, visited by Pope (1737), iv. 84.
The Post-man, i. 71, 350 n.
Pouilly, Levesque de, ii. 221 n.
Poussin, Nicolas, iv. 20.
Poyntz, Stephen: he and his wife expected at Bevis Mount, iii. 426, 488; a friend of Mrs. Knight, iii. 491; Mrs. P. (Anna Maria Mordaunt, niece of Lord Peterborow) was Croxall's 'Fair Circassian', iii. 426 n.
Pratt, Benjamin, i. 223.
Pratt, Mrs. (John): account of, iv. 21 n.; attends Edmund, Duke of Buckingham, iv. 21; doubtless surprised at the will of the Duchess of Buckingham, iv. 446.
Pretender, The ('James III'), i. 26 n., 235; the invasion of 1715, i. 273, 308, 310, 311, 320; the treatment of rebels by Londoners, i. 322 n. 2.
Price, Uvedale (grandfather of Sir Uvedale), iv. 212.
PRICE, Mrs. UVEDALE (Ann Somerset): letter to (from Pope), iv. 266, (from Martha Blount), 265; — a sister of Mrs. Greville, iv. 188 n.; a friend of Lord Cornbury, iv. 212, 265, 266; her death, iv. 350.
Price, Lucy, Curll's 'Lucasia', ii. 440 n.
Price, Robert, a judge, iii. 150.
Prince (a postillion?), i. 481.
Princeton University Library Chronicle, iv. 137.
PRIOR, MATTHEW: letter to, ii. 30; letter from, i. 521; a lost letter, i. 165; his *Adriani Morientis*, i. 178; his *Conversation* read in MS. by Pope, ii. 30; his libel on Atterbury forgiven, ii. 85; — Pope wishes to include *Jinny* in the *Miscellanies*, ii. 466; Curll projected an ed. of P.'s letters, iii. 459; Curll announces the publication of P.'s State Papers, iii. 471; — P. is quoted by Pope, ii. 336–7, 355; by T. Edwards, iv. 352 n.; P. revised too much, Fenton thinks, ii. 398; his 'cook maid', i. 27; he invites Pope to a *convivium poeticum*, i. 521 n.; P.'s death, ii. 84; Lord Edward Harley

PRIOR, MATTHEW (*cont.*)
asks Pope to read P.'s 'remains', ii.
193; Pope does so, ii. 203; portrait
by Rigault, ii. 204; Pope dislikes
P.'s monument, ii. 525; P.'s lamp at
Wimpole, iii. 114.
Prior Park (or 'Widcombe'): under construction, iv. 74 n.; its lofty site, iv.
173; Pope's life there, iv. 230; called
(1741) a 'new abode', iv. 354. *See*
Allen, Ralph.
Propertius, ii. 481.
Proudfoot, Mr., an agent for Swift, ii.
414 n.
Prussia, Frederick William I, King of,
iii. 208, iv. 212.
Prynne, Sam: one of Allen's clerks, iv.
417; his marriage to 'Betty', iv. 247,
253; Prynne writes for Allen to Pope,
iv. 479.
Pulham (Norfolk), Broome's new parish,
ii. 519, iii. 496.
Pulteney, Mrs. William (Anna Maria
Gumley): at Bath, ii. 133; she approves of Swift, iii. 194; her beauty, i.
451.
Pulteney, Daniel, ii. 502.
Pulteney, Elizabeth ('Betty'), friend of
Martha Blount, iii. 232.
PULTENEY, WILLIAM (later Earl of
Bath): letters from, ii. 247, 254, 443;
— account of, ii. 247 n.; — his places
of residence, ii. 392 n.; at Twickenham, iii. 474, v. 14, 15, 17; at Petersham, iv. 4 n.; has no country seat,
iv. 179; hopes vainly for a son, ii. 443,
475; has a son, iii. 162; friendship
with Gay, i. 388; they go abroad
together, i. 411, 416, 438, 449–50; —
P. is out of favour, i. 450; wrongly
said to be caballing with Bolingbroke,
ii. 291; subscribes to Buononcini's
Cantate, ii. 99; relations with Pope, ii.
247, 254, 392; sollicited by Pope for
aid to Dennis, iii. 171; Pope seldom
sees him, iv. 179; is reported as leasing
Ladyholt, i. 518; — relations with
Caryll, iii. 70, 74; helps to welcome
Swift (1726), ii. 373; is pleased by a
letter from Swift, ii. 395, 400; wrote
part of the Cheddar letter to Swift,
ii. 403 n.; Swift hesitates to com-
mence a useless correspondence with
P., ii. 408, 412–13; as a Whig, P. is

PULTENEY, WILLIAM (*cont.*)
objectionable to Swift, ii. 419;
becomes one of Swift's stock-healths,
iii. 97; he has written to Swift, iii. 182,
and always drinks Swift's health, iii.
194; — P. mentions Robert and
Horatio Walpole with disfavour, ii.
444; is dismissed as Privy Councillor,
iii. 206; his duel with Lord Hervey,
iii. 206 n.; Swift comments on P.'s
'disgrace', iii. 220; his friendship with
Bolingbroke, iii. 251; Swift thinks P.
has saved England from slavery, iii.
380; reported to Swift as against the
Test Act, iv. 4; Swift loves P. for his
patriotism, iv. 12; — recovers from a
serious illness, iv. 11, 12, 16; Swift
sent a signed letter and fears P. failed
to get it, iv. 45; P. plotted against by
others in the Opposition, iv. 142; his
reply to a joke by Sarah, Duchess of
Marlborough, iv. 163; informs Pope
of illness of T. Watts, iv. 343; — is
created Earl of Bath, iv. 414; Pope is
sick of 'great ones' who have been his
intimate acquaintance (P.? Spencer
Compton?), iv. 431; Pope ironically
hears 'good things' of P., iv. 459.
Purcell, J., Dr., i. 278.
Purchas, Samuel, i. 427.
Puttick and Simpson (dealers), iv. 345 n.
Pyne, Mr., Postmaster at Bath, iv. 462,
468.
Pythagoras, i. 321 n., 323–4.

Quarles, Francis, ii. 109.
Quarterly Review, cited on Borlase and
his letters, iv. 222, 228, 245.
Queensberry, 3rd Duke of, *see* Douglas,
Charles.
Quevedo, Don F. Gomez (y Villegas),
iii. 247.
Quintilian, i. 24, 25, iii. 140.

Rabelais, François, i. 28.
Racan, Honorat de, i. 18.
Racine, Jean, ii. 222.
RACINE, LOUIS (author of *La Religion*,
1742): letter to, iv. 415; letter from,
iv. 422; he mistakes Pope's principles
in religion, iv. 416; history of Pope's
letter to R., iv. 416 n.; R.'s apology,
iv. 422–3.

Racketts of Hallgrove, Charles, Magdalen, *et al.*: approve Mr. Weston's treatment of his wife, i. 119 n., 143; Pope is to visit them, i. 418; leaves because the Westons are coming, i. 426; sends his service, i. 403, 445; Pope is charged with their affairs, ii. 429.

RACKETT, CHARLES, Pope's brother-in-law: letters to, i. 424, ii. 181; sells Pope's palfrey, i. 404; Pope will arrive on Monday, i. 424; R. has the gout, ii. 4; he calls at Twickenham, ii. 29; he and his wife invited to Twickenham, ii. 181; his will (d. 1728), iii. 6 n.

RACKETT, HENRY, son of Charles; nephew to Pope: letter to, iii. 339; his difficulty as a Non-Juror in practising law, iii. 52 n., 56, 150, 153; Pope tries to get him employment, iii. 154; Pope's request for a statement as to John Rackett's debts, iii. 339; Pope arranges through Henry to lend Mrs. Rackett £300, iii. 407; Henry sends to his brother Michael Pope's account of the Rackett family finances, iv. 160–1; Pope sends his love to 'Cousin Harry', iv. 365; Harry's address, iii. 340.

Rackett, John, son of Charles; nephew of Pope; a sailor: wants to be second or third mate in an East India merchantman, ii. 246; in trouble over debts, iii. 339–40; again at sea, iii. 421; knows the Codrington estates in Barbados, iv. 168–9.

RACKETT, MAGDALEN, Pope's half sister; wife of Charles; mother of Michael, Henry, John, and others: Pope's letters to her, ii. 9, iii. 6, 39, iv. 203, 365; her letters to her stepmother, ii. 4; — Pope visits her, i. 113; mentioned, i. 135 n.; visits at Chiswick, i. 519; her small dau. dies, ii. 4; invites Mrs. Pope to Hallgrove, ii. 4, 5; her will, ii. 29 n.; — her troubles with her trustee, Essington, iii. 5, 112, 196; her administration of her husband's will, iii. 6; Fortescue attempts to clarify her affairs, ii. 530; *The Athenaeum* (1857) cited on her history, ii. 530 n., iii. 173 n.; her annuity from Lady Carrington, iii. 30, 39; Pope gives her financial advice, iii.

RACKETT, MAGDALEN (*cont.*)
39; Fortescue asked to investigate delays in her affairs, iii. 91; her lawsuit calls Pope often to Town, iii. 173; — she lives (1731) with her son Henry in Town, iii. 223 n.; unable to lease Hallgrove without legal consent of her eldest son, Michael, iii. 224; she asks Pope's aid for her son John, arrested for debt, iii. 339; Pope lends her £300, iii. 407; Pope asks news of three of her sons, iii. 421; loses her lawsuit and thus the money Pope has lent her, iv. 21; — cannot afford to buy her son Michael a commission in the army, iv. 161; Pope reports to her the qualities of Bristol and Bath waters, iv. 203; — Mr. Brown will not purchase Hallgrove, iv. 203; Murray might buy, iv. 203; she is in Chancery, iv. 214–15, 245, 258; Pope tells her of his plans to go to Bath, iv. 365; she is annoyed by Pope's bequest to Martha Blount, iv. 160 n.

RACKETT, MICHAEL, eldest son of Charles and Magdalen; Pope's nephew: letter to, iv. 160; Pope promises to write to M. giving financial advice, iii. 39; M. is living abroad, iii. 224; is actually in debt to his mother, iii. 224; his debts impoverish the family estates, iv. 160–1; his creditors have taken out an outlawry against him, iv. 160 n.; his need of £150 may force Pope to return from Bath in Jan., iv. 215.

Radcliffe, James, 3rd Earl of Derwentwater: his former war-horse drew Pope from Stowe, ii. 513; his dau. marries the 8th Lord Petre (1732), iii. 284 n.

Radcliffe, John, M.D.: orders Martha Blount to go to Bath, i. 257; his death, i. 268 n.; his bequests, i. 269; they include funds for the Radcliffe Camera, i. 269; his will, i. 429.

Radnor, 3rd Earl of, *see* Robartes, Henry.

Raines, Mrs. (subscribes to Homer), i. 296.

Raleigh (or Ralegh or Rawleigh), Sir Walter, ii. 192, 236, iv. 351.

Ralph, James, iv. 255.

Ramsay, Andrew, 'Chevalier', i. 123 n., ii. 294 n., iii. 6 n., iv. 416.

Rand, B., cited on Berkeley, i. 175 n., ii. 104 n.

Ranelagh, Lady, subscribes to the *Iliad*, i. 300.

Rapin, Réné, i. 18.

Rawdon, Lady, ii. 483.

Rawleigh, Sir Walter, *see* Raleigh.

Rawlinson, Christopher, his MSS. in Bodley, i. 36 n., ii. 439 n.

Rawlinson, William, *see* Rollinson.

Raymond, Sir Robert, iv. 494.

Read's Weekly Journal, iii. 155 n.

Reade, A. L., iv. 183 n.

Reading (Berks.), i. 15, 134.

Recorder of London, i. 78.

Rees, Mr., iv. 344.

Reeves, Edward, ii. 313.

Reeves, Thomas, ii. 300, 313, iv. 355.

Reeves (or Ryves), William, iii. 277, 289, 296.

Register House, Edinburgh, ii. 425.

Rehearsal, The (play), i. 161, ii. 23.

Rehearsal, The (newspaper), i. 70.

Rémond, Mr., friend and enemy of Lady Mary, ii. 52.

Rentcomb (Gloucestershire), ii. 85.

Reuchlin, Johann, i. 122 n.

Review, The, i. 70.

RES (*The Review of English Studies*): ii. 166 n., 168, 390, iv. 342.

Reynolds, Sir Joshua, painted C. Smart holding a Pope letter, iv. 483 n.

Reynolds, Myra, i. 203.

Ricci (painter), iv. 20.

Rich, Charlotte, Countess of Warwick, *see* Addison, Charlotte.

Rich, Edward Henry, 7th Earl of Warwick (Addison's stepson), i. 361, 438, 450, 516, ii. 88.

Rich, Elizabeth, Lady, wife of Sir Robert Rich, Bt.: letter to, i. 345-6; her sister Anne a Maid of Honour, i. 407 n.; Lady R. is 'brought to bed', i. 370; Lady Mary's adieu to her, i. 387; she and Lady Mary correspond, i. 405, 514; Fenton wishes data on Waller from her [the same Lady Rich ?], ii. 244, 278.

Rich, John, theatrical manager: i. 71, ii. 473; clears near £4,000 from *The Beggar's Opera*, ii. 478, 482; on Pope's recommendation he accepts for Covent Garden Dodsley's *Toy Shop*, iii. 346 n.

Rich, Sir Robert, husband of Elizabeth (Griffith), i. 345 n., 442; he admires Lady Mary, i. 442, 470.

Richardson, Jonathan (father and son): letters to, ii. 61, 93, 100, 106, 140, 177, 272, 284, 297, iii. 160, 231, 240, 269, 326, 330, 331, 345, 350, 351, 352, 374, 402, 410, 457, 485, iv. 54, 58, 78, 79, 80, 81, 91, 118, 123, 127, 147, 151, 194, 374, 399, 400, 408, 409, 427, 484, 487, 489, 513; — letter to Pope from R. jr., iii. 330; letter to R. conflated with one to Fenton, ii. 45 n., 46 n.; a lost letter to R., ii. 195 n.; — Pope invites the R.'s to Twickenham, ii. 61, 62, iv. 78, 408; R. invites Pope to a Shakespeare party, ii. 106; sends Judith Cowper's verses on Pope to Pope, ii. 93; the amity of the R.'s, father and son, ii. 141; R. slightly indisposed, ii. 177; — the death of Mrs. R. sr. (1725), ii. 272 n., iv. 372 n.; Pope compliments R. sr. as friend, husband, and father, ii. 272; R. goes occasionally to Bushey, ii. 298; has taken a house in Holborn Row, Lincoln's Inn Fields, ii. 298; — sends Pope complimentary verses on the *Essay on Man*, iii. 326-7; is cautioned to keep the authorship of the *Essay* still secret, iii. 350; Pope at Cirencester (1734) hopes to see R. in a fortnight, iii. 410; Pope by letter introduces a young gentleman about to go on the Grand Tour (possibly young Newsham ?), iii. 457; returning from Southampton, Pope hopes to see R. in town, iii. 486; Pope jokes R. about their orthodoxy, iv. 81; — R. likely to be up at sunrise, iv. 119; he has Pope and Warburton in for breakfast at 10 a.m., iv. 380; Cheselden is to show R. Pope's letter, iv. 372; R. wishes to see Chiswick House and the pictures, iv. 409; Pope hopes to see R. on return from Bath (1742) in about 3 weeks, iv. 427; Pope hopes to spend winter evenings with R., iv. 484; whenever Pope comes to Town he will surely see R., iv. 487; is asked to come to Murray's to see Pope, who is ill there, iv. 489; — Pope sits to R. for various portraits, iii. 160, 402; R. does a sketch of Mrs. Pope, dead, iii.

RICHARDSON, JONATHAN (*cont.*)
374; engraves the plate for the title-page of Pope's (1737) *Letters*, iv. 54, 58; paints Pope for Dr. Mead, iv. 91; has pictures ready for Pope, iv. 147–8; one portrait of Pope with his garden and obelisk as background, iv. 150; is told to keep the 'blue' picture, iv. 151; Pope cancels a sitting, iv. 399; — he thanks R. for his drawing of Bolingbroke, iii. 326; copies a portrait of Bolingbroke for Pope, iv. 118–19; Bolingbroke may be well enough to sit to R. soon, iv. 119; R. has engraved Bolingbroke's portrait, iv. 123, 128; has three portraits of Bolingbroke, iv. 150; is again painting Bolingbroke for Pope, iv. 400; — Pope sends R. an ed. of Milton, iii. 231; the *Explanatory Notes on Paradise Lost*, iii. 231 n.; the book is to be published, iii. 327; R. asks Pope's opinion on an epithet, iii. 331; Pope and Chesterfield play a joke on R. with some 'new' lines supposedly by Milton, iv. 80 n.; — R. jr. is indisposed, ii. 61; his marginalia to *The Dunciad*, ii. 496 n.; he collates Pope's varying texts: hence Pope sends him a special copy with wide margins, iv. 78; Pope sends his papers (MSS.) to R. jr., iv. 374.

Richardson, Samuel, author of *Pamela*: his people do not forward properly Hill's mail, iv. 128; he is well disposed to Pope, but prints *The Daily Gazetteer* which is not, iv. 168; Pope's pleasure in reading *Pamela*, iv. 335 n.

Richardsoniana (1776), by Jonathan Richardson, jr., iv. 400 n.

Richmond, Duke of, *see* Lennox, Charles, 2nd Duke.

Richmond (Surrey), residence of the Prince of Wales (later King George II), ii. 14, 178; his gardens done by Bridgman, ii. 372; Miss Howe there, ii. 143, 174, and Mrs. Howard, ii. 178; the Mrs. Blounts have a house there (1725), ii. 305; the removal of the Court in June 1727, ii. 435 n.; its arrival in Aug. 1727, ii. 442; the place a 'soft retreat' in summer, iii. 123; recommended to Hill, iii. 201; Fortescue has a small house there

Richmond (Surrey) (*cont.*)
('The Vineyard' or 'Shepherd's Hut'), iv. 18.

Richmond (Yorkshire), i. 20, Walsh's borough (1706).

Riders Almanack, ii. 531–2.

Rigault (or Rigaud), Hyacinthe, his portrait of Prior, ii. 204.

Ripley, Thomas, architect at Houghton, iv. 124.

Riskins (Lord Bathurst's house): Atterbury urged to come there, ii. 120, 132; Pope's visits, ii. 207, 260, 299, 302 n., 304, 464–5, iii. 120–1; Pope to get lime trees from Riskins, ii. 263; in Apr. 1735 given to Lord Bathurst's son Benjamin, iii. 504 n.; in 1737 sold to Lord Hertford, iv. 179 n.

Robari, Dr., his medicine helped H. Bethel, iv. 473.

Robartes, Henry, 3rd Earl of Radnor, Pope's neighbour, iv. 230; Pope said to meet Warburton in Radnor's garden, iv. 236 n.; he subscribes to Buononcini's *Cantate*, ii. 99.

Robartes, John, 4th Earl of Radnor, iv. 230, 434.

Robert, Pope's discharged servant, ii. 257.

Roberts, Major, of Plas-Newydd: from him Martha Blount has purchased an annuity, iii. 33; no news of him, iii. 139; Bethel writes to R., iii. 197; Bethel has receipts, which for action in the case Fortescue needs, iii. 210, 227; — the Major's father dies and the estate is liable for the Major's debts, iii. 233; legal action planned, iii. 225, 271; the Major does not pay Martha, iii. 283, 355, 427, 441.

Roberts, James, bookseller, iii. 34.

Robinson, Mr., Fenton's London landlord, ii. 122, 148, 152, 232; he suddenly dies, ii. 234.

Robinson, Anastasia, professional singer, later Countess of Peterborow: her benefit, ii. 30, 31; she is said to haunt Buononcini, ii. 123; sings at Buckingham House, ii. 135 n.; her secret marriage to the Earl of Peterborow, ii. 123 n., 178 n., 474, iii. 425; is acknowledged as Countess, iii. 468 n., 487; — she and her sister dine with Peterborow and Dr. Arbuthnot, ii.

Robinson, Anastasia (*cont.*) 196; the Robinsons move to Fulham, ii. 196, 329 n.; she is a friend of Dr. Towne, ii. 424; her sister Margaret (*c.* 1728) marries George Arbuthnot, ii. 474; her Catholicism mentioned, iii. 218, 281; — Peterborow's last days, iii. 490; Pope visits her twice in 1736 at Bevis Mount, iv. 1, 21; he works on the gardens there, iv. 34, 41; she plans a visit to Bath, iv. 37; forwards Pope's order to the Duchess of Portland, iv. 83; Pope hopes to see her at Bath, iv. 350; she visits London, iv. 358.

ROBINSON, Mrs. D., mother of Anastasia: letter from, ii. 329; she asks for goods left with Pope, ii. 329.

Robinson, Jacob, bookseller: is concerned with Watson in a piracy of Pope's letters, iv. 87; he publishes Warburton's *Vindication*, iv. 171, 182, 196; his death, iv. 219 n.; Pope inquires at his shop for Warburton's arrival, iv. 233–4.

Robinson, Margaret, sister of Anastasia, married to George Arbuthnot (1728), ii. 474.

Roboton (or Robethon, &c.), M., Secretary to King George I, translates the *Essay on Criticism*, i. 193 n.

Rochefoucauld, *see* LaRochefoucauld.

Rochester, Earl of, *see* Wilmot, John.

Rochester, Countess of, *see* Hyde, Jane (Leveson-Gower), Countess of Rochester and of Clarendon (4th Earl of Clarendon), i. 417.

Rochester (Kent), Atterbury at Bromley, i. 378, 418.

Rock, Mr., Lord Harcourt's secretary, ii. 126.

'Roffen, Fra', *see* Atterbury, Francis: 'Fra Roffen' is his signature in many letters, e.g. i. 378, 452, to iii. 248.

Rogers, Mr. [?Samuel], i. 334 n.

Rolle, Samuel, his dau. marries Sir R. Walpole's son, ii. 183.

ROLLINSON, WILLIAM: letter from, i. 240; annoyed with Gay, i. 300; an unknown letter to, i. 433; his high opinion of Swift, ii. 410; death of his wife Sarah, iii. 132; his friendship with Pope and Bolingbroke, iv. 471 n.

Romulus Three-points, i. 49.

Rook, George, i. 359.

Roper, Edward, i. 155–6.

Roscoe, W., his ed. of Pope cited, i. 345, ii. 294, iv. 200.

Roscommon (Wentworth Dillon), 4th Earl of, i. 503.

Rose, Sir G. H., his *Marchmont Papers* cited, iv. 327, 364.

Ross, The Man of, *see* Kyrle, John.

Roubiliac, Louis François, sculptor: his work for Prior Park, iv. 354, 360; does heads for £20 each, iv. 360.

Rousham (Oxfordshire), home of James and Robert Dormer, iii. 216 n.; Pope visits there, ii. 510, 513, &c.; the *Odyssey* given by Pope to Mrs. Caesar is preserved there, ii. 293 n.

Rousseau, Jean Baptiste, i. 385.

ROWE, NICHOLAS: letters from, i. 184, 186; an ardent Whig, i. 27, 102; his Lucan defended by Pope, i. 102, 104, 105, 108; his *Jane Grey*, i. 138 n., 288, 290; witticisms about it, i. 288, 290; his *Jane Shore*, i. 211; Pope's Epilogue for it, i. 205; *Observations* on it by Sewell, i. 374 n.; R. asks to see a Prologue by Pope, i. 184; is laureate, i. 328; — his Shakespeare used as Pope's basic text, ii. 214 n.; asks Pope to dine, i. 186–7; visits Binfield, i. 190, 329; Swift appealed to Lord Oxford for R., ii. 67; Pope's character of, i. 330; his death, ii. 23 n.; Pope's epitaph for, ii. 23 n., 25, 51, iv. 176 n.

Roxburghe, 1st Duke of, *see* Ker, John.

Royal Academy of Music, ii. 474, 478.

Royal Society, ii. 412 n.

Royston Bargain, The, a ballad on the Caesar-Long wedding, iii. 56 n.

Rubens, Peter Paul, ii. 237.

Rudel, Jeffrey, i. 440.

Ruffhead, Owen: his life of Pope cited: on the Southcote abbey, iii. 6 n.; on the collaboration in the *Odyssey*, iii. 507; on Chesterfield's intentions for Warburton, iv. 356; on the quarrel of Warburton and Bolingbroke, iv. 498; — R. prints letters in part, usually: to Allen, iv. 68; to Hugh Bethel, iii. 209, 227, 287, 435, iv. 21, 225, 269, 339, 377, 396, 415, 445, 499; to Savage, iv. 392; from Voltaire, ii. 399; to Warburton, iv. 164, 429.

Ruhe, Edward, iv. 37 n., 38 n.
Rundle, Thomas, Bishop of Derry, iii. 436 n.; Swift's good opinion of him, iii. 492, v. 17; his failure to get the see of Gloucester, iii. 492 n., 508 n.; Pope's high opinion of him, iii. 508, iv. 3; Swift thinks Rundle 'a most excessive Whig but much liked', iv. 3; is to bring to Swift his special copies of Pope's *Letters* (1737), iv. 75; a man of taste, iv. 140.
Russel, Israel, leases a house to Lady Gerard, iv. 183 n., 186, 191.
Russell, Edward, Earl of Orford, iii. 199.
Russell, Wriothesley, 3rd Duke of Bedford, invites Pope to Woburn, ii. 309.
Ruston (Yorkshire), Mrs. Pope's rent-charge, i. 325, ii. 5 n.
Rutland, 3rd Duke of, *see* Manners, John.
Rutupiae (Richborough, Kent), iv. 450.
Rymer, Thomas: his *Short View*, i. 441 n.; his *Foedera*, iv. 51 n.
Rysbrack, Andreas, iii. 477.
Rysbrack, Michael: Pope sits to him, ii. 298; his bust of Pope, ii. 298, iii. 100.
Ryves, William, *see* Reeves, iii. 277, 289, 296.

S—, Mr. Baron, ii. 521.
S. E., sends to Curll Voiture letters ascribed to Pope, iii. 487, 501.
S., R., *see* (Rev.) R. Smith, iii. 461–7.
Sacchette, Marchese, iv. 163.
Sacheverell, Henry, D.D., hostile to Bishop Burnet, i. 287, 291.
Sackville, Charles, 2nd Duke of Dorset: author of a poem about the Abergavenny scandal, iii. 110 n.; the *Collection of Pieces . . . on the Dunciad* dedicated to him, i. 467 n., iii. 241 n.; he travels with Spence on the Continent, iii. 241 n.
Sackville, Charles, 6th Earl of Dorset, ii. 358; Pope's epitaph for him, iii. 241 n.
Sackville, Lionel Cranfield, 1st Duke of Dorset, an enemy of Pope's talks at his house on *Three Hours after Marriage*, i. 388; his letter to the Countess of Suffolk about Pope, iii. 241; — appointed Lord Lieut. of Ireland, iii. 108; his early preferments of

Sackville, Lionel Cranfield (*cont.*) others thought unwise, iii. 161–2; he must choose a new Bishop of Cork, v. 17; his arrival in Ireland awaited, iii. 191; wishes to confer with Pope on the epitaph for his father, iii. 241; his remarks about the *Essay on Man*, iii. 439.
Sackville, Thomas, 1st Earl of Dorset, author of *Gorboduc*: Pope's interest in the play, i. 408, 467, iv. 37 n.
Sacy, Louis de, translator of Pliny the Younger, ii. 218, 226.
Saffold, Mr., employed by Mrs. Howard at Marble Hill, iii. 34.
Saggioni, Mrs., a singer, ii. 136, iii. 434.
St. André, Nathaniel, surgeon: examines Pope's cut hand for glass splinters, ii. 403; may help Wise to a scholarship, iii. 140; at Bath with Peterborow, iii. 468; dined with Kent, Pope, *et al.*, iv. 154 n.
St. Aubyn, Sir John: sends his service to Allen, iv. 392; has seen Borlase's name in Pope's grotto, iv. 245 n.; his honesty, iv. 434; he and the 3rd Earl of Oxford dine with Pope, who seemed on the point of death, iv. 520 n.
St. Christophers (St. Kitts), Leward Islands, iv. 120.
St. James's Chronicle (1776) prints Pope letters, i. 29, 344, ii. 93, 140.
St. James's Evening Post, Curll advertises in it, iii. 468, 472 n.
St. James's Journal, ii. 104 n., 144.
St. John, Henry, Lord St. John, Bolingbroke's father, ii. 475, iii. 249, iv. 484, v. 12, 17.
ST. JOHN, HENRY, Viscount Bolingbroke: his correspondence, letters from Pope to him, ii. 226, iv. 260, 490 (to B. and Marchmont); letters from him to Pope, ii. 218, 249, 383; letters from Swift to B., iii. 63, 98, iv. 115; letters from him to Swift, ii. 186, 348 (with Pope), 383, 402, iii. 47, 70, 98, 163, 183 (with Pope), 210, 274 (with Pope), 404; letters from B. to Lord Harcourt, ii. 290; to Lord Bathurst, iii. 139; to Lord Marchmont, iv. 456, 498, 503, 519; — a letter from him to Prior quoted, i. 307; his 1723 letter to Swift a post-

ST. JOHN, HENRY (*cont.*)
script to Pope's letter, ii. 186 n., iv. 50; a letter from Pope (14 Jan. 1723/4) now unknown, ii. 218; so also a letter from Swift, ii. 324; B. writes from the Severn to the Three Yahoos, ii. 383; will accept letters from Swift to Pope or Gay as to himself, ii. 389; sends a letter to Swift by a bookseller rather than by post, ii. 402; writes the first part of the (lost) Cheddar letter, ii. 403; writes to Swift as he journeys to France, iii. 47–50; Swift addresses him under cover to Lord Bathurst, iii. 97; — B. speaks of 'the diligent Inspectors of private men's correspondence' in the Post Office, iii. 411; some of his letters appear in the clandestine vol. of Pope–Swift letters, iv. 263, 286–7; it was felony to correspond with him during his exile, iv. 286–7; no letters for that period to him are known, iv. 313 n.; B. on epistolary fame, iii. 102; he cites Pliny, Seneca, Balzac, and Voiture who wrote for publication: Cicero did not, iii. 102.
Biographical data: *To 1715*: he told Pope of a plot (1712) against B.'s life by Whig leaders, iii. 199; his gift to Booth for acting Cato, i. 175; he sends wine to Swift at Letcombe, i. 234; his Bill of Schism, i. 235 n.; his withdrawal to the country (15 Jan. 1715), i. 252, 275 n.; he escapes to France, i. 287 n.; his impeachment overshadows the publication of *Iliad*, vol. i, i. 295; his unhappy first marriage, i. 444 n.
To 1725: not at Dawley in 1722, ii. 120 n.; is pardoned in 1723, ii. 151, 175, 184; his pardon aided by Lord Harcourt, ii. 175; his arrival in England (June 1723), ii. 175 n.; his return to France in Aug., ii. 183 n., 186; is invited to Parson's Green (Peterborow?), ii. 183; — Pope's fondness for him (1723), ii. 184; B.'s friendship for Swift, ii. 186; B. contrasts his life (1714–23) with Pope's, ii. 186–8; B.'s second wife (Marquise de Villette), ii. 187; Swift fears for B.'s complete pardon, ii. 200, 221; B.'s quiet retreat at LaSource, ii. 187, 188; has a week with Pouilly and Voltaire, ii.

ST. JOHN, HENRY (*cont.*)
221; — doubts if he ever comes to England again, ii. 249; thinks the Jubilee Year may bring Pope to the Continent, ii. 249; his retirement not like that of Servilius Vatia, ii. 252; — his second return to England: settles at Dawley, ii. 282, 290 n., 327 n.; reported thrown from his hunter, ii. 327, 332; he wishes to see Bridgeman for his gardens, ii. 327.
To 1735: Swift (1726) goes to Dawley for a week, ii. 372; Voltaire writes to Pope from B.'s house, ii. 399; he has a house in Pall Mall, ii. 399; he entertains the Queensberrys and Gay at dinner (1726) at Cranford, ii. 400; — Pope's accident, coming from B.'s, in the river Crane, ii. 401; B. is repairing Dawley as 'an agreeable sepulchre', ii. 403; visits Sir W. Wyndham, ii. 410, iii. 139 n.; visits Lord Bathurst at Riskins, ii. 465; urges Swift to care for his health, ii. 472; Swift grieves that ill health drives B. to Bath, ii. 498, 503; — the bucolic life at Dawley, ii. 503; the walls of B.'s hall to be painted with farm implements, ii. 503, 525; Swift worries over B.'s lavish expenditures, ii. 505; B. visited Pope during Mrs. Pope's long illness, iii. 3; his suit over the 1st Lady B.'s property, iii. 27 n.; — the 2nd wife (Marquise de Villette) is improved in health, ii. 525; B. takes her back to France, and returns alone to England, iii. 48; his wife's health may compel him to live in France, iii. 103; thinks the Marquise would make a good nurse for Swift, iii. 163; — regrets Swift's plan to build on Drapier's Hill, iii. 50; has a project to bring Swift to an English parish, iii. 183, 211; tries to get Swift the living at Burghfield, iii. 303 n.; has expected because of Gay's news Swift's coming (1731) to England, iii. 210; warns Swift against recommending undeserving people like Pilkington (1734), iii. 405; — has put Pope at work on a philosophical poem (*Essay on Man*), iii. 71–72; they talk metaphysics, iii. 139; he quotes Pope on passions as the gales of life, iii. 183–4;

ST. JOHN, HENRY (*cont.*)
on rewards and punishments in
another life, iii. 210–11; sketches the
contents of the *Essay on Man*, iii. 213–
14; spoken of (?) as Pope's chief
critic in Swift's absence, iii. 349; the
Essay, though touching metaphysics,
is to be approved, iii. 405; B. and
Swift approve Pope's Moral Essays,
iii. 414; — 'Duke' Disney leaves B.
£500, iii. 249; B. is angry at the
attacks on him and Pulteney, iii. 214–
15; Swift approves the friendship with
Pulteney, iii. 251; Swift deplores the
longevity of B.'s father, iii. 363, v. 12;
B. healthy and happy in retirement,
iii. 404; will write for posterity (i.e.
for posthumous publication?), iii.
404–5; often wishes himself out of
England, iii. 405; his acquaintance
with Mallet, iii. 177, 330, 408; B.'s
opinion of the ineffectuality of Robert,
Earl of Oxford, iii. 412; he plans to
take Pope to Bath, iii. 433.
To 1739: B. goes to France in May
1735, iii. 470, v. 14; Pope misses his
conversation, iii. 483; Swift asks
where B. is, iii. 505; B.'s absences from
England, iii. 515 n.; — sends from
France to Pope unidentified writings
by himself, iv. 6; Swift is glad B. is
writing, iv. 12; Swift is reproached
for spreading gossip about him, iv.
27; Pope thinks his title to fame will
be his friendships with Swift and B.,
iv. 28; — Swift laments B.'s squander-
ing of health and fortune, iv. 45; B.,
seems a 'settled philosopher' in France,
iv. 50; is soon (June 1738) expected in
England, iv. 106; arrives 8 July 1738,
to sell Dawley, iv. 113; as Pope's
guest he keeps Pope from going to
Bath, iv. 108 n.; his arrival noted in
the newspapers, iv. 109; wishes to sell
Dawley, iv. 113; stays at Twickenham with Pope, iv. 113, 119, 146,
149, 177; in his absence Pope and T.
Gordon drink Walpole's health, iv.
114; A. Hill wishes B.'s approval of
a tragedy in MS. (*The Roman Revenge*), iv. 105, 110 n., 111, 126–7; B.
declines to have it dedicated to him,
iv. 166, 168; B. is briefly ill, iv. 117,
118; Pope asks Allen to send Bath

ST. JOHN, HENRY (*cont.*)
waters for B., iv. 119, 134; — B. tried
to help Hooke's son in France, iv.
119; he visited (?) Sir W. Wyndham,
iv. 119 n.; the sale of Dawley is slow,
iv. 124, 153, 177; B. does not write to
Swift when Pope does, iv. 134; almost never goes to Town, iv. 154; —
wishes to take Robert Arbuthnot back
to France with him, iv. 171; he plans
to sail, iv. 171; he would like to dine
with Burlington before sailing, iv.
172; he sails from Greenwich, 14 Apr.
1739, iv. 172 n.; his life at LaSource,
iv. 177; his wife's son-in-law is
governor of the Forest of Fontainebleau, iv. 177.
1740–4: B. would return from
France, Pope says, to serve his country, iv. 260; fears for B.'s health, iv.
261; B. is commended in Pope's lines
on his grotto, iv. 262; B.'s affection
for Hugh, 3rd Earl of Marchmont,
iv. 327; B.'s career 'tost by whirls of
fortune', iv. 364; Pope thinks him
badly treated by his country, iv.
364–5; B. begs that Lyttelton will not
forget him, iv. 369; Brinsden's ill
health worries B., iv. 372; B. has a
bilious fever, iv. 390, 398; he may go
to Bath to see Brinsden, iv. 393; his
stay in England will be brief, iv. 393;
— his father, Lord St. John, dies, iv.
393 n., v. 12; is expected to arrive to
settle his father's estate, iv. 393; goes
for some days to Twickenham with
Pope, iv. 394; stays in England from
late Apr. to 14 June 1742, iv. 394 n.;
H. Bethel is told of B.'s presence in
England, iv. 395; — his return to
France, iv. 400, 401, 402; Pope gives
him Warburton's books to read, iv.
402; B. and Marchmont are expected
at Twickenham for a few days (Feb.
1743), iv. 442, 451, 453; the date of
his arrival in 1743 from France, iv.
451 n.; has been with Pope for 5
weeks, iv. 455; — is to embark for
France 25 May 1743, iv. 456; now
lives at Argeville in France, iv. 456 n.;
Pope hopes politics might bring B.
back again, iv. 459; is in England
'for a month or two' towards the end
of 1743, iv. 483; was not at Battersea

ST. JOHN, HENRY (*cont.*)
in 1739, iv. 484 n.; the alleged quarrel with Warburton at Murray's, iv. 488, 498; he plans to 'stay a month yet', iv. 495; is with Lord Stair, iv. 498; he is alarmed by the beginning of the war with France, iv. 498; — is to take Pope to Battersea tomorrow, iv. 498; called Pope's 'old and long experienced friend', iv. 499; Pope's printing of the *Idea of a Patriot King*, iv. 499 n.; Cheselden comes to Battersea to bleed Pope, iv. 501; B. and Marchmont go to Twickenham, iv. 503, 511, 514; B. is at Chetwynd's in Dover Street, iv. 518; will be at Twickenham Sunday, iv. 519; is much worried about the national crisis, iv. 519; sobs over Pope's chair as Pope is dying, iv. 525-6; his portraits as done by Richardson, iii. 326, iv. 119, 123, 148, 400.

Bolingbroke's character, chiefly as seen by Pope: his traits, ii. 327; his 'improved mind', ii. 332; now above trifling, is grown a great divine, ii. 350; but B. loves trifling, ii. 350; B.'s anecdote of the Irish thief, ii. 350-1; B. labours to be unambitious — but in an unwilling soil, ii. 395; dislikes the denigration of Man in *Gulliver*, ii. 413; — Swift lectures B. on economy, iii. 28; Swift is invited to come and see how frugally B. lives, iii. 48; B. says his career has been a mixed theatrical *genre*, iii. 48; on fame, iii. 49; he was Swift's hero, not Oxford, iii. 63; Swift warns, 'Retrenchment is not your talent', iii. 64; B. replies that one can live with dignity on any income, iii. 71; Swift thinks that unlike B. Pope would not laugh at precepts on thrift, iii. 363, v. 14; on the validity of maxims, iii. 411-12; — B. thinks knaves preferable to fools, ii. 188; on lost friends, ii. 188; on long friendships, iii. 71; on appropriate conduct in the decline of life, iii. 183; the steady life B. now lives, ii. 186-7; his former debauchery admitted and regretted, iii. 184, v. 14-15; on retirement and exercise, iii. 275; Pope's superlative estimates of B., iii. 326, iv. 6, 153, 261, 395-6, 505.

ST. JOHN, HENRY (*cont.*)
Bolingbroke's politics: his views on 'party', ii. 187; on 'incivilities' in politics, ii. 188; 'National corruption must be purged by national calamities', iii. 163; provocative letter to *The Craftsman* (22 May 1731), iii. 215 n.; his *Final Answer*, iii. 215 n.; Pope calls him a creature of this world, not of the Universe (not a philosopher), iii. 445; Swift praises his *Dissertation upon Parties*, iii. 456, v. 14; his plan for revivifying the Opposition, iv. 142-4; is called disinterested in politics since barred from office, iv. 261; wants Pope to stimulate Marchmont to political action, iv. 271, 272; on Walpole's luck in losing leaders of an Opposition, iv. 272.

Bolingbroke's philosophical ideas: he seems (1723) a philosopher, ii. 184; professes no system of philosophy, ii. 220; adores the Creator of the world, ii. 220; on the unequal dispensations of Providence, iii. 214; on the problem of evil is an optimist, ii. 220, iii. 211; on judicial astrology, ii. 221; Pope thinks B. has given up ambition for philosophy, ii. 331; on business and philosophy, iii. 412-13; dislikes the definition of *animal rationis capax*, ii. 351; on hating the world: contra Swift and Pope, ii. 351; thinks Swift and Pope great wits, but bad philosophers, ii. 351; on men as seen by the public and as they actually are, iii. 103; cites Mencius and Confucius, iii. 413; disparages the Stoics, iii. 413; he has engrossed philosophy, Lyttelton says, iv. 348; disapproves of Delany's theology, iii. 211, 212, 275; at Pope's urging has written a philosophical vol. (1732), iii. 275; his antimetaphysical views, iii. 275, 433, 434, 440; — is voluminous to destroy vols., iii. 445; possible allusion to his 'Letter to Pope' or his 'Fragments', iii. 275 n.; has written six and a half letters on philosophy to Pope (1734) and plans one and a half more, iii. 433; will be on the same shelf with Locke and Malebranche, iii. 433; will publish his philosophy posthumously, iii. 404-5, 433.

St. John, Henry (*cont.*)
Bolingbroke as historian: his reading in history, ii. 187; remarks on historical writing, ii. 219–20; plans a large historical work, ii. 249–52; on the treaties of Utrecht and Baden, ii. 251; his projected history, iii. 28 n., 71; urged by Swift to work on his history, iii. 98; his project on the history of his times, iii. 212–13, 274–5, 372, iv. 177.
Authors mentioned by Bolingbroke: Seneca's *Epistles*, ii. 187–8; Pliny's *Letters*, ii. 220–1; he adapts Pliny in quoting, ii. 220–1; Cicero, *De Natura Deorum*, ii. 351; LaBruyère on relaxation and health, ii. 472; gave Swift Graevius and Gronovius, iii. 30; he quotes Montaigne, iii. 48; Paolo Sarpi ('Father Paul'), iii. 213.
Remarks on the Prestige of English: its richness, ii. 218; wishes Pope to leave translation for original writing, so as to 'fix' the language, ii. 218; on the spread of languages, ii. 219; on writing necessary to 'fix' the language, ii. 219; on the small prestige of English writers on the Continent, ii. 219–20; lack of a perfect work in English hinders prestige, ii. 220; translation will not do it, ii. 220; on the tragedy of Voltaire, Racine, and Corneille, ii. 222.
St. John, Frances (Winchcombe), 1st wife of Lord Bolingbroke, i. 300, 444.
St. Mawes (Cornwall), iv. 344.
Salisbury (Wilts.), iv. 464.
Salisbury Primer, i. 163.
Salkeld, Mr., tutor to Orrery's sons, iv. 309.
Sallust, ii. 531, iii. 66.
Salmond, Hon. Monica Margaret (Grenfell), Lady, ii. 496 n.
Salter, F. M., iv. 137.
Salvini, Antonio Maria, i. 447.
Sanders, Mr., Lord Bathurst's porter, iii. 131.
Sandwich, Lady, *see* Montagu, Elizabeth (Wilmot), wife of the 3rd Earl of Sandwich, i. 261.
Sandys, Samuel, iv. 143.
'Sappho', early used of Mrs. Nelson and others, i. 42, 47, 65, 99–100.
Sarpi, Paolo, iii. 213, 248.

Savage, Richard: letters to, iv. 37, 392, 417; he dedicates to the Earl of Middlesex (later Duke of Dorset), i. 467 n.; tells of the presentation of *The Dunciad* to the King and Queen, iii. 26 n.; publishes 'An Author to be Let', iii. 37 n.; tells Pope of Mallet's *Verbal Criticism*, iii. 66; fails to get the laureateship, iii. 158; — told Pope that 'A. H.' was taken for Aaron Hill, iii. 170; Pope sends service to Savage by Mallet, iii. 189; Savage tells Pope Booth and Mrs. Porter are unable to act in *Athelwold*, iii. 232; — gets aid from Lord Tyrconnel, Pope, *et al.*, iii. 238 n.; encourages Gilliver to hope to publish *Athelwold*, iii. 238; Pope disapproves of S.'s *Progress of a Divine*, iii. 504; S. gets Pope to help on a life of Gay, iv. 37–38; retires to Bristol in 1739, iv. 157; goes, supposedly, to Wales with £10 from Pope payable quarterly and another £10 from Allen, iv. 180; leaves London in July 1739, iv. 180 n.; — at S.'s trial (1729) Judge Page was insolent and severe, iv. 189 n.; S. got Pope's help for Dr. Johnson, iv. 194 n.; in a high tone objects to being put into 'a state of infancy', iv. 210; the subscription for his retirement, iv. 210, 331; his captious tone offensive to Pope, iv. 331, 392; Pope fears S. got an extra £10, iv. 344, 347; exasperated, Pope sends him £5, iv. 417; — S. determines to return to London, iv. 417; Pope hears S. is in prison, iv. 417; if S. returns to London, his friends will withdraw support, iv. 418; S. apparently appeals directly to Allen, iv. 431; Pope thinks him a 'wrong-headed fool', iv. 431, 432.
Savile, George, Marquess of Halifax, iii. 303 n., 328, 341.
Savile, Henry, iii. 303, 328, 341.
Scaliger, J. J., i. 225.
Scarborough, 2nd Earl of, *see* Lumley, Richard.
Scarborough (Yorkshire), iii. 197.
Schaub, Sir Luke, ii. 157.
Schism, Bill of, i. 235.
Schomberg, Frederick, Duke of, his monument in St. Patrick's, iii. 191, 208, 287.

Schulemberg, Mme von, i. 427 n.

Schutz, Augustus (Col.), ii. 476, iii. 409 n., iv. 188.

Scipio Africanus, his *ingrata patria*, i. 371, iv. 166.

Scot, Mr., Lord Burlington's gardener, iv. 118, 360, 449.

Scots Magazine, iv. 422 n.

Scott, Anne, Duchess of Monmouth, i. 169, 288 n., iv. 38.

Scott, Henry, ii. 513.

Scott, Temple, cited on Swift portraits, iv. 233 n.

Scott, Sir Walter, iv. 321 n.

SCRIBLERUS CLUB, THE: verse invitations to Lord Oxford, i. 216, 217, 228, 230, 478; members of the Club, i. 205, ii. 91; its project for *The Works of the Unlearned*, i. 195 n.; the *Memoirs* of Martin, i. 216; its last meeting in 1714, its dispersal regretted, i. 230, 233, 249–50; the meeting in 1718, i. 478–9; later references to the Club, ii. 90, 91, 292 n.; it was the origin of *Peri Bathous*, ii. 468 n.

Scrope, Mrs., a friend of Martha Blount, i. 435.

Scudamore, Frances (Digby), Viscountess, a cousin of Robert Digby, i. 473 n.; her manner of life in town, i. 473; she stays in the country all winter, ii. 58; she like others wishes R. Digby were in Town, ii. 44; she may visit Sherborne, ii. 48; T. Southerne her guest in 1724, ii. 234; — she returns to Holm Lacy, ii. 240; Holm Lacy is to be improved by Lord Bathurst, ii. 314; *The Dunciad Variorum* (1729) given out from her house by Edward Digby, iii. 27; her dau. the scandalous Duchess of Beaufort, iv. 266 n.

Scudamore cider, ii. 45.

Scudery, Mlle de: *Grand Cyrus* sent to Martha Blount, i. 375, 379; cited by Pope, iv. 397.

Seaforth, Countess of, *see* Mackenzie, Frances (Herbert).

Seaforth, 4th Earl of, *see* Mackenzie, Kenneth.

Seaforth, 5th Earl of, *see* Mackenzie, William.

Searle, John, Pope's gardener (*c.* 1724–44), ii. 263 n.; an expert on pineapples, iv. 186, 405, 449; jokingly

Searle, John (*cont.*)
called Johannes Serlius, iv. 459; told to meet Martha Blount and take her back to London from Bath, iv. 463; becomes Allen's gardener in 1744, iv. 429 n.; his *Plan of Mr. Pope's Garden* cited, iv. 451 n.

Secker, Thomas, iii. 358.

Secundus, Johannes, i. 331.

Sedley, Sir Charles, i. 145.

Selkirk, 2nd Earl of, *see* Hamilton, Charles.

Selkirk, Alexander, ii. 13.

Selwyn, Mr., groom of the Bedchamber of the Prince of Wales, ii. 324.

SELWYN, GEORGE: letter to (on the project of translating Cicero's letters), iv. 130–1.

Seneca: his *Oedipus* quoted, i. 99; his *Thyestes*, ii. 109, 140, 302, iii. 479; his *Epistles* quoted, i. 147, 195, ii. 187–8, 253; his letters written for publication, Bolingbroke says, iii. 102; quoted by Bolingbroke, iii. 214, 413; Seneca was a slave to the Court, Bolingbroke says, ii. 351.

Senesino, opera singer, iii. 484.

Senior, Dorothy, iii. 435 n.

Septimius, i. 172.

Septimuleius, i. 27.

Sequel of Mr. Pope's Law Case, The, iii. 355 n.

Severus, i. 49.

Sewall, Samuel, will take Pope's *Works* to Byles in New England, ii. 527.

Sewell, George: his work on Lucretius, i. 374; writes observations on *Jane Shore*, i. 374 n.

Seymour, Algernon, Earl of Hertford; later 7th Duke of Somerset: purchases Riskins (1739), iv. 179 n.; mentioned, ii. 269.

Seymour, Berkeley, i. 298; also Mrs. Seymour.

Seymour, Charles, 6th Duke of Somerset, his dau., wife of Sir Wm. Wyndham, dies (1731), iii. 194 n.

Shadwell, Sir John, M.D.: on Dr. Radcliffe's death, i. 269 n.; his copy of vol. i of the *Iliad*, i. 297; discusses the secret disease with Pope, i. 428; his idiom in physiology, iv. 220.

Shakespeare, William: Pope has his portrait in his chamber, i. 120; Atterbury

Shakespeare, William (*cont.*)
  thinks S. obscure and bombastic, ii.
  78, 87; S. quoted by Pope, i. 60, 186,
  202, 427, iv. 208; by Atterbury, ii.
  129; by Orrery, iv. 82; S. gives H.
  Brooke rapture, iv. 199; quoted by
  A. Hill, iv. 105; Swift recalls the
  Wife of Bath 'in Shakespeare', iii. 72;
  — *Pope's Edition of Shakespeare*: in
  process, ii. 63; Tonson makes an initial
  payment of £60 on the ed., ii. 81;
  Pope has found (1721) men at Oxford
  to help on the ed., ii. 81; the work
  progresses, ii. 93, 117, 142, 213; Pope
  wishes the division of scenes determined, ii. 81; his 'dabbling' in the
  text, ii. 87–88; asks Cheselden to put
  conjectures on paper, ii. 101; — Pope
  advertises for 4tos antedating 1620, ii.
  102 n.; he mistakes the date of the
  first folio, ii. 102; on what eds. are
  useful, ii. 102; arranges parties for
  collating the texts, ii. 106, 118;
  Richardson and Cheselden help in
  collating, ii. 177 n.; — reports the
  ed. one-fourth printed, ii. 142; Tonson asks for copy on *The Merchant of
  Venice*, ii. 212; the Index of the ed. is
  planned, ii. 81, 130, 213, 214; one
  volume is proof-read by Fenton, ii.
  222; Fenton's work on the ed., ii. 244;
  Pope will proof-read vol. vi, ii. 222;
  Pope wants the three parts of *Henry
  VI* to work on, ii. 214; the Preface is
  finished, ii. 270; it is circulated among
  noble critics, ii. 279–80; work on the
  ed. is finished, ii. 270; the Stratford
  monument is engraved for the ed., ii.
  279–80; the wording of the title-
  pages, ii. 282; the ed. is advertised for
  publication, ii. 282, 285 n., 286; —
  the possibility of an 8vo ed., ii. 302;
  no report from Knapton on a further
  projected ed., iv. 393; the ed. of
  Nicholas Rowe, ii. 214; a new ed. projected by Pope and Warburton, iv.
  417; Pope sees one sheet of Hanmer's
  ed. at Oxford, iv. 475.
Shannon, Lord, writes for Congreve to
  Pope, ii. 12.
Shawford, near Winchester (Hants), iii.
  66 (the Duke of Montrose, David
  Mallet).
Sheers, Sir H., i. 17.

Sheffield, Mr., *see* Sheffield, Charles
  (Herbert).
Sheffield, *né* Charles Herbert: not in
  favour with Duchess of Buckingham,
  ii. 303; his bequests from John, Duke
  of Buckingham, iv. 65.
Sheffield, Edmund, 2nd Duke of
  Buckingham: Coste his tutor, ii. 88 n.,
  89; he dines with a party at Bromley,
  ii. 121 n.; he subscribes for five sets
  of the *Odyssey*, ii. 276; Ward is his
  rascally agent, ii. 287 n.; — a protégé of Lord Strafford, ii. 314; his
  majority (7 years off) awaited, ii. 525
  n.; he goes to Oxford, iii. 296, 299;
  his death, iv. 21 n.; Pope sees some of
  his papers and has a good opinion of
  the man, iv. 65.
SHEFFIELD, JOHN, Duke of Buckingham: letters to, i. 492, 508, v. 5;
  letters from, i. 386, 387, 485; he read
  Pope's Pastorals in MS., i. 17; Lord
  Oxford is invited to leave him for
  Scriblerus, i. 217; Pope quotes the
  Duke's 'Reconcilement', i. 343, iii.
  105; the Duke's contributions to
  Pope's 1717 Miscellany, i. 386–7; —
  he arranges a party with Pope, 'the
  Doctor', and Atterbury, i. 387; Pope
  helps revise the *Essay on Poetry*, i. 387;
  attends the Duke's levee, i. 435; the
  Duke is ill, i. 452; his approbation of
  Lady Mary Wortley Montagu, i. 442,
  470; Pope sends similar letters to His
  Grace and to Lady Mary, i. 505 n.; —
  the Duke's opinion on the French controversy over Homer, i. 485–7; some
  account of Buckingham House, i.
  508 n.; the Duke has Prior and his
  friends at his House, i. 521, ii. 30;
  takes Pope to Tunbridge, ii. 48; puts
  up a tomb for Dryden in the Abbey,
  ii. 51, 55; his own tomb, ii. 217; his
  epitaph, ii. 73; he was no suicide, ii.
  74; his will upheld over the protest of
  the Duchess, iv. 65 n.; — Pope edits
  the Duke's *Works*, ii. 63 n., 81; without monetary profit, Pope says, ii. 81,
  93; he gets Lord Edward Harley's
  opinion of the Duke's tragedies, ii.
  101; Atterbury wishes to see the
  Works in sheets (before publication),
  ii. 123; the Duke's plays performed
  privately, ii. 134 n., 135 n.; Pope's

SHEFFIELD, JOHN (*cont.*)
choruses for, i. 386, v. 5; the inscription for his *Works*, ii. 124-5, 127-8; Pope tells Caryll of the contents of the Duke's *Works*, ii. 117; Pope is asked by Tonson to cancel their agreement concerning the Duke's *Works*, ii. 211; — the Duchess is difficult concerning the *Works*, ii. 100; concerning the inscription for the *Works*, ii. 127-8; concerning the Dedication, ii. 123; Pope is pained by the suppression of the *Works*, ii. 145 n., 151; the *Works* are printed by Ald. Barber and paid for by Tonson, ii. 158; the licence to print was secured by Barber, ii. 160; — Pope is paid £197 for the editing of the Duke's *Works*, ii. 211; the Works are republished after suppression, ii. 218 n.; Pope wishes to get shares in the *Works* for Lintot, ii. 217-18; the other booksellers concerned, ii. 222.

SHEFFIELD, KATHERINE (Darnley), wife of John, Duke of Buckingham: letters to, ii. 99, 225; letters from, ii. 286, 303; she goes (1721) to Bath, ii. 84, 100; Atterbury does not advise her about the Duke's *Works*, ii. 85; she gets Pope's opinion as to the Duke's monument, ii. 99; — makes difficulties over the Duke's *Works*, ii. 100, 123, 127-8; dines at Bromley, ii. 121 n.; arranges for the performance of the Duke's plays at Buckingham House, ii. 135; Pope has promised to visit her at Leighs, ii. 259, 260; she subscribes for five sets of the *Odyssey*, ii. 276; — in her lawsuit against John Ward she is aided by Lord Harcourt, Lord Bathurst, and Pope, ii. 282, 286-7; — she expects Pope tomorrow, ii. 287; Pope visits her at Leighs, ii. 297, 299; her dislike of 'Mr. Sheffield', ii. 303; at Leighs she meditates improvements suggested by Lord Bathurst, ii. 525; — has sold Pope an annuity, ii. 525; attempts to 'pay' Pope £100 for a friendly act, iii. 91, 110; Pope indignantly returns the £100, iii. 116, 122; the Duchess makes a sudden and mysterious trip to France, iii. 296; Curll advertises his intention of printing Pope's letters to her, iii. 477, 481; — goes to Spa

SHEFFIELD, KATHERINE (*cont.*)
with her son and Mrs. Pratt, iv. 21; vainly sues to break her husband's will, iv. 65; possibly referred to as 'the Duchess', iv. 149 n.; ill, iv. 232; thinks Orrery her best friend, iv. 232; sits in her coach at Pope's door and pays him her annuity, iv. 406; — is seriously ill, iv. 440-1; her state is deplorable, iv. 442; her expensive funeral, iv. 446; her will makes Walpole her trustee and Lord Hervey her executor, iv. 446; — Pope's final comment on her character, iv. 446; her 'character' revised but not written by Pope, iv. 460; her annuity still payable to Pope from the estate, iv. 467; her grandson by her first husband (C. Phipps) marries Lepell Hervey, iv. 482 n.

Sheffield, Robert (nearest relative of the late Duke, John Sheffield), ii. 303 n.

Shelburne, 1st Earl of, a friend of Hugh Bethel, *see* Fitzmaurice (later Petty), John.

Shelley, Sir John, i. 312.

Shepherd, Mrs., housekeeper in Fortescue's house (The Vineyard, called 'Shepherd's Hut'), Richmond: *see* Fortescue, Martha Blount, and Pope; Mrs. Shepherd cares for Martha Blount at the Hut, iv. 34; Pope tells her to read Milton against worldly disappointments (i.e. having no guests), iv. 114; mentioned, iv. 169, 183.

'Shepherd's Hut', a cant name for The Vineyard, Fortescue's place at Richmond: *see* Mrs. Shepherd, Fortescue, Martha Blount, Pope, *et al.*

Sherborn, Bridget, wife of Sir Clement Cottrell, ii. 463 n.

Sherborne (Dorset), seat of Lord Digby: visited by Pope, ii. 115, 213; his description of the place, ii. 191, 192 n., 236-9.

Sherburn, George: *The Early Career of Pope* cited, on the reaction of Oxford dons to Pope's *Iliad*, i. 294 n.; on Curll's punishment by the Westminster boys, i. 350 n.; on the licence to publish the Duke of Buckingham's *Works*, ii. 81; on Pope's supposed marriage, ii. 134 n.; on the profits from the *Odyssey*, ii. 214 n.

SHERIDAN, THOMAS: letters to, ii. 442
(from Swift), 445, 523; — S. informs
Swift of Stella's illness, ii. 445; he
can get wines for Pope and Gay, ii.
462; he praises the Holyhead Journal
of Swift, ii. 468; sends Pope his translation of Persius, ii. 523; his account
of *The Intelligencer*, ii. 523 n., iii.
22, 292, 324; is the only Irish friend of
Swift who wishes to visit England, iii.
439; Swift plans to spend the winter
of 1735/6 with S., iii. 505; S. sends
his young son to England, v. 13.
Sherlock, Thomas, Bishop of Salisbury,
i. 462 n., iv. 140, 345 n., 371.
Shippen, William, ii. 465.
Shirley, Lady Fanny, dau. of Earl
Ferrers, and friend of Martha Blount,
iv. 167, 212, 457.
Shirley, Sir Robert, 1st Earl Ferrers, iv.
167 n.
Shrewsbury, Duke of, *see* Talbot,
Charles.
Shrewsbury (Shropshire), William Wy-
cherley, i. 14, 40, 61, 82.
Shropshire, *see* Mawley (Edward
Blount) and Shrewsbury (Wycher-
ley).
Sibley, Agnes, iii. 499 n.
Sidney, Algernon, iii. 328, 341.
Sidney, Sir Philip, iii. 125.
Sidney, Robert, 4th Earl of Leicester, i.
94.
'Signior', a nickname for William Kent,
iv. 164, &c.
Silhouette, Étienne de: translates the
Essay on Man into French prose, iv.
172 n., 484; translates Warburton's
Vindication, iv. 172 n., 216 n., 219.
Silius Italicus, ii. 219.
Simon of Cyrene, i. 130.
Sitwell, Edith, iv. 134 n.
SLOANE, Sir HANS: letters to, iv. 391,
397; — gives Pope a specimen from
the Giant's Causeway, iv. 391, 397.
SMART, CHRISTOPHER: letters to, iv.
478, 483; — wishes to translate the
Essay on Man into Latin, iv. 288 n.,
478; his pride in his letter from Pope,
iv. 483 n.
Smedley, Jonathan, ii. 523.
Smith, David Nichol, his ed. of the
Swift–Ford letters cited, i. 223 n., 234
n., 249 n., 258, iii. 366 n.; *Essays* . . .

Smith, David Nichol (*cont.*)
presented to D.N.S. cited, iii. 155,
iv. 5.
Smith, R., Pope's agent with Curll
(1735), *see* Smythe, R.
Smith, Tom, ii. 3.
Smollett, Tobias, iv. 339 n.
Smythe, James Moore, *see* Moore,
James.
'Smythe, R.': his role in the publication
of Pope's letters, iii. 461–7; only a
pretended clergyman, iii. 494.
Snape, Andrew, i. 462 n., ii. 183.
Snyder, Edward D., i. 425 n.
Socrates, i. 458: the 'ghostly father' of
Sarah, Duchess of Marlborough, iv.
413, 445, 459.
Solomon, The Wisdom of, i. 148.
Somers, John, Lord, ii. 68, iii. 191, 471.
Somerset, 6th Duke of, *see* Seymour,
Charles, iii. 194 n.
Somerset, 7th Duke of, *see* Seymour,
Algernon, ii. 269, iv. 179 n.
Somerset, Lord Arthur, father of
Mmes Price and Greville, iv. 188 n.,
265 n.
Somerset, Frances (Scudamore), Duchess
of Beaufort, ii. 330; her scandalous
behaviour, ii. 330 n., iv. 266.
Somerset, Henry, 3rd Earl of Beaufort,
iv. 266.
Somerset (County), *see* Bath, Bathamp-
ton Manor, Frome, Longleat, Mar-
ston, Orchard Wyndham, Prior Park,
Widcombe.
Sotheby Catalogues cited: for a lost
letter from Pope and Gay to R.
Digby, ii. 304 n.; for a letter from
Lord Bathurst, iii. 299 n.; for a letter
from Dr. Oliver, iv. 229; for fragments of letters, i. 340 n., iii. 409,
iv. 324, 348, 372; for an untraced
order to pay, ii. 110; for information
on the Duchess of Buckingham's concert, ii. 135 n.
South, Robert, D.D., iii. 495.
Southcote, Sir Edward, i. 123.
Southcote, (Abbé) Thomas, i. 122 n.,
123, v. 2 (his abbey secured by Walpole's aid), ii. 294 n., iii. 6; he tells
Pope of the attack on Caryll in *The
Flying Post*, i. 151–2; zealous in
defence of Caryll, i. 155; S. aids the
Iliad subscription, i. 233 n., 236; he

Southcote, (Abbé) Thomas (*cont.*)
asks Pope to pay for Mrs. Cope's 'last necessities', iii. 18.
Southerne, Thomas: he read Pope's Pastorals in MS., i. 17; a friend of Lady Trumbull and Lady Scudamore, ii. 234; invited to Sturston, ii. 234; wants a prologue from Broome for his *Money the Mistress*, ii. 340; the play is rejected at Drury Lane but produced at Lincoln's Inn Fields, ii. 352; read aloud at Sir C. Cottrell's, ii. 358; — S. helps Fenton's *Marianne*, ii. 340 n.; also helps Madden's *Themistocles*, iii. 25; is hospitably entertained in Dublin, iii. 378.
South Sea Company: stock ratings, ii. 32 n., 33 n.; its books closed, ii. 48; Pope's purchases, ii. 38, 39, 42, 48; he sells, ii. 49; he advises Lady Mary to buy, ii. 52; he still has stock, ii. 53; Warburton's statement on Pope's holdings, ii. 58; Pope thinks selling is good policy, ii. 57; his reflections on the whole affair, ii. 53–54, 57, 60.
Southwell, Mr., iv. 464.
Spain, war declared on, iv. 207 n.
Spanheim, Mlle, mentioned as over-dressed, i. 22.
Spanheim, Ezechiel, i. 22 n.
Spanioletta, a painter, i. 487.
Spectator, The: its influence, i. 1; its comment on the *Essay on Criticism*, i. 139; Pope refers to No. 192, i. 162; his project (No. 457) for *Works of the Unlearned*, i. 195; Bond's continuation disparaged, i. 276.
Speed, Henrietta Jane, iv. 185, 188.
Spence, Joseph: letters to, iii. 380, 491, 498; letter from S. to Pope, iii. 132; from S. to C. Pitt, ii. 507; from S. to his mother (about Pope), iii. 493; — S. for Pitt asks Pope about printing Pitt's translation of a part of the *Odyssey*, ii. 382; visits Pope, ii. 507; asks Pitt about the authorship of some verses, ii. 507; writes to Pope about Stephen Duck, iii. 132; travels on the Continent with the Earl of Middlesex, iii. 241 n.; is invited to Twickenham, iii. 380; his account of Pope's arrival at Oxford from Southampton, iii. 493; Pope grateful for S.'s hospitality at Oxford, iii. 498; S.

Spence, Joseph (*cont.*)
is asked to return Pope's letters, iii. 498; held against H. Brooke that Pope is the greatest of all poets, iv. 198–9; — S.'s Anecdotes cited: on Pope's seeing Dryden, i. 2 n.; on the friendship with Sir W. Trumbull, i. 10 n.; on Pope's visit to Abberley (Walsh), i. 29 n.; on Pope as a painter, i. 187 n.; anecdotes secured from Pope's cousin Mannock, i. 426 n., ii. 29 n.; — on Bathurst's pleasure in the verse of Prior and the prose of E. Lewis, ii. 258 n.; on the Southcote abbey, iii. 6 n.; on Cornbury's refusal of a pension, iii. 277 n.; on Swift's letter about Coote, iii. 376 n.; on Pope's notion that Swift was born in Leicester, iv. 63 n.; S.'s account of Warburton's first dinner with Pope, iv. 236; his record of Pope's last days, ii. 100, iv. 501 n., 525–6; — cited on Pope's *Works*: on *Alcander*, i. 467 n.; on Halifax and Pope's *Iliad* I, i. 270 n.; on the character of 'Orsini', ii. 461; on the collaboration in the *Odyssey* translation, iii. 507 n.; on the composition of the *Essay on Man*, iii. 155 n.; on the composition of the *Imitation of Horace*, Satire II. 1, iii. 348 n.; on Pope's large ethical plan, iii. 401 n., iv. 5 n.; on the 'death-bed' ed. of the Moral Essays, iv. 504 n.; on a leaf supposedly from *The Dunciad* sent to Cibber, iv. 448–9 n.; Spence's *Essay on Mr. Pope's Odyssey*, ii. 357, 379; Spence's 'Account of Lord Buckhurst' in his ed. of *Gorboduc*, i. 467 n., iv. 37 n.
Spencer, Albert Edward John, 7th Earl, iv. 149 n.
Spencer, Charles, 3rd Earl of Sunderland, iii. 199.
Spencer, Dorothy, wife of Henry, 1st Earl of Sunderland, also celebrated by Waller as 'Sacharissa', iii. 341.
Spencer, Robert, 2nd Earl of Sunderland, iii. 191.
Spenser, Edmund: mentioned by Walsh, i. 21; a favourite of Pope's, i. 316, 385; Gay reads *The Faerie Queene*, ii. 410; Pope thinks his letter to Hughes about S. too trivial to print, iii. 441.
Spinoza, B., iv. 416.

Spondanus, Johannes, i. 225.
Spooner, John (marries Fortescue's dau.), iv. 114.
Spooner, Mary (Fortescue: Mrs. John Spooner), iv. 84, 90.
Stafford, 2nd Earl of, *see* Stafford-Howard, William.
Stafford, John (father of the 2nd Earl of Stafford), i. 164, 195, iii. 346.
Stafford-Howard, William, 2nd Earl of Stafford, i. 164 n., ii. 293, iii. 346.
Staines (Middlesex), i. 428 (Miss Griffin).
Stair, 2nd Earl of, *see* Dalrymple, John.
Stanhope, Philip Dormer, Lord Stanhope, and after 1726 4th Earl of Chesterfield: Craggs sends service to him by Pope, i. 361; Gay has written to S., i. 450; he helps to welcome Swift (1726), ii. 373; Swift compliments C., ii. 407; is made Knight of the Garter, iii. 111 n.; may take a house in Twickenham, ii. 416; a friend of Wm. Cleland, iii. 144 n.; postpones aid for Swift's cousin Lancelot, iii. 162; supported the pall at Gay's funeral, iii. 338; after the Excise is in the Opposition, iii. 339; — at Bath in 1734, iii. 436; a patron of James Hammond, iv. 49 n.; with Pope plays a Miltonic joke on Richardson, iv. 80 n.; goes on a ramble with Pope, iv. 80 n.; is urged to confirm Wyndham in a 'new' patriotism, iv. 143; — at Bath in 1738, iv. 139; arrives in town, iv. 149; his admiration for Lady Fanny Shirley, iv. 167 n.; from Bristol Pope uses C. franks for Martha Blount, iv. 202, 205; he sponsors *Common Sense*, iv. 209 n.; writes scandalously about Lady Thanet, iv. 212; gave out an incorrect libel by Pope against pride and covetousness, iv. 212; he is Marchmont's servant, iv. 251; despondent but active for his country, iv. 261; — goes to Bath (1740) before Pope can, iv. 273; leaves town with Pope and Lord Orrery (1741), iv. 338 n.; intends to help Warburton to a living near London, iv. 356–7; ill at Pope's house, iv. 411; from Pope's house sends service to Orrery, iv. 413; plans to take Pope to Windsor Lodge, ʻowe, and towards Bath, iv. 419 n.;

Stanhope, Philip Dormer (*cont.*)
spends a week at Gosfield, iv. 419 n.; leaves Pope at Windsor Lodge, iv. 420; — at Bath (1743) he studies gardening, iv. 459; he promises franks for Martha Blount, iv. 464; serves as Pope's Bath address after the quarrel at Prior Park, iv. 465; Pope wants C. to have a gift copy of the final 4to ed. of the *Essay on Criticism* and *Essay on Man*, iv. 502.
Stanislaus I, King of Poland, iii. 418, 503.
Stanley, Sir John, i. 253, 262.
Stanley, Thomas, his *History of Philosophy*, i. 323 n.
Stanstead (Sussex), seat of the Earl of Scarborough, iii. 15 n.
Stanton Harcourt (Oxfordshire), *see* John Hewet, Sarah Drew, John Gay, A. Pope, Edith Pope, *and* the Harcourts.
Stonor Park (Oxfordshire), Thomas Stonor, i. 429.
Stanyan, Abraham: forwards Pope's letters to Lady Mary Wortley Montagu, i. 370, 407; a friend to Pope, ii. 158; in the Foreign Office, ii. 285.
Stanyan, Temple, franks a letter, ii. 130.
Stapylton, Sir W., Pope postpones an appointment with him, ii. 27.
Statius: Pope translates a part of Book I, i. 36–38; thinks Statius next to Virgil as versifier, i. 37; condemned for poetical indiscretions, i. 37; discussed, i. 63–64; Pope has done the rest of Book I, i. 56; he writes 'Arguments' to Book I, i. 91; Statius tells of a spotty tiger, ii. 345 n.
Stawell, William, 3rd Lord, to be host to the intending (1715) trippers, i. 312.
Stebbing, Henry, ii. 234.
STEELE, Sir RICHARD: letters to, i. 139, 146, 147, 149, 153, 158, 159, 165; letters from, i. 131, 141, 145, 152, 159; S. works with Tonson, i. 56, 195; writes the *Gazette*, i. 56, 59, 61; — is known as author of *The Tatler*, i. 59, 61; it is written under the name of Bickerstaff, i. 59, 87; its popularity, i. 59, 70; Bickerstaff's bills of mortality, i. 87; his opinions of women, i. 93; praises Philips's Pastorals, i. 101;

STEELE, Sir RICHARD (*cont.*)
and his winter piece, i. 101 n., 168;
Bolingbroke likes *The Tatler*, ii. 187;
Bickerstaff's upholsterer, i. 188; Pope
quotes *The Tatler*'s intention of being
dull, ii. 369; — Caryll introduces
Pope to S., i. 113, 134; S. and Caryll
connected through Lord Cutts's
affairs, i. 120 n.; S. to write to Pope, i.
120; asks Pope for a libretto for
Clayton, i. 131, 132; the Censorium
and Pope, i. 131 n., 152 n.; — Pope
thanks S. for *Spectator* paper on the
Essay on Criticism, i. 139; S. will in-
troduce Pope to Addison, i. 141 [for
The Spectator see under its own name];
S. proves friendly, i. 141; praises
Messiah, i. 146; prints a letter from
Pope in *The Guardian*, i. 147; prints
Pope's Hadrian verses in *Spectator*
No. 532, i. 149, 157; asks Pope for an
Ode of a cheerful dying spirit, i. 159;
Pope defends Hadrian, i. 159; — S.
asks Pope's help on a design (either
The Guardian or the Censorium), i.
152; reads in MS. and approves *The
Temple of Fame*, i. 149 n., 152;
quotes Rochester on Sedley, i. 145;
Pope helps S., i. 174, 177, 180; *The
Guardian* lacks Addison's help, i.
180; reasons for dropping *The
Guardian*, i. 193, 197 n., 198; Pope's
contributions readily known, i. 193,
198; S. begins *The Englishman*, i. 193,
198; — Pope stops writing for him, i.
197; S. intends to be more political
perhaps in his writing, i. 194, 198; S.
expresses, for Addison, displeasure at
Pope's *Narrative* concerning Dennis,
i. 184; is a friend of Whiston, i. 185
n.; his hostility to *The What D'ye Call
It*, i. 287; is patentee of Drury Lane, i.
287; he reports Addison's opinion on
vol. i of Pope's *Iliad*, i. 305; S.
thought Addison translated for
Tickell, i. 305 n.; the argument over
The Conscious Lovers, ii. 144; Dennis
attacks S., ii. 144; S.'s 'Verses to the
Author of . . . Cato', i. 175 n.; becomes preoccupied in politics, i. 170;
his party violence, i. 177, 210, 215; his
contested election, i. 189; though
witty he is too political for Pope, i.
194; *The Crisis* hurts him, i. 210; his

STEELE, Sir RICHARD (*cont.*)
expulsion from Parliament, i. 210 n.,
215, 286; — is knighted (1715), i.
290; Swift had appealed to Lord
Oxford for him, ii. 67, 68; S.'s
natural good humour and good
nature, i. 185, 202, 215.
Steeves, Edna L., cited on *Peri Bathous*,
ii. 468 n.
Stephen, employed by Lord Burlington,
iv. 151, 163.
Stephens, Dr., physician (?) to the
Duchess of Marlborough, iv. 381.
Sternhold, Thomas (and Hopkins),
psalm-writers, i. 483, ii. 334.
Stoke Ash (Suffolk), ii. 352 n.
Stonor, Thomas: subscribes to Pope's
Iliad, i. 221; Pope tries to visit him
at Stonor Park, i. 411, 429; he resides
in Twickenham at times, i. 417; his
wife's death, ii. 117; his own death, ii.
253.
STOPFORD, JAMES: letters to, ii. 421,
425, 527; Swift introduces S. by
letters to Gay and Pope, ii. 310, 407;
he does not present himself, ii. 321,
324, 410; Swift's 'character' of him,
ii. 310-11; he goes to the Continent,
ii. 310; is invited to spend a few days
at Twickenham, ii. 421; the dates
of his journey (1726), ii. 421 n.; Pope
writes him an affectionate farewell, ii.
425; S. carries letters from Bolingbroke, Gay, and Pope to Swift (1726),
ii. 425; and a letter from Pope (1735)
to Swift, iii. 456, v. 13; Pope likes
Stopford, ii. 427; he approves a
learned conjecture, ii. 527; S. is promoted by Carteret, iii. 151.
Stourhead (Wilts.), Richard Hoare, iii.
300 n.
Stowe (Bucks.): Lord Cobham, ii. 302
n.; Pope's visits there, ii. 310, 388,
510 n., iv. 179, 185; the place is
celebrated in Pope's *Epistle to the Earl
of Burlington*, iii. 112 n.
Stowell (Glos.), *see* Howe, John Grubham.
Strabo, ii. 219.
Strada, Faminiamus, i. 60, 103.
Strafford, 2nd Earl of, *see* Wentworth,
Thomas.
Strafford, 4th Earl of, *see* Wentworth,
William.

Strand, near Brentford, *see* Mallet, David, iv. 522.
Stratford, William, D.D., ii. 121 n., 502.
Straus, Ralph, cited on Curll, ii. 434 n.
Strickland, Lady, iv. 21.
Stuart-Wortley, John, 2nd Baron Wharncliffe, ii. 52, 62.
Studies in Philology, ii. 257 n.
Sturston (Norfolk), *see* Mrs. Marriot, Wm. Broome, E. Fenton.
Sturston Hall (Norfolk), the Marriots.
Suetonius, i. 90, 503, ii. 80, iii. 420.
Suffolk, *see* Stoke Ash (R. Pack), ii. 352 n.
Suffolk, Countess of, *see* Howard, Henrietta.
Suffolk Correspondence, cited on Bathursts, iii. 137 n.; on Pope and Martha Blount at Bath, iii. 435 n.
Sunderland, 2nd Earl of, *see* Spencer, Robert.
Sundon, Charlotte, Viscountess, *see* Clayton, Charlotte.
Sunning Hill (Berks.), i. 121.
Supplemental Volume of Pope's *Works* (1825), i. 305, 443.
Surrey, *see* Albery Place (Southcote), Ashley (Lord Shannon, Congreve, Pulteney), Bagshot (Rackett), Barns (Tonson), Cheam (Lady Gerard), Epsom (H. Cromwell), Farnham (iii. 485), Godalming (Mary Tofts), Guildford (Caryll, Mary Tofts), Hallgrove (Bagshot, the Racketts), Ham (the Blount ladies), Marshgate, J. Knapton, Petersham (3rd Duke of Queensberry), Richmond (the Court, Mrs. Howard, Miss Howe, Fortescue, *et al.*), Sutton (J. Weston), Thistleworth (Chesterfield).
Sussex, *see* Finden (Caryll, J. Stafford), Grinsted West (Caryll, the Misses Blount, Pope), Harting (Ladyholt: Caryll), Lewes assizes, Midhurst (Ladyholt), Parham (Sir C. Bishop), Stanstead (Earl of Scarborough).
Sutherland, Countess of, ii. 99, iv. 93. *See* Gordon, Elizabeth (Wemyss).
Sutherland, James R., i. 35 n., iii. 31 n., iv. 377 n.
Sutton, Robert, 2nd Lord Lexington, iv. 493.

Sutton, Sir Robert: involved in the Charitable Corporation scandal, iii. 280, 282, 283; is defended by Warburton, iv. 492–4; omitted from Pope's satires to please Warburton, iv. 495.
Swansea (Glamorgan), Richard Savage supposed to retire to Swansea, iv. 210 344.
Swift, Deane (cousin of Dean Jonathan Swift, and son-in-law of Mrs. Whiteway): visits London and meets Pope, iv. 174, 241, 248; Pope pretends to suspect him of publishing the Swift–Pope letters, iv. 214; S. offers to correct the proofs for Faulkner, iv. 256; Orrery fans suspicion of Deane, iv. 280, 286, 306, 308; his projected Preface stopped, iv. 133 n., 283, 317–18; his *Essay upon . . . Swift*, iv. 174 n.
SWIFT, JONATHAN, D.D., Dean of St. Patrick's, Dublin: letters from Pope to S., i. 198, 230, 341, ii. 183, 321, 331, 348, 387, 394, 411, 426, 447, 454 (with Gay), 467, 472 (with Bolingbroke), 479, 503, 521, iii. 57, 79, 95, 101, 117, 183 (with Bolingbroke), 248 (with Gay), 274 (with Bolingbroke), 334 (with Arbuthnot), 347, 365, 372, 383, 400, 431 (with Bolingbroke), 444, 503, iv. 5, 27, 49, 62, 134, 176, 242, 336 (with Orrery); — letters from S. to Pope, i. 358, ii. 64, 198, 310, 324, 342, 384, 393, 406 (also to Gay), 417, 419, 451, 460, 491, 497, 504, iii. 15, 20, 27, 42, 64, 89, 92, 107, 160, 190, 207, 291, 343, 360, 367 (cf. v. 10), 376, 377, 438, 456 (cf. v. 13), 491 (cf. v. 16), 505, iv. 3, 11, 44, 55, 71, 76, 115 (also to Bolingbroke), 174, 175, v. 6, 10, 13, 16; letters from S. to Gay, ii. 152, 406 (also to Pope), 475, 481, iii. 72, 96, 147, 202, 218, 285; letters from Gay to S., ii. 399, 403, 409, 413, 454 (with Pope), 472 (with Bolingbroke), 478, iii. 68, 94, 119, 185, 194, 276, 288; — letters from S. to Gay and the Duchess of Queensberry, iii. 151, 179, 250, 296, 303, 319; letters from Gay and the Duchess of Queensberry to S., iii. 145, 204, 300, 307, v. 8; from Gay and the Duke, iii. 238; — letters from Dr. Arbuthnot to S., iii. 36, 334 (with

Swift, Jonathan (*cont.*)

Pope); letters from Bolingbroke to S., ii. 186, iii. 47, 70, 101, 163, 183 (with Pope), 210, 274 (with Pope), 404, 411, 431 (with Pope); letters from S. to Bolingbroke, iii. 63, 98; letters from S. to Martha Blount, ii. 475, 490, 504; from S. to Pilkington, v. 10; from S. to Sheridan, ii. 442; from the 2nd Earl of Oxford to S., ii. 506; from the 5th Earl of Orrery to S., iv. 60, 75, 81, 277; S. keeps all letters written to him, but not in very good order, he confesses, iii. 72; defects of the post: delay, ii. 409; the officers of the post open and read letters, iii. 149, 432, 439, iv. 115; letters sent by private hands are safer, iii. 109, 456.

The publication of Swift letters: letters to and from Anne Long published (1718) by Curll, ii. 439 n.; S. asks Faulkner (*c.* 1735) to print some of his letters, iii. 492 n., iv. 321 n.; he is told of the 'New Letters' to him published (1736) by Curll, iv. 50; Pope would put his and S.'s letters in a vol. to preserve the memory of their friendship, iii. 101; — assures Pope that all his letters are preserved but at S.'s death will be burnt, iii. 492, v. 16; Pope fears his letters may get into wrong hands, iv. 50; S. says their letters are 'mere innocent friendship'; i.e. not publishable, iii. 492, v. 16; assures Pope Curll shall not get his letters, iii. 505; promises Pope may have his letters back after S.'s death, iv. 11; has Pope's letters 'well sealed' and 'locked in a cabinet', iv. 11–12; has been urged to deposit the letters in Orrery's hands, iv. 42; insists he has every scrap that Pope ever wrote, iv. 42, 52; — remains silent after repeated requests for the return of Pope's letters, iv. 58–59; Pope advises S. never to lend letters, iv. 50; Pope's continuing uneasiness about his letters, iv. 61; S. reports a chasm (1717–22) in Pope's letters to him, iv. 72; — he finds nothing in Pope's letters to be omitted (i.e. he anticipates publication), iv. 72; he will return Pope's letters (June 1737) by Orrery,

Swift, Jonathan (*cont.*)

iv. 76, 81; S. praises the morality of Pope's printed *Letters* (1737), iv. 77; strangely forgetting (?) that he returned Pope's letters in 1737, S. writes to Pope in 1738 that Mrs. Whiteway has them all safe, iv. 115–16; at his death all his letters are supposed to go to Pope, iv. 243; — receives the printed 'clandestine' vol. of letters, authenticates the letters and gives them to Faulkner to print, iv. 242, 243, 270; his 'excessive earnestness' for publication alleged by Pope, iv. 274; S. is thought to have revised the text of his letters in 1741, iii. 344 n.; he did annotate them, iii. 456 n.; Pope wishes to hear from S. directly on the matter, iv. 275; — S. is thought to understand Pope's intrigues in the matter, iv. 276 n.; is said to be firm in wishing the vol. published, iv. 277; is careless of his MSS., iv. 283; the new letter added by him to the clandestine vol. is probably an unpublished pamphlet, iv. 283 n.; Orrery thinks S. will not tolerate revisions of the clandestine vol., iv. 306; Mrs. Whiteway says S. has quite forgotten the clandestine vol., iv. 307; — after publication of the vol. Pope sends word that in spite of the publication he still loves S., iv. 312; S. is treated 'with tenderness' in Pope's 'Narration', iv. 313, 316; S.'s varying accounts of the number and disposition of Pope's letters to him, iv. 314–15; — Pope's letters *in part* returned in 1737, iv. 315; Mrs. Whiteway had Faulkner write to Pope about the clandestine vol. since she was forbidden to do so, iv. 318; Mrs. W. said to allege S.'s positive command for publishing, iv. 319; S. never wrote directly to Pope about the vol., iv. 319; — Mrs. W. says S. never kept copies of his letters to Pope, iv. 320–1; S. feared his rulers, civil or ecclesiastic, might make an ill use of his letters, iv. 321; letters better than those from Pope have not been stolen, iv. 321; Mrs. W. speaks of a 'stitched volume' of famous letters to S., iv. 321; S. allows Mrs. W. to have and

SWIFT, JONATHAN (*cont.*)
to return to writers such letters as she chooses, iv. 321; — S. should not be involved in any publicity over the publication of the letters, so Pope and Orrery think, iv. 328; Pope believes S. has changed his mind about leaving his papers to Pope, iv. 332; Pope says S. published the letters without consulting him, iv. 334; Pope's last letter to S., iv. 337.

S. on letter-writing, ii. 198, iii. 92; his letters are a counterpart of his heart, ii. 342; approves informal, unstudied letter-writing, ii. 406; he cares little for letters written to be published, iii. 92; his favourable opinion of Voiture, Tully, Pliny, and Balzac as letter-writers, iii. 505; his own letters, 'nothing but Nature and friendship', not comparable with those of great letter-writers, iii. 505.

Biographical data to 1726: S. is painted (badly) by Pope three times, i. 187, 189; Vertue engraves a Swift portrait, after Jervas, i. 262. S.'s grandfather was impoverished by Cromwell's hellish crew, iv. 174; S. wrongly calls himself a younger son, iii. 63; Ireland his birthplace in spite of Pope's idea to the contrary, iv. 63; — S. (1714) retires to Letcombe, i. 205, 228, 230, 231, ii. 65; returns to Ireland, i. 205; leaves without notice to Parnell or Pope, i. 249, 250; Pope wonders when S. will return from Ireland, i. 259; S. said to plan a visit in 1716, i. 347; — finds Dublin depressing, i. 360; once considered for the place of historiographer, ii. 65; his income as Dean, ii. 68; Gay (1722) reports on S.'s health, ii. 149; — in 1723 S. 'awakes', ii. 151; nostalgic memories of London, ii. 152, 153; returns (1723) to Dublin after a long journey in southwest Ireland, ii. 198; — his sorry manner of life, ii. 199–200, 311; urges Pope (1725) to come and spend months in the Deanery, ii. 311; in spite of deafness he now (1725) plans a visit to England, ii. 311, 322, 331; S. has spent the summer at Quilca, ii. 324, 325; his decanal civil duties, ii. 325;

SWIFT, JONATHAN (*cont.*)
all his English friends eager to welcome him, ii. 350.

1726–7: arrives in London (Mar. 1726), ii. 357, 372; lodges at the Royal Chair, Bury Street, ii. 372–3; summer hospitality offered, ii. 357; goes to Dawley for a week, ii. 372; is anxious to see Lord Oxford, ii. 372; persons important for him to meet are enumerated, ii. 373 (Lords Oxford, Bathurst, Sir R. Walpole, Mrs. Howard); sleeps under a bad roof at Cirencester, iii. 136; difficult to arrange times with Lord Oxford, ii. 381; — Pope has S. and Gay as guests in June 1726, ii. 381, iv. 179; Peterborow arranges a dinner for S., v. 6; S. prepares to return to Ireland, ii. 384, v. 6; Pope's grief at S.'s departure, ii. 387–8; S. got from London to Dublin in 7 days, ii. 393; dreams of Twickenham, ii. 393; begged presents, but not expensive ones, ii. 394; paid for his lodging at Twickenham with wit, ii. 394; forgave Walpole £1,000, ii. 394; — his arrival (1726) in Ireland like that of a Lord Lieut., ii. 401, 414; the return like that from light back to a coal pit, ii. 406–7; he wants a recipe for chicken from Mrs. Howard, ii. 408; the spectacles left behind are for two old cousins, ii. 408; a present of Irish silk sent to Mrs. Howard is worn by the Princess, ii. 412; — is expected in London in 1727 early, ii. 414; considers the drawback of returning to Ireland, ii. 417; he and the Archbishop degrade a parson, ii. 418; is again (Apr. 1727) at Twickenham with Pope, ii. 430; 'the idle Dean's great businesses', ii. 431; goes a-fishing with Gay, ii. 431; is good-natured amid the Pope household illnesses, ii. 435; — in London, invited to Twickenham, ii. 436; rambles in Cambridgeshire with Lord Oxford, ii. 442; plans for sake of privacy to leave Twickenham, ii. 442; his deafness and giddiness worse than ever, ii. 442; his health may delay his return to Ireland, ii. 442, 445; plans to leave the middle of Sept., ii. 443; is abstemious

SWIFT, JONATHAN (*cont.*)
with regard to fruit, ii. 443; his
health a worry to Pope, ii. 443, 444;
S. left Twickenham the end of Aug.,
ii. 445; — no word of his arrival in
Dublin, ii. 447; last seen by Pope at
Hammersmith, ii. 448; his sudden
departure, ii. 448; the delay at the inn
in Holyhead, ii. 454–5; his reasons for
returning to Ireland, ii. 451–2.
1728–33: a New England newspaper
mentions Jonathan Gulliver, ii. 479–
80; Pope thinks S. socially 'destitute'
(now that Stella has died), ii. 481; S.
hopes to lure Pope to Ireland, ii. 492;
his house-keeper, Mrs. Brent, ii. 492;
his teasing chapter, a *Lutrin* possible on it, ii. 498; spends time with
the Achesons at Market Hill, ii. 522;
— hears reports of false remarks about
him at Court, ii. 523; cannot come to
England, as planned, this winter, ii.
526; Pope suggests that they might
go to the south of France, iii. 1;
account of life at Market Hill, iii.
15, 20–21; hopes Pope really will
come to Ireland in the spring, iii. 21;
rejects the idea of going to the south
of France, iii. 21; — ill health keeps S.
from London, iii. 21; lives like a hermit, iii. 29, 42, v. 12; on the present
state of Ireland, iii. 42, 48, 65, 72; S.'s
behaviour with bidential forks — and
knives, iii. 69; he plans but finally
decides not to build on Drapier's Hill,
iii. 57, 65, 70–71, 78, 79; — is expected
in London (1730) in the spring, iii.
71; had eleven summons from the
Queen before he went to her, iii. 74;
his present to the Queen does not
compare with that of the outlaw
Knight, iii. 80; talks of coming over
(1730) in the summer, iii. 78; — has
received bad burgundy from R.
Arbuthnot, iii. 81, 93–94, 97; has
tried to aid in getting Pope a pension,
iii. 81; has payment in full from
Motte, iii. 90; complains of a bad
memory, iii. 92; defends his 'oeconomy', iii. 92; his quarrel with Lord
Allen, iii. 92, 108; S. sues to recover
£1,600, iii. 92; his lawsuit may keep
him from England, iii. 93, 102–3;
S.'s lawyers give varying reports of

SWIFT, JONATHAN (*cont.*)
his suit, iii. 107, 109, 182, 202, 220,
248–9, v. 14; — unwillingly he pays
for Buckley's Thuanus, iii. 96; boasts
of his riding and walking, iii. 97;
might die 'like a poisoned rat in a
hole', iii. 99; — hopes expressed for a
good living in England for S., iii.
101, 103; Bolingbroke has a project
for a living for S., i. 183, 249; S.
finds the living of Burghfield inadequate by £300, iii. 303–4; his sure
income from lands, iii. 108; — may
give up wine soon, iii. 108; only
deafness keeps him from England, iii.
108; S. reported to be in the North of
Ireland, iii. 126; is expected at Bath
(1730–1) in the winter, iii. 145; once
numbered the stones of Stonehenge,
iii. 147; at Amesbury he will find
three-pronged forks, iii. 146, 148; —
confirmed giddiness will keep him
from Bath, iii. 148, 179, 204, 377;
the Duchess of Queensberry would be
a poor nurse for him, iii. 203; thinks
of going to France in the summer of
1731, iii. 148; complains of Lord
Burlington's lack of interest in the
Chapter's request that he endow the
family monument in St. Patrick's, iii.
149; — his solitary evenings, iii. 160–
1; boasts of his physical exercise, iii.
161; Gay manages S.'s finances in
England, iii. 69, 96, 185, 194, 204,
277; S. puzzled as to proper investments, iii. 192, 298; will take his
£100 to Ireland, iii. 303, 439; S.
when ailing likes friends who can be
ordered about, iii. 191; his fruit
ruined by the late spring, iii. 192; —
law permitting, S. may come to
England (1731), iii. 192, 297; is urged
to come to Amesbury, iii. 204–5, 210;
grief at his non-arrival, iii. 238, 249,
289; a fall has lamed one leg badly,
iii. 277, 285, 297, 298; — S.'s hermit
life, iii. 287, 297; feels 'out of favour'
because of failure to send medals promised, iii. 304; unnamed verses attack
S., Pope, and Gay, iii. 304; S. thinks
of death and the disposal of his 'little
fortune to a publick use', iii. 361; —
now wishes to come to England in
Aug. 1733 and spend the winter

SWIFT, JONATHAN (*cont.*)
there, iii. 362; drinks no malt beverage, only wine, iii. 362; rides almost 12 miles a day, iii. 363; sketches his state in *ambitiosa paupertate*, iii. 369, v. 12; would like to be a critic to both Pope and Bolingbroke, iii. 369; — is disappointed that Pope refused to come to Ireland with the Cottrells, iii. 378; Irish hospitality and poverty, iii. 378; the advantages of Dublin, iii. 379; S.'s powers as Dean of St. Patrick's, iii. 379; is doleful about his health, iii. 438; realizes that he will never get to England again now, iii. 439.
1733–43: Pope commends S. for his compassion for idiots, iii. 502, 509; S. plans (1735–6) to spend the winter with Sheridan, iii. 505; his lonely days, v. 14; will not be buried in 'a country of slaves', iii. 505; — Pope hopes to see S. again, iii. 470; he invites S. to give all to the Irish and come to live with him, iv. 6, 63–64, 81–82, v. 14; S. rides often a dozen miles a day, in spite of being only skin and bones, iii. 505, iv. 4, 44; only deafness keeps him from England, iv. 11, 71; Pope fears for S.'s health, iv. 11, v. 14; is pleased at S.'s recovery, iv. 12, 15; S. is certain his English friends cannot support him in the style to which he is accustomed, iv. 13, v. 12; — for him Dublin is a perfect retirement, iv. 45; his birthday causes more joy than a king's, iv. 49; offended by the habit of colonials of registering their births in English parishes and thus being English (whereas he is 'Irish'), iv. 77; — Pope sends S. 10 new lines for *The Dunciad*, iv. 178; Mrs. Whiteway now S.'s best friend, Pope tells her, iv. 248; S.'s liking for Dr. Francis Wilson, iv. 305; reports of S.'s ill health, iv. 42, 44, 49, 71, 73, 92, 124; his bodily health (deafness apart) reported good, iv. 240, 326; deafness and giddiness are trying, iv. 184; his ill health makes Pope melancholy, iv. 248; — his mind still competent in 1738; iv. 129 n.; also in 1740, iv. 240 n., 308 n.; reports on his later days

SWIFT, JONATHAN (*cont.*)
from Orrery: reported well, iii. 482, 502, iv. 55, 56 n., 226; his memory decaying, iv. 54; 'designing people' swarm about S., iv. 54, 62; S. is seldom cheerful except when talking of Pope, iv. 73; — Pope is alarmed by Orrery's reports, iv. 92; Orrery reports that 10 out of 13 MS. vols. by S. are lost, iv. 276, 283; Orrery blames S.'s carelessness about MSS., iv. 308, 322; Orrery sends Pope the melancholy news of S.'s senility, iv. 483.
S.'s relations with his friends: his memory is green in England, ii. 184; S. wants old friends in heaven to be acquainted, ii. 452; sends his 'service' to a list of English friends normally the same, ii. 200, 282, 331, 468, 475, iii. 23, 74, 94, 109, 149, 162, 192, 289, 363, 380, v. 15; enumerates to Pope the early friends they had in common, iv. 44; recalls 27 great ministers or wits whom he knew, all now dead, iv. 44; Pope lists S.'s remaining English friends, iv. 135, 178; — *S.'s chief friends (alphabetically commented upon)*: Dr. Arbuthnot, ii. 322, 326, 401, v. 14; Atterbury wants S. to have his *Vindication*, iii. 247; Alderman John Barber's will, iii. 74; Mary Barber (poet), iii. 89, 107; she should not have asked Pope to revise her poems, iii. 191; S. summarizes his acquaintance with Mrs. Barber and shrugs off 'his' letters to the Queen, iii. 207–9; on Berkeley's *Alciphron*, iii. 286; — writes jokingly to Martha Blount, ii. 475–6, 477; wishes her and Pope to come and live in Dublin, ii. 477; his esteem for Martha, iv. 45, 115, v. 17; Eustace Budgell wants S. to get him into Parliament, iii. 162; — S. fears Bolingbroke will not get complete pardon, ii. 200; their correspondence, ii. 342, 348, 408; iii. 97; eager to have Bolingbroke work on his projected history, iii. 27–28, 63, iv. 12, 116; answers Bolingbroke's travel letter, iii. 63; S. inquires as to B.'s estate, v. 17; thinks Bolingbroke's contempt for outward things is Stoic, not ecclesiastic, iii. 64; — finds Bolingbroke and Pope not young

SWIFT, JONATHAN (*cont.*)

enough for companionship to his age, iii. 293; approves Bolingbroke's attack on metaphysics, iii. 440; he praises B.'s *Dissertation upon Parties*, iii. 456, v. 14; Pope reproaches S. for gossip about Bolingbroke, iv. 27; S. is shy as to B.'s moral frailty, v. 15; S. feels neglected by Bolingbroke, iv. 28; his gratitude to Bolingbroke, iv. 115, 116; Lady Bolingbroke mentioned, ii. 478, 481-2, iii. 298; — S. offended by Burlington's failure to endow the family monument in St. Patrick's, iii. 73; threatens to write to Burlington 'with a vengeance'; dissuaded by Pope, iii. 94, 102; remains angry, iii. 287; his unfavourable opinion of Queen Caroline, iii. 109, 149 n., 152 n., 208, 209, v. 16; his inquiry after Cheselden, iv. 4, 12; sends compliments to Lord Chesterfield, ii. 407; Chesterfield does nothing for Cousin Lancelot, iii. 162; S.'s loss in Congreve's death, iii. 15; Thomas Coote introduced to Pope by S., iii. 376; S. writes to Charles Ford, i. 251, iii. 23; the man Fox in S.'s choir, ii. 479, 483.

S. and John Gay: S. suggests Gay do a Quaker or Newgate pastoral, i. 360; since S. writes to Gay, Pope ventures to write to S., ii. 184; S. thinks Gay might well come to Ireland with a Lord Lieut., ii. 326; the mice that ate Gay's buttons, ii. 407; S. is impatient to see Gay's *Fables*, ii. 417; urges frugality upon Gay, ii. 460; approves Gay's refusal to be Gentleman Usher, ii. 460; approves of Gay's account of S.'s journey to Dublin, ii. 460; cheapness of living in Dublin, ii. 461; — a business note for Motte sent via Gay, ii. 468; S. approves of *The Beggar's Opera*, ii. 475, 482, 493; advises Gay as to finances, ii. 475, 482, 505, iii. 21; Gay reproaches S. for writing only to Pope, iii. 68, 72, 145; on Gay's losing his lodgings in Whitehall, iii. 73-74; S. had complained that Gay gave him no chance to talk, iii. 145-6; — protests he does not know where to address Gay, iii. 147; a letter dictated by Pope for Gay to send to

SWIFT, JONATHAN (*cont.*)

S. is lost, iii. 182 n.; S. thinks Gay loves coaches too much, iii. 251; complains of Gay's inattention, iii. 304; likes Gay's *Fables*, iii. 297; thinks Gay and Pope dupes of the Queen and Mrs. Howard, iii. 321; — S.'s endorsement on the letter announcing Gay's death, iii. 334 n.; S. now expects to die poor and friendless, iii. 343; Pope's epitaph for Gay criticized, iii. 360-1, v. 12; S. dislikes *Achilles*, iii. 361; finds the deaths of Gay and Arbuthnot 'terrible wounds', iii. 456, v. 14; on Gay's posthumous papers, v. 12.

Lady Betty Germain mentioned, iii. 109, 363; Richard Glover ('Leonidas') unknown to S., iv. 72; Archbishop (John) Hoadly, iii. 147-8; N. Hooke's *Roman History*, iii. 191; — Henrietta Howard, Countess of Suffolk, celebrated by Pope in lines 'On a Certain Lady at Court', ii. 326, 343; S. tells her his troubles, ii. 446; S.'s character of Mrs. Howard is commented upon, ii. 461; she 'forbade' S. to go to France in 1727, ii. 472; his remedy for deafness may not suit her, ii. 481; has nothing to say to Mrs. Howard or to the Queen, iii. 23, 43; — S.'s 'character' of Mrs. Howard thought extreme, iii. 58; S. meditates a moral letter to her, iii. 93; Pope discourages the letter, iii. 101, 108, 109; his letter reproaching Mrs. Howard is disapproved of by Pope, iii. 161; other friends disapprove of his attitude towards Mrs. Howard, iii. 194, 363; S. expresses violent hostility to Mrs. Howard, iii. 203, 208, 219-20, 251, 363; — did not know John Hughes, iii. 492; gets the Prince of Wales to nominate M'aulay for the Irish parliament, iv. 175; has not yet seen Lady Mary's and Lord Hervey's attack on Pope (1733), iii. 362; his poor view of it later, iii. 368; — Orrery asked to take only kind messages to S., iv. 332; S. highly commends Orrery to Pope, iv. 78; — Edward, 2nd Earl of Oxford, corresponds with S., ii. 316, 334, 342; Oxford's gold cup outshines S.'s silver,

SWIFT, JONATHAN (*cont.*)

ii. 470; S. sends Oxford some medals, ii. 496; sends also his service, iv. 45; thinks Robert, 1st Earl of Oxford his superior in scholarship, ii. 67; a portrait of the 1st Earl sent to S., ii. 342; Bolingbroke says the 1st Earl sent S. to Dublin, iii. 211; — Thomas Parnell, i. 292; Lord Peterborow, ii. 198–9, 413, iii. 281, 363; Ambrose Philips, ii. 342–3; the Rev. Matthew Pilkington, iii. 293, 344, 405, v. 10.

Pope and S.: Pope states conditions for changing his religion, i. 198–201; Pope easily talks or sleeps in S.'s company, i. 204; Pope's indebtedness to S. for furthering the subscription to the *Iliad*, i. 245; his ties with S. are non-political, i. 245; S. is Pope's patron saint, i. 342; Pope wishes they might be together so as to *divert* themselves, ii. 321; S. inquires as to a London address for Pope, ii. 327; — gives Pope silver cups, ii. 388, 393; plans a visit of Pope to Dublin, ii. 394; Pope sends S. broccoli seeds, ii. 425; Pope offers condolence over misfortunes and griefs, ii. 447; S., Pope, and Bolingbroke called a triumvirate expecting nothing, ii. 497; Pope wishes to live with S., ii. 522; — S. wishes Pope to come to Dublin when Mrs. Pope dies, iii. 43; Pope's inadequate table forks, iii. 74; S. sends Pope usquebaugh, iii. 93, 97, 102; has tried to get Pope a pension, iii. 81, 94; Pope's early frugality with regard to wine, iii. 97; at death all S.'s papers are to go to Pope, iii. 291; iv. 305 n.; he would like to see Pope's papers and those of Bolingbroke, iii. 362; — Pope wishes S. would come over to help on Gay's papers, &c., iii. 365; S. condoles on the death of Mrs. Pope, iii. 378; tenderness of heart keeps Pope from writing, iii. 431–2; Irishmen come over and pretend intimacy with S., iii. 432; separation is Pope's greatest sorrow, iii. 432; — S. approves of Pope's summer rambles, iii. 438; regrets that Irish friends pester Pope, iii. 439, v. 15; letters from now on to be regarded as addressed to Pope and Bolingbroke jointly, iii. 440, iv. 115; Pope

SWIFT, JONATHAN (*cont.*)

wishes a reunion with S., iii. 444; — Pope's title to permanent fame, he thinks, will be his intimacy with S. and Bolingbroke, iv. 28; his affection for S., iv. 42, 59–60, 62, 64, 92, v. 18; a lost letter from S. expresses his feelings for Pope and Orrery, iv. 154–5; his affection for Pope stated by Mrs. Whiteway, iv. 184; his will did not leave his papers to Pope, iv. 305 n.; Pope's last letter to S., iv. 337; S.'s anxiety for Pope's health, ii. 384, 393, 408, 411–12, iii. 190.

S.'s interest in Pope's writings: the *Iliad*, i. 245, 259; inquires what Pope is at, ii. 154; regrets Pope's second voyage to Homerland, ii. 311, 325; hopes the veal when cooked will be better than the versified recipe, ii. 408; — *The Dunciad* impatiently awaited, ii. 475, 484, 492, 498; insists Pope print names in full in *The Dunciad*, ii. 504; Pope calls S. 'properly the author of *The Dunciad*', ii. 523; S. has received five copies of the poem, iii. 64; — S. has been told nothing of Pope's projected programme of epistles except by rumour, iii. 343–4; wishes an epistle addressed to him, iii. 203, 348–9, 492, v. 15, 17; Pope says that his second book of epistles, when written, will be dedicated to S., iv. 5; S. grieved at the lack of an epistle addressed to him, iv. 12, 45; his comment on the *Epistle to Bathurst*, iii. 343; — is eager to see himself in Pope's *Imitation of Satire II. ii* (1733), iii. 369; is not pleased with his role there, iii. 429; regards Pope's praise in the *Epistle to Augustus* as 'the greatest honour I shall ever receive', iv. 56, 70, 72; grateful for praise, still wants an epistle addressed to him, iv. 71–72; his recognition (or not) of Pope's hand in the *Essay on Man*, iii. 372, 432, 439, v. 11–12.

S.'s comments on Pope's friends and enemies: the foolish enemies listed, i. 358; Pope is cautioned against giving fame to scribblers by mentioning them, ii. 199, 343; S. is libelled with Pope in *One Epistle*, iii. 59 n.; — Pope's enemies thought stupid, iii.

SWIFT, JONATHAN (*cont.*)
362; Pope disapproves of S.'s reproaches to Mrs. Howard, iii. 161;
Pope (1731) seldom sees Gay, iii. 179;
Pope reproves S. for gossip about
Bolingbroke, iv. 27; S. asks if any
new friends replace for Pope those now
gone, iv. 45; suggests that Mrs. Pope
is praying for his conversion, ii. 394.
*S.'s hesitant correspondence with
Wm. Pulteney*, ii. 395, 408, 419;
values Pulteney since P. is now in
'disgrace', iii. 220; a patriot in corrupt
times, iv. 12; — the Duchess of
Queensberry's beauty is not harmed
by smallpox, ii. 483; S. wishes he had
known her, iii. 74; thinks of her (and
forks) when he dines, iii. 96; is pained
that she excels her mother in beauty,
iii. 148; S. likes to command; hence
hates Duchesses, iii. 151; his other
witticisms to the Duchess, iii. 152,
180, 181; he lays down conditions
for a visit to Amesbury, iii. 181; his
social standing declines when she
does not write, iii. 204; he is puzzled
by the handwriting of Gay and the
Duchess, iii. 218-19, 220; her Coptic
lines at the end of a letter, iii. 239, 252-
3; — S. graciously resumes correspondence with the Duchess, iii. 298;
wishes to hear from His Grace also,
iii. 219; sends by Pope a message to
the Duchess, iii. 344; sends compliments to Christopher Rawlinson, ii.
407; approves of Bishop Rundle, iii.
492, iv. 3; — the Duke of Schomberg's
relatives do not like S.'s inscription on
the Duke's monument, iii. 191; S.'s
opinion of the Duke of Shrewsbury,
ii. 65; S. not friendly with Steele during the Tory régime, ii. 68; — recommends Rev. James Stopford to
Pope, ii. 310, 321, 324, v. 13; introduces Deane Swift by letter, iv. 174,
who makes a good impression, iv.
180; introduces Mrs. Sykins by letter,
iii. 89, 101; his dislike of R. Tighe, iii.
292; — can get no subscribers for
Wesley's *Job*, iii. 109; subscribes to S.
Wesley's *Poems* (1735), iii. 504; is
grateful for Pope's kindness to
Whalley, iii. 21; Chief Justice Whitshed is S.'s enemy, ii. 64, 66; Sir Wm.

SWIFT, JONATHAN (*cont.*)
Wyndham fails to reply to S.'s letter,
ii. 479, 483.
S.'s character and opinions: Pope
jokes about S.'s salvation, i. 201; S.
thinks one's worst enemy is a 'book-
selling rogue', i. 359; his *mot* about
Arbuthnot's dislike of walking, ii.
253; — S. is a swan that does not sing,
i. 347; he does not counsel, ii. 67; is
cynical about the views of Pope and
Bolingbroke on retirement, ii. 199;
confesses he is splenetic, i. 230; —
lectures Bolingbroke on economy, iii.
28; Bolingbroke lectures in return, iii.
71; S. thinks he does not value money
excessively, iii. 64; one should live
suitably to one's own mind, iii. 64;
S.'s necessary 'figure of living', iii. 65;
the pleasure of giving, iii. 65; expects
good interest on his money from
Lord Bathurst, iii. 73; pessimistic
about Irish incomes, iii. 108; — his
hope of advancement long since at an
end, iii. 161; thrift 'brings ease and
liberty', iii. 363; discusses the incomes of Orrery and Bolingbroke, iv.
45; is worried about Gay's finances, ii.
153, 326, 505, iii. 43, 58, 107; — is
said to behave arrogantly, i. 231; is a
cheerful host at home, i. 371; his life
in Dublin innocuous, ii. 65; is loved
by the lower classes, iv. 56; is acquainted with no lord temporal or
spiritual in Ireland, iv. 56; — would
never knowingly form a friendship
with a sickly person, iii. 161; in
human nature prefers beef and mutton to partridges, ii. 492; on the best
kind of friends, ii. 492; is urged by
Pope to be quiet and happy, iv. 135;
cannot pardon inattention, which is
mortal to conversation, iii. 298;
wishes to do as little hurt and as much
good as possible in the scrap of life
left to him (1733), iii. 361; views on
fame: the desire 'to see and be seen', iii.
29; fame means more in youth, iii. 29;
no one looks at him when he walks
with his betters, iii. 30; lack of title
and fortune spurred Swift, iii. 30, 63-
64; S.'s notions of fame countered by
Bolingbroke, iii. 49; — Swift's
frustrations: complains of unjust

SWIFT, JONATHAN (*cont.*)

attacks, ii. 68–69, 71–72; wishes to be an avenging angel, ii. 332; Boys, he says, meaning Pope, should not talk of millenniums, ii. 343; would never seek redress from power, iii. 107; his frustrations as seen by Bolingbroke, ii. 221; the great fish he lost as a boy symbolizes later disappointments, iii. 29; — would anger the world, if he could with safety, ii. 342; on his hatred of the world, ii. 419; his dislike of Congreve's idea that all times are equally virtuous or vicious, iii. 29; believes there was a golden age, iii. 29; Bolingbroke's criticism of S.'s 'philosophical spectacles', iii. 48; — S. says he is ever more angry and revengeful, iii. 98; tells of throwing down a badly built wall, iii. 99; his own temper displeases him completely, iii. 99; 'life is a ridiculous tragedy', iii. 190; — describes his own misanthropy, ii. 325; the years, he thinks, have changed him more than they have Pope, ii. 343; has thought Rochefoucauld his favourite, ii. 343; Pope reproaches him on his bitterness against man, ii. 333; S. and *la bagatelle*, ii. 384, iii. 98; has never practised mere civility, ii. 408; oppression tortures him, iii. 492; posterity will be monsters, iv. 44–45; — on the evils of patronage, ii. 153; poets are not good flatterers, ii. 153–4; on genius and friendship, ii. 199; a bad poet is a public enemy to mankind, iii. 21; Swift's appetite for having works dedicated to him, iii. 203 n.; — on the decline of his talents (1729), iii. 22; fortune forsakes one as age takes over, iii. 28; his facility in writing declines, thanks to a lonely life, iii. 93; imagination and judgement cease to agree (1731), iii. 221; — is vain of the condescension of the Queensberrys to him, iii. 252; his creative powers decline, iii. 293; is as fit for matrimony as for invention, iv. 4; incapable of revising his writing, iv. 240; at his age, so says Mrs. Whiteway, 'people can hear no reason', iv. 277; S. thinks of death constantly, iii. 368, v. 11.

SWIFT, JONATHAN (*cont.*)

Swift's politics: his political career and views summarized, ii. 64–72; is said to persuade Pope to write against Whigs, i. 229; jokes about 'Whig' and 'Tory', i. 358, ii. 69; regrets he could not reconcile Bolingbroke and Oxford, ii. 67; tried to intervene with Tories for Whig friends, ii. 67; — is for annual parliaments, ii. 70, against standing armies, ii. 70; suggests a quarterly Political Catechism, ii. 71; is against any suspension of *habeas corpus*, ii. 70; is for the landed classes, ii. 70; against South Sea and Funds, ii. 70; — his friends are called traitors, ii. 198; the political temper in England is bitter, ii. 426; the present reign shamefully forgets its early promises, iii. 28; his hero was always Bolingbroke, never Oxford, iii. 63; is cured of Irish politics by despair, iii. 93; a change of government thought possible, iii. 97; S. would like to help drive Walpole out of office, iii. 98; would summon the Dictator (Bolingbroke) from the plough, iii. 99; Carteret talks favourably of S., iii. 145, 151; — S. pictures himself as expecting nothing since 1714 and so content, iii. 152; the desolation and beggary in Ireland, iii. 182, v. 17; is strong for the Test Act, iv. 4; in Ireland there are no young patriots, iv. 12–13; is against tyranny, ii. 71, 72, v. 14; S.'s bad opinion of Courts and Ministers of State, ii. 68, 344, 461, 484, v. 16; — caustic on the taste of a Court that makes Cibber laureate, iii. 192; S.'s outcry against corruption, iii. 80, 98–99, iv. 56, 57, 77; he hates power, v. 16; S. should now, Pope thinks, be above all parties, ii. 412–13; he is too old to change, 419, 497; Pope thinks S. now is above parties, iii. 250; S. rejoices that bad government brings virtuous persons together, iii. 251; S., Pope thinks, is the only patriot not hated for serving his country, iii. 384.

Swift's Works: he is pleased that Pope wishes him to record their friendship in verse, iii. 30; S.'s conception of proper materials for poetry,

SWIFT, JONATHAN (*cont.*)

iii. 72–73; on poets as creators, iii. 73; — says he writes follies — and burns them, iii. 161; complains of English trash in verse and prose, badly written, iv. 77; is absolutely done with poetry: his best verses only trifles, iv. 115; years ago burnt most of his writings, iv. 240; is (1734) done with writing, except letters, a few, iii. 438; — his collected *Works* (4 vols. 1735), iii. 366, 369; S.'s aloofness to Faulkner's project, iii. 369, 377–8, v. 12; Pope eager to receive the vol., iii. 429, 433; Pope wishes to have a vol. of *selected* pieces by S., iv. 259; — the Pope–Swift *Miscellanies*: Motte's slow payments, iii. 92; the involvement with Bowyer over copyright assignments, iii. 321, 323; S. is pleased that Pope approves his pieces for the *Miscellanies*, ii. 419; — urges Pope to revise them, ii. 420; Pope asks if *Cadenus and Vanessa* is to go into the *Miscellanies*, ii. 425, 438; S., so Pope says, wishes Prior's *Jinny* to appear in the *Miscellanies*, ii. 466; S. must be consulted (?1729) before the size of vol. iii of the *Miscellanies* can be determined, iii. 8; S. will send verses for the 1732 vol., but Pope must correct them, iii. 162, 291–2; the prose pieces by S. in the 1732 vol., iii. 292; the poems, iii. 293 n.

Individual pieces: S.'s fondness for his *Riddles*, ii. 420; the 'family jests' written at Market Hill, not for publication, iii. 22, 292–3; arrests due to the publication of the *Epistle to a Lady . . . in the Heroick Style*, iii. 401, 402, 405 n.; *Bounce to Fop* ascribed to S., iv. 1; 'To Mr. Gay on his being Steward to . . . Queensbery', iii. 180; S.'s 'Journal of a Dublin [Modern] Lady', iii. 22; — the 'Libel on Dr. Delany' embarrasses Pope, iii. 85, 90; it is taken by C. Caesar as an attack on S., iii. 149; its eulogy of Pope, iii. 107, 362, iv. 337 n.; — S. disowns 'The Life and Genuine Character of Dr. Swift', iii. 367–8, 432, v. 10–11; 'Pandora' in *The Grub-street Journal* thought to be S.'s, iii. 173; S. thinks lightly of 'Sir Ralph the Patriot' (not

SWIFT, JONATHAN (*cont.*)

his), iii. 22; S.'s verses upon the accidents (1726) to his four friends in England ('Upon four dismal stories'), ii. 408–9; 'On Poetry', ii. 154 n., iii. 401; 'Verses on the Death of Dr. Swift', iii. 251, iv. 130 n.

Swift's Prose Works: Directions to Servants, iii. 293, 438–9; fears it will never be completed, iii. 439 n., iv. 240; *Drapier's Letters*, iii. 80, 108, 219 n.; *Journal to Stella* cited, i. 437 n., 439 n.; — *Gulliver's Travels*, 'the most trifling subjects', ii. 199; Ford talks about *Gulliver* to Pope, ii. 321; the book is completed, ii. 325; its theme is man as *rationis capax*, ii. 325; the book is published after S. leaves for Ireland, ii. 357, 400 n., 409; on its early reception: *see under* Arbuthnot, Gay, Pope, Queen Caroline, Sarah, Duchess of Marlborough, Lord Harcourt, Bolingbroke, B. Motte; — Arbuthnot tells of forthcoming poems about *Gulliver*, ii. 411, 417; S. recounts early critiques of *Gulliver*, ii. 417; complains that the text has been mangled, ii. 417, 418; R. Sympson's letter in *Gulliver*, ii. 418 n.; — a Gulliver lost his case for lying at Salisbury assizes, ii. 441, 491; S. still coy about admitting authorship of *Gulliver*, ii. 468 n.; is pleased with Jonathan Gulliver of New England, ii. 491; wishes Motte to send his balance to Dublin, iii. 23; Capt. Gulliver ruined by winning a suit with costs, iii. 249; quoted by Pope, iv. 497; — S.'s *History of the Four Last Years*, incomplete, ii. 65, iii. 439; completed, ii. 187 n.; sent in MS. to Lord Oxford, ii. 387; when transcribed, it is to go to Daniel Pulteney, ii. 502; the *History* and *Gulliver* thought to be money-makers, iv. 240; — 'The Holyhead Journal', ii. 468; *The Intelligencer*, iii. 22, 292; *Polite Conversation*, may never be completed, iii. 439; S. at work on it, iii. 219, 293; *Proposal for the Use of Irish Manufactures*, ii. 65, 66; Pope wishes S. would finish some of his 'tracts', iii. 445, iv. 240; — S., at Letcombe, said in joke to be working

SWIFT, JONATHAN (*cont.*)
on the *Memoirs of Scriblerus,* i. 231;
Some Free Thoughts, ii. 64 n., 65; S.'s
Vindication of Lord Carteret, iii. 108;
S.'s project of writing Robert Harley's life, ii. 374 n.; approves the project of *Works of the Unlearned,* i. 195;
— his 'great designs' all in prose, ii.
311; complains of ascription of
others' works to him, ii. 67; is reported by Pope to intend writing
penny story-books of the good men
of the age, iii. 228; is thought the
author of a pamphlet about Richard
Norton's will, iii. 432; a 'Memorial'
by S. printed in *Mist's Weekly Journal,*
ii. 493.
    Swift's reading: he quotes *Don
Quixote,* iii. 21, 251; Cicero, ii. 68–69,
310, iii. 220; Graevius and Gronovius, iii. 29 n.; Horace, *Odes,* ii. 152,
153, iii. 148, 303; Horace, *Epistles,* ii.
152, 311, 453, iii. 303, iv. 44; Horace,
Satires, i. 358, ii. 493, iii. 190, 191;
Plautus, iii. 251; thinks the Wife of
Bath may be in Shakespeare, iii. 72;
subscribes grudgingly to Thuanus,
iii. 73; approves an anonymous piece,
Conversation, iv. 73; quotes the
epitaph of Fulke Greville, iii. 30.
Swinburne, Sir John (3rd Bt.), iv. 464.
Swinburne, Mary (Englefield), Lady
(wife of the 2nd Bt.), aunt of Teresa
and Martha Blount, i. 327, iii. 91 n.
Swinburne, Sir William (2nd Bt.), i.
327 n.
Sydney, Robert, 4th Earl of Leicester, i.
94 n.
Sykins (or Sican), Mrs., a Dublin poet
introduced to Pope by Swift, iii. 89,
101, 107.
Symonds, E. M., cited on Lady Mary
Wortley Montagu, ii. 21, 197.
Sympson, Richard, ostensible publisher
of *Gulliver,* ii. 412 n., 418.

T—, Lord [?Tyrconnel], iii. 162.
T., P., *see* 'P. T.'
Tacitus, iii. 89 n., 420.
Talbot, Miss (or Mrs.), falls into the
Thames with Pope, iv. 28 n.
Talbot, Adelhida, dau. of the Marquis
of Palleotti, and Duchess of Shrews-
bury, i. 278.

Talbot, Charles, only Duke of Shrews-
bury: a friend of Pope's, i. 306, 417;
his opinion of Blenheim, i. 432; Pope
gave him his 'Prayer to God' *c.* 1715,
iv. 31; a projected visit to his former
estate, iv. 347.
Talbot, Charles, 1st Lord, Lord Chan-
cellor, iii. 436 n.
Talbot, William, 2nd Lord (cr. Earl
Talbot, 1761), iv. 335.
Talbot, William, Bishop of Durham, ii.
269; earlier of Sarum, i. 286.
Tallemant, Abbé, iv. 425.
Tallow, Dr., of Marston (Somerset), iv.
508.
Tanner, Mr., i. 340, 443.
Tasso, Torquato, i. 18, 19.
Tate, Nahum (and Brady), i. 307, 326.
Taylor, Mr. (? overseer at Binfield), i.
524.
Taylor, Mr. (lawyer), iii. 59.
Taylor, Jeremy, i. 277.
Taylor, Jo (clerk of Bridewell), ii. 483.
Taylor, John G., iv. 456 n.
Taylor, Dr. Robert, iv. 236 n.
Taylor, William, bookseller, ii. 218 n.,
222.
Tedbury (Glos.), iv. 84.
Teem, Mr., iv. 354.
Tempest, Miss, i. 22.
Tempest, Mr., London agent for Caryll,
i. 414, 518.
Temple, Anne (Halsey), Viscountess
Cobham, iii. 216, iv. 185.
TEMPLE, Sir RICHARD, Viscount Cob-
ham: letters from, iii. 391, 393; Pope
says he has written to C. three letters
in 10 years, iii. 474; C. is the uncle of
Gilbert West and G. Lyttelton, iii.
244; subscribes to Buononcini, ii. 99;
Pope's visits to Stowe, ii. 257, 302, 310,
314, 388, 510 n., iii. 244, 375, iv.
179 (Pope usually goes to Stowe every
summer, he says), 404 n.; C. dines
with Pope and Mrs. Howard, iii. 377;
dines with Pope and Argyle and
Marchmont, iv. 341; Gay calls on C.,
ii. 324; C.'s witticism about *The
Beggar's Opera,* ii. 474; the moral of
Congreve's 'Letter' to C. distasteful
to Swift, iii. 29; after Excise C. is in
the Opposition, iii. 339; Pope wrote
to C. about Lord Bathurst, iii. 503;
C. met Warburton, iv. 239 n.; March-

TEMPLE, Sir RICHARD (*cont.*)
mont rivals C. as gardener, iv. 459;
C. reads Pope's Preface to Shakespeare, ii. 279; Pope's *Epistle to Cobham,* iv. 158 n., 339 n., 504.

Temple, Sir William: his three wishes,
ii. 522 n., iii. 53, 62, 291; he is quoted
by Swift, iv. 12.

Tenby (Wales), iii. 422, iv. 450.

Tenison, Mrs., becomes Mrs. Delany
(1732), iii. 304.

Tenison, Edward, Bishop of Ossory,
iii. 162 n.

Terence (Publius Terentius Afer),
comic poet, i. 492, ii. 487.

Tessier (or Teissier), Dr., iv. 395–6.

Thanet, Mary (Savile), Countess of, iv.
212.

Theatres: to close in royal mourning
(1708), i. 53; Haymarket called vic-
torious, i. 71; Drury Lane silenced, i.
71–72.

Theobald, Lewis: his ed. of Wycherley,
i. 32 n., 86 n., 147 n., iii. 59; helped
write the *Compleat Key to the What-
d'ye-Call-It,* i. 288 n; attacks Pope in
Mist's *Journal,* ii. 486; — is considered a candidate for the laurel, iii.
151; his Shakespeare would have been
published even if not taken by Tonson, iii. 242, 243; possibly helped on
the life of Gay for the *General Dictionary,* iv. 38 n.; Hill reproaches Pope
for his bias against T. in the *Bathos,*
iv. 100, 102.

Theocritus, i. 101, 116.

Thirlby, Styan, of Jesus College, Cambridge, i. 496 n., 497.

Thistleworth (the Earl of Chesterfield),
iv. 420.

Thomas, Elizabeth: called 'Sappho' or
'Corinna', i. 57 n., ii. 440; she sells the
Pope–Cromwell letters to Curll, i. 139
n., ii. 437, 439 n.; she conceals her
whereabouts, ii. 438; her story concerning the Cromwell letters, ii. 437–
8, iii. 458–9.

Thomas, Moy: his ed. (with Lord
Wharncliffe) of Lady Mary Wortley
Montagu's *Works* (1861) cited, i. 460,
469, ii. 83 n.

Thomas, Timothy, chaplain to the 2nd
Earl of Oxford, ii. 364, iii. 187,
193.

Thompson (or Thomson), Dr.: Pope's
last physician, iv. 499 n.; he is recommended by Bethel, iv. 512; he
becomes Pope's doctor, iv. 514, 521;
his severe regimen for Pope, iv. 522.

Thompson, Aaron, his translation of
Geoffrey of Monmouth, i. 425.

Thompson, Francis, cited on the date of
a letter, iii. 341 n.

Thomson, Dr., *see* Thompson.

Thomson, James: uses the episode of the
Stanton Harcourt lovers in *Summer,*
i. 479; his *Sophonisba,* iii. 86; Pope has
not recently heard from him, iii. 158;
Dr. Johnson's story of an Epistle
from Pope to T., iii. 226 n.; — Pope
will not do an epilogue for *Edward
and Eleonora,* iv. 132; the play is not
licensed, iv. 145; only two acts of it
written, iv. 151; the play is taken to
Covent Garden, iv. 151 n., 166, 167;
Hill suggests improvements in T.'s
Agamemnon, iv. 146, 152; Pope sends
good wishes to T., iv. 210; T. tries to
help Savage, iv. 418.

Thomson, K., her ed. of the *Memoirs of
Viscountess Sundon* cited, iii. 132 n.

Thornhill, Thomas (or Richard), i.
298.

Thorold, Sir George, ii. 16.

Thorold, Thomas, tobacconist, i. 82,
117, 134.

Thorpe, Thomas (antiquarian bookseller *c.* 1833), iv. 81, 254, 489.

Thory, Mr., partner or employee of
Fortescue, iii. 129, 139, 198, 283.

Thou, Jacques Auguste de, *see* Thuanus.

Thuanisi's, Kent and B. Fairfax dine
there, iv. 150.

Thuanns, keeps a dinner, Kent says, iv.
163.

Thuanus, Buckley's fine ed. of the *History,* ii. 471, 529 n., iii. 70 n., 73 n.

Thucydides, ii. 219.

Thurston, Mr. (Master in Chancery),
iii. 7.

Thurston, Joseph, a poet, friend to
Broome, iii. 24.

Thynne, Thomas, 1st Viscount Weymouth, i. 261 n.

Tiberius, ii. 483.

Tibullus, i. 173, 369, v. 3.

Tichborne, Sir Henry, i. 313 n., 464.

Tickell, R. E., ii. 157.

Tickell, Thomas: his 'Phaenix', i. 109; his verses in *Spectator* No. 532, i. 157; the subscription for his Lucan, i. 262; his *Iliad*, Book I, i. 196; critics on it, i. 294, 296, 299, 305, 306, 423; it is called a specimen in preparation for a translation of the *Odyssey*, i. 296; a copy of T.'s *Iliad* annotated by Pope is at Hartlebury, i. 296 n.; — T. is Addison's executor, i. 139; Pope (1723) inquires as to T.'s intention with the *Odyssey*, ii. 158, 159, 164; T.'s ed. of Addison's *Works*, i. 264 n., ii. 88 n.; T. and Pope are reconciled, ii. 223 n., iv. 3 n.; T. has a good 'place' in Ireland, ii. 326; brings a letter from Budgell to Swift, iii. 163; called a follower of Addison, iii. 191 n.; is concerned (1736) to hear that Pope is ill, iv. 3.

Tidcombe, John, Major-General: mentioned as a Whig, i. 26, 27; as Major-General, i. 109; as a man of pleasure, i. 47; as sad over the death of Prince George of Denmark, i. 53; as rough, rude or nasty, i. 56, 71, 79; as a patron of nonsense, i. 185, 202; values Pope's atheistical jests, i. 269; is popular at Will's, i. 288, 290; Pope sends service to, i. 43, 48, 68.

Tighe, Richard, iii. 292.

Tillard, John, iv. 404 n.

Tillotson, Geoffrey, i. 151 n., ii. 90 n., iv. 65 n.

Tillotson, John, Archbishop of Canterbury, iv. 278.

Times Literary Supplement, iv. 91 n.

Timothy, Sir (? nickname), iv. 381, 382, 412.

Tipping, H. Avray, iv. 125 n., 149 n., 162 n.

Tiverton (Devon), iii. 504 n.

Tofts, Mary (the rabbit woman), ii. 403 n., 418.

Tom the water fool (Swift's name for Pope's Bowry ?), ii. 407.

Tomlinson, Col., iv. 475.

TONSON, JACOB, sr. (1656 ?–1736): letters to, iii. 243, 290, 513; letters from to Pope, i. 17; from T. to his nephew (Jacob II), iii. 269; the youthful Pope has been in T.'s shop, i. 17; T. a notable publisher, i. 26, 52; publishes Pope's *Pastorals*, i. 50;

TONSON, JACOB, sr. (*cont.*) publication delayed, i. 51; has grown rich from poetry, i. 61; — his *Miscellaneous Poems* VI, i. 56, 60, 62, 102–6; his printer spoken of, i. 128; Pope's pieces in T.'s (Steele's) miscellany (1714), i. 191 n.; Parnell also contributes, i. 195; T. agrees with Tickell for the entire *Iliad*, i. 196 n.; — agrees with Pope as to all copyrights, i. 191–2; was to have published a miscellany for A. Philips, i. 276; refuses to have Tickell's *Iliad* I reprinted with three other translations, i. 298; visits Cambridge, i. 372; his good social standing envied by Lintot, i. 372; is a cautious man, i. 406; goes to Prior's house to talk of Prior's *Poems*, i. 521; — would like to see Pope attack Bentley's Milton, iii. 269; T.'s character in old age, iii. 176; is to dine as a 'phenomenon' with Pope *et al.* (1731), iii. 178; Lords Oxford and Bathurst with Pope and Gay dine with T. at Barnes, iii. 185; is asked for data on the 'Man of Ross', iii. 244; — Pope urges him to call at Cirencester when returning to London, iii. 244; lives at Ledbury, iii. 243 n.; T. sr. is 80 when his nephew (52) dies, iii. 513; Pope wishes to talk with him about a difficulty with the deceased nephew, iii. 513; T.'s deafness, iii. 513; Knapton is to approach T. about a new ed. of Shakespeare, iv. 417.

TONSON, JACOB II (1683 ?–1735), nephew to the preceding, whose partner he was: letters to, ii. 63, 80, 117, 118, 130, 213, 215, 217, 222, 282, 285, 288, 424, iii. 241, 243, 399; letters from him to Pope, i. 191, ii. 7, 211, 222, 279, iii. 242, 244; one letter from his uncle to Jacob II, iii. 269; he forgets a book Pope wanted, ii. 7; is invited to Twickenham, ii. 63, 117, 118, 223; the copyrights on Shakespeare and Milton, ii. 124; owns a Milton MS., ii. 124; T.'s connexion with the Duke of Buckingham's *Works*, ii. 158, 211; — does not wish to contract for the *Odyssey*, ii. 214; advises on paper for the *Odyssey*, ii. 217; Broome sends copy for the

TONSON, JACOB II (*cont.*)
Odyssey in care of T., ii. 264; his payments to Pope for editing Shakespeare, ii. 81; asks Pope for copy, ii. 212; sends back Pope's Preface to Shakespeare but wishes it returned soon, ii. 279–80; corrects the title-page of the ed., ii. 282; — publishes Fenton's *Mariamne*, ii. 145; kept a letter for Fenton too long, ii. 384; has a project of a translation of Virgil by Fenton and Broome, ii. 429; Fenton uses T. as a town address, ii. 486; forgot to send Pope the copy of Waller expected, ii. 80; has (Fenton says) a 'money-catching hand', ii. 234; wants Fenton to edit Waller, ii. 244; a copy of Fenton's ed. for Broome, iii. 37; — T. publishes Arbuthnot's *Tables* (1727), ii. 401, 424–5; explains why he publishes Theobald's Shakespeare, iii. 242; Pope expects T. to protect him from any slander from Theobald in the ed., iii. 243; T.'s fear of a vanishing copyright, iii. 242–3; — T. will consult Pope in reprinting any of Pope's pieces, iii. 245; T. sends an extraordinary reply to a simple letter (missing) from Pope, iii. 482; the death of Jacob II (Nov. 1735), iii. 513; has no copyright in Pope's early works, iv. 223–4; claims to copyrights in Shakespeare are vanishing, iv. 439.

Tooke, Benjamin (d. 1716): account of, i. 284; goes to Ireland, i. 284, ii. 154.

TOOKER, JAMES: letter to, v. 3–4; account of, v. 3 n.; he translated an elegy from Tibullus, v. 3–4; a friend of Pope and Caryll, i. 189; writes verses on Fort Knocke, v. 3.

Torbay, seat of Edward Blount, ii. 176.

Tottenham (Wilts.), seat of Lord Bruce, visited by Pope, iii. 417–18, iv. 14.

Toulon, the siege of, i. 28.

Tourreil, Jacques de, i. 275.

Towers, John, iii. 219, 439.

TOWNE, Dr. Richard: letter to, ii. 424; Pope owes him for service, ii. 424.

Townley (pseud.), ii. 144.

Townshend, Charles, 2nd Viscount, i. 217, ii. 269; Secretary of State, ii. 285 n.; allows visitors to Atterbury

Townshend, Charles (*cont.*)
in the Tower, ii. 173 n.; subscribes to the *Odyssey* (10 sets), ii. 276; Pope thanks him, ii. 286; possibly mentioned as 'Lord T—', iii. 162 n.; retired after 1730, iii. 498 n.

Townshend, Charles, Lord Lynn, later 3rd Viscount Townshend, ii. 182 n.

Trapp, Joseph, i. 105, 106.

Travels through Denmark (1707), cited, i. 75 n.

Treby, Sir George, i. 78 n.

Trefusis, Robert, ii. 488.

Tregaskis Catalogue, i. 165.

Trenqualéon, Max de, cited on the Carylls, i. 93 n.

Trent, Council of, ii. 221.

Trevor, Thomas, 1st Baron Trevor, ii. 287, iv. 65 n.

Tripoli, Countess of (and Jeffrey Rudel), i. 440–1.

Tripsack, Mr., a priest in Essex, iii. 218.

Trombold, —, *see* Trumbull, Sir W.

Trowbridge, Hoyt, i. 229 n.

Trumbold, Sir Wm., *see* Trumbull, Sir W.

Trumbull, Lady Judith (Alexander), dau. of the Earl of Stirling and 2nd wife of Sir William Trumbull, ii. 119 n.; Fenton is tutor to her son, i. 275 n., ii. 204, 208, 302; she expects Southerne (1724) for a visit at Easthampstead, ii. 234.

TRUMBULL, Sir WILLIAM: letters to, i. 176, 212, 281, 323; letters from, i. 10, 17, 45, 212, 281, 327; a letter to Caryll printed as if to Sir W. (1735), i. 174, 176; Sir W. approved of Dryden as a man, i. 2; Pope's note on Sir W., i. 10, 328 n.; his second marriage, i. 70; — values Pope's conversation, i. 17; reads Pope's Pastorals in MS., i. 17; mentions Pope's visit to Walsh at Abberley, i. 29; his diffident comment on Pope's 'Sarpedon', i. 45; urges Pope to translate Homer, i. 45; wishes to see Pope's translation of Statius, i. 77; praises *The Rape of the Lock*, i. 212; — urges Pope to avoid taverns, i. 212; is glad the *Iliad* subscription is a success, i. 212; thanks Pope for *The Temple of Fame*, i. 281–2; regrets Pope's absence all the winter, i. 282; uses Pope's imitation of

TRUMBULL, Sir WILLIAM (*cont.*)
Martial, i. 328; his connexion with *Windsor Forest*, i. 328 n.; — Pope's farewell to Sir W., i. 337; his epitaph for Sir W., i. 133 n.; Jervas paints the Trumbull family, i. 227, 282, 296; Sir W. interprets the 8th Enigma of Pythagoras, i. 327–8; he complains of the bitter weather, i. 328; his anecdote of Charles I, i. 75; Wycherley sends his service to Sir W. frequently, i. 54 ff., *passim*, to 85; the death of Sir W., i. 337 n.; later Fenton dies at Sir W.'s seat in Berkshire, iii. 325.

Trumbull, William, son of Sir William: Fenton is his tutor, i. 119 n.; he is accompanied to Cambridge by Sir Clement Cottrell and Fenton, ii. 377; W. intends (1728) to spend three months in Twickenham, ii. 486; his estate in bad shape, iii. 100; he gives Fenton's effects to Fenton's brothers, iii. 156.

Tucker, Gertrude: niece of Ralph Allen, spoken of (?) as 'Mrs. Gatty', iv. 432 n.; marries (1746) Warburton, iv. 448 n.

Tudway, Thomas, famous as a punster, ii. 380.

Tully, *see* Cicero.

Tunbridge Wells (Kent): Pope goes there with the Duke of Buckingham (1720), ii. 48; Gay (1723) is there, ii. 181; Cleland, Arbuthnot, and Sarah, Duchess of Marlborough (1730) there, iii. 126.

Turkish Spy, The, ii. 355.

Turnebus, Adrianus, i. 25.

Turnham Green, iv. 349.

Turrick (Bucks.), *see* Thomas Edwards, iv. 352.

Tuscany, Duke of, ii. 394.

Twickenham: Pope's villa chosen before 3 Feb. 1718–19, ii. 2; Atterbury visits Pope there, ii. 109, 115, 116; Pope's neighbours, ii. 117; the Twickenham Coach leaves from the White Horse Inn, iv. 506; — for residents of Twickenham mentioned in the letters *see* Rev. Penyston Booth, R. Cambridge, James Craggs, the Earl and Countess of Denbigh, Mr. — Hutchins (Fenton's Twickenham landlord), James Johnstone, Sir

Twickenham (*cont.*)
Godfrey Kneller, Lady Mary and Mr. Wortley Montagu, Robert Morris, Henry, 2nd Earl of Radnor, Thomas Reeves, the Countess of Seaforth, Thomas Stonor, Thomas Vernon (of Twickenham Park), Robert Vyner, Daniel Waterland, D.D., Thomas, Earl of Strafford, Mrs. Whitworth (her tomb).

Tycho Brahe, i. 104, 105.

Tyrconnel, Viscount, *see* Brownlow, John.

Tyrrel, General, iv. 473.

Ulrick, Mr., 'the Young Turk', iii. 503 n.

Universal Magazine, The, iv. 389.

Universal Museum, The, i. 436 n.

Universal Spectator, The: tells of Queensberry's departure (1729) for Scotland, with Gay, iii. 36 n.; Gay's success against piracies of *Polly*, iii. 37 n.; its early announcement of *One Epistle*, iii. 59 n.; — Eusden's death tardily announced, iii. 143 n.; the death of John Roberts, father of the Major, iii. 233 n.; Lord Petre's marriage, iii. 284; on the disposition of Atterbury's papers, &c., iii. 296; on Mrs. Pope's funeral, iii. 374 n.

Upton, John, iii. 86 n.

Ursines, Princesse des, a parallel for Mrs. Howard, ii. 461.

V—, Madam, has first claim on the services of A. Schutz, iv. 188.

Valterie, Abbé, his prose translation of the *Iliad*, i. 225, 492.

Vanbrugh, Sir John: mentioned as architect, i. 71 n.; his plays have bad priests, i. 106.

VANDEPUT, Sir PETER: a letter from him, ii. 232; 'Welsted's lie' thought connected with Lady Vandeput, ii. 232 n.

VAN DER BEMPDEN, Mr.: letter to, i. 325; he considers purchase of Mrs. Pope's rent-charge, i. 325, ii. 5 n.

Vanderpoel, H. B., ii. 37 n., 72.

Vandiest, Johan: some painting by him planned for Pope's grotto, iv. 340, 343; he works for Allen and Prior Park, iv. 13, 23, 195; he paints a fine portrait of N. Hooke, iv. 239;

Vandiest, Johan (*cont.*)
does statues for Allen's library, iv. 247, 253; he is soon to visit Wid-combe and view his works there, iv. 340, 343, 360.

Van Lennep, W., ii. 523.

Vanloo, Jean Baptiste, paints a portrait of Pope, iv. 500, 512.

Vanneck, Sir Joshua, thought of buying Dawley, iv. 136, 148.

Vatia, Servilius, symbol of ignoble re-tirement, ii. 252 n., iii. 413.

Vaughan, Mr., chairmaker employed by Pope, iv. 361.

Vaughan, John, 3rd Earl of Carbury, iii. 215.

Vernon, Sir Charles, interested in an offer for Pope's villa, iv. 467.

Vernon, Admiral Edward: news of him from the West Indies awaited, iv. 339; his busto commissioned by Sarah, Duchess of Marlborough, iv. 421.

VERNON, THOMAS, Pope's landlord: letter from, ii. 15; he will take Pope visiting, ii. 15; mentioned as land-lord, ii. 82; brings news of Lord Harcourt, ii. 126; trouble over Mrs. Howard's road, ii. 259, v. 5; Mrs. Howard wants more of his land, ii. 323; his death (1726), iv. 421 n.

Vernon, Mrs. Thomas: subscribes to Buononcini, ii. 99; wishes an exces-sive payment from Mrs. Howard, ii. 446; wishes to eject Mrs. Howard from some land, iii. 34; her death in 1742 makes Pope's villa for sale, iv. 387, 433, 446, 467; on the trouble with Mrs. Howard *see* v. 5, 19.

Verses address'd to the Imitator of Horace, see Lady Mary Wortley Montagu *and* John, Lord Hervey.

Vertue, George: engraves Swift and Pope, i. 262; engraves Jervas's por-trait of Pope, i. 310; he engraved the Stratford monument for Pope's ed. of Shakespeare, ii. 280 n.; his *Notebooks* cited, ii. 18, 242, 298, iv. 80.

Verrio, Antonio, iii. 268.

Vida, Marcus Hieronymus, i. 23, 317 n., ii. 383.

Vienna, Treaty of (1735), iii. 503 n.

Villette, Marquise de (2nd wife of Lord Bolingbroke): is about to visit Eng-land (1724), ii. 221; in London, ii.

Villette, Marquise de (*cont.*)
249; values Pope's conversation, ii. 249; writes Swift a long letter, ii. 427; is ill (1728) at Dawley, ii. 478; goes to Aix la Chapelle (1729), iii. 21; — Swift plans a gift of usquebaugh to her, ii. 482; he regrets her ill health, iii. 28; she will regret that at her return to England Swift is not there, iii. 50; in France, not well, iii. 103; her re-turn to England longed for by Bolingbroke, iii. 139 n., 163; though frail she would gladly nurse Swift at Dawley, iii. 184; she has a new promising remedy, iii. 214; Swift much concerned for her health, iii. 293; her life near Fontainebleau (1739), iv. 177; is a friend of the Countess of Denbigh, iv. 397 n.

Villiers, George, Duke of Buckingham, author of *The Rehearsal*, i. 26.

Villiers, William, 2nd Earl of Jersey, i. 411.

Vincent, Mother (unidentified), iii. 217.

Vincent Howard, P., i. 70, 328.

Virgil (Publius Virgilius Maro): his arrival at Rome, i. 508; Pope and the youthful V. compared, i. 7; V. was a borrower, i. 20; suits sound to sense, i. 23, 107, 109; is supreme in versifica-tion, i. 37, 44; — Dryden's transla-tion criticized, i. 102, 124; V. goes well in the blank verse of Trapp, i. 105; his debt to Homer, i. 192; Pope's Elzevir V., i. 372, ii. 336 n.; Atterbury compares V. with Milton, i. 452; French translation by F. Catrou, ii. 79; both Whigs and Tories read V., ii. 199; — Pope should avoid V.'s error in giving Maevius fame, ii. 343, 349; Gay reads V., ii. 410; Tonson considers a translation by Broome and Fenton, ii. 433; Caxton's Preface to be in *The Dun-ciad Variorum*, ii. 498; V. exemplifies the rythmus, iii. 140; he was once an Opposition poet, iii. 420; Atterbury's *Iapis*, iv. 55 n.; the *Culex* cited by Pope, i. 103, 376; the *Eclogues*: Cromwell advised to read one daily, i. 116; Steele thinks the *Pollio* inferior to Pope's *Messiah*, i. 146; — the *Eclogues* quoted by Pope, i. 28, 337, ii. 13, 190, 293, iii. 118; by Atter-

Virgil (*cont.*)
bury, i. 503, ii. 76, 123; by Edward
Blount, i. 338; by Broome, ii. 77; by
Fenton, iii. 55; the *Georgics* quoted
by Pope, i. 167, 411; by Atterbury,
ii. 123; by Bolingbroke, ii. 219; by
Cromwell, i. 96; by Lady Mary
Wortley Montagu, i. 397; by Swift,
iii. 99; — the *Aeneid* quoted by Pope,
i. 122, 317, 453, 464, 466, ii. 24, 302,
364, 380, 465, 532, iii. 118, 142, 255,
iv. 448, 521; quoted by Atterbury, ii.
74; by Lord Bathurst, i. 488; by
Mather Byles, ii. 495; by Fenton, ii.
487, 518, iii. 44; by Lady Mary
Wortley Montagu, i. 412; by Swift,
iii. 99; by Sir W. Trumbull, i. 212,
328.
Virgil the Magician's Life engrosses Lord
Oxford, iii. 187.
Vitruvius (Marcus Vitruvius Pollio), i.
45, ii. 44.
Voiture, Vincent, i. 1; imitated in
Pope's letters, i. 4 n.; cited by
Wycherley, i. 34, 53; *Pour le moins*
quoted, i. 89; *Ou vous savez* imitated by Pope, i. 90, 98, 129; V.'s
letters, Pope thinks, are artificial, ii.
41; so also Swift thinks, but he likes
them, iii. 92, 505; also Bolingbroke,
iii. 102; four of V.'s letters ascribed
to Pope by Curll, iii. 487; Pope's
alleged borrowings from V., iii. 495.
Volkra, Count, i. 363.
VOLTAIRE: a letter from, ii. 399; he is
spoken of as Bolingbroke's 'imagination', ii. 221–2; his *Mariamne*, ii. 222,
354; *La Ligue* discussed by Pope, ii.
228–9; Pope's notion of V.'s religion,
ii. 229; *La Henriade* published in
England, ii. 354 n.; he writes to
Pope condoling over the cut hand
(1726), ii. 399; Gay tells General
Dormer about V., ii. 416; V. dis-
credited Pope's letter to L. Racine, iv.
416 n.; is a friend of Dr. Towne, ii.
424 n.
Vossius, Gerhard Johann, ii. 487.
Vyner, Charles J., cited on the family, i.
476 n.
VYNER, M. (Mrs. R.), letter from, i. 476.
VYNER, R.: letter from, i. 476, inviting
Pope to call and see Miss Marriot, i.
476.

W—, Mr., lives near Holm Lacy, ii.
240.
W—y, Lady, became a great-grand-
mother last week, iii. 434.
Wade, George, General and (1743)
Field Marshal, father of the 1st Mrs.
Ralph Allen, iv. 68 n.; his special
copy of Pope's *Letters* (1737), iv.
68, 74; made Field Marshal, iv.
490; he might help young Thomas
Hooke get into the army, iv. 353,
357–8.
Waghorne, John, in Swift's choir, ii.
483.
Wake, William, Archbishop of Canter-
bury, ii. 269.
Waldegrave, Sir James, 2nd Baron and
(later) 1st Earl, i. 282.
Wales, Prince of (later George II) and
Princess (later Queen Caroline), enjoy
the *What-d'ye-Call-It*, i. 282–3. *See
also under* George II *and* Caroline,
Queen; *also under* Frederick, Prince
of W—.
Wales, famous for oysters, iv. 450.
Walker, Tom, actor, iv. 124.
Waller, Edmund, poet: quoted by
Pope, i. 23, 107, 147; quoted by
Atterbury, i. 503 n., ii. 84; Fenton's
ed. (1729), ii. 80 n., 213, 244, 278,
339; his verse Dedication, ii. 398;
Fenton quotes W. on 'monsters', ii.
488; the ed. published, iii. 24; the
plates wrought off too late, iii. 55.
Waller, Edmund, M.D., of St. John's,
ii. 449 n.
Walpole, Mrs., i. 364, iii. 39.
Walpole, Catherine (Shorter), Lady, 1st
wife of Sir Robert: Pope to act concerning her laver, iii. 140.
Walpole, Lady Mary, natural dau. of
Sir Robert; marries Charles Churchill
(1746), iv. 124 n.
Walpole, Horace (1717–97), son of Sir
Robert: his letters cited, ii. 56 n., iv.
167 n., 348 n.
Walpole, Horatio (or Horace, 1678–
1757), 1st Baron Walpole of Wolter-
ton, brother of Sir Robert: he comes
to see Vernon's land that Mrs. Howard
wants, ii. 323; mentioned as govern-
ing France, ii. 444; Pope's thanks to
him delayed by illness of Mrs. Pope,
iii. 6; mentioned, iv. 124.

Walpole, Sir Robert: Pope urged to praise him in his next Preface as he did Bolingbroke in 1715, i. 300; Sir R.'s eldest son looking for a wife, ii. 183 n.; Pulteney and Bolingbroke join in Opposition, ii. 247 n.; — Sir R. subscribes for 10 sets of the *Odyssey*, ii. 276; has done Pope a great favour, ii. 294; has visited Pope, ii. 323; Pope now has no favours to ask, ii. 323; dining at Sir R.'s Pope made an unfortunate remark, ii. 368; Pope frequently dines at Sir R.'s 'Sunday tables', ii. 441, 530, iii. 112; Pope would like to go to Sir R.'s with Fortescue, iii. 11; Sir R. is Fortescue's patron, iii. 52 n.; presents *The Dunciad Variorum* to the King, iii. 26 n.; Pope complains of Lady Mary's libels, iii. 53; Sir R.'s confidential remark about Lady Mary (not specified), iii. 357; Pope quotes Dodington's *Epistle to W.*, v. 2; Pope's relations with Sir R. embarrassed by Swift's 'Libel on Dr. Delany', iii. 91 n.; — wavering relations with Sir R. in 1730, iii. 85, 113, 125, 139; friendliness declines, iii. 159; Sir R.'s injustice to Pope's friends, iv. 377–8; a young student would like to see Sir R.'s pictures, iii. 457; Sir R. is complimented in both Dialogues of *1738*, iv. 114; — Swift regards Sir R. as not an object of anger, ii. 343 n.; Swift claims Sir R. owes him £1,000, ii. 394; Pope talks with Sir R. (1726) about Swift, ii. 395; Swift is ironical about Sir R.'s magnanimity towards Gay, iii. 73; Swift speaks of Sir R. as the 'wild boar in the garden', iii. 98; — Broome praises Sir R. in his *Epistle to Fenton*, ii. 398; Sir R.'s mice thought to have eaten Gay's buttons, ii. 407; Sir R. mentioned jocosely by Pulteney, ii. 444; Pope says the Court party feel they need no better writers than Cibber and the 'British Journalist', ii. 473; Swift asks if Sir R. is affronted by *The Beggar's Opera*, ii. 475; — Swift likens Walpole to a sharper at hazard, ii. 475; an attack on Pope is dedicated to Sir R., iii. 12; Gay despises him, iii. 120; the corruption of his régime,

Walpole, Sir Robert (*cont.*)
iii. 280 n.; the Duchess of Buckingham explains to him her sudden journey to France, iii. 296 n.; the Excise Bill cost him supporters, iii. 339; — Fortescue suggests that Sir R. would be pleased by changes in Pope's *Imitation of Satire II. i*, iii. 354; the Excise Bill is withdrawn, iii. 355; Sir R.'s famous remark ('not one Englishman') to the Queen, iii. 418 n.; his luck in losing leaders of the Opposition, iv. 272; he is too credulous to informers, iv. 378; his resignation, iv. 386; his praise of Sir John St. Aubyn's honesty, iv. 434 n.

Walpole, Robert (1701–51), son of Sir Robert, cr. Lord Walpole of Walpole (1723): he seeks a wife, ii. 183 n.

Walpole Society, The, cited on Kneller, ii. 18 n.; on Guelfi, ii. 242 n.; on Rysbrack, ii. 298 n.

Walsh, Victoria, lacks 2 vols. of Pope's *Iliad*, ii. 11.

WALSH, WILLIAM: letters to, i. 18, 22; letters from, i. 18, 20, 21, 29; Pope's account of, i. 7 n.; W. approves of poems by Pope sent to him by Wycherley, i. 7; wishes to make Pope's acquaintance, i. 7; praises the Pastorals, i. 17; wishes Pope to write a pastoral comedy, i. 18; is thanked for his criticisms, i. 18; W.'s remarks on 'borrowing', i. 20, also on too much wit, on the ancients, i. 20; on Virgil, Lucan, Ovid, i. 21; disparages 'mechanical rules', i. 21; his remarks on 'correctness', i. 21; on naturalness, i. 21; on wit, i. 21–22; on simplicity, on Walsh's 'Delia', i. 22; W. visits his corporation of Richmond (Yorks.), i. 20, 22; is thought a Socinian and a Whig, i. 200; Pope's tribute in the *Essay on Criticism* is valued by W.'s family, ii. 11.

Walsingham, Francis, a pseudonym for Wm. Arnall, iv. 179 n.

Walter, Peter, a symbol of dishonest attorneys, ii. 452, iii. 363.

Walton, Miss, possibly Lady Margaret Harley's governess, iii. 83 n.

WANLEY, HUMPHREY: letters to, ii. 304, 312; W. was librarian to the two Earls

WANLEY, HUMPHREY (*cont.*)
of Oxford, ii. 304 n.; Pope asks him
to get him some port wine, ii. 304,
312; W. as a stylist, ii. 364; after W.'s
death Lord Oxford wishes to have
Hearne as librarian, iii. 111 n.

WARBURTON, WILLIAM: letters to, iv.
163, 171, 182, 195, 215, 219, 233,
236, 237, 238, 243, 251, 288, 334,
339, 341, 345, 346, 356, 361, 370,
373, 379, 380, 384, 385, 386, 387,
388, 393, 399, 402, 403, 410, 424,
425, 427, 429, 434, 438, 447, 454,
455, 471, 474, 480, 491, 495, 500,
505, 506, 515, 518, 520; letter from,
iv. 492; in editing Pope's letters W.
combines two or three letters into one,
iv. 144 n., 234 n., 434 n., 455 n., 481;
misdates a letter in printing, iv. 403
n., 505 n.
In *The History of the Works of the
Learned* W. publishes his defence of
the *Essay on Man*, iv. 163 n.; to be
collected as *A Vindication of the Essay
on Man*, iv. 157; two more parts of it
sent to Pope, iv. 171; Pope thanks W.
for the defence, iv. 163–4; — suggests that flattery of him be cut out of
the collected ed., iv. 182; W. commends Pope in the *Vindication of the
Author of The Divine Legation*, iv.
182; his defence of the *Essay on Man*
to be translated into French, iv. 196.
W. is invited to Twickenham for
the spring of 1740, iv. 196; Pope is
eager to make his acquaintance, iv.
195–6; Pope and his friends are very
grateful to W., iv. 215; Henry
Brooke calls W. the Newton of Pope's
system, iv. 213; — later eds. of the
Vindication augmented, iv. 215 n.,
219, 361; W.'s *Commentary* on the
Essay is effusively dedicated to Ralph
Allen, iv. 400; attacks the charity
and candour of Crousaz, iv. 402–3; —
spends a pleasant week at Twickenham, iv. 237 n.; he and Pope are invited to Lyttelton's, iv. 238; W. during
his second week at Twickenham finds
himself among anti-ministerial men,
iv. 238 n.; is not a party man, iv. 238 n.;
W. knows Burlington's protégé the
Rev. Thomas Wood, iv. 237; —
W. arrived in London 21 Apr. 1740,

WARBURTON, WILLIAM (*cont.*)
iv. 236 n.; his first dinner at Pope's
house, iv. 236 n.; is told he can easily
read his proofs at Twickenham, iv.
233; is asked to notify Robinson of the
day of his arrival, iv. 233; left London on 24 May, iv. 243; — the next
year Pope is eager to see him in
Town, iv. 334; W. has read parts of
Lyttelton's *Henry II*, iv. 348; arrives
in London the night of 27 May 1741,
iv. 346 n.; his later quarrel with T.
Edwards, iv. 342 n.; Pope welcomes
W., iv. 341; W. thanks Pope for
attempts to get him a living nearer
London, iv. 361; — the fiasco of the
Oxford degrees, iv. 357, 437; the
efforts of Lords Arran and Orrery
towards the degree ineffectual, iv.
440, 442; Chesterfield considers getting preferment for W., iv. 356–7; W.
drops his dispute with Middleton,
iv. 369; — is urged by Pope to join
him at Widcombe for a month, iv.
370, 371; possibly best to come via
London, iv. 373 (to see Gyles's executors); Pope's service in making W.
acquainted with Allen, iv. 373 n.;
Allen's niece becomes (1746) W.'s
wife, iv. 373 n., 448 n.; — W. has
been ill, iv. 374; Pope recommends
Knapton to W. as successor to Gyles,
iv. 370; W.'s troubles with Mawhood,
Gyles's executor, iv. 379 n., 383, 385,
386, 387–8, 400, 402, 404, 409, 410,
411; W. shifts from Wright as
printer to Bowyer, iv. 402; — W. in
Town is invited to Orrery's and to
Richardson's, iv. 380; Hooke wishes
to meet W., iv. 381; W. plans to leave
London 11 Feb. 1742, iv. 386, 388;
Pope's superlative praise of Bolingbroke to W., iv. 394; W. will go to
Widcombe with Pope in the autumn
of 1742, iv. 398, 410, 412; Pope wants
a fortnight with W., iv. 420; he hopes
for W.'s health, iv. 421; W. injures his
leg in returning from Bath, iv. 424,
425, 431; — Carteret (?) now thinks
of preferment for W., iv. 433; W.'s
suspicions as to Hanmer's use of his
data on Shakespeare, iv. 438; as yet
W. is unaware of Allen's financial
intentions towards him, iv. 452; W.

Wardlaw, Lady, ii. 427 n.

Ware, Isaac, iv. 151.

Warren, Austin, ii. 390 n., 450 n., iv. 342 n.

Warton, Joseph: on Crashaw's influence on Pope, i. 110 n.; on Flatman, 159 n.; on Pope's use of the Alexandrine, i. 23–24 n.; he redates a letter, ii. 417 n., iii. 163 n.; on Pope's calling his young friends 'weeds', iv. 51 n.; on the first meeting of Pope and Warburton, iv. 233 n.

Warton, Thomas, sr. (1688–1745 ?): lends *Gorboduc* to Pope, i. 408, 467 n.; not the first to interest Pope in Milton's smaller poems, i. 408; a friend of Pope's at Basingstoke, iv. 37 n.

Warton, Thomas, the younger (1728–90), iii. 128 n., iv. 37 n.

Warwick, Charlotte (Rich), Countess of, *see* Addison.

Warwick, 7th Earl of, *see* Rich, Edward Henry.

Warwick, Sir Philip, i. 75.

Warwickshire, *see* Chadshunt (Newsham), Coleshill (Digby), i. 144 n.

Wasse, Joseph, i. 294.

Waterland, Daniel, D.D., iii. 280 n., iv. 334, 335 n.

Waters, —, *see* Walter, Peter.

WATERS, FRANCIS (or Frank), servant of Jervas in London: letters from, i. 501; his wife is Betty, ii. 24; forwards letters to Pope, i. 501; mentioned, i. 347, 500 n., ii. 18 n.

Watson, J. S., iv. 233 n.

Watson, James, bookseller and pirate, iii. 494, iv. 87.

Wattleton Park (for Watlington ?), i. 417 n.

Watts, John, printer, ii. 217, 223, iv. 224.

Watts, Thomas, of the Sun Fire Company: in this company Pope wishes to invest £1,000 in shares, iv. 340; W. is ill, iv. 343, 350, 363; W.'s death, iv. 387.

Way, Elizabeth Ann, owner of a Pope portrait, iv. 91 n.

Webb, Mr. Pope's schoolmate, ii. 428; he marries the widow of Englefield, i. 171 n., iii. 274.

Webb, John, architect, son-in-law of Inigo Jones, iii. 418 n.

Webb, M. I., cited on Rysbrack, ii. 298 n., iii. 477 n.

Webster, E., ii. 154 n.

Weekly Journal, i. 375 n.

Weekly Journal; or, British Gazetteer, i. 345 n.

Weekly Journal; or, Saturday's Post, see *Mist's Weekly Journal.*

Weekly Miscellany, iii. 337 n., iv. 182 n.

Weekly Packet, i. 375 n., 420 n., 479 n., 481 n., ii. 243 n.

Welch, Joseph, his *List of Scholars of Westminster*, ii. 108 n.

Weller, John, dealer in autographs, iii. 323.

WELSTED, LEONARD: letter from to Pope, iii. 355; writes the Prologue for Southerne's *Money the Mistress*, ii. 352; collaborates in *One Epistle*, iii. 59 n., 106 n.; his 'testimony' in favour of the *Essay on Man*, iii. 355–6.

Welwyn (Herts.), *see* Edward Young, J. Jones.

WENTWORTH, THOMAS, 3rd Earl of Strafford: letters to, ii. 300, 308, 313, 327; letter from, ii. 303; he is impeached, i. 298; is informed of Pope's trouble over the Kneller monument, ii. 300; his aid asked concerning the monument, ii. 301, 303, 307; Pope reports to him on the hearing about the monument, ii. 308–9, 313, 314, 328; his small dau.'s opinion of Pope's age, ii. 329.

Wentworth, William, 4th Earl of Strafford, iv. 341 n.

Wentworth Papers (1883) cited, 89 n., ii. 309 n.

Wesley, Samuel, the elder (1662–1735): his character and worth, iii. 95; aid for a subscription to his *Job* asked, iii. 102, 109.

WESLEY, SAMUEL, the younger (1691–1739): letters to, iii. 104, 504, v. 6; some account of, iii. 504 n.; Pope wishes his aid in the affair with Thomas Cooke, ii. 509, 515, 519, 529, iii. 8, 9, 10, v. 7; is invited to Twickenham, iii. 104, v. 7; Pope praises his *Elegy* on Mrs. Morrice, iii. 104; his verses on the marriage of Lady Margaret Harley, iii. 407 n.; Pope aids the subscription for W.'s *Poems* (1736), iii. 504.

West, Gilbert: his poem on Stowe (1731), iii. 244; he visits Pope with Lyttelton (his cousin), iii. 480; sends 'service' to Pope, iv. 331, 368; late annual visits to Pope, iv. 354, 403, 451.

West, John, 1st Earl of Delawarr, iii. 465, 466.

Westminster Abbey *Registers* cited, ii. 443 n.

Weston, Elizabeth: estranged wife of John Weston, i. 113, 119 n., 123, 132, 142; to be with her aunt, Lady Aston, for a week, i. 142–3; she suspects Pope's service, i. 151, 171, 173; a letter possibly addressed to her, ii. 367 n.

Weston, John, husband of Elizabeth: is called a tyrant, i. 123; complains of Caryll, i. 129; Pope tries to aid Mrs. Weston, i. 132; the husband is favoured over the wife by the Racketts, i. 143–4; Weston is hostile to Pope, i. 151; his letter about dinner at the Rackett's, i. 424, 426, 428; Pope departs, i. 426.

Weymouth, 1st Viscount, *see* Thynne, Sir Thomas.

Whaley, Rev. Nathaniel, Pope aids his suit, ii. 523, iii. 21, 102, 104.

Wharncliffe, 2nd Baron, *see* Stuart-Wortley, John.

Wharton, Philip, Duke of Wharton: he reads Pope's *Pastorals* in MS., i. 17, 21; aids the subscription for the *Iliad*, i. 226; a patron to Edward Young, ii. 154; his *Authentic Pieces* cited, ii. 166 n.; asks after Fenton, ii. 245.

Wharton, Thomas, 1st Marquis of, iii. 199.

Whiston, William, i. 26, 202; his *Memoirs* cited, i. 185 n.; his heterodoxy and his lectures on astronomy, i. 185 n.; he lectures at Will's coffeehouse, i. 288, 290; his comment on Bentley's learning, i. 294 n.

White, Mr., an acquaintance of H. Bethel's, iii. 33.

White, John (d. 1729), possibly mentioned, iii. 52.

White, Sir Thomas, iv. 450.

Whitehall Evening Post, The, ii. 428 n., iii. 516 n.

Whiteknights, *see* Englefield.

Whiteway, Martha: letter to her from Pope, iv. 248; letters from her to Pope, iv. 184, 240; from her to Lord Orrery, iv. 277, 307, 320; from Lord Orrery to her, iv. 308, 325, 327; — is suspected of secreting some of Pope's letters to Swift, iv. 73 n.; Swift says she has all of Pope's letters to him, iv. 115–16; she agrees, iv. 116; later she says not she but another 'safe hand' has Pope's letters, iv. 130; she has no Pope letters, she tells Orrery, iv. 133; she says Pope's letters are in a safe hand, but whose she does not know, iv. 316; — she writes to Pope for Swift about Macaulay, iv. 184; also about the 'tracts' Pope wants finished, iv. 240; she says Swift has burnt many MSS., iv. 276 n.; Pope pretends she will hardly protest against the publication of the Pope–Swift letters, iv. 256; she concealed the clandestine vol. for a time, iv. 277, 285, 319; she made Faulkner write to Pope for permission to print, iv. 277, 312; — her position with regard to these letters, iv. 277; seems to quote Faulkner's title-page for the vol. of letters, iv. 277; believes the clandestine vol. comes from Pope, iv. 279; blames Faulkner for printing it, iv. 280; Orrery says she has no fears of perjury, iv. 280; Pope thinks she protests extremely, iv. 285; she is sure the clandestine vol. comes from England, iv. 320, 321; from Pope's thieving servants, she thinks, iv. 321, 329; — Orrery tells her the vol. is sure to be published, iv. 328; she quotes from the clandestine vol., which she says she never read, iv. 321; she still regrets inability to prevent publication, iv. 321; no letter of hers admits opening and stopping of letters to Swift, iv. 286 n.; letters to her may be opened, she says, by Swift, iv. 319; — the history of the Bath covering letter, iv. 305, 307; Orrery thinks she had the clandestine vol. printed, iv. 308; her vehement protest against publication, iv. 319; — she will entrust Pope's MS. letters to Orrery, iv. 308; she had offered to return this second

WHITEWAY, MARTHA (*cont.*)
lot of Pope letters by Nugent, iv. 230–1, 233, 316; she dare not return these letters by post, iv. 320; Pope suggests she is a long time in returning the letters, iv. 330; he assures her of the same justice from him that she has given her, iv. 330; — Swift now allows her to return any letters that he has, iv. 321; she is the only relative Swift can endure, iv. 116; Swift's affection for Pope reported, iv. 184; Mrs. W. is an object of suspicion by Pope, iv. 214; her supervision of Swift reported by Orrery, iv. 226; Pope thinks her in part mad and impertinent, iv. 232; she will do Pope any appropriate service, iv. 241; she is jealous perhaps of legacies to Pope, iv. 305; — Orrery pretends that she is a conspirator, iv. 54, 306; her low opinion of Faulkner, iv. 318; she seems interested in the commercial value of Swift's writings, iv. 240; she wishes Swift's *Four Last Years* printed without change, iv. 130; her opinion of the *Directions to Servants* and *Four Last Years*, iv. 240; Dr. King's heirs should not think they have rights to *Four Last Years*, iv. 240, 248, 306.

Whitford, Mr., i. 156.

Whiting, B. J., i. 169.

Whitley, W. T., iv. 91 n.

Whitrow, Joan, i. 436.

Whitshed, William, Lord Chief Justice of Ireland, ii. 64, 66.

Whitton, Middlesex: Pope's accident there, ii. 357, 399. *See also* Edward Caryll, Lord Islay, Sir G. Kneller, Nathaniel Pigott.

Whitworth (or Whitrow), Mrs., i. 436.

Whitworth, Richard, i. 437 n.

Wickham, Kent, *see* Gilbert West.

Wicksted, Mr., iv. 469.

Widcombe, Somerset, *see* Ralph Allen.

Wight, Isle of, iii. 427, iv. 84.

Wilcocks, Joseph, iv. 140.

Wild-brat, i. 75.

Wiley, Margaret L., iii. 132 n.

Wilford, J., printer, iii. 401 n., 464.

Wilks, Robert, i. 136, 138, iii. 86, 223.

Willes, Sir John, iv. 507 n.

Willet, Mr., iv. 38.

William III, King of England, i. 10 n., ii. 63, iii. 471, iv. 205.

William, Duke of Cumberland, ii. 257, 340, 350, iii. 111 n.

Williams, Folkstone, i. 459, ii. 106 n.

Williams, Sir Harold, i. 288 n., ii. 496 n., 522, iii. 22 n., 292 n., 367.

Williams, William, ii. 425.

William's Coffeehouse (? Will's), i. 288.

Williton, Somerset, *see* Orchard Wyndham, i. 312.

Will's Coffeehouse, i. 11, 288, 290.

Wilmington, Earl of, *see* Compton, Spencer.

Wilmot, John, Earl of Rochester: quoted by Steele, i. 145; his lines 'On Nothing' mentioned by Fenton, ii. 385; imitated in Pope's 'Silence', i. 87 n.; called the greatest wit of the last age, ii. 385; quoted on knaves, iii. 502; Pope sleeps in his bed at Adderbury, iv. 189 n.

Wilson, Charles, *Memoirs of Congreve* cited, ii. 75.

Wilson, Francis, D.D., iv. 305, 309.

Wilson, James S., *Studies in Honor of Wilson* cited, iii. 132 n.

Wilton, Wilts., ii. 240.

Wiltshire, *see* Amesbury (Queensberry), Corsham (Pulteney), Salisbury, Stourhead, Wilton.

Wimpole, Cambridgeshire, *see* Oxford, 2nd Earl of, and Pope.

Wimsatt, W. K., jr., iv. 91 n.

Winchelsea, Earls and Countesses of, *see* Finch.

Winchester (Winton), Hants, iii. 133.

Windham, *see* Wyndham.

Windsor, Berks. i. 310; Windsor Castle, iii. 126, 131, 353; Kent's work there, iv. 154 n.; Windsor Park, residence of Henrietta, Duchess of Marlborough, and Congreve, ii. 400 n., 402; Windsor Lodge, residence of Sarah, Duchess of Marlborough, iv. 405, 419 n.

Windsor Forest: early home of Pope, i. 11, ii. 233; home of Lady Judith Trumbull, ii. 204, 231–2, 296.

Winnington, Salway, iv. 51 n.

Winton, *see* Winchester.

Wintringham, Dr. Clifton, iv. 338.

Wise, Mr., iii. 140 n., 141.

Wise, T. J., iv. 89 n.

Wollaston, William, ii. 179 n.

Wood, Robert, i. 247 n.

Wood, Rev. Thomas, iii. 329, 333, iv. 140–1, 237.

Woodfall, Henry, iii. 489 n.

Woodford, Rev. Richard, ii. 477–8.

Woodward, Dr. John, ii. 514.

Woodward, T., bookseller, iv. 410.

Wootton, Sir H., i. 10.

Wootton, John, artist, ii. 416, iii. 11, 115.

Worcestershire, *see* Abberley (Walsh, Pope, Edward Blount).

Worrall, John, ii. 442.

Worsborough, York, iii. 117 n.

Worsdale, James, iii. 476 n.

Worsley, Lady, ii. 191.

Wright, goldsmith and banker, ii. 37, 42, 72, 428.

Wright, John, printer: helps print the *Works* (1723) of the Duke of Buckingham, ii. 222; will send Pope's *Works* (1735) to Caryll, iii. 474; prints the 1737 *Letters* of Pope, iv. 58; his arrangements with Lintot, iv. 333; is Pope's printer, iv. 361; allows *The New Dunciad* to be pirated, iv. 392; has printed the 8vo ed. of the *Essay on Man*, iv. 502.

Wright, Sir Nathan, i. 12 n.

Wyat, John, ii. 391.

WYCHERLEY, WILLIAM: letters to, i, 1, 5, 8, 9, 11, 15, 31, 33, 60, 83, 86; letters from, i. 3, 5, 6, 12, 13, 14, 25, 29, 32, 34, 38, 40, 49, 50, 52, 54, 58, 61, 62, 64, 78, 82, 84; the correspondence suspected, i. 1; two letters omitted in eds. of 1735, i. 1; excessive compliments in the letters, i. 5, 6, 8, 9, 14, 34; — W.'s epistolary style, i. 52 n., 58 n., 69; failure to write to Pope, i. 52, 53, 72, 76, 96, 101; kind letter to Pope, i. 77; Pope's 'last' note, i. 84 n.; correspondence resumed after coolness, i. 134; W. threatens to print Pope's fine letters, i. 66; Pope's publication of letters in 1729, iii. 80, 469, 494 n., iv. 321, 330.

W.'s age, i. 8; his death-bed marriage, i. 70, 328–9, ii. 350; his estate impaired by his father, iii. 363; his bad fall, i. 58; illness, i. 40, 54, 73, 108; journeys to Shrewsbury, i. 14, 38, 52, 58, 61, 65, 80, 82; to Bath, i. 15, 134;

WYCHERLEY, WILLIAM (*cont.*)

visits (mainly projected) to Binfield, i. 11, 13, 33, 35, 39, 40, 43, 47, 52, 59, 61, 65, 82, 85.

W.'s friendship with Pope, i. 1, 40, 53; resentments implied, i. 55, but forgiven, i. 58, 67; Gildon's slanders, i. 73; estrangement, i. 86, 102; reconciliation, i. 113, 134; — W. invites Pope to Town, i. 53, 136; meets Pope at Bath (1714), i. 256; approves Pope's witty compliments, i. 79, his vigorous mind, i. 54–55, prescribes cure for P.'s headaches, i. 65; — on Pope's 'Pastorals', i. 41, 49–50, 59; on the 'Essay on Criticism', i. 134; W.'s high opinion of Sir W. Trumbull, i. 55; Pope's revisions of W.'s poems, i. 3, 13, 15, 30, 31, 33; advice to recast in form of prose *pensées*, i. 34; end of the revisions, i. 79, 82, 83, 84, 85, 147 n., iii. 55; — W.'s MSS. deposited by Pope in the Harley Library, i. 31, 130; W.'s *Posthumous Works*, i. 13 n., 16 n., 54 n., iii. 1, 54, 55 n., 459; — W.'s lines 'To Mr. Pope', i. 41, 50, Welsted's lie about it, iii. 106; *Plain Dealer* quoted by Pope, i. 187; W. calls himself a plain dealer, i. 34, 55, 66, 98; commended by Pope for wit, i. 38, 48; his good nature, i. 38, 55; other mentions, i. 27, 62, 97.

Wyndham, Sir William (of Orchard Wyndham): visited by Lord Bathurst, ii. 207, by Bolingbroke, iii. 139 n., iv. 119 n., by Gay, iii. 321; Lord Harcourt and Pope have cider with him, ii. 359; Swift pleased by Sir W.'s (political ?) friendship with the Queensberrys, iii. 251; — Pope confers with him on politics, iv. 138, 142–4; served as interpreter between Pope and Mme de Villette (Lady Bolingbroke), ii. 249; his health improved, ii. 333; Curll wrongly inserts Sir W.'s name in a letter, ii. 395 n.; — Sir W. knows Swift expects more than 'mere civility', ii. 408; gout kept him (1½ years) from answering Swift's letter, ii. 479; — the death (1731) of his wife (Lady Catherine Seymour), iii. 194; his son gets £500 by the will of Duke Disney,

Wyndham, Sir William (*cont.*)
iii. 249; attended first performance of *Athelwold*, iii. 253; Pope writes to Curll for him, iii. 359; died at Wells (1740), iv. 249 n.; reputedly led by Bolingbroke and seconded by Lord Marchmont, iv. 250; commended in Pope's lines on his grotto, iv. 262.

Xenophon, cited by Cromwell, i. 95, 96.

YORK, city and co.: Pope visits York, i. 370; H. Bethel's address, iii. 114, &c. *See also* Beverley, Beswick, Lanesboro (Londesborough), Richmond, Ruston, Scarborough, Worsborough.
Yorke, Charles (1722–70), cited on Warburton's visits to Pope, iv. 243 n.
Yorke, Philip, 1st Earl of Hardwicke: letters to him about Pope, iv. 243 n.; as Lord Chancellor rendered judgement on the right of publishing letters, iv. 343 n.

YOUNG, EDWARD: letters from, i. 294, ii. 171; Fellow of All Souls, i. 294; reports Oxford's preference of Pope's *Iliad*, i. 294; distributed *Iliad*, vol. i, for Pope in Oxford, i. 294; — his pension from the Duke of Wharton, ii. 154; *The Brothers*, ii. 171 n.; asks Pope for a Prologue, ii. 171; his opinion of *Mariamne*, ii. 162 n.; — sent Pitt's 23rd *Odyssey* to Pope for use in translating, ii. 382; introduced Aaron Hill to Pope, iii. 235; friend of J. Jones, iii. 376 n.; his tragic majesty, i. 223; not merry enough for Swift, iii. 372, v. 11–12; in Dublin (1733) thought to be the author of the *Essay on Man*, v. 11–12.
Younger, Miss, actress, friend of Pope and Gay, i. 283 n.

Zaman (for Seeman, Enoch), painted at Cannons, iii. 268.
Zoilus, a terror to critics, i. 333.
Zolicoffre, Mr., a banker, i. 274.

PRINTED IN
GREAT BRITAIN
AT THE
UNIVERSITY PRESS
OXFORD
BY
CHARLES BATEY
PRINTER
TO THE
UNIVERSITY